History of the American Economy

History of the American Economy

ELEVENTH EDITION

GARY M. WALTON

University of California, Davis

HUGH ROCKOFF

Rutgers University

SOUTH-WESTERN
CENGAGE Learning

Australia • Brazil • Japan • Korea • Mexico • Singapore • Spain • United Kingdom • United States

History of the American Economy: Eleventh Edition
Gary M. Walton and Hugh Rockoff

Vice President of Editorial, Business:
  Jack W. Calhoun

Acquisitions Editor: Steven Scoble

Managing Developmental Editor:
  Katie Yanos

Marketing Specialist: Betty Jung

Marketing Coordinator: Suellen Ruttkay

Content Project Manager: Darrell E. Frye

Frontlist Buyer, Manufacturing:
  Sandee Milewski

Production Service: Cadmus

Sr. Art Director: Michelle Kunkler

Internal Designer: Juli Cook

Cover Designer: Rose Alcorn

Cover Images: © Ross Elmi/iStockphoto;
  © Thinkstock Images

For product information and technology assistance, contact us at
Cengage Learning Customer & Sales Support, 1-800-354-9706

For permission to use material from this text or product, submit all requests online at **www.cengage.com/permissions**

Further permissions questions can be emailed to
permissionrequest@cengage.com

Package ISBN-13: 978-0-324-78662-0
Package ISBN-10: 0-324-78662-X
Book only ISBN 13: 978-0324-78661-3
Book only ISBN 10: 0-324-78661-1

South-Western, Cengage Learning
5191 Natorp Boulevard
Mason, OH 45040
USA

Cengage learning products are represented in Canada by Nelson Education, Ltd.

For your course and learning solutions, visit **www.cengage.com**
Purchase any of our products at your local college store or at our preferred online store **www.ichapters.com**

Printed in Canada
2 3 4 5 6 7 13 12 11 10 09

Douglass C. North   Robert W. Fogel

In honor of our dissertation advisors,
Douglass C. North and Robert W. Fogel,
Nobel Laureates in Economics, 1993

Brief Contents

Contents

PART 3   The Reunification Era: 1860–1920

PART 4   War, Depression, and War Again: 1914–1946

PART 5   The Postwar Era: 1946 to the Present

Preface

This new edition of *History of the American Economy* was deemed necessary because of the brisk advance of research in economic history and the rapid changes unfolding in the U.S. and global economies. The struggle of many nations to convert from centrally planned to market-led economies after the collapse of communism, the rapid economic expansion of India and China, and the growing economic integration in Europe invite new perspectives on the historical record of the American economy. Moreover, the terrorist attacks of September 11, 2001, on the World Trade Center and the Pentagon and the subsequent wars in Afghanistan and Iraq have spread a blanket of uncertainty on the future of the United States. The importance of understanding the sources of economic growth and change, the main subject of this book, is greater than ever.

To properly convey the speed of change of American lifestyles and economic well being, chapter 1 begins with a focus on twentieth-century American life, mostly but not entirely economic. The purpose is to show how dramatically different the way we live today is compared with the times of our grandparents and great-grandparents. The remarkable contrasts in living standards, length of life, and how we work and consume from 1900 to 2000 provide a "wake-up call" for the nation on the changes soon to unfold in our lives and in the lives of generations to come. This wake-up call serves a vital purpose: preparation for the future. As Professor Deirdre McCloskey admonishes us in her book *Second Thoughts*, in preparing for the future we best arm ourselves with a good understanding of the past.

Boxed discussions called "New Views" draw explicit analogies between current issues and past experiences—drug prohibition today and alcohol prohibition in the 1920s, and war finance today and war finance in the past, to name two. Economic historians, of course, have always made these connections for their students, but we believe that by drawing attention to them in the text, we reinforce the lesson that history has much to teach us about the present, and the perhaps equally important lesson that detailed study of the past is needed to determine both the relevance and the limitations of historical analogies.

We have retained the presentation of material in chronological order, albeit not rigidly. Part One, "The Colonial Era: 1607–1776," focuses on the legacies of that era and the institutions, policies, economic activities, and growth that brought the colonies to a point at which they could challenge the mother country for their independence. Part Two, "The Revolutionary, Early National, and Antebellum Eras: 1776–1860," and Part Three, "The Reunification Era: 1860–1920," each begin with a chapter on the impact of war and its aftermath. The other chapters in these parts follow a parallel sequence of discussion topics—land, agriculture, and natural resources; transportation; product markets and structural change; conditions of labor; and money, banking, and economic fluctuations. Each of these parts, as well as Part Four, "War, Depression, and War Again: 1914–1946," closes with a chapter on an issue of special importance to the period: Part One, the causes of the American Revolution; Part Two, slavery; and Part Three, domestic markets and foreign trade. Part Four closes with a discussion of World War II. All the chapters have been rewritten to improve the exposition and to incorporate the latest findings. Part Five, "The Postwar Era: 1946 to the Present" moreover, has been extensively revised to reflect the greater clarity with which we can now view the key developments that shaped postwar America.

Throughout the text, the primary subject is economic growth, with an emphasis on institutions and institutional changes, especially markets and the role of government, including monetary and fiscal policy. Three additional themes round out the foundation of the book: the quest for security, international exchange (in goods, services, and people), and demographic forces.

Finally, this edition further develops the pedagogical features used in earlier editions. We provide five basic rules of analysis called "economic reasoning propositions," in Chapter 1. We repeatedly draw attention in the text to these propositions with explicit text references and a marginal icon for easy reference. A list of historical and economic perspectives precedes each of the five parts of the book, providing a summary of the key characteristics and events that gave distinction to each era. Furthermore, each chapter retains a reference list of articles, books, and Web sites that form the basis of the scholarship underlying each chapter. Additional sources and suggested readings are available on the Web site. In addition to these pedagogical aids, each chapter begins with a "Chapter Theme" that provides a brief overview and summary of the key lesson objectives and issues. In addition to the "New Views" boxed feature described above, we have retained the "Economic Insights" boxes that utilize explicit economic analysis to reveal the power of economic analysis in explaining the past and to show economic forces at work on specific issues raised in the chapters. We have also retained the "Perspectives" boxes that discuss policies and events affecting disadvantaged groups.

We are pleased to introduce an improved technology supplement with this edition: *Economic Applications* (**http://www.cengage.com/sso**). This site offers dynamic Web features: EconNews Online, EconDebate Online, and EconData Online. Organized by pertinent economic topics, and searchable by topic or feature, these features are easy to integrate into the classroom. EconNews, EconDebate and EconData deepen a student's understanding of theoretical concepts through hands-on exploration and analysis of the latest economic news stories, policy debates, and data. These features are updated on a regular basis. The *Economic Applications* Web site is complimentary via an access card included with each new edition of *History of the American Economy*. Used book buyers can purchase access to the site at **http://www.cengage.com/sso**.

A Test Bank and Power Point slides accompany the *History of the American Economy*, 11th edition, and are available to qualified instructors through the Web site (**http://www.cengage.com/econmics.walton**).

Acknowledgments

We are especially grateful to the reviewers of this edition: Phil Coelho, Martha L. Olney, David Mitch, Michael R. Haines, Daniel Barbezat, and David Mustard. Farley Grubb, Pamela Nickless, and John Wallis were of special help with ideas for the first half of text. Richard England provided a detailed list of comments on and criticisms of the Tenth Edition that was extremely helpful.

This edition, moreover, reflects the contributions of many other individuals who have helped us with this and previous editions. Here we gratefully acknowledge the contributions of Lee Alston, Terry Anderson, Fred Bateman, Diane Betts, Stuart Bruchey, Colleen Callahan, Ann Carlos, Susan Carter, Phil Coelho, Raymond L. Cohn, James Cypher, Paul A. David, Lance Davis, William Dougherty, Richard A. Easterlin, Barry Eichengreen, Stanley Engerman, Dennis Farnsworth, Price Fishback, Robert W. Fogel, Andrew Foshee, Claudia Goldin, Joseph Gowaskie, George Green, Robert Higgs, John A. James, Stewart Lee, Gary D. Libecap, James Mak, Deirdre McCloskey, Russell Menard, Lloyd Mercer, Douglass C. North, Anthony O'Brien, Jeff Owen, Edwin Perkins, Roger L. Ransom, David Rasmussen, Joseph D. Reid Jr., Paul Rhode, Elyce Rotella, Barbara Sands, Don Schaefer, R. L. Sexton, James Shepherd, Mark Siegler, Austin Spencer, Richard H. Steckel, Paul Uselding, Jeffrey Williamson, Richard Winkelman, Gavin Wright, and Mary Yeager. The length of this list (which is by no means complete) reflects the extraordinary enthusiasm and generosity that characterizes the discipline of economic history.

Gary Walton is grateful to the Foundation for Teaching Economics and for the research assistance of Lisa Chang and to his colleagues at the University of California, Davis for advice and encouragement, especially Alan Olmstead, Alan Taylor, Greg Clark, and Peter Lindert.

Hugh Rockoff thanks his colleagues at Rutgers, especially his fellow economic historians Michael Bordo, Carolyn Moehling, and Eugene White. He is greatly indebted to Nuttanan Wichitaksorn for his able research assistance. Hugh owes his largest debt to his wife, Hope Corman, who provided instruction in the subtleties of labor economics and unflagging encouragement for the whole project. Hugh also owes a special debt to his children, Jessica and Steven, who have now reached an age at which they no longer provide a plausible excuse for not finishing the revision on time.

GARY WALTON
HUGH ROCKOFF

About the Authors

Gary M. Walton became the Founding Dean of the Graduate School of Management at the University of California, Davis in 1981 and is Professor of Economics Emeritus at the University of California, Davis. In addition, he is President of the Foundation for Teaching Economics, where he has designed and administered highly acclaimed economics and leadership programs (domestically and internationally) for high school seniors selected for their leadership potential, as well as for high school teachers.

He credits much of his personal success to his coach at the University of California, Berkeley, the legendary Brutus Hamilton (U.S. Head Coach of Track and Field in the 1952 Olympics), and his success as an economist to his doctoral dissertation advisor, Douglass C. North (1993 Nobel Laureate in Economics).

Hugh Rockoff is Professor of Economics at Rutgers University and a research associate of the National Bureau of Economic Research. He has written extensively on banking and monetary history and wartime price controls. He enjoys teaching economic history to undergraduates, and credits his success as an economist to his doctoral dissertation advisor, Robert W. Fogel (1993 Nobel Laureate in Economics).

CHAPTER 1

Growth, Welfare, and the American Economy

AMERICANS 1900–2009

When Rutgers and Princeton played the first intercollegiate football game in 1869, it is doubtful any person alive could have foreseen the impact football would have on twenty-first-century American life. From the weekly money and passion fans pour into their favorite teams, to the media hype and parties linked to season-ending bowl games, football is truly big business, both in college and in the pros. And how the game has changed!

By the turn of the twentieth century, some of the land grant colleges of the Midwest were also fielding teams, one of the earliest being the University of Wisconsin–Madison. The Badgers, as they are popularly called today, enjoy a long-standing sports tradition, and thereby provide some historically interesting facts. As shown in Figure 1.1 on page 2, in 1902, UW's football team was made up of players whose average size was 173 pounds. Most of the athletes played "both sides of the ball," on offense as well as defense, and substitutions were infrequent. Economists today would say they were short on specialization. By 1929, the average size had increased modestly to 188 pounds, and players were increasingly, though not yet exclusively, specializing on offense or defense. By 2008, the average weight of Wisconsin football players was 238 pounds, and players routinely specialized not just on defense or offense, but by particular positions and by special teams, and sometimes by types of formations. Even more dramatic size changes are revealed by comparing the weight of the five largest players. UW's five biggest players in 1902 averaged 184 pounds, hardly more than the average weight of the whole team. As shown in Figure 1.2 on page 2, in 1929 the five biggest players averaged 199 pounds. By 2008, the five largest offensive players averaged 315 pounds, just shy of a sixty percent jump over 1929.

UW alumni and students have also been big-time basketball enthusiasts, favoring players with speed, shooting and jumping skills, and height. In 1939, the Badgers' starting five had a considerable range of heights by position just as they do today. Figure 1.3 on page 3 conveys not only the consistent differences among guards, forwards, and centers but also the dramatic gains in height by players at every position taking the court today. The 1999 guards were taller than the 1939 forwards. Indeed, one of the 1999 guards was taller than the 1939 center. Such dramatic height gains are partly a result of the growing college entrance opportunities that exceptionally talented players enjoy today compared with young players long ago. But the height gains also reflect more general increases in average heights for the U.S. population overall, and these gains in turn indicate improvements in diet and health.

Changes in average height tell us quite a lot about a society; nations whose people are becoming taller, as they have in Japan over the last 50 years, are becoming richer and eating better. Because of genetic differences among individuals, an individual woman

FIGURE 1.1
University of Wisconsin
Starting Football Players'
Average Weight

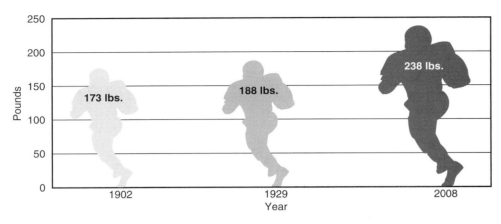

Source: *Sport Information Office, University of Wisconsin–Madison.*

FIGURE 1.2
University of Wisconsin
Football: Average
Weight of Five Largest
Players

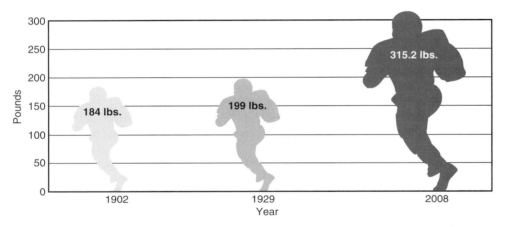

Source: *Sport Information Office, University of Wisconsin–Madison.*

who is short cannot be considered to be poor. Such a conclusion would not be unreasonable, however, especially along with other evidence, for a society of short people. Adult heights reflect the accumulative past nutritional experience during the growing years, the disease environment, health care, as well as genetic factors (which change very slowly). Americans are the heaviest people in the world; the Germans are second. Dutchmen are the world's tallest, with male adults averaging 6 feet 1 inches. Americans today, with adult males averaging 5 feet 10 inches and 172 pounds, are nearly 2 inches taller than their grandparents. The average height gain of Americans during the twentieth century was a little more than 3 inches. We are richer and eat more and better than Americans did 100 years ago, sometimes to excess, with a third of the population currently measured as obese or overweight.

Another, and arguably even better measure of a society's vitality and well-being is the length of life of its citizens. Throughout most of history, individuals and societies have fought against early death. The gain in life expectancy at birth from the low 20s to nearly 30 by around 1750 took thousands of years. Since then, life expectancy in advanced countries has jumped to 75, or 150 percent, and in 2002 in the United States it was

FIGURE 1.3
University of Wisconsin
Basketball Players'
Heights

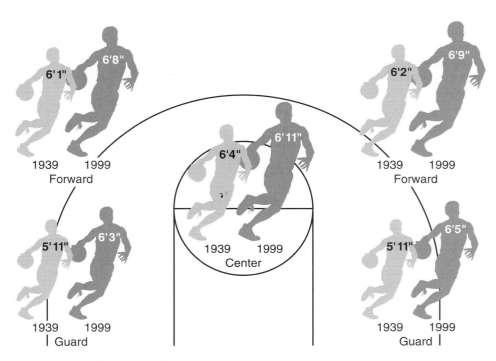

Source: *Sport Information Office, University of Wisconsin–Madison.*

79 years. This phenomenal change is not merely a reflection of decline in infant mortality; as Table 1.1 below shows for the United States, the advances in length of life are spread across all age-groups. As a consequence, in 2007, 302 million people were living in the United States, up from 76 million in 1900.

The gains in population size and in length of life stem primarily from economic growth, because such growth leads to better diets and cleaner water, to sewage disposal, and other health-enhancing changes. The broadest and most commonly used measures of overall economic performance are the levels and the rise in real gross domestic product (GDP). The U.S. real GDP increased from $0.5 trillion in 1900 to more than $11.5 trillion in 2007, measured in constant real purchasing power of 2000 dollars. When divided by the population, GDP per capita averaged $4,900 (in 2000 constant dollars) in 1900. In 2007 it was $28,000, almost eight times higher. Average yearly increases of 2 percent, which for any given year appear small, have compounded year after year to realize this sevenfold advance. These gains have not been exclusive to the few, the middle class, or the very rich.

TABLE 1.1 LIFE EXPECTANCY BY AGE IN THE UNITED STATES

AGE	1901	1954	2000	2005
0	49	70	77	77.8
15	62	72	78	78.6
45	70	74	79	80.3
65	77	79	83	83.7
75	82	84	86	86.9

Sources: *Data for 1901, U.S. Department of Commerce 1921, 52–53; and data for 1940–1996, National Center for Health Statistics, selected years.*

The rise in material affluence in the United States in this century has been so great that citizens whom the government labels "officially poor" currently have incomes surpassing those of average middle-class Americans in 1950 and higher than all but the richest Americans (top 5 percent) in 1900. The official poverty income level in the United States is based on the concept of meeting basic needs. The measure starts with a minimum amount of money needed to feed a person properly. This amount is then multiplied by three to meet needs for shelter, clothing, and other essentials. This widely used poverty threshold measure for Americans was about $8,500 at the end of the century, almost exactly one-quarter the income of the average American, but higher than average incomes for most of the rest of the world, and above the world average per capita income.

Despite gains for people labeled "poor" in the United States, the gap between the rich and the poor remains wide. This gap is an important element in drawing conclusions about the success or failure of an economic system. It bears on the cohesion, welfare, and security of a society. A useful starting point from which to consider this issue is to view a snapshot of the division of income in the United States. Figure 1.4 shows this distribution in fifths for all U.S. households for 2007. As in other years, a large gap existed between the top fifth and the bottom fifth. In fact, the richest fifth of the population received half the income (49.7 percent), about the amount the remaining four-fifths received. The poorest fifth U.S. households received only 3.4 percent of total income in 2007 (not including food stamps, assisted housing, Medicaid, and other such assistance). Figure 1.5 shows changes in average real income received by these five groups since 1966. By the end of the century, the top fifth of the households earned incomes averaging more than 13 times the average incomes of those in the bottom fifth.

In Figure 1.5, the income gap appears to have grown in recent years: The two top lines drift upward, while the lower three remain level. In percentage terms, for example, for 1975 the lowest fifth received 4.2 percent of total income; as noted, in 2001 it was down to 3.5 percent. In 1975 the top group received 43.7 percent but claimed 50.1 percent of the total in 2001.

The important question, however, is whether the people in the bottom fifth in 1975 were also in that category in 2001? If all of the people in the top category in 1975 had switched places by 2001 with all the people in the bottom category (the bottom fifth rising to the top fifth by 2001), no change would be observed in the data shown in

FIGURE 1.4

The American Income Pie by Fifths, 2007

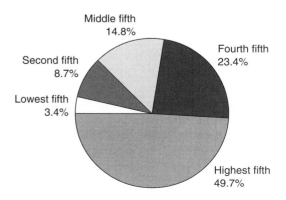

Source: *U.S. Census Bureau. "Share of Aggregate Income Received by Each Fifth and Top 5 Percent of Households, All Races: 1967to 2007" (www.census.gov/hhes/www/income/histinc/h02AR.html).*

FIGURE 1.5

The Income Gap, 1967–2003

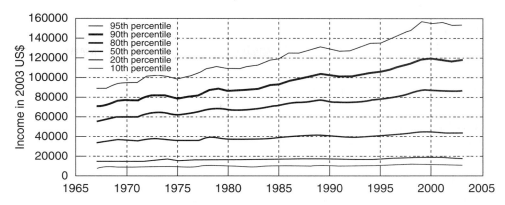

Source: *U.S. Census Bureau. "United States Income Distribution 1967-2003" (http://en. wikipedia.org/wiki/Image:United_States_Income_Distribution_1967-2003.svg).*

Figures 1.4 and 1.5. Surely such a switch would be considered a huge change in the distribution of income among people.

The best available data on the movement of people in these classifications come from a study undertaken by the University of Michigan Panel Survey on Income Dynamics covering 1975–1991. The conventional view of widening income disparity suggested by Figures 1.4 and 1.5 stands in sharp contrast to the evidence in Table 1.2. Reading along the bottom line, we find only 5.1 percent of those in the bottom quintile in 1975 were there in 1991; 29 percent had moved into the top fifth. Reading along the top line indicates that 0.9 percent of those in the top fifth in 1975 had fallen into the bottom fifth by 1991; 62.5 percent remained in the top category.

Further analysis of the data has shown that the rise in income and upward movement into higher categories were frequently swift. In any given year, many of those identified in the bottom fifth were young and in school. With gains in education and job opportunities, many advanced readily into higher rankings.

Another perspective on the economic gains that Americans experienced during the twentieth century comes from looking at the availability, ownership, and use of new goods. Figure 1.6 shows a virtual explosion in the array of goods routinely owned and

TABLE 1.2 CHANGES AMONG INCOME RANKINGS

INCOME QUINTILE IN 1975	PERCENTAGE IN EACH QUINTILE IN 1991				
	1ST	2ND	3RD	4TH	5TH
5th (highest)	0.9	2.8	10.2	23.6	62.5
4th	1.9	9.3	18.8	32.6	37.4
3rd (middle)	3.3	19.3	28.3	30.1	19.0
2nd	4.2	23.5	20.3	25.2	26.8
1st (lowest)	5.1	14.6	21.0	30.3	29.0

In 1991, only 5.1 percent who were in the lowest income quintile in 1975 were still there. Of the lowest quintile in 1975, 29 percent had progressed to the top one-fifth by 1991.

Source: *Cox and Alm 1995.*

FIGURE 1.6

Household Ownership and Use of Products

The past 100 years have brought a virtual explosion in the array of goods Americans routinely enjoy. At the turn of the century, nobody—not even society's wealthiest—could travel by air, wear comfortable tennis shoes, or even take an aspirin, yet the majority of modern-day Americans regularly do so. From cars to computers to cell phones, our ancestors would gawk at the products almost all Americans take for granted.

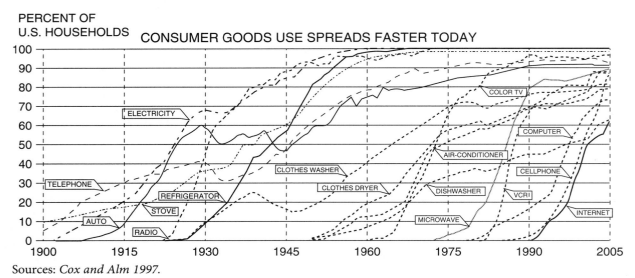

Sources: *Cox and Alm 1997.*

used in U.S. homes. Most of the items shown were not even available to the richest Americans alive in 1901.

A STUDY WITH A PURPOSE

Nation Building

Why should you study economic history? The best short answer is to better prepare you for the future. Economic history provides you with a clear perspective on the forces of change and a good understanding of the lessons of the past. The study of economic history also provides lessons on nation building and ways to analyze policies and institutions that affect the nation as well as you personally.

One hundred years ago, citizens of Great Britain enjoyed the highest standards of living in the world, and the British Empire was the leading world power. In 1892, the dominant European powers upgraded the ranks of their diplomats in Washington, D.C., from ministers to ambassadors, thereby elevating the United States to first-division status among nations. On economic grounds, this upgrading should have occurred much earlier, because in 1892, output per capita in the United States was much higher than in France and Germany and not far below that in Great Britain.

In 1950, the United States was the most powerful nation in the world, and Americans enjoyed standards of living higher, by far, than those of any other people. Another "super power," however, was intensely challenging this supremacy. As the cold war unfolded and intensified after World War II, nations became divided into two clusters: communist nations emphasizing command, control, and central planning systems, and free nations emphasizing markets, trade, competition, and limited government. This division into clusters was especially apparent in Europe and Asia, and many other nations sat on the sidelines pondering their futures and which system to follow. By all appearances, the Soviet Union displayed levels of economic, technological, and military strength rivaling those of the United States. It launched its space satellite, called Sputnik, in 1957, placing the first vehicle constructed on Earth in space. The cold war ended in 1989, and many satellite nations of the Soviet Union (e.g., Eastern Germany, the former Czechoslovakia, etc.) broke free. By the mid-1990s, the Russian Federation desperately needed aid just to feed its people. The life expectancy of men in Russia plummeted from the low 60s (mid-1980s) to 56 (mid-1990s). The economic and political collapse of the Soviet Union and the overwhelming relative success of market-driven systems provide another example of the importance of studying economic history.

Such swings in international power, status, and relative well-being are sobering reminders that the present is forever changing and slipping into the past. Are the changes that all of us will see and experience in our lifetimes inevitable, or can destinies be steered? How did we get where we are today?

It is unfortunate that history is often presented in forms that seem irrelevant to our everyday lives. Merely memorizing and recalling dates and places, generals and wars, presidents and legislative acts misdirects our attention to what happened to whom (and when) rather than the more useful focus on how and why events happened. One of the special virtues of the study of economic history is its focus on how and why. It provides us a deeper understanding of how we developed as a nation, how different segments of the population have fared, and what principal policies or compelling forces brought about differential progress (or regress) among regions and people. In short, the study of economic history enriches our intellectual development and provides an essential perspective on contemporary affairs. It also offers practical analytical guidance on matters of policy. The study of economic history is best suited for those who care about the next 1 to 1,000 years and who want to make the future better than the past.

This is no empty claim. Surely one of the primary reasons students major in economics or American history is to ultimately enhance the operation and performance of the American economy and to gain personally. Certainly instructors hope their students will be better-informed citizens and more productive businesspeople, politicians, and professionals. "If this is so," as Gavin Wright recently properly chastised his economic colleagues,

> *if the whole operation has something to do with improving the performance of the U.S. economy, then it is perfectly scandalous that the majority of economics students complete their studies with no knowledge whatsoever about how the United States became the leading economy in the world, as of the first half of the twentieth century. What sort of doctor would diagnose and prescribe without taking a medical history? (1986, 81)*

Too often, students are victims of economics textbooks that convey no information on the rise and development of the U.S. economy. Rather, textbooks convey the status quo of American preeminence as if it just happened, as if there were no puzzle to it, as if growth were more or less an automatic, year-by-year, self-sustained process. Authors of such textbooks need an eye-opening sabbatical in Greece, Russia, or Zimbabwe.

Economic history is a longitudinal study but not so long and slow as, say, geology, in which only imperceptible changes occur in one's lifetime. In contrast, the pace of modern economic change is fast and accelerating in many dimensions. Within living memory of most Americans, nations have risen from minor economic significance to world prominence (Hong Kong, China; Japan; the Republic of Korea) while others have fallen from first-position powers to stagnation (Russia in the 1990s and Argentina after 2002).Whole new systems of international economic trade and payments have been developed (the North American Free Trade Agreement, European Union). New institutions, regulations, and laws (1990 Clean Air Act, 1996 Welfare Reform Act) have swiftly emerged; these sometimes expand and sometimes constrain our range of economic choices.

The role of government in the economy is vastly different from what it was only 60 or 70 years ago; undoubtedly, it will be strikingly different 50 years from now. The study of economic history stresses the role of institutional change, how certain groups brought about economic change, and why. The study of history, then, is more than an activity to amuse us or sharpen our wits. History is a vast body of information essential to making public policy decisions. Indeed, history is the testing grounds for the economic theory and principles taught in economics classes, as well as for the theories taught in other subjects.

To simplify the vast range of economic theory, we rely primarily on five Economic Reasoning Propositions, as given in Economic Insight 1.1. These Economic Reasoning Propositions can be summarized for referral purposes throughout the text, as follows:

1. Choices matter.
2. Costs matter.
3. Incentives matter.
4. Institutions matter.
5. Evidence matters.

ECONOMIC INSIGHT 1.1

FIVE PROPOSITIONS FOR ECONOMIC REASONING

As John M. Keynes has said,

[E]conomics does not furnish a body of settled conclusions immediately applicable to policy. It is a method rather than a doctrine, an apparatus of the mind, a technique of thinking which helps its possessor to draw correct conclusions.

This "apparatus of the mind," or economic way of thinking, follows logically from *five basic propositions* of human nature and well-accepted truths.

1. *People choose, and individual choices are the source of social outcomes.* Scarcity compels us to compete in some form and it necessitates choice. People make choices based on their perceptions of the expected costs and benefits of alternatives. Choices involve risk; outcomes cannot be guaranteed because the consequences of choices lie in the future.
2. *Choices impose costs.* People incur costs when making decisions. Choices involve trade-offs among alternatives. People weigh marginal gains against marginal sacrifices. Ultimately, the cost of any decision is the next-best alternative that must be forgone. Reasoned decision making leads to an increase in any activity in which expected benefits exceed expected costs, and a decrease in any activity in which expected costs exceed expected benefits.
3. *Incentives matter.* Incentives are rewards that encourage people to act. Disincentives discourage actions. People respond to incentives in predictable ways; when incentives change, behavior changes in predictable ways.
4. *Institutions matter, and the "rules of the game" influence choices.* Laws, customs, moral principles, ideas, and cultural institutions influence individual choices and shape the economic system.
5. *Understanding based on knowledge and evidence imparts value to opinions.* The value of an opinion is determined by the knowledge and evidence on which it is based. Statements of opinion should initiate the quest for economic understanding, not end it.

Next time you are in a discussion or argument, recall Economic Reasoning Proposition 5. Evidence comes from history and tests the soundness of an opinion. An opinion is a good way to start a discussion, but it should not end one.

As Economic Reasoning Proposition 5 (evidence matters) emphasizes, not all opinions are equal, not when we want to understand how and why things happen. Two of the great advantages of economic history are its quantitative features and use of economic theory to give useful organization to historical facts. In combination, use of theory and evidence enhances our ability to test (refute or support) particular propositions and recommendations. This helps us choose among opinions that differ.

Policy Analysis for Better Choices

Consider, for instance, the run up of prices in early 2008, especially in gas and oil and food stuffs; additionally, prices on an average basket of goods purchased increased by nearly 4 percent in the United States and by 5.5 percent for the global economy. Such rates harken back to the 1970s. How could we assess a recommendation for mandatory wage and price controls as a means to combat inflation? Figure 1.7 traces a decade of inflation and reveals our experience with wage and price controls during the Nixon years. President Nixon's opinion at the time was that the controls would benefit the economy.

As shown in Figure 1.7, Nixon's controls (a choice made within his administration) were imposed in August 1971, when the inflation rate was 3.5 percent. The precontrol peak rate of inflation was 6 percent in early 1970 and was actually falling at the time controls were imposed. The rate of inflation continued to drift downward and remained around 3 percent throughout 1972; it started to rise in 1973, and by the time the controls were completely lifted in early 1974, the rate was 10 percent and rising.

On the face of it, controls did little to stop inflation. But what explains this dismal record? Were the controls themselves to blame, or were other factors responsible? Only a careful study of the period can identify the role of controls in the acceleration of inflation. A contrast between Nixon's price controls and those imposed during the Korean War (which were not followed by a price explosion after controls were lifted) suggests two important things to look at: monetary and fiscal policies.

Price controls, moreover, disrupted the smooth functioning of the economic system. For example, to circumvent the Nixon controls, the U.S. lumber industry regularly

FIGURE 1.7
Inflation and Nixon's Price Controls

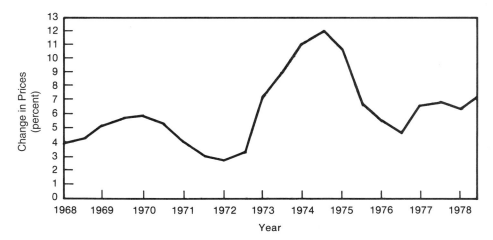

Source: *U.S. Department of Commerce 1978, 483.*

exported lumber to Canada and then reimported it for sale at higher prices. (Refer to Economic Reasoning Proposition 4: institutions [rules] matter.) As fertilizers and chemical pesticides became more profitable to sell abroad than at home, agricultural production suffered for want of these essential inputs. (Recall Economic Reasoning Proposition 3: incentives matter.) These and many other similar disruptions to production decreased the growth rate of goods and services and, therefore, the inflation was worse than it otherwise would have been. We cannot explore this issue in depth here. Our point is simply that to evaluate policy proposals, we must inevitably turn to the historical record.[1]

The use of wage and price controls during World War II provides another example adding to our understanding of their effectiveness. One important lesson this episode teaches is the need to supplement quantitative studies with historical research. An economist cannot naively assume that price statistics always tell the truth. During the war, controls were evaded in numerous ways that were only partly reflected in the official numbers despite valiant efforts by the Bureau of Labor Statistics. One form of evasion was quality deterioration. Fat was added to hamburger, candy bars were made smaller and had inferior ingredients substituted, coarser fabrics were used in making clothes, maintenance on rental properties was reduced, and so on. Sometimes whole lines of low-markup, low-quality merchandise were eliminated, forcing even poor consumers to trade up to high-markup, high-quality lines or go without any new items. And, of course, black markets developed, similar to current ones in controlled substances, such as marijuana, have done. The job of the economic historian is to assess the overall effect of these activities.[2]

CRITICAL SKILLS FOR PERSONAL DEVELOPMENT

Granted that economic history is important to the professional economist or economic policy maker, but is there any practical reason for studying it if a student has other long-term goals? The answer is yes. See Black, Sanders, and Taylor (2003), who show that undergrad economics majors do better financially than do business, math, or physics majors. The skills developed in studying economic history—critically analyzing the economic record, drawing conclusions from it based on economic theory, and writing up the results in clear English—are valuable skills in many lines of everyday work. The attorney who reviews banking statutes to determine the intent of the law, the investment banker who studies past stock market crashes to find clues on how to foretell a possible crash, and the owner-operator of a small business who thinks about what happened to other small businesses that were sold to larger firms are all taking on the role of economic historian. It will help them if they can do it well.[3]

Besides the importance of historical study for its vital role in deliberating private and public policy recommendations, knowledge of history has other merits. For one thing, history can be fun—especially as we grow older and try to recapture parts of our lives in nostalgic reminiscence. For another, history entertains as well as enriches our self-consciousness, and, often, because of television, the historical account is provided almost instantly (e.g., news coverage of the 2003 war in Iraq). A sense of history is really a sense

---

[1]An attempt to compare and contrast American experiences with wage and price controls is presented in Rockoff (1984).

[2]For one exploration of this issue, see Rockoff (1978).

[3]For further insights into the gains of studying economic history, see McCloskey (1976).

of participation in high drama—a sense of having a part in the great flow of events that links us with people of earlier times and with those yet to be born.

We conclude this section with the reminder that two of the principal tasks of economic historians are to examine a society's overall economic growth (or stagnation or decline) and to find out what happens to the welfare of groups within the society as economic change occurs. Our primary purpose in the following pages is to explain how the American economy grew and changed to fit into an evolving world economy. We study the past to better understand the causes of economic change today and to learn how standards of living can be affected by policies and other forces stemming from technological, demographical, and institutional change.[4]

The Long Road out of Poverty

Before diving into the chronology of American economic history emphasizing the forces of economic growth, it is essential to place the present-day circumstances of Americans and others in proper historical perspective. As Winston Churchill is credited with saying, "The longer back you look, the farther into the future you can see" (1956). However, we rarely see the distant past clearly, let alone the future.

Reflecting on some historical episode—perhaps from the Bible, or Shakespeare, or some Hollywood epic—is an interesting exercise. For most of us, the stories we recall are about great people, or great episodes, tales of love, war, religion, and other dramas of the human experience. Kings, heroes, or religious leaders in castles, palaces, or cathedrals—engaging armies in battles, or discovering inventions or new worlds—readily come to mind, often glorifying the past.[5]

To be sure, there were so-called golden ages, as in Ancient Greece and during the Roman Era, the Sung Dynasty (in China), and other periods and places in which small fractions of societies rose above levels of meager subsistence and lived in reasonable comfort, and still smaller fractions lived in splendor. But such periods of improvement were never sustained.[6] Taking the long view, and judging the lives of almost all of our distant ancestors, their reality was one of almost utter wretchedness. Except for the fortunate few, humans everywhere lived in abysmal squalor. To capture the magnitude of this deprivation and sheer length of the road out of poverty, consider this time capsule summary of human's history from Douglass C. North's 1993 Nobel address:

> Let us represent the human experience to date as a 24-hour clock in which the beginning consists of the time (apparently in Africa between 4 and 5 million years ago) when humans became separate from other primates. Then the beginning of so-called civilization occurs with the development of agriculture and permanent settlement in about 8000 B.C. in the Fertile Crescent—in the last 3 of 4 minutes of the clock [emphasis added]. For the other 23 hours and 56 or 57 minutes, humans remained hunters and gatherers, and while population grew, it did so at a very slow pace. Now if we make a new 24-hour clock for the time of civilization—the 10,000 years from development of agriculture to the present—the pace of change appears to be very slow for the first 12 hours.... Historical demographers speculate that the rate of population growth may have doubled as compared to the previous era but still was very slow. The pace of change accelerates in the past 5,000 years with the rise and then decline of economies

---

[4]For examples of institutional change, see Alston (1994) and Siniecki (1996).

[5]Such glorification has a long tradition: "The humour of blaming the present, and admiring the past, is strongly rooted in human nature, and has an influence even on persons endued with the profoundest judgment and most extensive learning" from Hume (1742/1987, 464).

[6]For example, see Churchill's (1956) description of life in Britain during and after the Roman era.

and civilization. Population may have grown from about 300 million at the time of Christ to about 800 million by 1750—a substantial acceleration as compared to earlier rates of growth. The last 250 years—just 35 minutes on our new 24-hour clock [emphasis added]—are the era of modern economic growth, accompanied by a population explosion that now puts world population in excess of 6.8 billion (2008). If we focus on the last 250 years, we see that growth was largely restricted to Western Europe and the overseas extensions of Britain for 200 of those 250 years. (North 1994, 364–365)

Evidence supporting North's observation that 1750 was a major turning point in the human existence is provided in Figure 1.8.

This graph of the world population over the past 11,000 years, along with noteworthy inventions, discoveries, and events, conveys its literal explosion in the mid-eighteenth century. Just a few decades before the United States won its independence from Britain, the geographic line bolts upward like a rocket, powering past 6 billion humans alive. The advances in food production from new technologies, commonly labeled the second Agricultural Revolution, and from the utilization of new resources (e.g., land in the New World) coincide with this population explosion. Also noteworthy is the intense acceleration in the pace of change in vital discoveries. Before 1600, centuries elapsed between them. Improvements in and the spread of the use of the plow, for example, first introduced in the Mesopotamian Valley around 4000 B.C., changed very little until around 1000 A.D. Contrast this with air travel. The Wright brothers were responsible for the first successful motor-driven flight, in 1903. In 1969, a mere 66 years later, Neil Armstrong became the first human to step foot on the moon. In short, the speed of life's changes.

FIGURE 1.8
World Population and Major Inventions and Advances in Knowledge

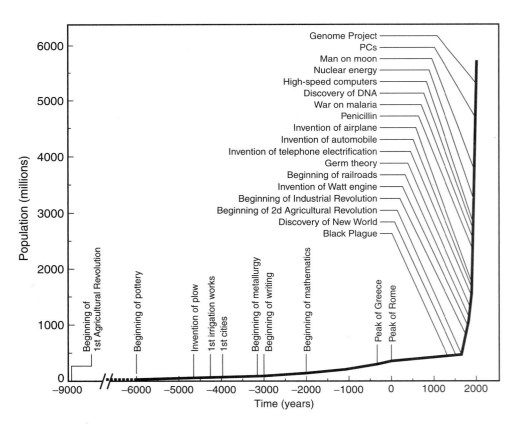

Source: *Fogel 1999.*

which many of us take for granted, has been accelerating, especially in the last two and a half centuries.

Before 1750, chronic hunger, malnutrition, disease, illness, and resulting early death were the norm for almost all people everywhere. Even wealthy people ate poorly; as Nobel Laureate Robert Fogel reports:

> *Even the English peerage, with all its wealth, had a diet during the sixteenth and seventeenth centuries that was deleterious to health. Although abundant in calories and proteins, aristocratic diets were deficient in some nutrients and included large quantities of toxic substances, especially alcoholic beverages and salt. (Fogel 1986)*

Exceedingly poor diets and chronic malnutrition were the norm because of the absence of choices, or the fact of scarcity. Food production seldom rose above basic life-sustaining levels. People were caught in a food trap: Meager yields severely limited energy for all kinds of pursuits, including production. Inadequate diets were accompanied by high rates of disease and low rates of resistance to them.

The maladies of malnourishment and widespread disease are revealed in evidence regarding height and weight. As late as 1750, the average height of adult males in England, the world's most economically advanced nation, was about 5 feet 5 inches, and shorter in France and Norway (Fogel 2004, 13). The average U.S. man today stands 5 inches taller. In the 1750s, typical weight was 130 pounds for an Englishman and 110 pounds for a Frenchman. Compare this with the weight of U.S. males today at about 190 pounds. It is startling to see the suits of armor in the Tower of London that were worn for ancient wars; they vividly remind us of how small even the supposedly largest people of long-ago really were.

The second Agricultural Revolution, beginning in the mid-eighteenth century, soon followed by the Industrial Revolution (first in England, then France, the United States and other Western countries), initiated and sustained the population explosion, lifting birth rates and lowering death rates. Table 1.3 summarizes research findings on life expectancy at birth for various nations, places, and times. From this and other empirical evidence we find that for the world as a whole, the gain in life expectancy at birth took thousands of years to rise from the low 20s to approximately 30 around 1750 (Preston 1995). Nations of Western Europe led the breakaway from early death and the way out of the malnutrition, poor diet, chronic disease, and low human energy of the past. Data in Table 1.3 for example, indicate that by 1800, life expectancy in France was just 30 years, and in the United Kingdom about 36. By comparison, India's rate was still under 25 years in the first decade of the twentieth century, and China's ranged between 25 and 35 two decades later. By 1950, life expectancy in the United Kingdom and France

TABLE 1.3 YEARS OF LIFE EXPECTANCY AT BIRTH

PLACE	MIDDLE AGES	SELECT YEARS	1950–1955	1975–1980	2002
France		30 (1800)	66	74	79
United Kingdom	20–30	36 (1799–1803)	69	73	78
India		25 (1901–1911)	39	53	64
China		25–35 (1929–1931)	41	65	71
Africa			38	48	51
World	20–30		46	60	67

Sources: *Lee and Feng 1999; Wrigley and Schofield 1981; World Resources Institute; and United Nations Development Program 1999.*

TABLE 1.4 REAL GROSS DOMESTIC PRODUCT PER CAPITA (1990 DOLLARS)

AREA	1000	1500	1700	1820	1900	1950	2003
Western Europe	$427	$772	$997	$1,202	$2,892	$5,513	$19,912
USA			527	1,257	4,091	9,561	29,037
India			550	533	599	619	2,160
China	450	600	600	600	545	439	4,609
Africa	425	414	421	420	601	893	1,549
World	450	566	615	667	1,262	2,114	6,477

Source: *Maddison 1995, 23, 24; 2007. http://www.ggdc.net/maddison/.*

was in the high 60s, while in India and China it was 39 and 41, respectively, comparable to rates in other low-income, developing countries.

In the period before 1750, children and infants, in particular, experienced high death rates globally. At least 20 to 25 percent of babies died before their first birthday. By 1800, infant mortality in France, the United States, and probably England had broken through the 20 percent level, comparable to rates that prevailed in China and India and other low-income, developing nations in 1950. For Europe, the United States, and other advanced economies, this rate is currently below 1 percent, but that rate is 4 percent in China, 6 percent in India, and 9 percent in Africa (Maddison 2007).

To provide another long-term perspective on the escape from poverty, Tables 1.4 and 1.5 provide evidence, albeit inexact, on real income per person, for various periods. Europe led the gradual rise of real income over a 1,000-year period. By 1700, it had risen

TABLE 1.5 GDP PER CAPITA FOR 56 COUNTRIES IN 1990 DOLLARS

	1820	1870	1900	1950	1973	2003
Western European Countries						
Austria	$1,218	$1,863	$2,882	$3,706	$11,235	$21,232
Belgium	1,319	2,692	3,731	5,462	12,170	21,205
Denmark	1,274	2,003	3,017	6,943	13,945	23,133
Finland	781	1,140	1,668	4,253	11,085	20,511
France	1,135	1,876	2,876	5,271	13,114	21,861
Germany	1,077	1,839	2,985	3,881	11,966	19,144
Italy	1,117	1,499	1,785	3,502	10,634	19,150
Netherlands	1,838	2,757	3,424	5,996	13,081	21,479
Norway	801	1,360	1,877	5,430	11,324	26,033
Sweden	1,198	1,662	2,561	6,739	13,494	21,555
Switzerland	1,090	2,102	3,833	9,064	18,204	22,242
United Kingdom	1,706	3,190	4,492	6,939	12,025	21,310
Western Offshoots						
Australia	518	3,273	4,013	7,412	12,878	23,287
New Zealand	400	3,100	4,298	8,456	12,424	17,564
Canada	904	1,695	2,911	7,291	13,838	23,236
United States	1,257	2,445	4,091	9,561	16,689	29,037

(continued)

TABLE 1.5 CONTINUED

	1820	1870	1900	1950	1973	2003
Selected Asian Countries						
China	600	530	545	439	838	4,609
India	533	533	599	619	853	2,160
Bangladesh				540	497	939
Burma	504	504		396	628	1,896
Pakistan				643	954	1,881
Selected African Countries						
Côte d'Ivoire				1,041	1,899	1,230
Egypt	475	649		910	1,294	3,034
Eritrea & Ethiopia				390	630	595
Ghana		439		1,122	1,397	1,360
Kenya				651	970	998
Nigeria				753	1,388	1,349
Tanzania				424	593	610
Zaire				570	819	212

Source: *Maddison 1995, 23, 24; 2007. http://www.ggdc.net/maddison/.*

above the lower level of per capita income it had shared with China (the most advanced empire/region around 1000 A.D.). While the rest of the world slept and remained mostly unchanged economically, Europe continued to advance. By the early 1800s, the United States had pushed ahead of Europe, and by the mid-1900s, U.S. citizens enjoyed incomes well above those of people residing in Europe and many multiples above those of people living elsewhere. One thousand years ago, even just 500 years ago, Europe and the rest of the world lived at levels of income similar to today's poorest nations: the Democratic Republic of Congo (formerly Zaire), Ethiopia, Tanzania, Myanmar (formerly Burma), and Bangladesh (see Table 1.5).

An Institutional Road Map to Plenty

From the preceding per capita income estimates, other evidence, and North's fascinating time capsule summary of human existence, the road out of poverty clearly is new. Few societies have traveled it: Western Europe, the United States, Canada, Australia, and New Zealand (Britain's offshoots), Japan, Hong Kong (China), Singapore, and a few others. What steps did Western Europe and Britain's offshoots take to lead humanity along the road to plenty? Why is China, the world's most populous country (more than 1.3 billion), now far ahead of India (second with 1.1 billion) when merely 50 years ago both nations were about equal in per capita income and more impoverished than most poor African nations today? Is there a road map leading to a life of plenty, a set of policies and institutional arrangements that nations can adopt to replicate the success of the United States, Europe, and other advanced economies? An honest answer to this question is disappointing. Economic development organizations such as the International Monetary Fund and the World Bank, as well as countless scholars who have committed their professional lives to the study of economic growth and development are fully aware of the limited theoretical structure yet pieced together.

The fact is well known that a nation's total output is fundamentally determined (and constrained) by its total inputs—its natural resources, labor force, stock of capital, entrepreneurial talents—and by the productivity of its inputs, measured as the output or service produced by a worker (or unit of capital, or acre of land, etc.). To measure standards of living, however, we rely on output (or income) per capita, rather than total output. For changes in income per capita, productivity advance dominates the story. For example, if a nation's population increases by 10 percent, and the labor force and other inputs also increase by 10 percent, output per capita remains essentially unchanged unless productivity increases. Most people (80 to 90 percent of the labor force) everywhere 250 years ago were engaged in agriculture, with much of it being subsistence, self-sufficient, noncommercial farming. Today that proportion is less than 5 percent in most advanced economies (3 percent in the United States). During this transition, people grew bigger, ate more, and worked less (and lived in more comfort). The sources of productivity advance that have raised output per farmer (and per acre) and allowed sons and daughters of farming people to move into other (commercial) employments and careers and into cities include advances or improvements in the following:

1. Technology (knowledge)
2. Specialization and division of labor
3. Economies of scale
4. Organization and resource allocation
5. Human capital (education and health)

These determinants are especially useful when analyzing a single nation's rate and sources of economic growth; however, they are less satisfactory for explaining the reasons that productivity advances and resource reallocations have been so apparent and successful in some parts of the world but not in others.

To explain why some nations grow faster than others, we need to examine the ways nations apply and adapt these sources of productivity change. To use this perspective, we need to assess the complex relationships of a society's rules, customs, and laws (the institutions) and its economic performance. For clarification, consider just one source of productivity change, technology. A new technology can introduce an entirely new product or service such as the airplane (and faster travel) or a better product such as a 2009 BMW automobile compared with a 1930 Model A Ford. A new technology can also lead to new materials, such as aluminum, that affect the cost of production. Aluminum provided a relatively light but strong material for construction of buildings and equipment.

In short, technological changes can be thought of as advances in knowledge that raise (improve) output or lower costs. They often encompass both invention and modifications of new discoveries, called *innovation*. Both require basic scientific research, trial and error, and then further study to adapt and modify the initial discoveries to put them to practical use. The inventor or company pursuing research bears substantial risk and cost, including the possibility of failure and no commercial gain. How are scientists, inventors, businesses, and others encouraged to pursue high-cost, high-risk research ventures? How are these ventures coordinated and moved along the discovery-adaptation-improvement path into commercially useful applications for our personal welfare?

This is how laws and rules—or institutions as we call them—help us better understand the causes of technological change. Institutions provide a society's incentive framework (Economic Reasoning Proposition 3: incentives matter), including the incentives to invent and innovate. Patent laws, first introduced in 1789 in the U.S. Constitution, provided property rights and exclusive ownership to inventors for their patented inventions. This path-breaking law spurred creative and inventive activity, albeit not immediately. Importantly, this exclusive ownership right includes the right to sell it, usually to people specialized in finding commercial uses of new inventions. The keys here are the laws and rules—the institutions that generate dynamic forces for progress in some societies and stifle creativity and enterprise in others. In advanced economies, laws provide positive incentives to spur enterprise and help forge markets using commercial legal and property right systems that allow new scientific breakthroughs (technologies) to realize their full commercial-social potential. Much more could be added to describe in detail the evolving and intricate connections among universities, other scientific research institutions, corporations, and various business entities (and lawyers and courts), all of which form interrelated markets of production and exchange, hastening technological advances (see Rosenberg and Birdzell, Jr. 1986).

Developing and sustaining institutional changes that realize gains for society as a whole are fundamental to the story of growth. The ideologies and rules of the game that form and enforce contracts (in exchange), protect and set limits on the use of property, and influence people's incentives in work, creativity, and exchange are vital areas of analysis. These are the key components paving the road out of poverty.

Examining the successful economies of Europe, North America, and Asia suggests a partial list of the institutional determinants that allow modern economies to flourish:

- *The rule of law, coupled with limited government and open political participation*
- *Rights to private property that are clearly defined and consistently enforced*
- *Open, competitive markets with the freedom of entry and exit, widespread access to capital and information, low transaction costs, mobile resource inputs, and reliable contract enforcement*
- *An atmosphere of individual freedom in which education and health are accessible and valued*

North admonishes that, "it is adaptive rather than allocative efficiency which is the key to long-term growth" (1994). The ability or inability to access, adapt, and apply new technologies and the other sources of productivity advances points directly to a society's institutions. Institutional change often comes slowly (customs, values, laws, and constitutions evolve), and established power centers sometimes deter and delay changes conducive to economic progress. How accepting is a society to risk and change when outcomes of actions create losers as well as winners (Schumpeter 1934)?

In the following pages, we retrace the history of the American economy, not simply by updating and recounting old facts and figures, but also by emphasizing the forging of institutions (customs, values, laws, and the Constitution). The end of the cold war and the growing body of knowledge about the importance of institutions to economic progress give solid reasons for recasting the historical record and bearing witness to the strengths and shortcomings of an emerging democracy operating within the discipline of markets constrained by laws and other institutions.

SELECTED REFERENCES AND SUGGESTED READINGS

Alston, Lee J. "Institutions and Markets in History: Lessons for Central and Eastern Europe." In *Economic Transformation in East and Central Europe: Legacies from the Past and Policies for the Future*, ed. David F. Good, 43–59. New York: Routledge, 1994.

Avery, Dennis. "The World's Rising Food Productivity." In *The State of Humanity*, ed. Julian L. Simon, 379–393. Boston: Basil Blackwell, 1995.

Black, Dan A., Seth Sanders, and Lowell Taylor. "The Economic Reward for Studying Economics." *Economic Inquiry* 41, no. 3 (July 2003): 365–377.

Blank, Rebecca M. "Trends in Poverty in the United States." In *The State of Humanity*, ed. Julian L. Simon, 231–240. Boston: Basil Blackwell, 1995.

Churchill, Winston S. *A History of the English Speaking People*. Vols. 1–4. New York: Dorset Press, 1956.

Cox, W. Michael, and Richard Alm. "By Our Own Bootstraps: Economic Opportunity and the Dynamics of Income Distribution." Dallas: Federal Reserve Bank of Dallas, 1995.

_____. "Time Well Spent: The Declining Real Cost of Living in America." Dallas: Federal Reserve Bank of Dallas, 1997.

Fogel, Robert W. *The Escape from Hunger and Premature Death, 1700–2100.* Cambridge: Cambridge University Press, 2004.

_____. "Nutrition and the Decline in Mortality since 1700: Some Preliminary Findings." In *Long-Term Factors in American Economic Growth*, eds. Stanley L. Engerman and Robert E. Gallman, 439-555. Chicago: University of Chicago Press (for the National Bureau of Economic Research), 1986.

_____. "Catching Up with the Economy." *The American Economic Review* 89 (1999): 1–21.

Historical Statistics of the United States, Series F1. Washington, D.C.: Government Printing Office.

Hume, David. "Of the Populousness of Ancient Nations." In *Essays, Moral, Political, and Literary,* ed. Eugene F. Miller (first published 1742). Indianapolis, Ind.: Liberty Fund, Inc, 1987.

Johnston, Louis D., and Samuel H. Williamson. "What Was the U.S. GDP Then?" Measuring Worth, 2008. http://www.measuringworth.org/datasets/usgdp.

Kennedy, Paul. *The Rise and Fall of the Great Powers.* New York: Random House, 1987.

Maddison, Angus. *Monitoring the World Economy 1820-1992.* Paris: Development Centre of the Organisation for Economic Co-Operation and Development (OECD), 1995. Updated 2007.

McCloskey, Donald N. "Does the Past Have Useful Economics?" *Journal of Economic Literature* 14 (1976): 434–461.

Lee, J., and W. Feng, "Malthusian Models and Chinese Realities: The Chinese Demographic System, 1700–2000." *Population and Development Review* 25 (1999): 33–65.

National Center for Health Statistics. *Vital Statistics of the United States.* Hyattsville, Md.: National Center for Health Statistics, Department of Health, Education, and Welfare, selected years.

North, Douglass C. "Economic Performance Through Time." *The American Economic Review* 84 (1994): 364–365.

Preston, S. H. "Human Mortality throughout History and Prehistory." In *The State of Humanity*, ed. Julian L. Simon, 30–36. Boston: Basil Blackwell, 1995.

Rockoff, Hugh. "Indirect Price Increases and Real Wages in World War II." *Explorations in Economic History* 15 (1978): 407–420.

_____. Drastic Measures: A History of Wage and Price Controls in the United States. New York: Cambridge University Press, 1984.

Rosenberg, Nathan, and L. E. Birdzell, Jr. *How the West Grew Rich.* New York: Basic Books, Inc., 1986.

Schumpeter, Joseph A. *The Theory of Economic Development.* Cambridge, Mass.: Harvard University Press, 1934.

Siniecki, Jan. "Impediments to Institutional Change in the Former Soviet System." In *Empirical Studies in Institutional Change*, eds. Lee J. Alston, Thrainn Eggertsson, and Douglass C. North, 35–59. New York: Cambridge University Press, 1996.

United Nations Development Program. *Human Development Report 1999.* New York: Oxford University Press, 1999.

U.S. Census Bureau. "The Changing Shape of the Nation's Income Distribution, 1747–2001." **http://www.census.gov**.

U.S. Census Bureau. "Mean Income Received by Each Fifth and Top 5 Percent of Families (All Races) 1966–2001." **http://www.census.gov/hhes/income/histinc/f03.html.**

U.S. Department of Commerce. *U.S. Life Tables, 1890, 1901, and 1901–1910.* Washington, D.C.: U.S. Government Printing Office, 1921.

U.S. Department of Commerce. *Statistical Abstract.* Washington, D.C.: U.S. Department of Commerce, 1978.

U.S. Department of Commerce, Bureau of Economic Analysis. "U.S. Real GDP Per Capita (Year 2000 Dollars." **http://www.measuringworth.org/graphs/graph.php?year_from=1900&year_to=2007&table=US&field=GDPCP&log.**

Wrigley, E. A., and R. S. Schofield. *The Population History of England, 1541–1871: A Reconstruction.* Cambridge, Mass.: Harvard University Press, 1981.

Wright, Gavin. "History and the Future of Economics." In *Economic History and the Modern Economists*, ed. William N. Parker. New York: Blackwell, 1986.

The Colonial Era: 1607–1776

ECONOMIC AND HISTORICAL PERSPECTIVES *1607–1776*

1. The American colonial period was a time when poverty was the norm throughout the world and wars among nations were frequent. The earliest English settlements in North America were costly in terms of great human suffering and capital losses.

2. The nations and city-states of Europe that emerged from the long, relatively stagnant period of feudalism rose to prominence in wealth and power relative to other leading empires in the Middle East and the Orient and quickly dominated those in the Americas.

3. Spain, Portugal, Holland, England, and France each built international empires, and England and France especially further advanced their relative economic and military strength while applying mercantilist policies. Great Britain ultimately dominated the colonization of North America and was the nation that launched the Industrial Revolution, beginning in the second half of the eighteenth century.

4. Innovations in trade and commerce, the spread of practical learning, new and expanding settlements that added land and adapted it to best uses, and falling risks in trade and frontier life raised living standards in the New World. By the time of the American Revolution, the material standards of living in the colonies were among the highest in the world and comparable to those in England. However, the distribution of wealth and human rights among the sexes, races, and free citizens was vastly unequal.

5. Although Americans sustained their long English cultural and institutional heritage, even after independence, their strong economic rise ultimately placed them in a position of rivalry with the mother country. The period from 1763 to 1776 was one of confrontation, growing distrust, and, ultimately, rebellion. Throughout the colonial era, the Native American population declined through disease, dislocation, and war.

CHAPTER 2

Founding the Colonies

From the perspective of European colonists in America, the New World was a distant part of a greatly expanded Europe, a western frontier, so to speak. The New World presented new opportunities and challenges for settlers, but their language and culture, laws and customs, and basic institutions were fundamentally derived and adapted from the other side of the Atlantic. In the colonies that would first break free of Europe and become the United States, these ties were primarily to Great Britain, for in the race for empire among the European nation-states, it was ultimately Britain that prevailed in North America. Britain dominated because of its institutions and its liberal policies of migration and colonization. Accordingly, our legacy as Americans is principally English—if not in blood, at least in language, law, and custom.

To understand this legacy it is important to have at least a brief background in the rise of western Europe, the voyages of discovery, and key developments of empire building in the New World. This will place in clearer perspective the demographic transition that led to British domination of North America relative to the native population and to other colonists from rival European nation-states.

EUROPEAN BACKGROUND TO THE VOYAGES OF DISCOVERY

More than 10 centuries passed from the fall of Rome to the voyages of discovery that led to the European expansion into the "New World." Toward the end of that period, the feudal age had passed, and by the late 1300s, many nation-states had emerged throughout Europe. In Russia, Sweden, England, France, and Spain, national rulers held the allegiance of large citizenries, and sizable groups of German-speaking peoples were ruled by their own kings and nobles.

The center of European wealth and commerce rested in the Mediterranean. That economic concentration was based primarily on long-distance trade among Asia, the Middle East (mainly Persia), and Europe. Because of their locational advantage and superior production and commercial skills and knowledge, the Italian city-states of Milan, Florence, Genoa, and Venice had dominated most of the Old World's long-distance trade for centuries.

European Roots and Expanding Empires

By the end of the fifteenth century, however, northern Europe had experienced substantial commercial growth, especially in the Hanse cities bordering the North Sea and the Baltic. Greater security of persons and property, established in law and enforced through courts and recognized political entities, spurred commerce and economic investments. Growing security in exchanges and transactions opened up whole new trades and routes of commerce, especially in the northern and western regions of Europe. This rise often augmented the old trades in the Mediterranean, but the new trades grew faster than the old.

Noteworthy as well was the rapid increase in Europe's population, which was recovering from the famines of the early fourteenth century and, most important, from the Black Death of 1347 and 1348. In England, for example, the population had fallen from 3.7 million in 1348 to less than 2.2 million in the 1370s; France probably lost 40 percent of its population; and losses elsewhere vary in estimates from 30 to 50 percent. During the fifteenth and sixteenth centuries, the demographic revival from that catastrophe added to the commercial growth and shifting concentrations of economic activity. The rapid growth of populations and growing commercialization of Europe's economies were significant building blocks in the strengthening of Europe's fledgling nation-states. Expansion in Europe and elsewhere—including, ultimately, America—was also part of the nation-building process.

For centuries, Catholic Europe had been pitted in war against the Muslim armies of Islam with one Crusade following another. By the fifteenth century, the age of Renaissance, Europe forged ahead in many political, commercial (and seagoing), and military areas. This century was a turning point, speeding the pace of an arms race among competing nations and empires. The year 1492 is as celebrated in Christian Spain for its capture of Granada from the Moors, ending seven centuries of Muslim rule there, as it is in the United States for Christopher Columbus's voyage to America.

PORTUGAL AND THE FIRST DISCOVERIES

It was somewhat of a historical accident that Christopher Columbus—a Genoese sailor in the employ of Spain—made the most vital and celebrated of the landfalls. Neither Spain nor the great Italian city-states were the world's leaders in long-distance exploration. Tiny, seafaring Portugal was the great Atlantic pioneer, and by the time Columbus embarked, Portugal could claim more than seven decades of ocean discoveries.

Having already driven the Muslims off Portuguese soil in the thirteenth century, Portugal initiated Europe's overseas expansion in 1415 by capturing Cuenta in North Africa. Under the vigorous and imaginative leadership of Prince Henry the Navigator, whose naval arsenal at Sagres was a fifteenth-century Cape Canaveral, Portugal—from 1415 to 1460—sent one expedition after another down the western coast of Africa. The island of Madeira was taken in 1419 and the Canary Islands shortly thereafter. The Portuguese colonized the Azores from 1439 to 1453 and populated most of these islands with slaves imported from Africa to grow sugar. These ventures had commercial as well as military aims. Europeans had first become familiar with sugar during the early Crusades, and the Mediterranean islands of Cypress, Crete, and Sicily had long been major sugar-producing areas. The commercial development and sugar plantations of the Iberian-owned islands reflected the fifteenth-century Western shift of economic strength and activity. In addition, the Portuguese and others sought to circumvent the Turk-Venetian collusion to control trade and prices over the eastern Mediterranean trade routes. Europeans hungered for Asian goods, especially spices. In an age before refrigeration, pepper, cloves, ginger, nutmeg, and cinnamon were used with almost unbelievable liberality by medieval cooks, whose fashion it was to conceal the taste of tainted meat and embellish the flavor of monotonous food. Accompanying the discoveries of new places and emergence of new trades was the accumulation of knowledge. New methods of rigging sails and designing ships (from one- to three-masted vessels) and other navigational advancements were learned by trial and error. These new technologies were vital in overcoming the difficult prevailing winds of the mighty Atlantic.

Commercial Splendor: Venice (rendered here by Caneletto) was almost as much an Eastern as a Western city, and for hundreds of years its commercial and naval power was a great sustaining force of Western civilization.

PORTUGAL AND SPAIN: EXPANDING EMPIRES

As shown in Map 2.1, the greatest of the sea explorations from Europe took place within a little less than thirty-five years. The historical scope of it is astonishing. In 1488, Bartholomeu Dias of Portugal rounded the Cape of Good Hope and would have reached India had his mutinous crew not forced him to return home. In September 1522, the *Vittoria*—the last of Ferdinand Magellan's fleet of five ships—put in at Seville; in a spectacular achievement, 18 Europeans had circumnavigated the globe. Between these two dates, two other voyages of no less importance were accomplished. Columbus, certain that no more than 2,500 miles separated the Canary Islands from Japan, persuaded the Spanish sovereigns Ferdinand and Isabella to finance his first Atlantic expedition. On October 12, 1492, his lookout sighted the little island of San Salvador in the Bahamas. Only a few years later, Vasco da Gama, sailing for the Portuguese, reached Calicut (Kozhikode) in India via the Cape of Good Hope, returning home in 1499. Following Dias's and Columbus's discoveries, Portugal and Spain, with the pope's blessing, agreed in the treaty of Tordezillas (1494) to grant Spain all lands more than 370 leagues (1,100 miles) west of the Cape Verde Islands (a measurement accident that ultimately established Portugal's claim to Brazil). Thus, the sea lanes opened, with Portugal dominant in the East (to East Africa, the Persian Gulf, the Indian Ocean, China, and beyond) and Spain supreme in the West.

By the early sixteenth century, the wealth and commerce of Europe had shifted to the Atlantic. The Mediterranean leaders did not decline absolutely; they were simply overtaken and passed by. In an international context, this was a critical first phase in the relative rise and eventual supremacy of key Western nation-states.

After Spain's conquest of Mexico by Hernando Cortez in 1521, American silver and gold flowed into Spain in ever-increasing quantities. When the Spanish king Philip II

MAP 2.1

Exploration

Spain and Portugal came first; then France, Holland, and England. All these nations explored vast amounts of territory in North America, giving rise to new economic opportunities, but England's exploration gave rise to the most extensive permanent settlements in the New World.

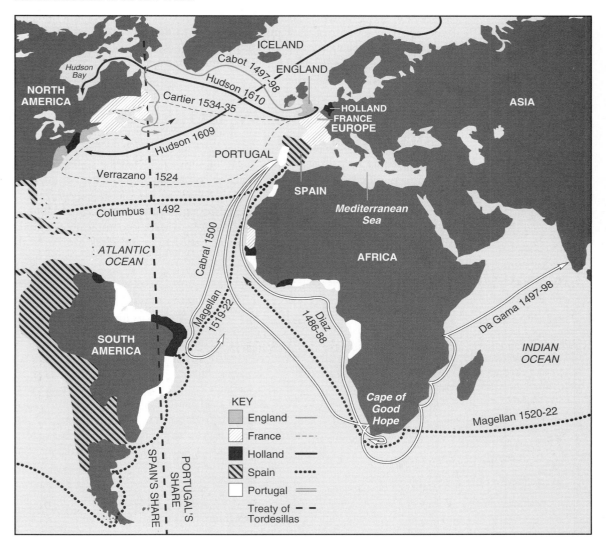

made good his claim to the throne of Portugal in 1580, Spanish prestige reached its zenith. By royal decree, Spain simply swallowed Portugal, and two great empires, strong in the Orient and unchallenged in the Americas, were now joined. When we reflect that no other country had as yet established a single permanent settlement in the New World, it seems astonishing that the decline of Spanish power was so imminent.

Although Spain was a colonizer, Spanish attempts to settle in the Americas lacked a solid foundation. Spain's main interests, for both the conquistadors and the rulers at home, were treasures from America's mines (especially silver) and Christianity for the conquered. To be sure, attempts were made to extend agriculture and to establish manufacturing operations in the New World, but the Spaniards remained a ruling caste, dominating the natives who did the work and holding them in political and economic bondage. Their religious, administrative, military, and legal institutions were strong and lasting, but the Spanish were more like occupying rulers than permanent settlers.

Meanwhile, the Protestant Reformation radically altered the nature of European nation building and warfare. When, toward the end of the sixteenth century, Spain became involved in war with the English and began to dissipate its energies in a futile attempt to bring the Low Countries (Holland and Belgium) under complete subjection, Spain lost the advantage of being the first nation to expand through explorations in America. Also harmful to Spain was the decline in gold and silver imports after 1600 as the mines of better-grade ores became exhausted.

THE LATECOMERS: HOLLAND, FRANCE, AND ENGLAND

Holland, France, and England, like Spain, all ultimately vied for supremacy in the New World (see Map 2.2). English and Dutch successes represented the commercial revolution sweeping across northern and western Europe in the 1600s. Amsterdam in particular rose to preeminence in shipping, finance, and trade by midcentury. But Holland's claim in North America was limited to New York (based economically on furs), and for the most part its interest lay more in the Far East than in the West. Moreover, the Dutch

MAP 2.2
European Colonies

European possessions and claims in America fluctuated. Shown here are those territories and the major cities toward the end of the seventeenth century.

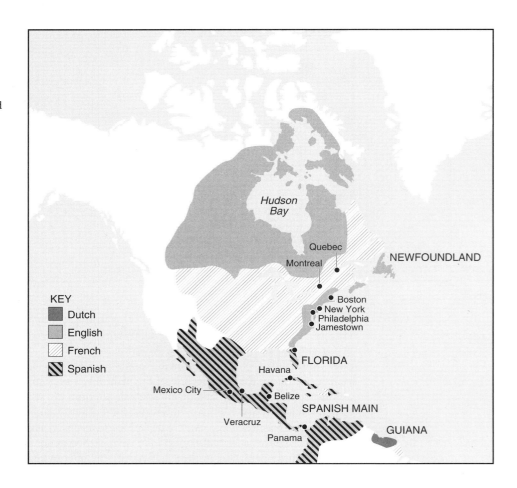

KEY
- Dutch
- English
- French
- Spanish

Hudson Bay

Quebec
Montreal
NEWFOUNDLAND
Boston
New York
Philadelphia
Jamestown
FLORIDA
Havana
Mexico City
Belize
SPANISH MAIN
Veracruz
Panama
GUIANA

placed too much emphasis on the establishment of trading posts and too little on colonization to firmly establish their overseas empire.

As it turned out, France and England became the chief competitors in the centuries-long race for supremacy. From 1608, when Samuel de Champlain established Quebec, France successfully undertook explorations in America westward to the Great Lakes area and had pushed southward down the Mississippi Valley to Louisiana by the end of the century. And in the Orient, France, although a latecomer, competed successfully with the English for a time after the establishment of the French East India Company in 1664. In less than a century, however, the English defeated the French in India, as they would one day do in America. The English triumphed in both India and America because they had established the most extensive permanent settlements. It is not without significance that at the beginning of the French and Indian War in 1756, some 60,000 French had settled in Canada and the Caribbean compared with 2 million in the English North American colonies.

For our purposes, the most important feature of the expansion of Europe was the steady and persistent growth of settlements in the British colonies of North America. Why were the English such successful colonizers?

To be sure, the English, like the French and the Dutch, coveted the colonial wealth of the Spanish and the Portuguese, and English sailors and traders acted for a time as if their struggling outposts in the wilderness of North America were merely temporary. They traded in Latin America, while privateers such as Francis Drake and Thomas Cavendish plundered Spanish galleons for their treasures as they sailed the Spanish Main. English venturers, probing the East for profitable outposts, gained successive footholds in India as the seventeenth century progressed. Yet, unlike the leaders of some western European countries, Englishmen such as Richard Hakluyt advocated permanent colonization and settlement in the New World, perceiving that true colonies eventually would become important markets for manufactured products from the mother country as well as sources of raw materials.

It was not enough, however, for merchants and heads of states to reap the advantages of the thriving colonies: Commoners had to be persuaded of the benefits of immigrating to the New World for themselves and their families. The greatest motivations to immigrate were the desires to own land—still the European symbol of status and economic security—and to strive for a higher standard of living than could be attained at home by any but the best-paid artisans. These economic motivations were often accompanied by a religious motivation. Given the exorbitant costs of the transatlantic voyage (more than an average person's yearly income), the problem remained how to pay for moving people to the New World.

FIRST BRITISH SETTLEMENTS IN NORTH AMERICA

Perilous Beginnings

Two half-brothers, Sir Humphrey Gilbert and Sir Walter Raleigh, were the first Englishmen to undertake serious ventures in America. Gilbert, one of the more earnest seekers of the Northwest Passage, went to Newfoundland in 1578 and again in 1583 but failed to colonize the territory either time and lost his life on the return voyage to England after the second attempt. Raleigh, in turn, was granted the right to settle in "Virginia" and to have control of the land within a radius of nearly 600 miles from any colony that he might successfully establish. Raleigh actually brought two groups of colonists to the new continent. The first landed on the island of Roanoke off the coast of what is now North Carolina and stayed less than a year; anything but enthusiastic about their new home, these first colonists returned to England with Sir Francis Drake in the summer of 1586. Undaunted, Raleigh solicited the financial aid of a group of wealthy Londoners and, in the following year, sent a second contingent of 150 people under the leadership of Governor John White. Raleigh had given explicit instructions that this colony was to be planted somewhere on the Chesapeake Bay, but Governor White disregarded the order and landed at Roanoke. White went back to England for supplies; when he returned after much delay in 1590, the settlers had vanished. Not a single member of the famed "lost colony" was ever found, not even a tooth.

After a long war between England and Spain from 1588 to 1603, England renewed attempts to colonize North America. In 1606, two charters were granted—one to a group of Londoners, the other to merchants of Plymouth and other western port towns. The London Company received the right to settle the southern part of the English territory in America; the Plymouth Company received jurisdiction over the northern part.

So two widely separated colonies were established in 1607: one at Sagadahoc, near the mouth of the Kennebec River, in Maine; the other in modern Virginia.[1] Those who survived the winter in the northern colony gave up and went home, and the colony established at Jamestown won the hard-earned honor of being the first permanent English settlement in America.

Hard earned indeed. When the London Company landed three tiny vessels at the mouth of the Chesapeake Bay in 1607, 105 people disembarked to found the Jamestown Colony. Easily distracted by futile "get-rich-quick" schemes, they actually sent shiploads of mica and yellow ore back to England in 1607 and 1608. Before the news reached their ears that their treasure was worthless "fool's gold," disease, starvation, and misadventure had taken a heavy toll: 67 of the original 105 Jamestown settlers died in the first year.

The few remaining survivors (one of whom was convicted of cannibalism) were joined in 1609 by 800 new arrivals, sent over by the reorganized and renamed Virginia Company. By the following spring, frontier hardships had cut the number of settlers from 838 to 60. That summer, those who remained were found fleeing downriver to return home to England by new settlers with fresh supplies, who encouraged them to reconsider. This was Virginia's "starving time," to use Charles Andrews's (1934) vivid label, and a time of environmental degradation (Earle 1975).

Inadequately supplied and untutored in the art of colonization, the earliest frontier pioneers routinely suffered and died. In 1623, a royal investigation of the Virginia experience was launched in the wake of an Indian attack that took the lives of 500 settlers. The investigation reported that of the 6,000 who had migrated to Virginia since 1607, 4,000 had died. The life expectancy of these hardy settlers upon arriving was two years.

The heavy human costs of first settlement were accompanied by substantial capital losses. Without exception, the earliest colonial ventures were unprofitable. Indeed, they were financial disasters. Neither the principal nor the interest on the Virginia Company's accumulated investment of more than £200,000 was ever repaid (approximately $22 million in today's values). The investments in New England were less disappointing, but overall, English capitalists were heavy losers in their quest to tame the frontier.

---

[1] At this time, the name Virginia referred to all the territory claimed by the English on the North American continent. Early Charters indicate that the area lay between the 34th and 45th parallels, roughly between the southern portion of the Carolinas and the northernmost boundary of New York.

EARLY REFORMS

The economic and institutional lessons of these first settlements, though negative, proved useful in later ventures, and colonization continued with only intermittent lapses throughout the seventeenth and eighteenth centuries. Because North America rendered no early discoveries of gold or silver mines or ancient populations prepared to exchange exotic wares, trading post establishments characteristic of the European outposts in South America and the Orient proved inadequate. North America's frontier demanded a more permanent form of settlement. For this to result without continuous company or Crown subsidization, the discovery of "cash crops" or other items that could be produced in the colonies and exchanged commercially was essential. Consequently, the production of tobacco and rice and the expansion of many other economic activities discussed in chapter 3 proved vital in giving deep roots and permanent features to British settlement in North America. In addition, substantial organizational changes were made to increase production efficiency. The joint-stock company arrangement, which facilitated the raising of capital and had served the British well in other areas of the world, faltered when forced to conform to the conditions in North America. Modeled after such great eastern trading companies as the East India Company, new companies—including the London Company, the New Plymouth Company, the Massachusetts Bay Company—must receive credit for establishing the first British settlements in the New World. But their success was limited merely to securing a colonial foothold. With the exceptions of the Hudson Bay Company (founded in 1670 and still in operation today) and the unique Georgia experiment in the late colonial period, the joint-stock company (with absentee direction from England) survived less than two decades in British North America.

The ordeals of the Jamestown experience forcefully accent the difficulties encountered and the adjustments required by the early settlers. The early Jamestown settlers were brought over by the company and given "planter shares," with profits to be divided five years later. Meanwhile, they were to live at the company's expense and work wholly for the company. In effect, the colony originally operated as a collective unit, in which both production methods and consumption were shared. But collectivity encouraged individuals to work less and resulted in much discontent. Unmarried men complained of working without recompense for other men's wives and children. Stronger, more able workers were embittered when they did not receive larger amounts of food and supplies than others who could or would not work as hard. In addition, common ownership stifled incentives to care for and improve lands and to make innovations in production.

In addition, absentee direction from England created problems, because successful production required local managerial direction. Futile insistent demands from England for quick profits sidetracked productive efforts and added to the settlers' discouragement.

Jamestown residents gained greater control over local matters in 1609 when small garden plots of land were given to individuals and again in 1612 when various institutional reforms were undertaken. To generate more flexible leadership and local autonomy in that hostile environment, a deputy governor was stationed in Virginia. Steadily thereafter, centralized direction from England became less and less frequent.

As private landholdings replaced common ownership, work incentives improved; the full return for individual effort became a reality, superseding output-sharing arrangements. In 1614, private landholdings of 3 acres were allowed. A second and more significant step toward private property came in 1618 with the establishment of the headright system. Under this system, any settler who paid his own way to Virginia was given 50 acres and another 50 acres for anyone else whose transportation he paid. In 1623—only 16 years after the first Jamestown settlers had arrived—all landholdings were converted to private ownership. The royal investigation of that year also ushered in the dissolutions of the corporate form of the colony. In 1625, Virginia was converted to a Crown colony.

Many of the difficulties experienced in early Jamestown were also felt elsewhere in the colonies. But the Puritan settlements of New England, first at Plymouth (the Plymouth Company in 1620) and then at Boston (the Massachusetts Bay Company in 1630), avoided some of the problems faced by the Jamestown settlers. For instance, because the Massachusetts Bay Company actually carried its own charter to the New World, it avoided costly direction and absentee control from England. Stronger social and cultural cohesion and more homogeneous religious beliefs may have contributed to a greater success of communal arrangements there, but as noted in Economic Insight 2.1, the Plymouth colonies also reverted to private holdings. Town corporations prolonged the use of common landholdings, but private landholdings steadily replaced land held in common. By 1650, privately owned family farms were predominant in New England.

Another noteworthy colony established by a joint-stock venture was New York, first settled by the Dutch West India Company (1620) but taken in a bloodless confrontation in 1664 by the British. Maryland and Pennsylvania were initiated through proprietary grants, respectively, to Lord Baltimore in 1634 and to William Penn in 1681. The former's desire was to create a haven for Roman Catholics, profitably if possible, and the latter's was the same for Quakers and other persecuted religious groups. Rhode Island's settlement was also religiously motivated because of Roger Williams's banishment from Puritan Massachusetts in 1644. These, the Carolinas, and the last mainland colony to be settled, Georgia (1733), benefited from the many hardships and lessons provided by the earlier settlements. Despite each colony's organizational form, the Crown assured all settlers except slaves the rights due English citizens. The British empire in North America extended from French Canada to Spanish Florida and through to the sugar plantation islands of the Caribbean.

Bringing in Settlers

The Atlantic Ocean posed a great barrier to settlement in North America. In the early seventeenth century, the cost of the Atlantic passage was £9 to £10 per person, more than an average English person's yearly income. Throughout most of the later colonial period, the peacetime costs of passage were £5 to £6. Consequently, in the seventeenth century, a majority of British and European newcomers could not and did not pay their own way to America. By 1775, however, more than half a million English, Scotch, Irish, German, and other Europeans had made the transatlantic voyage. More than 350,000 of them paid their way by borrowing and signing a unique IOU, an indenture contract.

The indenture contract was a device that enabled people to pay for their passage to America by selling their labor to someone in the New World for a specified future period of time. Often mistakenly referred to today in the press as quasi-slavery, indenture opportunities were really an expansion of individual freedoms. These contracts were written in a variety of forms, but law and custom made them similar. Generally speaking, prospective immigrants would sign articles of indenture binding them to a period of service that varied from three to seven years, although four years was probably the most common term. Typically, an indentured immigrant signed with a shipowner or a recruiting agent in England. As soon as the servant was delivered alive at an American port, the contract was sold to a planter or merchant. These contracts typically sold for £10 to £11 in the eighteenth century, nearly double the cost of passage. Indentured servants, thus bound, performed any work their "employers" demanded in exchange for room, board,

ECONOMIC INSIGHT 2.1

PROPERTY RIGHTS AND INCENTIVES

The problems of collective ownership and equally shared consumption have existed from ancient times to today. Colonial America and communist Russia attempted such organizational forms of production and distribution, and these attempts ultimately failed. Some have termed the problem the "tragedy of the commons" (common property), which leads to overuse and speedy exhaustion of a resource commonly owned.

You are encouraged at this point to briefly review the five Economic Reasoning Propositions in Economic Insight 1.1 on page 8. These propositions explain how collective ownership and shared (equal or fixed-share) consumption of the output create a "free rider" problem. To illustrate this, consider 10 workers who share ownership of the land and who collectively produce 100 bushels of corn, averaging 10 bushels each for consumption. Suppose that one worker begins to shirk and cuts his labor effort in half, reducing output by 5. The shirker's consumption, like the other workers', is now 9.5 (95 ÷ 10) bushels thanks to the shared arrangement. Though his effort has fallen 50 percent, his consumption falls only 5 percent. The shirker is free riding on the labors of others. The incentive for each worker (Economic Reasoning Proposition 3, incentives matter), in fact, is to free ride, and this lowers the total effort and total output.

Conversely, suppose that one worker considers working longer daily hours (12 instead of 10) to raise total output from 100 to 102. The gain in consumption to each individual is 0.2 bushels, a 2 percent consumption increase for each person based on a 20 percent effort increase by one. Would you make the extra effort?

With private property for each, there is no free riding. Any effort cut is borne in proportion by the individual's output decline. Any effort increase places all the rewards of the extra effort in the lap of the one working harder (or smarter). More generally, with private property for each, any change in output (DQ) from more effort goes to the person extending the extra effort. With common property, the gain is not DQ but DQ divided by the number in the group. The larger the group, the less the gain from working harder and the less the loss from working less—from the individual's perspective. In other words, the larger the group, the greater the incentive to free ride. These incentive effects (Economic Reasoning Proposition 3, incentives matter) are telling, as Governor Bradford noted in 1623 at the Plymouth Colony in New England:

So they begane to thinke how they might raise as much corne as they could, and obtaine a beter crope then they had done, that they might not still thus languish in miserie. At length, after much debate of things, the Governor...gave way that they should set corne every man for his owne perticuler, and in that regard trust to them selves; in all other things to goe on in the generall way as before. And so assigned to every family a parcell of land, according to the proportion of their number for that end, only for present use (but made no devission for inheritance), and ranged all boys & youth under some familie. This had very good success; for it made all hands very industrious, so as much more corne was planted then other waise would have bene by any means the Governor or any other could use, and saved him a great deall of trouble, and gave farr better contente. The women now wente willingly into the feild, and tooke their litle-ons with them to set corne, which before would aledg weaknes, and inabilitie; whom to have compelled would have bene thought great tiranie and oppression. The experience that was had in this commone course and condition, tried sundrie years, and that amongst godly and sober men, may well evince the vanitie of that conceite of Platos & other ancients, applauded by some of later times;— that the taking away of propertie, and bringing in communitie into a comone wealth, would make them happy and flourishing; as if they were wiser then God. For this comunitie (so farr as it was) was found to breed much confusion & discontent...For the yongmen that were most able and fitte for labour & service did repine that they should spend their time & strength to worke for other mens wives and children, with out any recompence. The strong, or man of parts, had no more in devission of victails & cloaths, then he that was weake and not able to doe a quarter the other could; this was thought injuestice...Let none objecte this is men's corruption, and nothing to the course it selfe. I answer, seeing all men have this corruption in them, God in his wisdome saw another course fiter for them. (Bradford 1962, 90-91)

Clearly, getting the institutional arrangements right (Economic Reasoning Proposition 4) is very important.

and certain "freedom dues" of money or land that were received at the end of the period of indenture. This system provided an active trade in human talent, and the indenture system should be viewed as an investment in migration as well as in job training (or apprenticeship).

The first indentured immigrants were sent to Jamestown and sold by the Virginia Company: about 100 children in their early teens in 1618, a like number of young women in 1619 for marital purposes, and a young group of workers in 1620. Soon thereafter, private agents scoured the ports, taverns, and countryside to sign on workers for indenture. The indentured servants were drawn from a wide spectrum of European society, from the ranks of farmers and unskilled workers, artisans, domestic servants, and others. Most came without specialized skills, but they came to America voluntarily because the likelihood of rising to the status of landowner was very low in Britain or on the Continent. They were also willing to sign indenture contracts because their opportunity cost, the next best use of their time, was typically very low—room and board and low wages as a rural English farm worker, a "servant in husbandry." Children born in English cottages usually went to work at the age of 10, moving among families and farms until good fortune (often inheritance or gifts) allowed them to marry. For many, a period of bondage for the trip to America seemed worth the risk.

Whether the life of a servant was hard or easy depended primarily on the temperament of the taskmaster; the courts usually protected indentured servants from extreme cruelty, but the law could be applied quickly to apprehend and return servants who ran away. The usual punishment for runaways was an extension of the contract period.

Studies by David Galenson (1977–1978), Robert Heavener (1978), and Farley Grubb (1994) reveal many of the intricacies of this market in bonded labor. For example, the indenture period for women was originally shorter than for men because of the greater scarcity of women in the colonies, but by the eighteenth century, the periods of service were comparable for both sexes. The indentured servants' work conditions and duration of service also depended on location. Generally, the less healthful living areas, such as the islands of the Caribbean, offered shorter contractual periods of work than did the mainland colonies. Skilled and literate workers also obtained shorter contracts, as a rule. Overall, it was a highly competitive labor market system steeped in rational conduct.

Immigrants from continental Europe, mainly Germans, usually came as redemptioners, immigrants brought over on credit provided by ship captains. Sometimes the redemptioners prepaid a portion of the costs of passage. After arrival, they were allowed a short period of time to repay the captain, either by borrowing from a relative or a friend or by self-contracting for their services. Because they usually arrived with no ready contacts and typically could not speak English, the contract period for full cost of passage was sometimes longer than for indentures, up to seven years. In addition, German immigrants usually came over in families, whereas English immigrants were typically single and more likely to enter into indentured servitude. The longer period of service for German redemptioners was in part a consequence of their preference to be highly selective in choosing their master-employers, a right indentured servants did not have. Migrating in family groups encouraged this preference, and most Germans settled in Pennsylvania. Alternatively, when the families had paid a portion of their passage costs before disembarking, their redemptioners' time could be much shorter.

As the decades passed, the percentage of European immigrants arriving as indentured servants or redemptioners declined. By the early nineteenth century, the market for indentures had largely disappeared, done in by economic forces rather than legislation. Alternative sources of financing, according to Farley Grubb, largely from residents in the United States paying for their relatives' passage from the Old World, were the main cause of this market's disappearance (Grubb 1994).

The drop in the costs of passage over this time and the rise of earnings of workers in Europe also contributed to this market's disappearance. In addition, slavery was a viable cost-cutting alternative labor source compared with indentured servants or free labor.

The counterpart to white servitude or free labor, namely slavery, did not become an important source of labor until after 1650, although slaves were imported in increasing numbers after 1620. By 1700, slavery had become a firmly established institution from Maryland southward (for an economic analysis of the transition from indentures to slavery in the Chesapeake, see Grubb and Stitt 1994). Slaveholding was not unknown in New England and the Middle colonies, but it was less popular there for several reasons. Rarely was a slave in the South unable to work due to the rigors of bad weather, whereas working outdoors in the North could be impossible for days at a time. Also important was the fact that tobacco, then rice, and finally indigo (a blue dye native to India) were the staple crops of the South. Because raising them required much unskilled labor that could be performed under limited supervision in work groups, these cash crops were especially suited to cultivation by slaves. Although not nearly as large as the huge sugar plantations of the Caribbean islands, large-scale farm units made slavery particularly profitable, and the size of farms became much larger in the South than in the Middle or New England colonies. The crops, especially rice and indigo, and the slave system itself generated economies of scale and fostered larger production units of team labor under supervision. Economies of scale occur when output expands relative to inputs (land, labor, and capital) as the production unit gets larger. As we have learned from Christopher Hanes, another advantage of slavery compared with free labor, and to a lesser extent indentured servants, was the reduction in turnover costs (Hanes 1966). Slave owners did not face the possibility of slaves leaving the fields at planting or harvest times or switching to other employers for higher pay. Finally, the mere momentum of the growth of slavery in the South was accompanied by moral and institutional adaptations to strengthen and sustain it. For example, the purchase of imported slaves in the South triggered the headright to land of 50 acres per slave purchased, reinforcing the growth in the size of farm units there. Also, primogeniture, a form of inheritance in which the land is transferred to the oldest son, prevailed in the southern colonies. In the Middle and New England colonies (except in Rhode Island and New York), multigeniture was typically followed, with an equal division of property among the sons. Over time, primogeniture perpetuated and built comparatively larger estates.

Unlike the indentured whites, African slaves were not protected in the colonies as British subjects. Terms of service were for life, and children of female slaves were born slaves, regardless of who fathered the children. Only by self-purchase or benevolence could a slave become free. In 1774, there were nearly half a million blacks in the colonies, 18,000 of whom were free.

As we have emphasized, those coming to America through their own resources received 50 acres of land from headright land grants in most colonies. However, not only land but also relatively high wages attracted workers to the colonies. Especially in the seaports, craftsmen and artisans of all sorts, merchants, seamen, and even scholars gave vibrance to the commercial life on western Atlantic shores. Finally, prisoners, too—perhaps as many as 30,000—avoided death sentences or indefinite imprisonment in England by voluntarily transporting themselves to the New World. After 1718, it was customary for convicts to serve seven years of indenture for minor crimes and 14 years for major ones.

DEMOGRAPHIC CHANGE

Underpopulation Despite High Rates of Population Growth

One major fact of American economic life—underpopulation and labor scarcity—persisted throughout the entire colonial period. Another extremely important aspect of British colonization and a crucial factor in securing and maintaining Britain's hold on the North American frontier was the extremely high rate of population growth in the colonies. What generated the characteristic of apparent underpopulation was the vast amount of available land, which "thinned" the population spatially and established high population densities in only a few major port towns. This occurred despite the exceptionally high rate of growth, which was so high—the population approximately doubled every 25 years—that Thomas Malthus worrisomely referred to it as "a rapidity of increase, probably without parallel in history" (Potter 1960). Malthus and others pointed to the American colonies as a prime example of virtually unchecked population growth. Wouldn't such a rate of increase, which was twice the population growth rate in Europe, ultimately lead to famine, pestilence, and doom?

Such European polemics were far from the minds of the colonists. Indeed, Benjamin Franklin wrote an essay in 1751 extolling the virtues of rapid population increases in the colonies. Overpopulation never occurred in the colonies, despite the various methods that were used to encourage or force (in the case of African captives) population relocation to the New World. Nor did the high natural rate of population increase create population pressures in the colonies; population growth was generally viewed as a sign of progress and a means of reducing the uncertainties, risks, and hazards of a sparsely populated frontier region.

Population Growth in British North America

The population growth from both migration and natural causes is illustrated by region and race in Table 2.1. Note the remarkable similarity in the timing, rise, and levels of the total populations in New England and the Upper South. The latecomers—the Middle colonies and the Lower South—displayed slightly higher growth rates, which allowed them to catch up somewhat. The rate of population expansion was quite steady for the colonies as a whole, slightly over 3 percent per year. From 300 settlers in Virginia in 1610, 1.7 million people of European origin and half a million of African origin resided in the 13 colonies by 1770.

The period of greatest absolute migration occurred in the eighteenth century—particularly after 1720, when between 100,000 and 125,000 Scotch-Irish and about 100,000 Germans arrived in North America. Most immigrants in the seventeenth century were British, and another strong surge of British migration occurred between 1768 and 1775. Perhaps as many as 300,000 white immigrants came to the New World between 1700 and 1775, and a somewhat smaller number of blacks came as well. Plenty of highly fertile land and a favorable climate attracted Europeans and provided motives for securing African slaves. Nevertheless, migration was the dominant source of population growth in only the first decades of settlement in each region.

In New England, immigration virtually halted in the late 1640s, and natural causes became the source of population growth after 1650. For areas settled later, such as Pennsylvania, the forces of migration remained dominant later, but natural forces swiftly took over even there. Even the enslaved black population grew swiftly and predominantly

TABLE 2.1 POPULATION BY REGION FOR THE 13 NORTH AMERICAN COLONIES (IN THOUSANDS)

YEAR	NEW ENGLAND			MIDDLE COLONIES		
	WHITES	BLACKS	TOTAL	WHITES	BLACKS	TOTAL
1620	0.1	0.0	0.1	0.0	0.0	0.0
1640	13.5	0.2	13.7	1.7	0.2	1.9
1660	32.6	0.6	33.2	4.8	0.6	5.4
1680	68.0	0.5	68.5	13.4	1.5	14.9
1700	90.7	1.7	92.4	49.9	3.7	53.5
1710	112.5	2.6	115.1	63.4	6.2	69.6
1720	166.9	4.0	170.9	92.3	10.8	103.1
1730	211.2	6.1	217.3	135.3	11.7	147.0
1740	281.2	8.5	289.7	204.1	16.5	220.5
1750	349.0	11.0	360.0	275.7	20.7	296.4
1760	436.9	12.7	449.6	398.9	29.0	427.9
1770	565.7	15.4	581.1	521.0	34.9	555.9
1780	698.4	14.4	712.8	680.5	42.4	722.9

YEAR	UPPER SOUTH			LOWER SOUTH			TOTAL OF 13 COLONIES		
	WHITES	BLACKS	TOTAL	WHITES	BLACKS	TOTAL	WHITES	BLACKS	TOTAL
1620	0.9	0.0	0.9	0.0	0.0	0.0	1.0	0.0	1.0
1640	8.0	0.1	8.1	0.0	0.0	0.0	23.2	0.5	23.7
1660	24.0	0.9	24.9	1.0	0.0	1.0	62.4	2.1	64.6
1680	55.6	4.3	59.9	6.2	0.4	6.6	143.2	6.7	149.9
1700	85.2	12.9	98.1	13.6	2.9	16.4	239.4	21.1	260.4
1710	101.3	22.4	123.7	18.8	6.6	25.4	296.0	37.8	333.8
1720	128.0	30.6	158.6	24.8	14.8	39.6	412.0	60.2	472.2
1730	171.4	53.2	224.6	34.0	26.0	60.0	551.9	97.0	648.9
1740	212.5	84.0	296.5	57.8	50.2	108.0	755.6	159.2	914.7
1750	227.2	150.6	377.8	82.4	59.8	142.2	934.3	242.1	1,176.5
1760	312.4	189.6	502.0	119.6	94.5	214.1	1,267.8	325.8	1,593.6
1770	398.2	251.4	649.6	189.4	155.4	344.8	1,674.3	457.1	2,131.4
1780	482.4	303.6	786.0	297.4	208.8	506.2	2,158.7	569.2	2,727.9

Source: Compiled from Tables 5.1, 9.4, 6.4, and 8.1 on the respective regions in McCusker and Menard 1985, 103, 203, 136, and 172.

from natural sources after 1700. On the eve of the Revolution, only one white in 10 was foreign born; the figure for blacks was between two and three in 10.

Commercial successes, favorable economic circumstances, and the high value of labor powered a high rate of reproduction in the colonies. White birthrates in North America per 1,000 women ranged between 45 and 50 per year, compared with near 30 in Europe or 12 in the United States today. The colonial population was exceptionally young. By the 1770s, 57 percent of the population was under the age of 21. Moreover, a higher percentage of the colonial population was of childbearing age. Typically, colonial women tended to marry rather early, between the ages of 20 and 23, which was a couple of years younger than the average marriage age of European women. The cheapness of land encouraged early marriage in the colonies, and it was generally easier for colonists than for Europeans to strike out on their own, acquire land, and set up a household. Child-bearing was a major cause of death for women, and many men remarried to sustain their families. The average European married man produced four or five children, but earlier marriages and higher proportions of mothers in their childbearing years resulted in an average colonial family of about seven to eight children. Greater emphasis on rural economic activity also encouraged higher birthrates in the colonies. Children were more costly to raise in urban areas, and their labor contribution tended to be less there.

Also of great significance was the fact that once the first few years of starvation had passed, the colonies experienced rather low mortality rates. The annual death rate in Europe was about 40 per 1,000 people; in the colonies, it was 20 to 25 per 1,000.

The lower age structure of the colonial population accounts in part for this, but the exceptionally low rate of child mortality was an even more impressive statistic. On average, white mothers in the colonies were better fed and housed than mothers in Europe. Consequently, colonial babies were healthier. The harsh winters of North America and the inferior medical technology of the frontier were more than offset by plentiful food supplies, fuel, and housing. And because the population was predominantly rural, epidemics were rare in the colonies. Once past infancy, white colonial males typically lived to be 60 or older. Because of the hazards of childbirth, however, the comparable age for early colonial women was normally slightly over 40.[2]

The Racial Profile

Six percent of all slaves imported into the New World came to areas that became the United States. As shown in Figure 2.1, migration was the initiating force of population growth of blacks. By the eighteenth century, however, natural forces dominated the growth of the black population. By midcentury, the birthrate of blacks, like that of

FIGURE 2.1

Foreign-Born Blacks as a Percentage of the U.S. Black Population, 1620–1860

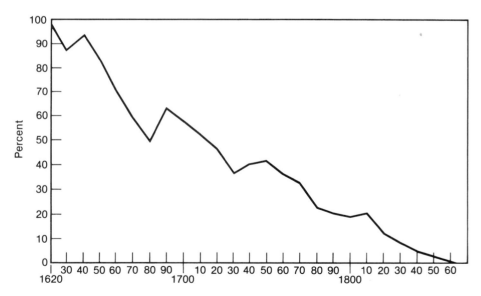

Source: *From TIME ON THE CROSS: The Economics of American Negro Slavery by Robert William Fogel and Stanley L. Engerman. Copyright © 1974 by Robert William Fogel and Stanley L. Engerman. Used by permission of W.W. Norton & Company, Inc.*

[2]Although perhaps atypical, evidence presented by Graven (1966) shows women also living into their sixties in that area.

whites, was near the biological maximum. Death rates were also similar to those of whites in North America. Because the natural rate of increase was comparable for both races—which resulted in a doubling of the population nearly every 20 to 25 years—and because the actual number of imported slaves practically equaled the number of white immigrants, the proportion of the total population that was black increased significantly after 1700. As shown in Table 2.1, in 1680, only about 3 percent of the total population was black. A century later, this proportion had increased to about 20 percent, and the black population was near half a million. Of course, regional differences were great, and more than 90 percent of the slaves resided in southern regions. As Figure 2.2 illustrates, however, relatively small proportions of the total population of the mainland colonies were composed of blacks, compared with the Caribbean islands. In New England, the proportion of blacks was in the neighborhood of 2 percent; in the Middle colonies, 5 percent. In Maryland in the late colonial years, 32 percent of the total population comprised blacks; in Virginia, 42 percent. The more limited commercial development in North Carolina, resulting from inadequate harbors, generated a black population proportion of only 35 percent. In contrast, South Carolina contained the largest concentration of blacks—60 percent. This especially high proportion in South Carolina resulted from the special advantages of slave labor and economies of scale in rice and indigo production. Consequently, the social profile of South Carolina suggested by its high concentration of enslaved blacks was similar to the profiles of the British and French West Indies sugar islands. Although Virginia's population profile did approach this proportion, South Carolina's profile of a majority of slaves controlled by a minority of plantation owners was unique among the mainland colonies. In contrast to their Caribbean counterparts, blacks typically remained a minority race on the mainland of North America.

Finally, the pattern of change for the Native American population was in sharp contrast to that of whites and blacks. The actual number of people in North America in 1491 is unknown, with guesses ranging tenfold from 1.8 million to 18 million.[3] At the

FIGURE 2.2

Blacks as a Percentage of the Total Population, 1650–1780

The population profile was much different on the North American continent from that on the islands of the Caribbean. Only in South Carolina did the black population outnumber the resident white population.

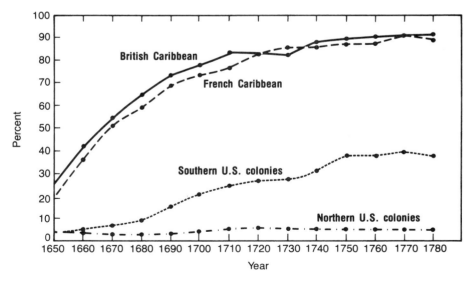

Source: *From TIME ON THE CROSS: The Economics of American Negro Slavery by Robert William Fogel and Stanley L. Engerman. Copyright © 1974 by Robert William Fogel and Stanley L. Engerman. Used by permission of W.W. Norton & Company, Inc.*

[3]For the most recent review of estimates of the Native populations in the Americas and their livelihoods, see Mann (2002).

time Jamestown was founded, it was likely that more than 300,000 native American Indians lived within 150 miles of the Atlantic seaboard. By the mid–eighteenth century, the impact of battle, and especially the devastation of communicable diseases such as smallpox and measles, against which the natives had developed no immunity, reduced their population to between 50,000 and 100,000. This depopulation was unique among mainland North Americans, whatever their origin. This topic is further discussed in Economic Insight 2.2.

ECONOMIC INSIGHT 2.2

EARLY EUROPEAN—AMERICAN ECONOMIC RELATIONS AND DEMOGRAPHIC CHANGES

The population data on native Americans in North America in early periods are notoriously speculative (see Mann 2002). Table 2.2 gives the best current estimates available of the total population of Native Americans in North America at the time of arrival of Europeans and of the population sizes of several northeastern regions and tribes. In the northern regions, the French formed political and economic alliances with the Huron and Algonquian tribes early in the seventeenth century. The early Dutch, mostly fur traders like the French, also linked themselves to the native Americans, soon after arriving in 1620. After the British took over New York in 1644, they also took over the economic and political relations with the Iroquois Confederacy (the "Six Nations" of the Cayuga, Mohawk, Oneida, Onondaga, Seneca, plus the Iroquois) that the Dutch traders had formed. Similar relationships were formed in the southeast:

French-Choctaw, and British-Chickasaw. Beaver furs were the key economic element of these relationships in the Northeast, deer skins in the southeast. Indians specialized in hunting and skinning, and the Europeans exchanged wholesale trading cloth, gunpowder, and other manufactured items.

These early relationships were fundamental to the first settlements, and the long-standing hostilities between the Huron and Mohawk tribes added force to the longtime rivalry between the French and the British (see Roback 1992, 14–16).

The economic gains from these relationships were soon overwhelmed by the effects of disease (epidemics against which the native Americans had no natural resistance), violence, and dislocation. Figure 2.3 shows very approximately the timings of the demise of the Native American population relative to the rise of Europeans and Africans. In the Southeastern regions the nonindigenous population became the majority before 1715 (see Wood 1989). In all likelihood, the crossover to a nonindigenous majority had occurred by a similar early date in the northeastern British colonies.

TABLE 2.2 POPULATION ESTIMATES FOR VARIOUS REGIONS OR TRIBES AT TIME OF ARRIVAL OF FIRST EUROPEANS IN NORTH AMERICA

REGION OR TRIBE (NOT MUTUALLY EXCLUSIVE)	POPULATION ESTIMATE	SOURCE(S)
North America (excluding present-day Mexico)	3,790,000	Denevan (1992), Table 1
New England	72,000–144,000	Cook (1976b), Snow (1980), Salisbury (1996)
Mohawk	13,700–17,000	Snow (1980)
Algonquian	14,300–22,000	Feest (1973)
Arikara	30,000	Holder (1970)
Iroquoi	20,000–110,000	Trigger (1976), Englebrecht (1987), Clermont (1980)
Huron	23,000–30,000	Trigger (1985), Dickinson (1980)
Micmac	12,000–50,000	Snow (1980), Miller (1976, 1982)

Source: *Summarized from Denevan 1992, xix–xx and xxviii; Table 1 as given in Barrington 1999, 2.*

ECONOMIC INSIGHT 2.2

EARLY EUROPEAN–AMERICAN ECONOMIC RELATIONS AND DEMOGRAPHIC CHANGES, Continued

FIGURE 2.3
Indigenous and Nonindigenous Composition of Population, United States and Canada

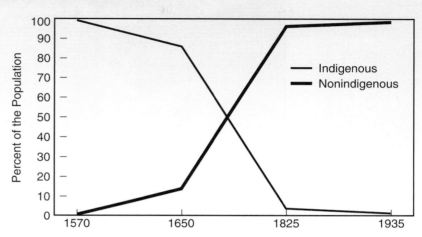

Source: *Population data from Rosenblot 1954, 1:21, 37, 59, and 88, as given in Barrington 1999, 2.*

Imperial European Rivalries in North America

The rivalry of European empires persisted for a long time, and the growth in population and the colonization of new territory were not restricted to the eastern coast of North America (see Map 2.3). During the sixteenth century, Spain had occupied northern Mexico and Florida, and while English settlement was taking place, the Spanish were moving northward into Texas, southern Arizona, and southern California. As we have already mentioned, in the seventeenth century, France established bases in the Lesser Antilles and in Canada; from Canada, French explorers and traders pushed into the Mississippi Valley and on to the Gulf of Mexico. The three rival states were bound to clash in America, even if they had not been enemies in other parts of the world. To the general historian we must leave the descriptions of these bitter rivalries and of the resulting complex, if small-scale, wars. Following intermittent conflict between the French and the English in the Northeast and along most of the western frontier, the French and Indian War resulted in the temporary downfall of the French in North America. By the treaty of Paris in 1763, only Spain and England were left in possession of the North American continent. Spain took all the territory west of the Mississippi, and England secured everything to the east, with the exception of certain fishing rights and small islands retained by the French off Newfoundland. According to this agreement, England acquired all of Florida, thereby settling perennial disputes with Spain that had long disturbed the colonies of South Carolina and Georgia. It is difficult to remember that Spain, not France, harassed the pioneers who moved out of the original 13 colonies and into the southern interior. Not until 1800 did France again own the Territory of Louisiana and its vital port of New Orleans, and that control did not last long.

MAP 2.3

Territorial Claims

Territorial possessions and claims in North and Central America toward the end of the eighteenth century.

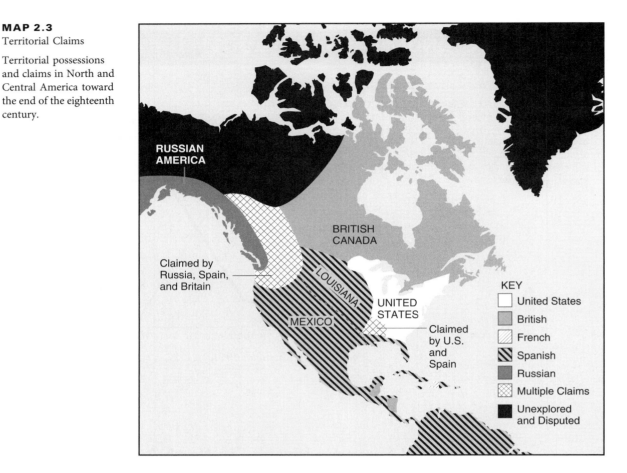

Two institutional arrangements particularly favored British dominance in North America. First was the open labor market of indentured servitude, used by the British but not by the Spanish or French, to facilitate migration. Of the 500,000 British immigrants (1610–1775), 350,000 came as indentured servants. Second was the establishment of permanent British settlements, which fostered privately owned farms and families and, ultimately, towns. Thanks largely to these two market-based, government-supported institutions, British settlers in North America outnumbered the French nearly 20 to 1 by 1750. High levels of English migration, encouraged by wide-ranging economic opportunities, forged the beginnings of an American identity cloaked in English language, customs, and common law (rather than the French civil law).[4]

---

[4]For further analysis and comparisons of the differential paths of development among regions in the New World, see Engerman and Sokoloff (1996).

SELECTED REFERENCES AND SUGGESTED READINGS

Andrews, Charles M. *The Colonial Period of American History*. New Haven, Conn.: Yale University Press, 1934.

Barrington, Linda, ed. *The Other Side of the Frontier*. Boulder, Co.: Westview, 1999.

Bradford, William. *Of Plymouth Plantation*. New York: Capricorn Books, 1962.

Denevan, William, ed. *The Native Population of the Americans in 1492,* 2nd ed. Madison: University of Wisconsin Press, 1992.

Earle, Carville. *The Evolution of a Tidewater Settlement System: All Hallow's Parish, 1650–1783*. Chicago: University of Chicago Press, 1975.

Engerman, Stanley L., and Kenneth L. Sokoloff. "Factor Endowments, Institutions, and Differential Paths of Growth Among New World Economics: A View From Economic Historians of the United States." In *How Did Latin America Fall Behind?* ed. Stephen Haber. Palo Alto, Calif.: Stanford University Press, 1996.

Fogel, Robert, and Stanley Engerman. Chapter 1 in *Time on the Cross: The Economics of American Negro Slavery*. Boston: Little, Brown, 1974.

Franklin, Benjamin. "Observations Concerning the Increase of Mankind." Philadelphia, 1751. In *The Papers of Ben Franklin*, ed. Leonard Laberee. New Haven, Conn.: Yale University Press, 1961.

Galenson, David W. "Immigration and the Colonial Labor System: An Analysis of the Length of Indenture." *Explorations in Economic History* 14 (1977): 361–377.

_____. "British Servants and the Colonial Indenture System in the Eighteenth Century." *Journal of Southern History* 44 (1978): 41–66.

_____. "The Market Evaluation of Human Capital: The Case of Indentured Servitude." *Journal of Political Economy* 89 (1981): 446–467.

_____. *White Servitude in Colonial America*. Cambridge: Cambridge University Press, 1981.

_____. "The Rise and Fall of Indentured Servitude in the Americas: An Economic Analysis." *Journal of Economic History* 44 (1984): 1–26.

_____. "The Settlement and Growth of the Colonies: Population, Labor, and Economic Development." In *The Cambridge Economic History of the United States*, Vol. I, eds. Stanley L. Engerman and Robert E. Gallman, 135–207. Cambridge: Cambridge University Press, 1996.

Graven, Philip. "Family Structure in Seventeenth Century Andover, Massachusetts." *William and Mary Quarterly* (April 1966): 234–256.

Grubb, Farley. "Colonial Labor Markets and the Length of Indenture: Further Evidence." *Explorations in Economic History* 24 (1987): 101–106.

_____. "The End of European Immigrant Servitude in the United States: An Economic Analysis of Market Collapse 1772–1835." *Journal of Economic History* 54 (1994): 794–824.

Grubb, Farley, and Tony Stitt. "The Liverpool Emigrant Servant Trade and the Transition to Slave Labor in the Chesapeake, 1697–1707: Market Adjustments to War." *Explorations in Economic History* 31 (1994): 376–405.

Hanes, Christopher. "Turnover Cost and the Distribution of Slave Labor in Anglo-America." *Journal of Economic History* 56 (1966): 307–329.

Heavener, Robert. "Indentured Servitude: The Philadelphia Market, 1771–1773." *Journal of Economic History* 38 (1978): 701–713.

Mann, Charles. "1491." *The Atlantic Monthly* 289, no. 3 (March 2002): 41–53.

McCusker, John J., and Russell Menard. *The Economy of British America 1607–1789*. Chapel Hill: University of North Carolina Press, 1985.

Potter, Jim. "The Growth of Population in America, 1700-1860." In *Population in History: Essays in Historical Demography* eds. D. V. Glass and B. E. C. Eaversley. Chicago: Aldine, 1960.

Roback, Jennifer. "Exchange Sovereignty, and Indian-Anglo Relations." In *Property Rights and Indian Economies: The Political Economy Forum*, ed. Terry Anderson. Lanham, Md.: Rowman & Littlefield, 1992.

Rosenblot, Angel. *La Poblacion Indigena yel Mestizaje en America*. Buenos Aires, Argentina: Nova, 1954.

Salisbury, Neal. "The History of Native Americans from Before the Arrival of the Europeans and Africans Until the American Civil War." In *The Cambridge Economic History of the United States,* Vol. I, eds. Stanley L. Engerman and Robert E. Gallman, 1–52. Cambridge: Cambridge University Press, 1996.

Wood, Peter. "The Changing Population of the Colonial South: An Overview by Race and Region, 1685–1760." In *Powhatan's Mantle: Indians in the Colonial Southeast,* eds. Peter Wood, Gregory A. Waselkov, and Tomas M. Hartley. Lincoln: University of Nebraska Press, 1989.

CHAPTER 3

Colonial Economic Activities

CHAPTER THEME

After the discovery of "cash crops" such as tobacco, market production and trade grew rapidly and gave permanent features to the English settlements in North America. In this chapter, we present the economic activities of the colonists in terms of their regional and occupational specializations.

These specializations were fundamentally determined by comparative advantages in production, and the advantages varied significantly among the colonies. Overwhelmingly, however, the abundance of land and natural resources determined the path of development and particular economic activities in the various colonies. The regional specializations based on land (and natural resource) abundance relative to capital and labor contrasted sharply with the much higher labor-to-land and capital-to-land ratios in Britain and Europe. The colonial specializations that emerged, for market trade in particular, also enabled the young economy to grow and fit itself into the British imperial economy and the world economy.

LAND AND NATURAL RESOURCE ABUNDANCE, LABOR SCARCITY

Throughout the colonial period, most people depended on the land for a livelihood. From New Hampshire to Georgia, agriculture was the chief occupation, and the industrial and commercial activity that was there revolved almost entirely around materials extracted from the land, the forests, and the ocean. Where soil and climate were unfavorable to cultivating commercial crops, it was often possible to turn to fishing or trapping and to the production of ships, ship timbers, pitch, tar, turpentine, and other forest products. Land was seemingly limitless in extent and, therefore, not highly priced, but almost every colonist wanted to be a landholder. When we remember that ownership of land signified wealth and position to the European, this is not hard to understand. The ever-present desire for land explains why, for the first century and a half of our history, many immigrants who might have been successful artisans or laborers in someone else's employ tended instead to turn to agriculture, thereby aggravating the persistent scarcity of labor in the New World.

Like labor, physical capital was scarce relative to land, especially during the first century of settlement. Particular forms of capital goods that could be obtained from natural resources with simple tools were in apparent abundance. For instance, so much wood was available that it was fairly easy to build houses, barns, and workshops. Wagons and carriages were largely made of wood, as were farm implements, wheels, gears, and shafts. Shipyards and shipwares also were constructed from timber, and ships were built in quantity from an early date.

ECONOMIC INSIGHT 3.1

SOCIAL ENGINEERING AND ECONOMIC CONSTRAINTS IN GEORGIA

In 1732, plans for the last British colony to be settled in North America were being made. The colonization of Georgia provides a vivid example of good intentions pitted against the economic realities of opportunities and restraints. Here again, we observe the impact of relative factor (input) scarcities of abundant land (and natural resources) relative to labor and capital as well as observing the importance of institutions.

Like Pennsylvania and Massachusetts, Georgia was founded to assist those who had been beset with troubles in the Old World. General James Edward Oglethorpe persuaded Dr. Thomas Bray, an Anglican clergyman noted for his good works, to attempt a project for the relief of people condemned to prison for debt. This particular social evil of eighteenth-century England cried out to be remedied because debtors could spend years in prison without hope of escape except through organized charitable institutions. As long as individuals were incarcerated, they were unable to earn any money with which to pay their debts, and even if they were eventually released, years of imprisonment could make them unfit for work. It was Oglethorpe's idea to encourage debtors to come to America, where they might become responsible (and even substantial) citizens.

In addition to their wish to aid the "urban wretches" of England, Bray, Oglethorpe, and their associates had another primary motivation: to secure a military buffer zone between the prosperous northern English settlements and Spanish Florida. Besides their moral repugnance to slavery, they believed that an all-white population was needed for security reasons. It was doubtful that slaves could be depended on to fight, and with slavery, rebellion was always a possibility. Therefore, slavery as an institution was prohibited in Georgia—initially.

In 1732, King George II obligingly granted Dr. Bray and his associates the land between the Savannah and Altamaha Rivers; the original tract included considerably less territory than that occupied by the modern state of Georgia. By royal charter, a corporation that was to be governed by a group of trustees was created; after 21 years, the territory was to revert to the Crown. Financed by both private and public

funds, the venture had an auspicious beginning. Oglethorpe himself led the first contingent of several hundred immigrants—mostly debtors—to the new country, where a 50-acre farm awaited each colonist. Substantially larger grants were available to free settlers with families, and determined efforts were made, both on the Continent and in the British Isles, to secure colonists.

Unfortunately, the ideals and hopes of the trustees clashed with economic reality and the institutions used in Georgia. Although "the Georgia experiment" was a modest success as a philanthropic enterprise, its economic development was to prove disappointing for many decades. The climate in the low coastal country—where the fertile land lay—was unhealthful and generated higher death rates than in areas farther north. As the work of Ralph Gray and Betty Wood (1976) has shown, it was impossible without slavery to introduce the rice and indigo plantations in Georgia that were so profitable in South Carolina, and the 50-acre tracts given to the charity immigrants were too small to achieve economies of scale and competitive levels of efficiency for commercial production.

Failing to attract without continuous subsidy a sufficient number of whites to secure a military buffer zone and given the attractive potential profits of slave-operated plantation enterprises, the trustees eventually bowed to economic forces. Alternatively stated, the opportunity costs of resources (Economic Reasoning Proposition 2, choices impose costs, in Economic Insight 1.1 on page 8) were too high under the nonslave small farm institutional structure to attract labor and capital without continued subsidies. By midcentury, slavery was legalized, and slaves began pouring into Georgia, which was converted to a Crown colony in 1751. By 1770, 45 percent of the population was black.

This particular example of social-economic engineering reveals a wider truth. The most distinctive characteristic of production in the colonies throughout the entire colonial period was that land and natural resources were plentiful, but labor and capital were exceedingly scarce relative to land and natural resources and compared with the input proportions in Britain and Continental Europe. This relationship among the factors of production explains many institutional arrangements and patterns of regional development in the colonies.

Crowded prisons in seventeenth-century England held many debtors. The colonization of Georgia, in part, had a purpose of relieving debtor-filled jails.

Alternatively, finished metal products were especially scarce, and mills and other industrial facilities remained few and small. Improvements of roads and harbors lagged far behind European standards until the end of the colonial period. Capital formation was a primary challenge to the colonists, and the colonies always needed much more capital than was ever available to them. English political leaders promoted legislation that hindered the export of tools and machinery from the home country. Commercial banks were nonexistent, and English or colonials who had savings to invest often preferred the safer investment in British firms. Nevertheless, as we shall see in chapter 5, residents of the developing American colonies lived better lives in the eighteenth century than most other people, even those living in the most advanced nations of the time, because high ratios of land and other natural resources to labor generated exceptionally high levels of output per worker in the colonies.

AGRICULTURE AND REGIONAL SPECIALIZATIONS

At the end of the eighteenth century, approximately 90 percent of the American people earned a major portion of their living by farming (compared with about 3 percent today). Most production in the New World was for the colonists' own consumption, but sizable proportions of colonial goods and services were produced for commercial exchange. In time, each region became increasingly specialized in the production of particular goods and services determined by particular soil types, climate, and natural bounties of the forests and ocean.

The Southern Colonies

The southern colonies present a good example of the comparative advantage that fertile new land can offer. Almost at the outset, southern colonials grew tobacco that was both cheaper to produce and of better quality than the tobacco grown in most other parts of the world. Later, the South began to produce two other staples, rice and indigo. For nearly two centuries, the southern economy was to revolve around these few export staples because the region's soil and climate gave the South a pronounced advantage in the cultivation of crops that were in great demand in the populous industrializing areas of Europe.[1]

Tobacco   Within a decade after the settlement of Jamestown, Virginia began exporting tobacco to England. The weed had been known in Europe for more than a century; sailors on the first voyages of exploration had brought back samples and descriptions of the ways in which natives had used it. Despite much opposition on moral grounds, smoking had increased in popularity during the sixteenth century; thus, even though James I viewed it "so vile and stinking a custom," it was a relief to the English to find a source of supply so that tobacco importation from the Spanish would be unnecessary. Tobacco needed a long growing season and fertile soil. Furthermore, it could be cultivated in small areas, on only partly cleared fields, and with the most rudimentary implements. All this suited the primitive Virginia community. But tobacco production had two additional advantages in the colonies: As successive plantings exhausted the original fertility of a particular plot, new land was readily available, and ships could move up the rivers of the Virginia coast to load their cargoes at the plantation docks. One challenge that lingered for most of the seventeenth century was that the colonists had much to learn about the proper curing, handling, and shipping of tobacco, and for many years the American product was inferior to the tobacco produced in Spain. Nevertheless, colonial tobacco was protected in the English market, and the fact that it was cheaper led to steady increases in its portion of the tobacco trade. The culture of tobacco spread northward around the Chesapeake Bay and moved up the many river valleys. By the end of the seventeenth century, there was some production in North Carolina.

The highly productive American tobacco regions swelled the supply of tobacco in British and European markets and, as will be discussed in great detail in chapter 5, tobacco prices fell precipitously until the last quarter of the seventeenth century. By the turn of the eighteenth century, it was apparent that the competition in colonial tobacco production would be won by large plantations and that if the small planters were to succeed at all, they would have to specialize in high-quality tobacco or in the production of food and other crops. From the work of David Klingaman (1969) we have learned that, in the eighteenth century, substantial areas around the Chesapeake (especially in Maryland) turned to the production of wheat.

Larger production units were favored in tobacco cultivation because slaves worked in groups could be supervised and driven. To achieve the best results, a plantation owner needed enough slaves to ensure the economical use of a plantation manager. Supervision costs did not grow in proportion to the number of slaves owned and used; therefore, per-unit costs fell as plantations grew in size (at least up to a point). A plantation with fewer than 10 slaves intermittently prospered, but only larger units earned substantial returns above cost, provided they were properly managed and contained sufficient acreage to

---

[1]There were failures, too. For example, every effort was made to encourage the production of wines then being imported from France and Spain, but the quality of American wines was so poor that serious attempts to compete with established wine-producing areas were abandoned. Similarly, it was hoped that silk and hemp could be produced in quantity, and bounties and premiums were offered for their production; but again, quality was inferior, and high wage rates resulted in a high-cost product.

avoid soil exhaustion. Thus, the wealthy or those who were able to secure adequate credit from English and Scottish merchants attained more efficient scales of tobacco production and, in so doing, became even wealthier and further improved their credit standing. We should not conclude that slaves were held only by the largest plantation owners, however; the crude statistics available today indicate that in pre-Revolutionary times, as later, large numbers of planters owned fewer than 10 slaves. Nonetheless, there was persistent pressure in the southern colonies to develop large farms favored by lower per-unit costs.

Rice   Around 1695, the second of the great southern staples was introduced. Early Virginia colonists had experimented with rice production, and South Carolina had tried to cultivate the staple in the first two years after settlement, but success awaited the introduction of new varieties of the grain (Gray 1933). By the early 1700s, rice was an established crop in the area around Charleston, although problems of irrigation remained.

It is possible to grow rice without intermittent flooding and draining, but the quality of the grain suffers. Rice was first cultivated in the inland swamps that could be flooded periodically from the rivers, but the flooding depended on uncertain stream flows. Besides, such a growing method could not be used on the extremely flat land that lay along the coast itself. Before long, a system of flooding was devised that enabled producers to utilize the force of tidal flows. Water control, originally a Dutch specialty, had grown in importance and sophistication in England (to drain marshes), and this knowledge was transferred to America. Dikes were built along the lower reaches of the rivers, and as the tide pushed back the fresh water, it could be let through gates into irrigation ditches crossing the fields.

Flooding near tidewater remained capital was worthwhile because proper engineering permitted the two major tide-propelled floodings to occur at precisely the right times, and the water could be removed just as accurately. Such fixed costs added to the prospects of scale economies in rice production, and much labor was needed to build the dikes and to plant and harvest.

Slaves were imported in great numbers during the eighteenth century for these purposes. The "task" system of working slaves, which gave each slave a particular piece of ground to cultivate, was utilized. The work was backbreaking, similar to the "gang system" used in sugar production in the Caribbean, and it was carried out in hot, mosquito-infested swamps. Although contemporary opinion held that Africans were better able to withstand the ravages of disease and the effects of overexertion than were Europeans, the mortality rate among blacks in this region was high. Recent scholarship provides evidence that bears out this contemporary view. Blacks had disproportionately high rates of mortality in the northern mainland colonies, and whites had disproportionately higher death rates in the far southern and Caribbean colonies. Phil Coelho and Bob McGuire (1997) explain these differences in terms of the races coming into contact with pathogens for which they had little or no prior geographic exposure. Tropical diseases were particularly devastating to Europeans, less so to Africans (Coelho and McGuire 1997). Despite production difficulties, rice output steadily increased until the end of the colonial period, its culture finally extending from below Savannah up into the southern regions of North Carolina.

Indigo   To the profits from rice were added those from another staple—indigo, so named from a plant native to India. The indigo plant was first successfully introduced in 1743 by Eliza Lucas, a young woman who had come from the West Indies to live on a plantation near Charleston. Indigo almost certainly could not have been grown in the colonies without special assistance, because its culture was demanding and the preparation of the deep blue dye required exceptional skill. As a supplement to rice, however, it was an ideal crop, both because the plant could be grown on high ground where rice

The cultivation of rice required advanced engineering techniques and much slave labor, but it remained a profitable crop for South Carolina and Georgia during the colonial period.

would not grow and because the peak workloads in processing indigo came at a time of year when the slaves were not busy in the rice fields. Indigo production, fostered by a British subsidy of sixpence a pound, added considerably to the profits of plantation owners, thereby attracting resources to the area.

Other Commodities   In emphasizing the importance of tobacco, rice, and indigo, we are in danger of overlooking the production of other commodities in the southern colonies. Deerskins and naval stores (pitch, tar, and resin) were exported from the Carolinas, and bulk unfinished iron in quantity was shipped from the Chesapeake region. Throughout the South, there was a substantial output of hay and animal products and of Indian corn, wheat, and other grains. These items, like a wide variety of fruits and vegetables, were grown mostly to make the agricultural units as self-sufficient as possible. Yet upland farmers, especially in the Carolinas and Virginia, raised livestock for commercial sale and exported meat, either on the hoof or in cured form, in quantity to other colonies. In all the colonies, food for home consumption was a main economic activity.

The Middle Colonies

The land between the Potomac and the Hudson Rivers was, on the whole, fertile and readily tillable and therefore enjoyed a comparative advantage in the production of grains and other foodstuffs. As the seventeenth century elapsed, two distinct types of agricultural operations developed there. To the west, on the cutting edge of the frontier, succeeding generations continued to encounter many of the difficulties that had beset the

Colonial agriculture depended heavily on such cash crops as indigo—shown here being processed in South Carolina from fresh cut sheaves to final drying—and rice, shown previously in a plantation setting.

first settlers. The trees in the forests—an ever-present obstacle—had to be felled, usually after they had been girdled and allowed to die. The felled trees were burned and their stumps removed to allow for the use of horse-drawn plows. The soil was worked with tools that did not differ much from the implements used by medieval Europeans. A living literally had to be wrested from the Earth. At the same time, a stable and reasonably advanced agriculture began to develop to the east of the frontier. The Dutch in New York and the Germans in Pennsylvania, who brought skills and farming methods from areas with soils similar to those in this region, were encouraged from the first to cultivate crops for sale in the small but growing cities of New York, Philadelphia, and Baltimore. Gradually, a commercial agriculture developed.

Wheat became the important staple, and although there was a considerable output of corn, rye, oats, and barley, the economy of the region was based on the great bread grain. During the latter part of the seventeenth century, a sufficient quantity of wheat and flour was produced to permit the export of these products, particularly to the West Indies.

The kind of agricultural unit that evolved in the Middle colonies later became typical of the great food belts of the midwestern United States. Individual farms, which were considerably smaller in acreage than the average plantation to the south, could be operated by the farmer and his family with little hired help. Slaveholding was rare (except along the Hudson in New York and in Rhode Island) because wheat production was labor intensive only during planting and harvest periods and because there were no apparent economies of large-scale production in wheat, corn, or generalized farming as there were in the southern plantation staples, especially rice. It was normally preferable to acquire an indentured servant as a hand; the original outlay was not great, and the productivity of even a young and inexperienced servant was soon sufficient to return the owner's investment. The more limited growing season in the North also lowered the economic gains of slave labor in the fields. Finally, as Coelho and McGuire (1997) show, the northern climates had negative biological consequences for blacks relative to whites.

New England

Vital as the agriculture of New England was to the people of the area, it constituted a relatively unimportant part of commercial output for sale. Poor soils, uneven terrain, and a severe climate led to restricted commercial farming. The typical farm emphasized subsistence farming, growing only those crops necessary for family maintenance. Because it could be produced almost anywhere and because its yield even on poor land was satisfactory, Indian corn was the chief crop. Wheat and the other cereal grains, along with the hardier vegetables, were grown for family use. Partly because of climate and partly because of the protection from wild predators that natural barriers furnished, the Narragansett region, including the large islands off its coast, became a cattle- and sheep-raising center. By the eve of the Revolution, however, New England was a net importer of food and fiber. Its destiny lay in another kind of economic endeavor, and from a very early date, many New Englanders combined farming with other work, thereby living better lives than they would have had they been confined to the resources of their own farms. Homecraft employments of all varieties were common features of rural life in all the colonies, especially in New England. Shipping and fishing were also major economic activities of this region.

THE EXTRACTIVE INDUSTRIES

Although most colonial Americans made their livings from agriculture, many earned their livelihoods indirectly from the land in what we will call *extractive pursuits*. From the forest came the furs and wild animal skins, lumber, and naval stores. From the coastal waters came fish and that strange mammal, the whale. From the ground came minerals, although only in small quantities during the early colonial years.

Furs, Forests, and Ores

The original 13 colonies were a second-rate source of furs by the late colonial period, because the finest furs along the seaboard were processed quickly and the most lucrative catches were made long before the frontier moved into the interior (Bridenbaugh 1971). It was the French, with their strong trade connections to Native Americans (who did most of the trapping), not the English, who were the principal furriers in North America (see Perspective 3.1 on page 50). Nonetheless, farmers trapped furs as a sideline to obtain cash, although they caught primarily muskrats and raccoons, whose pelts were less desirable then, as now.

The forest itself, more than its denizens, became an economically significant object of exploitation. The colonials lived in an age of wood. Wood, rather than minerals and metals, was the chief fuel and the basic construction material. Almost without exception, the agricultural population engaged in some form of lumbering. Pioneers had to fell trees to clear ground, and used wood to build houses, barns, furniture, and sometimes fences. Frequently, they burned the timber and scattered the ashes, but enterprising farmers eventually discovered that they could use simple equipment to produce potash and the more highly refined pearlash. These chemicals were needed to manufacture glass, soap, and other products and provided cash earnings to many households throughout the colonies.

From the forests also came the wood and naval stores for ships and ship repair. White pine was unmatched as a building material for the masts and yards of sailing ships, and white and red oak provided ship timbers (for ribbing) of the same high quality. The pine trees that grew abundantly throughout the colonies furnished the raw material for the manufacture of naval stores: pitch, tar, and resin. In the days of wooden vessels, naval stores were indispensable in the shipyard and were used mostly for protecting surfaces and caulking seams. These materials were in great demand in both the domestic and British shipbuilding industries. Considerable skilled labor was required to produce naval stores, and only in North Carolina, where slaves were specially trained to perform the required tasks, were these materials produced profitably without British subsidy.

PERSPECTIVE 3.1

AMERICAN INDIAN HUNTERS AND THE DEPLETION OF THE BEAVER

Early forms of territorial hunting rights (property rights) among North American tribes sustained stocks of game, because hunters, especially in forested areas, had incentives (Economic Reasoning Proposition 3, incentives matter) to limit their takings. In forested areas, game generally remained in a fixed area, so tribes or groups established rules, giving hunting areas to particular tribes or groups. Only in the case of exceptional circumstances, such as famine, fire, or the like, would hunters from another tribe be allowed to hunt in another's territory. When the English-owned Hudson Bay Company was established early in the seventeenth century, its demand for beaver furs for the markets of England and Europe encouraged Indian hunters to harvest larger quantities of beaver pelts. The French, along with the Hudson Bay Company, competed to set prices for furs and for axes, cloth, and other manufactures exchanged for the furs.

When the French entered the market in competition with the English, fur prices moved upward, encouraging more intensive hunting. Figures 3.1 and 3.2 show an index of prices at two major English trading forts, 1700 to 1763, and regional beaver population

estimates. Greater competition alone did not deplete the beaver population, which, though declining, remained above self-sustaining levels.

The maximum sustained yield (the horizontal Pmsy line in the figures) indicates the amounts that could be taken consistent with the forest habitat being able to sustain the population. In the 1720s and 1730s, this maximum yield, just consistent with a sustained beaver population, was maintained, as shown in Figures 3.1 and 3.2. In the 1740s, however, a rise in demand and prices for furs in Europe plus greater competition between the French posts and England's Hudson Bay Company forts, combined to deplete the stock. Higher prices encouraged greater takings and overharvesting (Economic Reasoning Proposition 3, incentives matter), and because of increasing tribal migrations and dislocations, the Native American groups were unable to generate communally based or closed-access property rights systems.

The tragedy of the commons arose with all its negative consequences. Intense and growing competition in the absence of appropriate property rights fails (Economic Reasoning Proposition 4, institutions matter). By the late colonial period, the colonies contained few beavers, and even farther west the beaver population was moving toward extinction.

(For more analysis, see Carlos and Lewis 1999.)

FIGURE 3.1

Fur Prices and Simulated Beaver Population: York Factory, 1716–1763

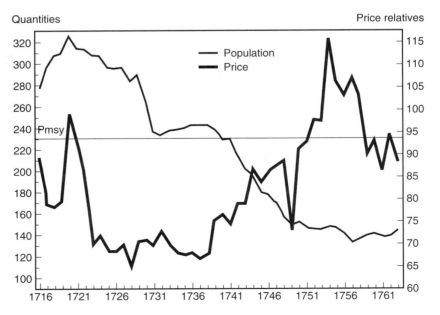

Source: *Carlos and Lewis 1999.*

PERSPECTIVE 3.1

AMERICAN INDIAN HUNTERS AND THE DEPLETION OF THE BEAVER, Continued

FIGURE 3.2

Fur Prices and Simulated
Beaver Population: Fort
Albany, 1700–1763

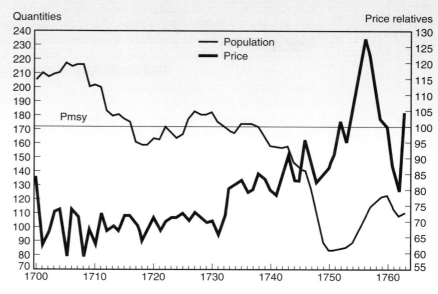

Source: *Carlos and Lewis 1999.*

The only mineral obtained by the colonials in any significant quantity was raw iron. The methods used in the colonial iron industry did not differ greatly from those developed in the late Middle Ages, although by the time of the Revolution, furnace sizes had increased greatly. In the seventeenth century, the chief source of iron was bog ore, a sediment taken from swamps and ponds. When this sediment was treated with charcoal in a bloomery or forge until the charcoal absorbed the oxygen in the ore, an incandescent sponge of metal resulted. The glowing ball of iron was removed from the forge and in a white-hot condition was hammered to remove the slag and leave a substantial piece of wrought iron.

Rich rock ores were discovered as the population moved inward, and during the eighteenth century, a large number of furnaces were built for the reduction of these ores. Pig iron could then be produced in quantity. A mixture of rock ore, charcoal, and oyster shells or limestone was placed in a square or conical furnace and then ignited. Under a draft of air from bellows worked by water power, the iron ore was reduced to a spongy metal, which as it settled to the bottom of the furnace alloyed itself with large amounts of carbon, thereby becoming what we call "cast iron." Poured into molds called "pigs" or "sows," the resulting metal could be either remelted and cast into final form later or further refined and reworked in a mill or blacksmith shop. The discussion of these rudimentary processes provides an important background that will help us understand the later development in the American iron and steel industry.

Because of the simple processing required and an abundance of charcoal, the colonial iron industry was able to compete with that of the British Isles in the sale of bars and pigs. The number of forges and furnaces in the colonies just before the Revolution probably exceeded the number in England and Wales combined, and the annual output of wrought and cast iron by then was about 30,000 tons, or one-seventh of the world's output. But the colonies remained heavy net importers of finished iron products.

Sea Products

Although restricted primarily to the northern colonies, the occupations of fishing and whaling were of major importance in the development of the entire early colonial economy. The sea provided New Englanders a commodity for which there was a ready market, and there were also many splendid harbors to house small fishing vessels and plenty of timber with which to build them. But most important was the sizable market for the magnificent cod. The large, fat, hard-to-cure cod were consumed at home. The best cod were exported to Catholic Europe; the poorer grades were sent to the West Indies, where they were fed to slaves. Gloucester, Salem, Boston, and Marblehead became the chief home ports for the great fishing fleets.

In colonial times, whale oil was highly prized as both an illuminant and a lubricant, ambergris was prized as a base for perfumes, and whalebone as a material for stays. Whaling was, therefore, a profitable and vigorous, if small, industry. Before 1700, whalers operated near the New England coast, but their take was small. During the eighteenth century, however, whalers ranged far and wide, and by 1775, more than 300 vessels of all sizes sailed from the Massachusetts ports, of which Nantucket was the great whaling center.

THE MANUFACTURING INDUSTRIES

The abundance of land and natural resources in the colonies and the sparse and scattered populations there discouraged manufacturing. Nevertheless, household production, mostly for self-sufficiency and outside the market, was pervasive, and craftshops, mills, and yards also deserve mention.

Household Manufacture and Craftshops

The first concern of the colonial household was the manufacture of food and clothing, and most colonial families had to produce their own. Wheat, rye, or Indian corn grown on the farm was ground into flour at the local gristmill, but the women of the family made plentiful weekly rations of bread and hardtack. Jellies and jams were made with enough sweetening from honey, molasses, or maple syrup to preserve them for indefinite periods in open crocks. The men of the family were rarely teetotalers, and the contracts signed by indentured servants indicate that nearly a third of the feeding costs of indentures was for alcoholic beverages. Beer, rum, and whiskey were easiest to make, but wines, mead, and an assortment of brandies and cordials were specialties of some households.

Making clothing—from preparing the raw fiber to sewing the finished garments—kept the women and children busy. Knit goods such as stockings, mittens, and sweaters were the major items of homemade apparel. Linsey-woolsey (made of flax and wool) and jeans (a combination of wool and cotton) were the standard textiles of the North and of the pioneer West. Equally indestructible, though perhaps a little easier on the skin, was fustian, a blend of cotton and flax used mostly in the South. Dress goods and fine suitings had to be imported from England, and even for the city dweller, the purchase of such luxuries was usually a rare and exciting occasion.

Early Americans who had special talents produced everything from nails and kitchen utensils to exquisite cabinets. Throughout colonial America the men of the family participated in the construction of their own homes, although exacting woodwork and any necessary masonry might be done by a specialist. Such specialists, of widely varying abilities, could be found both in cities and at country crossroads. Urban centers especially exhibited a great variety of skills, even at a rather early date. In 1697, for example, 51 manufacturing handicrafts, in addition to the building trades, were represented in Philadelphia.

Whaling was a hazardous but profitable industry in early America and an important part of New England's seafaring tradition. New Bedford, where Captain Ahab started his quest for Moby Dick, and Nantucket were the main whaling centers of New England.

The distinction between the specialized craftsman and the household worker, however, was not always clear in colonial America. Skilled slaves on southern plantations might devote all their time to manufacture; this made them artisans, even though their output was considered a part of the household. On the other hand, the itinerant jack-of-all-trades, who moved from village to village selling reasonably expert services, was certainly not a skilled craftsman in the European sense. Because of the scarcity of skilled labor, individual workers often performed functions more varied than they would have undertaken in their native countries; a colonial tanner, for example, might also be a currier (leather preparer) and a shoemaker. Furthermore, because of the small local markets and consequent geographic dispersal of nearly all types of production, few workers in the same trade were united in any particular locality.

For this reason, few guilds or associations of craftsmen of the same skill were formed. As an exception, however, we note that as early as 1648, enough shoemakers worked in Boston to enable the General Court to incorporate them as a guild, and by 1718, tailors and cordwainers were so numerous in Philadelphia that they, too, applied for incorporation (Bridenbaugh 1971).

Mills and Yards

To colonials, a mill was a device for grinding (grains), cutting (wood), or forging (iron). Until around the middle of the eighteenth century, most mills were crude setups, run by water power that was furnished by the small streams found all along the middle and north Atlantic coast. Throughout most of this period, primitive mechanisms were used; the cranks of sawmills and gristmills were almost always made of iron, but the wheels themselves and the cogs of the mill wheels were made of wood, preferably hickory. So little was understood about power transmission at this time that a separate water wheel was built to power each article of machinery. Shortly before the Revolution, improvements were made

The spinning wheel, the starting tool for homemade clothing, was a common utensil in the homes of colonial America.

in the application of power to milling processes, and at that time, the mills along the Delaware River and Chesapeake Bay were probably the finest in the world. In 1770, a fair-size gristmill would grind 100 bushels of grain per day; the largest mills, with several pairs of stones, might convert 75,000 bushels of wheat into flour annually.

We can only suggest the variety of the mill industries. Tanneries with bark mills were found in both the North and the South. Paper-making establishments, common in Pennsylvania and not unusual in New England, were called "mills" because machinery was required to grind the linen rags into pulp. Textiles were essentially household products, but in Massachusetts, eastern New York, and Pennsylvania, a substantial number of mills were constructed to perform the more complicated processes of weaving and finishing. The rum distilleries of New England provided a major product for both foreign and domestic trade, and breweries everywhere ministered to convivial needs.

Shipbuilding

Although large-scale manufacturing was not characteristic of colonial economic activity, shipbuilding was an important exception. As early as 1631, barely a decade after the Pilgrims landed at Plymouth, a 30-ton sloop was completed in Boston.

During the seventeenth century, shipyards sprang up all along the New England coast, with Boston and Newport leading the way. New York was a strong competitor until the

Navigation Act of 1651 (see chapter 4) dealt its Dutch-dominated industry a crippling blow, but the shipbuilding industry in New York again grew rapidly after 1720. By this time, Philadelphia boasted a dozen large shipyards along the banks of the Delaware River, and of the five major towns, only Charleston relied on ships produced by others. In the first half of the eighteenth century, the output of colonial shipyards reached its peak.

By 1700, the New England fleet exceeded 2,000 exclusive of fishing boats. American industry not only furnished the vessels for a large domestic merchant fleet, but also sold a considerable number of ships abroad, chiefly to the English. An uncontradicted estimate attributes nearly one-third of the ships in the British Merchant Marine in 1775 to American manufacture (Price 1976).

Many of the ships constructed were small. But whether they were building a square-rigged, three-masted vessel of several hundred tons or a fishing boat of 10 tons, Americans had a marked and persistent advantage. The basis for success in colonial shipbuilding was the proximity of raw materials, mainly lumber. Although labor and capital costs were lower in England, the high costs of transport of bulky materials from the Baltic—or the colonies—made shipbuilding more expensive in England. Higher wages encouraged sufficient numbers of shipwrights and artisans to migrate from Holland and England to the colonies, where they built colonial vessels with low-cost materials for about two-thirds of British costs. Consequently, shipbuilding in the colonies was exceptional: Though most other manufacturers did not generate raw material cost savings enough to offset the much higher labor costs in the colonies, in this case, the high costs of transport of the bulky raw materials ensured a comparative advantage of production in favor of the colonies. In addition, the Navigation Acts (discussed in chapter 4) equally encouraged shipbuilding, both in the colonies and in England. However, an important distinction arose between England and North America in the first century of manufacturing development. In England, raw materials were typically imported or brought to the craftsmen, but in the New World, workers located near raw materials.

The Merchant Marine Finally, as the sizable New England fleet suggests, shipping services and other distribution services associated with the transportation, handling, and merchandising of goods were important commercial activities in the colonies. The merchant marines in New England and the Middle colonies, which employed thousands of

© BETTMANN/CORBIS

Thanks to their ready supplies of first-class timber and naval stores, colonial shipbuilders enjoyed an early comparative advantage in shipbuilding.

men, were as efficient as the Dutch and English merchants in many trades throughout the world. Indeed, by the end of the colonial period, the colonies could boast of a sizable commercial sector, and as a source of foreign exchange earnings, monies earned from the sale of shipping services were second only to those earned from tobacco exports. Shipping and overseas trade as commercial activities were vital to the colonial economy.

OCCUPATIONAL GROUPS

Although the colonies established a rich diversity of economic activities, from a functional occupational standpoint, daily life was fairly stable. Occupational roles changed little over the years in settled areas; from today's perspective, occupational opportunities remained narrow and rigid. Most people expected the future to replicate the past, and most young people followed in the employment footsteps of their parents. Perspective 3.2 shows the traditionalism in the Native American culture.

The male population generally fit into one of several employment categories, the most predominant being family farmers. Other significant categories or classes were slave, indentured servant, unskilled laborer, and seaman. Upper-middle classes included artisans, merchants, and landowning farmers, but the richest occupational groups included merchants in New England and the Middle colonies and large landholding planters in the South. As Edwin Perkins (1988) and Alice Hanson Jones (1992) inform us, the very wealthy were classified as esquires, gentlemen, or officials.

Most women participated in work to complement the work of the male head of the household. Child care, domestic service, livestock tending, and household production dominated women's duties. Family farm life in particular, the most typical lifestyle of the period, had women and children engaged in handicraft production within the home. During harvest times, they usually turned to outdoor work to help the men. In seventeenth-century Maryland, for instance, Lois G. Carr and Lorena Walsh (1977) have shown that wives routinely spent the spring and summer months in the tobacco fields. In the Middle colonies, according to Joan Jensen (1986), women typically helped

PERSPECTIVE 3.2

NATIVE AMERICAN FAMILY STRUCTURE

In contrast to the patriarchical family, social-economic structure of European settlers, the Iroquois and other eastern tribes developed a matrilinear family structure. As hunters, men were frequently absent from the household for long periods, often for months and sometimes even years at a time. This disengaged them from fatherly (and husbandly) responsibilities; therefore, the husband-wife relationship was not the most basic social relationship. Instead, the most fundamental foundation of the family was mother-daughter.

Women were the planters and harvesters, with corn the primary food source. Although all land was commonly owned by the nation, or tribe, loose ownership rights to individual plots could occur. From Anthony Wallace, we learn the following:

An individual woman might, if she wished, "own" a patch of corn, or an apple or peach orchard, but there was little reason for insisting on private tenure: the work was more happily done communally, and in the absence of a regular market, a surplus was of little personal advantage, especially if the winter were hard and other families needed corn. In such circumstances hoarding led only to hard feelings and strained relations as well as the possibility of future difficulty in getting corn for oneself and one's family. (1970, 24)

The long-term relationships of mothers, daughters, granddaughters, and neighbors living communally minimized shirking and bad behavior, and the sharing provided a form of insurance against poor individual harvests and bad times.

in the easier tasks of spreading hay to dry, digging for potatoes, gathering flax, and picking fruit. Most away-from-home work for women, especially younger women, was in other people's homes. Such domestic service for extra income was common for women under the age of 25.

Alice Hanson Jones (1992) reminds us to take special note of the inferior legal and political status of women and the fact of male dominance and patriarchal authority within the family. A woman was expected to be obedient to her husband, and marriage was accepted unquestionably as her proper destiny, regardless of class or status. For those who did not marry, the outlook for work was bleak.

To spin fiber or help in the household tasks of parents or relatives was likely for an unmarried woman (hence the term *spinster*, meaning an unmarried woman). Some women, with education and special connections, might teach music, reading, or other skills.

Children began helping their parents at about the age of 7 or 8; by the age of 12, they were usually important apprentice-type workers in the home or fields. Child labor was very important, and maintaining the allegiance of children to labor on behalf of parents was a special problem for parents in the nonslave areas. Indeed, the problem was reflected even in the law. The laws of inheritance varied among the colonies but were consistent with the goals of economic efficiency and the maintenance of a reliable rural labor force. Southern colonies used primogeniture (the oldest son inherits the estate) because slaves supplied labor on the plantations, while the Middle and New England colonies typically used multigeniture (splitting estates among the sons) to better ensure work allegiance by sons.

SELECTED REFERENCES AND SUGGESTED READINGS

Bridenbaugh, Carl. *Cities in the Wilderness: The First Century of Urban Life in America, 1625–1742.* New York: Oxford University Press, 1971.

Carlos, Ann M., and Frank D. Lewis. "Property Rights and Competition in the Depletion of the Beaver: Native Americans and the Hudson Bay Company." In *The Other Side of the Frontier,* ed. Linda Barrington, 131–149. Boulder, Co.: Westview, 1999.

Carr, Lois G., and Lorena Walsh. "The Planter's Wife: The Experience of White Women in Seventeenth Century Maryland." *William and Mary Quarterly* 34 (1977): 542–571.

Coelho, Philip R., and Robert A. McGuire. "African and European Bound Labor in the British New World: The Biological Consequences of Economic Choices." *Journal of Economic History* 37 (1997): 83–115.

Gray, Lewis C. *History of Agriculture in the Southern United States to 1860.* Washington, D.C.: Carnegie Institution of Washington, 1933.

Gray, Ralph, and Betty Wood. "The Transition from Indentured Servant to Involuntary Servitude in Colonial Georgia." *Explorations in Economic History* 13 (October 1976): 353–370.

Jensen, Joan. *Loosening the Bonds: Mid-Atlantic Farm Women 1750–1850.* New Haven, Conn.: Yale University Press, 1986.

Jones, Alice Hanson. "The Wealth of Women, 1774." *Strategic Factors in Nineteenth Century American Economic History,* eds. Claudia Goldin and Hugh Rockoff. Chicago: University of Chicago Press, 1992.

Klingaman, David. "The Significance of Grain in the Development of the Tobacco Colonies." *Journal of Economic History* (1969): 267–278.

Perkins, E. J. Section 1 in *The Economy of Colonial America,* 2nd ed. New York: Columbia University Press, 1988.

Price, Jacob. "A Note on the Value of Colonial Exports of Shipping." *Journal of Economic History* 36 (1976): 704–724.

Wallace, Anthony C. *The Death and Rebirth of the Seneca.* New York: Knopf, 1970.

CHAPTER **4**

The Economic Relations
of the Colonies

CHAPTER THEME

The economic relations of the colonies with England and other overseas areas are a central part of the story of economic progress in the colonies. Overseas areas were economically important as markets for colonial products, as sources of manufactured goods and other items demanded by American consumers, and as sources of labor and capital. Additional investment came from England for the provision of defense. This chapter analyzes the commercial relations and commodity exchanges of the colonies, the legal and business aspects of their shipping and trade, and the special problems of money, capital, and debt in overseas and domestic commerce. It shows how the colonies fit into the world economy and into the English trading realm.

ENGLISH MERCANTILISM AND THE COLONIES

In the long period from 1500 to 1800, western European nation-states were all influenced by a set of ideas known as the mercantile system or mercantilism. Mercantilist doctrine and institutions were not created by a particular group of thinkers, nor were they ever set forth in systematic fashion by a "school" of economists, but the ideas were important because they were held by practical businesspeople and heads of state who—at different times in different countries—strongly influenced public policy and institutional change.

The primary aim of mercantilists was to achieve power and wealth for the state. Spain's experience in the sixteenth century had led most observers to conclude that an inflow of gold and silver was potent in attaining needed goods and services and in prosecuting wars. To generate an inflow of gold or silver through trade, the value of exports should exceed the value of imports. The gold or silver paid for the differences between exports and imports. With such additions to amounts of money, called *specie*, domestic trade would be more brisk and tax revenues higher. It was further held that the state could attain great power only if political and economic unity became a fact. In a day when productivity depended so greatly on the skills and knowledge of workers, it was crucial to keep artisans at home. If all the materials necessary to foster domestic industry were not available, they could best be obtained by establishing colonies or friendly foreign trading posts from which such goods could be imported. A strong merchant marine could carry foreign goods, thereby helping to secure favorable trade balances, and merchant ships could be converted for war if the need arose.

Mercantilists believed that these means of achieving national power could be made effective by the passage and strict enforcement of legislation regulating economic life.

58

England had begun to pass such laws by the end of the fifteenth century, but its mercantilist efforts did not fully flower until after the British, together with the Dutch, had successfully turned back Spanish power. Indeed, it was largely a consequence of England's desire to surpass Holland—a nation that had reached the zenith of its power during the first half of the seventeenth century—that British legislation was passed marking the beginning of an organized and consistent effort to regulate colonial trade.

Adherence to mercantilist principles was implicit in the colonizing activity that the English began in the early 1600s. Almost as soon as Virginia tobacco began to be shipped in commercial quantities to England, King James I levied a tax on it while agreeing to prohibit the growth of competing tobacco in England. Taxes, regulation, and subsidies were all used as mercantile policies, but the primary ones that affected the colonies were the Navigation Acts.

The Early Navigation Acts

During the English Civil War, which began in 1642 and ended in 1649, the British had too many troubles of their own to pay much attention to regulating trade with the colonies. In this period, Americans had slipped into the habit of shipping their goods directly to continental ports, and the Dutch made great inroads into the carrying trade of the colonies. In 1651, Parliament passed the first of the so-called Navigation Acts, directed primarily at prohibiting the shipping of American products in Dutch vessels. Not until after the Restoration, however, was England in a position to enforce a strict commercial policy, beginning with the Navigation Acts of 1660 and 1663.

These acts were modified from time to time by hundreds of policy changes; at this point, it is sufficient to note the three primary categories of trade restriction:

1. All trade of the colonies was to be carried in vessels that were English built and owned, commanded by an English captain, and manned by a crew of whom three-quarters were English. English was defined as "only his Majesty's subjects of England, Ireland, and the Plantations." Of great importance to colonists was the fact that colonists and colonial ships were both considered "English" under the law.
2. All foreign merchants were excluded from dealing directly in the commerce of the English colonies. They could engage in colonial trade only through England and merchants resident there.
3. Certain commodities produced in the colonies could be exported only to England (or Wales, Berwick-on-Tweed, or other English colonies—essentially any destination within the Empire). These "enumerated" goods included sugar, tobacco, cotton, indigo, ginger, and various dyewoods (fustic, logwood, and brazilletto). The list was later amended and lengthened, and Scotland was added as a legal destination after 1707.

It is important to keep these three categories of restrictions firmly in mind. Although they were the cause of occasional protests on the part of the colonists, they caused practically no disruption of established trade patterns during the remaining decades of the seventeenth century. Indeed, the acts were only loosely enforced throughout most of the seventeenth century. When in 1696 a system of admiralty courts was established to enforce the Navigation Acts, their impact became somewhat more pronounced. Indeed, from the beginning of the eighteenth century, most spheres of colonial commercial activity were regulated. One relaxation of the regulations in the 1730s is noteworthy. At that time, some enumerated goods were allowed to be shipped directly to ports south of Cape Finisterre, in Northern Spain.

EXPORTS, IMPORTS, AND MARKETS

The enumeration of certain products requiring direct shipment to England suggests their special importance from the perspective of the mother country. Table 4.1 confirms this importance also from the perspective of the colonies. Tobacco, rice, and indigo accounted for more than half the value of the top 10 exports, and these were predominantly from southern soils. The dominance of the southern staples as a proportion of total colonial exports was greater in the seventeenth century than in the eighteenth, but their lead and importance were maintained right up to the decade of independence. These top 10 exports made up 77 percent of the total commodity exports on average between 1768 and 1772.

Miscellaneous manufactured goods of all varieties composed the lion's share of imports from England; a Philadelphia merchant provided a contemporary description of his import trade from Britain:

> [A]ll kinds of British manufactories in great abundance and India goods, etc. In the last of the winter or early spring [we] choose to import our linens and other things fit for summer, the latter end of which we should have our woolen goods of all kinds ready for fall sale to use in winter. The spring is the best time for iron mongery, cutleryware, furniture for furnishing houses, and all other brass and iron work. Our imports of those articles are very large, the people being much employed in agriculture, husbandry, clearing and improving lands, but slow progress is made in the manufactories here.[1]

Wine and salt came from southern Europe, and sugar, molasses, and rum imports from the West Indies.

A useful summary of the relative importance of the various trading partners of the colonies is shown in Figure 4.1. Great Britain was the main overseas region to receive colonial exports (56 percent of the total) and to supply colonial imports (80 percent of the total).[2] Nevertheless, the West Indies and southern Europe were important trading partners, especially as markets for American exports.

TABLE 4.1 TOP 10 COMMODITY EXPORTS FROM THE 13 COLONIES (AVERAGE ANNUAL VALUES, 1768–1772, IN THOUSANDS OF POUNDS STERLING)

Tobacco	£766
Bread and flour	410
Rice	312
Fish	154
Wheat	115
Indigo	113
Corn	83
Pine boards	70
Staves and headings	65
Horses	60

Source: *Derived from Walton and Shepherd, 1979, Table 21, 194–195.*

---

[1]Letter from Thomas Clifford, Philadelphia, to Abel Chapman, Whitby, England, July 25, 1767, as quoted from Bezanson et al. (1935, 263).

[2]Because of reshipment allowed by the Navigation Acts, not all of these amounts were actually consumed or produced in the British Isles.

FIGURE 4.1

Percentage Distribution of Total Colonial Trade

The United Kingdom was colonial America's dominant trading partner in exports and imports, followed by the West Indies and southern Europe.

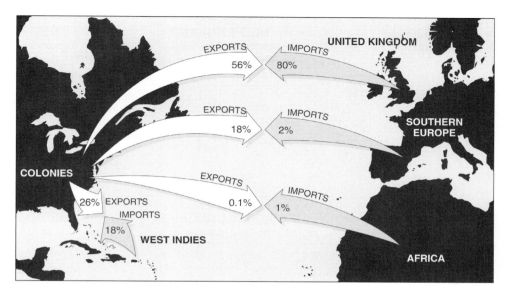

Source: *Shepherd and Walton 1972, 160–161.*

Another feature of colonial trade is revealed in Figure 4.2 (page 62). Here we see the sharp difference among the regions' ties to various overseas markets. Commerce in the southern regions was overwhelmingly dominated by the trades to Great Britain. Alternatively, the trades of the Middle colonies were more evenly balanced among Great Britain, southern Europe, and the West Indies. New England's most important trading partner was the West Indies. Colonial imports in each region arrived predominantly by way of Great Britain. Few products were imported from southern Europe, and commodity trade with Africa was insignificant.

OVERSEAS SHIPPING AND TRADE

Although urban residents numbered little more than 5 percent of the total population in the late colonial period, the major port towns with safe harbors and accessible productive hinterlands became key locations for trade and commerce. Map 4.1 (page 63) shows the 10 most populated towns in 1776. Philadelphia, with 40,000 people, was second only to London in population within the Empire, slightly less in number than San Bruno, California, or Bennington, Vermont, today. New York (25,000), Boston (16,000), Charleston (12,000), and Newport (11,000) were the only other towns in excess of 10,000 residents. Note that all of the top 10 urban centers were port towns. Because these were both readily accessible and points of change in transportation modes, from sea- to rivercraft or land vehicles and animals, they were greatly advantaged as trade centers. In an age when bluff-bowed sailing ships typically took six weeks to cross the Atlantic and relaying news to the interior took additional weeks, the port towns also had a special communication advantage. Lastly, travel and shipment were always much less expensive by water than by land, especially for bulky, weighty items typical of the colonies. Landlocked cities were a rarity in history before the railroad age.

Advantages of location and communication also went far in determining overseas shipping and trade patterns. For example, British ships almost completely dominated the trades of the southern colonial regions, whereas New England shippers dominated the New England–West Indies trade route.

FIGURE 4.2

Percentage Distribution
of Colonial Trade by
Region

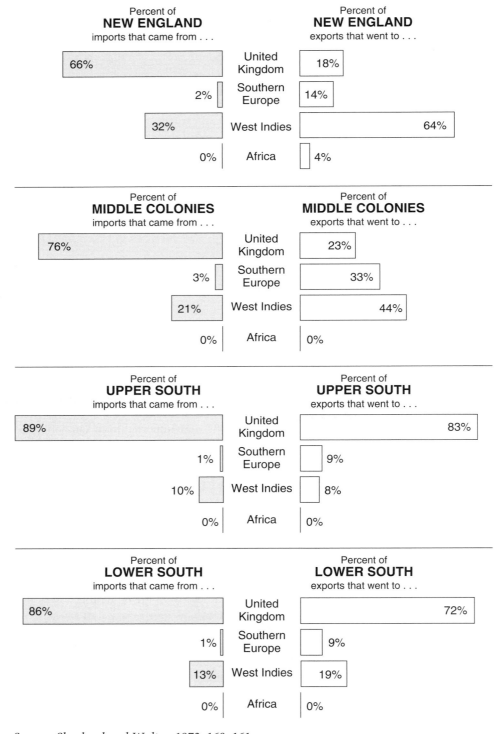

Source: *Shepherd and Walton 1972, 160–161.*

MAP 4.1

Safe harbors and productive hinterlands were the conditions favoring these 10 leading urban centers in the colonies.

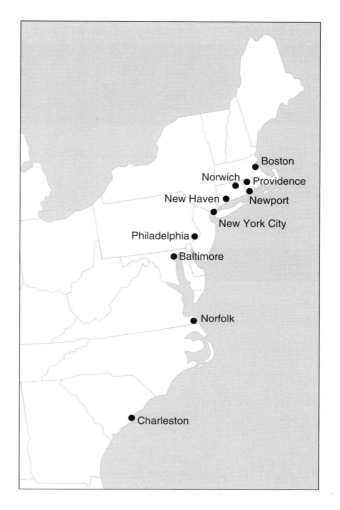

Table 4.2 on page 64 shows ownership proportions of shipping on several key routes of commerce. It is clear that neither British nor colonial shippers dominated or had a comparative advantage in shipping on all routes. For example, colonists owned 96 percent of the tonnage clearing New England to the West Indies and 85 percent to Great Britain, but only 12 percent of the tonnage clearing the Upper South to Great Britain. Why did British shippers dominate the southern trades to England but get left behind in the trades between New England and Great Britain, and between New England and the West Indies? Three critical factors provide the answer: (1) the high risks of maritime trade, (2) the problems of acquiring and responding to information about markets (prices and trade opportunities), and (3) the opportunities to lower labor costs by discharging crews in home ports.

Consider first the problem of trading and marketing goods. New England and other colonial merchants typically consigned their goods either to ship captains or selling agents, called factors, who were stationed in overseas markets and took delivery of the goods. Because these relationships necessitated placing a high degree of trust in a third party, it is not surprising that colonial merchants favored colonial ship captains. After all, greater familiarity and more frequent contact between merchant and agent lowered the risks of trade. So colonial merchants most often favored colonial shippers to gain trust and better ensure higher revenues in their exchanges.

TABLE 4.2 MID-EIGHTEENTH CENTURY OWNERSHIP, PROPORTIONS OF SHIPPING

SHIPS CLEARING	COLONIAL OWNED	BRITISH OWNED	WEST INDIAN OWNED	COLONIAL OWNED	BRITISH OWNED	WEST INDIAN OWNED	COLONIAL OWNED	BRITISH OWNED	WEST INDIAN OWNED
	TO GREAT BRITAIN			TO SOUTHERN EUROPE			TO WEST INDIES		
From New England	85	15	0	93	7	0	96	3	1
From Middle Colonies	72	28	0	75	25	0	80	20	0
From Upper South	12	88	0	88	12	0	85	0	15
From Lower South	23	77	0	0	100	0	51	23	26
SHIPS ENTERING	FROM GREAT BRITAIN			FROM SOUTHERN EUROPE			FROM WEST INDIES		
Into New England	68	32	0	84	16	0	96	1	3
Into Middle Colonies	63	37	0	76	24	0	84	16	0
Into Upper South	9	91	1	33	67	0	61	23	16
Into Lower South	12	88	0	20	80	0	30	43	27

Source: *Walton 1968, 368.*

Due to the rudimentary forms of communication and transportation at the time, proximity to a market was an important advantage. For example, British shippers and merchants in the tobacco trade could acquire information about changing market conditions in the Chesapeake Bay area and in Europe more easily than New England shippers could. In trades to and from the West Indies, however, colonial shippers and merchants were nearer to their markets and could respond more quickly to fluctuations. Being close to a market reduced the time and cost of obtaining market information, allowing merchants to respond with more timely cargo arrivals and reduce the risks of trade. As British shipowner Michael Atkins stated in a 1751 letter to his colonial colleague, "Traders at the Northern Colonies have all the West India business to themselves, Europeans can have no encouragement for mixing with them in the commodities of provisions and lumber. You time things better than we and go to market cheaper" (Pares 1956, 8).

Finally, the efficient use of labor time was always an important factor. It was general practice in colonial times for crews to be paid while a vessel was docked in foreign ports, and crews were normally discharged only at the end of the voyage in the home port. This meant that British crews in the tobacco trade were paid for the time they spent at sea and in southern colonial ports, but not for their port time in England. Therefore, New England shippers were at a disadvantage on this trade route, because they paid wages both in British ports and in the Chesapeake Bay. Conversely, colonial shippers faced lower labor costs on trade routes between their home ports and the Caribbean.

These same considerations played a large role in determining the routes of trade. It was not too long ago that students of American colonial history were taught that shuttle routes (out and direct return) were common and typical of the southern colonial trades—mainly to England—but that the New England and Middle colonial shippers usually engaged in triangular and other more complex patterns.[3] It has been shown, however, that shuttle patterns were the dominant pattern for all colonial regions (see table 4.2 and its source). For most trades, shuttle patterns cut costs. Although the desire to keep vessels as fully loaded as possible encouraged "tramping" from port to port to take advantage of differences in demand and cargo availability, such a practice often incurred major offsetting costs. For example, a New England ship captain in the West Indies trade, acting on behalf of his merchant, would attempt to locate the best markets for the commodities he carried. This might require several voyages among the islands before agreeing on prices, the medium of exchange, and even the question of past debts. Transactions were often complex, even when the merchants and captains were acquainted with each other. Of course, in unfamiliar markets, poor communications, credit limitations, and other vexatious details compounded the difficulties. For all these reasons, arrivals at strange ports often resulted in delays and costly extensions of port times; therefore, captains usually maintained regular runs between a limited number of familiar destinations. The practice of discharging crews only in their home ports further supported the growth of shuttle trade routes, because such routes increased the percentage of total port time that was home port (wage-free) time.

INTERCOLONIAL COMMERCE

For similar reasons, colonials dominated the great volume of coastwise commerce. Early in the seventeenth century, the Dutch of New Amsterdam had anticipated the profit potential in distributing European products along the colonial coast in exchange for tobacco, furs, grain, and fish, which were then sent to Holland. After the Dutch lost power in North America in 1664, their hold on these trades declined, and New Englanders—together with enterprising merchants in New York and Philadelphia—dominated the coastal trades of North America.

In terms of the money value of products exchanged, coastal commerce was less than overseas trade with either Britain or the West Indies, but it was equal to each of these major trade branches in physical volume. As James Shepherd and Samuel Williamson (1972) have shown, just before the Revolution, coastwise trade accounted for about one-third of the volume of total overseas trade. Compared with the North, the coastwise commerce of the South was much less important, but even there it contributed perhaps one-fifth of the tonnage that entered and cleared southern ports (Johnson et al. 1915).

With regard to commerce within the interior and between the countryside and towns, we can say little in quantitative terms. Thanks to recent work by a host of scholars, including James A. Henretta, Winifred B. Rothenberg, and Thomas M. Doerflinger, much of it based on probates, tax lists, and other original sources, we know much more about the rich diversity of rural trade and activity (see their chapters in Hoffman et al. 1988). Statistical estimates of volume still elude us, however. Backcountry people traded their small agricultural surpluses for goods they could not produce themselves—salt, medicines, ammunition, cotton yarn, tea or coffee, and the like. In the villages and towns, households were less self-sufficient, although even the wealthiest homes produced some goods for everyday consumption.

---

[3]American history college textbooks in the 1960s and before commonly emphasized these descriptions. Some high school history texts still do. Famous triangles included New England–Africa–West Indies (to New England); New England–southern Europe–England (to New England); and New England–West Indies–England (to New England). For examples, see Dillard (1967, 197–198); Robertson (1964, 80–81); Williamson (1951, 50–51); Kirkland (1960, 111–112); and Wright (1941, 153–154).

Boston's natural endowments helped the city attain a place of prominence as a trading and shipping center; but the mountains to the west inhibited access to the hinterland, and Boston ultimately fell behind New York in the commercial rivalry between these two great ports.

In the complex of colonial domestic trade between country and town, it became common practice for the town merchant to extend credit to farmers, either directly or through the so-called country traders who served as intermediaries. Advances were made for the purposes of obtaining both capital equipment, such as tools and building hardware, and the supplies necessary for day-to-day existence. At the end of the growing season, farmers brought their produce to town to discharge their debts.

MONEY AND TRADE

One of the most persistent problems in the colonies was establishing and maintaining an acceptable currency. Among friends and acquaintances especially, barter trade and exchanges on account were common. Money was needed for impersonal commerce, however, to facilitate exchange among merchants and farmers. Money also served as a unit of account and as a liquid form of wealth.

Commodity Money

One of the earliest forms of money, borrowed from the Indians, was wampum, black and white polished beads made from clam shells. Wampum circulated as legal tender for private debts in Massachusetts until 1661 and was used as money in New York as late as 1701. In Maryland and Virginia, tobacco was initially the principal medium of exchange, while other colonies designated as "country pay" (acceptable for taxes) such items as hides, furs, tallow, cows, corn, wheat, beans, pork, fish, brandy, whiskey, and musket balls. Harried public officials were often swindled into receiving a poor quality of "country pay."

Because it was in an individual's self-interest to make payments whenever possible with low-quality goods, one of the major problems in using commodity money—besides inconvenience, spoilage, and storage difficulties—was quality control. One of the earliest domestically initiated regulations, the Maryland Tobacco Inspection Act of 1747, addressed this issue. The act was mainly designed to increase the value of tobacco exports from Maryland.[4] This move toward quality control ultimately did raise the value of Maryland's tobacco exports, but it also set firm standards of quality control for tobacco as money. In fact, because paper certificates called inspection notes were given on inspected tobacco, the circulation of money became easier. A Maryland planter in 1753 reported on

> [T]he Advantage of having Tobacco Notes in my pocket, as giving me credit for the quantity mentioned in them wherever I went, and that I was thereby at large to dispose of them when, to whom, and where I pleased; whereas, before this Act, my credit could not be expected to go beyond my own Neighborhood, or at farthest, where I might be known. (Maryland Gazette, April 5, 1973, as reported in Schweitzer 1980, 564)

Despite the problems, commodity money was extensively used in the colonies in the seventeenth century. By the early eighteenth century, however, both specie (gold or silver) and paper currency were common in the major seaboard cities, and by the end of the colonial period, commodities—particularly furs—were accepted only in communities along the western frontier.

Coins, Specie, and Paper Money

Because of the sizable colonial trades with many overseas areas, the gold and silver coins of all the important commercial countries of Europe and their dependencies in the Western Hemisphere were freely exchanged throughout the eastern seaboard. More important than English coins, which could not be legally exported from Britain to the colonies, were the silver coins of the Spanish mint. These were struck for the most part in Mexico City and Lima and introduced into the colonial economy via vigorous trading with the Spanish colonies. English-speaking people referred to the "piece of eight" (as the old Spanish peso was called) as a "dollar," probably because it was about the size of the German thaler. Spanish dollars were so common in the colonies that the coin was eventually adopted as the monetary unit of the United States. The fractional coin, known as the "real" or "bit," was worth about 12 1/2 cents, or one-eighth of a Spanish dollar, and was important in making change.[5]

Massachusetts was the first colony to mint coins of low bullion content in 1652, and in 1690, Massachusetts again was the first to issue paper money, as bills of credit to pay soldiers. During the next 65 years, at least eight other colonies followed this example to meet financial emergencies, especially payments of war-related efforts. Bills of credit were issued with the proviso that they were to be redeemed in specie at some future date; in the meantime, they were accepted for taxes by the issuing colony. Such redemption provisions, although restricted, facilitated the free circulation of these bills as money. In some states—notably Rhode Island, Massachusetts, Connecticut, and South Carolina—the bills were commonly overissued, thereby depreciating their value relative to specie. The same difficulty was encountered with the paper of the publicly owned "banks"

---

[4]For an excellent analysis of the impact of the act and evidence on tobacco prices, see Schweitzer (1980).

[5]The "piece of eight" was so called in colloquial language because of the numeral VIII impressed on one side to indicate its value of eight reales. In many parts of the United States, the expressions *two bits*, *four bits*, and *six bits* are still used today.

FIGURE 4.3

Annual Rate of Exchange in London for Pennsylvania Currency

The exchange rates between English sterling and Pennsylvania's paper currency moved upward between 1720 and 1739, taking more Pennsylvania money to buy an English pound. In later periods, the sterling rate fell.

Source: Historical Statistics *1976, Series Z585.*

established by colonial governments. These institutions, unlike anything we call a bank today, issued "loan bills" to individuals, usually based on the security of land or houses. Borrowers used the bills to meet their obligations and were usually required to repay the debt, with interest, in annual installments.

Historically, most paper issues in the colonies invited little attention from England, but settlements of account among merchants in the colonies and in England (and elsewhere) required legal scrutiny. Figure 4.3 traces the exchange rate of Pennsylvania paper currency for English sterling in London. Clearly, Pennsylvania paper money did not exchange at 1 to 1, but was discounted. English merchants sometimes complained of payments being made in depreciated money, especially when the par rate of 1 to 1.67 was exceeded, as in the 1740s when nearly 180 was needed to equal 100 sterling. Court settlements in Pennsylvania, however, of contracts written in sterling used current market values of the currency (as shown in Figure 4.3) rather than the par rate. This protected English merchants from being paid in unanticipated, depreciated paper currency. Finally, other colonies using paper money had different exchanges and par rates (i.e., Maryland was 133 to 1).[6]

A paper currency that was widely acceptable stands as one of the great legacies of the colonists. Occasionally, despite public issues of paper, private remedies were still undertaken, as exemplified by one merchant's April 1761 announcement in the *Maryland Gazette*:

> *As I daily suffer much inconvenience in my Business for Want of small Change, which indeed is a universal Complaint of almost everybody in any Sort of Business, I intend to...Print...a Parcel of small Notes, from Three Pence to Two Shillings and Six Pence each, to pass Current at the same Rate as the Money under the Inspecting Law, and to be Exchanged by me...for good Spanish Dollars at Seven Shillings and Six Pence each Dollar. (Ernst 1973, 154–155)*[7]

Despite their risks, such issues lowered transaction costs, especially on retail and small-lot exchanges. It is noteworthy that paper money at that time was uniquely American. Although invented and used in ancient China, paper money was not used anywhere in the world after 1500 until it was reintroduced by the mainland colonists.

---

[6]See Grubb (forthcoming [2009]), for a brief overview of money in the colonies.

[7]For more on this issue, see Hanson (1984).

TRADE DEFICITS WITH ENGLAND

It is important to reemphasize here that mercantilist measures were implemented by the Crown to regulate trade and generate favorable trade balances for England. In addition, because European manufactured goods were in great demand in the New World, colonists faced chronic deficits, especially in their trade with England. Trade deficits in the colonies resulted in a continual drain of specie from colonial shores and encouraged the use of paper money substitutes. Table 4.3 shows the size and trend of these trade deficits with England over much of the eighteenth century. As highlighted in Table 4.4, most of these deficits were incurred by New England and the Middle colonies, but even the southern colonies frequently faced deficits in their commodity trade with England.

How did the colonists pay for their trade deficits? Benjamin Franklin's reply to a Parliamentary committee in 1760 explaining Pennsylvania's payment of its trade deficit with England was as follows:

> The balance is paid by our produce carried to the West Indies, and sold in our own islands, or to the French, Spaniards, Danes, and Dutch; by the same carried to other colonies in North America, as to New England, Nova Scotia, Newfoundland, Carolina and Georgia; by the same carried to different parts of Europe, as Spain, Portugal and Italy: In all which places we receive either money, bills of exchange, or commodities that suit for remittance to Britain; which, together with all the profits of the industry of our merchants and mariners arising in those circuitous voyages and the freights made by their ships, center finally in Britain to discharge the balance and pay for British manufactures continually used in the province or sold to foreigners by our traders. (Faulkner 1960, 81)

As emphasized by the esteemed Franklin, colonial trade deficits to Britain could be paid by surpluses earned in trades to other overseas areas as well as by earnings from shipping and other mercantile services.

Other sources of foreign exchange, such as payments by the British forces stationed in the colonies, also affected the inflow of sterling. To determine the relative importance of these and other sources of exchange earnings (and losses), we need to assess the various components of the colonies' overall balance of payments. (See Economic Insight 4.1 on page 70.)

TABLE 4.3 VALUES AND BALANCES OF COMMODITY TRADE BETWEEN ENGLAND AND THE AMERICAN COLONIES (ANNUAL AVERAGES BY DECADE, IN THOUSANDS OF POUNDS STERLING)

	IMPORT	EXPORT	DEFICIT
1721–1730	£ 509	£ 442	£ 67
1731–1740	698	559	139
1741–1750	923	599	324
1751–1760	1,704	808	896
1761–1770	1,942	1,203	739

Source: *Shepherd and Walton 1972, 42.*

ECONOMIC INSIGHT 4.1

A BALANCE OF PAYMENTS FOR THE 13 COLONIES

A balance of payments study clarifies many critical issues. It can determine how the deficits to England were paid and show the size of net specie drains from the colonies or indicate the magnitude of growing indebtedness of colonists to British creditors. It can show the inflows of capital into the colonies and suggest the magnitude of possible British subsidization of colonial economic development. A balance of payments is an accounting framework in which debits and credits always balance. In short, one way or another, things get paid for, with goods, money, or IOUs (debt). This is true for people and true for nations (and colonies) as well.

Surviving information on the myriad of exchanges for the years from 1768 to 1772 gives us a reasonably clear picture of the colonies' balance of payments in the late colonial period. A breakdown of the colonies' commodity trade balances with the major overseas areas during this period is provided in Table 4.4. These data confirm the findings presented earlier in Table 4.3, indicating that sizable deficits were incurred in the English trade, especially by New England and the Middle colonies. Somewhat surprisingly, even the colonies' commodity trade to the West Indies was unfavorable (except for the trade of the Lower South). However, trades to southern Europe generated significant surpluses (augmented slightly by the African trades), which were sufficient to raise the southern colonial regions to a surplus position in their overall commodity exchanges.

TABLE 4.4 AVERAGE ANNUAL COMMODITY TRADE BALANCES OF THE 13 AMERICAN COLONIES, 1768–1772 (IN THOUSANDS OF POUNDS STERLING)

	GREAT BRITAIN AND IRELAND	SOUTHERN EUROPE	WEST INDIES	AFRICA	ALL TRADES
New England	£−0,609	£+048	£−36	£+19	£−0,577
Middle Colonies	−0,786	+153	−10	+01	−0,643
Upper South	−0,050	+090	−09	00	+0,031
Lower South	−0,023	+048	+44	0	+0,069
Total	−1,468	+339	−11	+20	−1,120

Notes: (1) A plus sign denotes a surplus (exports exceed imports); a minus sign, a deficit (imports exceed exports). (2) Values are expressed in prices in the mainland colonies; thus, import values include the costs of transportation, commissions, and other handling costs. Export values are also expressed in colonial prices and, therefore, do not include these distribution costs.

Source: Shepherd and Walton 1972, 115.

Although commodity exchanges made up the lion's share of total colonial exchanges, the colonies did have other sources of foreign exchange earnings (and losses) as well. Table 4.5 begins with colonial commodity exchanges indicating the £1,120 aggregate deficit in that category.

The most important source of foreign exchange earnings to offset that average deficit was the sale of colonial shipping services. Shipping earnings totaled approximately £600,000 per year in the late colonial period. In addition, colonial merchants earned more than £200,000 annually through insurance charges

and commissions. Together, these "invisible" earnings offset more than 60 percent of the overall colonial commodity trade deficit. Almost 80 percent of these invisible earnings reverted to residents of New England and the Middle colonies. Thus, the mercantile activities of New Englanders and Middle colonists, especially in the West Indian trade, enabled the colonies to import large quantities of manufactured goods from Great Britain. When all 13 colonies are considered together, invisible earnings exceeded earnings from tobacco exports—the single most important colonial staple export.

ECONOMIC INSIGHT 4.1

A BALANCE OF PAYMENTS FOR THE 13 COLONIES, Continued

TABLE 4.5 BALANCE OF PAYMENTS FOR THE 13 COLONIES, 1768–1772 (IN THOUSANDS OF POUNDS STERLING)

	DEBITS	CREDITS
Commodities		
Export earnings		£2,800
Imports	£3,920	
Trade deficit	1,120	
Ship sales to foreigners		140
Invisible earnings		
Shipping cargoes		600
Merchant commissions, insurance, etc.		220
Payments for human beings		
Indentured servants	80	
Slaves	200	
British collections and expenditures		
Taxes and duties	40	
Military and civil expendituresa		440–460
Payments deficit financed by specie flows and/or increased indebtedness		20–40

Notes: Gwyn's estimates of total expenditures for military and civil purposes for 1768–1772 are £365, but Thomas's study suggests higher arms payments by nearly £100,000 yearly for the same period. Neither accounts for savings by men stationed in the colonies who returned some of their earnings home; thus, the £440–460 range; £460 assumes no savings sent home.

Sources: Data compiled from Walton and Shepherd 1979, Table 9, 101; Gwyn 1984, 74–87, fn. 7; and Thomas 1988, 510–516.

Another aspect of seafaring, the sale of ships, also became a persistent credit item in the colonies' balance of payments. As Jacob Price (1976) has shown, colonial ship sales averaged at least £140,000 annually from 1763 to 1775, primarily to England. Again, the lion's share of these earnings went to New England shipbuilders, but the Middle colonies also received a portion of the profits from ship sales. Taken together, ship sales and "invisible" earnings reduced the colonies' negative balance of payments to only £160,000.

In contrast to these earning sources, funds for the trade of human beings were continually lost to foreign markets. An average of approximately £80,000 sterling was spent annually for the 5,000 to 10,000 indentured servants who arrived each year during the late colonial period. Most of these servants were sent to Pennsylvania and the Chesapeake Bay area. A more sizable amount was the nearly £200,000 spent each year to purchase approximately 5,000 slaves. More than 90 percent of these slaves were sent to the southern colonies, especially to the Lower South in the later colonial period.

Finally, expenditures made by the British government in the colonies on defense, civil administration, and justice notably offset the remaining deficits in the colonists' current account of trade. Table 4.5 does not indicate the total amount of these costs to Great Britain. Instead, it shows how much British currency was used to purchase goods and services in the colonies and how much was paid to men stationed there. The net inflow for these expenditures averaged between £440,000 and £460,000 from 1768 to 1772, reducing the net deficit in the colonial balance of payments for these years to £40,000 per year at most, and probably less.

Interpretations: Money, Debt, and Capital

Having assessed the colonies' balance of payments, we turn now to its impact on the colonial economy. The estimated remaining annual colonial deficit of £20,000 to £40,000 was paid either by an outflow of specie or by growing indebtedness to Britain. Temporary net outflows of specie undoubtedly did occur, thereby straining trade and prices in the colonies. Certainly, contemporary complaints of money scarcity, especially specie, indicate that this often happened. But no significant part of this normal deficit could have been paid with precious metals. The colonists could not sustain a permanent net outflow of specie because gold and silver mines were not developed in colonial North America. Typically, then, the outflow of specie to England was matched by an inflow from various sources of colonial exchange earnings. Nevertheless, the erratic pattern of specie movement and the issuance of paper money of uncertain value caused monetary disturbances, as reflected in price movements and alterations in rates of exchange among the currencies. But most colonists preferred to spend rather than to accumulate a stock of specie. After all, limited specie was simply another manifestation of a capital-scarce economy. To the colonists, it was more desirable to receive additional imports—especially manufactures—than to maintain a growing stock of specie.

The final remaining colonial deficits were normally financed on short-term credit, and American merchants usually purchased goods from England on one-year credit. This was so customary, in fact, that British merchants included a normal 5 percent interest charge in their prices and granted a rebate to accounts that were paid before the year ended. And in Virginia, Scottish firms generally established representatives in stores to sell or trade British wares for tobacco and other products. Short-term credit was a normal part of day-to-day colonial exchanges in these instances.

The growth of short-term credit reflected the expanding Atlantic trades and represented a modest amount of increasing colonial indebtedness to Britain. Sizable claims against southern planters by British merchants after the Revolution[8] have encouraged some historians to argue that the relationship between London merchants and southern planters was disastrous at that time and even to argue that increasing colonial indebtedness to Britain provided impetus for the Revolution. But was this, in fact, so?

By adding the "invisible" earnings and ship sales to the regional commodity trade deficits (and surpluses), we obtain these rough averages of the regional deficits (−) and surpluses (+) in the colonies:[9]

New England − £50,000; Middle colonies − £350,000; Southern colonies + £350,000

Clearly, the major deficit regions were north of the Chesapeake Bay area, primarily in the Middle colonies. The southern regions were favored with more than a sufficient surplus in their current accounts of trade to pay for their purchases of slaves and indentured servants.

---

[8]Of the approximately £5,000,000 claimed by British merchants in 1791, more than £2,300,000 was owed by Virginia, nearly £570,000 by Maryland, £690,000 by South Carolina, £380,000 by North Carolina, and £250,000 by Georgia. However, nearly one-half of these amounts represented accumulated interest on deficits that had been in effect since 1776. Moreover, Aubrey Land argues that these claims were exaggerated by as much as 800 percent and that the Americans honored only one-eighth of such claims (see Land 1967).

[9]The regional division of shipping earnings and other "invisibles" is derived from chapter 8 in Shepherd and Walton (1972). Because the ownership of vessels is not given separately for the Upper South and Lower South, we have combined these two regions here, but undoubtedly, the Upper South earned the greater portion of the combined £240,000 surplus. All ship sales have been credited to the northern regions; £100,000 to New England and £40,000 to the Middle colonies.

A fair number of planters availed themselves of greater credit from abroad. Nevertheless, it appears there was no growing indebtedness on average in the South at this time, and British expenditures for military and administrative purposes eliminated the negative New England balance and reduced most of the Middle colonies' balances as well.[10]

Nevertheless, England's claims were real enough, even if exaggerated. But remember that British merchants and their colonial representatives normally extended credit to southern planters and accepted their potential harvests as collateral. Usually, of course, the harvests came in, and the colonists' outstanding debts were paid. But with the outbreak of the Revolution, this picture changed radically. Colonial credit, which normally was extended throughout the year, was still outstanding at the end of the year because agents or partners of British firms had retreated home before the crops were harvested and the debts were paid. But the mere existence of these debts did not indicate growing indebtedness—nor did it provide motivation for colonial revolt.

The capital inflows that did occur were rarely channeled directly into long-term investments in the colonies, and British merchants held few claims on such investments. Nevertheless, because commercial short-term credit was furnished by the British, colonial savings were freed for other uses: to make long-term investments in land improvement, roads, and such physical capital as ships, warehouses, and public buildings. For the purposes of colonial development, British short-term credit represented a helping hand, and its form was much less important than its amount.

However, with the highly important exception of military and civil defense, the colonies apparently were not subsidized by Britain to any great extent. For the most part, the formation of capital in the New World depended on the steady accretion of savings and on investment from the pockets of the colonists themselves. It is impossible to determine precisely how much was annually saved and invested during the late colonial period. According to our estimates, which will be elaborated in chapter 5, annual incomes probably averaged at least £11 sterling per person in the colonies. Because nearly 2.5 million people were living in the colonies on the eve of the Revolution, if we assume a savings rate of not less than 9 percent (£1 out of £11), total capital accumulation per year would have exceeded £2.5 million at that time. Thus, the capital inflow from Britain probably accounted for 1 or 2 percent of capital formation in the colonies.

The sizable estimates of British military expenditures in North America between 1763 and 1775 (Thomas 1988) and of civil and military expenditures for the longer period from 1740 to 1775 (Gwyn 1984) support these general conclusions of small net deficits in the colonies' balance of payments throughout much of the late colonial period. Only the substantial British expenditures for military and administrative purposes reveal a form of British subsidization or colonial dependency in the decades just before the Revolution.

---

[10]Further alteration of the regional deficits and surpluses would have resulted from coastal trade among the regions. Surprisingly, however, the major regions in the 13 colonies appear to have earned surpluses in coastal trade. Florida, the Bahamas, and the Bermuda Islands and the northern colonies of Newfoundland, Nova Scotia, and Quebec were the deficit areas in coastal trade. See Shepherd and Williamson (1972).

SELECTED REFERENCES AND SUGGESTED READINGS

Bezanson, Ann, et al. *Prices in Colonial Pennsylvania.* Philadelphia: University of Pennsylvania Press, 1935.

Dillard, Dudley. *Economic Development of the North Atlantic Community.* Englewood Cliffs, N.J.: Prentice Hall, 1967.

Ernst, Joseph A. *Money and Politics in America, 1755–1775.* Chapel Hill: University of North Carolina Press, 1973.

Faulkner, Harold U. *American Economic History*, 8th ed. New York: Harper & Row, 1960.

Grubb, Farley. "Money Supply in the British North American Colonies." In *Palgrave Dictionary of Economics* [online version], 2009.

Gwyn, Julian. "British Government Spending and the North American Colonies, 1740–1775." *Journal of Imperial and Commonwealth History* 8 (1984): 74–84.

Hanson, John R. "Small Notes in the American Economy." *Explorations in Economic History* 21 (1984): 411–420.

Historical Statistics. Series Z585. Washington, D.C.: Government Printing Office, 1976.

Hoffman, Ronald, et al., eds. *The Economy of Early America: The Revolutionary Period, 1763–1790.* Charlottesville: University Press of Virginia, 1988.

Johnson, E. R., et al. *History of Domestic and Foreign Commerce of the United States.* Washington, D.C.: Carnegie Institution of Washington, 1915.

Kirkland, Edward. *A History of American Economic Life.* New York: Appleton-Century-Crofts, 1960.

Land, Aubrey C. "Economic Behavior in a Planting Society: The Eighteenth Century Chesapeake." *Journal of Southern History* 32 (1967): 482–483.

Pares, Richard. *Yankees and Creoles.* Cambridge, Mass.: Harvard University Press, 1956.

Price, Jacob. "A Note on the Value of Colonial Exports of Shipping." *Journal of Economic History* 36 (1976): 704–724.

Robertson, Ross M. *History of the American Economy*, 2nd ed. New York: Harcourt, Brace & World, 1964.

Schweitzer, Mary McKinney. "Economic Regulation and the Colonial Economy: The Maryland Tobacco Inspection Act of 1747." *Journal of Economic History* 40 (1980): 551–570.

Shepherd, James F., and Gary M. Walton. *Shipping, Maritime Trade and the Economic Development of Colonial North America.* Cambridge: Cambridge University Press, 1972.

Shepherd, James F., and Samuel Williamson. "The Coastal Trade of the British North American Colonies 1768–1772." *Journal of Economic History* 32 (1972): 783–810.

Thomas, Peter D. G. "The Cost of the British Army in North America, 1763–1775." *William and Mary Quarterly* 45 (1988): 510–516.

Walton, Gary M. "New Evidence on Colonial Commerce." *Journal of Economic History* 28 (September 1968): 363–389.

Walton, Gary M., and James F. Shepherd. *The Economic Rise of Early America.* Cambridge: Cambridge University Press, 1979.

Williamson, Harold F. ed. *The Growth of the American Economy*, 2nd ed. Englewood Cliffs, N.J.: Prentice Hall, 1951.

Wright, Chester W. *Economic History of the United States.* New York: McGraw-Hill, 1941.

CHAPTER 5

Economic Progress and Wealth

CHAPTER THEME

Because of high levels of migration and rapid population growth, total output in the colonies grew at high rates throughout the colonial period. Standards of living for the average colonist also grew at rates that were high by contemporary standards and comparable to gains in Britain, Holland, and France. The sources of growth of per capita income form an important part of the story of economic development, because these sources of progress lifted the colonial economy to a position from which it could become independent from England. These sources are found principally in case (or sectoral) studies of productivity change. Although the economy grew and prospered, people and regions did not gain equally, and already, substantial inequality of wealth (and income) existed among people and places as settlements in the wilderness grew into towns and centers of trade.

GROWTH AND CHANGE IN THE COLONIAL ECONOMY

The many local and regional economies that composed the total colonial economy were always in a state of flux. Because the colonies began literally as settlements in the wilderness, and because war and other frontier disturbances were frequent, it is particularly difficult to systematically portray the economic growth of the colonies. The data are simply too scant to provide any systematic and comprehensive measures of economic growth.

In 1964, George R. Taylor triggered a debate that still demands attention. In his presidential address to the Economic History Association, Taylor argued that before 1710, very little economic growth, in terms of sustained increases in real per capita income, occurred in the colonies (it was "slow and irregular"), but that then, between 1710 and 1775, it averaged "slightly more than 1 percent per annum" (Taylor 1964, 437). A handy rule of thumb, known as the Rule of 70, shows the impact of annual growth rates. If r is the rate of growth in percentage terms and t is the number of years that the growing quantity takes to double, then $r \times t = 70$. Taylor's assertion of 1 percent implies a doubling of income per capita in 70 years: $t = 70/1$, or 70 years. Did Taylor's claim of an early eighteenth-century acceleration really take place, and did per capita incomes really almost double between 1710 and 1775, as the 1 percent claim implies? Did such economic advances continue indefinitely thereafter, or did periods of stagnation reappear?

Because of data limitations on real per capita income, firm answers elude us.[1] Through recent scholarly efforts, however, fragments of information have appeared to

---

[1] In measuring changes of income, we often neglect other factors that affect the quality of life, such as the amount of leisure time enjoyed, conditions of health, environment, personal attributes, and even the distribution of wealth.

significantly advance our understanding of the pace and main sources of growth in the colonies.

Productivity Change in Agriculture

The major economic activity in the colonies was agriculture, and progress in this sector had a particularly strong bearing on total colonial production. Because agriculture was such a significant part of total output, total average gains were significantly influenced by advances (or lack of advances) in this sector. Moreover, it is important to remember that economic progress in real per capita terms stems primarily from human efforts to raise productivity—the increase of output relative to the inputs of labor, capital, and land. Therefore, we will devote particular attention to periods of change in productivity and to the agricultural improvements that were introduced.

Tobacco in the Upper South   An obvious starting point is the dominant colonial staple, tobacco. Information on tobacco prices in the Chesapeake Bay area, as shown in Figure 5.1, suggests that most of the increases in the productivity of tobacco occurred very early in the colonial period. Ranging between 20d. and 30d. sterling per pound in the early 1620s, tobacco prices fell to less than 3d. per pound around 1630. A second phase, lasting approximately four decades, followed that precipitous decline. This time, the average price decreased to about a penny per pound. Of course, short-term periods of cyclical variations occurred, but tobacco prices stayed at that low price throughout most of the remaining peacetime years. Open competitive markets ruled out monopoly pricing.

FIGURE 5.1
Chesapeake Farm
Tobacco Prices,
1618–1710

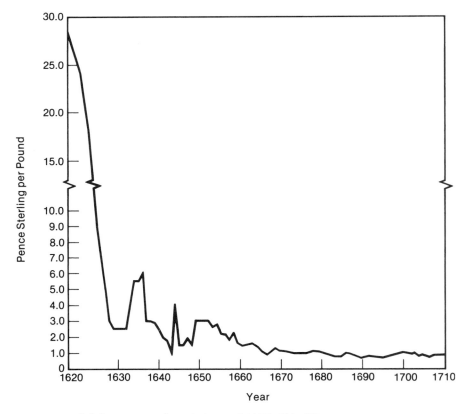

Sources: *Compiled from Menard 1973, 85; and 1976, 401–410.*

Little doubt exists that these two early periods of declining tobacco prices represented major surges in productivity. According to Allan Kulikoff (1979), tobacco output per worker doubled between 1630 and 1670. The demand for tobacco in Europe was persistently growing, and the costs of the labor and land required to produce tobacco did not decrease over these years. Therefore, declining wages or rents cannot explain the lower costs of tobacco; these declines must have been largely caused by increases in output per unit of input (land, labor, and capital in combination)—that is, by gains in productivity. Terry Anderson and Robert Thomas (1978) also estimate very high productivity advances in tobacco: Over the last three quarters of the seventeenth century, the advance was nearly 1.5 percent per year on average. Very little productivity advance occurred in tobacco in the eighteenth century, however, and undoubtedly, the major period of progress in tobacco cultivation was during the seventeenth rather than the eighteenth century.

This characteristic of rapid early gains and subsequent periods of slower advance has always been common to the growth patterns of production in firms and industries. In colonial times, before the age of widespread technological advances, productivity gains stemmed primarily from trial and error and learning by doing. In agriculture, the fruits of these efforts generally materialized within a few decades of crop introduction. Sometimes, as in the case of tobacco, the introduction of a new seed type generated a surge of crop productivity. Also, in the early phases of experimentation, the colonists found ways to combine and adjust soils, seeds, labor implements, and other agricultural inputs to their optimum uses. In later stages of agricultural development, improvements were more gradual, based on a slower-paced accumulation of knowledge about the most productive uses of available soils and resources. In some instances, such as the colonists' futile attempts at wine production and silk cultivation, these efforts ceased in the experimentation phase.

Grain and Livestock in the Middle Colonies   In grain and livestock production, as in tobacco, gains in productivity appear to have been modest, indeed low, throughout most of the eighteenth century. The most visible change in Pennsylvania farms was the sharp decline in average farm size, from about 500 acres in 1700 to about 140 acres at the end of the century. But this decrease did not indicate a fall in the ratio of "effective land" to labor. Instead, it was the consequence of population expansion and the subdivision of uncleared acres into new farms. Because the amount of uncleared land per farm exceeded the minimum needs for fuel and timber, these acreage reductions had no noticeable effect on agricultural output. Because the average number of cleared acres per farm changed little, the effective input of land per farm remained almost constant throughout the entire eighteenth century.

Alternatively, additional implements, structures, and accumulated inventories raised the amount of capital inputs per farm. Meanwhile, the average family size was shrinking. Consequently, in the predominantly family farm areas such as Pennsylvania, the amount of labor per farm decreased. Therefore, both the capital–labor ratio and the cleared land–labor ratio rose. Given the increase of inputs per worker, we would expect output per worker to expand.

Indeed, the evidence reveals that output per farm was increasing (see Ball and Walton 1976). Not only were farms producing more livestock and grains (mainly wheat and maslin, a combination of wheat and rye), but also by the late colonial period, a small but growing portion of farm labor time was being diverted to nonagricultural production, including milling, smithing, cabinet making, chair making, and tanning. Overall, average output per farm increased by about 7 percent between the first and third quarters of the eighteenth century. When the gain in output is compared with

The tranquility of this eighteenth-century rural colonial setting belies the hard work and varied daily tasks of family farming.

the change in total input,[2] it appears that total productivity advanced approximately 10 percent during these decades. Expressed in terms of rates of change, total productivity expanded by 0.1 to 0.2 percent per year, with the most rapid change (0.3 percent) occurring in the first decades of the eighteenth century. Finally, the growth of output per worker was somewhat higher (approximately 0.2 to 0.3 percent per year) over the first three quarters of the century.[3]

Specific evidence on the precise sources of these advances is almost entirely lacking. The low measured rate of advance, however, does reinforce historical descriptions. For

---

[2]With land per farm nearly constant, labor per farm declining, and capital per farm rising, total input per farm changed according to the relative importance of labor and capital and the relative degree of change of each. Because labor comprised such a high percentage of total costs, total combined input per farm actually declined by a few percentage points during the eighteenth century.

[3]Labor productivity (output per worker) increased more than total productivity (output per total combined input) because the amounts of capital and cleared land per worker increased during this period. Increases in these other inputs enabled labor to produce more.

Additions of capital and the specialization of tasks raised productivity per worker in colonial tobacco production.

instance, in their classic study of agriculture, Bidwell and Falconer assert that in the colonies north of the Chesapeake, "The eighteenth century farmers showed little advance over the first settlers in their care of livestock," and "little if any improvement had been made in farm implements until the very close of the eighteenth century" (Bidwell and Falconer 1925, 107, 123). Another study of Pennsylvania agriculture specifically concludes that "economic conditions throughout the century prohibited major changes and encouraged a reasonably stable and uniform type of mixed farming that involved fairly extensive use or superficial working of the land" (Lemon 1972, 150–151). It seems reasonable to conclude that farmers were probably beginning to learn to use the soil and their implements more effectively. But there is little indication of input savings, either from technological improvements or from economies of scale in terms of larger farms. Better organized and more widespread market participation, however, may have contributed somewhat to gains in agricultural productivity.

These findings and conclusions come as no surprise when examined in the light of agricultural developments in later periods. For instance, investigations by Robert Gallman indicate total productivity gains of approximately 0.5 percent per year over the nineteenth century (Gallman 1972, 1975). However, in the first half of the century, combined output per unit of land, labor, and capital advanced at a rate of 0.1 to 0.2 percent. In the second half of the century, the productivity rate rose to 0.8 percent. Undoubtedly, the lower-paced first half of the nineteenth century—before the transition to animal power and increased mechanization—would be more suggestive of the eighteenth-century experience. In short, agricultural progress throughout most of the colonial period was sporadic, limited, and slow paced.

Productivity Gains in Transportation and Distribution

Although productivity advances in agriculture were slow and gradual, substantially higher gains were registered in the handling and transportation of goods. Such gains were extremely important because transportation and other distribution costs made up a large portion of the final market price of products. This was especially true of the bulky colonial products, which were normally low in value relative to their weight or volume (displaced cargo space). For example, transportation and handling costs would double the value of a barrel of pitch between Maryland and London. Even the distribution costs of expensive lightwares represented a significant fraction of their value.

During the eighteenth century, the differential between English and colonial prices for manufactures shipped to the colonies was declining at a fairly steady rate. In the early decades of the century, it was not uncommon for English goods to sell for 80 to 140 percent more in the colonies than in England. By midcentury, prices on British wares were 45 to 75 percent higher in the colonies. Finally, just before the Revolution, this price spread had been reduced to a range of only 15 to 25 percent. As late as the 1770s, however, colonial staples such as pitch, tar, lumber, rice, and other space-consuming exports were still commanding more than double their domestic price in normal English and European markets.

Table 5.1 shows evidence of improvements in the marketing and distribution of transatlantic tobacco shipments. The average differential between the Amsterdam and the colonial price of tobacco (given as a percentage of the Amsterdam price) declined (Shepherd and Walton 1972).

A series of advances in transatlantic tobacco distribution stemmed from improvements in packaging and merchandising, from declining costs of information on prices and markets, and from reductions of risk in trade. By far, however, the most important improvements were in shipping. Although freight rates fluctuated and varied according to route, and between periods of war and peace, the long-run trend was persistently downward. During the 100 years preceding the Revolution, the real costs of shipping were almost halved. Expressed in terms of productivity gains, shipping advanced at a rate of approximately 0.8 percent per year. For that period—and specifically compared with changes in agriculture—these increases suggest that shipping was a strategic factor in the overall economic advance of the colonies.

TABLE 5.1 TOBACCO PRICE RATIOS

PRICE IN EUROPE—PRICE IN AMERICA
PRICE IN EUROPE

YEARS	RATIOS MEASURES
1720–1724	82%
1725–1729	76
1730–1734	82
1735–1739	77
1740–1744	77
1745–1749	76
1750–1754	67
1755–1759	72
1760–1764	70
1765–1769	65
1770–1774	51

Source: *Shepherd and Walton, 1972, 60.*

Sources of Productivity Change in Shipping What caused these productivity gains? In cases in which trades were well organized and markets reasonably large and safe, economies of scale in shipping were usually realized. In the Baltic timber trades, for instance, the use of larger vessels generated labor savings per ton shipped. Although larger ships necessitated larger crews, the increased cargo capacity more than compensated for the additional labor costs. As vessels increased in size, their carrying capacity per unit of labor also increased. In other words, on larger ships, fewer men were needed to transport a given volume of goods.

Despite these possibilities, the average size of vessels employed in the western Atlantic and in the Caribbean failed to increase significantly over the 100-year period. The potential labor savings of the larger ships were offset by greater occurrences of low utilization in these waters. In fact, in those numerous small and scattered markets, the port times of large vessels were usually as much as twice as long as those for small vessels. Therefore, in colonial waters, schooners and sloops normally traveled a larger number of miles per ton than did large ships or brigs. Nevertheless, because crew sizes decreased as vessels remained unchanged in size, the number of tons per man increased. For example, a Boston vessel of 50 tons employed an average of seven men early in the eighteenth century, but by the late colonial period, the same ship required only five crew members. Over this same time span, the crew size of a typical New York vessel of 50 tons decreased from 11 to 7 members. Paralleling this reduction in labor was the reduction or elimination of armaments on vessels that traded in colonial waters. Guns had been commonplace on seventeenth-century vessels trading in the western Atlantic, but cannons had all but disappeared on ships there by the end of the colonial period.

Although the average useful life of vessels changed little over the period, insurance rates decreased due to the declining risks in ocean travel. In contrast to earlier times, by 1720, insurance rates for most one-way transatlantic passages had reached the rock-bottom common peacetime level of 2 percent. Of course, rates for voyages into pirate-infested waters were quite another matter. Between New York and Jamaica, for example, the prevailing rate of 5 percent in 1720 had dropped to 4 percent by the 1770s. On routes from New England to various other islands in the West Indies, peacetime insurance rates were halved between 1700 and 1775.

Faster ship speed was not a positive force in raising productivity. Vessels from New England and the Middle colonies that sailed to the West Indies and back showed no gains in speed on either leg of the journey during this period, as shown in Figure 5.2. Nevertheless, round-trip voyage times declined from 1700 to 1775. As Figure 5.3 shows,

FIGURE 5.2
Average Ship Speeds (knots)

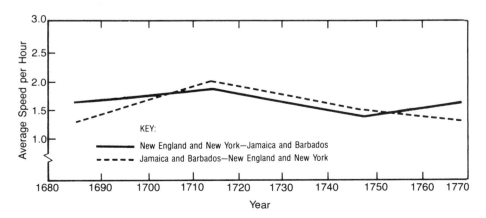

Source: *Walton 1967, 74.*

FIGURE 5.3
Average Port Times

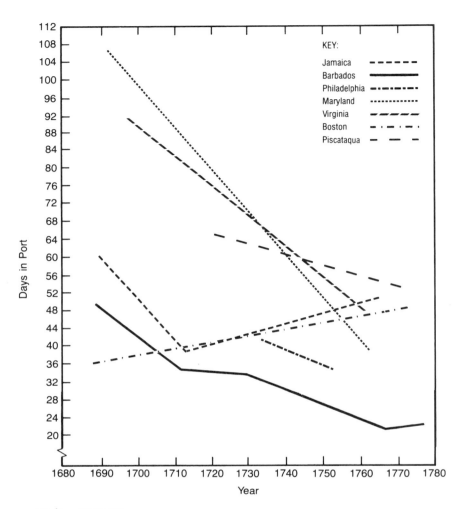

Source: *Walton 1967, 75.*

with the single exception of Boston, layover times fell markedly in many key ports in the New World. Because a very large portion of a sailing ship's life was spent in port, such declines contributed greatly to higher productivity. For example, in the Chesapeake trade, vessels were in port more than twice as long at the end of the seventeenth century as they were in the 1760s. An important contributor to this change was the introduction of Scottish factors (representatives of Scottish merchant firms) into the Chesapeake Bay area after 1707. Undoubtedly, their methods of gathering and inventorying the tobacco crop in barns and warehouses for quick loading significantly shortened port times in the Chesapeake Bay.

Similarly, port times in Barbados were halved during this period. In the early colonial days, port times were extraordinarily long because exchanges were costly to transact. The many scattered markets were small and remote, and prices varied widely among islands and even within the same island. The shipmaster, acting on behalf of a merchant, might have to visit several islands on one trip to find the best market for his cargo. Difficulties in negotiating prices and determining the medium of exchange, as well as possibly settling past debts, all tended to lengthen the transaction period. Often, bartering was practiced, but even when money was used, prices were not easy to determine because

PERSPECTIVE 5.1

THE HORSE AND INSTITUTIONAL CHANGE IN INDIAN CULTURE

Like an invention, the northward diffusion of the horse, 1601 to 1740, first introduced in the New World by the Spanish in the sixteenth century, imposed dramatic changes on the daily lives of North American Indians. This was especially true of Indians living on the Great Plains. Before the horse, they were seminomadic, living much of the year in communal earthen lodges and cultivating gardens of beans, squash, and corn. Summers and falls found them on the move, on foot with dogs dragging teepees, following and hunting buffalo, thereby adding meat to their diet.

On foot and with dogs, a good day's journey was about 5 miles. In winter a few hunters could succeed in stalking a few bison; in good weather, larger bands of hunters used tactics of surrounding small herds and killing them with arrows. Given appropriate terrain, the "pedestrian drive" was used where herds were driven into traps or over cliffs.

The most immediate impact of the horse was to reduce the amount of agricultural work plains Indians had done. This changed the balance of their diet. It also led to more extensive killing and less intensive use of the meat on the carcass—"light butchering," as it was called.

From 5 miles a day, the hunting groups on horses could cover 20 miles. Instead of a 50-mile hunting area in a season, they were soon able to extend their range to 500 miles. Hunting groups became smaller and more independent since communal schemes (a type of insurance) were less needed: Less time was spent in fixed locations in communal earthen lodges, and horse power enabled the movement of larger teepees that dogs could pull on travois (wheelless carts).

Pasturage and water sources took on greater importance, intensifying the problem of campsite selection. Before the horse, intertribal warfare was rare; afterward, intertribal alliances were few and warfare was frequent.

Finally, like land to the Europeans, the horse became the symbol of wealth and prestige for Native Americans. It was a form of personal property (including right to inheritance, trade, use, and exclusion of use). Especially on the plains, the institutional changes brought about by the horse were so great that the number of horses owned often meant the difference between survival, starvation, and conquest (see Anderson and LaCombe 1999 for elaboration).

different currencies and bills of exchange (with varying degrees of risk) were afforded no set value. Finally, the problem of collecting cargoes extended port times, especially when harvests were poor.[4] As a more systematic market economy and other institutional changes evolved, long layovers in the Caribbean became less common.

Decreasing port times produced savings not only in capital but also in labor costs, because crews were customarily fed and paid while they were in foreign ports. Such savings more than offset other sources of cost increases. Although wages and ship repair costs remained fairly constant over the period, the costs of shipbuilding and victualing (obtaining food for the crew) increased. Overall, however, the productivity gains countervailed, and freight costs were cut in half between 1675 and 1775.

TECHNOLOGICAL CHANGE AND PRODUCTIVITY

Among the most powerful engines of modern economic growth have been technological changes that raise output relative to inputs. But compared with those of the nineteenth century, technological changes remained minor and sporadic in the colonial period. It preceded the era of the cotton gin, steam power, and the many metallurgical advances that vastly increased the tools available to workers. Even in iron production, we hear

---

[4]As discussed in chapter 4, many of these factors also explain the generality of shuttle patterns of shipping and of route dominance by the colonists vis-à-vis the British on particular routes.

Acts of piracy in the western Atlantic, the Caribbean, and elsewhere thrived before 1720. The long-term effects of actions by the Royal Navy to eliminate piracy were to change the characteristic of ships and reduce freight rates on ocean transport.

from Paul Paskoff (1980), learning by doing and adapting remained the key source of labor and fuel savings in the late colonial period. In the decade preceding the Revolution, iron output per man increased nearly 50 percent, and charcoal use per ton decreased by half. Learning to reduce the fuel input to minimal levels saved on labor needed to gather charcoal and work the forges. Technology remained static and forge sizes constant, however. The evidence in agriculture also indicates no significant leaps in technology.

In shipping, the same conclusion is reached. This period preceded the era of iron ships and steam, and both ship materials and the power source of ships remained unchanged. Even increasingly complex sails and rigs and the alterations of hull shapes failed to increase ship speed and, in any case, did not represent fundamental advances in knowledge.

It might be argued that crew reductions stemmed from advances in knowledge. During the early seventeenth century, however, Dutch shipping had already displayed many of the essential characteristics of design, manning, and other input requirements that were found on the most advanced vessels in the western Atlantic in the 1760s and 1770s. In fact, the era's most significant technological change in shipping had occurred in approximately 1595, when the Dutch first introduced the flyboat, or flute, a specialized merchant vessel designed to carry bulk commodities. The flyboat was exceptionally long compared with its width, had a flat bottom, and was lightly built (armament, gun platforms, and reinforced planking had been eliminated). In addition, its rig was simple, and its crew size was small. In contrast, English and colonial vessels were built, gunned, and manned more heavily to meet the dual purpose of trade and defense. Their solid construction and armaments were costly—not only in materials but also in manpower. Larger crews were needed to handle the more complex riggings on these vessels as well as their guns.

NEW VIEWS

With friendly observers tipping off pirates operating out of lawless and largely governmentless Somalia, pirates in October 2008 captured a Ukranian cargo ship laden with 33 T-72 Russian-built tanks, antiaircraft guns, grenade launchers, and assorted other heavy weapons. Captures of smaller craft by seafaring bandits in the Red Sea and Gulf of Aden occasionally drew the attention of international observers, but this large prize brought the U.S. navy into quick action and the Russian navy as well. Fully surrounded, the pirates bargained coolly, "give us $20 million and we'll turn over the crew, cargo, and vessel fully intact." Months later, on February 4th, 2009, the pirates accepted $3.2 million in cash dropped by parachute offshore; hence the *Faina*, and its crew and cargo, were freed.

Because these seas are free of any regular government protection, pirates have been thriving ruinously for years, particularly aiming for privately owned yachters, small commercial vessels, and tourist cruise vessels. The market rather than government agencies handled these captures. "Pay the ransom, go free" was the order of the seas there atop the western portion of the Indian Ocean. With France leading the charge to the United Nations to take action against the pirates off Somalia, there was hope that the record of 67 pirate attacks and 26 ships hijacked from January through October 2008 would be a lot less in 2009. If a concerted policing of those seas was undertaken, one could also predict a fall in maritime insurance costs and many fewer panicky calls from hostages seeking ransom money to get free. (recall Economic Reasoning Proposition 4, Economic Insight 1.1, p. 8)

It quickly became evident that the flyboat could be used advantageously in certain bulk trades where the danger of piracy was low. However, in the rich but dangerous trades into the Mediterranean and the West Indies, more costly ships were required. In general, high risks in all colonial waters led to one of the most notable features of seventeenth-century shipping—the widespread use of cannons and armaments on trading vessels. Such characteristics were still observed in certain waters throughout much of the eighteenth century. Until about 1750 in the Caribbean, especially near Jamaica, vessels weighing more than 100 tons were almost always armed, and even small vessels usually carried some guns.

The need for self-protection in the Caribbean was self-evident:

There the sea was broken by a multitude of islands affording safe anchorage and refuge, with wood, water, even provision for the taking. There the colonies of the great European powers, grouped within a few days' sail of one another, were forever embroiled in current European wars which gave the stronger of them excuse for preying on the weaker and seemed to make legitimate the constant disorder of those seas. There trade was rich, but settlement thin and defense difficult. There the idle, the criminal, and the poverty-stricken were sent to ease society in the Old World. By all these conditions piracy was fostered, and for two centuries throve ruinously, partly as an easy method of individual enrichment and partly as an instrument of practical politics. (Barbour 1911, 529)

Privateering also added to the disorder. As a common practice, nation-states often gave private citizens license to harass the ships of rival states. These privateering commissions or "letters of marque" were issued without constraint in wartime, and even in peacetime they were occasionally given to citizens who had suffered losses due to the actions of subjects from an offending state. Since privateers frequently ignored the constraints of their commissions, privateering was often difficult to distinguish from common piracy.

It should be emphasized that piracy was not confined to the Caribbean. Pirates lurked safely in the inlets of North Carolina, from which they regularly raided vessels trading at Charleston. In 1718 it was exclaimed that "every month brought intelligence of renewed outrages, of vessels sacked on the high seas, burned with their cargo, or seized and converted to the nefarious uses of the outlaws" (Hughson 1894, 123). Local traders, shippers, and government officials in the Carolinas repeatedly solicited the Board of Trade for protection. In desperation, Carolina's Assembly appropriated funds in 1719 to support private vessels in the hope of driving the pirates from their seas. These pleas and protective actions were mostly in vain, but finally, as the benefits of ensuring safe trade lanes rose relative to the costs of eliminating piracy, the Royal Navy took action. By the early 1740s, piracy had been eliminated from the western Atlantic.

The fall of piracy was paralleled by the elimination of ship armaments and the reduction of crew sizes. As such, this was a process of technical diffusion, albeit belated. Without piracy, specialized cargo-carrying vessels similar to the flyboat were designed, thereby substantially reducing the costs of shipping.

In summary, the main productivity advances in shipping during the colonial period resulted from institutional changes associated with the growth of markets, and the rules of law, namely, (1) economies of scale in cargo handling, which reduced port times; and (2) the elimination of piracy, which had stood as an obstacle to technical diffusion, permitting the use of specialized low-cost cargo vessels.[5]

SPECULATIONS ON EARLY GROWTH RATES

All such measures of productivity advance suggest that while improvements in colonial standards of material well-being occurred, the pace was slow and irregular, as George Taylor proposed. However, the measures do not support his assertion of an acceleration of growth of real income per capita to 1 percent annually between 1710 and 1775 (recall Economic Reasoning Proposition 5, evidence and theory give value to opinions, in Economic Insight 1.1 on page 8). Before the modern age of rapid technological change and widespread investments in schooling to generate a highly skilled and adaptive labor force, the effective sources of growth were much more limited. This is revealed in the analysis of sources of productivity advances, emphasizing the importance of learning by doing, adapting and utilizing economies of scale where possible, and diffusing existing technologies.

Wealth Holdings

Additional evidence, based on probated wealth holdings of deceased colonists, also portrays slow and irregular growth rates throughout the period from 1630 to 1775. Per capita wealth included land, buildings, physical possessions, money, debts receivable minus debts owed, and, often, slaves and indentured contracts. Allan Kulikoff 's (1979) analysis of wealth holdings in Maryland over the eighteenth century suggests a long-run trend

---

[5]Other similar productivity gains deserve at least a brief mention here. As port times decreased, so did inventory times. This reduced the time in which a planter's capital (crop) lay idle in storage barns or warehouses. Decreased inventory times saved colonial capital. Similarly, declining risks and insurance rates reduced the costs to owners of insuring their shipments or bearing the risks of personal shipments. And considerable progress was made in packaging, as tobacco and sugar hogsheads, rice barrels, and other containers increased in size. Although larger hogsheads and barrels demanded more input in construction, their carrying capacity grew relatively more because the surface area of such containers expanded less in proportion to their capacity. Finding the point at which increased difficulties in handling roughly offset the productivity gains from using larger containers provides us with a good example of the learning-by-doing, trial-and-error procedure.

TABLE 5.2 MALE PER CAPITA PROBATE WEALTH IN SOUTHERN NEW ENGLAND, 1638–1774

YEARS	TOTAL WEALTH
1638–1654	£227.3
1655–1674	251.9
1675–1694	263.5
1695–1714	248.9
1715–1734	272.4
1735–1754	275.8
1765–1774	364.7

Note: For estates of males only; weighted for age and area. Estates from 1755 to 1764 are not included due to incomplete sample for area weighting.

Source: Adapted from Main and Main 1988, 27–46.

rate of growth of 0.4 percent per year.[6] His evidence shows contrasting periods: a slight fall in the first quarter of the century, a sharper decline in the second, and a very strong advance in the third quarter. Recalling the strong productivity growth period of 1630 to 1670 in the tobacco colonies, with little or no change in the late seventeenth century, it appears that most of the growth bracketed a long period of no growth (or possibly some decline) in per capita well-being in the Upper South. Work by Terry Anderson (1975, 1979) on New England also shows very strong advances in wealth holdings per person from 1650 to 1680, and then very little growth up to 1710. The trend from 1650 to 1710 was unusually high, perhaps 1.6 percent per year.

Evidence provided by Gloria and Jackson Main (1988) on southern New England between 1640 and 1774 is shown in Table 5.2 on page 87. This evidence of growth in total wealth per male indicates a trend in yearly average income advance of 0.35 percent in this region. Note, however, the spurt following the 1638–1654 period, relative stagnation until the turn of the century, then another 20-year spurt followed by another 20-year flat period, and finally yet another rapid spurt. This evidence further supports the view that regions differed greatly in the timing of their growth phases. Over a very long period, however, the trend growth rates of regions were probably fairly similar.

It seems reasonable to conclude that over the last 100 to 150 years of the colonial period, the growth rate trend was slightly below 0.5 percent per year. Based on evidence of wealth gathered from samples of probated estates for all the colonial regions, Alice Hanson Jones concludes that—

> [d]espite possible local or regional spurts or lags or even declines in some subperiods after 1650, it seems likely that, for all regions combined, fairly steady intensive growth accompanied accumulating experience in the New World, learning by doing, increasing knowhow in shipping within the Atlantic community, and the enlargement in size of the market that came with growth of population and trade. (Jones 1980, 305)

By her calculations, Jones suggests growth rates for three distinct periods: 0.3 percent, 1650–1725; 0.4 percent, 1725–1750; and 0.5 percent, 1750–1775 (Jones 1980, 78). Although the acceleration of growth implied by her figures may be challenged, the range

---

[6]Deceased people's wealth exceeded average wealth per capita substantially, but not everyone who died had an estate probated. However, if the distribution of wealth did not change dramatically over the period, trends of probated wealth holdings probably reflected the trend in wealth holdings per person. Furthermore, if the ratio of output (or income) to physical nonhuman wealth (capital) stayed fairly consistent, trends in such wealth per person would mirror trends in income per person.

seems reasonable in light of the improvements we have already noted and in light of England's estimated annual economic growth rate of 0.3 percent throughout most of the eighteenth century (Deane and Cole 1964).

PER CAPITA WEALTH AND INCOME, 1774

Reflection upon the ordeals of first settlement, such as "the lost colony" at Roanoke and the "starving time" in early Jamestown, projects a stark contrast to the economic conditions of colonial life on the eve of the Revolution. From distant Scotland in 1776, Adam Smith declared in his *Wealth of Nations*:

> *There are no colonies of which the progress has been more rapid than that of the English in North America. Plenty of good land, and liberty to manage their affairs their own way, seem to be the two great causes of the prosperity (Bruchey 1966).*

Contemporaries in the colonies also supported this view. As early as 1663, the Reverend John Higginson of Boston could observe, "We live in a more plentifull and comfortable manner than ever we did expect" (Bruchey 1966). By the 1740s, Benjamin Franklin could remark, "The first drudgery of settling new colonies, which confines the attention of people to mere necessities, is now pretty well over; and there are many in every province in circumstances that set them at ease" (Bruchey 1966, 1). Indeed, by most any standards of comparison, the quality of life and standards of material well-being were extraordinarily high for free Americans by the end of the colonial period. They lived longer and better than populations of other nations and places at the time, and better than most people throughout the world today.

THE DISTRIBUTION OF INCOME AND WEALTH

As Economic Insight 5.1 and Tables 5.3 and 5.4 on page 89 illustrate, the high levels of material well-being for colonial Americans were not equally distributed regionally. By far the richest area was the South, where wealth and incomes per free capita were far above those in the Middle colonies and in New England.

Evidence from probate records of the time also permits us to estimate the distribution of wealth among individuals. It is widely believed that wealth and income in North America were fairly equitably distributed until the onset of industrialization in the early nineteenth century. However, the estimates in Table 5.5 on page 90 (which includes holdings in slaves and indentured contracts) suggest that widespread inequalities of wealth and income existed much earlier. For instance, the wealthiest 20 percent of all New Englanders owned 66 percent of the total wealth there. In the Middle colonies, the wealthiest 20 percent held 53 percent of the total wealth. In the South, 70 percent of the wealth was held by the top fifth. In short, the South had the most concentrated distribution of wealth, and the Middle colonies had the least. The greater southern concentration was primarily due to the dominance of wealthy plantations enjoying advantages of economies of scale in production. Slavery also added to the South's high concentrations of wealth, but New England had concentrations almost as high, and wealth inequalities were notably high in the port towns. It also merits emphasis that the degree of inequality reflected in these numbers was minor by comparison with the gaping wealth inequalities in the sugar islands of the Caribbean and throughout Brazil and Spanish America.

ECONOMIC INSIGHT 5.1

PER CAPITA INCOME ESTIMATE, 1774

The quantitative basis for accepting the sweeping conclusions reported previously also stems from the work of Alice Jones. Her wealth estimates for 1774 are shown in Table 5.3. These are nonhuman physical wealth holdings (excluding financial debts and slavery and indenture contracts) per capita and per free person in the separate regions. Table 5.4 shows several income estimates per capita and per free person derived from the wealth figures in Table 5.3 by using capital–output ratios. Actual incomes estimated from wealth holdings would depend on the prevailing ratio of capital to output, but the range of ratios (3 to 1, 3.5 to 1, and 4 to 1) used is likely to bracket the true incomes earned in 1774.

Using a capital–output ratio of 3.5:1 generates an estimate of income per free person in 1774 of £13.8, or £12.1 if the ratio was 4:1. These estimates compare approximately with $1,500 and $1,300 in 2000 prices, less than half the official U.S. poverty level, but obviously, the range of goods and other conditions of life

and the errors of estimation make any such comparisons extremely crude. Nevertheless, we can safely guess that free colonials enjoyed surprisingly high standards of living for the world at that time. Because taxes in the colonies were much lower than in England, after-tax incomes of free persons in the colonies were probably above those in the mother country on the eve of the Revolution.

Even today, relatively few countries generate average income levels that approach the earnings of free Americans on the eve of the Revolution. In fact, more than one-half of the current world population lives in countries where the average income is below the level of the typical free American's income of more than 200 years ago. This is true of most people of the developing world, including India, Pakistan, Indonesia, and large parts of Africa and South America. Relatively speaking, free colonial Americans lived very well, both by today's standards in many areas of the world and in comparison with the most advanced areas of the world in the late eighteenth century.

TABLE 5.3 PRIVATE NONHUMAN PHYSICAL WEALTH, 1774 (IN POUNDS STERLING)

REGION	PER CAPITA	PER FREE CAPITA
New England	£36.4	£38.0
Middle colonies	40.2	44.1
Southern colonies	36.4	61.6
Thirteen colonies	37.4	48.4

Source: *Adapted from Jones 1980, 54, 58.*

TABLE 5.4 ESTIMATES OF REGIONAL INCOMES, 1774 (IN POUNDS STERLING)

REGION	CAPITAL OUTPUT RATIOS					
	PER CAPITA			PER FREE CAPITA		
	(3:1)	(3.5:1)	(4:1)	(3:1)	(3.5:1)	(4:1)
New England	£12.1	£10.4	£9.1	£12.7	£10.9	£9.5
Middle colonies	13.4	11.5	10.0	14.7	12.6	11.0
Southern colonies	12.1	10.4	9.1	20.5	17.6	15.4
Thirteen colonies	12.5	10.7	9.4	16.1	13.8	12.1

Note: These estimates of income per capita and for the free population are derived from Alice Hanson Jones's wealth estimates by using her assumption of a capital–income ratio of 3.5:1 and two others (3:1 and 4:1) to widen the analysis somewhat. These income estimates are only approximate. Estimates of wealth stocks can be converted into income flows by dividing the wealth estimates by a capital–output ratio, but the relationship between capital and output (the capital–output ratio) is influenced by many factors and varies both over time and among countries and regions. Nevertheless, under normal peacetime conditions, the capital–output ratio is seldom lower than 3 or higher than 5.

Source: *Adapted from Jones 1980, 63.*

TABLE 5.5 TOTAL PHYSICAL WEALTH, 1774: ESTATE SIZES AND COMPOSITION FOR FREE WEALTH HOLDERS (IN POUNDS STERLING)

	ALL COLONIES	NEW ENGLAND	MIDDLE COLONIES	SOUTH
Mean average	£252.0	£161.2	£189.2	£394.7
Median average	108.7	74.4	152.5	144.5
Distribution				
Bottom 20%	0.8%	1.0%	1.2%	0.7%
Top 20%	67.3	65.9	52.7	69.6
Composition				
Land	53.0	71.4	60.5	45.9
Slaves and servants	22.1	0.5	4.1	33.6
Livestock	9.2	7.5	11.3	8.8
Consumer-personal	6.7	11.2	8.4	5.1

Source: *Adapted from Jones 1978; presented in Perkins 1988, 219.*

Thanks to the pioneering efforts of Jackson T. Main (1965) and James Henretta (1965), we have learned that a growing inequality in wealth and income accompanied the very process of colonial settlement and economic maturity. As development proceeded, frontier areas were transformed into subsistence farming areas with little specialization or division of labor, then into commercial farming lands, and finally, in some instances, into urban areas. In Main's opinion, this increasing commercialization resulted in greater inequality in the distribution of colonial wealth and income (Main 1965).

Other studies by James Henretta and Bruce D. Daniels also suggest a growth in the inequality of colonial wealth distribution within regions over time (Henretta 1965; Daniels 1973–1974). Comparing two Boston tax lists, Henretta found that the top 10 percent of Boston's taxpayers owned 42 percent of its wealth in 1687, whereas they owned 57 percent in 1771.[7] Daniels surveyed many New England probate records and, therefore, was able to tentatively confirm Main's contention (1988) that as economic activity grew more complex in the colonies, it tended to produce a greater concentration of wealth. Apparently, as subsistence production gave way to market production, the interdependence among colonial producers generated (or at least was accompanied by) a greater disparity in wealth. This was true both in older and in more recently settled agricultural areas. Alternatively, large established urban areas such as Boston and Hartford exhibited a fairly stable distribution of wealth throughout the eighteenth century until 1776. These urban centers also reflected the greatest degree of wealth inequality in the colonies. Smaller towns showed less inequality, but as towns grew, their inequality also increased.

Particularly high levels of affluence were observed in the port towns and cities, where merchant classes were forming and gaining an economic hold. Especially influential were the merchant shipowners, who were engaged in the export–import trade and who were considered to be in the upper class of society. In addition, urbanization and industrialization produced another class group: a free labor force that owned little or no property.

---

[7]Henretta's 1771 estimate was later revised downward to 48 percent by Gerard Warden, who found historical inconsistencies in the evaluation of assets in the tax lists on which Henretta's study was based. This adjustment modifies substantially the argument for rapidly rising inequality in Boston but not the overall picture of substantial inequality of wealth holdings there.

Probably one-third of the free population possessed few assets (according to estate records and tax rolls), but as Jackson Main (1965) has argued and Mary Schweitzer's (1987) work supports, these were not a permanent underclass of free poor people. These were mostly young people in their twenties, still dependent on parents or relatives. Through gifts, savings, and other sources, marriage usually tripled household wealth almost immediately. Without evidence on upward mobility to higher income levels, we cannot discern, as was shown in chapter 1, how frequently people moved up the economic ladder, escaping the poverty trap. Our speculation, because of land availability and less rigid social constraints in the colonies, is that free people in the colonies had much greater "class mobility" than did people in the Old World.

Not only occupation, marriage, and property ownership but also circumstances determined by birth greatly influenced a person's social standing. Race and sex were major factors. Some women were wealthy, but typically they owned far less property than men, and very few owned land. The rise of slave labor after 1675 furthered the overall rise of wealth inequality in the colonies.

Throughout most of the colonial period up to 1775, growing wealth concentration did not occur among free whites in the 13 colonies as a whole. Although growing inequality occurred within specific regions and localities, this did not occur in the aggregate. This is because the lower wealth concentration areas, the rural and especially the new frontier areas, contained more than 90 percent of the population. These grew as fast, or faster than, the urban areas, therefore offsetting the modest growth of inequality of the urban centers (Williamson and Lindert 1980). As an added statistical oddity, although rural wealth holdings (per free person) were less than urban holdings within each region, in the aggregate, rural wealth holdings averaged above urban holdings. This reversal in order happened because of the very high wealth holdings per free person in the South, which actually exceeded the average wealth holdings of northern urban residents. In any case, despite these peculiarities of aggregation, substantial wealth inequality was a fact of economic life long before the age of industrialization and the period of rapid and sustained economic growth that occurred in the nineteenth century. The absence of growing inequality of wealth among free Americans implies that the growth of per capita income and wealth was shared widely among these nearly 1.8 million people. On the eve of the Revolution, their sense of well-being and economic outlook was undoubtedly positive. British interference and changing taxation policies were threats that a powerful young emerging nation was willing and able to overcome.

SELECTED REFERENCES AND SUGGESTED READINGS

Anderson, Terry. *The Economic Growth of Seventeenth-Century New England: A Measurement of Regional Income.* New York: Arno, 1975.

_____. "Economic Growth in Colonial New England: 'Statistical Renaissance.'" *Journal of Economic History* 39 (1979): 243–257.

Anderson, Terry, and Steven LaCombe. "Institutional Change in the Indian Horse Culture." In *The Other Side of the Frontier*, ed. Linda Barrington. Boulder, Co.: Westview, 1999.

Anderson, Terry, and Robert Paul Thomas. "White Population, Labor Force, and Extensive Growth of the New England Economy in the Seventeenth Century." *Journal of Economic History* 33 (1973): 634–661.

_____. "Economic Growth in the Seventeenth Century Colonies." *Explorations in Economic History* 15 (1978): 368–387.

Ball, Duane, and Gary M. Walton. "Agricultural Productivity Change in Eighteenth-Century Pennsylvania." *Journal of Economic History* 36 (1976): 102–117.

Barbour, Violet. "Privateers and Pirates in the West Indies." *American Historical Review* 16 (1911): 529.

Bidwell, P. W., and J. I. Falconer. *History of Agriculture in the Northern United States, 1620–1860.* Washington, D.C.: Carnegie Institution of Washington, 1925.

Bruchey, Stuart, ed. *The Colonial Merchant: Sources and Readings.* New York: Harcourt Brace Jovanovich, 1966.

Daniels, Bruce. "Long Range Trends of Wealth Distribution in Eighteenth-Century New England." *Explorations in Economic History* 11 (1973–1974): 123–135.

Deane, Phyllis, and W. A. Cole. *British Economic Growth, 1688–1959: Trends and Structure.* Cambridge: Cambridge University Press, 1964.

Gallman, Robert E. "Changes in Total U.S. Agricultural Factor Productivity in the Nineteenth Century." *Agricultural History* 46 (1972): 191–210.

_____. "The Agricultural Sector and the Pace of Economic Growth: U.S. Experience in the Nineteenth Century." In *Essays in Nineteenth Century Economic History,* eds. David C. Klingaman and Richard K. Vedder, 35–76. Athens: Ohio University Press, 1975.

Henretta, James. "Economic Development and Social Structure in Colonial Boston." *William and Mary Quarterly* 22 (1965): 93–105.

Hughson, S. C. "The Carolina Pirates and Colonial Commerce." *Johns Hopkins University Studies in Historical and Political Science* 12 (1894): 123.

Jones, Alice H. *American Colonial Wealth: Documents and Methods,* 3 vols. New York: Arno, 1978.

_____. *Wealth of a Nation to Be: The American Colonies on the Eve of the Revolution.* New York: Columbia University Press, 1980.

Kulikoff, Allan. "The Economic Growth of the Eighteenth-Century Chesapeake Colonies." *Journal of Economic History* 39 (1979): 275–288.

Lemon, James T. *Best Poor Man's Country: A Geographical Study of Early Southwestern Pennsylvania.* Baltimore, Md.: Johns Hopkins University Press, 1972.

Main, Gloria, and Jackson T. Main. "Economic Growth and the Standard of Living in Southern New England, 1640–1774." *Journal of Economic History* 48 (1988): 27–46.

Main, Jackson T. *The Social Structure of Revolutionary America.* Princeton, N.J.: Princeton University Press, 1965.

Menard, Russell R. "Farm Prices of Maryland Tobacco, 1659–1710." *Maryland Historical Magazine* 58 (Spring 1973): 85.

_____. "A Note on Chesapeake Tobacco Prices, 1618–1660." *Virginia Magazine of History and Biography* (1976): 401–410.

Paskoff, Paul. "Labor Productivity and Managerial Efficiency against a Static Technology: The Pennsylvania Iron Industry, 1750–1800." *Journal of Economic History* 40 (1980): 129–135.

Perkins, Edwin. Chapter 1 in *The Economy of Colonial America,* 2nd ed. New York: Columbia University Press, 1988.

Schweitzer, Mary. *Custom and Contract: Household Government and the Economy in Colonial Pennsylvania.* New York: Columbia University Press, 1987.

Shepherd, James F., and Gary M. Walton. *Shipping, Maritime Trade, and the Economic Development of Colonial North America.* Cambridge: Cambridge University Press, 1972.

Taylor, George R. "American Economic Growth before 1840: An Exploratory Essay." *Journal of Economic History* 24 (1964): 437.

Walton, Gary M. "Sources of Productivity Change in American Colonial Shipping." *Economic History Review* 20 (April 1967): 67–78.

Williamson, Jeffrey G., and Peter H. Lindert. *American Inequality: A Macroeconomic History.* New York: Academic Press, 1980.

CHAPTER 6

Three Crises and Revolt

CHAPTER THEME

At the close of the French and Indian War (also called the Seven Years' War), when the French were eliminated as a rival power in North America, Britain's mainland colonies were on the brink of another wave of economic growth and rising prosperity. In accordance with British practices of colonization, the colonists remained English citizens with all rights due to the King's subjects under the laws of England. For financial, administrative, and political reasons, the Crown and Parliament in 1763 launched a "new order" (Economic Reasoning Proposition 4, laws and rules matter, in Economic Insight 1.1 on page 8). Misguided policies, mismanagement, and ill timing from England added political will to the economic circumstances of the colonies to steer an independent course. The American Revolution was the outcome.

THE OLD COLONIAL POLICY

Being part of the British Empire, and in accord with English laws and institutions, colonial governments were patterned after England's governmental organization. Although originally there were corporate colonies (Connecticut and Rhode Island) and proprietary colonies (Pennsylvania and Maryland), most eventually became Crown colonies, and all had similar governing organizations. For example, after 1625, Virginia was a characteristic Crown colony, and both its governor and council (the upper house) were appointed by the Crown. But only the lower house could initiate fiscal legislation, and this body was elected by the propertied adult males within the colony.

Although the governor and the Crown could veto all laws, power gradually shifted to the lower houses as colonial legislative bodies increasingly tended to imitate the House of Commons in England. The colonists controlled the lower houses—and, therefore, the purse strings—thereby generating a climate of political freedom and independence in the colonies. Governors, who were generally expected to represent the will of the Empire and to veto legislation contrary to British interests, were often not only sympathetic to the colonists but also dependent on the legislatures for their salaries (which were frequently in arrears). Consequently, the actual control of civil affairs generally rested with the colonists themselves, through their representatives.

Of course, the power that permitted this state of affairs to exist rested in England, and the extent of local autonomy was officially limited. After the shift in power in England from the Crown to Parliament in 1690, the Privy Council reviewed all laws passed in the colonies as a matter of common procedure. According to official procedure, colonial laws were not in effect until the Privy Council granted its approval, and sometimes the council vetoed legislation passed in the colonies. Time, distance, and bureaucratic apathy, however, often permitted colonial laws and actions to become effective before they were even reviewed in England; and if the colonists highly desired a vetoed piece of legislation, it could be reworded and resubmitted.

In short, British directives influenced day-to-day events in the colonies only modestly. Indeed, government activity—whether British or colonial—was a relatively minor aspect of colonial affairs. The burdens of defense, for example, fell on the shoulders of those in Britain, not on those in the colonies, and colonists were among the most lightly taxed people in the world. Furthermore, the colonists themselves held the power to resolve issues of a local nature. They had no central or unifying government,[1] but the colonial governments had organized themselves to the point in the early eighteenth century where they appointed officials, granted western lands, negotiated with the Indians, raised taxes, provided relief for the poor, and the like. In this way, British subjects in the New World enjoyed extensive freedom of self-determination throughout most of the colonial period (Economic Reasoning Proposition 1, scarcity forces us to make choices).

The main provisions of the early Navigation Acts, which imposed the most important restrictions on colonial economic freedom, formed the basis of the old colonial policy. Recall that these laws epitomized British mercantilism and that their aim was threefold: (1) to protect and encourage English and colonial shipping; (2) to ensure that major colonial imports from Europe were shipped from British ports; and (3) to ensure that the bulk of desired colonial products—the enumerated articles—were shipped to England.

The first Acts of Trade and Navigation (in 1651, 1660, and 1663) introduced these concepts concerning the colonies' relationship with the Empire. Colonial settlers and investors always had been aware of the restrictions on their economic activities. Rules were changed gradually and, until 1763, in such a way that American colonists voiced no serious complaints. Articles were added to the enumerated list over a long period of time. At first, the list consisted entirely of southern continental and West Indian products, most importantly tobacco, sugar, cotton, dyewood, and indigo. Rice and molasses were not added until 1704, naval stores until 1705 and 1729, and furs and skins until 1721. Whenever enumeration resulted in obvious and unreasonable hardship, relief might be granted. For example, the requirement that rice be sent to England added so much to shipping and handling costs that the American product, despite its superior quality, was priced out of southern European markets. Consequently, laws passed in the 1730s allowed rice to be shipped directly to ports south of Cape Finisterre, a promontory in northwestern Spain.

Commodities were enumerated if they were especially important to English manufacturers or were expected to yield substantial customs revenue. However, the requirements of shipping listed items to English ports were less onerous than we might initially suppose. First, because the Americans and the English shared general ties of blood and language (and, more specifically, because their credit contacts were more easily established), the colonists would have dealt primarily with English merchants anyway. Second, duties charged on commodities that were largely re-exported, such as tobacco, were remitted entirely or in large part to the colonies. Third, bounties were paid on some of the enumerated articles. Fourth, it was permissible to ship certain items on the list directly from one colony to another to furnish essential supplies. Finally, the laws could be evaded through smuggling; with the exception of molasses, such evasion was probably neither more nor less common in the colonies than it was in Europe during the seventeenth and eighteenth centuries.

With respect to colonial imports, the effect of the Navigation Acts was to distort somewhat—but not to influence materially—the flows of trade. The fact that goods had

---

[1]Ben Franklin had proposed a new unified colonial administration in 1754, but his idea was rejected.

to be funneled through England added to costs and restricted trade to the colonists. Again, however, traditional ties would have made Americans the best customers of British merchants anyway. Furthermore, hardship cases were relieved by providing direct shipment of commodities such as salt and wine to America from ports south of Cape Finisterre.

If English manufacturers were to be granted special advantages over other European manufacturers in British American markets, should restrictions also be placed on competing colonial manufacturers? Many British manufacturers felt that such "duplicate production" should be prohibited and tried to convince Parliament that colonial manufacturing was not in the best interest of the Empire. In 1699, a law made it illegal to export colonial wool, wool yarn, and finished wool products to any foreign country or even to other colonies. Later, Americans (many of Dutch origin) were forbidden to export hats made of beaver fur. Toward mid-century, a controversy arose in England over the regulation of iron manufactures; after 1750, pig and bar iron were admitted into England duty free, but the colonial manufacture of finished iron products was expressly forbidden. The fact that these were the only prohibitive laws directed at colonial manufacturing indicates Britain's lack of fear of American competition.

After all, England enjoyed a distinct comparative advantage in manufacturing, and the colonies' comparative advantage in production lay overwhelmingly in agriculture and other resource-intensive products from the seas and forests. Note that the important shipbuilding industry in the colonies was not curtailed by British legislation; indeed, it was supported by Parliament. Therefore, any piecemeal actions to prevent colonial manufacturing activities appear to have been taken largely to protect particular vested interests in England, especially those with influence and effective lobbying practices.

The laws prohibiting colonial manufactures were loosely enforced; they were restrictive and annoying, but they did not seriously affect the course of early American industrial development or the colonial quest for independence. Also, the economic controls that England imposed on the colonies were less strict than the colonial controls other European countries imposed, and these controls were less harsh for America than for Ireland and other colonies within the Empire. We should not, however, misapprehend the trend of enforcement of the old colonial policy. Regulation of external colonial trade was progressively strengthened. Beginning in 1675, governors were supplied with staffs of officials to help enforce trade regulations; after the general reorganization of 1696, the powers of these officials were sufficient to provide considerable surveillance and commercial regulation.

The only trade law flaunted with impunity was the Molasses Act of 1733—an act that, if enforced, would have disrupted one of the major colonial trades and resulted in serious repercussions, especially in New England. Before 1700, New England had traded primarily with the British possessions in the West Indies. In time, however, British planters failed to provide a sufficient market for northern colonial goods, and sugar and molasses from the increasingly productive French islands became cheaper than the English staples. During the same period, British planters in the sugar islands were hurt by the requirement that cane products be shipped to England before being re-exported. In an effort to protect British West Indian holdings, Parliament imposed high duties on foreign (predominantly French) sugar, molasses, and rum imported to the English colonies. The strict levying of these duties and the prevention of smuggling would have suppressed the market of northern staples in the West Indies and would have seriously curtailed all trade involving rum. New Englanders felt they had no feasible alternative because they had to sell their fish, provisions, lumber, and rum to pay for their imports. Rather than accept such hardships, the New Englanders continued to trade as usual; instead of facing the issue resolutely, English officials, many of whom were routinely bribed (10 percent being the custom for "looking the other way"), made no serious attempts to enforce trade regulations (Economic Reasoning Proposition 4, laws and rules matter). Some 30 years later, after the matter had been raised time after time, the Sugar Act of 1764 ruled against the American colonists in favor of the British West Indian planters. This decision to impose and collect the tax was a key factor in bringing on the first crisis leading to revolution.

THE NEW COLONIAL POLICY AND THE FIRST CRISIS

The events that led to the American Revolution are more clearly understood if we repeat and keep in mind their central underlying theme: New and rapid changes in the old colonial policy that had been established and imposed on an essentially self-governing people for 150 years precipitated a series of crises and, ultimately, war. These crises were essentially political, but the stresses and strains that led to colonial fear and hatred of British authority had economic origins. Britain's "new" colonial policy was only an extension of the old, with one difference: The new enactments were adopted by a Parliament and enforced by bureaucratic oversight that had every intention of enforcing them to the letter of the law, thereby sharply changing the atmosphere of freedom in the colonies. Furthermore, high British officials insisted—at almost precisely the wrong moments—on taking punitive actions that only compounded the bitterness they had already stirred up in the colonies.

The series of critical events that generated the first crisis began with the English victory over the French in 1763. The Seven Years' War had been a struggle for the empire, of course, but it also had been a fight for the protection of the American colonies. And the colonials had been of only limited help in furnishing England with either troops or materials—to say nothing of the hurtful trade they intermittently carried on with the French in both Canada and the West Indies. The English were in no mood to spare the feelings of an upstart people who had committed the cardinal sin of ingratitude. Besides, the war had placed a heavy burden on the English treasury, and British taxes per capita in the mid-1760s were probably the highest in the world (see Davis and Huttenback 1982). Interest on the national debt had soared to £5 million annually (nearly $500 million in today's values), and land taxes in England had doubled during the war. To many of the English, especially taxpayers, it seemed only fair that American colonists be asked to contribute to the support of the garrisons still required on their frontier. Despite their substantial wealth, the colonists at this time were still free riders of protection, receiving British defense at almost no cost. Taxes per capita in the colonies were among the lowest in the world, only 20 to 25 percent of taxes paid by the average English resident.

George Grenville, England's prime minister, proposed stationing a British force of some 10,000 men in the North American possessions. Although the actual number realized was closer to 6,000, their costs were more than £350,000 annually. To help meet these costs, Parliament passed two laws to generate approximately one-tenth of this revenue. Of the two laws, the Sugar Act of 1764 had more far-reaching economic implications for the colonists, because it contained provisions that served the ends of all major English economic interests and threatened many American businesses in the colonies. But the Stamp Act of 1765, although actually far less inclusive, incited political tempers to a boil that in a very real sense started the first step toward rebellion.

The most important clauses of the Sugar Act levied taxes on imports of non-British products of the West Indies. Although the duty on foreign molasses was actually lowered from 6d. to 3d. sterling a gallon—a marked reduction from the rate set by the old

Molasses Act—provision was made for strict collection of the tax in the belief that the smaller tax, if strictly enforced, would produce a larger revenue. (A similar argument is characteristic of today's supply-side economics.) A more important goal, however, was the protection of British West Indian planters—who were well represented in Parliament—from the competition of New England rum makers. Actually, more than half of the molasses imported by colonists was used in homes to make Boston baked beans, shoofly pie, apple pandowdy, and molasses jack (a kind of homebrewed beer); but the chief fear of the English sugar planters was that cheap molasses imports from the French West Indies would enable the New England rum distilleries to capture the rum market on the mainland as well as in the non-British islands.[2] And their concern was probably justified, despite the alleged inferiority of the New England product. Moreover, the Sugar Act added to the list of enumerated articles several raw materials demanded by British manufacturers, including some important exports of the Northern and Middle colonies. Finally, this comprehensive law removed most of the tariff rebates (drawbacks) previously allowed on European goods that passed through English ports and even placed new duties on foreign textiles that competed with English products. Nevertheless, the Sugar Act, in form and substance, was much like earlier acts passed to restrict and control trade.

The Stamp Act, on the other hand, was simply designed to raise revenue and served no ends of mercantile policy. The law required that stamps varying in cost from half a penny to several pounds be affixed to legal documents, contracts, newspapers and pamphlets, and even playing cards and dice.

According to Benjamin Franklin's argument to Parliament against the tax, the colonists objected on the grounds that the act levied an "internal" tax, as distinguished from the traditional "external" taxes or duties collected on goods imported to the colonies. When English ministers refused to recognize this distinction, the colonists further objected that the tax had been levied by a distant Parliament that did not contain a single colonial representative. Thus was born the colonial rallying cry, "No taxation without representation!" Colonists complained that both the Sugar Act and the Stamp Act required the tax revenues to be remitted to England for disbursement, a procedure that further drained the colonies of precious specie and constantly reduced the amount of goods that could be imported to America. When it became apparent that strict enforcement would accompany such measures, severe resistance arose in the colonies. Lawyers and printers—who were especially infuriated by the Stamp Act—furnished articulate, able leadership and communication for anti-British agitation.

The decade of trouble that followed was characterized by alternating periods of colonial insubordination, British concession, renewed attempts to raise revenues, further colonial resistance, and, at last, punitive action—taken by the British in anger at what was felt to be rank disloyalty. The so-called Stamp Act Congress met in New York in 1765, passed resolutions of fealty, and organized a boycott of English goods. "Nonimportation associations" were established throughout the colonies, and the volume of imports from Britain declined dramatically as docks and warehouses bulged with unsold British goods.

A concerted effort to boycott English goods did not develop in all regions. The Middle colonies—where the boycotts first centered—exhibited the greatest decrease in trade with England. The Upper South contributed effectively to the boycott, largely because of the Restraining Act of 1764, which curtailed Virginia's paper money issues and restricted their uses (see chapter 4). New England gave only slight support to these first nonimport agreements, and the Lower South failed to join the boycott. Yet overall, colonial efforts to boycott British imports were highly effective (Economic Reasoning Proposition 2,

---

[2]For the details of this controversy, see Ostrander (1956). See also Bruchey (1966).

choices impose costs). In fact, English merchants were so sharply affected that they demanded the repeal of the Stamp Act. They were joined by such political leaders as Edmund Burke and William Pitt, who sympathized with the colonists. Parliament promptly responded, repealing the Stamp Act and reducing the duty on foreign molasses from 3d. to 1d. per gallon. Thus, the first major confrontation between America and England ended peacefully, and a profound lesson had been learned. In the mercantilist scheme of things, the Empire had tilted. The American mainland colonies ultimately had become as important a market for English wares as they and the West Indian planters were a source of raw materials. Americans as consumers had found a new and powerful economic weapon—the boycott.

MORE CHANGES AND THE SECOND CRISIS

Although Parliament had responded to economic pressure from America by repealing the Stamp Act, England angrily and obstinately maintained its right to tax the colonies. The other sugar duties remained, and the Declaratory Act of 1766 affirmed the right of Parliament to legislate in all matters concerning Americans. Nevertheless, there was rejoicing both in the colonies and in England, and it was generally believed that the English and American differences would be reconciled. But even then, the Quartering Act of 1765 had been on the statute books a year, with its stipulations that the colonial assemblies provide barracks, some provisions, and part of the costs of military transport for British troops stationed within the colonies. This law proved to be especially problematic in New York, where soldiers were concentrated on their way to the West. Much worse was to come, however. George Grenville had been dismissed from the British ministry in 1765, largely because King George III (age 25) disliked him. Grenville was replaced as chancellor of the exchequer by Charles Townshend. Because the great English landowners were persistently clamoring for relief from their heavy property taxes, Townshend tried once again to raise revenues in America. He felt that if the colonials objected to "internal" taxes, he would provide them with some "external" duties levied on such important articles of consumption as tea, glass, paper, and red and white lead (pigments for paint). By 1767, the Townshend duties were imposed.

Although these dutied items were definitely important to colonial life, the colonists might have accepted their taxation calmly had the British not adopted measures to put real teeth into the law. One of the Townshend Acts provided for an American Customs Board, another for the issuance by colonial courts of the hated general search warrants known as writs of assistance, and another for admiralty courts in Halifax, Boston, Philadelphia, and Charleston to try smuggling cases. With a single stroke (Economic Reasoning Proposition 1, scarcity forces us to make choices), the British ministry succeeded once again in antagonizing a wide cross-section of the American populace, and again resistance flared—this time in the form of both peaceful petitions and mob violence, culminating in the 1770 Boston Massacre, which left five colonials dead. Once more the nonimportation agreements, especially effective in the port towns (see page 63, Map 4.1), were imposed. Only in the Chesapeake colonies—the one major colonial region spared a court of admiralty—was this boycott fairly unsuccessful.[3] Nevertheless, by late 1769, American imports had declined to perhaps one-third of their normal level. The

---

[3]Another contributing factor may have been that trade in the Chesapeake region was relatively decentralized, thereby reducing the possibility of blacklisting or boycotting colonial importers and others who failed to join the effort.

value of lost English sales in the colonies exceeded £1 million in 1768 and 1769 combined, and once again, English merchants exerted pressure to change trade policy. For the second time, Parliament appeared to acquiesce to colonial demands. In 1770, all the Townshend duties except the duty on tea were repealed, and although some of the most distasteful acts remained on the books, everyone except a few colonial hotheads felt that a peaceful settlement was possible. Trade was resumed, and a new level of prosperity was reached in 1771.

THE THIRD CRISIS AND REBELLION

Reasonable calm prevailed until 1773, when resistance flared up again over what now seems to have been an inconsequential matter. The English East India Company, in which many politically powerful people owned an interest, was experiencing financial difficulties. Parliament had granted the company a loan of public funds (such as Congress gave the Chrysler Corporation in 1981 and Bear Stearns in 2008) and had also passed the Tea Act of 1773, which permitted the company to handle tea sales in a new way. Until this time, the company, which enjoyed a monopoly on the trade from India, had sold tea to English wholesalers, who, in turn, sold it to jobbers, who sent it to America. There the tea was turned over to colonial wholesalers, who at last distributed it to American retailers. Overall, many people had received income from this series of transactions; besides, duties had been collected on the product when it reached English ports and again when it arrived in America. The new Tea Act allowed the East India Company to ship tea directly to the colonies, thereby eliminating the British duty and reducing handling costs. Consumers were to benefit by paying less for tea, the company would presumably sell more tea at a lower price, and everybody would be happy. But everybody was not happy. Smugglers of Dutch tea were now undersold, the colonial tax was still collected (a real sore point), and, most important, the American importer was removed from the picture, thus alarming American merchants. If the colonial tea

Angered colonists, disguised as Indians, invited themselves to a "tea party" to show the British how they felt about English mercantile policies. The damage to property was nearly £9,000 (about $1 million in 2008 values).

This illustration emphasizes the political antagonisms launched by the Intolerable Acts of 1774.

wholesaler could be bypassed, couldn't the business of other merchants also be undercut? Couldn't other companies in Great Britain be granted monopoly control of other commodities, until eventually Americans would be reduced to keeping small shops and selling at retail what their foreign masters imported for them? Wouldn't just a few pro-British agents who would handle the necessary distribution processes grow rich, while staunch Americans grew poor? The list of rhetorical questions grew, and the answers seemed clear to almost every colonist engaged in business. From merchants in Boston to shopkeepers in the hamlets came a swift and violent reaction. Tea in the port towns was sent back to England or destroyed in various ways—the most spectacular of which was the Boston Tea Party, a well-executed three-hour affair involving 30 to 40 men (Economic Reasoning Propositions 1, scarcity forces us to make choices; and 2, choices impose costs). Many colonists were shocked at this wanton destruction of private property, estimated at nearly £9,000 (or nearly $1 million in 2008 prices), but their reaction was mild compared with the indignation that swelled in Britain.

The result was the bitter and punitive legislation known as the Intolerable Acts. Passed in the early summer of 1774, the Intolerable Acts (1) closed the port of Boston to all shipping until the colonists paid the East India Company for its tea; (2) permitted British officials charged with crimes committed in an American colony while enforcing British laws to be tried in another colony or in Britain; (3) revised the charter of Massachusetts to make certain cherished rights dependent on the arbitrary decision of the Crown-appointed governor; and (4) provided for the quartering of troops in the city of Boston, which was especially onerous to the citizens after the events of the Boston Massacre four years earlier. In the ensuing months, political agitation reached new heights of violence, and economic sanctions were again invoked. For the third time, nonimportation agreements were imposed, and the delegates to the First Continental Congress voted not to trade with England or the British West Indies unless concessions were made. On October 14, 1774, the Continental Congress provided a list of grievances:

1. Taxes had been imposed upon the colonies by the "British" Parliament.
2. Parliament had claimed the right to legislate for the colonies.

 3. Commissioners were set up in the colonies to collect taxes.
  4. Admiralty court jurisdictions had been extended into the interior.
  5. Judges' tenures had been put at the pleasure of the Crown.
  6. A standing army had been imposed upon the colonies.
  7. Persons could be transported out of the colonies for trials.
  8. The port of Boston had been closed.
  9. Martial law had been imposed upon Boston.
 10. The Quebec Act had confiscated the colonists' western lands. (Hughes 1990, 59)

The Congress ultimately went on to demand the repeal of all the major laws imposed on the colonies after 1763 (Tansill, *Documents Illustrative of the Formation of Union of the American States,* 1927: 1–4). By this time, however, legislative reactions and enactments were of little importance. The crisis had become moral and political. Americans would not yield to the British until their basic freedoms were restored, and the British would not make peace until the colonists relented. The possibilities for peaceful reconciliation ebbed as the weeks passed. Finally, violence broke out with the shots of April 19, 1775, which marked a major turning point in the history of the world. On July 4, 1776, independence was declared. The Empire that had tilted in 1765 had now cracked.

Support in the Countryside

Although the events leading to the Revolution centered primarily on the conflicts between British authority and colonial urban commerce, the vast rural populace played an essential supporting role in the independence movement. How can we explain the willingness of wealthy southerners and many poor farmers to support a rebellion that was spearheaded by an antagonized merchant class? Though certainly no apparent allied economic interests were shared among these groups, each group had its own motives for resisting British authority. In rural America, antagonisms primarily stemmed from English land policy (Economic Reasoning Proposition 2, choices impose costs).

Before 1763, British policy had been calculated to encourage the rapid development of the colonial West. In the interest of trade, English merchants wanted the new country to be populated as rapidly as possible. Moreover, rapid settlement extended the frontier and thereby helped strengthen opposition to France and Spain. By 1763, however, the need to fortify the frontier against foreign powers had disappeared. As the Crown and Parliament saw it, now was the time for more control on the frontier. First, the British felt it was wise to contain the population well within the seaboard area, where the major investments had been made and where political control would be easier. Second, the fur trade was now under the complete control of the British, and it was deemed unwise to have frontier pioneers moving in and creating trouble with the Indians. Third, wealthy English landowners were purchasing western land in great tracts, and pressure was exerted to "save" some of the good land for these investors. Finally, placing the western lands under the direct control of the Crown was designed to obtain revenues from sales and quitrents for the British treasury.[4]

In the early 1760s, events on the frontier served to tighten the Crown's control of settlement. Angry over injustices and fearful that the settlers would encroach on their hunting grounds, the northern Indians rebelled under the Ottawa chief Pontiac. Colonial and British troops put down the uprising, but only after seven of the nine British garrisons west of Niagara were destroyed. Everyone knew that western settlement would come

---

[4]Quitrents were an old form of feudal dues seldom paid in any of the colonies except Virginia and Maryland. In Virginia, the quitrents went to the Crown (about £5,000 annually after 1765); in Maryland, they went to Lord Baltimore, the proprietor.

under continuing threat unless the native Indians were pacified. Primarily as a temporary solution, the king issued the Royal Proclamation of 1763, which, in effect, drew a line beyond which colonials could not settle without express permission from the Crown (see Map 6.1). Governors could no longer grant patents to land lying west of the sources of rivers that flowed into the Atlantic; anyone seeking such a grant had to obtain one directly from the king. At the same time, the fur trade was placed under centralized control, and no trader could cross the Allegheny Mountains without permission from England.

A few years later, the policy of keeping colonial settlement under British supervision was reaffirmed, although it became apparent that the western boundary line would not remain rigidly fixed. In 1768, the line was shifted westward, and treaties with the Indians made large land tracts available to speculators. In 1774, the year in which the Intolerable Acts were passed, two British actions demonstrated that temporary expedients had evolved into permanent policies. First, a royal proclamation tightened the terms on

MAP 6.1

Colonial Land Claims

The colonial appetite for new land was huge, as colonial land claims demonstrated. The Royal Proclamation of 1763 was designed to stop westward movement.

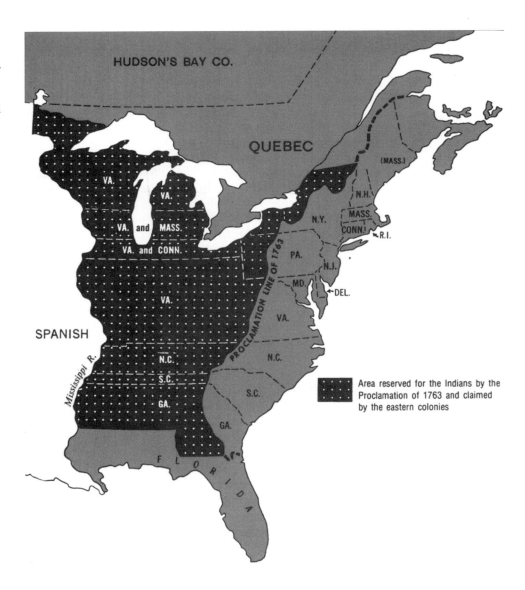

which land would pass into private hands. Grants were no longer to be free; instead, tracts were to be sold at public auctions in lots of 100 to 1,000 acres at a minimum price of 6d. per acre. Even more serious was the passage of the Quebec Act in 1774, which changed the boundaries of Quebec to the Ohio River in the East and the Mississippi River in the West (see Map 6.2). More important, the act destroyed the western land claims of Massachusetts, Connecticut, and Virginia. The fur trade was to be regulated by the governor of Quebec, and the Indian boundary line was to run as far south as Georgia. Many colonists viewed the act as theft.

Not all colonists suffered from the new land policy. Rich land speculators who were politically powerful enough to obtain special grants from the king found the new regulations restrictive but not ruinous. Indeed, great holders of ungranted lands east of the mountains, such as the Penns and the Calverts, or of huge tracts already granted but not yet settled, stood to benefit from the rise in property values that resulted from the British embargo on westward movement. Similarly, farmers of old, established agricultural areas would benefit in two ways: (1) the competition from the produce of the new

MAP 6.2

Reassignment of Claims

The Quebec Act of 1774 gave the Indians territories that earlier had been claimed by various colonies and, at the same time, nearly doubled the area of Quebec.

lands would now be less and (2) because it would be harder for agricultural laborers to obtain their own farms, hired hands would be cheaper.

Although many of the restrictions on westward movement were necessary, at least for a time because of Indian resistance on the frontier, many colonists resented these restrictions. The withdrawal of cheap, unsettled western lands particularly disillusioned young adults who had planned to set out on their own but now could not. Recall that from 1720 to 1775, about 225,000 Scotch-Irish and Germans had immigrated to America, mostly to the Middle colonies. These were largely men of fighting age with no loyalties to the English Crown. Now many had been denied land they saw as rightfully theirs. Similarly, even established frontier farmers usually took an anti-British stand because they thought that they would be more likely to succeed under a government liberal in disposing of its land. Although poor agrarians did not have dollar stakes in western lands that were comparable to those of large fur traders, land speculators, and planters, they were still affected. Those who were unable to pay their debts sometimes lost their farms through foreclosure; a British policy that inhibited westward movement angered the frontiersmen and tended to align them against the British and with the aristocratic Americans, with whom they had no other affiliation. The Currency Act (Restraining Act) of 1764 also frustrated and annoyed this debtor group because, although prices actually rose moderately in the ensuing decade, farmers were persuaded that their lot worsened with the moderate contraction of paper money that occurred (Economic Reasoning Proposition 4, laws and rules matter).

Economic Exploitation Reconsidered

It is sometimes alleged that the American Revolution was the result of the inevitable clash of competing capitalisms and of England's exploitation of the colonies. In the long run, such conjectures defy empirical testing. After all, how can one judge whether independence or British rule offered more promise for economic progress in North America?

Of course, the short-term consequences of independence can be assessed—a task that awaits us in chapter 7. But at this point, it is important to reconsider the question of colonial exploitation as a motive for revolt. Did British trade restrictions drain the colonial economy?

First, manufacturing restrictions had been placed on woolens, hats, and finished iron products. Woolen production in the colonies was limited to personal use or local trade, so this imposed no significant hardship. The colonists were quite satisfied to purchase manufactures from England at the lower costs made possible by the large-scale production methods employed there. This situation continued even after independence was achieved, and American woolens provided no competition for imported English fabrics until the nineteenth century.

A small portion of colonial manufacturing activity (predominantly New York producers) was hurt by the passage of the Hat Act in 1732. This one-sided legislation benefited London hatters by prohibiting the colonial export of beaver hats. For the overall American economy, however, the effects of the Hat Act were negligible. Similarly, parliamentary restrictions on iron proved moderately harmless. Actually, the colonial production of raw pig and bar iron was encouraged, but the finishing of iron and steel and the use of certain types of equipment were forbidden after 1750. Nevertheless, like the Molasses Act of 1733, restrictions on the manufacture of colonial iron were ignored with impunity: 25 iron mills were established between 1750 and 1775 in Pennsylvania and Delaware alone. Furthermore, the legislative freedom enjoyed by the colonists was amply displayed when the Pennsylvania assembly, in open defiance of the law, appropriated financial aid for a new slitting mill (nail factory). No matter how distasteful these British regulations were to the colonists, they were superfluous (woolen restrictions), ignored (the slitting mill), or inconsequential (hat production).

The generally liberal British land policy was designed to encourage rapid settlement. Only after the war with Chief Pontiac and the resulting Royal Proclamation of 1763 did land policy suddenly become less flexible. When land controls were tightened again by the Quebec Act of 1774, important political issues emerged. Western lands claimed by Massachusetts, Connecticut, and Virginia were redistributed to the Province of Quebec, and land was made less accessible. Territorial governments were placed entirely in the hands of British officials, and trials there were conducted without juries.

We have already assessed the economic implications of these land policies. Some people gained; others lost. But clearly, the climate of freedom changed swiftly, and the political implications of these new policies were hard for the colonists to accept. The major issue appears to have been who was to determine the policy rather than what the policy itself was to be. In fact, the British land policies proved to be largely necessary, and the same basic restraints were prescribed and adopted by the federal government after American independence was achieved. It seems unlikely that the new government would have adopted these restraints had they been economically burdensome (Economic Reasoning Proposition 2, choices impose costs).

The same thing was true of currency restrictions. After independence, the new government adopted measures similar to those England had imposed earlier. For instance, in 1751, Parliament passed the Currency Act, which prohibited New England from establishing new public banks and from issuing paper money for private transactions. A similar and supplemental Restraining Act appeared in 1764, in the wake of events in the Chesapeake area. Planters there were heavily in debt because they had continued to import goods during the Seven Years' War even though their own exports had declined. When Virginia issued £250,000 in bills of credit, to be used as legal tender in private transactions as well as for public sector payments (mainly taxes), British creditors stood to lose. To avoid uncertainties and avoid financial conflicts, Britain countered by extending the original Currency Act to all the colonies. This extension certainly hurt the hard-pressed Chesapeake region and stimulated its unusual support for the boycott of English imports in 1765. But the adoption of similar controls after independence indicates that the economic burden of currency restriction could not have been oppressive overall. The real point at issue was simply whether England or the colonists themselves should hold the reins of monetary control.

It appears that only with respect to the Navigation Acts was there any significant exploitation in a strict economic sense, as illustrated in Economic Insight 6.1. In the words of Lawrence A. Harper,

> The enumeration of key colonial exports in various Acts from 1660 to 1766 and the Staple Act of 1663 hit at colonial trade both coming and going. The Acts required the colonies to allow English middlemen to distribute such crops as tobacco and rice and stipulated that if the colonies would not buy English manufactures, at least they should purchase their European goods in England. The greatest element in the burden laid upon the colonies was not the taxes assessed. It consisted in the increased costs of shipment, transshipment, and middleman's profits arising out of the requirement that England be used as an entrepot. (Harper 1939)

While these burdens of more costly imports and less remunerative colonial exports amounted to nearly 1 percent of total colonial income, there were also benefits to the colonies: They were provided with bounties and other benefits such as naval protection and military defense at British expense.

ECONOMIC INSIGHT 6.1

THE SUPPLY AND DEMAND EFFECTS OF THE NAVIGATION ACTS

Supply-and-demand analysis is useful to illustrate explicitly the burdens on the colonists caused by the Navigation Acts. The requirement that England be used as an "entrepôt" burdened the colonists with extra handling and shipping costs—costs over and above those that would have occurred had commodities been shipped directly from continental Europe. A graph using supply-and-demand curves illustrates the case for imports:

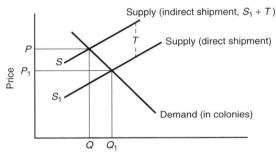

Commodities Imported from Europe via England

Let T represent these extra indirect routing costs on colonial imports from continental Europe. These extra costs may be viewed as a shift in the supply curve from S_1 to S. The effect of the higher transport costs is to cause prices of the affected imports to be higher in the colonies, at P rather than P_1, and quantities to be less, Q rather than Q_1.

The change in price $(P - P_1)$ times the quantities traded (Q) gives a lower bound to the burden on colonial imports from Europe. $(P - P_1)(Q_1)$ gives an upper-bound measure. A similar approach can illustrate the burdens of the laws on colonial exports to continental Europe. In this case, the export price in the colonies is lower because of the law. As the work of Roger Ransom (1968) has shown, these burdens were disproportionately large on southerners. Overall, however, the burdens on imports and exports from indirect routing were less than 1 percent of colonial income.[5]

In any case, the colonists had lived with these restrictions for more than a century. Even those hardest hit—the producers of tobacco and other enumerated products—almost never mentioned the restrictions in their lists of grievances against England. It is especially noteworthy that the acts of trade are not even mentioned in the Declaration of Independence.

Rather than exploitation, it was the rapidly changing and severely administered new colonial policies that precipitated the American Revolution. Before 1763, the colonists had been free to do pretty much as they pleased. An occasional new enactment or a veto of colonial legislation by Britain had caused little or no discord. After the Seven Years' War, however, conditions suddenly changed. A host of new taxes and regulations were effected and strictly enforced by Britain. The new taxes were light, but their methods of collection borne heavily.

Collectively, the acts after 1763 gave almost every colonist a grievance: Debtors objected to the Currency Act; shippers and merchants to the Sugar Act; pioneers to the Quebec Act; politicians, printers, and gamblers to the Stamp Act; retailers and smugglers to the Tea Act. As colonial resentments flared, Committees of Correspondence pressed forward to formally claim the rights they had long held de facto before 1763 (Economic Reasoning Proposition 4, laws and rules matter).

---

[5]For an assessment of the several studies and estimates of these costs, see Walton (1971). Also, for a more recent article and counterargument, see Sawyers (1992).

In many ways, it appears that the growing economic maturity of the colonies would soon have made American independence inevitable. Indeed, the gross product of the colonies was nearly £25 million at the time, or nearly one-third of England's gross national product, as compared with only about one-fourth at the beginning of the eighteenth century. Clearly, the colonies had matured economically to a point at which an independent course was feasible.

But was revolution necessary to break away from the Empire? After all, other English colonies subsequently gained independence without resorting to armed warfare. By 1775, according to Charles Andrews, the colonies had reached a point where they were

> *qualified to cooperate with the mother country on terms similar to those of a brotherhood of free nations, such as the British world is becoming today (1926). But England was unable to see this fact, or to recognize it, and consequently America became the scene of a political unrest which might have been controlled by a compromise, but was turned to revolt by coercion. The situation is a very interesting one, for England is famous for her ability to compromise at critical times in her history. For once, at least, she failed. (Andrews 1926, 232)*

The nature of that "failure" is nicely summarized by Lawrence Harper:

> *As a mother country, Britain had much to learn. Any modern parents' magazine could have told George III's ministers that the one mistake not to make is to take a stand and then to yield to howls of anguish. It was a mistake which the British government made repeatedly. It placed a duty of 3d. per gallon on molasses, and when it encountered opposition, reduced it to 1d. It provided for a Stamp Act and withdrew it in the face of temper tantrums. It provided for external taxes to meet the colonial objections and then yielded again by removing all except one. When finally it attempted to enforce discipline, it was too late. Under the circumstances, no self-respecting child—or colonist— would be willing to yield. (Harper 1942, 14)*

It would appear that the lessons the English learned from their failures with the American colonies served them well in later periods because other English colonies subsequently won their independence without wide-scale bloodshed. This colonial legacy was of paramount importance in the centuries to follow.

SELECTED REFERENCES AND SUGGESTED READINGS

Andrews, Charles. "The American Revolution: An Interpretation." *American Historical Review* 31 (1926): 232.

Bruchey, Stuart. *The Colonial Merchant.* New York: Harcourt Brace Jovanovich, 1966.

Davis, Lance E., and Robert A. Huttenback. "The Cost of Empire." In *Explorations in the New Economic History,* eds. Roger L. Ransom, Richard Sutch, and Gary M. Walton. New York: Academic Press, 1982.

Harper, Lawrence. "The Effects of the Navigation Acts on the Thirteen Colonies." In *The Era of the American Revolution,* ed. Richard Morris. New York: Columbia University Press, 1939.

_____. "Mercantilism and the American Revolution." *Canadian Historical Review* 25 (1942): 14.

Hughes, Jonathan. *American Economic History,* 3rd ed. Glenview: Scott, Foresman, 1990, 59.

Ostrander, Gilman M. "The Colonial Molasses Trade." *Agricultural History* 30 (1956): 77–84.

Ransom, Roger. "British Policy and Colonial Growth: Some Implications of the Burdens of the Navigation Acts." *Journal of Economic History* 27 (1968): 427–435.

Sawyers, Larry. "The Navigation Acts Revisited." *Economic History Review* 45, no. 2 (May 1992): 262–284.

Tansill, Charles C. *Documents Illustrative of the Union of the Formation of the American States.* Washington, D.C.: Government Printing Office, 1927.

Walton, Gary M. "The New Economic History and the Burdens of the Navigation Acts." *Economic History Review* 24, no. 4, 2nd series (1971): 533–542.

PART 2

The Revolutionary, Early National, and Antebellum Eras: 1776–1860

ECONOMIC AND HISTORICAL PERSPECTIVES *1776–1860*

1. Industrializing Great Britain and the newly revolutionized France under Napoleon stood as the world's two leading powers. Britain was dominant in naval forces and led in per capita income; France was dominant in land forces, strong in total output, and larger in population.

2. War broke out between Britain and France in 1793 and lasted until 1815. To help finance his war, Napoleon sold the Louisiana Territory to the United States in 1803, doubling the land size of the new nation. Trade and commerce soared in American ports as U.S. shippers served as neutrals to the belligerents. The suppression of U.S. shipping entangled the United States in a second war with Britain in 1812.

3. The Northwest Land Ordinances of 1785 and 1787 ensured that new U.S. territories could progress toward statehood and enter the Union having full equality with the older states.

4. The U.S. Constitution, adopted in 1789, is a landmark document, historically unprecedented for its scope and simplicity, for its constraint on government power, and as a model of political compromise. It provided assurances of protection of property consistent with individual freedoms (with the telling exception of slavery, which persisted in the South).

5. The cotton gin, invented in 1793 by Eli Whitney, allowed the seeds of short staple cotton to be economically removed. Thereafter, U.S. cotton production as a share of world production increased from 0.5 percent in 1791 to 68 percent in 1850. Southern slavery became increasingly entrenched and a growing threat to the Union as western migrations brought the proslavery and antislavery forces into continual dispute.

6. As the Industrial Revolution spread from England to the United States in the early nineteenth century, a transportation revolution also unfolded to create a strong national market linking the industrializing Northeast with the agrarian Midwest and the southern cotton kingdom.

7. By 1860, the United States was the second-leading industrial power in the world.

CHAPTER 7

Hard Realities for a New Nation

The years from 1776 to 1815 consisted of four distinct periods: 1) first was war (the Revolution), then 2) peace and independence, followed by 3) war again (Napoleonic wars) with the new United States acting as a neutral, and, finally, 4) the young nation's second war with England. These events caused economic fluctuations and imposed significant shocks on the economy, pressing resources into new areas of production as trade lanes opened and closed. Years of war generally reduced American trade and economic activity. However, during the years of war when U.S. neutrality gave American shipping and commerce the opportunities to fill the void of others who were engaged in combat, times were especially prosperous.

Even during peacetime, great economic adjustments occurred because the new nation was now outside the British Empire; severe peacetime trade restrictions added to the nation's difficulties.

Finally, the new nation faced the problems of paying the debts accumulated during the Revolutionary War years and of forging agreements among the states on how to form a government based on constitutional limitations. Recall Economic Reasoning Propositions 1, scarcity forces us to make choices; 2, choices impose costs; and 4, laws and rules matter, in Economic Insight 1.1 on page 8.

THE WAR AND THE ECONOMY

The Revolutionary War, which began officially on April 19, 1775, dragged on for more than six bitter years. From a vantage point more than two centuries later, we can see that the war foreshadowed a massive upheaval in the Western world—a chain reaction of revolutions, great and small, that would transform the world. But to the embattled colonials, it was simply a conflict fought for the righteous cause of securing freedom from intolerable British intervention in American affairs. Paradoxically, the Revolution was never supported by the substantial popular majority. Perhaps one-third of the colonists remained loyal to England; another third did little or nothing to help the cause, often trafficking with the enemy and selling provisions and supplies to American troops at profitable prices. In varying numbers and in widely scattered theaters, foot soldiers slogged wearily back and forth in heartbreaking campaigns that produced no military gains. Although there were relatively few seamen and sea battles were, for the most part, militarily indecisive, it is an irony of history that the Revolutionary War was finally won with naval strength, as the French fleet under its admiral, the Comte de Grasse, drove off the British men-of-war and bottled up Cornwallis at Yorktown.

Of course, maritime commerce was always an important factor in the war effort, and trade linkages were vital to the supply of arms and ammunitions. When legal restrictions were implemented by both the British and the colonists in 1775, nearly all American overseas commerce abruptly ceased. By mid-1775, the colonies faced acute shortages in such military essentials as powder, flints, muskets, and knives. Even salt, shoes, woolens, and linens were in short supply. Late in 1775, Congress authorized limited trade with the West Indies, mainly to procure arms and ammunitions, and trade with other non-British areas was on an unrestricted basis by the spring of 1776.

Nevertheless, the British maintained a fairly effective naval blockade of American ports, especially during the first two years of the war. Boston was pried open late in 1776, but most of the other major ports in New England and the Middle colonies were tightly sealed until 1778. As the British relaxed their grip on the North, they tightened it on the South. Savannah was taken late in 1778, Charleston in 1780.

Yet the colonies engaged in international trade despite the blockade. Formal treaties of commerce with France in 1778 and with Holland and Spain shortly thereafter stimulated the flows of overseas trade. Between 1778 and early 1782, American wartime commerce was at its zenith. During those years, France, Holland, Spain, and their possessions all actively traded with the colonies. Even so, the flow of goods in and out of the colonies remained well below prewar levels. Smuggling, privateering, and legal trade with overseas partners only partially offset the drastic trade reductions with Britain. Even the coastal trades were curtailed by a lack of vessels, by blockades, and by wartime freight rates. British-occupied ports, such as New York, generated some import activity but little or nothing in the way of exports.

As exports and imports fell, import substitution abounded, and the colonial economy became considerably more self-sufficient. In Philadelphia, for instance, nearly 4,000 women were employed to spin materials in their homes for the newly established textile plants. A sharp increase also occurred in the number of artisan workshops with a similar stimulus in the production of beer, whiskey, and other domestic alcoholic beverages. The rechanneling of American resources into import-competing industries was especially strong along the coast and in the major port cities (Economic Reasoning Propositions 1, scarcity forces us to make choices; and 2, choices impose costs). Only the least commercialized rural areas remained little affected by the serpentine path of war and the sporadic flows of wartime commerce.

Overall, the war imposed a distinct economic hardship on the new nation. Most goods rose in cost and were more difficult to obtain. Higher prices and severe commercial difficulties encouraged some investors to turn from commerce to manufacturing (Economic Reasoning Proposition 3, incentives matter). Then, once the trade lanes reopened with the coming of peace, even those who profited from the war were stung by the tide of imports that swept into American ports and sharply lowered prices. Although many Americans escaped the direct ordeals of war, few Americans were untouched by it—at least indirectly.

The strains of war and economic decline were complemented by the critical problem of forming a government. By 1780, all of the 13 colonies had their own individual constitutions, and legally they were unified by the Articles of Confederation, written as a source of early political agreement and to wage the war. The articles were ratified by the individual states, between 1777 and 1781, but proved inadequate as a permanent framework for national government. For example, the power to tax was left to the individual states, thus allowing any state to free ride on revenues supplied by others. Furthermore, after the colonies won independence, the great powers treated the new nation with a disdain that bordered on contempt. Britain, annoyed because Americans refused to pay prewar British creditors or restore confiscated Tory property as provided in the peace treaty, excluded the United States from valuable commercial privileges and refused to withdraw troops from its frontier posts on American soil. Spain tried to close the lower Mississippi to American traffic. Even France refused to extend the courtesies traditionally

PERSPECTIVE 7.1

NATIVE AMERICANS AND THE REVOLUTION

The American Revolution was not entirely a war of colonial fighters against soldiers and sailors of the mother country. During the war, the Iroquois confederation (Six Nations) initially strained to maintain a neutral status. Eventually, however, most Iroquois tribes joined in fighting alongside the British. After the war, many Americans viewed the Iroquois as a people conquered and some wanted them banished west. In addition, Indian lands were greatly desired as a means to pay colonial soldiers for their services and help pay down the debts the colonists had built up during the war.

Despite refusing to accept a conquered status, the Iroquois' power was greatly weakened by the war and further reduced and broken in subsequent forest wars that soon followed. Many Iroquois moved to Canada, and much of their land was taken by the United States through purchase and treaties. By 1794, the remaining Iroquois were confined to a small set of reservations in the state of New York.

offered a sovereign government. These and other problems too great to be surmounted by the states acting individually pressed inexorably for a strong rather than weak union. Under the Articles, the national government appeared too weak to negotiate improvements in its economic or military relations.

Internally, the most pressing problems were financial. Between 1775 and 1781, the war was financed by the issue of paper money in amounts great enough to result in a galloping inflation—the only one ever experienced in America except in the Confederate South. Nearly $200 million (at face value) in continental money, more than $150 million (face value) in quartermaster and commissary certificates of the central government, and another $200 million (face value) in paper money of the states was issued to defray wartime expenses. Throughout the war years and the 1780s, Congress and many of the states failed to make interest payments on their debts and failed also to redeem their paper monies at face value. The states' failures were due to economic distress and inadequate tax revenues. But for the central government there was no power to tax at all, a major shortcoming of the Articles of Confederation (see Calomiris 1988, 47–68). The decline in the value of the Continental (issued by the central government) was particularly steep because it had no taxation powers to back it.

By 1786 Virginia called for the Annapolis Convention, primarily to settle questions of trade regulations among the states, but the only action taken there was to recommend to Congress that another convention be called to address a broader range of issues. By the following year, strong central government advocates had persuaded weak government advocates to reconsider. Indeed, the convention that met in Philadelphia in 1787 was able to ignore its instructions to amend the Articles of Confederation and to create a new government instead only because the great constitutional questions debated so heatedly since 1775 were at least settled in the minds of the majority. In a little more than four months after the first meeting of the delegates, George Washington, president of the convention, sent the completed document to the states for ratification.[1] Delaware ratified it almost immediately, on December 7, 1787; on June 21, 1788, New Hampshire cast the crucial ninth vote in favor (Economic Reasoning Propositions 1, scarcity forces us to make choices; and 4, laws and rules matter). Congress declared the Constitution in effect beginning March 4, 1789, and two years later, the Bill of Rights was passed and put into effect.

---

[1]For an analysis assessing the economic vested interests of the delegates, see McGuire and Ohsfeldt (1986).

THE CONSTITUTION

With the adoption of the Constitution, the power to tax was firmly delegated to the federal government, which was empowered to pay a portion (10 to 20 percent face value) of past debts, including those incurred by the states. The assurance that public debts will be honored has proven critical to the development of a sound capital market in the United States. There have been failings—as in the late 1830s, when several states defaulted on loans—but even today, the United States benefits from this institutional heritage and is viewed as a haven by major investors seeking safety for their capital (Economic Reasoning Propositions 3, incentives matter; and 4, laws and rules matter).

The Constitution also gave the central government the sole right to mint coins and regulate coinage. States were not allowed such rights, and the Constitution also banned states and their legislatures from issuing paper money. States, however, were left empowered to charter private banks who could issue paper money.

Both these powers, to tax and to regulate money, brought into sharp focus the founders' concerns over conflicting factions, the limits of majority rule, and the ability to redistribute wealth and income by governmental means.[2] Consequently, federal taxes had to be uniform among all the states and, of course, U.S. dollars had to be exchangeable throughout the states. The concerns urging barriers to prevent significant and radical changes in the distribution of wealth through government formed the basis for a major section of the Fifth Amendment: "nor shall any person...be deprived of life, liberty, or property, without due process of law; nor shall private property be taken for public use without just compensation."

Another matter of great political and economic significance was the regulation of trade among the states. Although no substantial barriers to interstate commerce had emerged in the 1780s, the possibility for them was evident. Under the Constitution, the states were forbidden to enact tariffs, thus ensuring the toll-free movement of goods. The important "interstate clause" established a great national common market that reduced the potential of local monopolies and increased the gain from regional specialization and trade; in later decades, it also permitted the extension of federal authority to many areas of interstate economic activity.

The Constitution promoted trade and economic specialization in other ways. It authorized the federal government to maintain an army and navy, establish post offices and roads, fix standards of weights and measures, and establish uniform bankruptcy

---

[2]In Paper 10 of the Federalist Papers, James Madison demonstrates his preoccupation with these important matters:

The most common and durable source of factions has been the various and unequal distribution of property. Those who hold and those who are without property have ever formed distinct interests in society. Those who are creditors, and those who are debtors, fall under a like discrimination. A landed interest, a manufacturing interest, a mercantile interest, a money interest, with many lesser interests, grow up of necessity in civilized nations, and divide them into different classes, actuated by different sentiments and views. The regulation of these various and interfering interests forms the principal task of modern legislation, and involves the spirit of party and faction in the necessary and ordinary operations of the government....The inference to which we are brought is, that the causes of faction cannot be removed, and that relief is only to be sought in the means of controlling its effects.

If a faction consists of less than a majority, relief is supplied by the republican principle, which enables the majority to defeat its sinister views by regular vote. It may clog the administration, it may convulse the society; but it will be unable to execute and mask its violence under the forms of the Constitution. When a majority is included in a faction, the form of popular government, on the other hand, enables it to sacrifice to its ruling passion or interest both the public good and the rights of other citizens. To secure the public good and private rights against the danger of such a faction, and at the same time to preserve the spirit and the form of popular government, is then the great object to which our inquiries are directed.

laws. It also gave Congress the authority to set laws on patents: "To promote the progress of science and useful arts by securing for limited times to authors and inventors the exclusive right to their respective writings and discoveries." With greater assurances to the gains of their own ideas and creations, creative people would hasten technical change.

Another transfer of authority to the federal government was that of foreign affairs. The federal government alone could negotiate treaties or set tariffs. The power to regulate tariffs became a powerful lever in negotiations with foreign nations to reduce or eliminate duties on American goods abroad, as it remains today in the global negotiations within the World Trade Organization (WTO). Before this shift of power, competition among the states minimized the possibility of this leverage, and U.S. tariffs were very low. Once they were centralized, however, tariffs became the chief source of federal revenues throughout most of the nineteenth century.

For the delegates at the Philadelphia convention (and the individual states) to voluntarily release such powers to the central government was unprecedented—made possible only through compromise, which was epitomized in the question of slavery. The Constitutional compromise allowed slavery to continue but limited the importation of slaves to only 20 years, ending in 1808. A tax of up to $10 per imported slave was allowed. Furthermore, each state was ordered to recognize the laws and court orders of other states; thus, runaway slaves escaping to another state were to be returned, like stolen property (Economic Reasoning Propositions 3, incentives matter; and 4, laws and rules matter). Was a slave merely property, or was a slave a person? Oddly, the Constitution viewed slaves in two respects: First and foremost, slaves were property, just as in colonial times; second, each slave was counted as three-fifths of a person for the purpose of determining each state's membership in the House of Representatives, which was based on population.

The debates of the convention focused carefully on the question of state versus national interests, and it was temporarily left implicit that powers not delegated to the federal government or forbidden to the states were reserved to the states (or the people). To strengthen these reserved rights, the Tenth Amendment was added to the Bill of Rights, ensuring the states' powers to set local and state laws such as licensing, regulation of business, taxes, zoning laws, civil conduct, and the like, and to use police powers to enforce them.

In respect to relations among people, the new nation preserved the treasured English Common Law. This long string of rules based on court decisions had worked well for centuries, and the First Continental Congress of 1774 had formally proclaimed the Common Law of England as the right of Americans.[3] Many states repeated this claim, and legal interpretations were left to the states as long as their legal statutes and interpretations were consistent with the Constitution, the supreme law of the land. Any conflict or challenge was to be adjudicated by the courts and, if necessary, ultimately by the Supreme Court.

The Constitution laid the foundation of the private property rights we enjoy today. It curbed the arbitrary powers of government and fostered personal security required for the pursuit of all varieties of productivity-enhancing activities. Amazingly brief and clear, the Constitution has proven flexible through court interpretation and, on 16 occasions since the Bill of Rights, through amendment.

Probably no single original source exists from which the essential concepts of the Constitution were derived. And yet, in 1776, the same year that the Declaration of

---

[3]For the origins, development, and significance of the Common Law and trial by jury as contrasted with Roman law, see chapter 13 in Churchill (1990).

This painting of the formal closing of the Philadelphia convention and sending the Constitution to the states for ratification highlights the hot work of the delegates through the months of late July, August, and September before the age of air conditioning.

Independence rang its message of political freedom around the world, an odd-looking Scot, whose professorial mien belied his vast knowledge of economic affairs, offered a clarion rationale of economic freedom. *The Wealth of Nations* ultimately became a best-seller, and Adam Smith became admired and famous. Educated people everywhere, including American leaders, read his great work, marveling at the lucid language and its castigation of mercantilist constraints on economic processes. It does not diminish Adam Smith's great influence to say that he was the articulate commentator on forces that existed long before he began to write. Chief among these forces were a growing regard for the advantages of private property arrangements and an abiding conviction that law and order were essential to the preservation of property rights and to the opportunity for all people to acquire the things of this world. It follows, therefore, that matching the political guarantees of the Constitution with their ultimate assurance of personal freedoms would be norms, customs, and other laws establishing fundamental economic guarantees of protection of private property and enforcement of contracts, essential to a viable market economy. The United States was especially well tailored to Smith's concept of an economic order, directed by self-interest, that limited governmental rules and regulations but ensured the domestic tranquility and freedom from foreign interference that only a strong central government could provide.

AMERICAN INDEPENDENCE AND ECONOMIC CHANGE

The adoption of the Constitution in 1789 and the emergence of a stronger federal government did not have dramatic immediate effects. The crucial political decisions of that time were matched by challenging economic problems. The central problem was independence itself. All at once the young nation found itself outside the walls of the British Empire, and soon even the wartime trade alliances with France and Spain began to crumble.

In the Caribbean, U.S. ships were excluded from direct trade with the British West Indies. American merchants who tried to evade the law faced possible seizure by officials. Spain added to American woes by withdrawing the wartime privilege of direct U.S. trade with Cuba, Puerto Rico, and Hispaniola. In addition, Spain reinstituted its traditional policy of restricting trade with its possessions, permitting them to import goods only from Spain. U.S. trade with the French West Indies increased, but this was not enough to offset the declines in commercial trade with other Caribbean islands. Even in its lively trade with the French, the United States was not allowed to carry sugar from French islands, and only in times of severe scarcity did the French import American flour. In addition, the French imposed high duties on U.S. salted fish and meat, and these products were banned entirely from the British islands.

Restrictions and trade curtailments were not limited to the Caribbean. Now Americans were also cut off from direct trade with the British fisheries in Newfoundland and Nova Scotia. As a result, the New England states suffered severe losses in trade to the north in provisions, lumber, rum, and shipping services. To the east and into the Mediterranean, American shipping faced harassment by the Barbary pirates because the United States was no longer protected by the British flag and by British tribute to the governments of Tunis, Tripoli, and Algeria.

While American shipping rocked at anchor, American shipbuilding and the supporting industries of lumber and naval stores also remained unengaged. Britain now labeled all American-built vessels as foreign, thereby making them ineligible to trade within the Empire even when they were owned by British subjects. The result was the loss of a major market for American shipbuilders, and after 1783, U.S. ship production declined still further because American whale oil faced prohibitively high British duties. In fact, nearly all the activities that employed American-built ships (cod fishing, whaling, mercantile, and shipping services) were depressed industries, and New England—the center of these activities—suffered disproportionately during the early years of independence.

The states of the former Middle colonies were also affected. Pennsylvania and New York shared losses in shipbuilding. Moreover, their levels of trade in wheat, flour, salted meat, and other provisions to the West Indies were well below those of colonial peacetime years. By 1786, the Middle colonies had probably reached the bottom of a fairly severe business downturn, and then conditions began to improve as these products were reaccepted into the traditional West Indian and southern European markets.

Similar problems plagued the South. For instance, British duties on rice restricted the planters of South Carolina and Georgia primarily to markets in the West Indies and southern Europe. As the price of rice declined, further setbacks resulted from the loss of bounties and subsidies on indigo and naval stores. Having few alternative uses of their productive capacity, the Carolinas and Georgia faced special difficulties. Their economic future did not look bright. Similarly, Virginia and Maryland faced stagnating markets for their major staple—tobacco. In Britain, a tax of 15d. sterling was imposed on each pound of foreign tobacco. In France, a single purchasing monopoly, the Farmers-General, was created to handle tobacco imports. Meanwhile, Spain and Portugal prohibited imports of American tobacco altogether. These economic changes were the results of the colonies' choice to become independent (Economic Reasoning Propositions 1, scarcity forces us to make choices; 2, choices impose costs; and 4, laws and rules matter).

Offsetting these restrictions were a few positive forces. Goods that previously had been "enumerated" now could be traded directly to continental European ports. This lowered the shipping and handling costs on some items such as tobacco, thereby having an upward effect on their prices. Meanwhile, the great influx of British manufactures sharply reduced prices on these goods in American ports. Although American manufacturers suffered, consumers were pleased: Compared with the late colonial period, the terms of trade—the prices paid for imports relative to the prices paid for exports—had improved. This was especially true in 1783 and 1784, when import prices were slightly below their prewar level and export prices were higher. Thereafter, however, the terms of trade became less favorable, and by 1790, there was little advantage in the adjustments of these relative prices compared with the prewar period.

A QUANTITATIVE ANALYSIS OF ECONOMIC CHANGE

To convey these many changes more systematically and in a long-run perspective, it is essential to compare the circumstances of the late colonial period and the years immediately following independence. Of course, this does not entirely isolate the impact of independence on the economy because forces other than independence contributed to the shifting magnitudes and patterns of trade and to the many other economic changes that occurred. Nevertheless, comparisons of the late colonial period with the early 1790s provide important insights into the new directions and prospects for the young nation.

Table 7.1 on page 117 shows that by 1790, the United States had taken advantage of its new freedom to trade directly with northern European countries. Most of this trade was in tobacco to France and the Netherlands, but rice, wheat, flour, and maize (Indian corn) were also shipped there in large amounts. Despite the emergence of this new trade pattern, the lion's share of American exports continued to be sent to Great Britain, including items that were then re-exported to the Continent. Many have speculated on the reasons for this renewal of American-British ties. Part of the explanation may be that Britain offered the greatest variety of goods at the best price and quality, especially woolens, linens, and hardware. Moreover, British merchants enjoyed the advantages of a

TABLE 7.1 AVERAGE ANNUAL REAL EXPORTS TO OVERSEAS AREAS FROM THE 13 COLONIES, 1768–1772, AND THE UNITED STATES, 1790–1792 (IN THOUSANDS OF POUNDS STERLING, 1768–1772 PRICES)

DESTINATION	1768–1772	PERCENTAGE OF TOTAL	1790–1792	PERCENTAGE OF TOTAL
Great Britain and Ireland	1,616	58%	1,234	31%
Northern Europe	—	—	643	16
Southern Europe	406	14	557	14
British West Indies	759	27	402	10
Foreign West Indies	—	—	956	24
Africa	21	1	42	1
Canadian Colonies	—	—	60	2
Other	—	—	59	2
Total	**2,802**	**100%**	**3,953**	**100%**

Note: — = not applicable.

Source: *Shepherd and Walton 1976.*

common language, established contacts, and their knowledge of U.S. markets. Because American imports were handled by British merchants, it was often advantageous to use British ports as dropping-off points for U.S. exports, even those destined for the Continent.

At the same time, new patterns of trade were emerging in the Caribbean. Before the Revolution, trade with the British West Indies had been greater than trade with the foreign islands, but by 1790 the situation was reversed, largely due to the exclusion of American shipping from the British islands. Undoubtedly, many American ships illegally traversed British Caribbean waters, and Dutch St. Eustatius remained an entrepôt from which British islands were supplied as they had been during the war. Consequently, the statistics in Table 7.1 exaggerate this shift. Nevertheless, it would appear that U.S. trade with non-British areas of the Caribbean grew substantially during these years. This trend had been under way before the Revolution, but postwar restrictions on American shipping undoubtedly hastened it.

Lastly, it is worth noting that no new trades to romantic, faraway places emerged in any significant way during this period of transition. The changes in trade patterns were actually rather modest.

As trade patterns changed, so did the relative importance of the many goods traded. For instance, the most valuable export by the early 1790s was no longer tobacco, but bread and flour. Tobacco production grew slowly, but rising tobacco prices aided the recovery of the tobacco-producing areas of Virginia and Maryland. Other important southern staples, such as pitch, tar, rice, and indigo, fell both in value and in quantities produced. The decline of indigo was aggravated by the loss of bounties and by increased British production of indigo in the West Indies after the war. The most striking change of the period, however, was the increase in the export of foodstuffs such as salted meats (beef and pork), bread and flour, maize, and wheat. Of course, this increase accompanied the relative rise of the trades to the West Indies. Because the uptrend in food shipments to the West Indies was under way before the Revolution, not all of this shift in commodities can be attributed solely to independence.

Because of these changing patterns and magnitudes of trade, some states improved their economic well-being, while others lost ground. Table 7.2 shows exports per capita for each state during this period, after adjusting for inflationary effects. Compared with prewar levels, New England had returned to about the same per capita position by the early 1790s. The Middle Atlantic region showed improvement despite the depression felt so sharply in Pennsylvania in the mid-1780s. As indicated in Table 7.2, the trade of the southern regions did not keep pace with a growing population. Although the South's prewar absolute level of exports had been regained by the early 1790s, its per capita exports were significantly below those in colonial times, with the Lower South most severely affected. Once again, however, this decline was caused not so much by independence as by a decline in growth of demand in Europe for southern staples.

The wide variety of changes among the states makes it extremely hazardous to generalize nationally. Overall, a 30 percent decline in real per capita exports (per year) occurred. Total exports had climbed by 40 percent, but this fell far short of the 80 percent jump in population. Accompanying this change was a slowing in urbanization. The major cities of Philadelphia, New York, and Boston grew only 3 percent over this period, despite the large increase in the total population of the states. Both of these adjustments—the decline in per capita exports and the pause in urban growth—were extremely unusual peacetime experiences. Yet, as emphasized, such aggregate figures hide as much as they reveal. The southern declines were sharp; only New York and the New England states (except New Hampshire) fully recovered from trade disruptions.

TABLE 7.2 AVERAGE ANNUAL EXPORTS FROM THE 13 COLONIES, 1768–1772, AND THE UNITED STATES, 1791–1792 (IN THOUSANDS OF POUNDS STERLING, 1768–1772 PRICES)

ORIGIN	1768–1772			1791–1792		
	TOTAL EXPORTS	PERCENTAGE OF TOTAL	PER CAPITA EXPORTS	TOTAL EXPORTS	PERCENTAGE OF TOTAL	PER CAPITA EXPORTS
New England	477	17%	0.82	842	22%	0.83
New Hampshire	46	2	0.74	33	1	0.23
Massachusetts	258	9	0.97	542	14	1.14
Rhode Island	81	3	1.39	119	3	1.72
Connecticut	92	3	0.50	148	4	0.62
Middle Atlantic	560	20	1.01	1,127	30	1.11
New York	187	7	1.15	512	14	1.51
New Jersey	2	—	0.02	5	—	0.03
Pennsylvania	353	13	1.47	584	16	1.34
Delaware	18	1	0.51	26	1	0.44
Upper South	1,162	41	1.79	1,160	31	1.09
Maryland	392	14	1.93	482	13	1.51
Virginia	770	27	1.72	678	18	0.91
Lower South	604	22	1.75	637	17	0.88
North Carolina	75	3	0.38	104	3	0.27
South Carolina	455	16	3.66	436	12	1.75
Georgia	74	3	3.17	97	3	1.17
Total, all regions	**2,803**	**100%**	**1.31**	**3,766**	**100%**	**0.99**

Source: *Shepherd and Walton 1976.*

WAR, NEUTRALITY, AND ECONOMIC RESURGENCE

As we have seen, the economic setbacks experienced by the United States throughout the late 1770s and most of the 1780s were followed by years of halting progress and incomplete recovery. Then, in 1793, only four years after the beginning of the French Revolution, the French and English began a series of wars that lasted until 1815.[4] During this long struggle, both British and French cargo vessels were drafted into military service, and both nations relaxed their restrictive mercantilist policies. Of all nations most capable of filling the shipping void created by the Napoleonic wars, the new United States stood at the forefront.

Because of these developments, the nation's economy briskly rebounded from the doldrums of the preceding years. The stimulus in U.S. overseas commerce is graphed statistically in Figure 7.1. As indicated, per capita credits in the balance of payments (exports plus other sources of foreign exchange earnings) more than tripled between 1790 and the height of war between the French and English. Overseas trade as a proportion of national income during these years is discussed in Economic Insight 7.1. These were extraordinary years for America—a time of unusual prosperity and intense economic

---

[4]The Treaty of Amiens, signed late in 1801, provided a year and a half of uneasy peace.

FIGURE 7.1

Per Capita Credits in the
U.S. Balance of Payments,
1790–1815

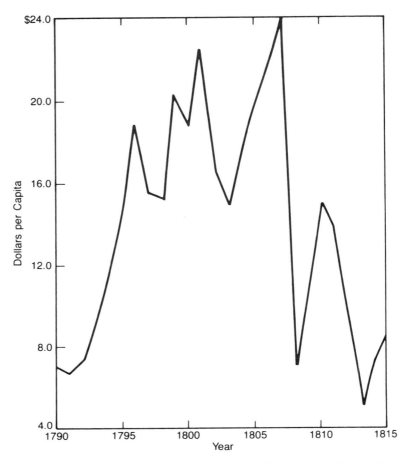

Source: *North 1961, 390. Reprinted by permission of the University of Chicago Press.*

activity, especially in the eastern port cities. It was a time characterized by full employment and sharply rising urbanization, at least until 1808. Famed entrepreneurs of New England and the Middle Atlantic region, such as Stephen Girard, Archibald Gracie, E. H. Derby, and John Jacob Astor, amassed vast personal fortunes during this period. These and other capital accumulations added to the development of a well-established commercial sector and eventually contributed to the incipient manufacturing sector.

It is important to recognize the significance of the commercial sector of the economy as well as the role of the merchant class during these decades. The growing merchant class, of course, had played an active role spearheading the move for national independence. Now the merchant class supplied the entrepreneurial talents required to take full advantage of the new economic circumstances. As the spreading European war opened up exceptional trade opportunities, America's well-developed commercial sector provided the needed buildings and ships as well as know-how. In short, both the physical and human capital were already available, and in many ways, the success of the period stemmed from developments that reached back to colonial times. It was exactly that prior development that singled out the United States as the leading neutral nation in time of war. Rather than the ports of the Caribbean, Latin America, or Canada, those of the United States emerged as the entrepôts of trade in the western Atlantic.

ECONOMIC INSIGHT 7.1

OVERSEAS TRADE AND TOTAL INCOME

How big was overseas trade as a proportion of national income? Was overseas trade large enough to merit the emphasis it has been given here? To answer these crucial questions, some calculations are in order.

Taking 1774 as a benchmark year, we see from Table 2.1 (page 35 that about 2.4 million people lived in the colonies. From Table 5.4 (page 89), we determine that average yearly incomes were about £10.7 (using the 3.5-to-1 capital output ratio). Total income was therefore £25.7 million (£10.7 × 2.4 million).

From Table 4.5 (page 71, we can sum commodity exports, plus ship sales, plus invisible earnings (but excluding British expenditures on military personnel) to show the average yearly values (1768–1772) of incomes from overseas trade and shipping activities. These were probably slightly below 1774's earnings, so we have a lower bound of £2,800,000 (exports) + £140,000 (ship sales) + £880,000 (invisible earnings) equaling £3.82 million. We can conclude, therefore, that income from overseas trade and shipping was nearly 15 percent of total incomes.

An added argument for stressing overseas economic activities is that these were market activities, ones that led the way in moving resources from lesser- to higher-valued uses. It was this commercial sector—not subsistence farming, hunting, woodcutting, and the like—that provided the chief stimulus to market expansion, economic specialization, technology transfer, capital accumulation, and advancing productivity and standards of living. Finally, if the coastal intercolonial trades are added to the overseas trade and shipping earnings (15 percent of total income), the combined proportion approaches one-fifth of total income.

The result of this quantitative analysis of the magnitudes of overseas (and coastal) trade, along with the arguments advanced here based on economic growth theory, urges our emphasis on this sector as a leading one for the economic progress of the colonies.

The western movement and the persistence of self-sufficient activities cushioned the downfall of incomes per capita. Undoubtedly, per capita internal trade did not decline to the same extent as per capita exports. (Unfortunately, we have no statistics on domestic trade during that hectic period.) Thus, the external relations probably exaggerated the overall setbacks of the period. It is safe to conclude, however, that the political chaos of the early national era was accompanied by severe economic conditions. Indeed, the problems of government contributed to the weakness of the economy, and economic events in turn clarified government failings under the Articles of Confederation.

These were the circumstances entering 1793, the year in which the Napoleonic wars erupted and Eli Whitney invented the cotton gin. The sweeping consequences of those events could never have been foreseen in colonial times. The colonies, however, had already developed a commercial base that now would prove crucial to further development. Because of its early efforts at overseas trade, the new nation was ready to take quick advantage of the economic opportunities available to a neutral nation in a world at war.

The effects of war and neutrality on U.S. shipping earnings are shown in Figure 7.2. In general, these statistics convey the same picture illustrated in Figure 7.1, namely, that these were exceptionally prosperous times for the commercial sector.

Although the invention of the cotton gin stimulated cotton production and U.S. cotton supplies grew in response to the growth of demand for raw cotton in English textile mills, commercial growth was by no means limited to products produced in the United States. As Figure 7.3 shows, a major portion of the total exports from U.S. ports included re-exports, especially in such tropical items as sugar, coffee, cocoa, pepper, and spices. Because their commercial sectors were relatively underdeveloped, the Caribbean islands and Latin America depended primarily on American shipping and merchandising services rather than on their own.

Of course, such unique conditions did not provide the basis for long-term development, and (as Figures 7.1, 7.2, and 7.3 all show) when temporary peace came between late 1801 and 1803, the U.S. commercial boom quickly evaporated. When hostilities

FIGURE 7.2
Net Freight Earnings of
U.S. Carrying Trade,
1790–1815

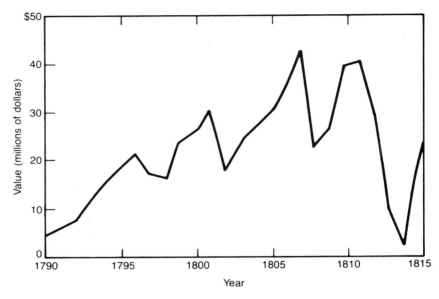

Source: *North 1961, 26, 28.*

erupted again, the United States experienced another sharp upswing in commercial activity. This time, however, new and serious problems arose with expansion. In 1805, the British imposed an antiquated ruling, the Rule of 1756, permitting neutrals in wartime to carry only those goods that they normally carried in peacetime. This ruling, known as the Essex Decision, was matched by Napoleon's Berlin Decree, which banned trade

FIGURE 7.3
Values of Exports and
Re-exports from the
United States,
1790–1815

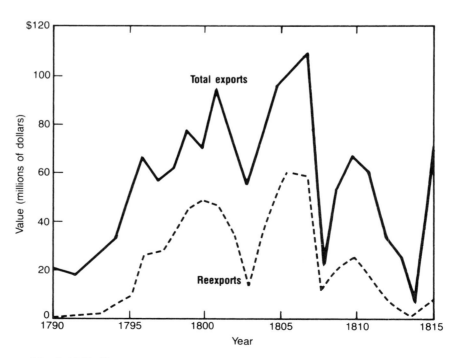

Source: *North 1961, 28.*

to Britain. As a result, nearly 1,500 American ships and many American sailors were seized, and some were forcefully drafted into the British Royal Navy. The Congress and President Thomas Jefferson, fearful of entangling the United States in war, declared the Embargo Act of 1807, which prohibited U.S. ships from trading with all foreign ports.

Basically, this attempt to gain respect for American neutrality backfired, and as the drastic declines in Figures 7.1, 7.2, and 7.3 convey, the cure was almost worse than the disease. As pressures in the port cities mounted, political action led to the Non-Importation Act of 1809. This act partially opened up trade, with specific prohibitions against Great Britain, France, and their possessions.

Nevertheless, continuing seizures and other complications between the United States and Britain along the Canadian border finally led to war—the second with England within 30 years. The War of 1812 was largely a naval war, during which the British seized more than 1,000 additional ships and blockaded almost the entire U.S. coast.

As exports declined to practically nothing, new boosts were given to the tiny manufacturing sector. Actually, stirrings there had begun with the 1807 embargo, which quickly altered the possibilities for profits in commerce relative to manufactures. As prices on manufactures rose, increasing possibilities for profits encouraged capital to flow into manufacturing. From 15 textile mills in 1808, the number rose to almost 90 by 1809. Similar additions continued throughout the war period, but when the Treaty of Ghent in 1814 brought the war to a close, the textile industry faltered badly. Once again, British imports arrived in massive amounts and undercut prices, which had been temporarily inflated by supply shortages resulting from the embargo and the war. Only large-scale U.S. concerns weathered the competitive storm, and there were few of these—most notably the Lowell shops using the Waltham system of cloth weaving (see chapters 10 and 11). Nevertheless, the war-related spurts in manufacturing provided an important basis for further industrial expansion, not only in textiles—the main manufacturing activity of the time—but also in other areas. This marked a time when the relative roles of the various sectors of the economy began to shift. Agriculture was to dominate the economy for most of the century, but to a lesser and lesser degree as economic growth continued.

The economic surge of the early Napoleonic war period (1793–1807) was unique, not so much by comparison with later years as by its striking reversal and advance from the two decades following 1772. Work by Claudia Goldin and Frank Lewis shows that during the decade and a half after the beginning of the Napoleonic wars, the growth rate of per capita income averaged almost 1 percent per year, with the foreign sector accounting for more than 25 percent of the underlying sources of growth (Goldin and Lewis 1980, 6–25, and especially page 22).[5]

In contrast, during the two decades preceding 1793, per capita exports fell (Table 7.2). Goldin and Lewis estimate that per capita income declined by a rate of 0.34 percent annually from 1774 to 1793 (Goldin and Lewis 1980, 22–23). Wealth holdings per capita also declined substantially over this period (Jones 1980, 82).

Several decades following independence were exceptionally unstable, not merely two decades of bust and then one and a half of boom. There were ups and downs within these longer bust-and-boom periods. Because of the importance of foreign trade at the time, export instability had strong leverage effects throughout the economy. Although external forces were always an important factor in determining economic fluctuations, as the influence of the Organization of the Petroleum Exporting Countries (OPEC) reminded U.S. consumers, workers, and businesses in the 1970s, their almost total dominance was now beginning to wane. By the turn of the century, internal developments—

---

[5]For an alternative interpretation of the role of neutrality, see Adams (1980).

This bustling dockside scene in the late-1800s shows the emergence New York City as a center of world trade.

especially those in the banking sector—had assumed a more pivotal role in causing economic fluctuations. As we shall see in chapter 12, both external forces (acting through credit flows from and to overseas areas) and internal forces (acting through changes in credit availability and the money stock) came to bear on the economy during the early nineteenth century. And some of the biggest challenges and opportunities for young Americans were settling and working new lands in the West.

SELECTED REFERENCES AND SUGGESTED READINGS

Adams, Donald R., Jr. "American Neutrality and Prosperity, 1793–1808: A Reconsideration." *Journal of Economic History* 40 (1980): 713–738.

Calomiris, Charles W. "Institutional Failure, Monetary Scarcity, and the Depreciation of the Continental." *Journal of Economic History* 48 (1988): 47–68.

Churchill, Winston S. *A History of the English-Speaking Peoples*, Vol. I. *The Birth of Britain.* New York: Dorset, 1990.

Goldin, Claudia D., and Frank D. Lewis. "The Role of Exports in American Economic Growth during the Napoleonic Wars, 1793–1807." *Explorations in Economic History* 17 (1980): 6–25.

Jones, Alice H. *Wealth of a Nation to Be.* New York: Columbia University Press, 1980.

McGuire, Robert A., and Robert L. Ohsfeldt. "An Economic Model of Voting Behavior over Specific Issues at the Constitutional Convention of 1787." *Journal of Economic History* 46 (1986): 79–112.

North, Douglass C. *American Economic Growth 1790–1860.* Englewood Cliffs, N.J.: Prentice Hall, 1960.

_____. *The Economic Growth of the United States, 1790–1860.* Englewood Cliffs, N.J.: Prentice Hall, 1961.

_____. "Early National Income Estimates of the United States." *Economic Development and Cultural Change* 9, no. 3 (April 1961).

Ohsfeldt, Robert L. "An Economic Model of Voting Behavior over Specific Issues at the Constitutional Convention of 1787." *Journal of Economic History* 46 (1986): 79–82.

Shepherd, James F., and Gary M. Walton. "Economic Change after the American Revolution: Pre-War and Post-War Comparisons of Maritime Shipping and Trade." *Explorations in Economic History* 13 (1976): 397–422.

CHAPTER 8

Land and the Early Westward Movements

The Treaty of Versailles, signed in September 1783, granted the Americans independence and the western lands they claimed by the ancient right of conquest. The western lands, first claimed by individual states but soon ceded to the federal government, were a valuable asset, collectively owned. How to use them best for the collective good was the problem and the challenge.

For the most part, the great Land Ordinances of 1785 and 1787 determined land policy through the guiding spirit of Thomas Jefferson. Throughout his career, Jefferson had three main goals for land policy: (1) to provide revenues to the federal government through sales, but not perpetual taxes; (2) to spread democratic institutions; and (3) to ensure clear property rights to the land owned by individuals, thereby enhancing their liberty and freedom and providing incentives (recall Economic Reasoning Proposition 3, incentives matter, in Economic Insight 1.1 on page 8) to utilize and make improvements on the land. Individual rights to buy, improve, work, and sell the land also inevitably created opportunities to speculate.

Fearing the potential threat of an excessively powerful, land-rich national government, Jefferson argued that the land should be transferred in a swift but orderly manner to the people. He advocated a process of privatization. First, surveys would be made and boundaries clearly marked. Sales from the federal government to private persons would transfer title completely. The federal government would not tax the land. As populations and settlements spread west, territories would be formed and then through application become states, entering the Union on an equal footing with the existing states. All this was fundamentally Jefferson's vision, part of his legacy that remains with us today.

THE ACQUISITION OF THE PUBLIC DOMAIN

One of the first truly national issues for the new government, after waging war and financing it, was the disposition of new lands in the West. The Articles of Confederation held that western lands could not be unwillingly taken from the states by the central government, and seven states held claims on western lands. These claims were based on the colonies' original grants from England and from dealings with the Native Americans. Many people argued, however, that the new western territories should belong to the national government and held or disposed in the national interest. Maryland, a state without western claims, brought the issue to a head by refusing to ratify the Articles until the land issue was resolved. In 1781, Maryland finally signed the Articles, after New York voluntarily gave its claims, based on treaties with the Iroquois, to the national government. Virginia promptly followed suit and relinquished its claims on western lands. The other five states with land claims soon followed their lead.

What land the new nation obtained from the British in 1783 is portrayed in the darkened area of Map 8.1. The United States began with a solid mass of land extending from the Atlantic coast to the Mississippi River and from the Great Lakes to, but not including, Florida.

Between 1802, when Georgia became the last state to relinquish its rights to western land, and 1898, when the formal annexation of Hawaii occurred, the United States very nearly assumed its present physical form as the result of eight main acquisitions (shown in Map 8.1):

1. The Territory of Louisiana, acquired in 1803 by purchase from France.
2. Florida, acquired in 1819 by purchase from Spain. A few years earlier, the United States had annexed the narrow strip of land that constituted western Florida.
3. The Republic of Texas, annexed as a state in 1845. The Republic of Texas had been established in 1836 after the victory of the American settlers over the Mexicans.
4. The Oregon Country, annexed by treaty with Great Britain in 1846. Spain and Russia, the original claimants to this area, had long since dropped out. By the Treaty of 1818, the United States and Great Britain agreed to a joint occupation of the Oregon Country and British Columbia; the Treaty of 1846 established the dividing line at the forty-ninth parallel.
5. The Mexican Cession, acquired by conquest from Mexico in 1848.
6. The Gadsden Purchase, acquired from Mexico in 1853.
7. The Alaskan Purchase, acquired from Russia in 1867.
8. The Hawaiian Annexation, formally ratified in 1898.

National acquisition of new land came either by a process of conquest and treaty or by purchase. The right of conquest was part of America's European heritage, rights claimed by the sovereigns of Europe and unquestioned by Christian societies when levied against non-Christian societies. This is seen clearly in early times in Europe, repeatedly against the Muslims, through the Crusades, and in Spain in 1492 against the Moors. The

MAP 8.1

U.S. Land Expansion

The purchase of Louisiana marked the beginning of the westward expansion of the United States, which culminated in the purchase of Alaska in 1867 and the annexation of Hawaii in 1898.

European belief in the right to conquer and rule non-Christian native societies in North America passed into American hands with independence. This legacy was ultimately extended in the nineteenth century, when the remaining Native Americans were forced onto reservations. These acts and their accompanying treaties are targets of continuous challenge in the courts by Native Americans today.

In half a century (1803–1853), the United States obtained a continental area of 3 million square miles, of which 1.4 billion acres, or 75 percent, constituted the public domain.[1] In 1862, two-thirds of this vast area was still in the possession of the government, but the process of disposal had been agreed on long before.

Disposing of the Public Domain

With rare exceptions, the land was valueless until settled. To give the land value, the Congress of the Confederation had addressed three questions:

1. How were land holdings and sales to be administered?
2. Should the government exact high prices from the sale of land, or should cheap land be made available to everyone?
3. What was to be the political relationship between newly settled areas and the original states?

Two major land systems had developed during the colonial period. The New England system of "township planning" provided for the laying out of townships, for the

Thomas Jefferson, the nation's third president, 1801–1809, had an earlier profound influence on the country for many of his leadership acts including his contribution to the momentous land ordinances of 1785 and 1787.

---

[1] Of the two later acquisitions, Alaska contained more than 586,400 square miles, most of it still in the public domain, and Hawaii added 6,423 square miles, none of it in the public domain.

subdivision of townships into carefully surveyed tracts, and for the auction sale of tracts to settlers. In the eighteenth century, it was usual to establish townships, which often were 6 miles square, in tiers. The opening of new townships proceeded with regularity from settled to unsettled land, gaps of unsettled land appeared infrequently, and no one could own land that had not been previously surveyed. In contrast, the southern system provided for no rectangular surveys. In the South, a settler simply selected what appeared to be a choice plot of unappropriated land and asked the county surveyor to mark it off. Settlers paid no attention to the relationship of their tracts to other pieces of property, and the legal description of a tract was made with reference to more or less permanent natural objects, such as stones, trees, and streams.

The Northwest Land Ordinance of 1785

No pressure was put on the Congress of the Confederation to provide a system for regulating public lands until 1784, after Virginia and New York had relinquished their claims to the southern part of the territory lying northwest of the Ohio River. In that year, a congressional committee of five, headed by Thomas Jefferson, proposed a system based on a rectangular survey. It is noteworthy that three of the five members were southerners who, despite their origins, recognized the value of the New England method of settlement. No action was taken, but a year later another committee, composed of a member from each state, reworked the 1784 report and offered a carefully considered proposal. With minor changes, this proposal was passed as the Northwest Land Ordinance of 1785.

Insofar as the ordinance set a physical basis for disposing of the public lands, its effects were permanent. Government surveyors were to establish on unsettled land horizontal lines called base lines and vertical lines called principal meridians, as shown in Map 8.2 on page 129. The first of the principal meridians was to be in what is now the state of Ohio, and the first surveys covered land north of the Ohio River. Eventually, all the land in the United States was included in the surveys except the original 13 states and Vermont, Kentucky, Tennessee, parts of Ohio, and Texas. These were literally celestial surveys, mappings by the stars.

As the surveys moved westward, other principal meridians were established—the second in what is now Indiana, the third in what is now Illinois, and so on. Map 8.2 indicates the other principal meridians and the base lines perpendicular to them. The insets show how tiers of townships, called ranges, were laid out to the east and west of each principal meridian. The ranges were designated by a number and a direction from the meridian, and the townships within each range were numbered north and south from the base line. Each township, being 6 miles square, contained 36 square miles numbered as shown in Map 8.2. In the Ordinance of 1785, a square mile was called a *lot*, but in later acts, the term *section* was used. Each square-mile section contained 640 acres, an acre being about the size of a football field (70 yards by 70 yards). In flying over the United States on clear days, you can see these checkerboard squares endlessly over the ground.

Two fundamentally different points of view emerged about the terms on which land should be made available, and a debate ensued that was not to end for several decades. Those who advocated a "conservative" policy were in favor of selling the public lands in large tracts at high prices for cash. The proponents of a "liberal" policy were in favor of putting land within the reach of almost everyone by making it available in small parcels at low prices on credit terms.

The Land Ordinance of 1785 reflected the prevalent conservative view that public land should be a major source of revenue, although in fact revenues from land sales never became a major source of federal revenues. Provisions relating to minimum size

MAP 8.2

Land Survey

Principal meridians and base lines made possible precise apportioning of newly opened territories into sections and easily described subdivisions of sections, thus simplifying later property transfers.

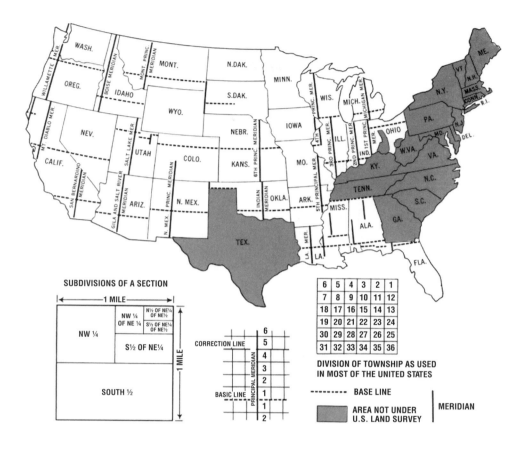

of tracts, prices, and terms were severe. Alternate townships were to be sold as a whole; the other half of the townships were to be sold by sections. All sales at public auction were to be for a minimum price of $1 per acre in cash. Thus, the smallest possible cash outlay was the $640 necessary to buy a section—an expenditure beyond the means of most pioneers. Moreover, a square mile of land was more than small farmers could normally utilize and work; they could barely clear and cultivate 10 acres in their first year, and a quarter section was the most a settler could handle without the aid of grown children. Only individuals of means and land companies formed by large investors could purchase land under the first law.

The Northwest Ordinance of 1787

The decision regarding the status of areas to be settled in the future also involved a great political principle. Were these areas to remain in colonial dependence, subject to possible exploitation by the original 13 states? Or were they to be admitted into a union of states on a basis of equality? The answers to these questions would test the foresight and self-lessness of Americans, who had themselves escaped the dominance of a ruling empire (Economic Reasoning Propositions 1, scarcity forces us to make choices; 3, incentives matter; and 4, laws and rules matter).

In 1787, Congress addressed the problems of establishing the political principles for western settlement. The Ordinance of 1787 provided that the Northwest Territory should be organized as a district to be run by a governor and judges appointed by Congress. As soon as it contained 5,000 male inhabitants of voting age, a territorial legislature was to be elected, and a nonvoting delegate was to be sent to Congress. At least three and not more than five states were to be created from this territory; when any one of the established divisions of the territory contained a population of 60,000 inhabitants, it was to be admitted to the Union as a state on a basis of complete equality with the older states. Contained in the ordinance were certain guarantees of civil and religious liberties, proper treatment of Native Americans, together with a prohibition of slavery in the territory.[2] *The main principle, however, was the eventual equality of status for the new areas.* The age-old source of trouble between colony and ruling country was thus removed by a simple, although unprecedented, device—making the colonies extensions of the empire that would be allowed to become socially and politically equal. Recall Economic Reasoning Proposition 4, laws and rules matter.

The Later Land Acts, 1796–1862

For a decade after the passage of the Land Ordinance of 1785, pioneering in the area north of the Ohio River was restricted as much by Indian troubles as by the high price of government land. The British, who persisted in maintaining posts on American territory in the Northwest, for years encouraged the Native Americans to make war on American settlers. By a treaty of 1794, the British agreed to evacuate the posts in the Northwest, and in August of that year, "Mad Anthony" Wayne and his forces defeated the Native Americans at the Battle of Fallen Timbers. The time was then ripe for the establishment of new land policies by the Congress of the United States.

The Land Act of 1796 represented another victory for the conservatives. A system of rectangular surveys substantially the same as the one established by the Ordinance of 1785 was made permanent. The minimum purchase allowed by the Act of 1796 was still 640 acres, but the minimum price per acre was raised to $2, the only concession to the cheap-land advocates being a credit provision that permitted half the purchase price to be deferred for a year. Only a small amount of land was sold under this act before Congress changed the minimum acreage to 320 in 1800 and permitted the buyer, after a cash payment of one-half the value, to pay one-fourth the value in two years and the final fourth in four years. A law of 1804 further lowered the minimum purchase to 160 acres. By 1820, the liberal forces had clearly won the battle: The minimum purchase was reduced to 80 acres and the price per acre to $1.25, but the credit provisions, which had resulted in losses to the government, were repealed. Twelve years later, the minimum purchase was reduced to 40 acres, so in 1832, a pioneer could purchase a piece of farmland for $50 (less than two months' wages for a common laborer). It merits emphasis that these prices were government-set prices. Actual prices paid by many settlers were undoubtedly less than these "list prices," however, because military veterans were often paid in "land warrants" to help them buy land at a discount. Because these warrants were transferable and were typically sold at discount, others as well as veterans paid less in cash than the official list prices suggest.

Settlers who were brave enough to risk their lives in a pioneering venture usually were not deterred from action by legal niceties. From the beginning, pioneers tended to settle past the areas that had been surveyed and announced for sale. As the decades passed and the West became "crowded," this tendency increased. Unauthorized settlement, or "squatting," resulted from the attempts of the pioneers to find better soils and the hope that they could settle on choice land and make it a going proposition before they were billed for it.

---

[2]Here again it is to Jefferson, who wanted slavery prohibited in all the western territories and states (even south of the Northwest Territory), that we owe these guarantees (see Hughes 1987).

Squatting was illegal, of course, but it was an offense that was hard to police. Moreover, there were those who argued that by occupying and improving the land, a squatter gained the rights to it—"cabin rights," "corn rights," or "tommyhawk rights," as they were variously called on the frontier. At first, federal troops tried to drive squatters from unsurveyed land, but successes were only temporary. Gradually, the government came to view this pioneer lawbreaking less and less seriously. Against those who would purchase the squatter's land when it became available for public sale, informal but effective measures were taken by the squatters themselves, who formed protective associations as soon as they settled in a particular locality. When the public auction of land in that locality was held, the members of the protective association let it be known that there was to be no competitive bidding for land preempted by them. The appearance of well-armed frontiersmen at the auction ordinarily convinced city slickers and big land buyers that it would be unwise to bid. Even in places where there was no organized action, squatters who found their farms bought out from under them often could charge handsomely for the "improvements" they had made, and frontier courts were inclined to uphold their "rights."

As early as 1820, Congress began to give relief to squatters, and scarcely a year went by after 1830 in which preemption rights were not granted to settlers in certain areas. In 1841, a general Preemption Act, called the "Log Cabin Bill" by its proponents, was passed. This law granted, to anyone settling on land that was surveyed but not yet available for sale, the right to purchase 160 acres at the minimum price when the auction was held. No one could outbid the settler and secure the land, provided the squatter could raise the $200 necessary to buy a quarter section. Technically, squatting on unsurveyed land was still illegal; because of this and because there was still no outright grant of land, the westerner (and anyone else who could make money by buying land and waiting for it to rise in value) was not satisfied. Nevertheless, the land policy of the country was about as liberal as could be consistent with the demand that the public domain provide a continuing source of revenue.

Pressure remained on Congress to reduce the price of "islands" of less desirable land that had been passed over in the first surges to the West. In 1854, the Graduation Act provided for the graduated reduction of the minimum purchase price of such tracts, to a point at which land that remained unsold for 30 years could be purchased for as little as $0.125 an acre. Settlers quickly purchased these pieces of land, attesting to the fact that people were willing to gamble a little on the probable appreciation of even the most unpromising real estate.

In the 1850s, as agitation for free land continued, it became apparent that the passage of a homestead law was inevitable. Southerners, who had at one time favored free grants to actual settlers, became violently opposed to this as time went on. The 160-acre farm usually proposed by homestead supporters was not large enough to make the working of slaves economical, and it seemed obvious to southern congressmen that homesteading would fill the West with antislavery people. On the other hand, many northern congressmen who normally might have had leanings toward a conservative policy joined forces with the westerners; they, too, knew that free land meant free states.

In 1860, a homestead act was passed, but President James Buchanan, fearing that it would precipitate secession, vetoed it. Two years later, with the Civil War raging and the southerners out of Congress, the Homestead Act of 1862 became law. Henceforth, any head of a family or anyone older than 21 could have 160 acres of public land on the payment of small fees. The only stipulation was that the homesteader should either live on the land or cultivate it for five years. An important provision was that settlers who decided not to meet the five-year requirement might obtain full title to the land simply by paying the minimum price of $1.25 an acre.

Although much land was to pass into private hands under the Homestead Act of 1862, it was not the boon that it was expected to be. Most of the first-class land had been claimed by this time. Furthermore, it was so easy to circumvent the provisions of the law that land grabbers used it, along with the acts that still provided for outright purchase, to build up great land holdings. By 1862, the frontier had reached the edge of the dry country, where a 160-acre farm was too small to provide a living for a settler and his family.

THE MIGRATIONS TO THE WEST

In discussing the colonial period, we noted that pioneers were moving across the Appalachian Mountains by the middle of the eighteenth century. By 1790, perhaps a quarter of a million people lived within the mountain valleys or to the west, and the trickle of westward movement had become a small stream. In the eighteenth century, there were two routes to the West. The more important one passed through the Cumberland Gap and then into either Kentucky or Tennessee; the other ran across southern Pennsylvania to Pittsburgh and on down the Ohio River. Even as the movement to the West was gaining momentum, pioneers were still settling in Pennsylvania and New York and to the north in Vermont, New Hampshire, and Maine.

An overview of population growth and the distributional impact of western migration and other demographic effects are shown in Table 8.1, and Figure 8.1, page 133. In 1812, on the eve of the second war with Great Britain, just over 1 million people (about 15 percent of the nation's total) lived west of the Appalachians. From this 15 percent, the western population grew to almost half of the total by 1860. On the eve of the Civil War, the center of the population was near Chillicothe, Ohio. The western population grew from 1 to nearly 13 million as the total grew from 7.2 to 31.4 million. In short, the rate of

TABLE 8.1 POPULATION IN THE TRANS-APPALACHIAN STATES[a]

STATE	1810	1850	1860
Ohio	231	1,980	2,340
Michigan	5	398	749
Indiana	25	988	1,350
Illinois	12	852	1,712
Minnesota	—[b]	6	172
Wisconsin	—	305	776
Iowa	—	192	675
Kansas	—	—	107
Kentucky	407	982	1,156
Tennessee	262	1,003	1,110
Alabama	9	772	964
Mississippi	31	607	791
Louisiana	77	518	708
Arkansas	1	210	435
Missouri	20	682	1,182
Texas	—	213	604
Total	1,080	9,708	14,831
Total U.S.	7,224	23,261	31,513
Trans-Appalachia Percentage of Total U.S.	15.0%	41.7%	47.1%

[a]Figures given in thousands of persons; excludes Far West and West Coast.
[b]No data.

Source: *Derived from* Historical Statistics, *1960.*

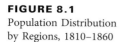

FIGURE 8.1

Population Distribution by Regions, 1810–1860

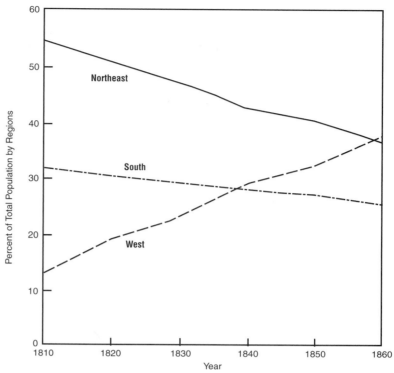

Note: *South—Alabama, Arkansas, Florida, Georgia, Louisiana, Mississippi, North Carolina, Texas, and Virginia; West—Illinois, Indiana, Iowa, Kansas, Kentucky, Michigan, Minnesota, Missouri, Nebraska, Ohio, Tennessee, Wisconsin, California, Nevada, and Oregon; Northeast—Connecticut, Delaware, Maine, Maryland, Massachusetts, New Hampshire, New Jersey, New York, Pennsylvania, Rhode Island, and Vermont.*

Source: *Walker 1872: 8–9. Reprinted from North 1961, 121.*

population growth was twice as high west of the Appalachian Mountains as in the East, more than 5.0 percent annually compared with 2.2 percent.

As the population expanded and pushed westward, the nation's frontier was pressed outward. The frontier, as technically defined in the census reports, was any area containing more than two and less than six people per square mile. In Map 8.3, page 134, the frontier lines for 1800, 1820, 1840, and 1860 have been drawn from census data. The line for 1800 indicates a wedge driven into the West, with its point in western Kentucky. Sixty years later, the line ran in a southerly direction from a point in the middle of Minnesota, with a noticeable bulge into the Nebraska and Kansas territories and a definite drift into Texas.

The Northwestern Migration and Hogs, Corn, and Wheat

During the early 1800s, the movement across the top of the country gained momentum and an initial lead over migration from the southern states (see Table 8.1 on page 132 and Map 8.3 on page 134). During the first quarter of the century, people from the New England and Middle Atlantic states were pouring into the northern counties of Ohio and Indiana and later into southern Michigan. By 1850, lower Michigan was fairly well settled, and the best lands in northern Illinois and southern Wisconsin had been claimed. On the eve of the Civil War, pioneers were pushing the northwestern tip of the frontier into

MAP 8.3

Moving Frontier

Census data from 1800 onward chronicled the constant westward flow of population. The "frontier," its profile determined by natural attractions and a few man-made and physiographic obstacles, was a magnet for the venturesome.

central Minnesota, most of Iowa was behind the frontier line, and the handsome country of eastern Kansas was being settled. Only in Texas did the frontier line of 1860 bulge farther to the west than it did in Kansas. By this time, California had been a state for a decade and Oregon had just been admitted, but the vast area between the western frontier and the coast was not to be completely settled for another half-century.

Southerners moving across the Ohio River were the chief influence in the lower part of the old Northwest. New Englanders, after the Erie Canal made transportation easier, were dominant in the Great Lakes region, but they were joined by another stream that originated in the Middle Atlantic states. For the most part, families moved singly, although sometimes as many as 50 to 100 would move together. As the frontier pushed westward, the pioneers on the cutting edge were frequently the same people who had broken virgin soil a short way back only a few years before. Others were the grown children of men and women who had once participated in the conquest of the wilderness.

Throughout this early period of westward expansion was an ever-increasing influx of land-hungry people from abroad. From 1789 to the close of the War of 1812, not more than a quarter million people emigrated from Europe. With the final defeat of Napoleon and the coming of peace abroad, immigration resumed. From half a million people in the 1830s, the flow increased to 1.5 million in the 1840s and to 2.5 million in the 1850s. For the most part, the newcomers were from northern Europe; Germans and Irish predominated, but many immigrants also came from England, Scotland, Switzerland, and the Scandinavian countries. Of these peoples, the Germans tended more than any

In the nineteenth century, wagon trains brought a steady stream of migrants to western America and its expansive lands.

others to go directly to the lands of the West. Some immigrants from the other groups entered into the agricultural migration, but most were absorbed into eastern city populations. The timing of the western migration is discussed in Economic Insight 8.1.

ECONOMIC INSIGHT 8.1

MIGRATION WAVES AND ECONOMIC OPPORTUNITY

Is there an economic explanation to the timing of the western migrations? Although the absolute numbers of western migrants from the eastern states and from abroad continued to swell, the decades of greatest western expansion, in terms of percentages, were the 1810s and 1830s. In absolute terms, the 1850s were the greatest. From Table 8.1 (see page 132, we can calculate percentage rates of increase of the western population for the five decades from 1810 to 1860: These were 6.9, 4.9, 5.6, 4.2, and 4.1 percent. Also from Table 8.1, we see the greatest increase in absolute numbers coming in the 1850s: nearly 4.3 million people.

As Douglass C. North has argued, in large measure, these surges are explained by the exceptional economic opportunities in the West (North 1961). Hogs, corn, and wheat became the great northwestern staples, and as shown in Figure 8.2, page 136, corn and wheat prices were unusually high in these decades. People came to the new lands in response to the profits to be made in the production of these important products.

Critics of North's "market opportunity response" argument have countered that land sales during these periods were based on pervasive speculation, not settlement and production for market (see, for example, Martin 1972; Temin 1969). Much of the land, however, was being put to use. The decades of greatest growth in "improved land" (for grazing, grass, tillage, or lying fallow) were also the 1810s, 1830s, and 1850s. The percentage rates of change in improved acres from 1810 to 1860, by decade, were 23.5, 6.5, 7.1, 5.4, and 7.8 (Haites, Mak, and Walton 1975, 113). In short, North's critics were wrong.

The only variable slightly out of step with North's general argument is the western population growth rate for the 1850s. This slowdown would be expected, however, from the general slowing of growth for the total population, the rise in the number of improved acres per person, and the rise in agricultural productivity—all of which occurred. The supply response to high staple prices is observed in terms of both population and improved acres in the 1810s and 1830s, but the supply response to the boom years of the 1850s was dominated more by improved acres than by population.

ECONOMIC INSIGHT 8.1

MIGRATION WAVES AND ECONOMIC OPPORTUNITY, Continued

FIGURE 8.2
U.S. Public Land
Sales in Several
Western States*
and Wheat and
Corn Prices,
1815–1860

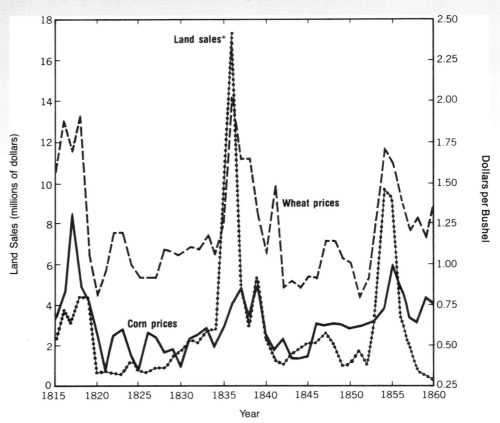

Source: *North 1961, 137.*

*Ohio, Illinois, Indiana, Michigan, Iowa, Wisconsin, and Missouri.

Agricultural Specialization and Regional Dislocation

The resulting surges in production in the Northwest (the Midwest as we know it today) did not immediately dislocate agriculture in the older states. Over the decades, however, the leading producers of hogs, corn, and wheat became western states.

Early in the 1800s, western hog production was greatly limited by high transportation costs; hogs were driven overland from Ohio to the urban centers of the East or were sent south by boat for sale to the plantations. Cattle, too, were driven in great herds to the East, where they were sold for immediate slaughter or for further fattening. But it was not long before pioneer farmers could market their hogs fairly close to home. Slaughtering and meat-packing centers arose in the early West, and by the 1830s, Cincinnati, nicknamed Porkopolis, was the most important pork-processing city in the country.

Commercial hog raising required corn growing. For a while, hogs were allowed into the forests to forage on the mast (acorns and nuts that fell from the trees). But regular feeding is necessary to produce a good grade of pork, and corn is an ideal feed crop. Corn can be grown almost anywhere, provided rainfall is adequate. It had been

The morning of the opening of the Oklahoma Land Rush, April 22, 1889. The people shown here are waiting for the gun shot that will signal their right to enter and claim land formerly held by Native Americans. Those who jumped the gun were known as "sooners."

cultivated in all the original colonies and throughout the South. As late as 1840, Kentucky, Tennessee, and Virginia led the nation in corn production. But within 20 years, it was apparent that the states to the northwest would be the corn leaders.[3] On the eve of the Civil War, Illinois, Ohio, Missouri, and Indiana led in corn production, and it appeared that Iowa, Kansas, and Nebraska would one day rank ahead of Kentucky and Tennessee, then in fifth and sixth place, respectively.

The attraction of new lands for wheat was also tremendous. Western wheat could not come into its own until facilities were available for transporting it in quantity to the urban centers of the East; even as late as 1850, Pennsylvania and New York ranked first and third, respectively, in wheat production nationally. Ohio, which had become a commercial producer in the 1830s, ranked second. During the next decade, the shift of wheat production to the West was remarkable. By 1860, Illinois, Indiana, and Wisconsin were the leading producers, and the five states carved from the Northwest Territory produced roughly half the nation's output. The major wheat-growing areas were still not firmly established, however; further shifts to the West in the production of this important crop were yet to come.

Ultimately, the western migration forced changes on the agriculture of the northeastern states. For a quarter of a century after the ratification of the Constitution, agriculture in New England, except in a few localities, remained relatively primitive; the individual farm unit produced practically everything needed for the household. With the growing industrialization of New England after 1810, production for urban markets became possible. Between 1810 and 1840, farmers in the Middle Atlantic states continued to grow the products for which their localities had traditionally been suited, and, as noted,

---

[3]For the advantages of corn growing to the western pioneer, see Gates (1960, 169). A single peck of seed corn, yielding as much as 50 bushels, planted an acre and could be transported far more easily than 2 bushels of wheat seed, which weighed 120 pounds but might bring in only 15 to 18 bushels per acre.

Pennsylvania and New York remained major wheat producers until midcentury. But the arrival of the steamboat in the West in 1811, the opening of the Erie Canal in the 1820s, and the extension of the railroads beyond the Alleghenies in the 1840s meant that products of the rich western lands would flow in ever increasing amounts to the East. Western competition caused the northeastern farmer to reduce grain cultivation, and only dairy cattle remained important in animal production. Specialization in truck gardens and dairy products for city people and hay for city horses came to characterize the agriculture of this region, and those who could not adapt to the changing market conditions moved to the city or went west.

THE SOUTHWESTERN MIGRATION AND COTTON

As discussed in chapter 7, the Lower South suffered serious setbacks during the early years of independence. Even the market for tobacco stagnated, especially after the Embargo Act of 1807 and again after the War of 1812 allowed tobacco from other regions to enter and gain greater shares of the world market.

The hope of the South was in cotton. Obtaining their supplies of raw cotton from the Orient, the English had increasingly turned to the manufacture of cotton cloth instead of wool in the late seventeenth century. The inventions that came a century later—the steam engine, the spinning jenny, the water frame, the spinning mule, and the power loom—all gave rise to an enormous demand for cotton fiber. The phase of the Industrial Revolution that made it possible to apply power to textile manufacturing occurred at just the right time to stimulate and encourage the planting of cotton wherever it could be grown profitably. In the southern United States, the conditions for profitable agriculture based on cotton were nearly ideal. Only some way of separating the green seed from the short-staple "upland cotton" had to be devised. One of the contributions of Yankee genius Eli Whitney was the invention of a gin that enabled a good worker to clean 50 pounds of cotton per day instead of only 1 pound by hand. With the application of power to the gin, the amount of fiber that could be produced appeared almost limitless.

On the humid coasts of Georgia and South Carolina, planters who had grown indigo turned to cotton. Even some rice fields were recultivated to produce the new staple. The culture moved up to North Carolina and Virginia and over the mountains to the beautiful rolling country of middle Tennessee. In the early 1800s, the piedmont of Georgia and South Carolina became the important cotton center; these states were vying for first place by 1820, with South Carolina slightly in the lead.

With the end of the War of 1812, the really important shift in cotton production to the west began (see Map 8.4). Almost unerringly, the settlers first planted the loamy, fertile soils that extended in an arc from Georgia through Alabama into northeastern Mississippi. A second major cotton-growing area lay in the rich bottom land of the lower Mississippi River and its tributaries. In this extremely fertile soil, the cotton even tended to grow a longer fiber. The culture spread into western Tennessee and eastern Arkansas. A jump into Texas then foretold the trend of cotton production.

By 1840, the early cotton-producing states had been left behind. In 1860, Alabama, Mississippi, and Louisiana were far in the lead, with Mississippi alone producing more cotton than Georgia and South Carolina combined. This shift in the realm of King Cotton was to have the most far-reaching consequences on the economy of the South.

Just before the Civil War, cotton was indeed king. As Douglass North has remarked, it is difficult to exaggerate the role of cotton in American economic growth between 1800 and 1850 (North 1961). The great staple accounted for more than half the dollar

MAP 8.4

Shifts in Cotton Cultivation

The tremendous growth of the world demand for cotton propelled the westward movement of cotton cultivation after the War of 1812 and up to the onset of the Civil War.

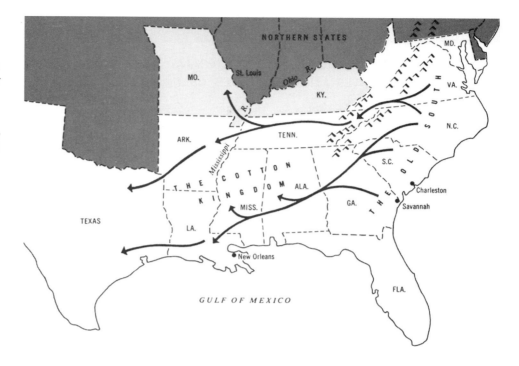

PERSPECTIVE 8.1

FORCED IMMIGRATION OF NATIVE AMERICANS IN THE SOUTHEASTERN UNITED STATES

Part of Jefferson's vision of western settlement as portrayed in the Northwest Land Ordinance was the fair and proper treatment of Native Americans. Except for the prohibition of slavery clause, southwestern settlement also followed the 1785–1787 ordinances, including Article 3 (1787):

> The utmost good faith shall always be observed toward the Indians; their land and property shall never be taken from them without their consent; and in their property, rights, and liberty, they shall never be invaded or disturbed, unless in just and lawful wars authorized by Congress, but laws founded in justice and humanity shall from time to time be made, for preventing wrongs being done to them, and for preserving peace and friendship with them.

Along the southwestern path of expansion lay the lands (see Maps 8.4 and 8.5) of the Cherokee, Creek, Choctaw, Chickasaw, and Seminole tribes. In spite of

Jefferson's words, many whites, both north and south, began calling for the removal of tribes to land farther west. White cravings for Cherokee lands, in particular, were intensified by the discovery of gold on Cherokee lands in 1828. President Andrew Jackson and other supporters of removal argued that the Cherokee would not be able to survive in the East because the game on which they mainly depended for food was disappearing. It was an opinion only (Economic Reasoning Proposition 5, evidence and theory give value to opinions). Research by David Wishart (1999) confirms that the Cherokee had achieved a remarkable degree of success beyond hunting and skinning deer and other animals. In fact, most Cherokee were farmers, practicing a diversified agriculture. Productivity in corn production was comparable with that on similar white lands. Other Cherokee earned their livings in market activities such as weaving and spinning, innkeeping, operating ferryboats, and so on. A minority engaged in large-scale plantation agriculture based on slavery. In economic terms, the Cherokee were similar to their white neighbors, but the facts were of no avail. Indeed, the improvements they had made on their land increased white demands for removal. In 1830, Congress passed the Indian Removal Act. The Choctaw, Chickasaw, and Creek signed treaties ceding

PERSPECTIVE 8.1

FORCED IMMIGRATION OF NATIVE AMERICANS IN THE SOUTHEASTERN UNITED STATES, Continued

their holdings for new lands west of the Mississippi, while the Cherokee resisted until finally forced, eight years later, to march in severe winter weather to what is now Oklahoma. An estimated 4,000 people, nearly one-fourth of the Cherokee, died on the "Trail of Tears." A few Cherokee remained in North Carolina through assimilation and special assistance. Approximately 50 families forsook their Cherokee citizenship to become citizens of North Carolina; other families from the Snowbird community bought back 1,200

acres of their land. State law prohibited Indians from owning land (until after 1864), but the purchase was made using names of sympathetic whites.

Farther south, in Florida, the Seminoles resisted both assimilation and removal. Ten thousand federal troops, 30,000 citizen soldiers, and $40 million in war expenditures finally prevailed (with 14 percent losses of life by action and disease over seven years). Nearly 3,000 Seminoles were removed to lands west of the Mississippi.

MAP 8.5

Tribal Lands of the Chickasaw, Cherokee, Choctaw, Creek, and Seminole before 1830

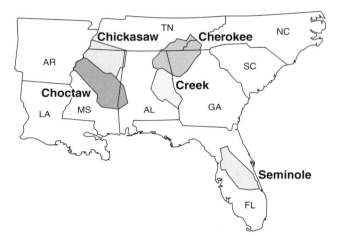

Source: *Weeks 1990, 20, as given in Barrington 1999, 17.*

value of U.S. exports—a value nearly 10 times as great in U.S. foreign trade as its nearest competitor, the wheat and wheat flour of the North. At home, cotton planters furnished the raw materials for textile manufacturers in the North, who by 1860 were selling half again as much cotton cloth as wool cloth. As we will see in chapter 10, cotton goods were the leading manufacture in the United States in 1860 when ranked by value added (second when ranked by employment). It was not surprising that even as antislavery forces strengthened in the late antebellum period, southerners could scarcely envisage a North, or even a world, without their chief product.

There was both a slight push and a major pull to the new lands of the South. The push had begun in colonial times as tidewater lands began to lose the natural fertility that staples grown there required. The small farmer, impelled by hardship, had moved into the piedmont. The shift had been especially pronounced in Virginia and North Carolina, from which struggling families tended to sift through the Cumberland Gap into Tennessee and Kentucky. The frontiersman—the professional pioneer—was then pulled into the rich new cotton country, mostly from Georgia and South Carolina, but partly from Tennessee and even Kentucky. Following closely came the yeoman farmer; almost

FIGURE 8.3
U.S. Public Land Sales
and Cotton Prices,
1814–1860*

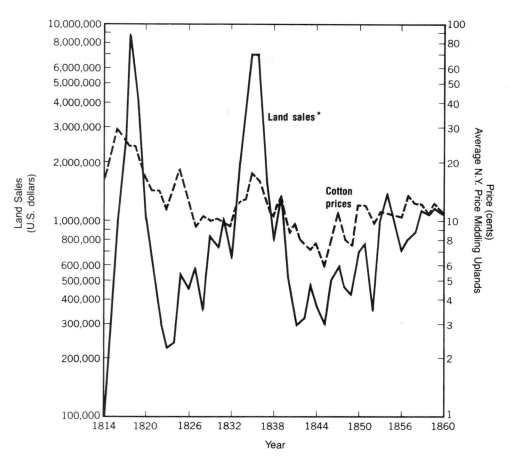

Source: *North 1961, 124.*

*Alabama, Florida, Louisiana, Mississippi, and Arkansas.

simultaneously—and this is what clearly distinguishes the southern migration—came the planter, the man of substance, with his huge household establishment and his slaves.

As with the surges in the Northwest, the 1810s, the 1830s, and the 1850s were the boom decades for the new southwestern areas. It was, of course, the favorable returns expected on cotton cultivation that brought the great, irregular surges of movement toward the southwest. As shown in Figure 8.3, there is close correlation between the price of cotton on the one hand and the volume of public land sales in Alabama, Florida, Louisiana, Mississippi, and Arkansas on the other. Here again, we observe the responsiveness of individuals to favorable economic opportunities.

THE FAR WESTERN MIGRATION

Although of only minor economic importance when compared with the southern and northwestern migrations, the California Gold Rush was one of the most widely discussed and emotionally charged of all the migrations in response to economic opportunity.[4] On

---

[4]Another fascinating western migration was that of the Mormons, driven by mob violence from Ohio, Missouri, and Illinois in the late 1830s and 1840s, plus the later gathering of the "saints" at Zion (Utah). (for descriptions of this special migration, see Stagner 1964; Arrington and Bitton 1979; Walton 1999; Carson 2002).

A KANSAS LAND-OFFICE.—[See Page 565.]

Land speculation—"holding for a rise"—became a lively offshoot of the westward population surge. Here, a Kansas land office provides a center for speculative activity.

January 24, 1848, only nine days before the war with Mexico ended, James W. Marshall discovered gold while building a sawmill for John Sutter on the South Fork of the American River.

Sutter and Marshall attempted to keep the discovery a secret while trying to secure for themselves stronger property rights on the area. However, a young boy told of the discovery to a man bringing supplies to the mill, and, coincidentally, the boy's mother gave the driver a small nugget as a present. When the man later used the nugget to buy a drink back at "Fort Sutter," the word was out.

As gold fever swept the land, people poured across the country and "around the Horn." In the first several months of 1849, almost 20,000 left the East Coast by boat destined for California, and nearly 40,000 arrived in San Francisco throughout 1849. From a population of about 107,000 near the end of 1849, California grew to more than 260,000 within three years.

Among the most fascinating aspects of the California Gold Rush was the initial absence of property rights to land and of a government capable of enforcing law and order. Despite stiff penalties for desertion, for instance, U.S. soldiers in California left their posts in droves to hunt for gold. (Enlisted men, who typically earned $7 a month plus room and board, numbered almost 1,059 in 1847 but only 660 in 1848.) Yet despite an initial absence of law and order, violence in the gold fields was surprisingly low. As John Umbeck, one of the leading authorities on the Gold Rush, reports:

> *During 1848, . . . nearly 10,000 people rushed to mine gold on property to which no one had exclusive rights. Furthermore, although nearly every miner carried a gun, little violence was reported. In July, when Governor Mason visited the mines, he reported that the miners were respecting Sutter's property rights and that "crime of any kind was very infrequent, and that no thefts or robberies had been committed in the gold district . . . and it was a matter of surprise, that so peaceful and quiet a state of things should continue to exist. (Umbeck 1977)*[5]

Only after new waves of miners entered the fields did gold land become troublingly scarce, thereby urging exclusive property rights or claims. Several firsthand accounts indicate the nature of those rights:

> *When the mines in and around Nevada City were first opened they were solely in the ravines...and there was no law regulating the size of a miner's claim, and generally a party that first went into a ravine had the exclusive right there too. . . . As population increased that rule did not long maintain. The miners saw that something must be done, and therefore a meeting was called and a rule was established that each miner could hold thirty feet square as a mining claim.*
>
> *All these bars on the Middle Fork of the American River, from Oregon Bar upwards, after the lowest estimate, employed in the summer of 1850 not less than 1,500 men; originally working on shares, and the assessment on the share paid out daily, so that those who had been drunk or absent did not get any part of it; but this after a while caused dissatisfaction and was the reason of breaking up the co-operative work and commencing work on claims. A claim was a spot of ground fifteen feet wide on the river front.*
>
> *In a comparatively short time we had a large community on that creek, which led to rows and altercations about boundaries, that eventuated in an agreement, entered into by unanimous agreement, that each person should have 10 square feet.*
>
> *Wood's Creek was filled up with miners, and I here for the first time after the discovery of gold, learned what a miner's claim was. In 1848, the miners had no division of the ground into claims—they worked where it was richest, and many times four or five could be seen at work in a circle of six feet in diameter; but . . . here they were now measuring the ground off with tape measures so as to prevent disputes arising from the division. (Umbeck 1977, 215)*

It was at the "miners' meetings" that contract specifications (Economic Reasoning Proposition 4, laws and rules matter) were determined to establish and enforce claims

---

[5]This does not mean there was an absence of violence in the Far West; indeed, there were ample brawls, shootings, and killings in saloons and bars.

and prevent claim jumping. Each "field" held its own meetings, and afterward, each miner marked his claim boundary with wooden stakes and frequently a notice such as this:

> *All and everybody, this is my claim, fifty feet on the gulch, cordin to Clear Creek District Law, backed up by shotgun amendments.*
>
> *Any person found trespassing on this claim will be persucuted to the full extent of the law. This is no monkey tale butt I will assert my rites at the pint of the sicks shirter if legally necessary to taik head and good warnin. (Umbeck 1977, 216)*

In this fashion, property rights and other institutions first emerged in the gold fields of California, and with them an outpouring of millions of dollars in gold.

The great California Gold Rush had effects far beyond the bossless mass employment and wealth creation it generated.[6] It was a tidal wave of hope for people who no longer were forced to know their place and be resigned to it. And the timing: Ireland's potato famine, China's Taiping Rebellion, and political uprisings in France and Germany all added great numbers to young Americans, many discharged from service at the end of the Mexican War, who sought their fortunes in the gold fields. Not everyone struck it rich like Leland Stanford, formerly a failed lawyer, or Lucius Fairchild, a store clerk from Wisconsin who returned home rich and became Wisconsin's governor. But the Gold Rush did guarantee dreams and adventure to match the towering Sierra.

SELECTED REFERENCES AND SUGGESTED READINGS

Arrington, Leonard J., and Davis Bitton. *The Mormon Experience.* New York: Knopf, 1979.

Barrington, Linda, ed. *The Other Side of the Frontier,* Boulder, Co.: Westview, 1999.

Carson, Scott A. "Industrial Migration in America's Great Basin." *Journal of Interdisciplinary History* 33, no. 3 (2002): 387–403.

Gates, Paul W. *The Farmer's Age: Agriculture, 1815–1860.* New York: Holt, Rinehart & Winston, 1960.

Haites, Eric F., James Mak, and Gary M. Walton. *Western River Transportation: The Era of Early Internal Improvements.* Baltimore, Md.: Johns Hopkins University Press, 1975.

Historical Statistics. Series A, 123–180. Washington, D.C.: Government Printing Office, 1960.

Holiday, J. S. *Rush for Riches: Gold Fever and the Making of California.* Berkeley: University of California Press, 1999.

Hughes, Jonathon R. T. "The Great Land Ordinances: Colonial America's Thumb Print on History." In *Essays on the Economic Significance of the Old Northwest,* eds. David C. Klingaman and Richard K. Vedder, 1–18. Athens: Ohio University Press, 1987.

Martin, Albro. Review of David H. Fischer, *Historians' Fallacies: Toward a Logic of Historical Thought.* New York: Harper & Row, 1971. In *Journal of Economic History* 32 (December 1972): 968–970.

North, Douglass C. *The Economic Growth of the United States 1790–1860.* Englewood Cliffs, N.J.: Prentice Hall, 1961.

Stagner, Wallace. *The Gathering of Zion.* New York: McGraw-Hill, 1964.

Temin, Peter. *The Jacksonian Economy.* New York: Norton, 1969.

Umbeck, John. "The California Gold Rush: A Study of Emerging Property Rights." *Explorations in Economic History* 14 (1977): 192–226.

Walker, Francis A. *A Compendium of the Ninth Census, June 1, 1870.* Washington, D.C.: U.S. Census Bureau, 1872.

Walton, Gary M. *Chills along the Sweetwater.* Salt Lake City, Utah: Origin Book Sales, 1999.

Weeks, Philip. *Farewell My Nation: The American Indian and the United States, 1820–1890.* Wheeling, Ill.: Harlan Davidson, 1990.

Wishart, David M. "Could the Cherokee Have Survived in the Southeast?" In *The Other Side of the Frontier,* ed. Linda Barrington, 165–189. Boulder, Co.: Westview, 1999.

---

[6]For the longer-term effects of the gold rush, with emphasis on California history, see Holiday (1999).

Transportation and Market Growth

The economic growth of the United States in the nineteenth century was strategically influenced by the spread of a market economy, by the shifting of resources from lower-valued (subsistence) to higher-valued uses (production for market), and by the growth of specialization and divisions of labor in production. As Adam Smith and early nineteenth-century contemporaries knew, levels of productivity were vitally dependent on the size of the market, especially in manufacturing. Of course, market size was limited by the costs of moving goods and negotiating exchanges. In this early era, transportation costs were the most important component of these costs. For these many reasons, special concentration on transportation, mode by mode, is warranted and, indeed, is vital to our understanding of long-term economic growth and the location of people and economic activity. A viable transportation system was key to forming a national market (as discussed in Economic Insight 9.1, on page 162). In combination, the improvements in transportation from 1800 to 1860 were so striking as to merit the description "a transportation revolution." The effects of this revolution are seen in the falling costs of obtaining information and moving people and goods, in settlement and production patterns, and in the forging of a national economy. There are many parallels between the transportation revolution of the nineteenth century and the information revolution we are observing today.

THE ANTEBELLUM TRANSPORTATION REVOLUTION

Once the western migrations were unleashed, the demand for improved transportation systems grew dramatically. Investments in steamboats, canals, and railroads were the most important internal transportation developments of the antebellum era. There can be little doubt that the host of improvements in transportation and the precipitous decline in freight rates (as shown in Figure 9.1) were truly revolutionary in impact as well as in form. Not only did they directly propel the process of westward expansion and the relocation of agriculture and mining discussed in chapter 8, but also they greatly altered various regions' comparative advantages in production. For example, they set the stage for New England to concentrate increasingly in manufacturing and to further the advance and application of new technologies and organizational forms of production in a factory setting (chapter 10). In turn, these changes set the stage for urbanization and heightening urban problems and labor unrest (chapter 11). The falling costs of transport—and communication—boosted market size and efficiency and forged a national market for many goods and services. Whereas the pattern of general price declines in the western markets of Cincinnati and St. Louis had followed those in New York and Philadelphia by 12 months near the turn of the century, the lag was reduced to only

FIGURE 9.1
Inland Freight Rates,
1784–1900

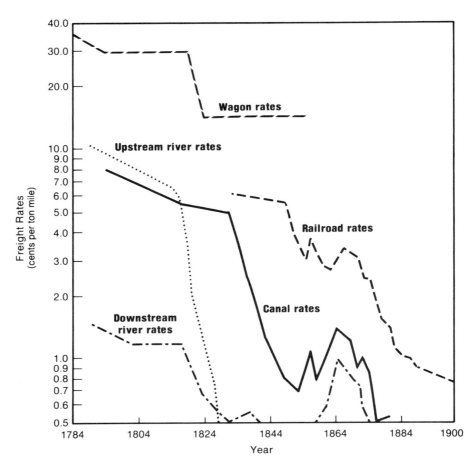

Freight rates declined dramatically during the nineteenth century.

Sources: *North 1965; 1973, 108.*

three or four months by the 1830s. By the 1850s, this lag had fallen even further to a mere week or so. Lastly, the transportation linkage by water and rail between the East and West would prove significant in binding these two regions—politically as well as economically—as interregional tensions mounted in the years preceding the Civil War. The term *transportation revolution* consequently implies far more than a mere series of new technological forms rapidly introduced.

An important part of the transportation story is the role of private versus public initiative during this critical period of growing economic unification. In England, private entrepreneurs built and operated railroads and canals, and government participation was slight. In the United States, however, there was a mixture of private and public enterprise. Government investments in canals and railroads as a percentage of total investment in these modes were large. Public investments included a smaller proportion for roads and a minimal amount for the natural waterways. A strong, active role in transportation for government had been planned as early as 1807, when Treasury Secretary Albert Gallatin was asked to develop "a plan for the application of such means as are within the power of Congress, to the purpose of opening roads and making canals" (Goodrich 1960, 27). Gallatin's ingenious plan had a projected total cost of $20 million ($400 million in today's money), but questions of legality—and politics, as always—prevented the federal government from undertaking it. Many viewed the Constitution as an agreement among sovereignties (the sovereign states), and "strict constructionism" throughout most of the antebellum period held the federal government to only a few projects, mainly those passing through several states at a time. Nevertheless, Gallatin's plan was carried out, not by the federal government but by private entrepreneurs and by state, local, and private enterprise mixtures. The sheer size of the capital requirements often necessitated these collaborations. Both public officials and private citizens promoted government intervention in transport investment. In some cases, private operators succeeded in obtaining public credit and special assistance just as special interest groups (such as farmers) do today. In other cases, local politicians who wanted transportation improvements for their town or region took advantage of private entrepreneurs.

THE ROUTES OF WESTERN COMMERCE

During the antebellum period, three natural gateways linked the western territories and states with the rest of the nation and other countries. The first ran eastward, connecting the Great Lakes to New York. The main arteries feeding this Northern Gateway were down the St. Lawrence River or along the Hudson or Mohawk river valleys. Major investments on this route included the Erie Canal, which opened in 1825, and the New York Central and New York and Erie Railroads, completed in 1852.

The second gateway, the Northeastern Gateway, was a network of roads, canals, and, later, rail systems that connected the river launching points at Pittsburgh (on the Ohio River) to Philadelphia and Wheeling (also on the Ohio River) to Baltimore. The National Road was completed west to Wheeling in 1817, and the Pennsylvania Turnpike—a toll road—reached Pittsburgh the next year. Competing canals on these two links created a rivalry in the 1830s. Then, in the 1850s, the rivalry of these cities was boosted again through rail linkages.

The Southern Gateway, at New Orleans, was the main southern entrepôt. The key event on the trunk rivers of the Mississippi, Missouri, Ohio, and other western river arteries to this gateway was the introduction of the steamboat in 1811.

Figure 9.2 shows the volume of shipments from the western interior to the East and abroad by each gateway.[1] The growth of total outbound shipments, from 65,000 tons in 1810 to nearly 4.7 million tons in 1860, documents the impressive development that was taking place in the West. We also see that the Northeastern Gateway played only a minor role, typically carrying less than 5 percent of the shipments from the West. The Northern Gateway was far more significant, but not until the late 1830s. Prior to 1825 and the opening of the Erie Canal, this gateway handled no outbound shipments. Even in the early 1830s, most of the shipments on the Erie Canal were from upstate New York. Therefore, it was primarily the Southern Gateway that handled western produce shipments, at least until the last few decades of the antebellum period. The dominance of the natural waterways, encompassing 16,000 miles of western rivers, led the contemporary James Lanman to say in 1841:

> Steam navigation colonized the west! It furnished a motive for settlement and production by the hands of eastern men, because it brought the western territory nearer to the east by nine tenths of the distance. . . . Steam is crowding our eastern cities with western flour and western merchants, and lading the western steamboats with eastern emigrants and eastern merchandise. It has advanced the career of national colonization and national production, at least a century! (1841, 124)

---

[1]The evidence on inbound shipments is more fragmentary and less complete, but it does not change the relative positions of each gateway in the movement of freight.

FIGURE 9.2
Freight Shipments from
the Interior by the
Western Gateways,
1810–1860

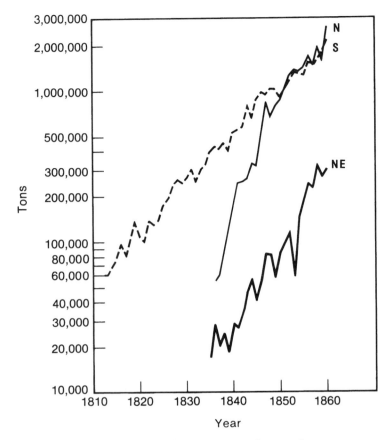

Source: *Haites, Mak, and Walton 1975, 7 and Appendix A.*

STEAMBOATS AND THE NATURAL WATERWAYS

Before the coming of the steamboat in the West, river travel was especially difficult, hazardous, and costly. Rafts and flatboats allowed downriver passage at reasonable cost, but the return upriver on foot or horseback was time consuming and dangerous. Typical voyages of 1,000 miles took one month downstream and three to four months to return. The keelboat, which made upstream journeys possible, was based on labor-intensive, backbreaking work. As shown in Figure 9.1, upstream travel costs were typically more than five times downstream travel costs.

In 1807, Robert Fulton, with the assistance of Robert R. Livingston, built the steamboat *Clermont*, which completed a historic voyage up the Hudson River from New York to Albany, a distance of 150 miles, in 32 hours. Following the initial trip, regular passenger service from New York to Albany was inaugurated, and the dependability of the steamboat was quickly demonstrated. A new era of transportation on the rivers of America had begun.

The steamboat's beginning in the West came at the northern terminus of Pittsburgh, where the junction of the Allegheny and the Monongahela forms the Ohio River and where plentiful supplies of timber and the local iron industry fostered a flourishing shipbuilding industry. Nicholas Roosevelt, under the Fulton-Livingston patents, constructed

TABLE 9.1 ANNUAL CONSTRUCTION (GROSS AND NET) AND TONNAGE OF STEAMBOATS IN OPERATION ON WESTERN RIVERS, 1811–1868

	SHIPS IN OPERATION			SHIPS IN OPERATION	
YEAR	NUMBER	TONNAGE	YEAR	NUMBER	TONNAGE
1811	1	400	1840	494	82,600
1815	7	1,500	1845	538	96,200
1820	69	14,200	1850	638	134,600
1825	80	12,500	1855	696	172,700
1830	151	24,600	1860	817	195,000
1835	324	50,100	1865	1,006	228,700
			1868	874	212,200

Source: *Haites, Mak, and Walton, 1975, 130–131.*

in Pittsburgh the first steamboat to ply the inland waters. Named the *New Orleans*, it left Pittsburgh on October 20, 1811, and completed its voyage to the Gulf of Mexico in a little over two and one-half months, despite an earthquake en route at New Madrid, Missouri. Six years passed before regular services upstream and downstream were established, but (as shown in Table 9.1) the tonnage of steamboats in operation on the western rivers by 1819 already exceeded 10,000. This figure grew to almost 200,000 tons by 1860. The periods of the most rapid expansion were the first two decades following 1815, but significant gains occurred throughout each decade. Not until the 1880s did steamboating on the western rivers register an absolute decline.

The appearance of the steamboat on inland waterways did not, by any means, solve all problems of travel. Variations in the heights of the rivers still made navigation uncertain, even dangerous. Ice in the spring and sand bars in the summer were ever-present

Inland shipping points like Cincinnati soon became major markets for an increasing variety of goods and services.

hazards; snags (trees lodged in rivers), rocks, and sunken vessels continually damaged and wrecked watercraft. In addition to these problems, the steamboat exposed westerners to some of the earliest hazards of industrialization; high-pressure boilers frequently exploded, accidentally killing thousands over the decades. This prompted the federal government to intervene: In 1838 and again in 1852, some of the first U.S. laws concerning industrial safety and consumer protection were legislated. The 1852 steamboat boiler inspection law was especially effective, significantly reducing boiler explosions and loss of life. (Refer to Economic Reasoning Proposition 4, laws and rules matter, in Economic Insight 1.1 on page 8.) Also, the federal government sporadically engaged in the removal of snags and other obstacles from the rivers. This also reduced losses of cargo, vessels, and people.

Competition, Productivity, and Endangered Species

One of the most significant characteristics of western river transportation was the high degree of competition among the various craft. This meant that the revolutionary effects of the steamboat, which were critical to the early settlement of the West, were transfused through a competitive market. Fulton and Livingston attempted to secure a monopoly via government restraint to prevent others from providing steamboat services at New Orleans and throughout the West (Walton 1992). Their quest for monopoly rights was ultimately defeated in the courts, reminding us again of the importance of Economic Reasoning Proposition 4, laws and rules matter. These and other associations failed to limit supply and block entry; and without government interference, the modest capital requirements needed to enter the business ensured a competitive market.

© HISTORICAL PICTURES STOCK MONTAGE

Robert Fulton's steamboat Clermont, *built in 1807, started a transportation revolution on America's rivers.*

Following an early period of bonanza profits (30 percent and more) on the major routes, a normal rate of return on capital of about 10 percent was common by 1820. Only on the remote and dangerous tributaries, where trade was thin and uncertain, could such exceptional returns as 35 or 40 percent be obtained.

Because the market for western river craft services was generally competitive, the savings from productivity-raising improvements ushered in by the steamboat were promptly passed on to consumers. And the cost reductions were significant, as the evidence in Table 9.2 illustrates.

Of course, a major cause of the sharp decline in freight costs was simply the introduction of steam power. However, the stream of modifications and improvements that followed the maiden voyage of the *New Orleans* provided greater productivity gains than the initial application of steam power. This assertion is verified in the fall of rates. The decrease in rates after 1820 was greater, both absolutely and relatively, than the decline from 1811 to 1820, especially in real terms. For example, in the purchasing power of 1820 dollars, the real-cost decline upstream on the New Orleans–Louisville run was from $3.12 around 1815 to $2.00 in 1820 to $0.28 in the late 1850s. Downstream, the real-cost changes were from $0.62 around 1815 to $0.75 in 1820 to $0.39 in the late 1850s.

Major modifications were made in the physical characteristics of the vessels. Initially resembling seagoing vessels, steamboats evolved to meet the shallow-water conditions of the western rivers. These boats became steadily lighter in weight, with many outside decks for cargo (and budget-fare accommodations for passengers), and their water depth (or draft) became increasingly lower despite increased vessel size. Consequently, the amount of cargo carried per vessel ton greatly increased. In addition, the season of normal operations was substantially extended, even during shallow-water months. This, along with reductions in port times and passage times, greatly increased the number of round trips averaged each year. Notably, the decline in passage times was only partially due to faster speeds. Primarily, this decline resulted from learning to operate the boats at night. Shorter stopovers at specified fuel depots instead of long periods spent foraging in the woods for fuel contributed as well. Lastly, as noted earlier, government activity to clear the rivers of snags and other natural obstacles added to the available time of normal operations and made river transport a safer business, as evidenced by a decline in insurance costs over the decades.

On reflection, it is clear that most of the improvements did not result from technological change. Only the initial introduction of steam power stemmed from advances in knowledge about basic principles. The host of modifications evolved from the process of learning by doing and from the restructuring of known principles of design and

TABLE 9.2 AVERAGE FREIGHT RATES (PER 100 POUNDS OF CARGO) BY DECADE BETWEEN LOUISVILLE AND NEW ORLEANS, 1810–1859

	UPSTREAM	DOWNSTREAM
Before 1820	$5.00	$1.00
1820–1829	1.00	0.62
1830–1839	0.50	0.50
1840–1849	0.25	0.30
1850–1859	0.25	0.32

Source: *Haites, Mak, and Walton, 1975, 32.*

engineering to fit shallow-water conditions. In effect, they are a tribute to the skills and ingenuity of the early craftsmen and mechanics.

In sum, the overall record of achievement gave rise to productivity advances (output per unit of input) that averaged more than 4 percent per year between 1815 and 1860. Such a rate exceeded that of any other transport medium over a comparable length of time in the nineteenth century (Haites, Mak, and Walton 1975).

With the steamboat's success, other forms of river transport either evolved or disappeared. The labor-consuming keelboat felt the strongest sting of competition from the new technology and was quickly eliminated from the competitive fray on the main trunk river routes. The keelboat made nearly 90 percent of its revenues on the upriver leg, where men labored to pole, pull, or row with backbreaking effort against the currents. As shown in Table 9.2, the steamboat's greatest impact was on the upstream rates. Only on some of the remote, hazardous tributaries did the keelboat find temporary refuge from the chugging advance of the steamboat.

Surprisingly, quite a different destiny evolved for the flatboat, which showed a remarkable persistence throughout the entire antebellum period. Because the reductions in downstream rates were more moderate, the current-propelled flatboat was less threatened. In addition, spillover effects from steamboating aided flatboating. First, there was the tremendous savings in labor that the steamboat generated by providing quick upriver transport to returning flatboat men. Not only were they saved the long and sometimes perilous overland journey, but access to steamboat passenger services led to repetitive journeys and, thus, to the acquisition of skills and knowledge. This led to the adoption of larger flatboats, which economized greatly on labor per ton carried. Because of these gains, there were more flatboats on the western rivers near the middle of the nineteenth century than at any other time.

In combination, these western rivercraft gave a romantic aura to the drudgery of day-to-day freight haulage and commerce. Sumptuously furnished Mississippi riverboats were patronized by rich and poor alike. Yeomen farmers also contributed their adventuresome flatboating journeys. Such developments were regional in character, however, and their impact was mainly on the Southern Gateway. On the waterways of the East or on the Great Lakes, the steamboat never attained the importance that it did in the Midwest. Canals and turnpikes furnished alternative means of transportation, and the railroad network had an earlier start in the East. Steamboats in the East were primarily passenger carriers—great side-wheelers furnishing luxurious accommodations for people traveling between major cities. On the Great Lakes, contrary to what might be expected, sailing ships successfully competed for freight throughout the antebellum years. Where human comfort was a factor, however, the steamship gradually prevailed. Even so, the number and tonnage of sailing vessels on the Great Lakes in 1860 were far greater than those of steamboats.

PUBLIC VERSUS PRIVATE INITIATIVE ON THE NATURAL WATERWAYS

Transportation developments on the natural waterways, especially on the rivers through the Southern Gateway, as well as along the Northern Gateway avenues, were predominantly a product of private initiative. Government investments as a proportion of total investments in vessels and river improvements were minuscule. Private entrepreneurs owned and operated the craft, and state and local government rendered few improvements in the rivers because many of the benefits to users could not be captured within state boundaries. Why should state or local governments appropriate funds for river improvements if most of the benefits went to vessel owners (and users) passing by? Calls for federal action to improve the rivers often went unheeded because of strict constitutional interpretations (Paskoff 2007). With the exception of sporadic but highly beneficial snag-removal programs, the public sector provided little capital to transportation on the natural waterways, no more than 1 or 2 percent of the total expenditures (Haites, Mak, and Walton 1975).

THE CANAL ERA

Although the natural waterways provided a substantial web of transport facilities, many productive areas remained regionally and economically disconnected until the canals were built and other internal improvements were made to link the areas. The first major undertaking began in 1816, when the New York legislature authorized the construction of the Erie and Champlain canals. With powerful canal commissioner DeWitt Clinton as its guiding spirit, the Erie Canal was promoted with enthusiasm, and sections were opened to traffic as they were completed. It quickly became apparent that the canal would have great success, and even before its completion in 1825, "canal fever" seized promoters throughout the country. In the tremendous building boom that followed, canals were constructed to link three types of areas. Some ran from the "back country" to the tidewater regions; some traversed, or attempted to traverse, the area between the older states and the Ohio valley; and some, the western canals, linked the Great Lakes with the waterways running to the East. The principal canals of the antebellum period are shown in Map 9.1. They were vital in developing the Northern and Northeastern gateways.

The Erie was the most important of the early canals, though by no means the only profitable one. This system, which still exists in an expanded and improved form as the New York Barge Canal, was a massive undertaking. Beginning at Albany on the Hudson River, it traversed the state of New York westward to Buffalo on Lake Erie, covering a distance of 364 miles. The work cost approximately $7 million (about $150 million in today's money) and took about nine years to complete. The builders overcame countless difficulties, not the least of which was their own ignorance. Hardly any of the engineers had ever worked in canal construction, and much experimentation was necessary. Some sections did not hold water at first and had to be lined with clay after work had been completed. The locks presented a special difficulty, but ingenuity and the timely discovery of water-resistant cement helped solve the problems of lock construction.

In its final form, the Erie system reached a fair portion of New York state. The Cayuga and Seneca, the Chemung, and the Genesee extensions connected important territory to the south with the canal. A branch to Oswego provided access to Lake Ontario, and the Champlain Canal gave access to the North. The system not only furnished transportation to much of the state but also tapped the Great Lakes areas served by the St. Lawrence route and the vast Ohio Territory. Beginning about 1835, a large part of the traffic from the West that had formerly traversed the Ohio and Mississippi rivers to New Orleans was diverted over the Erie Canal to the port of New York. This explains much of the convergence (catching up) of the Northern Gateway with the Southern Gateway revealed in Figure 9.2. Lumber, grain, and meat products were the chief commodities to move eastward; textiles, leather goods, machinery, hardware, and imported foods and drugs went west in exchange. Passengers, too, rode the horse-drawn boats in great numbers, with speeds of 100 miles in a 24-hour day compensating in part for the discomfort of cramped and poorly ventilated cabins.

Pennsylvania's answer to the competition of the Erie Canal was the Mainline of the Pennsylvania Public Works—a system of railroads and canals chartered in 1826 by the

MAP 9.1
Principal Canals of the Antebellum Period, 1800–1860

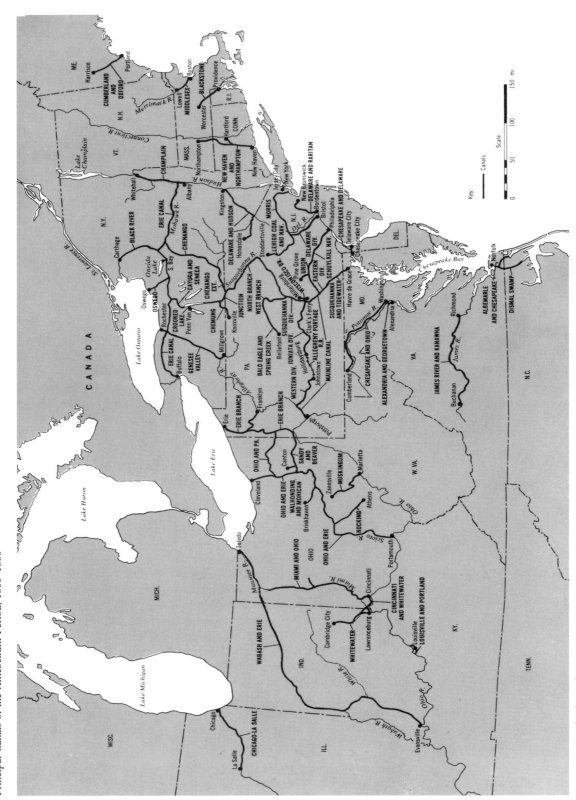

Sources: *Goodrich et al. 1961, 184–185.*

state legislature. But the fate of Pennsylvania's canals stood in sharp contrast with those in New York. A major disadvantage of the Pennsylvania canals was geographic. The terrain traversed by the Erie to reach the western frontier had been difficult enough for canal construction, rising as much as 650 feet above the Hudson at Albany and requiring many locks to raise the water. But the terrain of western Pennsylvania proved to be insurmountable by canal. The Mainline crossed the mountains, lifted passengers and freight to an altitude of more than 2,000 feet, and deposited both travelers and goods, westbound from Philadelphia, at Pittsburgh some 400 miles away. All this was accomplished by as fantastic a combination of transport as the country had ever seen. From Philadelphia, at tidewater, to Columbia, 81 miles westward on the Susquehanna River, a horse-drawn railroad carried both passengers and freight.[2] At Columbia the railroad joined the Juniata, or Eastern Division of the Pennsylvania Canal, from which passengers and freight were carried up a river valley by canal 173 miles to the Portage Railroad at Holidaysburg. Here, intrepid passengers saw their boat separated into front and rear sections, which were mounted on cars and run on underwater rails into the canal. A 36-mile trip on the Portage Railroad then began. The inclined tracks, over which cars were pulled by stationary steam engines winding cables on drums, accomplished a lift of 1,399 feet on the eastern slope to the summit and a descent of 1,172 feet on the western slope to another canal at Johnstown. From Johnstown to Pittsburgh, a distance of 105 miles, the water journey was comparatively easy.

The completion of this colossal work in 1834 was heralded by a celebration at Liberty Hall in Philadelphia. An old print depicts one of the halfboats decked with bunting and flags being drawn away from the hall by teams of prancing horses. In the sense that it carried all the traffic it could, the Mainline was successful, but the bottleneck of the Portage Railroad plus the fact that the system had twice as many locks as the Erie kept it from becoming a serious competitor for western business. Over the years, the Mainline carried 5 to 10 percent of the traffic volume of the Erie Canal, to the great disappointment of the people of a state that had spent more on waterways than any other.

This painting shows the junction of the Champlain Canal and the Erie Canal—an important point on the trade route that was to become the preeminent link between Midwest and East Coast urban centers.

---

[2]Although the steam locomotive was not employed in the United States until 1829, rails to permit smooth haulage had been used in both America and Europe for several years.

Other states as well expended large sums of money on canals to draw the trade of the new West. The Chesapeake and Ohio Canal was projected up the valley of the Potomac to Cumberland, Maryland, and on to the Ohio River. The canal company was chartered by the state of Virginia with the assent of the Maryland legislature, and the federal government contributed heavily to the venture. However, despite the political blessings of two states and the federal government, the generous financial backing of all three, and the aid of some local governments, technical difficulties resulted in the project's completion only to Cumberland.

The dazzling success of the Erie Canal and the competitive rivalry among cities and regions for commercial traffic generated many unprofitable investments in canals. The great canal-building era (1815–1843) totaled $31 million in investments, nearly three-quarters from government sources, mostly state governments. Despite the lack of profitability and the arrival and practical demonstration of the railroads, regional competitiveness spurred a second wave of investment in canals, totaling $66 million between 1843 and 1860. Nearly two-thirds of the financing was from the government, again mainly from state treasuries. More might have been invested. However, the commercial crises of 1837 and 1839 and the deep depression of the early 1840s caused financial chaos, and nine states had to suspend payments on their debts (mainly bonds, many sold to foreigners). Major canals in Pennsylvania, Maryland, Indiana, and Illinois never recovered.

Although most of the canal investments were financial failures and could not be justified by comparisons of benefits and costs, they did support the natural waterways in opening up the West. Some that have been considered preposterous mistakes might have turned out to be monuments to human inventiveness if the railroad had not developed at almost the same time. The canals posed problems, it is true. The limitations on horse-drawn vehicles for cargo transport were great except with regard to a few commodities. Canals were supposed to provide a system of waterways, but as often as not, the boats of larger canals could not move through the smaller canals. Floods and droughts often made the movement of the barges uncertain. Yet the chief reason for the eventual failure of the canals was the railroad, which could carry people and a wide variety of commodities at a much greater speed—and speed was requisite to a genuine transportation revolution.

THE IRON HORSE

Despite the clear-cut technological advantages of the railroad, natural waterways remained the primary means of transportation for nearly 20 years after the first pioneering American railroads were introduced in the early 1830s. Besides the stiff competition of water transport, an important hindrance to railroad development was public antipathy, which had its roots in ignorance, conservatism, and vested interest. People thought that speeds of 20 to 30 miles per hour would be physically harmful to passengers. At least one city in Massachusetts directed its representatives in the state legislature to prevent "so great a calamity to our town as must be the location of any railroad through it." Many honestly believed that the railroad would prove to be impractical and uneconomical and would not provide service as dependable as that of the waterways.

Unsurprisingly, the most vigorous opposition to railroads came from groups whose economic interests suffered from the competition of the new industry. Millions of dollars had been spent on canals, rivers, highways, and plank roads, and thousands of people depended on these transportation enterprises for their livelihood. Tavern keepers feared their businesses would be ruined, and farmers envisioned the market for hay and grain disappearing as the "iron horse" replaced the flesh-and-blood animal that drew canal boats and pulled wagons. Competitive interests joined to embarrass and hinder the railroads, causing several states to limit traffic on them to passengers and their baggage or to freight hauled only during the months when canal operations ceased. One railroad company in Ohio was required to pay for any loss in canal traffic attributed to railroad competition. Other railroads were ordered to pay a tonnage tax to support the operation of canals.

Despite the opinions and opposition of those who feared the railroads (recall Economic Reasoning Proposition 5, evidence and theory give value to opinions), construction went on. In sections of the country where canals could not be built, the railroad offered a means of cheap transportation for all kinds of commodities. In contrast to the municipality that wished to exclude the railroad, many cities and towns, as well as their state governments, did much to encourage railroad construction. At the time, the federal government was restrained by the prevailing political philosophy of strict constitutionalism from financially assisting and promoting railways. The government did, however, make surveys to determine rights of way and provided tariff exemptions on railroad iron.

By 1840, railroad mileage in the United States was within 1,000 miles of the combined lengths of all canals, but the volume of goods carried by water still exceeded that transported by rail. After the depression of the early 1840s, rail investments continued, mostly government assisted, and by 1850, the country had 9,000 miles of railroads, as shown in Table 9.3. Referring back to Figure 9.2, we see that by the late 1840s, the Northern Gateway had surpassed the Southern, and by the 1850s, the railroad's superiority was clear.

With the more than 20,000 miles of rails added to the transportation system between 1850 and 1860, total trackage surpassed 30,000 miles at the end of the decade, and the volume of freight traffic equaled that of canals.[3] All the states east of the Mississippi were connected during this decade. The eastern seaboard was linked with the Mississippi River system, and the Gulf and South Atlantic states could interchange traffic with the Great Lakes. Growing trunk lines such as the Erie, the Pennsylvania, and the Baltimore and Ohio completed construction of projects that had been started in the 1840s, and combinations of short lines provided new through routes. By the beginning of the Civil War, the eastern framework of the present rail transportation system had been erected, and it was possible to travel by rail the entire distance from New York to Chicago to Memphis and back to New York.

But the United States was still a long way from establishing an integrated railroad system. Although the "Stephenson gauge" of 4 feet 8 inches (distance between the rails) was preponderant in 1860, its final selection as the country's "standard gauge" was still a

TABLE 9.3 MILES OF RAILROAD IN OPERATION, 1830–1860

YEAR	MILEAGE
1830	23
1835	1,098
1840	2,818
1845	4,633
1850	9,021
1855	18,374
1860	30,626

Source: Historical Statistics, *1960.*

---

[3]Railroads had won from canals almost all passenger business (except that of poor immigrants coming across New York state) and the carriage of nearly all light, high-value goods.

TABLE 9.4 PRODUCTIVITY CHANGE IN RAILROADS, 1839–1859 (1910 = 100)

| | | INPUTS | | | | |
YEAR	(1) OUTPUT	(2) LABOR	(3) CAPITAL	(4) FUEL	(5) TOTAL INPUT[a]	(6) TOTAL FACTOR PRODUCTIVITY[b]
1839	0.08	0.3	0.8	0.07	0.5	16.0
1859	2.21	5.0	10.1	1.50	6.6	33.5

[a]Weighted average of labor, capital, and fuel; weights are proportions of costs.

[b](column 1 ÷ column 5) × 100.

Source: *Adapted from Fishlow, 1972, 499.*

quarter-century away. Because locomotives and cars were built for one gauge only, a multitude of gauges prevented continuous shipment, as did the lack of agreement among companies on such matters as the interline exchange of rolling stock, through bills of lading and passenger tickets, the division of through rates, and standard time (Taylor and Neu 1956).

Many modifications and improvements occurred, however, and, as shown in Table 9.4, total factor productivity in railroads more than doubled in the two decades before the Civil War. Alternately stated, railroad output grew relative to inputs by a factor of 2. Technological advances, according to Albert Fishlow, were reflected in the fact that the average traction force of locomotives more than doubled in these two decades. Freight car sizes also increased, with eight-wheel cars being common by 1859. Most of the productivity rise, however, resulted from increased utilization of existing facilities. The stock of capital—and other inputs—grew, but output grew much faster as the initial inputs became more fully utilized.

ROADS

Though technologically undramatic, roads and trails were part of the transportation network. Thanks to Hollywood and western movies, we are familiar with the trails followed by western settlers. These "highways" of long-distance land travel are shown in Map 9.2 on page 159. The overland routes of westward migration, settlement, and commerce usually followed the old Indian hunting and war paths, which in turn had followed stream valleys providing the easiest lines of travel. One of the most important paths was the Wilderness Road, pioneered by Daniel Boone. Penetrating the mountain barrier at Cumberland Gap, near present-day Middlesboro, Kentucky, the road then went north and west into the Ohio Territory. Over this road, which in many places was only a marked track, poured thousands of emigrants.[4] Although most of the overland roads turned into quagmires in the rainy season and into billowing dust clouds in the dry season, some of them were well constructed and well maintained through portions of their length.

---

[4]This same type of road or marked track appeared during the overland migration to the West Coast. The Oregon Trail, over which travel began in the early 1840s, was 2,000 miles long and carried settlers to the Pacific Northwest and California. The Mormon Trail, broken by Brigham Young in the late 1840s, paralleled the Oregon Trail along the south bank of the Platte for some distance. Earlier trails marked by the Spaniards, such as the Santa Fe Trail into present-day New Mexico and Arizona and El Camino Real (the King's Highway) in California, were valuable to early explorers and traders.

MAP 9.2

Westward Travel
The massive physical barriers faced by the pioneers could be minimized by following such famous routes as the Oregon, Mormon, or Santa Fe Trails. Note that the Mormons deliberately went north of the Platte River to avoid wagon trains hostile to them on the Oregon Trail south of the river.

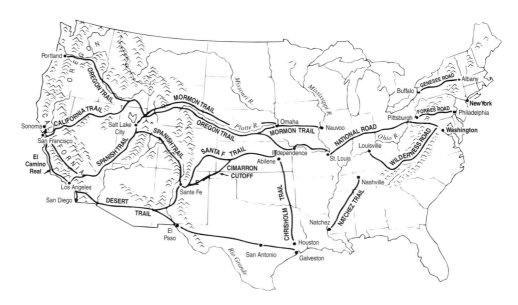

The most notable surfaced highway was the Cumberland Road, or "National Road," as it was often called, which was built by the federal government after much controversy. Begun at Cumberland, Maryland, in 1811, the road was opened to Wheeling on the Ohio River in 1818 and was later completed to St. Louis. This major government undertaking was part of Albert Gallatin's 1808 proposed plan for a system of federal roads. Despite support from many people for a comprehensive program of internal improvements, that was the only major road built in this early period by the federal government. Opposition to federal projects like this was based ostensibly on the assertion that federal participation in such an activity was unconstitutional. Recall Economic Reasoning Propositions 1, scarcity forces us to make choices; 2, choices impose costs, the highest valued alternative forgone; and 4, laws and rules matter. Sectional rivalries played a major role in blocking the proposed construction. The West, in particular, persistently and loudly called for a national road system, and at first, the Middle Atlantic states were inclined to agree. But after New York and Pennsylvania developed their own routes to the West, they did not wish to promote federally financed competition elsewhere. New Englanders, with fairly good roads of their own, were even less inclined to encourage further population drains or to improve the commercial positions of Boston's rivals. The South, although mired in the mud, was bitterly antagonistic to any program that would add to the government's financial needs or facilitate access to nonslave portions of the West. Despite all the opposition, Congress could not avoid appropriating increasing sums for post and military roads, but sectional rivalries over the geographic allocation of internal improvements permitted an incredibly primitive road system to survive well into the twentieth century.

Turnpikes

In many areas, especially where other transport modes were unavailable, roads were built by private turnpike companies. These companies collected tolls and used gates consisting of pikes or spears to let the toll payer pass to and from the road at selected points. The turnpike era began in 1789 with the construction of the Philadelphia and Lancaster Turnpike; it ended about 1830, after which only a few private highways were attempted as business ventures. During this period, Pennsylvania chartered 86 companies that built more than 2,000 miles of road. By 1811, New York had 1,500 miles of highways constructed by 135 companies, and New England had granted some 180 companies the right to build turnpikes. Despite toll collections, few of the companies that constructed roads for public use were profitable ventures; in fact, it is doubtful that even one earned close to the going rate of return on its capital. Teamsters avoided the tolls if at all possible, and dishonest gatekeepers often pocketed the receipts. But the chief difficulty—one unforeseen by most promoters—was that the only long-distance trade the roads attracted was stagecoach passengers and emigrants. Freight would not, for the most part, stand the cost of land carriage over great distances, and without freight traffic, turnpikes simply could not earn a profit. They eventually faced extensive competition from steamboats, canals, and railroads, but by this time returns on invested capital had already proved disappointing. Some turnpikes were abandoned and later acquired by the states for the rapidly growing public road system; others were purchased by local governments and made into toll-free highways.[5]

A special kind of toll road was the plank road, developed shortly after the decline in turnpike construction. Plank roads were built by laying wide, heavy planks or "rails" on stringers or ties placed in the direction of travel and were superior for all-weather use. The first plank road in the United States was built in Syracuse in 1837, and over the next 20 years, several thousand miles of plank roads were built, the heaviest concentration being in timber-abundant New York and Pennsylvania. Some were subsidized by the states, although most were privately and locally financed.[6]

THE ANTEBELLUM INTERREGIONAL GROWTH HYPOTHESIS

The antebellum interregional growth hypothesis provides another perspective on the importance of falling transportation costs to the early growth of a national market. Douglass C. North advanced the argument with quantitative evidence derived from earlier works (especially Callender 1930) and added theoretical specifications and structure. Briefly stated, North argues that U.S. growth from 1815 to 1843 was propelled primarily by the growth of British demand for southern cotton, which encouraged southern regional specialization in cotton. In turn, this raised the demand in the South for western foodstuffs and cheap northeastern manufactures, mainly boots, shoes, and coarse-fiber clothing for slaves. Growth in the size of the national market, through falling transport costs, realized economies of large-scale productions and greater regional economic specialization. As the Northeast became more specialized in manufacturing and more urbanized, the growing demand of the South for western foodstuffs was reinforced. Each region advanced along lines dictated by its respective comparative advantage in production, and each demanded goods produced in the other regions in increasingly greater amounts. After 1843, the primary initiating role of foreign demand for cotton diminished, and internal market forces ascended in importance. The railroad linking the West to the North also contributed to the lessening forces of the South. The evidence on the timing and waves of western migrations and land sales and prices of key regional staples supports North's argument. Evidence on Southern food production, however, for the years after 1840—the only years providing us with reliable food-production

---

[5]A few private roads continued into the twentieth century, but all that now remains of them is the name "turnpike" given to some important arteries of the highway system. These throughways differ from the older turnpikes in that the modern enterprises are owned by public corporations.

[6]For an excellent analysis of the building boom of plank roads, see Majewski, Baer, and Klein (1993).

data—suggests that the South was relatively self-sufficient in food (especially Gallman 1970; also Fishlow 1964 and the following discussion by Fogel 1964). Yet, as Lloyd Mercer has shown, pockets of food deficits in the South may have been sufficient to have a significant impact on western food production for market, especially before 1840 (Mercer 1982). Furthermore, the magnitude of self-sufficiency may hinge critically on how "the South" is defined. For example, should the border states of Kentucky and Tennessee, with their large meat surpluses, be considered southern or northern states (Sexton 1987)? Despite the inconclusiveness of the interregional linkages in this debate, the hypothesis provides a useful framework of analysis and an international perspective on the advances and linkages of the regions and of the formation of a national economy during that vital period of the transportation revolution.

OCEAN TRANSPORT

In addition to the many developments in internal transportation, great strides were being made in the long-traditional merchant marine. Thanks to bold entrepreneurship, the Black Ball line of New York instituted regularly scheduled transatlantic sailings in 1818. Beginning with only four ships, the line had a vessel sailing from New York for Liverpool the first week of each month, and a ship began the Liverpool–New York passage at the same time. Considerable risk was involved in pledging ships to sail "full or not full," as the line's advertising declared, because a ship might make three round trips a year (instead of the usual two made by the regular traders) with its hold far from full (Albion 1961). But by specializing in passengers, specie, mail, and "fine freight," the packets managed to operate successfully for more than 100 years. In the 1820s, the Black Ball line increased its trips to two a month each way, and other packet lines between New York and European ports were soon established. Henceforth, passengers could count on sailing at a particular hour on a given day, and merchants could book freight with something more than a vague hope that it would arrive in time to permit a profitable transaction. By ensuring a set schedule, the Black Ball line reduced risks and uncertainties in overseas commerce.

The transatlantic packets fully established New York as the predominant port in the United States. Coastal packets, running primarily to New Orleans but also to Charleston, Savannah, and Mobile, brought cotton to New York for eastbound ocean shipment and carried southward a considerable portion of the European goods brought from England and the Continent. In fact, trade between the cotton ports and New York was greater in physical and dollar volume than the ocean trade during most of the antebellum period (Albion 1938). These packets significantly complemented developments in the western rivers, which funneled produce from the interior through New Orleans, the Southern Gateway.

Between 1820 and 1860, remarkable design changes in sailing ships led to increases in tonnage and efficiency. From an average size of 300 tons in the 1820s, American sailing ships increased to 1,000 tons in the 1850s, and vessels of 1,500 tons' burden were not uncommon. There was a marked increase in length-to-beam ratios and spread of sail for the ordinary packet ship, and the centuries-old practice of making the widest part of the vessel forward of the center was abandoned. Borrowing from French designers, Yankee shipbuilders produced a special type of ship that was to dominate the seas for the three decades before the Civil War. This was the famed clipper ship, which, at some sacrifice of carrying capacity, attained unheard-of speeds. The clipper was a graceful ship with three masts, square-rigged but equipped with abundant fore-and-aft sails that gave it a great advantage going into the wind, thus increasing its speed. Manned by fewer hands than vessels of foreign register, a clipper was to be driven 24 hours a day, not put to bed for seven or eight hours at night.

The first American (or "Baltimore") clipper was the *Ann McKim*, launched in 1832. Its builder, Donald McKay, became a legendary figure, and some ships of his design bore names that are remembered even today: The *Flying Cloud*, the *Sovereign of the Seas*, the *Great Republic*, and the *Lightning* were spectacularly beautiful, with concave sides and bow and sails towering 200 feet above the deck. On its maiden voyage across the Atlantic, the *Lightning* logged a record 436 miles in one day with an average speed of 18 miles an hour. Even today, many ocean vessels do not approach this speed.

ECONOMIC INSIGHT 9.1

A NATIONAL MARKET FORMS

Surges of internal transportation developments solidly linked the interior western regions to the seaboard and abroad. Also contributing to market unification and falling costs of trade was the telegraph, invented by Samuel F. B. Morse in the 1840s. Telegraph wires were strung parallel to the railroads across the nation. By 1852, 23,000 miles of wire were in operation, speeding communications and reducing uncertainties. In 1866, an undersea cable was laid to Europe, further integrating the U.S. and European economies.

Although economic unification was far from complete, dramatic gains had been realized by the eve of the Civil War. As stated earlier, regional price movements portrayed these strides toward economic unification. As Thomas Berry states:

It is difficult to point to any consistent lag of the West behind the East during this early period (1788–1817) because of such diversity in general behavior; it is safe to state, however, that in such first magnitude movements as those of 1793–1797 and 1810–1817 there was a lag measuring somewhat more than a year in length. . . . Taking a later interval (1816–1860) weighted general indices of monthly prices in New York, New Orleans, and Cincinnati show agreement with each other to a surprising degree. . . . Cincinnati prices lagged the greater part of a year in their decline in 1819–1820, but they were only three or four months behind the seaboard markets in the turning-point of 1839 and reacted simultaneously at the time of the panic of 1857. (Berry 1943)

A viable transportation system was vital in perfecting a national market and linking regions. First the steamboats on the western rivers, then the canals, and finally the railroad revolutionized the costs of transport between the West and the seaboard. As Table 9.5 shows, western prices as a percentage of eastern prices grew dramatically. The figure here provides an analytical framework for interpreting the evidence in Table 9.5 on page 163.

Let S_1 represent the costs of production plus any local (short-distance) transportation costs of western wheat. Let S_2 reflect S_1 plus the cost of interregional transport in the early nineteenth century and S_3 equal S_1 plus these costs for the mid-1800s. Consumer costs P_2C fell to P_3C for a bushel of wheat, and farmers, receipts per bushel rose from P_2F to P_3F. Both consumers and producers gained.

Farmers gained larger and larger shares of the selling price of their crops. Moreover, consumers paid decreasing shares of the purchase price for transportation and other marketing costs. As freight costs fell, new unsettled areas were profitably cleared and added to the nation's economic activity. As Peter Lindert has shown, average land prices, adjusted for quality, more than doubled and possibly tripled from 1810 to 1860 (Lindert 1988). Improvements in transportation increased economic specialization and raised living standards dramatically. Today's "information revolution," globally, is realizing similar changes on the world in our time.

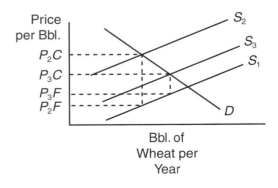

ECONOMIC INSIGHT 9.1

A NATIONAL MARKET FORMS, Continued

TABLE 9.5 CINCINNATI WHOLESALE PRICES AS A PERCENTAGE OF PHILADELPHIA, NEW YORK, AND NEW ORLEANS WHOLESALE PRICES, 1816–1860[a]

	COMMODITY											
	FLOUR (bbl.)			WHEAT (bu.)			CORN (bu.)			MESS PORK (bbl.)		
PERIOD	**PHIL.**	**N.Y**	**N.O.**	**PHIL.**	**N.Y.**	**N.O.**	**PHIL.**	**N.Y.**	**N.O.**	**PHIL.**	**N.Y.**	**N.O.**
1816–1820	63	66	72	45	48	—	51	48	—	56	58	63
1821–1825	52	52	56	39	38	—	38	32	30	63	67	76
1826–1830	68	67	67	50	48	—	49	41	29	67	68	78
1831–1835	73	74	76	57	56	—	55	49	36	77	77	85
1836–1840	73	73	77	59	61	—	56	51	47	87	85	86
1841–1845	77	73	86	68	65	90	53	47	65	82	79	84
1846–1850	78	71	87	68	63	88	51	48	62	81	90	88
1851–1855	82	79	90	73	61	90	61	59	74	85	90	92
1856–1860	88	95	89	79	70	86	70	66	72	91	94	93

[a]The "spreads" between prices in Cincinnati and the port cities narrowed dramatically between 1816–1820 and 1856–1860.

Source: *Haites, Mak, and Walton, 1975, 7 and Appendix A.*

Clippers were designed for the express purpose of carrying passengers and high-value cargo long distances. On the Atlantic runs, they were not profitable because of their limited capacity. But they dominated the China trade, and after 1849, they made fortunes for their owners by carrying passengers and freight during the gold rushes to California and Australia. On the New York–San Francisco trip around Cape Horn, a distance of 16,000 miles, the *Flying Cloud* set a record of just over 89 days, at a time when 100 days was about par for the clipper voyage.[7] This represented a time saving over ordinary ocean travel of up to three months, for which some merchants and travelers would pay a good price.

Clippers, however, were not the only vessels in the American merchant fleet. Broad-beamed and full-bowed freighting ships, much slower vessels than the clippers, were the backbone of the nation's merchant marine. Officered by men for whom seafaring was a tradition and a career of considerable social prestige, manned by crews of Americans bred to the sea, and owned by merchants of vision and daring like Stephen Girard of Philadelphia, the cheaply and expertly built ships from the marine ways of New York, Boston, and the Maine coast were the great ocean-freight carriers until the Civil War.

In the meantime, the British were making technical advances that enabled them to challenge American maritime supremacy and, finally, to overcome it. The major British innovation was the adaptation of the steamboat, originally invented for use on rivers and protected waters, to navigation on the open sea. The two principal changes made by the British were the use of iron instead of wood for the hull and the employment of the Archimedes' screw principle for propulsion instead of paddles. Iron hulls were necessary

---

[7]This record by sail was not broken until 1988.

to transport the heavy machinery of the early steam era safely, but they also had greater strength, buoyancy, and durability than wood. From the 1830s on, the British rapidly solved the problems of iron ship construction. The composite ship, with a frame of iron and a hull of wood, was tried for a while, but the acid in the oak timber corroded the iron. Once the British had perfected the techniques of riveting and working with sheet iron and steel, they had an absolute advantage in the construction of iron ships—as great an advantage as the United States had enjoyed in the making of wooden ones.

The inefficiency and slow speeds of early steam engines were a source of unending difficulty. For a long time, steamships had to carry a greater weight of coal than of cargo, and low engine speeds made the inefficient paddle wheel necessary despite its theoretical inferiority. After nearly 20 years of development, however, transatlantic steamships were making six voyages a year—twice as many as their sailing-packet competitors. Ten years later, Samuel Cunard's success in starting a line service was not entirely fortuitous; by 1848, engines were designed that could maintain higher speeds. The screw propeller was then rapidly adopted, and fuel consumption was cut greatly. During the 1850s, both the number and registered tonnage of steamships increased by leaps and bounds, and they almost entirely captured the passenger and high-value freight business.

In 1860, sailing ships still carried the greater part of the world's international freight. Yet by this time, the shape of the future was clear to all except die-hard American entrepreneurs, who—unable to comprehend the rapid obsolescence of their beautiful wooden ships—failed to take vigorous steps to compete with Britain. Recall Economic Reasoning Proposition 5, evidence and theory give value to opinions. Although government subsidies to American steamship builders began as early as 1845, these were both insufficient and poorly administered. Under the most favorable circumstances, however, builders in the United States could scarcely have competed on a cost basis with the vastly superior British iron industry. The signs were there for those who chose to read them. During the 1820s, American ships had carried close to 90 percent of the foreign trade of the United States; by the 1850s, this figure had declined to about 70 percent. The times had changed, and fortune's hand was laid on other shoulders.

SELECTED REFERENCES AND SUGGESTED READINGS

Albion, Robert G. *Square-Riggers on Schedule.* Princeton, N.J.: Princeton University Press, 1938.

_____. *The Rise of the New York Port, 1815–1860.* Hamden, Conn.: Archon, 1961.

Berry, Thomas S. *Western Prices before 1861.* Cambridge, Mass.: Harvard University Press, 1943.

Callender, Guy S. "The Early Transportation and Banking Enterprises of the States in Relation to the Growth of the Corporation." *Quarterly Journal of Economics* XVII (1930): 111–162.

Fishlow, Albert. "Antebellum Interregional Trade Reconsidered." *American Economic Review* 54 (May 1964): 352–364.

_____. "Internal Transportation." In *American Economic Growth*, ed. Lance E. Davis, et al., 499. New York: Harper & Row, 1972.

Fogel, Robert W. "Discussion." *American Economic Review* 54 (May 1964): 377–389.

Gallman, Robert E. "Self-Sufficiency in the Cotton Economy of the Antebellum South." *Agricultural History* 44 (1970): 5–23.

Goodrich, Carter H. *Government Promotion of American Canals and Railroads, 1800–1890.* New York: Columbia University Press, 1960.

Goodrich, Carter H., et al. *Canals and American Economic Development.* New York: Columbia University Press, 1961.

Haites, Erik F., James Mak, and Gary M. Walton. *Western River Transportation: The Era of Early Internal Development, 1810–1860.* Baltimore, Md.: Johns Hopkins University Press, 1975.

Historical Statistics. Series Q 15. Washington, D.C.: Government Printing Office, 1960.

Lanman, James H. "American Steam Navigation." *Hunt's Merchants' Magazine and Commercial Review* 4 (1841): 124.

Lindert, Peter H. "Long-Run Trends in American Farmland Values." *Agricultural History* (Summer 1988): 60.

Majewski, John, Christopher Baer, and Daniel B. Klein. "Responding to Relative Decline: The Plank Road Boom of Antebellum New York." *Journal of Economic History* 53 (1993): 106–122.

Mercer, Lloyd. "The Antebellum Interregional Trade Hypothesis: A Reexamination of Theory and Evidence." In *Explorations in the New Economic History*, eds. Roger L. Ransom, Richard Such, and Gary M. Walton, 71–96. New York: Academic Press, 1982.

North, Douglass C. "The Role of Transportation in the Economic Development of North America." A paper presented to the International Congress of the Historical Sciences, Vienna, August 1965, and published in *Les Grandes Voies Maritimes dans le Monde XVe–XIXe Siecles.* Paris: Ecole des Hautes Etudes en Sciences Sociales, 1965.

———. *Growth and Welfare in the American Past.* Englewood Cliffs, N.J.: Prentice Hall, 1973.

Paskoff, Paul. *Troubled Waters: Steamboats, River Improvements, and American Public Policy, 1821–1860.* Baton Rouge: Louisiana State University Press, 2007.

Sexton, Robert. "Regional Choice and Economic History." *Economic Forum* 16, no. 1 (Winter 1987).

Taylor, George R., and Irene Neu. *The American Railway Network, 1861–1890.* Cambridge, Mass.: Harvard University Press, 1956.

Walton, Gary M. "Fulton's Folly." In *Second Thoughts: Learning from American Social and Economic History*, ed. Donald McCloskey. London: Oxford University Press, 1992.

CHAPTER 10

Market Expansion and Industry in First Transition

CHAPTER THEME

Between the adoption of the Constitution and the outbreak of the Civil War, the economy of the United States was structurally transformed, and a solid foundation was laid for the United States to become an industrial power. Beginning with only a few small factories, mostly lumber mills, the new nation emerged by 1860 with a manufacturing sector second only to that of Great Britain. Yet in 1860, industrial firms were small by today's standards, and the United States was still predominantly an agricultural country. Nevertheless, many important changes had occurred that marked the advent of industrialization. Most significant was the evolution of new ways to combine factors of production, resulting in the substitution of capital for labor and requiring new forms of business organization. Business interests as a political force became evident, and New England and the Middle Atlantic states led the way in developing the industrial sector. Improvements in transportation played the main role in increasing regional specialization, and in many ways, transportation developments were instrumental to economic unification. What made the westward movement, the rise of King Cotton, and industrialization all the more remarkable is that all were unfolding simultaneously.

EARLY CHANGES IN U.S. MANUFACTURING

The Decline of Household Production

When Alexander Hamilton delivered his *Report on Manufacturers* to Congress in 1791, he estimated that from *two-thirds to four-fifths of the nation's clothing was homemade.* Most food processing was also done in the home. Water power had not yet been harnessed for textile production and was used mainly for milling grain and cutting lumber, among other uses. Artisans in the towns worked by hand, producing shoes, hats, pots, pans, and tools.

By 1830, however, household manufacture had exhibited a marked decline in the East and, thereafter, home manufacture and small artisan shops serving local markets continued to decline dramatically in all but the least accessible places. The major causes of this decline were the progress of industrial organization and modern means of transportation. Wherever steamboats ran or canals, highways, and railroads were built, home and artisan manufactures declined quickly. Even on the frontier, most households had access to the products of American or European factories after the middle of the nineteenth century. Map 10.1 shows the influence of transportation on homemade versus factory-made manufactures. The shaded areas in the two maps of New York show the counties in the one-third of the state having the highest per capita output of woolen goods made

MAP 10.1

Canal Impact

Household manufacture of woolen cloth (an index of isolation from commercial routes) underwent a drastic change between 1820 and 1845 along the Erie Canal. The shaded areas the counties in the one-third of the state with the highest home production of woolen goods during this period.

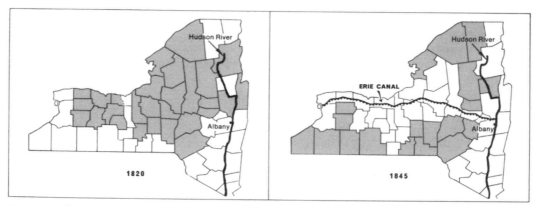

Source: *Cole 1926, 280. Reprinted by permission of the publisher; © 1926 by the President and Fellows of Harvard College.*

in the home in two different years, 1820 and 1845. Note that, in 1820, no county lying along the Hudson below Albany was in the top third. In 1845, the counties lying along the Erie Canal had similarly dropped in amount of home manufacture. In contrast, as late as 1865, nearly all the country people of Tennessee, especially those living in the mountain areas, wore clothing made at home. Primitive transport prolonged the wearing of homemade clothes. Recall Economic Reasoning Propositions 1, scarcity forces us to make choices; and 2, choices impose costs in Economic Insight 1.1 on page 8.

Craftshops and Mills

Until approximately 1815, the substantial increases in manufacturing output were effected by craftspeople operating independently or in craftshops. Craftspeople did "bespoke" work, making commodities only to order, maintaining the highest standards of quality, and selling through their own small retail outlets. But production by independent craftspeople declined rapidly after 1815. More important at that date and for some time afterward was the craftshop run by a master who employed several journeymen and apprentices. Sometimes, as in the case of the hatters of Danbury, Connecticut, an agglomeration of craftshops sold a quantity output to merchant wholesalers for distribution over wide market areas.

As in colonial days, the small mill was to be found in nearly all localities, and the national census of 1860 reported nearly 20,000 sawmills and 14,000 flour mills in the country. With few exceptions, tanneries, distilleries, breweries, and iron forges also produced for local markets. The decentralization of American industry before 1860, favored by the use of water power and commonly protected by high short-haul transport costs, produced small firms that often constituted effective local monopolies.

Before 1860, however, some mills had achieved large-scale production using methods of manufacture typical of the factory. Furthermore, large mills in two industries tended to concentrate in certain rather well-defined areas. Flour milling, which even in colonial days had been attracted to the Chesapeake area, continued to cluster there as farmers in Maryland and Virginia substituted wheat for tobacco. As cities grew larger and the demand for building materials increased, it became profitable for large lumbering firms to exploit timber areas located some distance from the markets. Typical were those situated by 1850 on the upper reaches of streams flowing through New England, New York, and Pennsylvania.

The Emergence of U.S. Factories

The term *factory* has been applied customarily to manufacturing units with the following characteristics:

1. A substantial output of a standardized product made to be sold in a wide, rather than a strictly local, market.
2. Complex operations carried on in one building or group of adjacent buildings. A considerable investment in fixed plant, the mechanization of processes, and the use of power are implied.
3. An assembly of workers under a definite organizational discipline.

In the United States, the factory developed first in the cotton textile industry. The mill of Almy, Brown, and Slater, in operation by 1793, is usually considered the first American factory. Moses Brown and William Almy were men of wealth in the New England mercantile tradition. Like many other American enterprisers, they had tried and failed to duplicate English spinning machinery. In 1789, a young mechanical wizard, Samuel Slater, came to Rhode Island after working for years in the firm of Arkwright and Strutt in Milford, England. Having memorized the minutest details of the water frames, Slater joined with Almy and Brown and agreed to reproduce the equipment for a mechanized spinning mill. Although small, the enterprise served as a training ground for operatives and as a pilot operation for managers.

A number of small cotton mills like the Slater mill soon followed, but most failed by the turn of the century because their promoters did not aim for a wide market. Not until the Embargo Act of 1807 and the consequent scarcity of English textiles that stimulated demand for domestic manufactures did spinning mills become numerous. Between 1805 and 1815, 94 new cotton mills were built in New England, and the mounting competition led Almy and Brown to push their markets south and west. By 1814, 70 percent of all consignments were to the Midwest via Philadelphia. Only two decades after Arkwright machinery was introduced into this country, the market for yarn was becoming national, and the spinning process was becoming a true factory operation as it was in England.

The Lowell Shops and the Waltham System

Two events propelled these changes. One was the successful introduction of the power loom into American manufacture; the other was the organization of production so that all four stages of the manufacture of cotton cloth could occur within one establishment. These stages were spinning, weaving, dying, and cutting.

After closely observing the workings of textile machinery in Great Britain, Francis Cabot Lowell, a New England merchant, gained sufficient knowledge of the secrets of mechanized weaving to enable him, with the help of a gifted technician, to construct a power loom superior to any that had been built to date. It was as an enterprise, however, that Lowell made a more significant contribution. He persuaded other men of means to participate with him in establishing a firm at Waltham that had all the essential characteristics of factory production (Economic Reasoning Proposition 1, scarcity forces us to make choices). This was the famed Boston Manufacturing Company, the forerunner

The complexity of mechanized factories and the substantial economies of scale related to them are illustrated here with a cotton manufacturing plant (circa 1839) where cotton is being carded, drawn, and roven (twisted into strands).

of several similar firms in which the so-called Boston Associates had an interest. Specializing in coarse sheetings, the Waltham factory sold its product all over America. Consolidating all the steps of textile manufacture in a single plant lowered production costs (Economic Reasoning Proposition 2, choices impose costs). A large number of specialized workers were organized into departments and directed by executives who were more like foremen than technical supervisors. The factory, by using power-driven machinery, produced standardized commodities in quantity.

At Lowell, where the Merrimack Manufacturing Company followed the Waltham pattern, and at Manchester and Lawrence, the factory system gained a permanent foothold. In the second leading center of New England textile manufacture—the Providence-Pawtucket region—a similar trend emerged, although the factories there were fewer and smaller. The third great district, located about Paterson and Philadelphia, contained mainly small mills that performed a single major process and turned out finer weaves. But by 1860, New England's industry had nearly four times as many spindles as the Middle Atlantic industry and accounted for nearly three-fourths of the country's output of cotton goods. The factory had demonstrated its superiority in the textile field.

It was simply a matter of time until other industries adopted the same organization. Because technological changes in wool production were slower, the production of woolen cloth tended to remain in the small mill longer than cotton production did. But after 1830, woolen factories began to adopt the Waltham system, and by 1860, the largest textile factories in the United States were woolen factories. Again, New Englanders far surpassed the rest of the country in combining factors of production in large units; two-thirds of America's woolen output in 1860 was made in New England.[1]

---

[1]It merits emphasis that cottage manufacture or putting-out system, where raw materials were taken to homes for processing (wool or cotton to be spun or yarn to be woven) and then to market, was prevalent in England but seldom used in the United States. U.S. manufactures for market came overwhelmingly from centralized plants. See Sokoloff and Dollar (1997).

Technological advances in iron and steel production, such as the blast furnace and rolling mill shown here, epitomized the "modern" nineteenth-century factory.

Iron and Other Factories

In most other industries as well, the decade of the 1830s was one of expansion and experimentation with new methods. In the primary iron industry, establishments by the 1840s dwarfed those of a quarter-century earlier. By 1845, for instance, the Brady's Bend Iron Company in western Pennsylvania owned

> *nearly 6,000 acres of mineral land and 5 miles of river front upon the Allegheny. It mined its own coal, ore, limestone, fire-clay, and fire-stone, made its own coke, and owned 14 miles of railway to serve its works. The plant itself consisted of 4 blast furnaces, a foundry, and rolling mills. It was equipped to perform all the processes, from getting raw materials out of the ground to delivering finished rails and metal shapes to consumers, and could produce annually between 10,000 and 15,000 tons of rails. It housed in its own tenements 538 laboring families. This company, with an actual investment of $1,000,000, was among the largest in America before the Civil War, though there were rival works of approximately equal capacity and similar organization.* (Clark 1916, 446)

In the anthracite region to the east, factory operation of furnaces and rolling mills had been achieved by 1850. Also by the 1850s, American factories were manufacturing arms, clocks and watches, and sewing machines.

How one industry could adopt new methods as a consequence of progress in another is shown by the fact that once the sewing machine was produced on a quantity basis, the boot and shoe industry developed factory characteristics. Carriages, wagons, and even farm implements were eventually produced in large numbers. Finally, where markets were more extensive, where there was a substantial investment in fixed plant, and where workers were subjected to formal discipline, some firms in the traditional mill industries other than the textile and iron industries achieved factory status. The great merchant flour mills of Baltimore and Rochester fell into this category, as did some of the large packing plants in New York, Philadelphia, Baltimore, and (after 1840) Cincinnati.

The Rise of Corporate Organization

In addition to size and organization, changes were also taking place in the legal concept of the business firm—the change from sole proprietorship and partnership organization to corporate organization (Economic Reasoning Proposition 4, laws and rules matter). The corporation gained prominence chiefly because some businesses required more capital than one person or a few people could provide. By 1810, the corporate form was commonplace for banks, insurance companies, and turnpike companies; in ensuing decades, canals and railroads could be financed only by tapping various sources of funds, from small merchants and professionals along proposed routes, to English capitalists thousands of miles away.

When it first appeared in the United States, the corporation lacked many of its present-day characteristics. Charters were granted by special acts of legislatures, and the question of the liability of stockholders was far from settled. Nevertheless, the corporation had a number of advantages over the sole proprietorship and the partnership, and its legal status came to be better defined than that of the joint-stock company. Of its unquestioned advantages, the most notable—in addition to the obvious one of attracting greater numbers of investors—were permanence and flexibility. The partnership and the sole proprietorship have one inescapable drawback: If one partner or the proprietor dies, the business is dissolved. The business can go on, of course, under a new partnership or proprietorship, but continuity of operation is contingent on the lives of particular individuals. The shares of a corporation, however, can be transferred, and investors, whether small or large, can enter and leave the business without destroying the structure of the corporation.

Early corporations did not have certain advantages that corporations have today, such as limited liability. Stockholders of the English joint-stock companies typically assumed "double liability"—that is, the stockholders were liable to the extent of their investment plus a like amount—and some states experimented with charters specifying either double liability or unlimited liability. After 1830, however, various states passed statutes providing for limited liability, and by 1860, this principle was generally accepted. Under limited liability, stockholders of a failed corporation could lose only the money they had invested in the venture.

The early requirement that incorporators of banks, insurance companies, canals, and railroads obtain their charters by the special act of a state legislature was not always a disadvantage. For those who had the political connections, this involved little uncertainty and expense, and obtaining a charter with exceptionally liberal provisions was always a possibility. Nevertheless, the politically unfavored could spend years lobbying futilely for corporate charters. As early as 1800, those who looked on incorporation by special act as "undemocratic" were agitating to secure "general" acts of incorporation—laws making it possible for any group, provided it observed and met prescribed regulations and requirements, to obtain a charter. Others, fearful that the corporation would spread too rapidly if their elected representatives did not review each application for charter, opposed general acts. In 1837, Connecticut passed the Connecticut General Incorporation Act, the first general act that made incorporation the right of anyone.

From that date, permissive general acts (acts allowing, but not requiring, incorporation under their provisions) were gradually placed on the statute books of most of the chief manufacturing states, and before 1861, the constitutions of 13 states required incorporation under general laws. In those states where permissive legislation had been enacted, incorporators continued until about 1870 to obtain special charters, which enabled the incorporators to secure more liberal provisions than they could under general laws.[2]

Leading Industries, 1860

The decline of household production and the rise in craftshops, mills, and factories dramatically changed the structure and location of manufacturing. By 1860, the total manufacturing labor force was nearly 1,530,000 (compared with almost 5,880,000 in agriculture). More than 96 percent of those engaged in manufacturing worked in 10 industries. These 10 industries are ranked in Table 10.1 by value added (value of total product minus raw material costs). Cotton goods ranked at the top, having grown from infancy 50 years earlier. Lumbering was a close second to cotton textiles. Looking now at ranking by number of employees, boots and shoes (third by value added) was the top employer, and men's clothing (fifth by value added) was nearly tied with cotton goods as the next highest employer. If iron products and machinery had been combined in a single category, their value added would have been the highest. Between 1850 and 1860, the doubling of the output of primary iron products and machinery forecast the shape of America's industrial future.

These industries were centered primarily in the Northeast. Cotton manufactures were located predominantly in New England, as were boots and shoes. Lumbering moved west and south but stayed strong in New England and the Middle Atlantic states. An overview of the location of industry, given in Table 10.2, demonstrates the primacy of the East in early manufacturing. Because the census counted even the smallest sawmills and gristmills as "manufacturing establishments," the large numbers for the West and the South are misleading. By any other criterion, New England and the Middle Atlantic states were

TABLE 10.1 UNITED STATES MANUFACTURES, 1860

ITEM	(1) NUMBER OF EMPLOYEES	(2) COST OF RAW MATERIAL	(3) VALUE OF TOTAL PRODUCT	(4) (3)–(2) VALUE ADDED BY MANUFACTURE	RANK BY VALUE ADDED
Cotton goods	114,955	$ 52,666,701	$107,337,783	$54,671,082	1
Lumber	75,595	51,358,400	104,928,342	53,569,942	2
Boots and shoes	123,026	42,728,174	91,889,298	49,161,124	3
Flour and meal	27,682	208,497,309	248,580,365	40,083,056	4
Men's clothing	114,800	44,149,752	80,830,555	36,680,803	5
Iron (cast, forged, rolled, and wrought)	48,975	37,486,056	73,175,332	35,689,276	6
Machinery	41,223	19,444,533	52,010,376	32,565,843	7
Woolen goods	40,597	35,652,701	60,685,190	25,032,489	8
Carriages, wagons, and carts	37,102	11,898,282	35,552,842	23,654,560	9
Leather	22,679	44,520,737	67,306,452	22,785,715	10

Source: Eighth Census of the United States: Manufactures, *1860.*

---

[2]In 1811, New York had passed a law that permitted incorporation, without special act, of certain manufacturing concerns with capitalization of less than $100,000.

TABLE 10.2 MANUFACTURING, BY SECTIONS, CENSUS OF 1860

SECTION	NUMBER OF FIRMS	CAPITAL INVESTED	EMPLOYMENT MALE	EMPLOYMENT FEMALE	ANNUAL VALUE OF PRODUCTS	VALUE ADDED BY MANUFACTURE
New England	20,671	$ 257,477,783	262,834	129,002	$ 468,599,287	$223,076,180
Middle Atlantic	53,287	435,061,964	432,424	113,819	802,338,392	358,211,423
Midwest	36,785	194,212,543	194,081	15,828	384,606,530	158,987,717
South	20,631	95,975,185	98,583	12,138	155,531,281	68,988,129
West	8,777	23,380,334	50,137	67	71,229,989	42,746,363
Territories	20,282	3,747,906	2,290	43	3,556,197	2,246,772
Totals	140,433	$1,009,855,715	1,040,349	270,897	1,885,861,676	$854,256,584

Source: Eighth Census of the United States: Manufactures, *1860.*

the leading regions. The figures for the Midwest reflect in part the rapid antebellum industrial growth of the Ohio Valley and the burgeoning of the Chicago area.

During the period from 1810 to 1860, the total value of manufactures increased from about $200 million to just under $2 billion, or roughly tenfold. Farming was still in first place as a means of earning a livelihood: The value added by manufacture in 1860 was markedly less than the value of three of America's major crops—corn, wheat, and hay—and capital investment in industry totaled less than one-sixth the value of farm land and buildings. Even then, however, the United States was second only to Great Britain in manufacturing.[3] Soon it would be the world's industrial leader as well as its agricultural leader. How was this remarkable achievement accomplished?

PREREQUISITES TO FACTORY PRODUCTION

The development of high-speed mass production required the introduction of machines and technology, standardization of items, continuous-process assembly lines of production, and new sources of power and energy. Advances in these areas increasingly led to the displacement of home manufactures and the craftshop. It was an evolutionary process, but in the longer view of history, it has been called the Industrial Revolution.

Machines and Technology

The Industrial Revolution that had begun in England in the late eighteenth century by no means guaranteed the immediate establishment of the factory system in America. In fact, the English sought to prevent dissemination abroad of the details of the new inventions. Parliament passed laws in 1774 and 1781 prohibiting the export of new industrial machinery, not unlike later laws that prohibited high-tech exports to Soviet bloc countries during the Cold War. In 1782, a law was passed to prevent labor pirating, the luring abroad of highly skilled British mechanics. Although these efforts possibly slowed the introduction of new machines and technologies in the United States, technology transfers occurred anyway. For example, on the eve of the Napoleonic wars, the Scofield brothers arrived in New England from Yorkshire and built water-powered wool-carding

---

[3]The *Twelfth Census of the United States,* quoting Mulhall's *Industries and Wealth of Nations,* placed the United States in fourth place after Great Britain, France, and Germany. But Douglass C. North shows convincingly that the United States ranked second (see North 1961, v).

machinery. They were preceded by Samuel Slater, who came to the United States in 1789 and, in cooperation with Moses Brown and William Almy of Providence, Rhode Island, built the first American spinning mill powered by water. More than a dozen small prototypes of their mill were built during the next decade in New England.

Largely because of the relatively high cost of labor in the United States, American managers tended to use the most nearly automatic machines available for a particular application. More important, they successfully innovated ways of organizing production that saved labor expense per unit of output. Their chief contributions—the two basic ideas that led to American preeminence in nineteenth-century manufacturing—were interchangeable parts and continuous-process manufacture. Both advances were allied with the development of machine tools and with changes in techniques of applying power.

Standardized Interchangeable Parts

The idea of standardizing a product and its various parts originated in Sweden in the early eighteenth century and before 1800 had been tried in France, Switzerland, and England. Through standardization, the parts of one product could be interchanged for the parts of a like product, facilitating manufacture and repair. The first permanently successful application of the idea in an important use was made in the American armament industry. At the turn of the nineteenth century, Eli Whitney and Simeon North almost simultaneously obtained contracts from the government to manufacture firearms by the interchangeable-parts method. It has long been customary to credit Whitney with the first successful manufacture by interchangeable parts, but the evidence does not substantiate his claim. Records suggest that North was using the "uniformity principle" as early as 1807 in making his pistols. Perhaps the first application of the idea in a way that would be followed later was made by John H. Hall, inventor and engineer at the Harper's Ferry Armory, who by 1817 was installing his system using metal-cutting and woodworking machines.[4] In any case, it took more than two years to make the essential innovations in the arms industry. Captain Hall's pattern turning greatly reduced the number of hours needed to shape asymmetrical rifle stocks. Drop-forging with dies was successfully introduced in about 1827. By 1855, Samuel Colt, who had invented his six-shooter years earlier, established an armory in which machine work of a high degree of accuracy was accomplished by skilled operators. From approximately mid-century on, the ultimate precision tool was no longer the craftsman's hand file.

Continuous Process and Assembly Lines

Although milling processes did not require assembly operations, continuous-process manufacture—production in which the raw materials move continuously through the factory—had its first successful application in the mills. One of the first to succeed was the American inventor Oliver Evans. In 1782, he built a flour mill in Philadelphia run by gravity, friction, and water power that moved grain through its processing with no human intervention other than guiding and monitoring. Continuous-process manufacture in its most significant form today, with motor-driven moving assemblies like those introduced by Henry Ford for automobile production, was an outgrowth of the successful interchangeable-parts production of firearms, clocks and watches, sewing machines, and agricultural implements. In the 1850s, agricultural implement companies actually used

---

[4]See Woodbury (1960). In Woodbury's view, interchangeable-parts manufacture involves four elements: (1) precision machine tools, (2) precision gauges or other measuring instruments, (3) uniform measurement standards, and (4) techniques of mechanical drawing.

conveyor belts to assemble the parts of major subassemblies in sequence, thus foreshadowing the mass production techniques of the early twentieth century.

Power and Energy

During the early years of manufacturing in the United States, water wheels furnished most of the motive power. Plentiful steadily moving rivers and streams ensured the availability of this dependable source of power, and readily available water power was further enhanced by technological improvements in water wheels.

A water wheel is always placed in a vertical position on a horizontal shaft and is moved at a comparatively low speed by direct action of the water. Wheels are classified by the way water is applied to turn them (see Figure 10.1). The undershot wheel, which was used in colonial times and for a while thereafter in frontier areas, was placed in the stream so that its blades were moved by the water passing underneath it. Although easy to install, the undershot wheel was inefficient, transmitting no more than 40 percent of the power applied to it. The overshot wheel was moved by water running from a flume across the top of the wheel into buckets covering its surface; the weight of the water in the buckets moved the wheel in the direction of the stream flow. The overshot wheel was more efficient, easy to install, and satisfactory wherever there was a good head of water, but the power it developed was not great enough for heavy industrial purposes. Consequently, the large manufacturing concerns almost invariably used the breast wheel. This type, too, was equipped with buckets, but the water struck the wheel short of its axle so that it rotated in an upstream direction; both the impulse of the water and its weight in the buckets enabled the wheel to utilize up to 75 percent of the applied power. Installed in multiples, the breast wheel developed sufficient horsepower to serve the largest early nineteenth-century industrial firms. The machinery of the Merrimack Manufacturing Company, for example, was run by eight breast wheels, each 30 feet in diameter with buckets 12 feet long.

The slow-moving and cumbersome water wheels could develop several thousand horsepower, but they had marked disadvantages. Power from a wheel was transmitted by wooden shafts and cogwheels and was limited by the strength of the entire mechanism. Furthermore, industrial location was restricted to stream sites, and the problem of finding sites, especially in industrialized areas, became a serious one. The first difficulty was partially overcome by making wheels and transmission parts of metal, the second by the improved engineering of dams and canals. The water turbine, which revolved on a vertical shaft, was much more efficient than a wheel and by the 1850s was adding rapidly to the power potential of the country.

Finally came steam power, although its introduction into U.S. manufacturing was slow for several reasons. In the beginning, the steam engine was extremely costly to operate. Breakdowns were frequent, and expert repair technicians were rare. In transportation, the

FIGURE 10.1

Water Wheel Designs

The three main engineering designs of water wheels that powered early textile and woodworking machinery are displayed here.

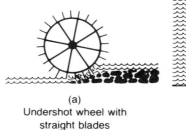

(a)
Undershot wheel with straight blades

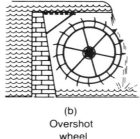

(b)
Overshot wheel

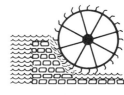

(c)
Crooked-blade undershot wheel (the "breast wheel")

steam engine could pull such heavy loads at such increased speeds that these disadvantages were more than offset, but in industry, water power remained cheaper than steam power for a long time. It has been estimated that, in 1812, only 11 engines of the high-pressure type developed by Oliver Evans were in use in this country (Clark 1916, 409).

During the next two decades, steam engines became more common in the South and West, but most of them were used in ironworks and glass factories that required fuel for other purposes or in mills that could not conveniently be located near water. Around 1840, manufacturers in New England and the Middle Atlantic states estimated the annual cost per horsepower of steam to be five or six times that of water. Within the next 20 years, improvements in metalworking technology lowered the cost of steam engines and improved both their efficiency and reliability. By the 1850s, steam engines were replacing water wheels in the heat-using industries and wherever stream flows were highly variable, as they were along the Ohio River. In New England, steam engines were being installed to power textile mills because of the serious lack of adequate power sites. As of 1860, water was still the chief source of power, but the years of the water wheel were clearly numbered.

Paralleling the rise of steam power, with a lag, was coal, which eventually became a major new source of energy. Because wood and, hence, charcoal were so cheap in the

© W. CODY/CORBIS

This fairly typical overshot water wheel was one used in the 20,000 sawmills and 14,000 flour mills reported in the 1860 national census.

United States, however, the increase in coal use was slowed in comparison with its rapid adoption in England. Coal, like water, had a major impact on the location of manufacturing. With adequate transportation facilities, coal power increasingly allowed factories to be built in urban centers, and after 1830, coal-powered factories increasingly became a feature of the rise of manufacturing in the United States.

Factor Proportions and Borrowing and Adapting Technology

Britain's head start in making machines gave the British a great advantage in manufacturing. Their machines typically embodied specific technological forms that reflected British relative costs of labor, capital, and raw materials. The relative costs of these inputs were different in the United States. Nineteenth-century Americans were short on labor and capital but long on raw materials and natural power sources (water). American industrialists had not only to copy English machines but also to adapt them to economize on labor, perhaps at the sacrifice of raw material usage. One example of their success is reflected in the comparison of the textile industries in each country. English textile firms averaged 17,000 spindles and 276 looms compared with 7,000 spindles and 163 looms in the United States. Robert Zevin's 1971 study of textiles reveals that the American cotton textiles industry had only 20 percent of Britain's spindles and 25 percent of its workers but processed 40 percent as much cotton. Clearly, the Americans had successfully adapted their equipment to save on scarce labor and capital.

The works of Lars Sandberg (1969) and later William Lazonick (1981) on the choice of techniques and their adoption reveals that technology was not uniform on both sides of the Atlantic. In textiles, the British became increasingly labor intensive and lowered the quality of their raw material inputs. Americans conserved labor by upgrading machinery and adopting higher grades of raw cotton or wool materials. Because Americans did not unionize as did British workers and were more mobile than British workers, American management could more easily substitute new machines to reduce its labor dependence and labor costs. Claudia Goldin and Kenneth Sokoloff (1982) add another consideration: Early manufacturers depended primarily on women and children. Where the opportunity costs of this labor were low, as in New England where farming produced a poor livelihood, women and children were relatively more available to supply factory labor. This encouraged the location of manufacturing there and supplied a labor force accepting of technological changes. These propositions by Goldin and Sokoloff have been scrutinized, tested, and supported by Lee Craig and Elizabeth Field-Hendry (1993).

In textiles, firearms, clocks and watches, and many other items, the ideas of standardization, interchangeable parts, and division of labor in assembly production processes were being widely applied. In 1851, at the Great Exhibition in London (in many ways like the World's Fair today), American products were a primary attraction. Though simple in design and not elegant or long lasting, they were practical, cheap, and functional. After all, they reflected the characteristics demanded by a population dominated by masses of farmers, pioneers, and workers who were, for the most part, unpretentious, practical people. Recall Economic Reasoning Proposition 1, scarcity forces us to make choices. In 1855, a British parliamentary committee visited the United States to determine the secret of the "American system," as it became known. They found, to their surprise, that American machinery was often technologically more sophisticated than its British counterpart. "Yankee Ingenuity" had become the wonder of the world.

But a paradox remains. Capital was relatively scarce in the United States—interest rates were high compared with those in Britain. Why, then, was it the Americans who built the ingenious machines, not the British? The answer is that skilled labor was even scarcer in the United States. In those industries that required skilled labor (firearms), it paid the Americans to substitute capital and natural resources (water power) for skilled labor. In industries that used less skilled labor, American industries used less capital per worker than their British counterparts. (James and Skinner 1985)

PRODUCTIVITY ADVANCES IN MANUFACTURES

The collective effects of the many and varied sources of productivity advance just discussed dramatically raised labor productivity in manufactures in the American Northeast. Estimates of the annual rates of growth of labor productivity by type of manufacture are given in Table 10.3 on this page. These ranges of percentage rates of advance are divided between capital-intensive industries and typically smaller-size firms of noncapital-intensive industries.

The comparable rates of advance of labor productivity by both categories of industries strongly suggest that capital deepening was not a prerequisite to higher output per worker, nor were these rates high for only a few select industries. A wide range of manufacturing industries exhibited high rates of productivity changes, even shops, mills, and small firms with limited mechanization and primitive power sources. This reinforces the perspective of economic growth as the cumulative impact of many incremental advances throughout the economy, similar to the pattern observed in chapter 9 in the analysis of productivity advance in steamboating.

TABLE 10.3 ANNUAL GROWTH RATES OF VALUE ADDED PER WORKER IN SELECTED MANUFACTURES IN THE NORTHEAST, 1820–1860

CAPITAL-INTENSIVE INDUSTRIES	CHANGE OF LABOR PRODUCTIVITY (%)
Cotton textiles	2.2–3.3%
Iron	1.5–1.7
Liquors	1.7–1.9
Flour/grist mills	0.6–0.7
Paper	4.3–5.5
Tanning	1.2–1.7
Wool textiles	2.7–2.8
OTHER INDUSTRIES	
Boots/shoes	2.0–2.1
Coaches/harnesses	2.0–2.4
Furniture/woodwork	2.9–3.0
Glass	2.5
Hats	2.4–2.5
Tobacco	0.1–2.4

Source: *Sokoloff, 1986, 698.*

PROTECTION FROM FOREIGN COMPETITION

After the peace of 1815, imports of English manufactured goods reached alarming proportions from the viewpoint of American businesses. Before 1815, duties on foreign goods had been set at rates that, although originally intended to protect, maximized government revenues in a hit-or-miss fashion. Growing protectionist sentiment in the Northeast gained enough support from the West and South to secure passage of the Tariff Act of 1816.

The tariff of 1816 levied ad valorem duties of 20 to 25 percent on most manufactured goods and 15 to 20 percent on raw materials. In general, the level of duties on manufactures did not prevent the entry of many goods at that time, although cheap cottons were shut out of the home market by specific duties (i.e., duties of so much per yard). Moreover, the tax on raw materials, particularly raw wool, lowered the expansion potential of domestic industries using raw wool inputs.

From 1816 until 1832, the protectionist tide rose; American producers of cottons, woolens, glass, and iron products received the greatest favors, with raw wool and hemp garnering their shares. Figure 10.2 traces the history of U.S. tariffs measured as rates, namely, duties collected as percentages of the values of dutiable imports. It shows the

FIGURE 10.2

Tariff Rates in the United States Since 1820

Tariff rates in the United States have bounced up and down, suggesting that in Congress, tariffs are a political football. Import-competing industries prefer high tariffs. The highest tariffs we have had were the Smoot-Hawley Tariff of 1930 and the "Tariff of Abominations" of 1828.

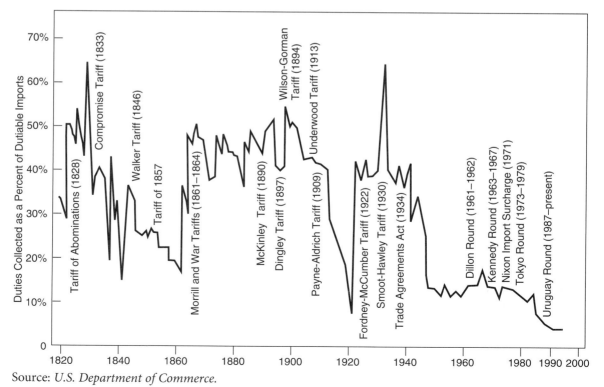

Source: *U.S. Department of Commerce.*

ECONOMIC INSIGHT 10.1

THE INCIDENCE OF THE TARIFF

As indicated by South Carolina's Nullification Ordinance in reaction to the "Tariff of Abomi-nations" (1828), the South had no enthusiasm for high tariffs. It fought against high tariffs just as the Northeast and Middle Atlantic states fought for them, with clear economic gains in mind.

The figure below illustrates the effect of a duty (d) on foreign cotton textiles. First, we derive total supply (S) as the horizontal sum of New England's supply (SNE) and Great Britain's (SGB). At price P, the quantity supplied by New England is QNE, equal to the line distance ab. And the amount supplied by Britain is QGB, equal to the line distance $aa1$. Total supply (s) at P is Q, the sum of QNE and QGB and equal to the line distance $ab1$, where the segment $a1b1$ is equal to $ab1$. Now we include the demand curve (D) and determine equilibrium at price P and quantity Q, where S and D intersect.

To see the effect of a duty (d) on British cotton textiles, we add it to SGB to get a new, higher cost supply curve SGBd inclusive of the tax. The tax, in effect, adds to the costs of going to the U.S. market for British producers. The result is a new supply schedule Sd above S by the amount of the duty. The new equilibrium quantity is Qd at price Pd. The government receives QGBd × d in revenues. Now we shall relate this changed equilibrium to the historical issues.

A *tariff* is a tax paid in part by consumers on dutiable imported goods. The tariff raised the price of all goods whether imported or not (P to Pd) and lowered the real income of consumers of these taxed goods. Since the duted items were largely imported manufactures, such as textiles, consumers had to pay more for manufactures when tariffs rose. Northeastern manufacturers, however, gained market shares and profits. (Check this by determining along the price line Pd the post duty quantities supplied by New England and Great Britain.) The losses of consumers outweighed the gains of manufacturers. But the manufacturers were better organized and could influence legislators.

The South lost because of high tariffs in another way. When the United States imported less, it placed fewer dollars in foreigners' hands. For example, with the English receiving fewer dollars for their textile exports to the United States, they had less foreign exchange (dollars) with which to purchase American exports. What was the leading U.S. export, and to whom? Cotton, to England.

Sending more cotton to New England only partially offset the reduction to England. Higher-priced cotton textiles meant lower quantities demanded overall (Qd rather than Q), which, in turn, meant lower quantities

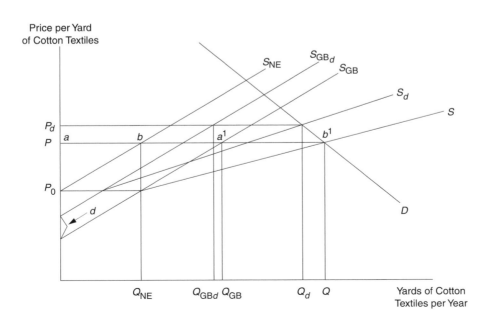

ECONOMIC INSIGHT 10.1

THE INCIDENCE OF THE TARIFF, Continued

demanded of raw cotton materials. Southern planters simply lost customers abroad faster than they gained them at home.

We see that the tariff transfers money to the protected industries, helping the owners of capital and the workers employed there. It takes money away from consumers and from foreign producers. The government gains from the tax revenues collected. In short, tariffs take money from one group and give it to another. As John James (1978) has shown, the high antebellum tariffs redistributed wealth and resources from the South to northeastern industries, a transfer southerners abhorred. From the southern perspective, the terms of trade deteriorated; prices of their exports fell, and prices of their imports rose.

Tariffs are noteworthy for their political popularity. They are often advocated, for example, by politicians to protect American workers from "cheap" foreign labor. But these were not the original arguments for U.S. tariffs. The political economy of tariffs was first expressed in the first Tariff Act in 1789:

Whereas it is necessary for the support of the government, for the discharge of the debts of the United States, and the encouragement of manufactures, that duties be laid on goods, wares, and merchandise imported.

So the original purposes of the tariff were clear: to generate government revenues and to protect infant American industry. Initially, tariffs successfully added revenue to government coffers. In 1790, 99.9 percent

of total federal revenue was derived from tariffs. In 1860, it was still 94 percent. (Today, it is less than 1 percent of federal revenues, and accordingly, we never hear this argument—or seldom do.) What about the other purpose, to protect infant industries? Success in that area appears dubious.

When peace came in 1815, ending the protection from foreign competition caused by war, low-grade British textiles flooded U.S. markets. In 1816, Francis Lowell went to Congress asking for a tariff on low-grade textiles competing with the ones his established mills produced. High-grade cotton cloth like that made in the infant firms in Rhode Island received no protection. In short, the Lowell mills gained, but Rhode Island's infant industry did not. The protection received was primarily a political matter. Who primarily paid the higher prices on the tariff-protected low-grade cloth? Again, it was the South, primarily for textiles going to slaves.

Were later higher tariffs a necessary condition for the rise of manufacturing? We note that in 1830, when the nullification controversy raged, the tariff rate on duties items exceeded 60 percent. By 1860, the tariff rate was just below 20 percent. In short, when manufacturing was growing rapidly (albeit faster in the 1830s and 1850s than in the 1840s), it did so over three decades while tariff protection was falling. But tariffs appear to have been important to U.S. cotton textiles. According to Mark Bils, Peter Temin, and Knick Harley, in independent studies, much of the U.S. cotton manufactures would have been competed away by the English without high tariffs (see Bils 1984; Temin 1988; Harley 1992).

Tariff Act of 1828 realizing a record high, not to be matched again until the Smoot-Hawley Tariff of 1930.

In general, the Northeast and Middle Atlantic states favored high tariffs; the South did not. The political shenanigans leading to the high tariff of 1828—the "Tariff of Abominations"—precipitated agitation in the South and necessitated a compromise within only a few years. In fact, a severe threat to the Union was South Carolina's Nullification Ordinance, which was legislated even after downward revisions in import duties had been made in 1832. The Compromise Tariff of 1833 provided that all duties would be reduced to a maximum of 20 percent ad valorem within a decade.

But only two months after the 20 percent maximum level was reached in 1842, the Whigs (the National Republicans who had just gained control of the White House) passed a bill in which rates reverted to about the protective level of 10 years before. President John Tyler, even though a southerner, accepted it because he felt this action would provide more revenue for the government. With the return of the Democrats to power in

1845, more moderate tariffs were rapidly secured, and the Walker Tariff of 1846 set an example that was followed until 1861.

The good times of the 1850s and the consequent increase in imports so swelled the revenues from tariffs that the government achieved great surpluses. The piling up of cash in U.S. Treasury vaults led to a general reduction in rates, and many items were placed on the free list. Just before the Civil War, it appeared that the United States might join the United Kingdom as a free-trade country. As shown in Figure 10.2, tariffs in 1860 averaged less than 20 percent of the value of dutiable imports (15 percent of the value of all imports), levels that had only moderate protective significance.

SELECTED REFERENCES AND SUGGESTED READINGS

Bils, Mark. "Tariff Protection and Production in the Early U. S. Cotton Textile Industry." *Journal of Economic History* 44 (1984): 1033–1045.

Clark, Victor S. *History of Manufactures in the United States 1607–1860.* Washington, D.C.: Carnegie Institution of Washington, 1916.

Cole, Arthur H. *American Wool Manufacture*, Vol. 1. Cambridge, Mass.: Harvard University Press, 1926.

Craig, Lee A., and Elizabeth B. Field-Hendry. "Industrialization and the Earnings Gap: Regional and Sectoral Tests of the Goldin-Sokoloff Hypothesis." *Explorations in Economic History* 30 (1993): 60–80.

Goldin, Claudia, and Kenneth Sokoloff. "Women, Children, and Industrialization in the Early Republic: Evidence from the Manufacturing Censuses." *Journal of Economic History* (December 1982).

_____. "The Relative Productivity Hypothesis of Industrialization: The American Case, 1820 to 1850." *Quarterly Journal of Economics* 69 (August 1984).

Harley, C. Knick. "International Competitiveness of the Antebellum American Cotton Textile Industry." *Journal of Economic History* 52 (1992): 559–584.

James, John A. and Jonathan, S. Skinner. "The Resolution of the Labor-Scarcity Paradox." *The Journal of Economic History* 45 (Sep., 1985): 513–540.

James, John. "The Welfare Effects of the Ante-Bellum Tariff: A General Equilibrium Analysis." *Explorations in Economic History* 15 (1978): 231–256.

Lazonick, William H. "Production Relations, Labor Productivity, and Choice of Technique: British and U.S. Cotton Spinning." *Journal of Economic History* 41 (1981): 491–516.

North, Douglass C. *The Economic Growth of the United States 1790–1860.* Englewood Cliffs, N.J.: Prentice Hall, 1961.

Sandberg, Lars G. "American Rings and English Mules: The Role of Economic Rationality" *The Quarterly Journal of Economics* 83 (Feb., 1969): 25–43.

Sokoloff, Kenneth L. "Productivity Growth in Manufacturing during Early Industrialization: Evidence from the American Northeast, 1820–1860." In *Long-Term Factors in American Economic Growth*, eds. Stanley L. Engerman and Robert E. Gallman, 698. Chicago: University of Chicago Press, 1986.

Sokoloff, Kenneth L., and David R. Dollar. "Agricultural Seasonality and the Organization of Manufacturing in Early Industrial Societies: The Contrast between England and the United States." *Journal of Economic History* (1997).

Temin, Peter. "Product Quality and Vertical Integration in the Early Cotton Textile Industry." *Journal of Economic History* 48 (1988): 891–907.

Woodbury, Robert S. "The Legend of Eli Whitney and Interchangeable Parts." *Technology and Culture* 2, no. 1 (1960): 235–253.

Zevin, Robert B. "The Growth of Cotton Textile Production after 1815." In *The Reinterpretation of American Economic History*, eds. Robert Fogel and Stanley Engerman. New York: Harper & Row, 1971.

_____. *The Growth of Manufacturing in Early Nineteenth-Century New England.* New York: Arno, 1975.

Labor during the Early Industrial Period

Before 1860, most of the U.S. population lived in rural areas, and most workers were self-employed on farms and in craftshops. Nevertheless, after the War of 1812, rapid industrialization and urbanization, especially in the Northeast and Middle Atlantic states, transformed the working conditions and living standards of many Americans who depended on their labor for a living. Real wages—monetary wages adjusted for the cost of living—rose between 1820 and 1860; unskilled workers' earnings fell relative to those of skilled workers as the supply of unskilled labor swelled through immigration; and working conditions became less personal as more and more workers changed from self-employment to working for an employer. It was a period when the first stirrings of a labor movement began in the United States and when the right to vote spread in the Western world. These changes occurred as economic growth increased and industrialization advanced and spread.

THE GROWTH OF THE POPULATION AND THE LABOR FORCE

The population of the United States grew rapidly during the first half of the nineteenth century. In 1800, there were 5,308,000 Americans; by 1860, there were 31,443,000, a growth rate of about 3 percent per year, an extremely high rate in comparison with other countries. Population grew rapidly because both the rate of natural increase and the rate of immigration were high.

Families were large in the early republic. Although the evidence is fragmentary, it indicates that the average woman in 1800 would marry rather young, before age 20, and would give birth to about seven children. Few men or women would remain unmarried. Fertility declined during the first half of the nineteenth century, a trend that began in rural areas well before industrialization and urbanization became the norm. Economic historians have offered a number of hypotheses to explain this rather puzzling decline in fertility. Yasukichi Yasuba (1962), who was one of the first to examine the problem, suggests the "land availability" hypothesis: As population and land prices rose, the cost to farmers of endowing their children with a homestead rose, and so parents chose to have smaller families to ensure a good life for their children. William A. Sundstrom and Paul A. David (1976, 1988) have described an interesting variation. The growth of nonfarm employment in rural areas forced farmers to provide more economic opportunities for their children to keep them "down on the farm." Maris A. Vinovskis (1972) notes that more conventional factors—especially the growth of urbanization, industrialization, and literacy—also played a role.

FIGURE 11.1

Additions to the U.S. Labor Force from Migration, 1800–1860

Laborers came in huge numbers during the post-1845 period to a nation rich in land and rapidly increasing its stock of capital.

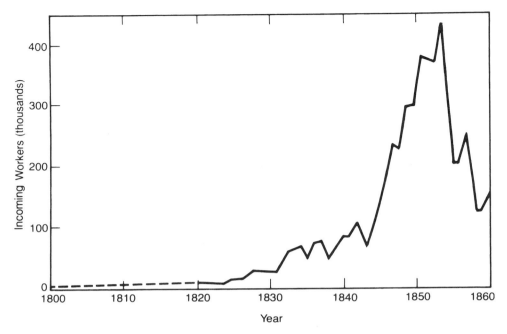

Source: *Historical Statistics, 1958.*

Mortality was also high in the early republic, near the 20 percent level for white infants below the age of one. Nevertheless, birthrates were so high that the increase in the population due to natural factors continued to be strongly positive despite declining fertility and high mortality.

Although the high birthrate dominates the story of rapid total population growth, immigration also had a significant impact, especially on labor markets because the flow of immigrants was rich in unskilled male workers in their prime working years. This is illustrated in Figure 11.1, which shows the number of workers coming to the United States. The huge increase toward the end of the period was created by events in Europe: the potato famine in Ireland (which also affected the continent of Europe, although to a lesser extent) and political unrest in Europe. While immigration accounted for only 3 percent of the total U.S. population growth from 1820 to 1825, it accounted for between 25 and 31 percent from 1845 to 1860.

THE CHANGING LABOR FORCE DISTRIBUTION AND COMPOSITION

Table 11.1 shows the continued dominance of agriculture throughout the period. It also shows how differently labor was allocated in 1860 compared with 1810. Mining took the biggest jump, largely because of the California Gold Rush, but more important is the twentyfold increase of workers in manufacturing. On the eve of the Civil War, 1.5 million workers labored in manufacturing, most of them in the Northeast and Middle Atlantic states. In absolute numbers, agricultural workers grew the most, but manufacturing workers grew relatively. The economy was changing its structure from one of agriculture to one of manufacturing, a normal pattern of modern economic growth and development.

TABLE 11.1 LABOR FORCE DISTRIBUTION, 1810 TO 1860 (IN THOUSANDS)

YEAR	TOTAL	AGRI-CULTURE	FISHING	MINING	CON-STRUCTION	MANU-FACTURES	TRANS-PORTATION	TRADE	SERVICES
1810	2,330	1,950	6	11	—	—	60	—	82
1820	3,135	2,470	14	13	—	—	50	—	130
1830	4,200	2,965	15	22	—	—	70	—	190
1840	5,660	3,570	24	32	290	500	112	350	285
1850	8,250	4,520	30	102	410	1,200	155	530	430
1860	11,110	5,880	31	176	520	1,530	225	890	715

Source: *Adapted from Lebergott 1964, 510.*

Factories and Workers

As the economy and especially urban centers grew, and as economic unification progressed, output was sold in larger, more integrated markets. In addition, as shown in Table 11.2, the size of firms grew, as reflected in the number of employees per firm. For example, the number of workers per firm in cotton textiles nearly tripled and more than doubled in wool textiles and in hats and caps between 1820 and 1850. Pressures were great to achieve volume at the expense of artistry, and the small artisanal shops were increasingly giving way to the factory. This change in firm size was apparent both in mechanized or mechanizing industries (cotton and wool textiles) and in nonmechanized industries (hats, books, and shoes). So mechanization was only part of the story of this trend toward larger production units. Another key change was the greater division of labor, diminishing the proportion and role of workers with general skills. A more intense workplace under careful supervision aimed for standardized products, an early form of quality control. Such a transition in a nonmechanized shop is described by an observer, B. E. Hazard:

> *He [Gideon Howard, a manufacturer of shoes in South Randolph, Massachusetts] had a "gang" over in his twelve-footer who fitted, made and finished: one lasted, one*

TABLE 11.2 EMPLOYEES PER FIRM IN NORTHEASTERN MANUFACTURING, 1820 AND 1850

	1820		1850		
	EMPLOYEES PER FIRM	NUMBER OF FIRMS OBSERVED	EMPLOYEES PER FIRM	NUMBER OF FIRMS OBSERVED	RATIO OF FIRM SIZE IN 1850 TO THAT IN 1830
Boots and shoes	19.1	15	33.6	72	1.76
Cotton textiles	34.6	92	97.5	5,856	2.82
Flour and grist milling	2.4	90	1.8	5,128	0.75
Glass	56.9	8	64.6	76	1.14
Hats and caps	8.4	32	17.0	812	2.02
Iron and iron products	19.5	73	24.2	1,562	1.24
Liquors	2.7	165	5.0	633	1.85
Paper	14.3	33	22.4	12	1.57
Tanning	3.8	126	4.2	3,233	1.11
Wool and mixed textiles	10.6	107	24.5	1,284	2.31

Source: *Adapted from the 1820 and 1850 Census of Manufactures, as provided in Sokoloff 1984, 354.*

pegged and tacked on soles, one made fore edges, one put on heels and "pared them up," and in cases of handsewed shoes, two or three sewers were needed to keep the rest of the gang busy…. These groups of men in a ten-footer gradually took on a character due to specialization demanded by the markets with higher standards and need of speed in output. Instead of all the men working there being regularly trained shoe-makers, perhaps only one would be, and he was a boss contractor, who took out from a central shop so many cases to be done at a certain figure and date, and hired shoemakers who had "picked up" the knowledge of one process and set them to work under his supervision. One of the gang was a laster, another a pegger, one an edge-maker, one a polisher. Sometimes, as business grew, each of these operators would be duplicated. Such work did away with the old seven-year apprenticeship system. (Sokoloff 1984, 357)

Another characteristic of this transition to larger firms, at least initially in most manufacturing firms, was the increase in the proportion of the labor force composed of women and children. Larger firms typically exhibited a proportionately large share of simple and relatively narrowly defined tasks, such as machine tending, starting materials in machines, carrying materials, and other simple tasks. A key problem for many firms was hiring unskilled but able workers. In New England, these were mostly women, especially before the large waves of immigration in the late 1840s and 1850s.

The Rhode Island and Waltham Systems

Mill and factory owners in the textile industry generally solved their employment problems in one of two ways. Under the *Rhode Island system*, they hired whole families, assigned father, mother, and children to tasks suitable to their strength and maturity, and housed the families in company-constructed tenements. South of Boston, the Rhode Island system was used almost exclusively, partly because child labor was first introduced there in imitation of English methods, and partly because the mule spinning typical of the area required both heavy and light work. A second system, called the *Waltham system*, was introduced in Waltham, Massachusetts, by Francis Cabot Lowell and the Boston Associates. It employed women in their late teens and early twenties who worked in large factories. Housed in dormitories or boarding houses, they remained under the careful supervision of matrons who kept any taint of disreputability from the young women. (Recall Economic Reasoning Propositions 1, scarcity forces us to make choices; 2, choices impose costs; and 4, laws and rules matter in Economic Insight 1.1 on page 8).

A key impetus to the Waltham system was the low female-to-male wage ratio in agriculture in the New England area. This argument was introduced by Claudia Goldin and Ken Sokoloff (1982), and it has been buttressed by Lee Craig and Elizabeth Field-Hendry (1993). By contrast, the female-to-male wage ratio was higher and more steady in the South, which did not industrialize until much later. In the North, using the Waltham system, rapid advances in productivity in the mills raised the value and earnings of the women working there. The initially low female-to-male wage ratio rose as industries dominated by female labor experienced above-average productivity increases from 1815 to 1860. During these 45 years, female earnings rose from about one-third to nearly one-half of male wages. In short, low-cost female labor contributed significantly to the initiation of industrialization, and in turn, women's earnings in New England rose relative to men's in the antebellum period because of industrialization. Moreover, by drawing women away from agriculture in the North, the Waltham system and other female work opportunities in industry increased the relative value and earnings of women who remained in farming. The weekly wage of farm women more than doubled from 1830 to 1860.

© AFL/CIO/PHOTO RESEARCHERS

Child labor in spinning was common, especially in areas south of Boston; a family-based labor system known as the Rhode Island system *developed there.*

Hours of work in the early factories were long. A 12-hour day was considered reasonable, and half an hour off for meals was standard. From sunrise to sunset, it was possible to operate machinery without artificial light, and in wintertime, candles furnished enough illumination to permit operation into the evening. Because of the slow speeds of the early machines, the work pace was not great; for this reason, women and children could work 72 hours per week without physical breakdown.

The life of a New England textile worker was tiresome and drab, although it was not noticeably worse than the life of a poor New England farmer, whose dawn-to-dusk regimen left little time for pleasure and other pursuits. As noted, the factory offered young women an escape from the low pay, boredom, and isolation of farm life. Their next best alternative for work (Economic Reasoning Proposition 2, choices impose costs) was typically farm work or to join their mothers in handweaving or making straw hats, palmleaf hats, or shoes. Taking another perspective, New England factory workers generally escaped the harshness subjected to English workers during the first decades of the factory system. Undoubtedly, largely because of greater labor scarcity, American manufacturers were compelled to maintain a certain standard of decency to attract and hold the labor they wanted. Nor does evidence show that American factory owners were as cruel to children as some English employers.

It was in the cities that the most negative aspects of industrialization were first witnessed, both in England and the United States. The worst conditions were in the so-called sweatshops, where workers worked 14 to 16 hours a day in the garment industries of New York, Philadelphia, and Boston. And common laborers who sold their services to transportation companies, urban building contractors, or factory and mill owners found themselves in an unenviable position when stiff competition from immigrant labor retarded the growth of real wages. For most workers, however, the antebellum period was one of rising wages and higher standards of material well-being.

THE IMPACT OF IMMIGRATION

Similar to current changes in the labor force, mainly from Asian and Hispanic immigrants, further composition changes came from immigration. As shown in Table 11.3, the large waves of immigrants who arrived in the 1840s and 1850s came principally from three countries: England, Ireland, and Germany. A steady stream of immigrants from England flowed into the United States until the decade of the Civil War; the Irish and the Germans came in ever-increasing numbers through the mid-1850s, repelled by conditions at home and attracted by economic opportunities in a new land. The tragic potato famine of 1845 to 1847 precipitated the heavy Irish emigration. Fleeing starvation and the oppression of hated absentee landlords, the Irish found employment as common laborers and factory hands. (As many American laborers moved west to join the gold rush, opportunities opened up for the new arrivals.) The census of 1850 reported nearly 1 million Irish in the United States, 40 percent of them in large cities, where their "shanty towns" became the notorious slums of the era. The Germans came a little later, following the failure of the democratic and nationalistic revolutions of 1848. Within 15 years, 1.3 million had arrived. Most Germans, having a little capital, settled on farms in the Midwest, but almost one-third of them swelled the populations of booming cities such as Cincinnati, Chicago, Milwaukee, and St. Louis.

Immigration was also having its effects on the sexual composition of the labor force. By 1860, women constituted only one-fifth of the manufacturing labor force, indicating the lessening relative importance of textile manufacture and the competition of cheap immigrant labor, most of which was male. As it is today, this was a period of significant change in women's social roles, but then the trend was toward domestic pursuits. The cotton textile industry still employed the most females (many of whom were children); the clothing and shoe industries were second and third in this respect, ahead of woolen textiles. Nevertheless, as Pamela Nickless has shown, despite the transition in the late 1840s from predominantly women workers to male Irish workers, the advance of labor productivity in the textile mills remained high and steady, averaging 4.5 percent annually between 1836 and 1860 (Nickless 1978, 288). Moreover, the slums and initial poor labor opportunities for Irish and other immigrants did not lock them into poverty. Upward mobility and wealth accumulation accompanying changes in jobs and location by the immigrants improved their well-being (see Ferrie 1994).

TABLE 11.3 AVERAGE YEARLY IMMIGRATION BY ORIGIN, 1845–1860 (IN THOUSANDS)

YEAR	TOTAL	GREAT BRITAIN	IRELAND	GERMANY	OTHER
1845–1850	233	34	107	66	26
1851–1855	350	47	139	129	35
1856–1860	170	38	44	61	27

Source: *Historical Statistics 1958.*

THE WAGES OF MALE LABOR IN MANUFACTURING

Although female earnings rose relative to men's in the antebellum period, the average wages of adult males working in manufacturing concerns in New England and the Middle Atlantic states grew dramatically between 1820 and 1860. Annual wage earnings of these workers averaged $267 in 1820, $292 in 1832, $341 in 1850, and $360 in 1860 (see Sokoloff and Villaflor 1992, 36). In today's money, it would take about $7,400 to purchase the same amount of goods and services with the 1860 earnings.

Consumer prices fell between 1820 and the mid-1830s; then they rose, passing slightly above the 1820 level by the late 1830s. By the mid-1840s, prices had fallen below the mid-1830s floor. Then they rose again in the early 1850s. To account for these fluctuations, we must adjust the money wages by a consumer price index; this will show the changes in wages of constant purchasing power. Table 11.4 provides these adjustments and shows indexes of real wages for adult males by geographic area, level of urbanization, and firm size. For all workers together (bottom row), real wages grew between 60 and 90 percent (101 to 159 or 191) from 1820 to 1860; on average, wages rose between 1.2 and 1.6 percent per year.

Inspection of Table 11.4 reveals many important features of workers' earnings. The period of fastest growth of real wages was between 1820 and 1832—a range of 2.2 to 3.7 percent per annum, depending on place and firm size. Between 1832 and 1850, the

TABLE 11.4 INDEXES OF REAL WAGES FOR ADULT MALES IN NORTHEASTERN MANUFACTURING BY GEOGRAPHIC AREA, URBANIZATION, AND SIZE OF FIRM, 1820 TO 1860

WEIGHTED[a]	1820	1832	1850	1860	PER ANNUM GROWTH RATE, 1820–1860
Middle Atlantic	100	122–143	159–202	157–188	1.2–1.6
Rural	90	118–139	131–166	166–199	1.6–2.1
Urban	111	150–176	165–209	154–185	0.8–1.3
Major urban	115	—	171–217	151–180	0.7–1.2
Small	81	93–108	129–163	140–168	1.4–1.9
Medium	106	128–151	142–180	163–195	1.1–1.6
Large	110	123–144	171–216	159–190	0.9–1.2
New England	101	131–154	149–188	164–197	1.3–1.7
Rural	95	133–156	143–181	156–187	1.3–1.8
Urban[b]	110	130–153	150–190	165–198	1.2–1.5
Major urban	122	170–200	154–195	182–218	1.0–1.5
Small[c]	90	125–147	159–201	172–206	1.7–2.2
Medium	99	127–149	152–193	163–195	1.3–1.8
Large	110	133–157	146–185	164–196	1.0–1.5
Total	101	128–150	155–197	159–191	1.2–1.6

[a]Weighted averages are weighted by number of employees in each group.
[b]Urban firms are those located in counties with a city of 10,000 or more; major urban, the same for 25,000 or more.
[c]Small firms, 1 to 5 workers; medium, 6 to 15; large, 16 or more.

Source: *Sokoloff and Villaflor 1992, 36.*

© BETTMANN/CORBIS

Women, whose wages were far below men's, made up a large portion of the early industrial labor force. Women's earnings began to close that gap by the end of the antebellum era.

pace of advance slowed to between 1.1 and 1.5 percent. Little gain in real wages in manufacturing occurred during the 1850s.

Wages were at about the same levels in New England as in the Middle Atlantic states, and they grew at about the same rate. This reveals a labor market of workers and employers who were responsive (as sellers and buyers at the margin) and who moved and/or offered terms that arbitraged away geographic wage differences. In monetary (not real) terms, annual manufacturing wages in New England were only about 1 percent higher than in the Middle Atlantic states in 1820. This difference was still only 5 percent by 1860.

As shown in Table 11.4, in 1820, manufacturing workers in rural areas earned less than those in urban areas, who in turn earned less than those in major urban areas. A similar relation for 1820 is seen in the earnings among workers by size of firm: the larger the firm, the more the pay. But this was no longer true by 1860. Rural manufacturing real wages grew faster than urban wages, and the earnings in smaller firms rose faster than in larger firms.

Here again we see the erosion of wage gaps. Improvements in transportation enhanced labor mobility and made both product and labor markets more competitive. As navigable waterways spread and improved and railroads advanced, markets became more integrated, and wage rates converged. These market forces had disproportionately large effects on the rural areas and outlying hinterlands, pulling them into the market and affording them opportunities for specialization.

English–American Wage Gaps

Although wage gaps among the industrializing states were low, transportation costs sustained significant wage gaps between England and the United States. When American industry started to develop in the early nineteenth century, the wages of adult laborers were much higher in the United States than in England or other countries. Table 11.5, based on work by Nathan Rosenberg (1967), shows pay differentials classified by various skills for the years 1820 through 1821. Across all skill categories listed, wages were higher in the United States than in England.

By and large, these pay differentials are attributable to the fact that a floor under the remuneration of labor in industry was set by rewards in agriculture. Well into the 1800s, there were no insuperable obstacles, either of distance or expense, to obtaining a fertile farm in the United States. Output per worker in agriculture was relatively high, and the course of agricultural technology in the early nineteenth century increased output per person. Moreover, farmers in America, who ordinarily owned their own land, received, in addition to their own wages and those of their families, elements of rent and profit that in England went to the landlord. Therefore, U.S. land abundance added to the apparent wage gap between American and English workers, making the income or wealth gap between typical workers larger than the wage gap.

International labor mobility, at least in the early nineteenth century, failed to close these observed wage differentials. Sharp increases in immigration in the late 1830s and throughout the 1840s and 1850s led to a narrowing of the wage differential between American and English labor; even so, the floor for U.S. industrial wages was, according to a consensus of voluminous testimony, still relatively high in 1860.

TABLE 11.5 WAGE DIFFERENTIALS BY SKILL BETWEEN ENGLAND AND THE UNITED STATES, 1820 TO 1821 (ENGLISH WAGE = 100)

WORKERS	U.S. WAGES
Skilled	
Carpenter	150
Mason	147
Best machine makers, forgers, etc.	77 to 90
Ordinary machine makers	114 to 129
Unskilled	
Common laborer	135
Farm laborer	123 to 154
Servant, maid	149 to 224
Common mule spinners in cotton mills	106 to 137
Common mule spinners in woolen mills	115
Weavers on hand looms	122
Women in cotton mills	102 to 153
Women in woolen mills	128
Boys 10 to 12 years old	115

Source: Adapted from Rosenberg 1967, 226.

TABLE 11.6 RATIOS OF DAILY WAGES OF MACHINISTS TO COMMON LABORERS IN URBAN MASSACHUSETTS, 1825–1860

YEAR	PERCENT
1825	150%
1831–1840	156
1837	185
1845	169
1841–1850	190
1851–1860	220

Source: *Wright 1889, 22, 54, and 55; as quoted in Williamson and Lindert 1980, 71.*

Skilled–Unskilled Wage Ratios

More important perhaps, from the perspective of free American workers, was the change in relative wages among various "grades" or skill levels. During the first decades of the nineteenth century, as throughout most of the colonial period, the premiums paid for artisan skills in the United States were typically less than those paid in England. "Premiums" reflect the extra amounts paid to skilled labor above wages paid to unskilled labor. Skilled American workers typically earned more than skilled British workers, but the skilled-to-unskilled U.S. wage ratio was lower than the skilled-to-unskilled English wage ratio. However, the evidence in Table 11.5 shows that this was not uniformly true. The lower ratio is most clearly evident in the machine makers skill category when compared with common or farm labor.

The relatively low premium paid for skilled labor in early nineteenth-century America resulted primarily from the greater pulling power of agricultural expansion on unskilled labor and the higher proportion of skilled British immigrants entering the United States before mass immigration began (see Habakkuk 1962).

By the 1820s, however, this skill premium began to advance. For example, Table 11.6 shows the ratio of machinists' daily wages to those of common laborers in urban Massachusetts during the antebellum period. See Economic Insight 11.1 on page 193 to explore questions raised by this trend. Although these widening pay differentials may have varied somewhat regionally, they generally represented a broad pattern of advance (for further evidence on this point see Williamson and Lindert 1980).[1]

GROWING INEQUALITY OF INCOME

Advancing pay differentials may have contributed to a growing sense of class consciousness. They certainly contributed to increased inequality of income and wealth. According to evidence on wealth trends provided by Jeffrey Williamson and Peter Lindert (1980), we find that between 1774 and 1860 wealth concentrations grew significantly. Growing inequality was a sharp break with the stable (but unequal) pattern of aggregate wealth concentration prevalent during the colonial period. In 1774, 12.6 percent of total assets were held by the top 1 percent of free wealth holders, and the richest 10 percent held slightly less than half of total assets. By 1860, the wealthiest 1 percent held 29 percent of U.S. total assets, while the top 10 percent held 73 percent (Williamson and Lindert 1980, 36). In short, the share held by the richest 1 percent more than doubled, and that of the

---

[1]For work challenging Williamson and Lindert's view and based on labor contracts at military installations, see Margo and Villaflor (1987).

ECONOMIC INSIGHT 11.1

THE ANTEBELLUM LABOR MARKET

Two features of the antebellum labor market beg for more explicit economic analysis: first, why did the rapid rise in early nineteenth-century real wages in U.S. manufacturing slow to nearly zero in the 1850s (Table 11.4)? Second, why did skilled wages rise relative to unskilled wages between 1830 and 1860 (Table 11.6)? Supply and demand will serve as our analytical guide, and we can add demographic evidence to support the hypotheses empirically.

Figure 11.2 addresses the first question. Before 1840, demand shifts exceeded the supply shifts, and wages rose. After 1840, the supply increase was larger than normal. The supply shift was approximately the same as the demand shift, and wages changed little if at all.

FIGURE 11.2
The Market for
Manufacturing Workers

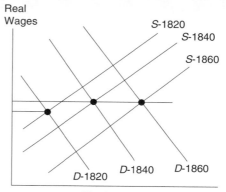

Figure 11.3 addresses the second question. While both the supply and demand for skilled and unskilled labor grew dramatically over the period, the growth in the supply of unskilled labor (*S*-1840 to *S*-1860, Figure 11.3B) accelerated in the 1840s and 1850s and grew relative to the supply of skilled labor (*S*-1840 to *S*-1860, Figure 11.3A). This lowered the wages of unskilled workers relative to those of skilled workers.

FIGURE 11.3
The Market for
Manufacturing Workers
Separated by Skill

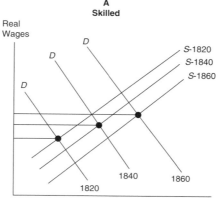

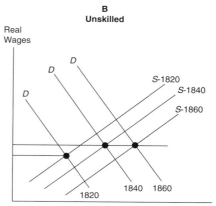

ECONOMIC INSIGHT 11.1

THE ANTEBELLUM LABOR MARKET, Continued

We now turn to the demographic evidence. The population data given in Table 11.7 reveal dramatic gains. The underlying rate of advance in the totals is 3.3 percent per annum. No European nation at the time showed anything like this rate of advance, not even by half. In addition, the bulge in immigration occurred after 1840 (see Figure 11.1, page 184). From Table 11.7 we see that immigration accounted for only 3.0 percent per annum of population growth, 1820–1825, but was 25–31 percent 1845–1860.

The combined effects of natural increases and immigration raised the average (median) age of the population from 16 to 19 and swelled the proportion of people in their working years and in the labor force. Between 1820 and 1860, the ratio of gainfully employed to total population grew from 33 to 36 percent—a gain of 9 percent (3/33rds). Moreover, the proportion of people living in urban places more than doubled between 1820 and 1850 and nearly doubled between 1840 and 1860 (Table 11.7). The demographic evidence is consistent with the wage changes observed. Consistency, however, is not proof of causation. Other hypotheses may also explain the record. Recall Economic Reasoning Proposition 5, evidence and theory give value to opinions.

TABLE 11.7 BASIC POPULATION DATA, 1790–1860

YEAR	POPULATION (IN MILLIONS)			PERCENTAGES		NET IMMIGRANTS' SHARE OF POPULATION CHANGE IN PREVIOUS DECADE
	TOTAL	WHITE	NONWHITE	NONWHITE	URBAN	
1790	3.9	3.2	0.7	17.9	5.2	n.a.
1800	5.3	4.3	1.0	18.9	6.1	n.a.
1810	7.2	5.9	1.3	18.1	7.3	3.3
1820	9.6	7.9	1.8	18.8	7.2	2.1
1830	12.9	10.5	2.3	17.8	11.7	3.8
1840	17.1	14.2	2.9	17.0	10.8	11.7
1850	23.3	19.6	3.6	15.5	15.2	23.3
1860	31.5	26.9	4.5	14.3	19.4	31.1

Source: *Historical Statistics 1960, Series A2, A45, A46, and A195.*

top decile jumped by almost half of its previous level. Williamson and Lindert emphasize their broad impact: "[T]he movement toward wealth concentration occurred within regions, just as it seems to have occurred within given age groups, among native and foreign born, and within rural and urban populations" (Williamson and Lindert 1980, 46). Further work by Jeremy Atack and Fred Bateman (1987) adds to this perspective, demonstrating that in 1860, wealth was more equally distributed in northern rural areas than in the cities or in the rural South.

Thomas Jefferson's egalitarian dream of a strong, free democratic nation of contented individualistic small farmers was a vision shared by others. But the forces of the Industrial Revolution had leaped the Atlantic from Great Britain. The famed traveler and commentator Alexis de Tocqueville warned in 1839 of the growing concentrations of wealth. He feared that the rise of an industrial elite would destroy the basis of American egalitarianism:

I am of the opinion...that the manufacturing aristocracy which is growing up under our eyes is one of the harshest that ever existed...the friends of democracy should keep their eyes anxiously fixed in this direction; for if a permanent inequality of conditions and aristocracy…penetrates into [America] it may be predicted that this is the gate by which they will enter. (Williamson and Lindert 1980, 37–38)

American egalitarianism in terms of economic end results (income or wealth) was only a dream, then as now. But the Industrial Revolution and advance in the rate of economic growth before the Civil War were engines of opportunity for many, albeit not equally. As with other economies undergoing the transformation from an agrarian to an industrializing society, the U.S. transition generated greater inequality. The poor did not get poorer, but their advance was slower than the gains of the richer members of society.

THE EARLY UNION MOVEMENT

The rise in the numbers of workers in manufacturing paralleled growing activities by workers to organize for their benefits. Some have argued that the origin of the labor movement and the original labor–management problem sprang from the separation of workers from their tools. It is claimed that artisans, who owned their trade implements, lost their identity and independence when employer capitalists furnished the equipment. Like most generalizations, this one has its uses, but it may lead to false inferences (Economic Reasoning Proposition 5, evidence matters, applies here). The Industrial Revolution placed great numbers of laborers in a position of uncertainty and insecurity, making them depend on the vagaries of economic fluctuations and the mercy of employers. Yet the first impetus to a genuine labor movement was furnished by workers who were by no means separated from their tools. Craftsmen in Philadelphia, New York, and Boston founded craft labor societies in the 1790s, the prototypes of modern unions. Most of these societies were established in the hopes of securing increases in real wages (i.e., of pushing up monetary wages faster than the prices of consumer goods), although attempts were also made to gain shorter working hours, to establish and maintain a closed shop, and to regulate the conditions of apprenticeship. Invariably, there was considerable fraternal motivation for these societies as well, as people who made a living in the same way easily forged a social bond. In nearly all the major cities, shoemakers (cordwainers) and printers were among the first to form "workingmen's societies"; carpenters, masons, hatters, riggers, and tailors also found it worthwhile to organize. Again, these organizations were separated by craft and initiated by skilled workers (Economic Reasoning Proposition 1, scarcity forces us to make choices).

Legal Setbacks and Gains

The early craft societies were typically transitory, the longest-maintained union being the Philadelphia Cordwainers (1794–1806). Cyclical economic downturns routinely dissolved worker collective actions, and wage reductions, though resisted, were common during downturns in the economy. Another deterrent to unionization came from court actions. Conservative judges, in their instructions to juries, contended that union action per se was illegal. Societies of workers were considered conspiracies under English common law, a conspiracy being defined as "a confederacy of two or more, by indirect means to injure an individual or to do any act, which is unlawful or prejudicial to the community." (Commons, 1910, p. 82) A doctrine developed in England during the late Middle Ages was thus applied some 500 years later to restrict the unionization of craftspeople. In the famous case of the Pittsburgh Cordwainers in 1815, the judge contended that both the master shoemakers and the journeymen were coerced:

> *No shoemaker dare receive one who worked under price, or who was not a member of the society. No master workman must give him any employment, under the penalty of losing all his workmen. Moreover, a conspiracy to prevent a man from freely exercising his trade, or particular profession, in a particular place, is endictable. Also, it is an endictable offense, to conspire to compel men to become members of a particular association, or to contribute towards it. (quoted in Commons 1910, 82–83.)*

The jury in this case agreed that the master shoemakers, the journeymen, and the public were endangered by the association of journeymen and returned a verdict of guilty of conspiracy, although the court fined the defendants only $1 each, plus prosecution costs.

Later judgments sustained this legal perspective until the famous case of *Commonwealth v. Hunt.* In the fall of 1840, Hunt and other members of the Boston Bootmakers' Society were hauled into municipal court for attempting to enforce a closed shop. Again, after a strict charge from a judge who felt that such union activities could lead only to a "frightful despotism," the accused were convicted. The case was appealed to the supreme court of the Commonwealth of Massachusetts, and in 1842, Chief Justice Lemuel Shaw handed down a monumental decision that set a precedent on one point and opened the way to more liberal decisions on another. First, he held that a combination of union members was not criminal unless the object of the combination was criminal; the mere fact of organization implied no illegal conspiracy. Second, he asserted the doctrine that union members were within their rights in pressing for a closed shop and in striking to maintain union security. Justice Shaw was not a radical, nor was he particularly sympathetic with labor's cause, but he was well aware of the economic realities that were pressing labor to act collectively. This decision did not mean that trade unions were free from further court confrontations, but no more serious efforts were made to make the mere fact of organization a criminal offense, and henceforth there would be some reticence about presuming that the use of any and all weapons of the trade unions were socially harmful.

Organizational Gains

Judge Shaw's decision brought no immediate revival of unions, however; the long, deep slump from the late 1830s through the early 1840s had wiped out most of the societies that had formed in the craft union resurgence of 1824 to 1837. Workingmen's societies made a comeback in the 1850s (with setbacks in the recession years of 1854 and 1857), but it is important to remember that before 1860, union members never exceeded 1 percent of the total labor force. Factory workers, field hands, slaves, and domestic workers were almost completely outside the union movement. The primary early beneficiaries of workingmen's organizations were labor's minority elite, the craftsmen. Their unions were important, however, in that they established two concrete organizational advances for labor as a movement, as well as a series of political advances.

First, labor learned the technique of bargaining collectively, and aggressive unions began to use the weapons of the strike and boycott with skill and daring. The closed shop—an agreement whereby membership in a recognized union is made a condition of employment—was soon tested as an instrument for maintaining union security. The benevolent and protective aims of labor organizations tended to disappear, and militancy replaced early hesitance and reluctance to act.

Second, the rapidly increasing number of individual societies began to coalesce. Local federations and then national organizations appeared. In 1827, unions of different crafts in Philadelphia federated to form a "city central" or "trades' union," the Mechanics'

Union of Trade Associations. Six years later the societies in New York established a General Trades' Union. In the next three years, city centrals were formed in several major cities—not, as might be supposed from the modern functions of such organizations, to exchange information or engage in political activities, but for the more pressing purpose of aiding individual unions engaged in battle with employers. Attempts at organization on a national scale followed. In 1834, the General Trades' Union, New York's city central, called a national convention of these city federations, which resulted in the foundation of a National Trades' Union. At the same time, some of the craft societies began to see the advantages to be gained from a national organization along strict craft lines, and in 1835 and 1836, no less than five national unions of this type were established. The strongest of these were formed by the shoemakers and the printers.

POLITICAL GAINS FOR COMMON WORKING PEOPLE

Suffrage

As discussed in Perspective 11.1, one of the most significant political gains for workers was the broadening of suffrage, the right to vote. In the first decades of U.S. history, a

GAINS IN THE RIGHT TO VOTE

When Margaret Thatcher, Britain's Prime Minister, was invited to Paris in 1989 to speak in celebration of the 200th anniversary of the French Revolution, her opening remarks shocked many of the revelers. She reminded the French that is the North American British colonies that initiated and led the war along the path to freedom and equality.

Nevertheless, France was the first democracy to grant the secret ballot for men and the first to realize 100 percent male suffrage (as shown in Table 11.8). In this regard, France led Germany and the United States by a couple of decades. With respect to women, France trailed the United States, United Kingdom, and Germany by two and half decades.

TABLE 11.8 LAWS ON SUFFRAGE*

	SECRET BALLOT OBTAINED	WOMEN GAIN VOTE	100% MALE SUFFRAGE	PROPORTION OF POPULATION VOTING IN 1900
United States	1849	1920	1870	18.4
United Kingdom	1872	1918	1948	16.2
Germany	1848	1919	1872	15.5
France	1831	1945	1848	28.2
Argentina	1912	1947	1912	1.8
Brazil	1932	1932	1988	3.0
Chile	—	1949	1970	4.2
Peru	1931	1955	1979	—
Venezuela	1946	1945	1946	—
Costa Rica	1925	1949	1913	—

*Special thanks to Elyce Rotella's student, Rachel Reed, for correcting an error in the 10th edition.

person had to own a minimum amount of real property or pay a certain amount in taxes to have a voice in political affairs. The struggle for voting privileges took place in the original 13 states; only four of the new states entering the Union placed no property or tax payment qualifications on the right for an adult male to vote. By the late 1820s, suffrage had been extended sufficiently to enable working men to participate in the elections of the populous states. First to disappear was the property-owning requirement; by 1821, only five states retained it. Five states still set a tax-paying restriction 30 years later, but it was purely nominal.[2] Generally speaking, by 1860, white male citizens of the United States could vote, black males could vote in New York and New England, and alien males could vote in the agricultural Northwest.

Public Education

Although she could not vote herself, Fanny Wright effectively worked tirelessly for reforms in education. Except in New England, children of the poor received little or no education; and even in New England the early training was of poor quality and exhibited a religious slant that many opposed. Wright and her followers proposed that the state establish boarding schools for the education of rich and poor children alike, where class distinction would be eliminated. Others, less radical, proposed a simple plan of free public schools. By the mid-1830s, progress had been made to broaden educational opportunity; Albert Fishlow (see 1966) has shown that by midcentury, nearly 1 percent of gross national product (GNP) was spent on education (compared with almost 8 percent today). Public common schools were most prevalent in the North, where political concern and efforts were greatest. Recall Economic Reasoning Proposition 1, scarcity forces us to make choices.

Debts, Military Service, and Jail

In the minds of the working people, the most needed reform, next to that of the educational system, was the abolition of imprisonment for debt. Thousands of citizens were jailed annually for failure to meet obligations of a few dollars, and there was understandably fierce resentment against this injustice. The unfairness of the militia systems of the several states, which favored the rich, rankled in the hearts of the poor who were faced with the alternatives of a term in the service or a term in jail. These and other objectives—removing the competition of convict labor and obtaining the right to file liens on the property of employers for back wages—inflamed the spirits of great numbers of laborers, small businessmen, and professional people with a high degree of social consciousness. The militia system did eventually become less onerous, mechanics' lien laws were passed in many states, and imprisonment for debt was outlawed in most jurisdictions. Recall Economic Reasoning Propositions 1, scarcity forces us to make choices; 2, choices impose costs; and 4, laws and rules matter. But this first movement lost momentum after 1832, as labor turned its energies during the ensuing period of prosperity to advancing the cause of unionization, which in turn collapsed in 1837.

The 10-Hour Day

Although later movements and colorful episodes of the 1840s and 1850s were characterized by impractical utopian schemes (proposed and led by Robert Owen, Charles

---

[2]Comparing the votes for president with the total population, we find that there were two large jumps in the electorate: from 1824 to 1828 (3.2 percent to 9.3 percent) and from 1836 to 1840 (9.6 percent to 13.6 percent).

Fourier, and George Henry Evans), one movement of the midcentury gained quick relief for workers: the struggle for the 10-hour day. That goal was set as early as 1835, but there was then no serious prospect of attaining it. Hope rose in 1840 when Martin Van Buren set a 10-hour day for federal employees. Craftspeople in some trades already worked no longer than 10 hours, but factory operatives still labored 12 to 14 hours a day. In the mid-1840s, New England factory workers added to the agitation for shorter hours. In 1847, the New Hampshire legislature passed the first regulatory law setting a 10-hour upper limit for a day's work, but there was a loophole in it. The law provided that if workers agreed to work longer hours, the 10-hour limit might be exceeded. Threatened with discharge if they did not agree, factory hands found themselves no better off. Statutes passed by other state legislatures followed the same pattern, except that laws limiting the workday of children to 10 hours did not contain the hated "contract" clause.

Perhaps the most important effect of the agitation for regulatory acts was the pressure of public opinion thereby exerted on employers. Many large factories voluntarily established 11-hour days. By 1860, a 10-hour day was standard in all the craft trades, and already a new standard of 8 hours was being timorously suggested.

SELECTED REFERENCES AND SUGGESTED READINGS

Atack, Jeremy, and Fred Bateman. *To Their Own Soil: Northern Agriculture and the Westward Movement.* Ames: Iowa State University Press, 1987.

Commons, J. R. *A Documentary History of American Industrial Society,* Vol. 4. 1910.

Craig, Lee A., and Elizabeth B. Field-Hendrey. "Industrialization and the Earnings Gap: Regional and Sectoral Tests of the Goldin-Sokoloff Hypothesis." *Explorations in Economic History* 30 (1993): 60–80.

Fishlow, Albert. "Levels of Nineteenth-Century American Investment in Education." *Journal of Economic History* 26 (1966): 418–436.

Ferrie, Joseph P. "The Wealth Accumulation of Antebellum Immigrants to the U.S., 1840–60." *The Journal of Economic History* 54 (1994): 1–33.

Goldin, C., and K. Sokoloff. "Women, Children, and Industrialization in the Early Republic: Evidence from the Manufacturing Censuses." *Journal of Economic History* 42 (1982): 741–774.

Habakkuk, H. J. *American and British Technology in the Nineteenth Century.* Cambridge: Cambridge University Press, 1962.

Historical Statistics. Washington, D.C.: Government Printing Office, 1960.

Lebergott, Stanley. *Manpower in Economic Growth: The American Record since 1800.* New York: McGraw-Hill, 1964.

Margo, Robert A., and Georgia C. Villaflor. "The Growth of Wages in Antebellum America: New Evidence." *Journal of Economic History* 47 (1987): 873–896.

Nickless, Pamela J. "Changing Labor Productivity and the Utilization of Native Women Workers in the American Cotton Textile Industry, 1825–1866." *Journal of Economic History* 38 (1978): 287–288.

Rosenberg, Nathan. "Anglo-American Wage Differences in the 1820s." *Journal of Economic History* 27 (1967): 221–229.

Sokoloff, Kenneth L. "Was the Transition from the Artisanal Shop to the Nonmechanized Factory Associated with Gains in Efficiency? Evidence from the U.S. Manufactures Censuses of 1820 and 1850." *Explorations in Economic History* 21 (1984): 351–382.

Sokoloff, Kenneth L., and Georgia C. Villaflor. "The Market for Manufacturing Workers during the Early Industrialization: The American Northeast, 1820 to 1860." In *Strategic Factors in Nineteenth Century American Economic History: A Volume to Honor Robert W. Fogel,* eds. Claudia Goldin and Hugh Rockoff. Chicago: University of Chicago Press, 1992.

Sundstrom, William A., and Paul David. "Socioeconomic Determinants of Interstate Fertility Differentials in the United States in 1850 and 1860." *Journal of Interdisciplinary History* 6 (1976): 375–396.

_____. "Old-Age Security Motives and Farm Family Fertility in Antebellum America." *Explorations in Economic History* 25 (1988): 164–197.

Vinovskis, Maris. "Mortality Rates and Trends in Massachusetts before 1860." *Journal of Economic History* 32 (1972): 184–213.

Williamson, Jeffrey G., and Peter H. Lindert. *American Inequality: A Macroeconomic History.* New York: Academic Press, 1980.

Wright, C. D. *Comparative Wages, Price, and Cost of Living.* Boston: Wright & Potter, 1889. In *American Inequality: A Macroeconomic History,* eds. Jeffrey G. Williamson and Peter H. Lindert. New York: Academic Press, 1980.

Yasuba, Yasukichi. *Birth Rates of the White Population of the United States, 1800–1860: An Economic Analysis.* Baltimore, Md.: Johns Hopkins University Press, 1962.

CHAPTER **12**

Money and Banking in the Developing Economy

CHAPTER THEME

After the Constitution was ratified, the new nation faced the problem of establishing a legal framework for its monetary system. But there was little agreement on how best to achieve the ultimate goals of a monetary unit of stable purchasing power and a banking system that was sound yet liberal in supplying credit. This chapter describes the many experiments tried by the young republic in the pursuit of these elusive goals. These experiments had at the time important consequences for the economy, and they permanently influenced Americans' beliefs about how the financial system should be regulated. The chapter also describes the macroeconomic fluctuations—inflation, depressions, and financial crises—that affected the course of economic development.

THE AMERICAN MONETARY UNIT

Because international trade had made the dollar (a common name for the Spanish peso) and its subdivisions more plentiful than any other coins in the commercial centers along the American seaboard, it became customary to reckon accounts in terms of dollars (although some merchants used pounds, shillings, and pence and continued to do so long after independence). The dollar, therefore, was adopted as the unit of account and, fortunately for all of us, a decimal system of divisions was adopted rather than the arithmetically troublesome old English system of pounds, shillings (20 = 1 pound), and pence (12 = 1 shilling). Thomas Jefferson, who along with Robert Morris and Alexander Hamilton was most responsible for our adopting the decimal system, made the following cogent argument in his 1783 report to Congress:

> *The easiest ratio of multiplication and division, is that by ten. Everyone knows the facility of Decimal Arithmetic. Everyone remembers, that, when learning Money-Arithmetic, he used to be puzzled with adding the farthings, taking out the fours and carrying them on; adding the pence, taking out the twelves and carrying them on; adding the shillings, taking out the twenties and carrying them on; but when he came to the pounds, where he had only tens to carry forward, it was easy and free from error. The bulk of mankind are schoolboys through life. (Ford 1894, 446–447)*

More important than the decision to decimalize the currency was the question of a standard. Would the currency's value be based on gold? Silver? Gold and silver? The inflationary experiences of the United States during the Revolution, and in some of the states under the Articles of Confederation, showed that paper issues without backing were liable to abuse: The government could print too much. But it was hard to choose between the two great monetary metals, gold and silver. Ultimately it was decided to use both. Gold would add its prestige to the monetary system and serve in higher-denomination coins; silver would serve for smaller denominations.

201

Alexander Hamilton, the first secretary of the treasury, pointed out that the dollar was, in fact, in general use in the states and that people everywhere would readily accept it as the monetary unit. The only difficulty, he said, was that Spanish dollars varied in their content of pure silver. He suggested that the pesos in circulation be assayed (tested) to see how much silver they contained. The number of grains of silver in the new U.S. dollar would simply be the average of that in the Spanish coins then circulating. Because gold was about 15 times as valuable as silver, gold coins need contain only one-fifteenth as much metal as silver coins of the same denomination. These ideas were ultimately translated into the Coinage Act of 1792. This decision for a bimetallic standard (both gold and silver) proved controversial over the three-quarters of a century during which it was maintained.

THE BIMETALLIC STANDARD

It is one thing to adopt a bimetallic standard and quite another to maintain it. The problem is that the relative values of gold and silver fluctuate. Thus, even though a mint ratio of 15 to 1 closely approximated the prevailing market ratio in 1792, world supplies of and demands for gold and silver were such that the ratio in the market rose gradually during the 1790s to about 15.5 to 1; by 1808, it was 16 to 1. A market ratio of 16 to 1 and a mint ratio of 15 to 1, technically, is a relationship in which gold is "undervalued" at the mint. Under such circumstances, it paid to export gold coins, exchange them for silver in Europe, import the silver, and convert it into new coins at the mint.

For centuries, observers had noted this tendency for undervalued coins to be hoarded for export. One naturally paid out debased coins whenever it was possible to pass them off at their nominal value and held on to the undervalued coins. Popular sayings to the effect that "bad money drives out good money" or "cheap money will replace dear" thus came into use in various languages. Sir Thomas Gresham, Elizabeth I's master of the mint, is credited with analyzing this phenomenon, which has become known as *Gresham's law*. For our purposes, we may best state the law as follows: Money overvalued at the mint tends to drive out of circulation money undervalued at the mint, providing that the two monies circulate at fixed ratio.

In a well-known paper entitled "Gresham's Law or Gresham's Fallacy?" Arthur Rolnick and Warren Weber (1986) pointed out that if people were willing to use coins at their market values, there would be no reason for one coin to drive another out of circulation. For example, if people were willing to value one gold dollar at, say, $1.05 in silver coins, reflecting the market values of the metallic contents of the coins, both gold and silver could circulate side by side, even though gold was undervalued at the mint. But as Robert Greenfield and Hugh Rockoff (1995) and George Selgin (1996) show, legal tender laws, custom, and convenience are powerful forces that tend to force the exchange of coins at their face (mint) values. In early nineteenth-century America, it was easier for holders of gold coins to hoard them for export rather than to try to use them in everyday transactions at more than their face values. Recall Economic Reasoning Propositions 1, scarcity forces us to make choices; 2, choices impose costs; 3, incentives matter; and 4, laws and rules matter in Economic Insight 1.1 on page 8.

The idea of Gresham's law incidentally is used (often somewhat loosely) in a wide variety of other situations. For example, some college professors worry that students will want to take easy courses because an A in an easy course counts just as much toward their grade point average as an A in a hard course: "Bad Courses

ECONOMIC INSIGHT 12.1

BAGEHOT'S RULE

While the United States had no central bank, Britain had the venerable Bank of England, the "Old Lady of Threadneedle Street." The Bank of England had begun life, and was still in some measure a private bank. It was not always clear that it could or should act as a lender of last resort. Ideas about central banking, however, were evolving. A major landmark was the famous book by Walter Bagehot: *Lombard Street* published in 1873.[1] Here Bagehot argued that it was crucial for the stability of the banking system that the Bank of England build up an adequate reserve of gold and announce its willingness to use that reserve during panics to lend to financial intermediaries who were in desperate need of funds. In times of panic, Bagehot wrote, "it [the Bank of England] must advance freely and vigorously to the public out of the reserve." Bagehot saw the need for some restrictions on emergency lending—it should be at a high interest rate to encourage prompt repayment and should be backed by assets that normally would be valuable—but above all the Bank had to stop the panic. Sixty years later during the banking panic of the 1930s the Federal Reserve had yet to learn this lesson.

THE QUANTITY THEORY OF MONEY

The quantity theory of money can be expressed by the following equation:

$$M = kPy$$

M stands for money (silver or gold coins, bank notes, bank deposits, and so on); k for the proportion of income held as money (a decision made by money holders), P for the price level, and y for real output. The equation is a tautology, made true by the way k is defined. But it still can provide important insights into how the economy works. An increase in M, for example because the government printed paper money or because new gold or silver mines were discovered, must produce an increase in one of the variables on the other side of the equation. If k and y are relatively stable, the main impact will be on P: "Inflation is the result of too much money chasing too few goods." Or, to take another example, if M and k are stable, and y is growing rapidly, then P must fall: Inadequate monetary growth could produce deflation.

Drive out Good." Gresham's law applies to college courses because of the difference between the way students and colleges value courses, just as it applies to coins when there is a difference between the way the market and the mint values the metal in the coins.

In June 1834, two acts were passed that changed the mint ratio to just a fraction over 16 to 1. Gold was then overvalued at the mint, and gold slowly began to replace silver, which was either hoarded or exported. The discovery of gold in California in 1848 accelerated the trend toward a pure gold circulation.

The international flows of metal under the bimetallic standard were a nuisance. Often coins in convenient denominations could not be had, and the coins that were available were badly worn. But the bimetallic standard also provided a major, if often overlooked, benefit. A change in the market ratio could reflect the slow growth of one metal, say, gold, relative to demand. If the country were tied solely to that metal, the general price level would fall. But under a bimetallic standard, the cheaper metal can replace the dear metal, thus helping to maintain the stock of money and the price level.

---

[1]Pronounced bad-jit, not baggy-hot, although the latter might be more fun.

BANK NOTES AS PAPER MONEY

Although the Constitution forbade the states from issuing paper money, they did retain the power to create corporations. After the commercial boom beginning in 1793, special state charters established a large number of banks. These were entirely new institutions on the American scene, for commercial banks had not existed in the colonies. Before 1790 there had been only three banks, but by 1800, there were 20, and by 1811 there were 88. All but two were private, state-chartered banks empowered to issue their own paper money, redeemable in gold or silver.

In many ways, a bank note was similar to a bank deposit. When a bank made loans to its customers, it gave them the proceeds either in the form of its own notes, which then circulated as cash, or as a deposit on which they could write checks. Today, of course, banks no longer issue notes, and the Federal Reserve issues the paper money that passes from hand to hand; moreover, whenever a firm borrows money today, it takes the proceeds as a credit to its account. But during the years before the Civil War, and even for some time after that in rural areas, a bank issued notes much more frequently than it made credits to customers' accounts.

Typically, only bank notes issued by nearby banks were accepted at par. People arriving from a distant city would have to exchange their "foreign" bank notes for local money, and typically they would be charged a discount. They might get only $0.97 in local money for each dollar of foreign money, a 3 percent discount. Note brokers specialized in buying notes from distant banks, and "bank note reporters," publications that listed the discounts, aided them and other local merchants. Gary Gorton (1996) and Howard Bodenhorn (2000) have studied these discounts and found that the notes were priced much like short-term bonds in today's money market. Distance from the point of issue was the main determinant of the discount, but other factors also played a role. Typically, the notes of new banks were discounted more, as might be expected, with the discount falling as the bank established a reputation for soundness.

The system encouraged counterfeiting. By 1860, more than 1,500 state banks were issuing, on an average, six different denominations of notes. Therefore, not fewer than 9,000 different types of notes were being passed. Some counterfeiters issued spurious counterfeits that imitated the notes of no particular bank; others concentrated on careful imitations of genuine bills. Perhaps the most successful ways of counterfeiting were to alter the notes of a broken bank to make them appear to be the issue of a solvent bank or to change bills from lower to higher denominations. Some counterfeiters specialized in the manufacturing end of the business; others, called utterers, were adept at passing the bogus money. To combat counterfeiters, banks formed anticounterfeiting associations, hiring men called snaggers to ferret out makers of spurious bills.

Clearly, it was often difficult to determine the genuineness of a bill and the discount at which a valid note should be accepted. If a bill was much worn, or if it was perforated many times by the bank

---

LOUISIANA.

Bank of Louisiana—New Orleans—Wm. W. Montgomery, Pres.; R. M. Davis, Cash

5s, alter.d from a broken bank, "Louisiana" defective.

20s, description hereafter, as we have not seen these bills.

50s, new plate, altered from 5s.

500s, let. A. Nov. 1, 1839—vig. Cybele & Mercury—on the right an Indian—the bank has issued nothing like it.

Citizens' Bank—New Orleans—E. W. Moise, Pres 3

Exchange Bank—New Orleans—H. Beard, Manager; J. E. Armor, Cash . . . 3

Louisiana State Bank—New Orleans—Samuel J. Peters, Pres.; Richard Relf, Cash 3

10s, L. Bihl cash., C. Clement, pres.—engraved by the "Western Bank note Company."

20s, v.g. a female, agricultural implements &c., her left hand rests on the figure 2, and her right hand on the 0—on the left, a view of the place d'arms and cathederal —not like genuine.

50s, the female in her right hand holds a sword, and her left arm rests on a sheaf of wheat—a train of cars, &c., on her right:—a broad, dark colored band on right and left margin, one having the figure 50, and the other the word FIFTY upon it. The note reads the "Louisiana State Bank will pay Fifty Dollars to the bearer on demand." All these particulars are different from the genuine note, although in their general appearance they are much the same.

100s, vig. locomotive and cars—Franklin on one end and Roman head on the other— not like genuine, and poorly done.

Louisiana State Bank—(Branch.) Wm. H. Avery, Pres.; R. J. Palfrey, Cash 3

Mech. & Trad. Bank—New Orleans—U. H. Dudley, Pres.; Gustavus Cruzat, Cash 3

5s, let. A. vig. steamboat, &c.—pay A. Brown Jan. 1, 1843.

10s, filling up in boy's hand, very bad—officers both in the same hand, in blue ink —engraving rather coarse.

100s, altered from tens—very well done.

New Orleans Canal & Banking Co.—R. W. Montgomery, Pres.; S. C. Bell, Cash 3

Union Bank—New Orleans—C. Adams, Pres.; F. Frey, Cash 3

50s, said to be in circulation—we have not seen this counterfeit.

An excerpt from Sheldon's North American Bank Note Detector and Commercial Reporter, *Chicago, July 2, 1853. Notes of Louisiana banks were at a 3 percent discount in Chicago. Descriptions of counterfeit notes are listed under the banks.*

teller's needlelike staple, one might presume it to be genuine. Anyone who regularly took in paper money, however, usually had more assistance in the form of a "bank-note reporter" and a "counterfeit detector." *Thompson's Bank Note and Commercial Reporter*, a weekly, contained alphabetical listings, by states, of the notes of banks and the discounts at which they should be received, together with descriptions of all known counterfeited bills. *Thompson's Bank Note Descriptive List*, published at irregular intervals, contained word descriptions of genuine bills of banks in the United States and Canada. *Nicholas' Bank Note Reporter* at one time listed 5,400 counterfeits. Only a small fraction of these were actually in circulation at any one time, but any of them might be. *Hodges' Bank Note Safeguard* contained 360 pages of facsimile reproductions of genuine notes.

Although this system seems strange to us today because our currency has the same value everywhere, it is easy to exaggerate the difficulties. Today, merchants must still contend with bad checks and stolen credit cards, and using an automated teller machine (ATM) often means paying a service charge analogous to the charge once made by note brokers. Indeed, today many individuals rely on check-cashing services, which perform an economic service quite similar to that performed by the note brokers before the Civil War. There can be little doubt, however, that many people of this period were dissatisfied with the currency and hankered for federal action to provide a uniform national currency.

THE FIRST BANK OF THE UNITED STATES

Robert Morris established and organized the first American bank in 1781, with Congress's approval, to help finance the war effort and provide financial organization in those troubled times. However, we usually think of the nation's first central bank as being established 10 years later. See a discussion of the definition of a central bank in Economic Insight 12.2 on page 208.

Shortly after becoming secretary of the treasury, Alexander Hamilton wrote a *Report on a National Bank* in which he argued for a Bank of the United States. Hamilton's report shows remarkable insight into the financial problems of the young republic. He argued that a "National Bank" would augment "the active or productive capital of a country." By this, he meant that the notes issued by the bank would replace some of the gold and silver money in circulation, which could then be exported in exchange for real goods and services. Normally, moreover, the stock of money must grow from year to year to accommodate increased business activity. With a note-issuing national bank in place, the United States would not be forced in future years to depend primarily on net exports to increase its stock of money.

As important to Hamilton as its salutary effects on the economy was the assistance the bank could give the government by lending money to the U.S. Treasury. Moreover, the bank could serve as a fiscal agent for the government by acting as a depository of government funds, making transfers of funds from one part of the country to another and (Hamilton hoped) serving as a tax collection agency. Finally, because the government and private shareholders were to jointly own the bank, it would cement the relationship between the fledgling government and leading men of business.[2]

---

[2]The federal government bought one-fifth of the $10 million initial capital stock. The government paid for its shares with the proceeds of a $2 million loan extended by the bank on the security of its own stock; the loan was to be repaid in 10 equal annual installments. At the start of operations, then, the government participated in the earnings of a privately financed venture without contributing a penny to the original capital.

*Alexander Hamilton (1775–1804) was one of the chief architects of the Con-
stitution and the economic policy of the new nation. He was killed in a duel
with Aaron Burr.*

The bill creating the bank followed Hamilton's report closely. It had substantial opposition, even in the predominantly Federalist Congress, on the grounds that (1) it was unconstitutional, (2) it would create a "money-monopoly" that would endanger the rights
and liberties of the people, and (3) it would be of value to the commercial North but not
to the agricultural South. The bill was carried on a sectional vote, and President
Washington signed it on February 14, 1791. The bank's charter was limited to 20 years,
so further battles lay ahead.

The notes of the Bank of the United States and its branches were soon circulating
widely throughout the country at, or very close to, par.[3] In other words, $1.00 notes of
the bank were always worth $1.00 in silver. Many state banks developed the habit of
using notes or deposits issued by the Bank of the United States as part of their reserves,
thus economizing on the use of silver, as Hamilton had predicted. At all times, the bank
held a considerable portion of the silver in the country; its holdings during the last three
years of its existence were probably close to $15 million, which practically matched the
amount held by all state banks.

The bank followed a conservative lending policy compared with those of the state
banks. As a result, it continually received a greater dollar volume of state-bank notes

---

[3]By 1800, the bank had branches in Boston, New York, Baltimore, and Charleston. Branches were added in
Washington and Savannah in 1802 and in New Orleans in 1805.

The first Bank of the United States issued these $10 notes, which were canceled by inking three or four Xs on their faces after they became worn. They were promises to pay dollars (most likely Mexican or American silver dollars) on demand immediately when brought to an office of the bank.

than state banks received of its obligations. It became, to put it differently, a creditor of the state banks. The bank was, therefore, in a position to present the notes of the state banks regularly for payment in specie, discouraging them from issuing as many notes as they would have liked.

Although there was no obligation on its part, legal or customary, to assist other banks in need, in practice, the Bank of the United States (like the Bank of England, which was also a private bank) became a lender of last resort. The bank also acted as fiscal agent for the government and held most of the U.S. Treasury's deposits; in return, the bank transmitted government funds from one part of the country to another without charge. After 1800, the bank helped collect customs bonds in cities where it had branches. It further facilitated government business by effecting payments of interest on the public debt, carrying on foreign-exchange operations for the U.S. Treasury, and supplying bullion and foreign coins to the mint. All in all, we can conclude that the bank was well on its way to being a central bank when Congress refused to recharter it in 1811.

In retrospect, the reasons for the continued operation of the Bank of the United States seem compelling. During the two decades of the bank's existence, the country enjoyed a well-ordered expansion of credit and a general stability of the currency. Compared with the difficulties before 1791, the money problems of the 1790s and early 1800s were insignificant. The first Bank of the United States helped to give the nation a better monetary system than it had any reason to hope for in 1791.

Political arguments based on economic facts often must compete, however, with those based on appeals to emotion and prejudice (Economic Reasoning Proposition 5, evidence and theory give value to opinions). Those who opposed the recharter of the bank made the same points that had been advanced when the matter had been originally debated nearly 20 years earlier. They argued that the bank was unconstitutional and that it was a financial monster so powerful it would eventually control the nation's economic life and deprive the people of their liberties. To these contentions was added a new objection: The bank had fallen under the domination of foreigners, mostly British. Foreign ownership of stock was about $7 million, or 70 percent of the shares. This was not unusual; foreigners owned about the same percentage of U.S. bonds. The bank's charter, moreover, attempted to prevent foreigners from exercising much influence over its policies: Only shareholding American citizens could be directors, and foreign nationals could not vote by proxy. Nevertheless, many people felt that the influence of English owners

ECONOMIC INSIGHT 12.2

A CENTRAL BANK

There is no precise definition of a central bank that all experts would agree to and, hence, no exact moment at which a big bank becomes a central bank. Typically, when speaking of central banking, economists have one or more of the following criteria in mind: (1) the bank serves as a lender of last resort to other banks or financial institutions by lending them money during crises. The idea is that by preventing a few major financial institutions from closing, the central bank can prevent a panic from taking hold. This function was analyzed by Walter Bagehot in his famous book *Lombard Street* (1873), in which he urged the Bank of England to declare its determination to be the lender of last resort and to acquire a gold reserve commensurate with that responsibility. *Bagehot's rule* is that during financial crises, the central bank should lend freely but at high interest rates (to encourage prompt repayment after the crisis). (2) The bank has considerable control over the stock of money and uses this control to moderate fluctuations in credit conditions, prices, or other aspects of the economy. If the country is on a metallic standard, the case we are examining here, the central bank cannot issue as much money as it might like because of the risk to its own metallic reserves. (3) The bank regulates other banks, punishing those whose behavior it considers imprudent. (4) Finally, we come to the modern definition of a central bank: It lends lots of money to the government.

---

was bound to make itself felt through those American directors with whom they had close business contacts.

Personal politics also mattered. On a number of occasions, Thomas Jefferson had stated his conviction that the bank was unconstitutional and a menace to the liberties of the people. Although Jefferson was no longer president when the issue of recharter arose, his influence was still immense, and many of his followers doubtlessly were swayed by his view. But the decisive votes were cast against the bank as a result of personal antagonism toward Albert Gallatin, who, although having served as Jefferson's secretary of the treasury, was a champion of the bank. In the House, consideration of the bill for renewal of the charter was postponed indefinitely by a vote of 65 to 64. In the Senate, Vice President George Clinton, enemy of both President James Madison and Gallatin, broke a 17–17 tie with a vote against the bank.

THE SECOND BANK OF THE UNITED STATES

Difficulties in financing the War of 1812 and the sharp inflation following the suspension of specie payments in 1814 convinced many people of the need for a second Bank of the United States. It took two years of congressional wrangling and consideration of no less than six separate proposals before a bill to charter such a bank was passed. The bank was finally chartered in 1816, again for a period of 20 years. And again, the renewal clause set the stage for future battles.

The charter of the second Bank of the United States resembled that of its predecessor. The capital was set at $35 million, four-fifths of it to be subscribed by individuals, firms, or states and the remaining one-fifth by the federal government. Most of the capital was to consist of government bonds, but one-fourth of the private subscription ($7 million) was to be paid in coin. The bank was to have 25 directors, 20 elected by private stockholders and 5 appointed by the president of the United States. The main office of the bank was to be located in Philadelphia, with branch offices to be established on the initiative either of the directors or of Congress.

President of the second Bank of the United States, archfoe of Andrew Jackson, and advocate of central-bank controls was Philadelphia aristocrat Nicholas Biddle (1780–1844). Some argued that his hauteur cost the bank its charter; others believed that Wall Street would have done in Chestnut Street anyway.

The greatest contributions of the second Bank of the United States came after 1823, the time of the appointment of Nicholas Biddle as its third president. Sophisticated, widely traveled, and well-educated, Biddle typified the early American aristocrat. He had wealth, power, and a mind that enabled him to successfully run the nation's largest enterprise. He was also arrogant and out of touch with the fears and aspirations of the average citizen.

Under Biddle, a conscious attempt was made to regulate the banking system according to certain preconceived notions of what ought to be done. In the first place, the bank soon became the lender of last resort to the state banks. State banks did not keep their reserves as deposits with the Bank of the United States, but they did come to depend on the second bank in times of crisis, borrowing specie from it to meet their obligations. The bank was able to meet such demands because it kept a much larger proportion of specie reserve against its circulation than other banks did. The second bank also assisted in times of stress by lending to business firms when other banks could not or would not. Because of these practices, many came to regard the bank as the holder of ultimate reserves of the banking system.

The bank developed a policy of regularly presenting the notes of state banks for payment. By presenting the notes of state banks for payment in specie, it kept their issues moderate. The bank not only furnished a currency of its own of uniform value over the entire country, but it also reduced to a nominal figure the discount at which the notes of state banks circulated. By the late 1820s, the paper money of the country was in a very satisfactory state. Biddle also tried to affect the general economic climate of the

A bank note issued by a private bank before the Civil War. Notes like this one circulated from hand to hand as money.

United States by alternate expansion and contraction of the bank's loans. Furthermore, he made the bank the largest American dealer in foreign exchange and was able to protect the country from severe specie drain when a drain would have meant a harmful contraction of monetary reserves. In the 1820s, the problem of making payments over considerable distances within the country was not much different from the problem of effecting remittances between countries. There was a flourishing business in "domestic exchange," and the bank obtained a large portion of it.

By 1829, the position of the second Bank of the United States seemed secure. It had grown and prospered. In many ways, it had become a central bank. It had attained a shining reputation abroad—so much so that when the Bank of Spain was reorganized in 1829, the Bank of the United States was explicitly copied. Although the bank had made enemies, the idea of a "national institution" was widely accepted, and even those who persistently opposed "the monster" grudgingly admitted that it had been good for business. Congress had made sporadic attacks on the bank, but these had been ineffective. Yet the apparent permanence of the bank was illusory.

In 1828, Andrew Jackson was elected to the presidency. Beloved by the masses, Jackson had the overwhelming support of the people during two terms in office. Long before taking office, he had decided against supporting banks in general and "The Bank" in particular. As a young man in Tennessee, Jackson had taken the notes of a Philadelphia merchant that passed as currency in payment for 6,000 acres. When he tried to use these notes, he found that they were worthless because the merchant had failed. To make his obligations good, Jackson suffered years of financial difficulty in addition to the loss of his land. Later, he and his business partners often found themselves victims of exorbitant charges by bankers and bill brokers in both New Orleans and the eastern cities (see Campbell 1932). On one occasion, Jackson bitterly opposed the establishment of a state bank in Tennessee, and as late as 1826, he worked against the repeal of a law prohibiting the establishment of a branch of the Bank of the United States in his home state.

In his first annual message to Congress, seven years before the charter of the bank was to expire, Jackson called attention to the date of expiration, stated that "both the constitutionality and the expediency of the law creating this bank are well questioned by a large portion of our fellow citizens," and speculated that

If such an institution is deemed essential to the fiscal operations of the Government, I submit to the wisdom of the Legislature whether a national one, founded upon credit of the Government and its revenues, might not be devised which would avoid all

In this cartoon, Andrew Jackson (left) attacks the many-headed serpent (the second Bank of the United States) with his walking stick (his veto). The largest head is Nicholas Biddle, the bank's president. The remaining heads represent other officials of the bank and its branches. Jackson is assisted by Martin Van Buren (center).

constitutional difficulties and at the same time secure all the advantages to the Government and country that were expected to result from the present bank.

We have the great Democrat's word for it that his statement was toned down by his advisers. It was the beginning of the "Bank War."

Biddle initially tried to win Jackson's support, but his efforts were unsuccessful. Henry Clay, charming and popular presidential candidate of the National Republicans (Whigs), finally persuaded Biddle to let him make the question of recharter a campaign issue in the election of 1832. During the summer, there was enough support in Congress to secure passage of a bill for recharter—a bill that Jackson returned, as expected, with a sharp veto message prepared by presidential advisers Amos Kendall and Roger Taney. In the veto, the president contended that (1) the bank was unconstitutional, (2) there was too much foreign ownership of its shares, and (3) domestic ownership was too heavily concentrated in the East. A central theme ran through the message: The bank was an instrument of the rich to oppress the poor; an institution of such power and so little responsibility to the people could undo democracy itself and should be dissolved.

Agrarians of the West and South felt that the bank's conservative policies had restricted the supply of credit to agriculture.[4] But Wall Street also opposed the bank; it

---

[4]The conviction in the West and South that interest rates are unnaturally high and that the government ought to do something about it is one of the hardy perennials of American politics. It would blossom again during the Populist era, as we will see in chapter 19. Indeed, politicians have continued to cultivate this issue to the present day.

wanted to supplant Philadelphia (where the home office of the bank was located) as the nation's financial center. Economics makes for strange bedfellows.

After a furious presidential campaign, Jackson emerged the victor by a substantial margin. He considered his triumph a mandate from the electorate on the bank question, and the acclaim he was receiving due to his masterful handling of the problem of nullification strengthened his resolve to restrict the bank's activities at once.[5] In the fall of 1833, the government discontinued making deposits with the bank, and editor Greene of the *Boston Post* was moved to write its epitaph: "Biddled, Diddled, and Undone."

Biddle was not through, however. Beginning in August 1833 and continuing into the fall of 1834, the bank contracted its loans sharply and continued its policy of presenting the notes of state banks for payment in specie. Biddle maintained that contraction was necessary to prepare the bank for liquidation, although there was doubtlessly a punitive motive in the vigor of his actions. In any case, his actions contributed significantly to the brief but definite financial stringency of 1834.

The administration, however, remained firm in its resolve to end the bank, which became a state bank chartered under the laws of Pennsylvania in 1836. Although stripped of its official status, the U.S. Bank of Pennsylvania remained the most powerful financial institution in America for several years. With its resources alone, Biddle engineered a grandiose scheme to support the prices of cotton and other agricultural staples during the nation's economic troubles of 1837 and 1838. Biddle, in other words, bet the bank on a final gamble that the price of agricultural products would rise. If they had, the bank would have made a tremendous amount of money, farmers would have credited the bank with raising farm incomes, and Biddle would have been a hero. But this last convulsive effort started a chain of events that led to the bank's failure in 1841, two years after Biddle's retirement.

ECONOMIC FLUCTUATIONS AND THE SECOND BANK

During the early years of Biddle's reign, the economy followed a relatively smooth course with no deep recessions or periods of significant inflation. As shown in Figure 12.1, during the 1820s, the price level slipped downward as the amount of specie in the economy remained roughly constant and the amount of money (specie plus bank notes plus bank deposits) rose modestly. Undoubtedly, the growth in the stock of money was less than the growth of the volume of goods exchanged.

Then entirely new conditions began to prevail: first inflation in the mid-1830s and then the Great Depression of 1839–1843. At one time, historians blamed these disturbances on the demise of the second bank. The argument was that the absence of the second bank unleashed irresponsible banking, that increases in the money supply and the price level were a direct result, and that the crashes of the late 1830s and the depression of the early 1840s were the inevitable result of the previous excesses. A glance at the upper two lines in Figure 12.1 seems to support this argument: The stock of money (remember that this includes bank notes and deposits as well as specie) rose sharply, as did prices.

Shortly after President Jackson vetoed the bank's recharter, he began withdrawing government funds from the second bank and placing them in so-called pet banks, which

---

[5]The principle of nullification, first enunciated by John C. Calhoun in 1828, was that any state could refuse to be bound by a federal statute it considered unjust until three-quarters of the states had agreed to the statute. South Carolina tried to apply the principle in 1832–1833 during a dispute over a tariff bill. Jackson's strong stand defeated the attempt.

FIGURE 12.1

U.S. Prices, Money, and Specie, 1820–1845

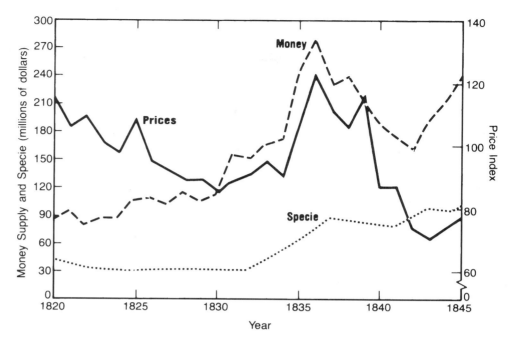

Source: *Rockoff 1971, Table 1, 45.*

the states charted. Allegedly, as Biddle's power to present the notes of state banks for redemption ebbed, many banks began to expand their paper note issues recklessly. Owners interested only in making a quick profit formed new banks. These disreputable banks came to be called "wildcat banks," and the name stuck. The origin of the term is somewhat obscure. One story, probably apocryphal, is that the banks were located in remote areas, wildcat country, to discourage people from trying to convert their notes into specie.

Subsequent research by George Macesich (1960) and Peter Temin (1969) showed, however, that Jackson's attack on the second bank deserves very little of the blame for the inflation. The United States was still greatly influenced by external events. Coincidentally, at the time of the demise of the second bank, the United States began to receive substantial amounts of silver from Mexico, which was undergoing its own political and economic turmoil. These and other flows into the United States from England and France sharply raised the amount of specie in the United States. In addition, a steady outflow of specie to China substantially declined at this time. Historically, China had run balance-of-payments surpluses with the rest of the world, but as opium addiction spread in China, China's balance-of-payments surplus disappeared, and Chinese merchants began to accept bills of credit instead of requiring payment in specie.[6]

As shown in Figure 12.1, the stock of specie substantially increased in between 1833 and 1837. Because the amount of money banks could issue was limited mainly by the amount of specie they could keep in reserve, the amount of paper money and deposits increased, step by step, with the new supplies of specie. To a considerable extent, the influx of specie explains the increase in money and prices. The ratio of paper money and bank deposits to specie actually increased only slightly. The banking sector, in other

---

[6]China's attempts to restrict foreign trade, particularly the opium trade, led to the Opium War with Britain (1839–1842).

ECONOMIC INSIGHT 12.3

HUME'S PRICE-SPECIE-FLOW MECHANISM

According to Hume's *Price-Specie-Flow mechanism* (named after the eighteenth-century Scottish philosopher David Hume), our story makes sense. A sudden increase in the stock of money in one country will raise prices in that country relative to those the rest of the world, but it will then set in motion forces that ultimately will restore the initial equilibrium. Imports will increase relative to exports as prices rise because imports become relatively cheaper and exports relatively more expensive, and specie will flow to the rest of the world. The loss of specie will reduce the stock of money and prices, and this will continue until prices fall back to a level consistent with balance in international trade.

Since Hume's day, economists have developed many qualifications and alternatives to his prediction.

Advocates of the monetary theory of the balance of payments, for example, believe that prices of internationally traded goods will be kept in equilibrium at all times by commodity arbitrage (buying something where it is cheap and selling where it is expensive). They would expect to find the explanation for the U.S. inflation in a general inflation in countries on the bimetallic standard. They would expect the stock of money to increase during an inflation but only because a larger stock of money was demanded at a higher price level.

New theories force the historian to look at information that might have been ignored (here, the world price level and the lags between changes in money and prices). At the same time, the examination of historical episodes can help economists choose among and refine their theories (Economic Reasoning Proposition 5, evidence and theory give value to opinions).

words, does not appear to have acted irresponsibly during the 1830s, even after Jackson's veto.[7]

This episode shows that facts that seem to fit one interpretation on the surface may support an altogether different conclusion when thoroughly analyzed. It seems natural to blame Jackson for the inflation that occurred on his watch, but the real sources of the inflation were very different. We have another illustration of Economic Reasoning Proposition 5, evidence and theory give value to opinions, and further explanation in Economic Insight 12.3.

Though the attack on the second bank was not the cause of the inflation, it did influence the economy in other ways. During Biddle's reign throughout the 1820s and early 1830s, people placed an increasing trust in banks, largely because of the leadership and sound banking practices of the second bank. As a result, the proportion of money that people normally held in specie declined (Temin 1969, 159). Their confidence in paper money reached unusually high levels in the 1820s and early 1830s. Then events changed. First came Jackson's veto in 1832. This was followed by the Specie Circular in 1836, which required that most federal land sales be paid in specie. As prices rose and confidence in paper monies waned, more and more people returned paper for specie at their banks. When large numbers of noteholders attempted to do this, the banks were unable to make the exchanges, and banking panics occurred. (A strong second bank might have been able to nip these panics in the bud by acting as a lender of last resort.) The result was a sharp but temporary recession in 1837 and, finally, one of the worst depressions of the century from 1839 to 1843.[8]

---

[7]For this evidence and a pathbreaking reinterpretation of the Bank War, see Temin (1969).

[8]In addition, the Bank of England, concerned over the continuing outflow of specie to the United States, began to call in specie (sell back bonds) in 1837.

EXPERIMENTS IN STATE BANKING CONTROLS

The variety of banking systems that the states established during the antebellum era is simply astonishing. Some prohibited banking, some established state banks, some permitted "free banking," and this list could easily be extended. For this reason, economic historians have been drawn to this era to learn what sorts of banking systems work well and which do not.

The Suffolk System and the Safety Fund

Country bank note issues circulated widely in Boston. In 1824, six Boston banks joined with the Suffolk Bank of Boston to create a system for presenting country banks with their notes in volume, thus forcing them to hold higher reserves of specie. Soon after, the country banks agreed to keep deposits in the Suffolk Bank, resulting in the first arrangement of a clearing house for currencies of remote banks.

These deposits, a costless source of funds, helped make the Suffolk Bank one of the most profitable in the country. The other Boston banks shared in this profit through their ownership of Suffolk stock, so the arrangement was hardly altruistic. As result, however, the prevailing discounts on country bank notes fell. By 1825, country notes passed through the *Suffolk system* at par. Consequently, New England was blessed with a uniform currency.

The Suffolk Bank continued as the agency for clearing New England notes until 1858, when some new Boston banks and country banks that resented the dictatorial policies of the Suffolk Bank organized a rival institution. Shortly afterward, national banking legislation did away with state bank notes and the need for such regional systems, but the Suffolk system was the predecessor to the modern practice of requiring reserve deposits of member banks in the Federal Reserve system.

In addition to this private regulatory effort, New York in 1827 invoked state regulatory power. To increase protection for depositors and noteholders, the state passed a law holding bank stockholders responsible for debts equal to twice the value of their stock holdings. In 1827, New York passed the Safety-Fund Act, requiring new banks and those being rechartered to hold 3 percent of their capital stock in a fund to be used as reserves for banks that failed. This first state deposit insurance scheme failed in the panic of 1837,

A note issued by one of New Jersey's free banks. The bank's name stresses the point that the note is backed by government bonds (stocks).

but others were tried again and again. State deposit insurance schemes, although generally unsuccessful, were the forerunner of Federal Deposit Insurance initiated in the 1930s.

Free Banking

The most important of the bank experiments was the free banking law. The New York Assembly passed the first such law in 1838. Actually, between the beginning of the agitation for the New York system and final passage of the act establishing it, a Michigan statute provided for a similar plan, but the chief influence on American banking derives from the New York law. The adjective *free* indicates the most important provision of the law, under which any individual or group of individuals, upon compliance with certain regulations, could start a bank. Under the old rule, the privilege of starting a bank had to be granted by a special legislative act. Increased competition promised improved services and a reduction of legislative corruption.

To protect noteholders and sometimes to boost the state's credit, the free banking laws required the banks to deposit bonds, usually federal bonds or those issued by the state where the bank was located, with the state banking authority. If a bank refused to redeem a note in specie, the holder could protest to the state banking authority, which would then sell the bonds and redeem all of the bank's notes. The rules governing the amount and type of bonds that had to be deposited had a great deal to do with the success or failure of the system. If too much backing was required for each note issued, no banks would be set up. If too little backing was required, the way might be opened for wildcat banking. If the required backing protected note holders while permitting the bankers a reasonable profit, however, the system would work well.

In New York, to take the most important example, free banking was successful. The system expanded rapidly, and there were few failures. Indeed, the free banking systems of New York and Ohio were probably the models for the national banking system adopted during the Civil War. But Michigan's free banking law of 1837 produced a famous episode of wildcat banking. Despite apparent safeguards, including a safety fund, the law permitted dubious securities to be put up as a guarantee of note redemption.

Under the Michigan law, all a bank had to do to start operation was to show that it had specie on hand. Enterprising bankers showed an amazing ingenuity in outwitting examiners. Moreover, specie payments at the time were suspended nationwide because of a banking crisis, so the would-be wildcat banker did not even have to fear immediate withdrawals. Two bank commissioners noted a remarkable similarity in the packages of specie in the vaults of several banks on their examination list and later discovered that a sleigh drawn by fast horses preceded them as they went from bank to bank. Specie, some observers said, flew about the backwoods of Michigan with the "celerity of magic." Nearly all banks operating on such a basis failed and disappeared by 1840, but not before a victimized public had been stuck with their worthless notes.

The Forstall System

Reasonably sound banking systems usually developed in states that had reached a degree of economic maturity. It was not by chance that Louisiana law of 1842 set up a system, called the *Forstall system*, that became a model of sound and conservative banking. With a port second only to that of New York, Louisiana had economic ties with both a great productive hinterland and the rest of the world.

The most notable feature of the Louisiana law required banks chartered under it to keep a specie reserve equal to one-third of their combined note and deposit liabilities.

Before 1863, several states came to require specie reserves against notes, ranging variously from 5 to 33 percent; however, except for Louisiana and Massachusetts, they did not require reserves against deposit liabilities as well. The notion that deposits as well as bank notes were money was not universally recognized. Partly as a result of the Forstall system, New Orleans banks developed a well-deserved reputation for soundness, and their notes circulated widely. According to one possibly apocryphal theory, the South became known as the Land of Dixie because $10 notes issued in New Orleans bore the French word *dix* (ten) on the back.

The financial upheavals that we have discussed so far were the work of politicians and businessmen. The financial upheaval that began in 1848 had a very different origin, however.

THE ECONOMIC CONSEQUENCES OF THE GOLD RUSH

In 1848, gold was discovered in California. Soon men (almost no women) from all over the world were on their way to California (see Holiday 1999). Initially, the methods used to take the gold were simple. The gold was found in riverbeds. The gravel was scooped up and washed in a pan; the heavier gold remained, and the lighter elements washed away. If no gold was found, it was said that the gravel didn't "pan out." The miners, however, began to build machines that could wash larger and larger amounts of gravel. They realized, moreover, that still larger deposits must lie in the mountains crossed by the streams they worked. Where, they asked, was the "mother lode"? Soon the source of gold was found, and conventional mining began.

Because gold was the basis of much of the world's monetary system, the outpouring of gold from California (and from Australia, where discoveries were soon made) increased the world's money supplies. Table 12.1 shows the results in the United States. An index of the stock of money in the United States rose from 100 in 1849 to a peak of 182 in 1856, a rate of increase of about 8.5 percent per year. The result was a long economic boom, as indicated by the increase in gross domestic product (GDP) shown in column 3 of Table 12.1, and a substantial increase in prices, as shown in column 4.

How do we know that the increase in the stock of money caused the inflation, not some other factor? We cannot know for sure: Correlation does not prove causation. In

TABLE 12.1 MONEY, INCOME, AND PRICES, 1849–1859

YEAR	MONEY	REAL GDP	GDP PRICE DEFLATOR	FARM PRICES	CHEMICAL AND DRUG PRICES
1849	100	100	100	100	100
1850	120	104	104	101	—
1851	129	112	103	115	101
1852	143	122	104	124	103
1853	160	135	108	134	111
1854	161	141	118	150	114
1855	169	142	122	158	117
1856	182	149	120	135	116
1857	151	150	123	153	113
1858	173	154	112	123	111
1859	179	162	113	132	111

Sources: *Money: Friedman and Schwartz 1970, Table 14, column 3, 232. GDP: Carter 2006, series Ca13. Prices: Carter 2006, series Ca13, Cc114, Cc121.*

this case, however, we have a "natural experiment." We know that the increase in the stock of money was mostly due to luck. Either the inflation that followed occurred by chance, or it was caused by the increase in the stock of money; the inflation could not have caused the increase in the amount of gold. Recall Economic Reasoning Proposition 5, evidence and theory give value to opinions.

All prices did not rise at the same rate during the inflation. An example is shown in the last two columns of Table 12.1. Farm prices rose sooner and further than the prices of chemicals and drugs. By 1855, farm prices had risen 58 percent compared to 17 percent for chemical and drug prices; chemical and drug prices had *fallen* 41 percent relative to farm prices. Why were there such disparities? Factors specific to individual markets are likely to affect relative prices: Good or bad harvests, technological progress, changes in consumer tastes, and so on must be brought into the story when we discuss relative prices. The monetary expansion also may have played a role. It may have been true, as the great British economist William Stanley Jevons suggested, that prices in more competitive markets, such as agriculture, responded faster to the monetary expansion.

The long expansion came to an end in the Crisis of 1857, which is clearly visible in Table 12.1 as a sudden decline in money and (a year later) in prices. The failure of the Ohio Life Insurance and Trust Company, a large bank with a reputation for sound investing (whose main branch was in New York despite its origins in Ohio) that had invested heavily in western railroad bonds, shocked the financial community. Distrust of banks spread. Soon there were runs, and the banks, desperate to protect themselves, called in loans and refused to make new ones. The result was a sharp recession. Unemployment rose, and New York experienced bread riots. The crisis, moreover, aggravated the tensions that were already pulling the country apart. In the North, the newly formed Republican Party argued that the crisis showed that traditional parties did not know how to manage the economy. In the South, advocates of secession argued that the relatively mild impact of the crisis on the South proved that cotton was king and that the South would be better off without the North.

SELECTED REFERENCES AND SUGGESTED READINGS

Bodenhorn, Howard. *A History of Banking in Antebellum America: Financial Markets and Economic Development in an Era of Nation-building.* Cambridge: Cambridge University Press, 2000.

Campbell, Claude A. *The Development of Banking in Tennessee.* Self-published, 1932.

Carter, Susan B. *Historical Statistics of the United States: Earliest Times to the Present.* Millennial ed. New York: Cambridge University Press, 2006.

Ford, Paul Leicester, ed. *The Writings of Thomas Jefferson.* New York: Putnam's 1894.

Friedman, Milton, and Anna J. Schwartz. *Monetary Statistics of the United States.* Chicago: University of Chicago Press, 1970.

Gorton, Gary. "Reputation Formation in Early Bank Note Markets." *Journal of Political Economy* 104 (1996): 346–397.

Greenfield, Robert L., and Hugh Rockoff. "Gresham's Law in Nineteenth-Century America." *Journal of Money, Credit & Banking* 27 (November 1995): 1086–1098.

Holiday, J. S. *Rush for Riches: Gold Fever and the Making of California.* Berkeley: University of California Press, 1999.

Macesich, George. "Sources of Monetary Disturbances in the U.S., 1834–1845." *Journal of Economic History* 20 (1960): 407–434.

Rockoff, Hugh T. "Money, Prices and Banks in the Jacksonian Era." Chapter 33 in *The Reinterpretation of American Economic History*, eds. R. W. Fogel and Stanley Engerman. New York: Harper & Row, 1971.

Rolnick, Arthur J., and Warren E. Weber. "Gresham's Law or Gresham's Fallacy?" *Journal of Political Economy* 94 (February 1986): 185–199.

Selgin, George. "Salvaging Gresham's Law: The Good, the Bad, and the Illegal." *Journal of Money, Credit & Banking* 28 (1996): 637–649.

Temin, Peter. *The Jacksonian Economy.* New York: Norton, 1969.

CHAPTER **13**

The Entrenchment of Slavery and Regional Conflict

CHAPTER THEME

Slavery, as an economic and social organization, was morally and legally accepted by peoples everywhere for thousands of years. However, once abolitionist forces took effect, slavery collapsed in the Americas in approximately a century, between 1776 and 1888. First in the Caribbean and then throughout South America, politicians yielded to abolitionists' arguments and pressures to free the enslaved. In the southern United States, however, slavery based on race became increasingly entrenched in the decades leading to the Civil War. Investments in slaves had proved profitable, slave labor productivity and plantation efficiency were high, and wealthy planters who dominated southern politics clearly saw the wealth loss implications from abolitionists' aims. The clash of abolitionists' moral objectives and southern economic interests intensified as the country grew westward, until the force of arms resolved the issue on the battlefield.

AFRICAN SLAVERY IN THE WESTERN HEMISPHERE

In the 1860s, the African slave trade ended, bringing to a close three and a half centuries of forced migrations of nearly 10 million Africans across the Atlantic. Their dominant economic activity, overwhelmingly, was sugar production. As Figure 13.1 on page 220 shows, most of the slaves were destined for Brazil (36 percent) and the Caribbean islands (40 percent), areas economically based on sugar production. The United States received only 6 percent of the total numbers crossing the Atlantic. By 1825, the distribution of slaves was noticeably different from the pattern of arrivals. As revealed in Figure 13.2 on page 220, in 1825 the United States was the leading slave nation, housing 36 percent of all slaves in the Western Hemisphere. Differences in natural rates of population growth, negative in Brazil and in the Caribbean for long periods and positive and high in the United States, account for this significant demographic adjustment. Although having only a peripheral role in the Atlantic slave trade, the United States ultimately became the bulwark of resistance to the abolition of slavery in the Western world. This resistance was almost entirely in the southern United States.

In one sense at least, it is astonishing how quickly slavery collapsed in the Americas. For thousands of years, statesmen, philosophers, theologians, and writers had accepted uncritically the legitimacy and utility of slavery as a "time-honored" form of economic and social organization. Popes and queens and commoners alike accepted it. Early voices against it, such as the Germantown Quakers (Society of Friends), who in 1688 condemned it as a violation of the Golden Rule, were ridiculed. No actions compelling conformity to abolitionist arguments were taken until 1758, when the Quakers in

FIGURE 13.1

The Distribution of
Slaves Brought into the
New World, 1500–1870

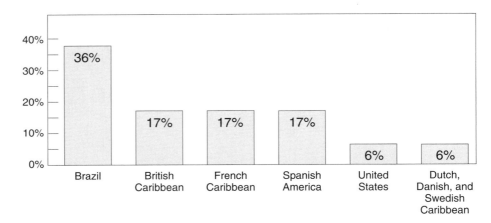

Source: *Fogel and Engerman 1974, 14. ©1974 by Robert W. Fogel and Stanley L. Engerman. Used by permission of W.W. Norton & Company, Inc.*

Philadelphia condemned both the slave trade and the owning of slaves. Members in violation were to be excluded from positions of responsibility in the Society of Friends.

Across the Atlantic, the English Society of Friends voted in 1774 to expel any member engaging in the slave trade. As shown in Table 13.1, a year later slavery was abolished in Madeira; the abolition fever strengthened and spread until Brazil, the last American bastion of slavery, abolished it in 1888.

FIRST U.S. CONSTRAINTS ON SLAVERY

In 1780, the enslaved populations in the United States totaled nearly 575,000. Nine percent of these resided north of the Chesapeake; the remainder lived in the South. As part of one of the great constitutional compromises, the nation's forefathers agreed in 1787 to permit the existence of slavery but not to allow the importation of slaves after 20 years. (In 1807, therefore, Congress prohibited the foreign slave trade, effective the following year.) Also in 1787, the Northwest Land Ordinance forbade slavery in the Northwest Territory.

FIGURE 13.2

The Distribution of
Slaves in the Western
Hemisphere, 1825

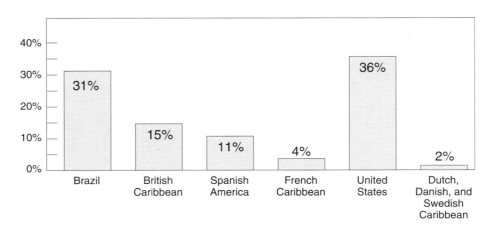

Source: *Fogel and Engerman 1974, 28. ©1974 by Robert W. Fogel and Stanley L. Engerman. Used by permission of W.W. Norton & Company, Inc.*

TABLE 13.1 A CHRONOLOGY OF EMANCIPATION, 1772–1888

1772	Lord Chief Justice Mansfield rules that slavery is not supported by English law, thus laying the legal basis for the freeing of England's 15,000 slaves.
1774	The English Society of Friends votes the expulsion of any member engaged in the slave trade.
1775	Slavery abolished in Madeira.
1776	The Societies of Friends in England and Pennsylvania require members to free their slaves or face expulsion.
1777	The Vermont Constitution prohibits slavery.
1780	The Massachusetts Constitution declares that all men are free and equal by birth; a judicial decision in 1783 interprets this clause as having the force of abolishing slavery. Pennsylvania adopts a policy of gradual emancipation, freeing the children of all slaves born after November 1, 1780, at their 28th birthday.
1784	Rhode Island and Connecticut pass gradual emancipation laws.
1787	Formation in England of the "Society for the Abolition of the Slave Trade."
1794	The French National Convention abolishes slavery in all French territories. This law is repealed by Napoleon in 1802.
1799	New York passes a gradual emancipation law.
1800	U.S. citizens barred from exporting slaves.
1804	Slavery abolished in Haiti.
	New Jersey adopts a policy of gradual emancipation.
1807	England and the United States prohibit engagement in the international slave trade.
1813	Gradual emancipation adopted in Argentina.
1814	Gradual emancipation begins in Colombia.
1820	England begins using naval power to suppress the slave trade.
1823	Slavery abolished in Chile.
1824	Slavery abolished in Central America.
1829	Slavery abolished in Mexico.
1831	Slavery abolished in Bolivia.
1838	Slavery abolished in all British colonies.
1841	The Quintuple Treaty is signed, under which England, France, Russia, Prussia, and Austria agree to mutual search of vessels on the high seas in order to suppress the slave trade.
1842	Slavery abolished in Uruguay.
1848	Slavery abolished in all French and Danish colonies.
1851	Slavery abolished in Ecuador.
	Slave trade ended in Brazil.
1854	Slavery abolished in Peru and Venezuela.
1862	Slave trade ended in Cuba.
1863	Slavery abolished in all Dutch colonies.
1865	Slavery abolished in the United States as a result of the passage of the Thirteenth Amendment to the Constitution and the end of the Civil War.
1871	Gradual emancipation initiated in Brazil.
1873	Slavery abolished in Puerto Rico.
1886	Slavery abolished in Cuba.
1888	Slavery abolished in Brazil.

Source: *Fogel and Engerman 1974, 33–34. ©1974 by Robert W. Fogel and Stanley L. Engerman. Used by permission of W.W. Norton & Company, Inc.*

It merits notice that the timing of the debates and discussions leading to the slavery restrictions in the Constitution and land ordinances coincided within days. In this way, the growth of slavery in the United States was limited and regionally restricted. Of course, the smuggling of human cargo was not uncommon, and various estimates suggest that as many as a quarter of a million blacks were illegally imported into the United States before 1860. But illicit human importation was only a minor addition to the total numbers held in bondage, and by 1860 foreign-born blacks were a small percentage of the enslaved population. Indeed, most blacks were third-, fourth-, and fifth-generation Americans. As mentioned earlier, natural sources of population expansion, averaging 2.4 percent per year between 1800 and 1860, were predominant in increasing the number of slaves. In 1863, the slaves numbered almost 4 million—all residing in the South.

Northern Emancipation at Bargain Prices

Even before the writing of the Constitution, some states had progressed toward the elimination of slavery. Between 1777 and 1804, the eight northeastern states individually passed measures to provide for the emancipation of their slave populations. In Vermont, Massachusetts, and New Hampshire, vague constitutional clauses left emancipation to the courts. Unfortunately, little is known about the results of this process; but in any case, these three states domiciled only a very small fraction of the northern blacks— probably 10 to 15 percent in 1780. As shown in Table 13.2, Pennsylvania, Rhode Island, Connecticut, New York, and New Jersey each passed laws of emancipation well before the year prohibiting slave importations. The process of emancipation used in these states was gradual, and the living population of slaves was not freed. Instead, newborn babies were emancipated when they reached adulthood (and were referred to as "free-born").

This form of emancipation demonstrates that many—perhaps most—of those who were politically dominant were more concerned with the political issue of slavery than with the slaves themselves. Besides not freeing the living slaves, there were no agencies in any of these states to enforce the enactments. In addition, the enactments themselves contained important loopholes, such as the possibility of selling slaves to the South.

The emancipation process, however, did recognize the issues of property rights and costs. These "gradual emancipation schemes" imposed no costs on taxpayers, and owners were not directly compensated financially for emancipated slaves. But curiously enough, owners were almost entirely compensated indirectly by maintaining the free-born in

TABLE 13.2 SLAVE EMANCIPATION IN THE NORTH FOR THE FREE-BORN

STATE	DATE OF ENACTMENT	AGE OF EMANCIPATION	
		MALE	FEMALE
Pennsylvania	1780[a]	28	28
Rhode Island	1784[b]	21	18
Connecticut	1784[c]	25	25
New York	1799[d]	28	25
New Jersey	1804[e]	25	21

[a]The last census that enumerated any slaves in Pennsylvania was in 1840.
[b]All slavery was abolished in 1842.
[c]The age of emancipation was changed in 1797 to age 21. In 1848, all slavery was abolished.
[d]In 1817, a law was passed freeing all slaves as of July 4, 1827.
[e]In 1846, all slaves were emancipated, but apprenticeships continued for the children of slave mothers and were introduced for freed slaves.

Source: *Fogel and Engerman 1974, 341.*

bondage until they had repaid their owner for their rearing costs. In most cases, these slaves were freed when they reached their mid-twenties. In the first several years after birth, a slave's maintenance cost was determined to be in excess of the value of his or her services (or output). Near the age of 10, the value of the slave's annual output usually just about matched the costs of food, clothes, and shelter. Thereafter, the value of output exceeded yearly maintenance costs, and normally by the age of 25 or 26, the slave had fully compensated the owner.

Thus, the slaves themselves bore nearly all the costs of emancipation in the North. Newborn slaves who eventually were freed fully paid back their owners for their rearing costs. Owners of males who were born before the dates of enactment suffered no wealth loss. Owners of females who were born before the enactments and who could or eventually would reproduce incurred some minor wealth losses in that they lost the value of their slaves' offspring. About 10 percent of the value (price) of a young female slave was due to the value of her offspring, and perhaps as many as 30 percent of the total enslaved population included females in their fertile or prefertile years.[1] Consequently, only 3 percent (10 percent of 30 percent) of the total slave wealth was lost to northern owners by abiding by these enactments, but the percentage was probably much closer to zero because of the loopholes of selling slaves to the South, working the slaves harder, and reducing maintenance costs.

The Persistence of Southern Slavery

Despite the constitutional restrictions on slave imports and the "gradual emancipation schemes" of the northern states, slavery did not die. Table 13.3 profiles the growth of the southern population, showing the slave population increasing slightly more rapidly than the free southern population. The proportion enslaved grew from about 49 percent in 1800 to 53 percent in 1860.

After Eli Whitney's invention of the cotton gin in 1793, mechanical means replaced fingers in the separation of seed from short-staple cotton varieties. The soils and climate of the South, especially the new Southwest, gave it a comparative advantage in supplying the massive and growing demand for raw cotton by the British and later by New England textile firms. Cotton quickly became the nation's highest-valued commodity export,

		BLACK		SLAVE AS A PERCENTAGE OF FREE
YEAR	**WHITE**	**SLAVE**	**FREE**	
1800	1.70	0.86	0.06	49%
1810	2.19	1.16	0.11	50
1820	2.78	1.51	0.13	52
1830	3.55	1.98	0.18	53
1840	4.31	2.43	0.21	54
1850	5.63	3.12	0.24	53
1860	7.03	3.84	0.26	53

TABLE 13.3 THE SOUTHERN POPULATION BY RACE, 1800–1860 (IN MILLIONS)

Note: Amounts rounded.
Source: Historical Statistics *1960.*

***

[1]Female slaves of all ages represented 37 percent of the total slave population.

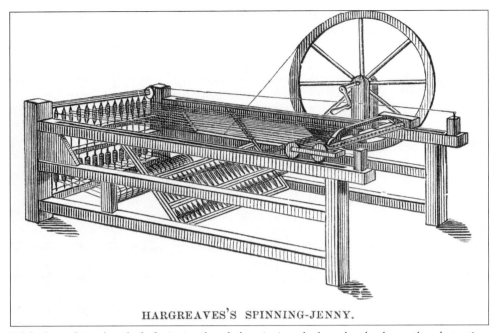

HARGREAVES'S SPINNING-JENNY.

While the traditional method of spinning thread, the spinning wheel, produced only one thread at a time, Hargreave's spinning jenny (1764) allowed an individual spinner to produce eight threads at once. Soon, as the engraving shows, the machine was improved so that even more threads could be spun at one time by one worker.

and output expanded as the southwestern migrations discussed in chapter 8 placed an army of slaves on new southwestern lands. According to estimates by Robert Fogel and Stanley Engerman (1974), nearly 835,000 slaves moved out of the old South (Maryland, Virginia, and the Carolinas, primarily), most of them going to the cotton-rich lands of Alabama, Mississippi, Louisiana, and eastern Texas. Three surges of movement and land sales occurred: the first in the years right after the end of the War of 1812, the second in the mid-1830s, and finally, the third in the early 1850s. (These are graphically shown in Figure 8.2, on page 136). The plantation based on slave labor was the organizational form that ensured vast economical supplies of cotton.

PLANTATION EFFICIENCY

In the heyday of King Cotton, the growth in the number and size of plantations in the South was dramatic. Of course, many small family farm units produced cotton and related items for market, but the really distinguishing characteristic of southern agriculture in the antebellum period was the plantation. Based on forced labor, the plantation represented both the economic grandeur and the social tragedy of the southern economy.

Although most of the condemnation of slavery was confined to moral and social issues, some of the damnation was extended to strictly economic aspects. In some instances, the forced labor of blacks was condemned as inefficient, either on racial grounds or because slavery per se was considered economically inefficient and unproductive. For example, the white contemporary observer Cassius M. Clay noted that Africans were "far less adapted for steady, uninterrupted labor than we are" (Clay 1848, 204). Another contemporary, Frederick Law Olmsted, reported that "white laborers of equal intelligence and under equal stimulus will cut twice as much wood, split twice as many rails, and hoe a third more corn a day than Negroes" (Olmsted 1953, 467–468).

There are sound reasons and growing evidence to reject these contemporary assertions and illustrate Economic Reasoning Proposition 5, evidence and theory give value to opinions, in Economic Insight 1.1 on page 8. For example, Gavin Wright (1978, 28) has shown that 86 percent of the South's cotton crop was grown on farm units of more than 100 acres containing 90 percent of the slaves, and cotton production increased by 1,100 to 1,200 percent between 1820 and 1860, while the slave population grew by 250 percent. This and additional evidence by Olmstead and Rhodes (2008) indicates more than a fourfold increase in cotton output per slave. Clearly, ample growth in agricultural productivity was based on slave labor.

ECONOMIC INSIGHT 13.1

CAPITAL ASSET VALUE OF A SLAVE

Writing in the first decade of this century, noted historian Ulrich Phillips (1905) claimed that antebellum southern slavery had become unprofitable by the 1840s and 1850s. This led some to believe, incorrectly, that slavery eventually would have died out because of market economic forces.

Phillips based his analysis on two time series: the price of prime field hands like that shown in the figure on the next page, and the trend of cotton prices. Cotton prices varied year to year, with $0.09 being typical in the 1840s and $0.10 being the average in the 1850s. With slave prices rising, especially between 1845 and 1859, but cotton prices hardly increasing, Phillips reasoned that investments in slaves increasingly were realizing losses. He further asserted that these losses surely occurred because slaves worked no harder in 1860 than in 1820 or 1830.

These conclusions were widely accepted until two economists, Alfred Conrad and John Meyer, took the pains in the late 1950s to actually measure the rates of return on investments in slaves. Their asset pricing model in its simplest form took into account the yearly expected output values (the price of cotton [Pc] times the marginal physical product of the slave [MPs], minus yearly maintenance costs (M) summed over the expected remaining length of life of the slave ($t = 0 \ldots 30$ years). This sum was discounted by (r) to equalize the price paid for the slave (Ps). Expressed as an equation,

$$P_s = \sum_{t=0}^{30} \frac{(P_c \times MP_s - M)_t}{(1 + r)^t}$$

As the equation illustrates, if the price of cotton should rise, or output per worker rise, or maintenance costs fall, profits would rise, sending the price of the slave upward. These calculations and a host of other estimates that followed showed a range of returns, typically 8 to 12 percent, that were competitive or above normal compared with returns on alternative investments at that time.

But how, then, did the prices of slaves rise if cotton prices did not? We now know the answer: more output per slave. Phillips erred in overlooking the productivity gains that arose over the period—from economies of scale as plantations grew, from other organizational advances such as assigning tasks, from moving into more productive areas (the southwestern migrations), new and improved cotton seeds (plants), and from other sources. Phillips's observation, perhaps correct, that slaves worked no harder in 1860 than earlier and used the same technology, overlooked other sources of productivity advance.

Furthermore, there is no evidence to suggest that slavery would have died out. Not even temporary periods of overcapitalization of slaves—that is, when prices of slaves were being bid too high—would support such a conclusion. Indeed, slave prices were apparently overcapitalized in the years from 1818 to 1820 and in the mid-1830s, and prices readjusted to lower levels, reducing losses on "overpriced slaves" to normal rate of return levels. The facts are that slaves produced more, much more, than it cost to rear and maintain them throughout the entire antebellum period. Only if the value of slave output had fallen below subsistence costs would owners have gained by setting slaves free.

ECONOMIC INSIGHT 13.1

CAPITAL ASSET VALUE OF A SLAVE, Continued

FIGURE 13.3
Price of a Prime Male
Slave, New Orleans,
1800–1860

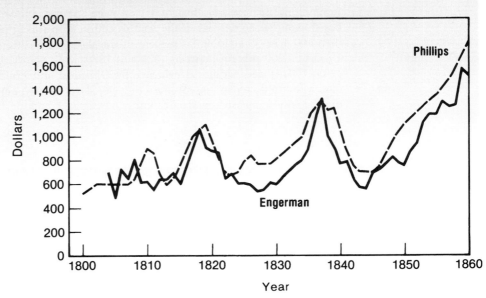

Source: *Ransom and Sutch 1988, 155. As reported there, the original sources to these two series are Phillips and Engerman, as follows. Phillips: Prices for 1800, 1801, and 1812 are estimated visually from Phillips 1929, 177. All other figures are from Conrad and Meyer 1958,
reprinted in Conrad and Meyer 1964, Table 17, column 6, 76. Engerman: Data were supplied by Stanley Engerman. They are mean values of the prices included in a sample of in-
voices of slave sales held in New Orleans. The sample size for each year ranged between 2.5
and 5 percent. The prices averaged refer to "males ages 18 to 30, without skills, fully guaranteed as without physical or other infirmity." Engerman "utilized only those cases in which
there was an individual price listed for a separate slave." For most years, about 15 to 20 observations were used in preparing the averages given.*

Another perspective is to compare plantations directly with free Southern farms.
Were plantations worked by masses of slaves more or less efficient than free-family
farm units? Did the South face increasing economic retardation as slavery became more
and more entrenched?

Before diving into the evidence, we must acknowledge certain caveats. The problems
of measuring efficiency comparatively have been a source of intense scholarly debate.
The agricultural output comparisons are really valued outputs rather than strictly physical output comparisons. Variations in soil type and location also pose problems of
measurement.

Of course, because of their size, plantations produced more cotton and other goods
and foodstuffs than the southern free-family farms. But when comparing output per
unit of input (capital, labor, and land in combination), and after adjusting at least in
part for variations in land quality, location, length of workday and work year, and other
factors, it is clear that the large plantations were considerably more productive than the

TABLE 13.4 COMPARISONS OF EFFICIENCY IN SOUTHERN AGRICULTURE BY FARM TYPE AND SIZE (INDEX OF FREE SOUTHERN FARMS = 100)

NUMBER OF SLAVES	INDEX OUTPUT PER UNIT OF TOTAL INPUT
0	100
1–15	101
16–50	133
51 or more	148

Source: *Fogel and Engerman 1977, 285.*

small or slaveless farms.[2] Table 13.4 shows these productivity comparisons for southern farms and plantations as well as for plantations worked by different numbers of slaves. By far the most efficient units were those using 50 or more slaves. Small-scale farming was less productive per unit of input employed, and there was little difference in efficiency between southern free-family farms and small farms employing only a few slaves. Therefore, it appears that racial factors had an insignificant effect on productivity. Black workers with their complementary but white-owned capital and land were about as productive in small units as white workers on single-family farms.

It was the large plantations with sizable numbers of slaves where exceptionally high productivity levels were witnessed. One contributing factor was the organization of the slaves into production units called *gangs*. Coupled with this was the careful selection of the slaves by strength and skill for particular tasks and the intensity per hour that the slaves were worked. Another factor was the improved varieties of seeds and plants developed (primarily) on the larger plantations, which radically improved the tasks of growing and picking cotton. Yet another was the superior lands occupied by the larger plantations, especially as cotton production expanded westward. The gang system was most pronounced on extremely large sugar plantations in the Caribbean and in South America (see Fogel 1989). These plantations were more like factories than farms, with the organization of slaves resembling an assembly line of workers. Though less striking in cotton, contemporary reports reveal a similar strong commitment to careful tasking and intensity.

> *The cotton plantation was not a farm consisting, as the farm does, in a multiplicity of duties and arrangements within a limited scope, one hand charged with half a dozen parts to act in a day or week. The cotton plantation labor was as thoroughly organized as the cotton mill labor. There were wagoners, the plowmen, the hoe hands, the ditchers, the blacksmiths, the wheelwrights, the carpenters, the men in care of work animals, the men in care of hogs and cattle, the women who had care of the nursery...the cooks for all...[n]o industry in its practical operation was moved more methodically or was more exacting of a nice discrimination in the application of labor than the Canebrake Cotton plantation.*

---

[2]For a lively but highly technical debate on the issues of measuring the relative efficiency of slavery, see the exchanges in the March 1979 and September 1980 issues of the *American Economic Review* between Paul David and Peter Temin; Gavin Wright, Donald Schaefer, and Mark Schmitz; and Robert Fogel and Stanley Engerman.

PERSPECTIVE 13.1

THE SLAVE FAMILY

In the 1930s the Works Projects Administration and Fisk University compiled nearly 2,200 interviews with ex-slaves. This unique source of information about life under slavery, though undoubtedly biased to various degrees, allows us valuable insights into the slave family (for greater detail and discussion, see Crawford 1992, the source of the following evidence).

Table 13.5 gives the distribution of family structure under slavery, showing more than half of those interviewed being children of two-parent families living together. Another 12 percent had two parents in their lives, but with the father resident in another plantation and normally allowed weekly visits. Official passes were given for those "approved visits," but many reported that dads often risked being whipped by sneaking other visits. Within the mother-headed households (33 percent) between 15 and 25 percent were formed because the father was white. Death of fathers and separation by sale

account for the rest of these single-mother families. Sexual contact between female slaves and whites was much more frequent on small than on large plantations. Once broken by death, desertion, or sale, slaves seldom remarried (stepfathers were very seldom mentioned in the narratives).

The average number of children per slave family are shown in Table 13.6 and the large numbers are consistent with the view that white owners preferred slaves in family formations.

Though slaves were sold, thus breaking marriages, such disruptions to the family were not costless to owners. The numbers of fathers being sold away are not known, but children were undoubtedly sold away more frequently than fathers or mothers. Table 13.7 shows the probability by age of a child's being sold away from the family. A child by the age of 16 had typically faced the risk of a 20 percent chance of being sold away from the family. Prudence, if not sensitivity, led to few small children being sold.

TABLE 13.5 DISTRIBUTION OF FAMILY TYPE FOR SLAVE'S FAMILY OF ORIGIN

FAMILY TYPE	ABSOLUTE FREQUENCY	PERCENTAGE WITHIN SAMPLE
Two-parent, consolidated	694	51.1%
Two-parent, divided residence	168	12.4
One-parent, female headed	451	33.2
One-parent, male headed	24	1.8
Orphan	20	1.5
Total	1,357	100.0%

Note: Family of origin is given by the structure at the time the slave was sold from the family or at emancipation.

Source: *Crawford 1992.*

TABLE 13.6 THE AVERAGE NUMBER OF CHILDREN PER SLAVE FAMILY

FAMILY TYPE	NUMBER OF CHILDREN
Two-parent, consolidated	7.2
Two-parent, divided residence	8.0
One-parent, female headed	5.7

Source: *Crawford 1992.*

PERSPECTIVE 13.1

THE SLAVE FAMILY, Continued

TABLE 13.7 PROBABILITY OF A CHILD'S SALE FROM THE FAMILY OF ORIGIN, BY AGE

AGE	PERCENTAGE SOLD[a] (1)	EXPECTED NUMBER SOLD[b] (2)	CUMULATIVE NUMBER SOLD (3)	SLAVES AT GIVEN AGE OR OLDER[c] (4)	CUMULATIVE PROBABILITY OF SALE[d] (5)
3	4.8%	5.23	5.23	1,833.6	.0028
4	7.1	7.74	12.97	1,764.6	.0073
5	7.1	7.74	20.71	1,695.6	.0122
6	7.1	7.74	28.45	1,599.9	.0178
7	14.3	15.59	44.04	1,519.4	.0290
8	14.3	15.59	59.63	1,423.6	.0419
9	2.4	2.62	62.25	1,308.6	.0476
10	9.5	10.36	72.61	1,222.4	.0594
11	11.9	12.97	85.58	1,118.9	.0765
12	2.4	2.62	88.20	1,021.2	.0864
13	4.8	5.23	93.43	915.8	.1020
14	4.8	5.23	98.66	785.6	.1256
15	4.8	5.23	103.89	705.1	.1473
16+	4.8	5.23	109.12	561.4	.1944
Total	100.0%	109.00			

[a]Derived from the percentage of ex-slaves who reported being sold at that age among all who gave age at sale.
[b]Derived by multiplying the percentages in column 1 by 109, the total number of ex-slaves in the entire sample sold from their families.
[c]Derived by applying the age distribution of the subsample of ex-slaves who gave their exact age, 1,167, to the entire sample, 1,916.
[d]Column 3 divided by column 4.

Source: *Crawford 1992.*

When the period for planting arrives, the hands are divided into three classes: 1st, the best hands, embracing those of good judgment and quick motion; 2nd, those of the weakest and most inefficient class; 3rd the second class of hoe hands. Thus classified, the first class will run ahead and open a small hole about seven to ten inches apart, into which the 2nd class [will] drop from four to five cotton seeds, and the third class [will] follow and cover with a rake.[3]

Exceptional levels of productivity for large-scale slave labor in the antebellum period was made possible in part by speeding up the work and demanding greater work intensity, not longer hours, and the efficiency gains stemmed also from worker-task selection and the intensity of work per hour. In fact, slaves on large plantations typically took longer rest breaks and worked less on Sundays than their white counterparts did. Indeed, these conditions were needed to achieve the levels of work intensity imposed on the slaves. It is apparent that these productivity advantages were not voluntary. Essentially, they required slave or forced labor. No free-labor plantations emerged during the period.

[3]These quotations by contemporaries are in reference to the Canebrake Plantation and the McDuffie Plantation, respectively. See Metzer (1975) for complete citations and other examples.

And as we will see, a significant reduction occurred in labor participation, work intensity, and organization after emancipation.[4]

New research by Olmstead and Rhodes (2008), however, has directed us to additional sources of productivity gains in cotton. Biological innovations—new seeds from Mexico and elsewhere—were used and adapted to soils as cotton cultivation moved west onto exceptional highly fertile soils. Picking was not performed by gangs, but plots were assigned to individual slaves so intensity of work was maintained, with the threat of the lash as the option for failure of assignment. New larger bolls and taller plants eased the task of picking, leading to a fourfold increase of cotton picked per day per slave. This implied a 2.3 percent per annum advance in labor productivity, well above average gains elsewhere (Olmstead and Rhodes 2008, 1153). Finally, the large plantation productivity

Invoice of a sale of slaves, 1835. The last two sentences are of special interest.

---

[4]Recent work on disease incidence differences between whites and blacks in the American South suggests another possible contributing factor to the productivity explanation. Blacks in adulthood had much less incidence of malaria and hookworm (the most common debilitating disease in the South) than whites (see Coelho and McGuire 1999). This difference likely affected the productivities of white versus black laborers, but by how much is not clear. The closeness of the productivity measures for free southern white farms and small plantations suggests these effects were small.

advance was in part, an East-West phenomenon. The virgin western soils held an advantage, but the western producers, which were the largest, also enjoyed the greatest advantage in the use of the new seed varieties. These biologically based cotton productivity boosters were invented and improved upon in the South West.

ECONOMIC EXPLOITATION

It hardly needs to be stressed that black slaves were exploited. They had no political rights, and the law of the plantation and the whim of the taskmaker was the web of confinement the slave directly faced. Owners did not carelessly mistreat their slaves, for obvious reasons. By our measure, a prime male field hand was worth close to $600,000 in 2007 prices (see Economic Insight 13.2).

Various forms of punishments and rewards pressured slaves to be obedient workers. Few failed to witness or feel the sting of the lash and fear combined with the hopelessness of escape in maintaining control. Slaves' standards of living were low but self-sustaining; these certainly would have been much higher if the value of their total output had been returned to them. However, because the property rights to their labor and their product resided with the white owner, their output accrued to the owner.

Richard Vedder (1975) has attempted to measure the economic exploitation of slaves in the South. His measure is based on the fundamental economic proposition that workers in competitive industries such as cotton production tend to be paid amounts that are equal to what labor contributes at the margin. An additional worker adds a certain value of output. Any sustained difference between the value of output the worker adds and what he or she receives may be reasonably termed economic exploitation.

ECONOMIC INSIGHT 13.2

1860 SLAVE PRICES IN TODAY'S VALUES

In 1860 a prime unskilled male field slave cost about $1,800. But how much is that in today's money? One way of answering the question is by using a cost of living index (consumer price index).

A good estimate is that in 2007 the consumer price index was about 25.7 times the level in 1860. So using the consumer price index to inflate (to use the economist's term) the cost of a slave gives a figure in today's money of about $46,000 ($1,800 × 25.7). There are other ways, however, of putting historical values into today's money. Wages of unskilled labor in 1860 were perhaps $0.10 per hour. Today the wage of unskilled labor, at least in some areas of the country, would be about $7.50 per hour. Using wages to inflate yields a figure in the neighborhood of $135,000 ($1,800 × [$7.5/$0.10]). A third way of putting $1,800 in 1860 into today's money is by using per capita income. In 1860, per capita income was about $128; in 2007, per capita income was about

$46,000. Therefore, using per capita income to inflate the value of a slave yields a value in today's money of almost $600,000.

As this example illustrates, there is no unique way of putting things into today's money. The best method to use in a particular circumstance depends on the reason for asking the question. Inflating by the consumer price index tells us what kind of consumption someone was forgoing by owning a slave. For example, if we wanted to get an idea of how much of a sacrifice someone made by freeing a slave, rather than selling him, the first calculation would be appropriate. The other calculations tell us something about how much power a slaveholder had within the society in which he lived, about how much "noise" (political, economic, and social leverage) slaveholders made in the world, to use Deirdre McCloskey's term. If we want to know how valuable an asset a slave was in the production process, perhaps the high figure of $600,000 is most appropriate.

For the average slave, this difference (the value of output added minus maintenance costs) divided by the value of the output added was at least 50 percent and may have been as high as 65 percent.[5]

Of course, there was much more to the exploitation issue than simply taking one-half of each worker's earnings. The mere entrapment of workers blocked their advance materially and otherwise by taking away their incentive for self-improvement and gain.

Perhaps the best thing that can be said about the economic conditions of American slavery is that typically they were not as bad as the conditions of slavery elsewhere. The drastic relative declines in the slave population in the Caribbean and in Brazil testify to the especially brutal conditions there. By comparison, the southern United States offered treatment that was life-sustaining. Slaves in the antebellum South experienced standards of material comfort that were low by today's standards but well above those of the masses in many parts of their contemporary world.

ECONOMIC ENTRENCHMENT AND REGIONAL INCOMES

Although the slave system proved efficient on the plantation, its economic advantages were not widely applicable elsewhere. As a result, the South experienced little structural change during the antebellum years. For instance, the South was slow to industrialize, partly because of the slave system. Some slaves did become skilled craftsmen, and slaves were employed in cotton factories, coal mines, ironworks, lumber mills, and railroads. There was little point in incurring the costs of training slaves for industrial occupations on a large scale, however, when they could readily and profitably be put to work in agriculture.

In addition, the South experienced little immigration from Europe or elsewhere. It was not the South's "peculiar institution" that kept European migrants away; immigration did not increase after emancipation. Europeans tended to settle in latitudes where the climate was like that of their former home. The main deterrent to locating in the South, however, was that outsiders perceived a lack of opportunity there; immigrants feared that they would become "poor whites." By 1860, only 3.4 percent of the southern population was foreign born, compared with 17 percent in the central states and 15 percent in New England.

When viewed as a business, plantation slavery was profitable. Extremely high net returns in parts of the cotton belt and rewards at least equal to those of alternative employments of capital in most areas of the Deep South were the rule. Nor were there economic forces at work making the slave economy self-destructive. There is simply no evidence to support the contention that slave labor was overcapitalized, and slaves clearly reproduced sufficiently to maintain a growing workforce. In addition, internal migration from the older southern states to the new cotton belt illustrated the flexibility of the southern economy.

This flexibility, exhibited in the western migrations, was especially important to the South. Table 13.8 shows income figures for various regions in 1840 and 1860. Note that the nearly 44 percent growth in income for the entire free South, from $105 to $150, was higher than the internal growth of any subregion in the South (about one-third for the old South, about 15 percent for the new South). The southern migrations, in contrast to those in the north, were from poorer to richer areas on average, and this leveraged up

---

[5]For further elaboration, see Vedder (1975). As Vedder notes, in New England cotton textile mills (a sample of 71 firms) in 1820, the comparable exploitation calculation was 22 percent; for iron workers in 1820 (101 firms), the rate was 28 percent. Similar levels of exploitation (24 and 29 percent, respectively) have been computed in Ransom and Sutch (1977, 3).

TABLE 13.8 PER CAPITA INCOME BEFORE THE CIVIL WAR (IN 1860 PRICES)

	TOTAL POPULATION		FREE POPULATION	
	1840	**1860**	**1840**	**1860**
National Average	$ 96	$128	$109	$144
North	109	141	110	142
Northeast	129	181	130	183
North Central	65	89	66	90
South	74	103	105	150
South Atlantic	66	84	96	124
East South Central	69	89	92	124
West South Central	151	184	238	274

Source: *Fogel and Engerman 1971, Table 8, 335. ©1971 by Harper & Row Publishers, Inc. Reprinted by permission of Pearson Education, Inc.*

the income growth for the South as a whole. As we shall see, the South was vitally concerned, for apparently sound economic reasons, with the right to extend slavery into western lands. Also noteworthy is the relative position of the West South Central region, where King Cotton and sugar reigned supreme. This was by far the highest income region in the country. And these high relative standings remain whether or not slaves are included in the population figures. When the incomes per capita of only the free population are compared, even the older, less wealthy southern areas show levels that were quite high.[6] There can be little doubt that on the eve of the Civil War, the South was a very rich area indeed.

From the moral, social, and political viewpoints, however, southern slavery imposed a growing source of self-destruction on the American people. The system epitomized a great barrier to human decency and social progress that was contrary to deeply felt ideals in many quarters. With almost religious fervor, abolitionist elements grew in strength, and national disunity grew proportionately.

As the moral arguments against slavery gained a greater hearing, the economic costs of emancipation grew as well. Table 13.9 shows the wealth held in slaves in the South by

TABLE 13.9 TOTAL VALUE OF SLAVES IN THE UNITED STATES, 1810–1860 (IN MILLIONS OF DOLLARS)

YEAR	TOTAL VALUE
1810	$ 316
1820	610
1830	577
1840	997
1850	1,286
1860	3,059

Source: *Ransom and Sutch 1988.*

---

[6]Fogel and Engerman (1974) used $20 per year as the average income of slaves to estimate the incomes of only the free population. Later work by them and others raised the yearly average values of slave consumption (income). Therefore, modest downward adjustments in the free population in the South are required, but they do not change significantly the conclusions given here.

decade. After 1830, the rise in value was dramatic, reaching almost $3.1 billion in 1860. According to Ransom and Sutch (1988), slaves represented 44 percent of the total wealth in the major cotton-growing states in 1859, and real estate accounted for another 25 percent (1988, 138–139). Could $3.1 billion in taxes be raised to compensate owners for slaves emancipated? Would owners give up such wealth voluntarily? As an additional consideration, southerners had witnessed, in the late 1830s, the outcome of rapid emancipation in the British West Indies. There, land values plummeted when the gang system disappeared and labor was withdrawn from the fields. The prospect of land value losses adding to the wealth losses of uncompensated emancipations stiffened the resolve of the South's slaveholding oligarchy.

Laws were passed in the southern states increasing the punishment for insurrection and for assisting runaways: Eleven states imposed the death penalty on slaves participating in insurrection, and 13 made it a capital crime for free men to incite slave insurrection. Several states began requiring legislative consent for manumission on a case-by-case basis. Seven required newly freed slaves to leave their territory. Freedoms to bear arms, assemble in public meetings, and sell liquor were frequently denied free blacks. In these and other ways, slavery became more entrenched, both economically and legally.

POLITICAL COMPROMISES AND REGIONAL CONFLICT

For a majority of Americans living at the time of slavery, the most significant issue was its containment, not its eradication. Indeed, the basis of political compromise on this issue was first established in the Northwest Ordinance, passed unanimously by Congress in 1787. Article six reads:

[T]here shall be neither slavery nor involuntary servitude in the said territory…provided always, that any person escaping into the same, from whom labor or service is

A familiar scene—slaves picking cotton as white overseers look on. Costs of supervision were higher in northern agriculture because the labor force often had to be dispersed.

© BETTMANN/CORBIS

claimed in any of the original states, such fugitive may be lawfully reclaimed and conveyed to the person claiming his or her labor or service as foresaid.

The 1787 ordinance, in effect, outlawed slavery in lands that became the states of Ohio, Indiana, Michigan, Illinois, Wisconsin, and Minnesota. This set the stage for controlling the expansion of slavery in other territories, allowing some new regions at least to be nonslave, but this important legislation did not provide a final solution.

The western migrations, both north and south, continued to bring the issue of slavery to a head. The key problem for the South, as a political unit, was to maintain at least equal voting power in the Senate. The South accomplished this objective and won a series of compromises that enabled it to extend the institution of slavery and counter abolitionist threats.

In 1819, the Senate was balanced: There were 11 slave and 11 free states. By the Missouri Compromise of 1820, Missouri was admitted as a slave state and Maine as a free state on the condition that slavery should thereafter be prohibited in the territory of the Louisiana Purchase north of the 36 × 30′ line (see Map 13.1). For nearly 30 years after this, states were admitted to the Union in pairs, one slave and one free, and by 1850, there were 15 free and 15 slave states. As of that year, slavery had been prohibited in the Northwest Territory, in the territory of the Louisiana Purchase north of 36 × 30′, and in the Oregon Territory—vast areas in which an extensive slave system would not have been profitable anyway. Violent controversy arose over the basis of admission for prospective states in the area ceded to the United States by Mexico. The terms of the Mexican Cession required that the territory remain permanently free, yet Congress in 1848 had rejected the Wilmot Proviso, which would have prohibited slavery in the Southwest, where its extension was economically feasible. In the end, California was admitted as a free state in 1850. In the territories of Utah and New Mexico, however, slaveholding could be permitted. The final decision on slavery was to be made by the territorial populations on application for admission to the Union.

Further events of the 1850s for a time appeared to portend ultimate victory for the South. The Kansas-Nebraska Act of 1854 (see Map 13.2 on page 236) in effect repealed

MAP 13.1

The Missouri Compromise of 1820

After this enactment, growing sectional acrimony was supposed to be a thing of the past. For a time, a truce did prevail.

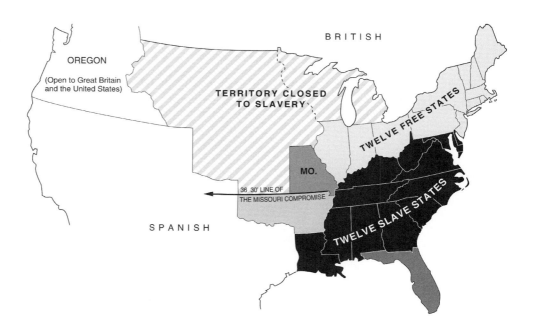

MAP 13.2

New Settlements

The Compromise of 1850 and the Kansas-Nebraska Act of 1854 were further attempts to keep sectional strife from erupting into war. The concept of "popular sovereignty" introduced in the latter act, however, led to conflict in Kansas.

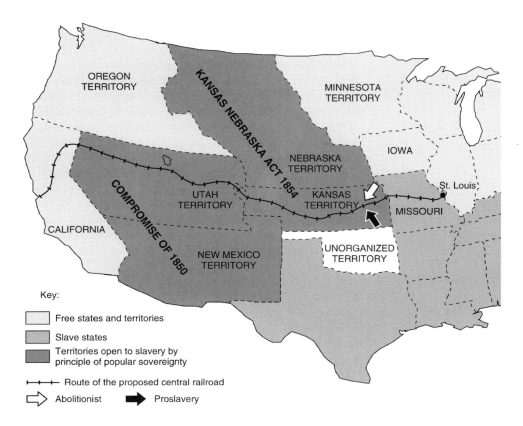

Key:

☐ Free states and territories

▨ Slave states

▨ Territories open to slavery by principle of popular sovereignty

├┼┼┤ Route of the proposed central railroad

⇨ Abolitionist   ➡ Proslavery

the Missouri Compromise by providing for "popular sovereignty" in the hitherto unsettled portions of the Louisiana Purchase. The result was gunfire and bloodshed in Kansas. In the *Dred Scott* decision (1857), the Supreme Court went even further, declaring that Congress could not prohibit slavery in the territories. And during this time, southerners, desperately eager to inhibit the movement of small farmers into territories where slavery could not flourish, successfully resisted passage of a homestead act that would have given free land to settlers.

Yet legislative successes could be achieved only as long as Democrats from the North and Northwest were willing to ally themselves with the South. Toward the end of the 1850s, the antislavery movement in the North became irresistible. In large part, the movement was led by those who opposed slavery on purely ethical grounds, but altruistic motives were reinforced by economic interests. Northwest farmers resisted the extension of the plantation system because they feared the competition of large units with their small ones. And as transportation to eastern centers improved, especially through the Northern Gateway, the products of the Northwest increasingly flowed into the Middle Atlantic states and Europe. In this way, the people of the Northwest found their economic interests more closely tied to the eastern industrialists than to the southern planters. The large migrations of Irish and Germans, who had no stake in slavery, added to the shift in economic and political interests near midcentury. The Republican party, founded in the mid-1850s, capitalized on the shift in economic interests. As old political alignments weakened, the Republican party rapidly gained strength, chiefly from those who opposed the extension of slavery into the territories.

In the opening speech of his sixth debate with Stephen A. Douglas on October 13, 1858, in Quincy, Illinois, Abraham Lincoln elaborated on slavery:

We have in this nation the element of domestic slavery….The Republican party think it wrong—we think it is a moral, a social, and a political wrong. We think it is a wrong not confining itself merely to the persons or the State where it exists, but that it is a wrong which in its tendency, to say the least, affects the existence of the whole nation….I suppose that in reference both to its actual existence in the nation, and to our constitutional obligations, we have no right at all to disturb it in the States where it exists, and we profess that we have no more inclination to disturb it than we have the right to do it….We also oppose it as an evil so far as it seeks to spread itself. We insist on the policy that shall restrict it to its present limits….We oppose the Dred Scott decision in a certain way….We propose so resisting it as to have it reversed if we can, and a new judicial rule established upon this subject.

Lincoln's advocacy of fencing in slavery as the South saw it violated the federal Constitution. Cotton was already flourishing in Texas. California and Arizona boded well for the extension of cotton cultivation. These promising lands had been acquired from Mexico in the 1840s. Were southerners to be excluded from them?

From the southern perspective, the election of Lincoln in 1860 presented only two alternatives: submission or secession. To a wealthy and proud people, submission was unthinkable.[7] To Lincoln, alternatively, the Union had to be preserved.

The war that maintained the Union cost the country more lives and human suffering than any other war in the history of the United States. Although initially, emancipation was not an objective of the northern war effort, it became the ultimate moral justification for the war.

SELECTED REFERENCES AND SUGGESTED READINGS

Clay, Cassius Marcellus. *The Writings of Cassius Marcellus Clay: Including Speeches and Addresses*, ed. H. Greeley. New York: Harper, 1848.

Coelho, Philip R. P., and Robert A. McGuire. "Biology, Diseases, and Economics: An Epidemiological History of Slavery in the American South." *Journal of Bionomics* 1 (1999): 151–190.

Conrad, Alfred, and John Meyer. "The Economics of Slavery in the Antebellum South." *Journal of Political Economy* 66 (1958): 95–130.

———. *The Economics of Slavery and Other Studies in Economic History*. New York: Aldine, 1964.

Crawford, Stephen. "The Slave Family: A View from the Slave Narratives." In *Strategic Factors in Nineteenth Century American Economic History: A Volume to Honor Robert W. Fogel*, eds. Claudia Golden and Hugh Rockoff, 331–350. Chicago: University of Chicago Press, 1992.

Engerman, Stanley L. "Slavery and Its Consequences for the South in the Nineteenth Century." In *The Cambridge Economics History of the United States*, Vol. II, *The Long Nineteenth Century*, eds. Stanley L. Engerman and Robert E. Gallman, 329–366. New York: Cambridge University Press, 2000.

Fogel, Robert W., *Without Consent or Contract: The Rise and Fall of American Slavery*. New York: Norton, 1989.

Fogel, Robert W., and Stanley L., Engerman. "The Relative Efficiency of Slavery: A Comparison of Northern and Southern Agriculture in 1860." *Explorations in Economic History* 8 (Spring 1971): 353–367.

———."Philanthropy at Bargain Prices: Notes on the Economics of Gradual Emancipation." *Journal of Legal Studies* 3, no. 2 (June 1974): 341.

———. *Time on the Cross: The Economics of American Slavery*, 2 vols. Boston: Little, Brown, 1974.

———. "Explaining the Relative Efficiency of Slave Agriculture in the Antebellum South." *American Economic Review* 67 (June 1977): 275–296.

---

[7]Recall the prewar scene from *Gone With the Wind* when eager southern warriors were predicting a short war and a decisive southern victory. Rhett Butler, alone, cautioned to the contrary.

_____. "Explaining the Relative Efficiency of Slave Agriculture in the Antebellum South: A Reply." *American Economic Review* 70 (September 1980): 672–690.

Historical Statistics. Washington, D.C.: U.S. Government Printing Office, 1960.

Metzer, Jacob. "Rational Management, Modern Business Practice, and Economies of Scale in the Antebellum Plantations." *Explorations in Economic History* 12 (April 1975): 123–150.

Olmstead, Alan L., and Paul W. Rhodes. "Biological Innovation and Productivity Growth in the Antebellum Cotton Economy." *Journal of Economic History* 68, no. 4 (2008): 1123–1171.

Olmsted, Frederick L. *The Cotton Kingdom: A Traveler's Observations on Cotton and Slavery in the American Slave States,* ed. A. M. Schlesinger. New York: Knopf, 1953.

Phillips, Ulrich B. "The Economic Cost of Slaveholding in the Cotton Belt." *Political Science Quarterly* (June 1905).

_____. *Life and Labor in the Old South.* Boston: Little, Brown, 1929.

Ransom, Roger L., and Richard Sutch. *One Kind of Freedom.* Cambridge: Cambridge University Press, 1977.

_____. "Capitalists without Capital: The Burden of Slavery and the Impact of Emancipation." *Agricultural History* (Summer 1988): 133–160.

Schmitz, Mark D., and Donald F. Schaefer. "Slavery, Freedom, and the Elasticity of Substitution." *Explorations in Economic History* 15 (July 1978): 327–337.

Sutch, Richard. "The Treatment Received by American Slaves: A Critical Review of the Evidence Presented in Time on the Cross." *Explorations in Economic History* 12 (October 1975): 335–438.

Vedder, Richard K. "The Slave Exploitation (Expropriation) Rate." *Explorations in Economic History* 12 (October 1975): 453–458.

Wright, Gavin. "Slavery and the Cotton Boom." *Explorations in Economic History* 12 (October 1975): 439–452.

_____. *The Political Economy of the Cotton South: Households, Markets, and Wealth in the Nineteenth Century.* New York: Norton, 1978.

PART 3

The Reunification Era: 1860–1920

ECONOMIC AND HISTORICAL PERSPECTIVES *1860–1920*

1. For nearly 100 years following 1815, there were no major wars between national coalitions. The U.S. Civil War, the nation's bloodiest war ever, was a violent exception in this long period of global peace.

2. After the Civil War, rapid industrialization in the North and renewed western expansion sustained a high overall growth rate for the nation. The large absolute fall in output in the South due to the war and emancipation and the slow pace of growth in the cotton belt ushered in an era of southern backwardness and regional disparity.

3. Emancipation redistributed wealth and incomes sharply from white slave owners to blacks but created a legacy of slavery that sustained black poverty, especially in the Deep South.

4. By the mid-1890s, the United States had become the world's leading industrial power, and by 1910, it was outproducing by nearly twice the nearest industrial rival, Germany, while England had slipped into third place.

5. Technological change, economies of scale, and mass production methods became the main engines of modern economic growth, powered by growth enhancing institutions.

6. The path of growth was far from smooth. Periods of deflation, financial crises, and fears of the concentration of wealth led to demands for reform of the economic and financial systems.

7. The U.S. population topped 100 million during World War I; 48 states were in the Union; and federal, state, and local expenditures combined reached a record high of nearly 10 percent of GNP.

CHAPTER **14**

War, Recovery, and Regional Divergence

CHAPTER THEME

The Democratic Party split in mid-1860, permitting the Republican candidate for president, Abraham Lincoln, to win the November election with a mere 40 percent of the popular vote. Lincoln carried the North and West solidly, but his name did not even appear on 10 state ballots in the South. The South's political strategy had been to control the Senate and the presidency. Both were lost in 1860.

By the time of Lincoln's inauguration on March 4, 1861, 10 southern states had followed South Carolina's decision to secede. One of Lincoln's first tasks was to counter threats to Fort Sumter in Charleston Harbor. His order to reinforce the fort gave South Carolinians the excuse they sought to begin shooting.

Slavery was the root cause of the Civil War. The United States had equivocated on the slave issue both in 1776 and in 1790. The last "slavery truce," in 1850, was based on popular sovereignty in the western territories, and it ended within a decade. By 1860, the South was prepared to fight to save its social order, based on plantation slavery. The North was prepared to fight to save the Union and to save the Republican victory that "finally had contained the slave power within the political framework of the United States" (Ransom 1989, 177). Permitting independence to the southern states would have divided the nation and allowed the South to pursue a separate foreign policy committed to the expansion of slavery.

Lincoln's key miscalculation, like the South's, was his belief that a strong show of force would bring the fighting to a speedy end. The South's victory at Bull Run, the first great battle of the Civil War, added to southern confidence and resolve to maintain the course of rebellion.

The war proved to be longer and more destructive than anyone in power imagined at its start. An estimated 620,000 American soldiers and sailors would lose their lives, nearly as many as in all the rest of America's wars combined. By the time the war ended, America's society and economy had been radically transformed. The most important change was the freeing of 4 million slaves. Moreover, the institutional framework (Economic Reasoning Proposition 4, laws and rules matter, in Economic Insight 1.1 on page 8) of nearly every aspect of economic life—including finance, education, land policies, and tariff policies—was altered in some way. In the North and parts of the South, recovery from the war was rapid. But in parts of the South, the institutional framework that developed after the Civil War prevented the former slaves and poor whites from being rapidly integrated into the mainstream of the American economy.

THE ECONOMICS OF WAR

Despite ample pride, talent, and faith in its cause, the South was woefully unprepared for a protracted war. Figure 14.1 provides a rough portrayal of the available human

FIGURE 14.1
Population of Males
10–49 Years of Age in
1860 (in thousands)

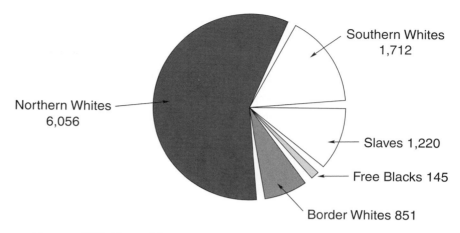

Southern Whites
1,712

Northern Whites
6,056

Slaves 1,220

Free Blacks 145

Border Whites 851

Source: *Ransom 1989, Figure 6.2.*

resources that each side possessed for potential combat. The reality of the situation, moreover, was that the 1.2 million military-age slaves in the South could not be used for fighting on the front, and probably fewer than 30 percent of eligible whites in the Border states sided with the southern cause.

Indeed, the South had to use some of its precious manpower to repress its slave labor force. And, when circumstances permitted, slaves and free blacks joined the Union forces, further tipping the balance in favor of the North. By the end of the war, blacks in the Union army alone outnumbered the Confederate forces. Conventional military wisdom of the day calculated a ratio of two to one for an attacking army to overcome a defending army. Ultimately, those calculations proved valid: The North could outman the South three or more to one.

In industrial capacity, the comparisons are even more lopsided. Value added in manufacturing in the North, according to Fred Bateman and Thomas Weiss (1981), totaled $1.6 billion in 1860. It totaled merely $193 million in the South, with half of it in Virginia. Richmond, Virginia, was also the site of the only cannon manufacturer in the South. (The original buildings are still there along the James River.) Initially, neither side had a significant advantage in arms production, and both depended heavily on imported arms. But the North was able to increase production quickly. The South was much less able to do this, and its lack of domestic manufacturing bore down heavily after the federal naval blockade during 1863 and 1864 shut off foreign supplies.

Particularly troubling to the South, especially after the North took control of the Mississippi River, was the lack of a transport network sufficient to move food and supplies to the troops. The South's limited rail network was strained to capacity, but the primary shortage was of horses and mules. Because the fighting was largely on southern soil, the South's animal stocks fell relative to the North's as the war wore on.

These comparisons, however, do not mean that the South's decision to fight was irrational. The South's hope was that the North would eventually tire of the enormous human costs of the war and agree to let the South go its own way. The Revolutionary War had provided a forceful example of a nation winning independence from an economically and militarily more powerful foe. (For Robert E. Lee, that example was part of the family history: His father, "Light-Horse Harry" Lee, had been an outstanding cavalry commander in the Revolution.) In the summer of 1864, even after numerous southern defeats, it still seemed possible that war weariness might defeat Lincoln in his bid for reelection—indeed, Lincoln himself doubted that he would win—and that Lincoln's successor might negotiate a peace that preserved slavery. However, General William Tecumseh Sherman's capture of Atlanta in September rekindled Lincoln's fortunes, and Lincoln's reelection sealed the South's fate.

Trade and Finance Policies South and North

With the exception of two new government-built and -operated munitions factories, the South maintained its emphasis on agriculture. The South's early confidence in the power of King Cotton and the likelihood of a quick end to fighting, moreover, encouraged it to adopt trade policies that reinforced its poor preparation for war.

The northern naval blockade did not become effective until 1863. Thus, for nearly two years, the South could produce and export specialty crops, particularly cotton, to England in exchange for munitions and manufactures. The Confederate government, however, discouraged exports in the hope of forcing England to support the southern effort; during 1861 and 1862, the South exported only 13,000 bales of cotton from a crop of 4 million bales. The southern government also imposed a ban on sales of cotton to the North. Although the "cotton famine" imposed severe costs on British employers and workers, England could not be moved from neutrality. In hindsight, it is clear that these policies weakened the southern war effort.

Besides production and trade problems, the South also faced financial difficulties. Although a few bonds backed by cotton were sold in Europe, foreigners for the most part were unwilling to lend to the Confederacy, especially after the North's naval blockade became effective. It also proved difficult, for both political and economic reasons, to develop an effective administrative machinery for collecting taxes. The South's war materials and support, therefore, were financed primarily by inflationary means—paper note issues. Only 40 percent of its expenditures were backed by taxes or borrowing.

Indexes of prices and money in the South (given in Figure 14.2) show clearly that prices rose further and faster than the stock of money and that the final months were ones of hyperinflation. There were two reasons for the gap that opened between prices and money: the decline in southern production and the decline in confidence in the southern currency.

FIGURE 14.2

Inflation in the Confederacy

The rate of inflation was not very great in the beginning of the Civil War, but the value of a Confederate dollar had depreciated to about 1 percent of its original value by the end of the war.

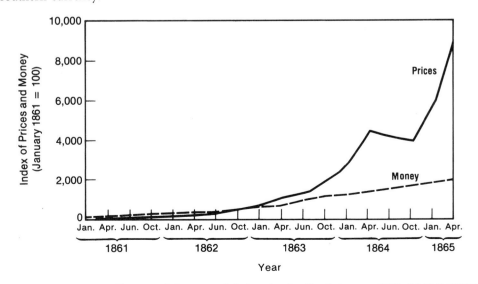

Source: *E.M. Lerner, "Money, Wages, and Prices in the Confederacy, 1861–1865," JOURNAL OF POLITICAL ECONOMY 63, February 1955): 29. Reprinted by permission of the University of Chicago Press.*

© BETTMANN/CORBIS

The South could not match the vast amount of munitions produced by northern industry.

A diary account of an exchange in 1864 reveals the decline in confidence in the Confederate paper money:

She asked me 20 dollars for five dozen eggs and then said she would take it in "Confederate." Then I would have given her 100 dollars as easily. But if she had taken my offer of yarn! I haggle in yarn for the million the part of a thread! When they ask for Confederate money, I never stop to chafer. I give them 20 or 50 dollar cheerfully for anything. (Chestnut 1981, 749)

Despite the heroism and daring displayed by the Confederates, Union troops increasingly disrupted and occupied more and more southern territory. By late 1861, Union forces controlled Missouri, Kentucky, and West Virginia; they took New Orleans in the spring of 1862, cutting off the major southern trade outlet. By 1863, thanks to the brilliant campaigning of Ulysses S. Grant, the entire Mississippi River basin was under Union control. Sherman's march through Georgia in 1864, in which he followed a deliberate policy of destroying the productive capacity of the region, splintered the Confederacy and cut off Lee's Army of Northern Virginia from an important source of supplies.

Once a Union victory appeared likely, confidence declined even more sharply, producing the astronomical rates of inflation experienced in the final months of the war.

The economic strain of the war was not as severe in the North as it was in the South, but the costs of the war were extremely high even there. A substantial portion of the labor force was reallocated to the war effort, and the composition of production changed with the disruption of cotton trade and the growing number of defaults on southern debts. At the outset, in 1861, a sharp financial panic occurred, and banks suspended payments of specie. With the U.S. Treasury empty, the government quickly raised taxes and sold bonds. The tax changes included the first federal taxes on personal and business incomes. But the most significant increases were in tariffs and internal taxes on a wide range of commodities—including specific taxes on alcohol and tobacco (which are still with us) as well as on iron, steel, and coal—and a general tax on manufacturing output. Despite these increases, however, bond sales brought in nearly three times the revenues of taxes.

The Union government also resorted to inflationary finance. Paper notes, termed "greenbacks" because of their color (and because they were backed by green ink rather than gold or silver), were issued. They circulated widely but declined in value relative to gold.[1] In 1864, one gold dollar was worth two and one-half greenbacks, and the northern price level in 1864 in terms of greenbacks was twice what it had been in 1860. Nevertheless, the North escaped the near hyperinflation that confounded the South.

THE CIVIL WAR AND NORTHERN INDUSTRIALIZATION

Writing in the years between World War I and World War II, Charles and Mary Beard (1927) and Louis Hacker (1940) provided a captivating economic interpretation of the Civil War—namely, that the war spurred northern industrial expansion. The *Beard-Hacker thesis* emphasized the transfer of political power from southern agrarians to northern industrial capitalists. With new power in Congress, northern legislators passed laws intended to unify markets and propel industrialization. The range of new programs established during the war was remarkable, including the establishment of the national banking system, an increase in tariffs (to protect American industry from foreign competition), the land-grant college act, and grants of land to transcontinental railroads.

The Beard-Hacker thesis also emphasized that the war stimulated the economy and increased investment. This part of the thesis, however, has been rejected in subsequent research, based on estimates of economic activity that were not available when the thesis was formulated (Economic Reasoning Proposition 5, evidence and theory give value to opinions, in Economic Insight 1.1 on page 8). Perhaps this is less surprising when we realize that nearly 1 million men—or almost 15 percent of the labor force of 7.5 million—were normally involved in the fighting each year. Of these working-age soldiers, 259,000 Confederate men and 360,000 Union men were killed and another 251,000 southerners and 356,000 northerners were wounded. One person was killed and another wounded for every six slaves freed and for every 10 southerners kept within the Union. Claudia Goldin and Frank Lewis (1975) have assessed these permanent losses of labor and human capital (Economic Reasoning Proposition 2, choices impose costs) to have had economic values approaching $1.8 billion ($1.06 billion in the North and $787 million in the South—all lost). In addition, the North spent $2.3 billion directly on the war effort; the South spent $1 billion through direct government outlays. Another $1.5 billion worth of property was destroyed, most of this in the South. These combined sums of

---

[1]The greenbacks were legal tender for paying private debts (including the obligations of banks to their depositors), but they were not legal tender for paying tariffs—these had to be paid in gold.

TABLE 14.1 AVERAGE ANNUAL RATE OF GROWTH OF COMMODITY OUTPUT, 1840–1899		
YEARS	**U.S. ECONOMY**	**MANUFACTURING SECTOR**
1840–1859	4.6%	7.8%
1860–1869	2.0	2.3
1870–1899	4.4	6.0

Source: *Gallman 1960.*

$6.6 billion were probably more than twice the size of our national income in 1860 and exceeded eight times the value added of total U.S. manufacturing that year.

The tragedy of the Civil War is compounded by the fact that in 1860, the total market value of slaves was approximately $3.06 billion (Ransom and Sutch 1988, 151). The costs of the war were more than twice the cost of purchasing the slaves. This does not mean that peaceful abolition was realistic before the war. After 1845, peaceful abolition like that undertaken by the British in the West Indies was viewed in the South as a complete disaster. Southerners were convinced that the economy of the West Indies was in shambles and that slave owners there had lost fortunes in the process of emancipation.

The work of Stanley Engerman (1971a and 1971b) and Robert Gallman (1960) provides further ground for rejecting the Beard-Hacker thesis that the Civil War stimulated postwar industrialization. As shown in Table 14.1, growth rates of total commodity output and manufacturing output were no higher, and possibly lower, after the Civil War than they were before the War.

Even within the various war industries of the North, there was no great spurt; by and large, the new dimensions of output in the North were modest adjustments in the various sectors. In fact, the most startling aspect of the war years was the minute stimulus to manufacturing. Iron production for small arms increased, but iron production for railroads declined. Although the demand for clothes and boots for servicemen stimulated manufactures, the loss of the southern market more than offset this. For example, in Massachusetts—the center of boot and shoe production—employment and output in that important industry decreased almost one-third during the war. Similarly, without raw cotton, the textile mills were underutilized. True, the enlistment and conscription of men ameliorated unemployment, and speculation offered opportunities for enrichment for a select few. Overall, however, expenditures by the federal government did not spur rapid industrialization or economic expansion.

We have considered the debate over the Beard-Hacker thesis in detail because it illustrates so clearly the importance of quantitative evidence. An argument may be persuasive, and it may be supported by numerous illustrative examples, but it can still be wrong (Economic Reasoning Proposition 5, evidence and theory give value to opinions).

ECONOMIC RETARDATION IN THE SOUTH

The economic outcome of the war was a distinct reversal in the relative positions of the North and South. As shown in Table 14.2, in 1860 the North's real commodity output per capita was slightly less than the South's ($74.8 compared with $77.8). By 1870, the North's per capita output exceeded the South's by nearly two-thirds ($81.5 compared

TABLE 14.2 COMMODITY OUTPUT PER CAPITA BY REGION (IN 1879 PRICES)

YEARS	OUTSIDE THE SOUTH	SOUTH
1860	$ 74.8	$77.7
1870	81.5	47.6
1880	105.8	61.5

Source: *Engerman 1966, 181.*

with $47.6). This advantage remained in 1880. The major source of this reversal was not the northern and midwestern advance, but the dramatic absolute decline in southern output during and shortly after the war.

It would be an error, however, to conclude that the entire southern economy remained stagnant. The commodity output per capita figures for 1870 and 1880 show that the South's growth rate was initially rapid and close to the North's growth rate of almost 2.6 percent yearly. Such high rates were not sustained, however, nor were they distributed evenly across the South. Table 14.3 shows estimates of the rate of growth of personal income per capita in real terms for the five most cotton-dependent states of the Deep South (Louisiana, Georgia, Mississippi, South Carolina, and Alabama) and for the remaining eight southern states from 1879 to 1899. Clearly, there was great variation among the southern states, with several growing more than twice as fast as those making up the Deep South.

TABLE 14.3 ANNUAL RATES OF GROWTH IN CONSTANT–DOLLAR VALUES OF PER CAPITA PERSONAL INCOME BY STATE BETWEEN 1879 AND 1899

STATE	ANNUAL PERCENTAGE RATES OF GROWTH PER CAPITA PERSONAL INCOME
Louisiana	0.44%
Georgia	0.81
Mississippi	0.96
South Carolina	0.98
Alabama	1.14
Five cotton states	**0.86**
North Carolina	1.38
Kentucky	1.42
Arkansas	1.43
Tennessee	1.89
Virginia	2.15
West Virginia	2.26
Texas	2.53
Florida	2.64
Total, 13 southern states	**1.54**
United States	**1.59%**

Source: *Derived from Easterlin 1960, 185.*

Richmond, Virginia, after the destruction caused in the Civil War.

As this evidence suggests, southern manufacturing rebounded from the war more quickly than southern agriculture. Southern manufacturing output had approached pre-war levels by the early 1870s, and the South's transportation network (based on steamboats, roads, and railroads) had been completely revitalized. This revitalization was accomplished with reasonable ease, requiring little more than repairs and replacements and modest additions of capital. In fact, as John Stuart Mill had noted shortly before the Civil War, rapid postwar recoveries have been quite common throughout history:

An enemy lays waste a country by fire and sword, and destroys or carries away nearly all the movable wealth existing in it; all the inhabitants are ruined, and yet in a few years after, everything is much as it was before. . . .The possibility of a rapid repair of their disasters, mainly depends on whether the country has been depopulated. If its effective population have not been extirpated at the time, and are not starved afterwards; then, with the same skill and knowledge which they had before, with their land and its permanent improvements undestroyed, and the more durable buildings probably unimpaired, or only partially injured, they have nearly all the requisites for their former amount of production. (Mill 1940 [1848], 75)

Rapid regeneration is propelled by eliminating bottlenecks. For example, the South's railroad network had almost ceased to function by the war's end, largely due to the lack of rolling stock and partially destroyed track; the roadbed, specialized labor expertise, and considerable track remained in good condition but were unusable. Prompt investment in the essential complementary resources (rolling stock and damaged track) reemployed the other existing resources (labor, roadbed, and usable track). This initiated a regenerative spurt, and other similar spurts in combination led to a temporary high-growth period. When these unusual investment opportunities had been fully exploited, the long-run slower rate of growth resumed (for elaboration on the theory of regenerative growth, see Gordon and Walton 1982). In agriculture, however, the prospects for southern recovery were quite different. Lincoln's Emancipation Proclamation altered the whole makeup of the South's agricultural society for both whites and blacks. The results were great reductions in agricultural output, especially during the late war years and the immediate postwar years. In the absence of emancipation, the South's agricultural sector surely would have restored itself within a few years; but the political, social, and economic adjustments stemming from emancipation delayed regenerative growth for many years.

The decline in southern output, especially in the cotton states of the Deep South, was much deeper than that precipitated by war destruction alone. Indeed, the growth of agricultural output in the Deep South averaged negative 0.96 percent per year from 1857 to 1879.

Decline in the Deep South

The five key cotton states of the Deep South have been shown to have experienced the greatest setbacks (Table 14.3). This precipitous decline occurred for three principal reasons.

First, the highly efficient plantation system was destroyed, and attempts to resurrect plantation methods proved futile. Free blacks shunned assembly-line methods employing gangs that were driven intensively from dawn to dusk, as they always had been by free whites. In place of the plantations, smaller units arose—some owned, many rented, and many sharecropped (the owner of the land and the tenant split the crop). Table 14.4 shows the alteration in farm sizes between 1860 and 1870 in the Deep South. Whereas 61 percent of the farms had been less than 100 acres in 1860, 81 percent were under 100 acres in 1870. Economies of scale based on the intense driving of slave labor were lost.

A second closely related reason was the significant withdrawal of labor from the fields, especially labor by women and children. This reallocation of human effort undoubtedly raised household production and improved the quality of life, but it nevertheless contributed to the decline in measured per capita agricultural output in the Deep South by 30 to 40 percent between 1860 and 1870.

Finally, the growth of the demand for southern cotton slowed because of competition from India, Brazil, and Egypt, and because the growth of world demand slowed. The U.S. South had dominated the world cotton market in 1860, commanding 77 percent of English imports (see Ellison 1968, in Gavin 1974; also see Wright 1978, 1986). During the war years, however, when the door to the new competition was opened, only 10 percent of England's cotton came from the South. The South's market share rebounded well in the late 1870s, but it never reached its 1860 high mark.

TABLE 14.4 FARM SIZE DISTRIBUTION IN FIVE MAJOR COTTON STATES

IMPROVED ACRES	PERCENTAGE OF FARMS IN SIZE CLASS		PERCENTAGE OF LAND IN SIZE CLASS	
	1860	1870	1860	1870
3–49	36.9%	60.9%	7.4%	20.2%
50–99	24.2	19.8	12.0	19.6
100–499	32.0	17.2	47.6	49.1
500+	6.9	2.1	33.0	11.0

Source: *Ransom and Sutch 1977, 71.*

The decline in the Deep South immediately after the Civil War was to be expected. The tragedy was that southern agricultural production remained depressed for decades afterward. The most puzzling aspect of the decline in the Deep South was the increased concentration on cotton. Unlike small prewar southern farms, small postwar farms, especially those operated by former slaves, became highly specialized in cotton. In the five main cotton-growing states, 82 percent of nonslave farms (85 percent of all farms) had grown cotton in 1860 compared with 97 percent of all farms there in 1870 (Ransom 1989, Table 7-3, 257). Moreover, a greater proportion of the land on each farm was devoted to cotton production in 1870 than in 1860. Indeed, whereas many slave plantations had been self-sufficient in food before the Civil War, the Deep South now became a food-importing region. Black farmers were the most cotton dependent, with 85 percent of their crop in cotton compared with 60 to 70 percent for white farmers. White owners placed the smallest proportion of their land in cotton; white tenant farmers produced nearly twice that of white owners, and black tenants nearly four times that of white owners. Increased dependency on cotton occurred despite declining cotton prices in the 1870s.

Concentration on cotton production was not irrational. Stephen DeCanio (1974a and 1974b) has shown that the South had a comparative advantage in cotton production and that southern cotton farmers were about as responsive to price changes as northern wheat farmers were to wheat prices (Economic Reasoning Proposition 3, incentives matter). Nevertheless, the limited economic alternatives provided by the cotton economy sentenced many former slaves to a life of grinding poverty. To see why this happened, we must explore the transition from slavery to freedom and the new economic institutions that replaced the old.

The Inequities of War

Men from lower-income groups primarily waged fighting in the Civil War. Once the need for mass mobilization was evident, both sides turned to the draft to acquire men, and both sides allowed conscripts to buy out their service by paying another to go in their place. From this time on, the war was widely and correctly viewed as a "rich man's war and a poor man's fight." While this policy shifted the burden of fighting to the poor, it arguably had efficiency advantages. The exchanges were voluntary, and if those with higher labor opportunity costs were replaced by those with lower opportunity costs, the overall costs of the war effort were reduced. The inequities, however, remained.

In the North, the cities witnessed the most heated discontent, especially New York, where large numbers of immigrants lived. The Irish, especially, felt that the burden of the draft was falling on them. In July 1863, mobs stormed through the streets of New York for four days; 20,000 federal troops were needed to quell the riots, which resulted in 105 deaths.

The recruitment and drafting of large numbers of men might have been expected to raise the real wages of those working on the home front by reducing the available supply of labor, but this did not happen.

As shown in Figure 14.3, prices rose more rapidly than wages in the North. Thus, real wages (wages/prices), the amount of goods and services that could be bought with an hour's work, fell. Wesley C. Mitchell, who first studied this problem, thought that workers bargained ineffectively because they (and their employers) were influenced by customary notions about wages. The wage lag, he believed, had produced a surge in profits that could be invested after the war, another reason for thinking that the war accelerated industrialization (Mitchell 1903, 347). Reuben Kessel and Armen Alchian (1971), however, pointed out that the fall in real wages could also be explained by rising taxes, rising

FIGURE 14.3
The Wage Lag in the North during the Civil War

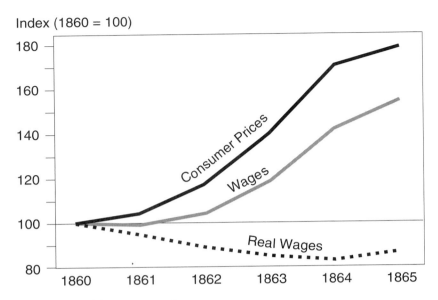

Index (1860 = 100)

Source: *Kessel and Alchian 1971, 460.*

prices of imported goods, and other real factors (Fogel and Engerman 1971). Subsequently, Stephen DeCanio and Joel Mokyr (1977) showed that failure to anticipate inflation explains about two-thirds of the fall in real wages and real factors about one-third. Northern labor, in other words, would have experienced a substantial decline in its income in any case, but the inability of labor markets to adapt rapidly to the inflation made things a lot worse than they otherwise would have been.

Inequality was even more glaring in the South. In October 1862, the southern draft law was altered to allow an exemption for anyone owning 20 or more slaves. Although this exemption benefited small numbers, it created great resentment. Small farmers were infuriated to see their farms, dependent on their own labor, deteriorate while rich plantations were maintained. R. M. Bradford of Virginia wrote the Confederate Secretary of War in October 1864:

> *The people will not always submit to this unequal, unjust, and partial distribution of favor and wholesale conscription of the poor while able-bodied and healthy men of property are all occupying soft places. (Escott 1978, 119)*[2]

The South did not use slaves for fighting because both masters and slaves knew the enemy provided a route to freedom.[3] Ironically, the efforts of slaves to grow cotton, spurred by the exceptionally high prices in the early 1860s, was negated by the South's trade policies to England. Most of this vital labor was simply wasted as high stockpiles of cotton rotted in the countryside and on the docks.

THE LEGACY OF SLAVERY

The Thirteenth Amendment to the Constitution freed all slaves; the Fourteenth Amendment ensured that no "state shall deprive any person of life, liberty or property, without

---

[2] R. M. Bradford to James Seddon, quoted in Escott (1978, 119).

[3] At the very end of the war, the South considered plans to employ slaves as soldiers.

due process of law" and guaranteed that "the right of citizens to vote shall not be abridged." These amendments were passed soon after the war but were not sufficient to ensure sustained progress for blacks. The first effects of the new freedoms surely helped blacks dramatically. Just as surely, many southern whites suffered in the late 1860s. The redistribution and changing levels of income by race are shown in Figure 14.4. In addition, average wealth holdings of whites in the Deep South in 1860 had been $81,400 for plantation owners, $13,300 for slave-owning small farmers, and $2,400 for nonslave-owning farmers. In 1870, the average for all white farmers in the Deep South was $3,200. Resentment against Yankees and blacks reflected the whites' slide in wealth and hatred of the northern occupation.

Land reform that broke up the plantations and gave the land to former slaves was pushed by Republicans in Congress. This might have set the South, and ultimately the whole country, on a different course. The House and Senate each passed a bill to give black heads of households 40 acres, but President Andrew Johnson vetoed it. Except in a few isolated areas such as the Sea Islands of Georgia and on the former plantation of Confederate President Jefferson Davis, where land reform proved to be a success in promoting stable farming communities, most of the land remained in the hands of the same people who had owned it before the war. Roger Ransom and Richard Sutch (1977, 79) show that the wealthiest fifth of the population still owned 73 percent of the land in 1870, a drop of only 2 percent from 1860. Moreover, the power of northern Republicans to ensure a solid political base in the South by protecting the civil rights of the former slaves was limited by economic conditions nationally and by an absence of effective local support in the South. When the courts upheld President Johnson's executive order of total amnesty to anyone willing to take an oath of allegiance, the old Confederates began to take power—aided by violence, including that of the newly formed Ku Klux Klan. The Constitutional amendments protecting black rights were subverted, and blacks ultimately became disenfranchised.

FIGURE 14.4
Distribution of Agricultural Output per Capita by Race in the Deep South, 1857 and 1879

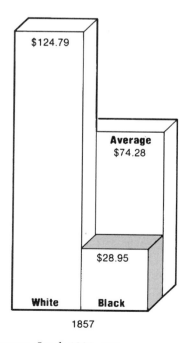

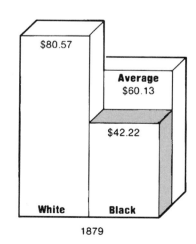

Source: *Sutch 1981, 145.*

ECONOMIC INSIGHT 14.1

THE LABOR MARKET IN THE NORTH DURING THE CIVIL WAR

This figure shows why real wages would have declined in the North during the Civil War even if inflation had been held in check. S-1860 is the supply of labor before the war, and D-1860 is the demand.

The expansion of the armed forces reduced the supply of labor to S-1864. Other things being equal, this would have raised real wages. But the demand for labor is derived from the demand for final products. Rising taxes on production (excise taxes) and rising costs of imported products reduced profits and the demand for labor from D-1860 to D-1864. The shift in demand was greater than the shift in supply and lowered equilibrium real wages from W-1860 to W-1864.

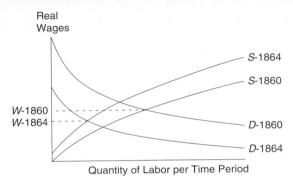

In the immediate aftermath of the war, there was considerable interstate migration of former slaves. Much of this movement can be explained by the efforts of former slaves to reunite families broken up during slavery. Perhaps also, many former slaves wanted to see more of the country in which they lived, a privilege denied to them by slavery. From 1870 to 1890, however, black migration within the South, as shown by Philip E. Graves, Robert L. Sexton, and Richard K. Vedder (1983), was reduced compared with migration during the antebellum period. While slaveowners would generally move or sell slaves whenever economic considerations dictated, the former slave could also weigh the costs of leaving behind family, friends, and familiar institutions (Economic Reasoning Propositions 1, scarcity forces us to make choices; and 2, choices impose costs). Black migration to the North did not become truly large until after 1910, when a combination of rising northern wages, rising expectations of a better life, and the information provided by earlier generations of migrants encouraged a mass exodus. This important wave of northern migration also opened new occupational opportunities for blacks and spurred their mobility into higher earnings categories (see Maloney 2001). Nevertheless, before 1910 most African Americans had to make their living in southern agriculture. Most were simply hired hands earning abysmally low wages. Many, however, worked the land as tenant farmers or in a small but surprising number as owners.

As shown in Figure 14.5 on page 255, blacks worked about 30 percent of the land in crops, and whites worked 70 percent. Blacks were close to 70 percent of the agricultural work force in 1880 but owned less than 10 percent of the land. (As can be seen in the figure, if 30 percent was occupied by blacks and 32 percent of that land was owned by blacks, then 0.3×0.32, or 9.6 percent, of all land was owned by blacks.) Given the resistance and hostility of white southerners and the absence of any federal redistribution

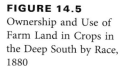

FIGURE 14.5

Ownership and Use of Farm Land in Crops in the Deep South by Race, 1880

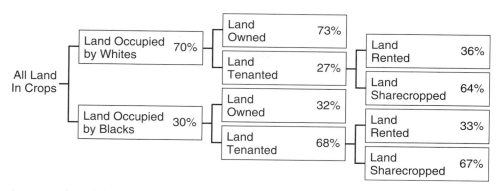

Source: *Adapted from Ransom and Sutch 1977, 84.*

program, it is a wonder that blacks owned even this much land. Of the two-thirds of the land that was tenanted by blacks, two-thirds was sharecropped.

Instead of paying a fixed annual sum in dollars for the use of the land, the basic idea of sharecropping was for the sharecropper to split the crop with the land owner after the harvest. Standard yearly contracts gave a 50-50 split to owner and tenant. Economic historians have hotly debated the benefits and costs of sharecropping. To Ransom and Sutch (1977), tenant farming, sharecropping in particular, was a disaster that forced the former slaves into dependency on cotton, and in some cases into a condition similar to slavery known as "debt peonage."

Others, however, have concluded that sharecropping offered a number of advantages, at least compared with the available alternatives. Former slaves and poor whites were provided independence from day-to-day bossing and given a chance to earn a living. The risk of a very bad year—due perhaps to poor growing conditions or unusually low prices—was shared with the owner. The sharecropping contract, moreover, as Joseph Reid (1973) has pointed out, also gave the owner an incentive to remain interested in the farm throughout the growing season and to share information such as changing crop prices with the tenant. On large plantations where such information sharing was difficult, renting predominated (Alston and Higgs 1982). Just as the sharecropper shared part of the risk of a bad harvest with the owner, he also shared part of any gain from his own hard work. Tenant farmers had an incentive to slight long-term investments. Competition among tenants and incentives built into rental contracts only partially offset the negative effects of renting on long-term investment.

Meanwhile, the credit system added to the cropper's burden. The source of rural credit was the white-owned country store. Here the farmer bought most of his supplies, including food. Typically, two sets of prices were common in country stores, one for goods bought for cash and one for goods bought on time to be paid after the harvest. The markups were steep, often implying an interest rate of 40 to 70 percent per annum for buying on time. The cropper who could not pay his debts after harvest often had to mortgage the next year's crop to receive continued credit. This transaction was made possible by "crop lien" laws passed in many states. The crop lien was a powerful means of control, and storekeepers (nearly 8,000 throughout the rural South) soon learned that by insisting on payment in cotton, they could maintain long-term control over their debtors. The tenant was thus "locked in" to cotton.[4]

---

[4] For further discussion of these and other issues in the postwar South, see *One Kind of Freedom* by Ransom and Sutch (1977) and the collection of papers in their book; Walton and Shepherd 1981; and the special issue of *Explorations in Economic History* 38 (January 1, 2001) in *One Kind of Freedom*.

TABLE 14.5 INCOMES OF SLAVES AND SHARECROPPERS

	SLAVE ON A LARGE PLANTATION IN 1859	SHARECROPPER IN 1879	ANNUAL RATE OF GROWTH (PERCENT PER YEAR)
Income (1879 dollars)	$27.66	$40.24	1.87%
Value of the increase in leisure time	—	33.90[a]	—
Total	$27.66	74.14	4.93%

[a]The average of the high and low estimates.

Source: *Ng and Virts 1989, 959.*

High interest rates were the result of the high costs of credit to the storeowner, the risks faced by the storeowner, and the exploitation of local monopoly power possessed by the storeowner. The slow recovery of southern banking in rural areas after the Civil War contributed to the storeowner's costs of doing business and protected his local monopoly. The National Banking Act had set a minimum capital requirement that made it hard to establish national banks in small towns and very hard to establish more than one.[5] Banking legislation had also made it impossible for state-chartered banks to issue bank notes and directed the funds that national banks received by issuing notes into federal bonds rather than local loans. After the turn of the century, the development of deposit banking, along with the easing of state and federal banking regulations, helped align southern interest rates with those in other parts of the country. There is some dispute about how much of the storeowner's high interest charges reflected his monopoly power and how much reflected his own high costs of supplying credit. In either case, the result for the farmer caught in the trap of debt peonage was extreme poverty and very little freedom of choice.

Table 14.5 shows estimates of the real income of slaves in 1859 and of sharecroppers in 1879. Evidently, in terms of real spendable income (available for food, clothing, shelter), emancipation was a moderate boon. Sharecroppers had more freedom to choose how they would spend their limited income, and between 1859 and 1879, blacks' real disposable income increased at an average rate of 1.87 percent per year. The 1879 figures, moreover, apply to all black sharecroppers. For some of those caught most firmly in the vise of debt peonage, the gains were smaller. When an allowance is made for the monetary value of increased leisure time (the reduction in hours spent working multiplied by the wage of agricultural labor), however, the material gain from emancipation appears to be truly large.[6]

The problem of debt peonage was not endemic to the entire South. To recall the evidence from Table 14.3, such states as Virginia, West Virginia, Texas, and Florida showed remarkable recoveries and sustained advances following the war. Research by Price Fishback (1989) has shown that Georgia sharecroppers, on average in the 1880s, were able to pay off their debts after the harvest and that their debt burdens were declining. Research by Robert Higgs (1982, 1984) and Robert Margo (1984) has shown that in some areas

---

[5]As late as 1880, there were only 42 national banks in the Deep South of 2,061 in the nation as a whole (126 in the 12 former Confederate states).

[6]One way to increase our understanding of postbellum southern poverty is to use data and methods drawn from other disciplines. For an excellent example, see Rose (1989). Rose uses skeletal remains to identify disease and nutritional problems in the black population.

© CORBIS

Typical of many blacks in the postwar South, the couple in this photograph taken in 1875—12 years after emancipation—remained entrapped in poverty.

blacks, despite the enormous difficulties they faced, were able to move up the agricultural ladder and become owners of their own farms.

A variety of factors gradually weakened the grip of debt peonage and helped transform southern agriculture. The boll weevil, an insect that attacked cotton and hit southern cotton in the last decade of the nineteenth century, spread for decades and brought utter ruin to impacted regions. Thanks to very recent work by Lange, Olmstead, and Rhodes (2009), data are now available at the local county level revealing declines in yields, acres planted in cotton, attempts to reallocate production to other crops, the uprooting of individuals and families, and local losses of population.

Improved roads and the automobile also eroded the monopoly power of the local storeowner (lenders). And the growth of the great mail-order houses in Chicago provided increased competition in the supply of certain kinds of merchandise. To look at things from the other direction, being a sharecropper was not necessarily the lowest rung on the agricultural ladder. In the Mississippi Delta, as James R. Irwin and Anthony Patrick O'Brien (2001) have shown, moving from agricultural laborer to tenant was a source of considerable economic progress. That it was indicates how low wages were in this region.

More important than these factors, however, were increasing urbanization and industrialization throughout the nation, which provided alternatives to agriculture. Southern industrialization was the goal of the "New South" movement proclaimed by southern politicians, newspapermen, and church leaders. There were some successes—a steel industry developed in Birmingham, the cigarette industry developed in North Carolina, and the cotton textile industry moved to the South—but the southern effort to industrialize progressed slowly. Ultimately, it was northern industrialization and its growing demand

The Monument to the Boll Weevil. When the boll weevil destroyed their cotton, farmers near Enterprise, Alabama, turned to peanuts, which proved profitable. The partly ironic plaque reads as follows: "In profound appreciation of the boll weevil and what it has done as the herald of Prosperity, this monument is erected by the citizens of Enterprise, Coffee County, Alabama, Dec. 11, 1919."

for labor that allowed many southern blacks to escape from tenant farming (see Bateman and Weiss 1981).

Despite a modest exodus of labor and limited advance of industrialization, the southern economy, especially that of the Deep South, remained a distinctive low-wage economy until the 1940s. Gavin Wright's book *Old South, New South* (1986) explains the slow pace of progress toward regional parity. In Wright's view, the South remained a separate labor market. Many people left, and few came in, but rapid natural increase kept labor abundant (see Vedder, Gallaway, Graves, and Sexton 1986). Cotton became increasingly labor intensive as farm sizes fell. By the late nineteenth century, most southern farms were smaller than northern farms, the reverse of the situation during the antebellum years. Mechanization was slowed, and wages and earnings kept low.

Southern whites attempted to protect their position by pushing African Americans even lower on the economic ladder. By the turn of the century, "black codes" and "Jim Crow" laws segregated blacks and maintained their impoverishment. Such laws determined where blacks could work, live, eat and drink, ride on public transport, and go to school. Northerners, as Wright emphasizes, shunned investments in the South. The result was that a striking wage gap remained between the North and South (for the importance of these initial institutions on twentieth-century developments, see Alston and Ferrie 1998). A considerable part of the South's relative backwardness can surely be attributed to its educational system. Public expenditures per pupil remained a mere fraction of those in the North. Wealthy southerners argued that educating the poor, especially blacks, merely encouraged their migration north in pursuit of higher wages. The Supreme Court held in *Plessy v. Fergusson* (1896) that separate education for blacks was constitutional as long as it was equal. "Separate" was adhered to religiously, but "equal" was not. As Robert Margo (1990) shows in his *Race and Schooling in the South*, far more money was spent on white students than on black students. Margo found, for example, that in 1910, spending on black pupils relative to white pupils ranged from 17 percent in Louisiana to 75 percent in Delaware.

Part of this discrepancy can be explained by discrimination against black school teachers; but other measures of the quality of schooling, such as class size, show similar differentials. Lack of spending on education may have served the interest of some wealthy southerners, but the result was a labor force ill prepared to participate in modern economic growth.

SELECTED REFERENCES AND SUGGESTED READINGS

Alston, Lee J., and Joseph P. Ferrie. *Southern Paternalism and the Rise of the Welfare State: Economics, Politics, and Institutions in the U.S. South 1865–1965.* Cambridge: Cambridge University Press, 1998.

Alston, Lee, and Robert Higgs. "Contractual Mix in Southern Agriculture since the Civil War: Facts, Hypotheses, and Tests." *Journal of Economic History* 42 (1982): 327–353.

Bateman, Fred, and Thomas Weiss. *A Deplorable Scarcity.* Chapel Hill: University of North Carolina Press, 1981.

Beard, Charles, and Mary. *The Rise of American Civilization.* Two volumes, New York: MacMillan, 1981.

Chesnut, Mary. *Mary Chesnut's Civil War,* ed. C. Vann Woodward. New Haven: Yale University Press, 1981.

Dated March 7, 1864, from *Mary Chesnut's Civil War,* ed. C. Vann Woodward, (New Haven, Conn.: Yale University Press,) 1981, 749.

DeCanio, Stephen. *Agriculture in the Postbellum South.* Cambridge, Mass.: MIT Press, 1974a and b.

———. "Productivity and Income Distribution in the Post-Bellum South." *Journal of Economic History* 34 (1974): 422–446.

DeCanio, Stephen, and Joel Mokyr. "Inflation and Wage Lag during the American Civil War." *Explorations in Economic History* 14 (1977): 311–336.

Easterlin, Richard. "Regional Growth of Income: Long-Term Tendencies, 1880–1950." In *Population Redistribution and Economic Growth, United States 1870–1950,* Vol. 2, *Analyses of Economic Change,* eds. S. Kuznets, A. R. Miller, and R. A. Easterlin, 185. Philadelphia: American Philosophical Society, 1960.

Ellison, Thomas. *The Cotton Trade of Great Britain.* Augustus Kelley, 1968. Cited in Gavin Wright. "Cotton Competition and the Post-Bellum Recovery of the American South." *Journal of Economic History* 34 (1974): 611.

Engerman, Stanley. "The Economic Impact of the Civil War." *Explorations in Economic History* 3 (Spring 1966): 181.

———. "The Economic Impact of the Civil War." In *The Reinterpretation of American Economic History,* eds. Robert W. Fogel and Stanley L. Engerman. New York: Harper & Row, 1971a and b.

———. "Some Economic Factors in Southern Backwardness in the Nineteenth Century." In *Essays in Regional Economics,* eds. John F. Kain and John R. Meyer. Cambridge, Mass.: Harvard University Press, 1971a and b.

Escott, Paul. *After Secession: Jefferson Davis and the Failure of Confederate Nationalism.* Baton Rouge: Louisiana State University Press, 1978.

Fishback, Price V. "Debt Peonage in Postbellum Georgia." *Explorations in Economic History* 26 (1989): 219–236.

Fogel, Robert W., and Stanley L. Engerman, eds. *The Reinterpretation of American Economic History.* New York: Harper & Row, 1971.

Gallman, Robert E. "Commodity Output, 1839–1899." In *Trends in the American Economy in the Nineteenth Century,* 24. Series on Income and Wealth. Princeton, N.J.: Princeton University Press, 1960.

Goldin, Claudia, and Frank Lewis. "The Economic Cost of the American Civil War." *Journal of Economic History* 35 (1975): 294–326.

Gordon, Donald F., and Gary M. Walton. "A New Theory of Regenerative Growth and the Post-World War II Experience of West Germany." In *Explorations in the New Economic History: Essays in Honor of Douglass C. North,* eds. Roger L. Ransom, Richard Sutch, and Gary M. Walton, 171–192. New York: Academic Press, 1982.

Graves, Philip E., Robert L. Sexton, and Richard K. Vedder. "Slavery, Amenities, and Factor Price Equalization: A Note on Migration and Freedmen." *Explorations in Economic History* 20 (1983): 156–162.

Hacker, Louis. *The Triumph of American Capitalism.* New York: Columbia University Press, 1940.

Higgs, Robert. "Accumulation of Property by Southern Blacks before World War I." *American Economic Review* 72 (1982): 725–735.

_____. "Accumulation of Property by Southern Blacks before World War I: Reply." *American Economic Review* 74 (1984): 777–781.

Kessel, Reuben A., and Armen A. Alchian. "Real Wages in the North during the Civil War: Mitchell's Data Reinterpreted." In *The Reinterpretation of American Economic History,* eds. Robert W. Fogel and Stanley L. Engerman. New York: Harper & Row, 1971.

Lange, Fabian, Alan L. Olmstead, and Paul W. Rhodes. "The Impact of the Boll Weevil, 1892–1932." *Journal of Economic History* (2009).

Lerner, Eugene. "Money, Wages, and Prices in the Confederacy, 1861–1865." *Journal of Political History* 63 (February 1955).

Maloney, Thomas N. "Migration and Economic Opportunity in the 1910s: New Evidence on African-American Occupational Mobility in the North." *Explorations in Economic History* 38, no. 1 (2001): 147–165.

Margo, Robert A. "Accumulation of Property by Southern Blacks before World War One: Comment and Further Evidence." *American Economic Review* 74 (September 1984): 768–776.

_____. *Race and Schooling in the South, 1880–1950.* Chicago: University of Chicago Press, 1990.

Mill, J.S., *Principles of Political Economy,* 1948, Book I, chapter 5, section 7.

Mill, John Stuart. *Principles of Political Economy.* London: Longman's Green, 1940 [1848].

Ng, Kenneth, and Nancy Virts. "The Value of Freedom." *Journal of Economic History* 49 (December 1989): 959.

Mitchell, Wesley C. A. *History of the Greenbacks* with special reference to the Economic Consequences of their issue: 1862-65. Chicago: University of Chicago Press, 1903.

Ransom, Roger L. *Conflict and Compromise: The Political Economy of Slavery, Emancipation, and the American Civil War.* New York: Cambridge University Press, 1989.

Ransom, Roger L., and Richard Sutch. *One Kind of Freedom: The Economic Consequences of Emancipation.* New York: Cambridge University Press, 1977.

_____. "Capitalists without Capital: The Burden of Slavery and the Impact of Emancipation." *Agricultural History* 62 (Summer 1988): 133–160.

Reid, Joseph. "Sharecropping as an Understandable Market Response: The Postbellum South." *Journal of Economic History* 33 (1973): 106–130.

Rose, Jerome C. "Biological Consequences of Segregation and Economic Deprivation: A Post Slavery Population from Southwest Arkansas." *Journal of Economic History* 49 (1989): 351–360.

Sutch, Richard. "Growth and Welfare in the American South." In *Market Institutions and Economic Progress in the New South 1865–1900,* eds. Gary M. Walton and James F. Shepherd, 145. New York: Academic Press, 1981.

Vedder, Richard, Lowell Gallaway, Philip E. Graves, and Robert L. Sexton. "Demonstrating Their Freedom: The Post-Emancipation Migration of Black Americans." *Research in Economic History* 10 (1986): 213–239.

Walton, Gary M., and James F. Shepherd. *Market Institutions and Economic Progress in the New South, 1865–1900.* New York: Academic Press, 1981.

Wright, Gavin. *The Political Economy of the Cotton South.* New York: Norton, 1978.

_____. *Old South, New South: Revolutions in the Southern Economy.* New York: Basic Books, 1986.

CHAPTER 15

Agriculture's Western Advance

CHAPTER THEME

During the 25 years following the Civil War, the American frontier moved steadily west. So dense was settlement by 1890 that people claimed the frontier had virtually disappeared. Spearheading the drive into the western territories were miners and cowboys. The miners were drawn by discoveries such as the famed Comstock Lode of silver in Nevada and the gold in the Black Hills of South Dakota. Though remembered in legend as hard-drinking tellers of tall tales, the miners were first of all businessmen who were able to evolve precise sets of efficient property rights from their crude mining camp rules (Libecap 1978).

The cowboys came to spur cattle on the long drives to market. Cattle drives from Texas began in 1866, and by the 1880s, cattle baronies of great wealth occupied the territories from Texas to Montana. The cattle drives were destined for the nearest railheads: in the earliest years Sedalia, Missouri, but later Abilene (the destination of the famous Chisholm Trail) and then Dodge City, Kansas (for transport to Chicago). The rise and decline of the great long-distance cattle drives is fascinating history and superb folklore.[1] The long drives ended abruptly in 1885, not because of the advent of barbed wire (as popularly believed) but because northern cattlemen organized and created new institutions to curb the overstocking of the northern ranges. The passage and enforcement of quarantine laws kept out the distant Texas herds.[2]

However important miners and cattlemen were as path breakers, the families who settled down to farm set the abiding economic pattern of the West. This chapter tells their economic history: how they got title to their land, what they grew and how they grew it, what prices they were paid for their products, and why many farmers became disillusioned with the economic system and demanded help from state governments and, ultimately, from Washington, D.C.

THE EXPANSION OF LAND UNDER CULTIVATION

Most of the participants in the final opening of new land came from places that only a few years before had been the object of settlement. People who moved into Kansas, Nebraska, the Dakotas, and, later, Montana and Colorado more often than not traveled

---

[1]The movie classic *Red River* starring John Wayne and Montgomery Clift and the 1989 CBS TV special "Lonesome Dove" are recommended. Also see Atherton (1961). Although the scions of wealthy eastern families such as Richard Trimble and Teddy Roosevelt could not resist the West, the men who started from scratch and became fabulously successful were, for the most part, country boys from the Midwest and South or cowboys only a few years away from the hard-drinking, roistering life of Newton or Dodge City.

[2]For an in-depth account of the reasons long drives were abruptly ended in 1885, see Galenson (June 1974).

TABLE 15.1 TOTAL NUMBER OF FARMS AND ACRES BY DECADE, 1860–1920				
YEAR	**NUMBER OF FARMS (IN MILLIONS)**	**PERCENT INCREASE**	**NUMBER OF ACRES (IN MILLIONS)**	**PERCENT INCREASE**
1860	2.0		407	
1870	2.7	35%	408	0.2%
1880	4.0	48	536	31
1890	4.6	15	623	16
1900	5.7	24	839	35
1910	6.4	11	879	5
1920	6.5	2	956	9

Source: *Historical Statistics 1975, Series K4 and J51.*

only short distances to get there. Some had settled previously in Missouri or Iowa, Minnesota or Wisconsin, Indiana or Illinois; others were sons and daughters of the pioneers of a previous generation. It was not uncommon for settlers to move from place to place within one of the new states. No matter how bitter previous pioneer experiences or how monotonous and unrewarding the life on virgin land, the hope persisted of better times if only new soil could be broken farther west.

Table 15.1 shows the total number of farms and farm acres by decade from 1860 to 1920. The decades of sharpest advance were the 1870s and 1890s. The addition of land input in these decades was extraordinary: Total land under cultivation more than doubled between 1870 and 1900.[3] This was made possible by a policy of rapidly transferring ownership of land to farmers and other users—by rapidly "privatizing" government land, to use modern jargon. (Several Economic Reasoning Propositions apply here; see Economic Insight 1.1 on page 8.)

FEDERAL LAND POLICY

During the Civil War, the absence of southern Democrats allowed the Republican Congress to pass the Homestead Act of 1862. Recall from chapter 8 that this act, which provided 160 acres per homestead (320 per married couple), continued the liberalization of the federal government's land policy. At the time of the act, prime fertile lands remained unclaimed in western Iowa and western Minnesota and in the eastern parts of Kansas, Nebraska, and the Dakotas; these were soon taken, however, leaving little except the unclaimed lands west of the hundredth meridian in the Great Plains (an area of light annual rainfall) or in the vast mountain regions. In most of these plains and mountain regions, a 160-acre homestead was impractical because the land, being suitable only for grazing livestock, required much larger farms. Consequently, between 1870 and 1900, less than 1 acre in 5 added to farming belonged to homesteads.

Mining and timber interests also pressed Congress to liberalize land policy, winning four more land acts:

- The Timber-Culture Act of 1873. *Passed ostensibly to encourage the growth of timber in arid regions, this law made available 160 acres of free land to anyone who would agree to plant trees on 40 acres of it.*

---

[3]During the 1860s, the number of farms increased sharply but total acreage not at all. As discussed in chapter 14, the 1860s were unusual because of the breakup of southern plantations.

- The Desert Land Act of 1877. *By the terms of this law, 640 acres at $1.25 an acre could be purchased by anyone who would agree to irrigate the land within three years. One serious defect of this act was its lack of a clear definition of irrigation.*
- The Timber and Stone Act of 1878. *This statute provided for the sale at $2.50 an acre of valuable timber and stone lands in Nevada, California, Oregon, and Washington.*
- The Timber-Cutting Act of 1878. *This law authorized residents of certain specified areas to cut trees on government lands without charge, with the stipulation that the timber be used for agricultural, mining, and domestic building purposes.*

The transfer of public lands into private hands also included purchases at public auctions under the Preemption Act. This act, as noted in chapter 8, encouraged "squatting" by allowing first rights of sale to settlers who arrived and worked the land before public sales were offered.[4] Furthermore, huge acreages granted by the government as subsidies to western railroads and to states for various purposes were in turn sold to settlers. Nearly 100 million acres from the Indian territories were opened for purchase by the Dawes Act of 1887 and subsequent measures, ignoring promises made to Native Americans.

Although steps were taken in the 1880s to tighten up on the disposition of public lands, Congress did not pass any major legislation until the General Revision Act of 1891, which closed critical loopholes. In addition, the Preemption Act and provisions defining irrigation were added to the Desert Land Act of 1877. Congress also repealed the Timber-Cutting Act of 1878, removing from the books one of the most flagrantly abused of all the land laws. Finally, the president was authorized to set aside forest preserves—a first milestone in the conservation movement, which had been gaining popular support.

After the turn of the century, the Homestead Act itself was modified to enable settlers to obtain practical-size farms. Beginning in 1904, a whole section (1 square mile, or 640 acres) could be homesteaded in western Nebraska. A few years later, the Enlarged Homestead Act made it possible to obtain a half-section in many areas free of charge. Still later, residence requirements were reduced to three years, and the Stock-Raising Homestead Act of 1916 allowed the homesteading of 640 acres of land suitable only for grazing purposes. Whereas only 1 acre in 5 added to farming before 1900 came from homesteading, the ratio jumped to 9 in 10 between 1900 and 1920.

From the findings of a commission that reported to President Theodore Roosevelt on the pre-1904 disposition of public lands, we may see how the land had been distributed. The total public domain in the United States from 1789 to 1904 contained 1,441 million acres. Of this total, 278 million acres were acquired by individuals through cash purchase. Another 273 million acres were granted to states and railroads, about which more will be said in chapter 16. Lands acquired by or available to individuals free of charge (mostly via the Homestead Act) amounted to 147 million acres. The rest of the public domain, aside from miscellaneous grants, was either reserved for the government (209 million acres) or unappropriated (474 million acres). Between 1862 and 1904, acres homesteaded exceeded government cash sales to individuals. If, however, we count purchases from railroads and states, ultimate holders of land bought twice as much between 1862 and 1904 as they obtained free through homesteading.

---

[4]As late as 1891, an individual could buy a maximum of 1,120 acres at one time under the public land acts. Unlimited amounts of land could be purchased from railroad companies and from states at higher, although still nominal, prices.

After 1904, U.S. land policy became less generous, but by that time, nearly all the choice agricultural land, most of the first-rate mineral land, and much of the timber land located close to markets had been distributed. Between 1904 and 1920, more than 100 million new acres of land were homesteaded in mainly dry and mountainous areas. During this same short period, the government reserved about 175 million acres. Of the original public domain, 200 million acres of land that remained to be disposed of were "vacant" in 1920.[5]

THE IMPACT OF FEDERAL LAND POLICY

The principal goals of federal land policy—namely, government revenues, wide accessibility (or fairness), and rapid economic growth—varied in importance over time, with the latter two gaining significance. Clearly, the most outstanding feature of American land policy was the rapidity with which valuable agricultural, mineral, and timber lands were transferred into private hands. In addition, the goal of making land widely accessible was largely achieved, especially in the second half of the nineteenth century. But by no means was the process, or the result, egalitarian. As we just emphasized, large tracts of lands went to corporations and wealthy individuals. Special interests were favored, and for a time, the granting of land to railroads was considered normal public policy. In addition, large grants to the states were rationalized as growth enhancing, either to support transportation ventures or for educational purposes (the land-grant universities).

Frequently, good land was fraudulently obtained by mining and lumber companies or speculators. Aided by the lax administration of the land laws, large operators could persuade an individual to make a homesteading entry or a purchase at a minimum price and then transfer the title. With the connivance of bribed land officials (Economic Reasoning Proposition 3, incentives matter), entries were occasionally made for people who did not even exist. As Gary Libecap and Ronald Johnson (1979) have shown convincingly, fraud ultimately served a positive economic purpose: It helped transfer resources to large companies that could take advantage of economies of scale. Resource laws that recognized economic realities and permitted sales of large acreages directly to final users would have reduced fraud and corruption.

Until the 1970s, the consensus among American historians was that federal land policy was economically inefficient and reduced total output. Because people of all sorts and circumstances settled on the land, there was a high rate of failure among the least competent—settlers who eventually lost their holdings and became either poor tenants or low-paid farmworkers. More important, it is alleged that the rapid distribution of the public domain laid the groundwork for modern agricultural problems by inducing too much capital and labor into agriculture, thereby impeding the process of industrialization.

Little doubt exists that specific errors were made and inefficiencies were imposed, yet it is difficult to make the case that federal policies were generally inefficient. Partially as a result of this rapid addition of resources, the new West produced crops at such a rate that consumers of foodstuffs and raw materials enjoyed 30 years of falling prices. Furthermore, according to Robert Fogel and Jack Rutner (1972), average rates of return on investments in land improvements, livestock, farm buildings, and machinery equaled or exceeded returns on other contemporary investments, and real incomes in the new

---

[5]Homestead entries were substantial in the 1920s and 1930s but fell to practically zero by midcentury. Some homesteading continues today in Alaska.

ECONOMIC INSIGHT 15.1

A NATIONAL MARKET

What price for federal land would have maximized real gross national product (GNP)? Surprisingly, the answer, in many areas, would have been zero. In the figure below, the vertical axis shows the price of land and the horizontal axis the quantity, arranged from high quality to low. In effect, *ACF* is the demand for farmland in a region of new settlement where the federal government initially owned all the land.

The government might set a relatively high price for federal land, *BD*, to maximize the government's revenues (*BCED*). This might seem the best policy because the revenues could then be redistributed fairly to the people—assuming, of course, that special interests did not get there first. But setting a price of *BD* reduces the land in production from a maximum of *DF* to *DE*. How do we measure the loss associated with keeping *EF* out of production? The distance between a point on the horizontal axis and the demand curve tells us the maximum that some farmer will pay for a piece of land, presumably because the farmer's resources would produce this much wealth in alternative uses. Therefore, the triangular area *CEF* measures the value of the future incomes that are lost if the price for the land is set at *BD* and *EF* is kept out of production. Setting the price at zero will eliminate the welfare loss triangle.

Concerns about fairness, about the rationality of farmers, or about the effect on the environment may lead one to reject the GNP-maximizing policy. But one should at least recognize the powerful economic argument that the right policy (Economic Reasoning Proposition 5, evidence and theory give value to opinions) was the one followed: getting federal land rapidly into the hands of those who could use it productively.

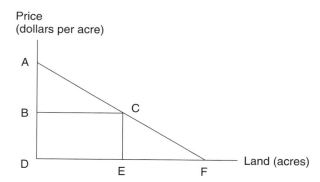

agricultural areas outside the South grew at rates comparable with those in manufacturing.[6] Once again we see the importance (as emphasized in Economic Reasoning Proposition 5, evidence and theory give value to opinions) of quantitative evidence. Instances of hard times in rural America were numerous, and political unrest characterized certain sections of the Midwest and the Plains in the late nineteenth century, but these should not be permitted to dominate our judgment of federal land policy.[7]

---

[6]For the evidence and more discussion of these issues, see Fogel and Rutner (1972); and Previant Lee and Passell (1979).

[7]For an assessment of the politics of federal land policy, see Gates (1976, 213–229).

GROWTH AND CHANGE IN AGRICULTURE

New Areas and Methods of Cultivation

As areas became settled, they tended to specialize in certain crops. These areas of geographic specialization are depicted for the principal crops in Map 15.1. The wheat and corn belt continued its western advance over the century, with spring wheat leading in western Minnesota and the Dakotas and winter varieties dominating the southern Midwest and Nebraska, Kansas, and Oklahoma.[8]

Although tobacco remained tied to the old South, cotton production leapfrogged the Mississippi River. By 1900, Texas was the leading cotton producer as well as a major source of cattle. Farmers around the Great Lakes found it profitable to turn from cereals to dairy farming, following a path traveled previously by farmers in New England. In California, Florida, and other warm-climate areas, fruits, vegetables, and specialty crops became important—especially after the refrigerated railcar, introduced in the 1880s, created a national market.

In addition, and contrary to conventional wisdom (as revealed in numerous writings including earlier editions of *History of the American Economy*), the nineteenth and early twentieth centuries witnessed a stream of biological innovations, many of which successfully modified the planting and growing environment. Thanks to the research of Alan L. Olmstead and Paul W. Rhode (2008) we have a greater appreciation of changes in plant varieties, irrigation systems, fertilizers, and other biological inventions that

MAP 15.1

Geographic Areas of Specialization in Major Cash Crops in the Late Nineteenth Century

Note that the boundaries between sections did change and that many crops were and still are grown within various belts.

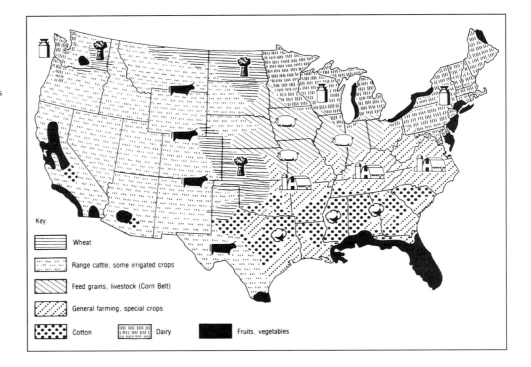

Key:

- Wheat
- Range cattle, some irrigated crops
- Feed grains, livestock (Corn Belt)
- General farming, special crops
- Cotton
- Dairy
- Fruits, vegetables

---

[8]Winter wheat is sown in the fall and harvested in late spring or early summer, depending on the latitude. Where the climate is too cold, spring wheat is grown. Modern varieties of winter wheat are hardy enough to be grown in the southern half of South Dakota, at least as far north as Pierre.

TABLE 15.2 CEREALS OUTPUT AND LAND INPUT, 1870–1910

YEAR	CORN[a]	LAND IN CORN[b]	BUSHELS OF CORN PER ACRE	WHEAT	LAND IN WHEAT	BUSHELS OF WHEAT PER ACRE
1870	1,125	38.4	29.3	254	20.9	12.1
1890	1,650	74.8	22.1	449	36.7	12.2
1910	2,853	102.3	27.9	625	45.8	13.7

[a]In millions of bushels.
[b]In millions of acres harvested.

Source: Historical Statistics 1975, Series K502, K503, K506, and K507.

greatly affected the use of land for planting. These changes worked along two lines: (1) the discovery of new wheat varieties (and hybrids), which allowed the North American wheat belt to push hundreds of miles northward and westward; and (2) researchers and farmers who found new methods of combating insects and diseases, some of which came from experimentation with new varieties (seeds) from Europe and elsewhere. This change in plant varieties is a good example of the positive and negative effects of globalization in an earlier era. Table 15.2 shows the growth of corn and wheat outputs and acreage harvested in each crop between 1870 and 1910. The evidence shows very little, if any, growth in land productivity as measured in bushels per acre. Nonetheless, labor productivity grew dramatically in wheat and corn over these decades. According to Robert Gallman (1975), labor productivity in these two crops grew at a rate of 2.6 percent annually between 1850 and 1900. In the first half of the nineteenth century, the comparable figure was 0.4 percent. Further evidence of output growth relative to inputs is shown in Figure 15.1, which plots total agricultural output relative to all inputs (land, labor, and capital). Figure 15.1 clearly shows the "miracles" of the scientific chemical and biological advances (see Olmstead and Rhode 2008). It also reveals the effects of mechanization that had such important influences, as Gallman's nineteenth-century findings reveal.

In 1848, Cyrus Hall McCormick, who had received a patent in 1834 for his reaper, boldly moved his main implement plant to Chicago, thereby ensuring a steady supply

FIGURE 15.1

Total Factor Productivity in Agriculture, 1869–1955

This figure shows a ratio of agricultural output relative to a price weighted average of land, labor, and capital inputs.

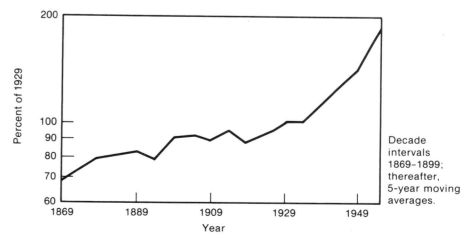

Decade intervals 1869–1899; thereafter, 5-year moving averages.

Source: *John W. Kendrick, PRODUCTIVITY TRENDS IN THE UNITED STATES (Princeton, N.J.: Princeton University Press, 1961), 362–364. Reprinted by permission of the National Bureau of Economic Research, Inc.*

of his harvesting machines to the Midwest. The day of the hand scythe and the one-horse plow had passed, as this editorial from an 1857 *Scientific American* suggests:

> *Every farmer who has a hundred acres of land should have at least the following: a combined reaper and mower, a horse rake, a seed planter, and mower…a thresher and grain cleaner, a portable grist mill, a corn-sheller, a horse power, three harrows, a roller, two cultivators, and three plows. (Danhof 1951, 150)*

Increased amounts of capital per worker, along with new technologies embodied in the capital equipment, raised labor's productivity. Even though yields per acre changed little, mechanization allowed farmers to add more acres to their farms, thus expanding output per farm. Although mechanized farming did not replace traditional farming instantaneously, advances were relentless.[9] After the Civil War, wages paid to grain cradlers (hand harvesters) increased, and acres per farm devoted to grains increased, hastening the introduction of mechanical reapers.

By 1857, John Deere's new plant in Moline, Illinois, was annually producing 10,000 steel plows, eclipsing the iron plow, which had proved ineffectual in the tough clay sod of the prairies as Olmstead and Rhode (1995, 27) report:

> *Between the censuses of 1850 and 1860, the number of firms producing reapers and mowers increased from roughly 20 to 73, and annual output rose about tenfold to roughly 25,000 machines. This expansion set the stage for an explosion in sales during the war years. By 1864 approximately 200 firms were making reapers and mowers with a total output of about 90,000 machines.*

Seed drills, cultivators, mowers, rakes and threshing machines, and myriad attachments and gadgets for harvesting machines added to the mechanization of farming in the second half of the century. Between 1860 and 1920, the number of mouths fed per farmer nearly doubled, freeing labor for industry, but not without economic dislocations and personal hardships.

HARD TIMES ON THE FARM, 1864–1896

The years from the close of the Civil War to the end of World War I include two contrasting periods in agricultural history. The first of these, from 1864 to 1896, was characterized by agricultural hardship and political unrest; the second, from 1896 until about 1920, represented a sustained period of improvement in the lot of the farm population. This improvement is reflected quantitatively in Table 15.3, which traces average annual percentage growth rates in real farm income over the last half of the nineteenth century. Note that real incomes did rise from 1864 to 1896, but the rate of increase seemed painfully slow, and the averages obscure the hardships suffered by many western farmers in the 1870s and 1880s.

American farmers, from the mid-1860s to the mid-1890s, knew that their lives were hard without being shown data to prove it. Conditions were especially hard on the frontier, where the combination of dreary surroundings and physical hardship compounded the difficulties of economic life, which included declining prices, indebtedness, and the necessity of purchasing many goods and services from industries in which there appeared to be a growing concentration of economic power.

---

[9]Paul David argues that one cause of slowness of adoption was the large minimum size of farm needed to employ a reaper profitably. But Alan Olmstead adduced evidence to show that farmers could hire the services of reapers or share them with neighbors. See David (1975) and Olmstead (June 1975).

TABLE 15.3 TRENDS IN FARM INCOME AND PRODUCTIVITY (AVERAGE ANNUAL PERCENTAGE CHANGE)

YEARS	REAL INCOME PER CAPITA	REAL INCOME PER WORKER
1849–1859	2.0%	2.0%
1859–1869	0.8	0.9
1869–1879	0.8	0.3
1879–1889	0.7	0.3
1889–1899	2.2	2.1
1849–1899	1.3	1.0
1869–1899	1.2	0.7

Source: *Fogel and Rutner 1972, Table 2, 396, adapted by permission of Princeton University Press. © 1972 by the Center for Advanced Study in the Behavioral Sciences.*

All prices were falling between 1875 and 1895, but as Table 15.4 shows, the price of farm products was falling relative to other prices. To put it slightly differently, the farmer's terms of trade—the price of the things the farmer sold divided by the price of things the farmer bought—were worsening. This did not mean that real farm income was falling (recall that Table 15.3 shows that it was rising), because the terms of trade refer only to price and do not take productivity into account (for more on these issues, see Bowman and Keehn 1974). It does mean, however, that the farmer had to run faster just to avoid losing ground. By 1895, to take the low point in Table 15.4, the farmer had to produce about 16 percent more than in 1870 just to offset the fall in his terms of trade.

Why were the farmer's terms of trade worsening? Part of the explanation is the rapid increase in the supply of agricultural products. All over the world, new areas were entering the competitive fray. In Canada, Australia, New Zealand, and Argentina as well as in the United States, fertile new lands were becoming agriculturally productive. In the United States alone (as Table 15.1 indicates), the number of acres in farming more than doubled between 1870 and 1900. Reinforcing this trend was the increased output made possible by mechanization.

TABLE 15.4 THE FARMER'S TERMS OF TRADE, 1870–1915

YEAR	WHOLESALE FARM PRICES	CONSUMER PRICES	TERMS OF TRADE
1870	100	100	100
1875	88	87	102
1880	71	76	94
1885	64	71	90
1890	63	71	89
1895	55	66	84
1900	64	66	97
1905	71	71	100
1910	93	74	127
1915	90	80	112

Source: Historical Statistics *1975, Series E42, E53, and E135.*

Notable changes occurred, too, on the demand side. One favorable influence on the domestic demand was the continued rapid increase in the population. After 1870, the rate of population growth in the United States fell, but until 1900, it was still high. In the decades of the 1870s and 1880s, the increase was just over 25 percent, and in the 1890s, it was more than 20 percent—a substantial growth in the number of mouths to feed. There was an offsetting factor, however: In 1870, Americans spent one-third of their current per capita incomes on farm products. By 1890, they were spending a much smaller fraction, just over one-fifth, and during the next few years this proportion dropped further. Thus, although the real incomes of the American population rose during the period, and although Americans did not spend less on food absolutely, the proportion of those incomes earned by farmers declined (in technical terms, the income elasticity of demand was less than 1 for most agricultural crops). See Economic Insight 15.2.

Offsetting these effects in part was the rise in the demand abroad for U.S. crops. Export demand for farm products increased steadily until the turn of the century. Wheat and flour exports reached their peak in 1901, at which time nearly one-third of domestic wheat production was sold abroad. Likewise, meat and meat products were exported in larger and larger quantities until 1900, when these exports also began to decline. Overall, the value of agricultural exports rose from $297 million in 1870 to more than $840 million in 1900. Exports of farm products during these decades helped expand agricultural markets, but they were far from sufficient to alleviate the hard times on the farm.

Farmers were not inclined to see their difficulties as the result of impersonal market forces. Instead, they traced their problems to monopolies and conspiracies: bankers who

ECONOMIC INSIGHT 15.2

THE ENGEL CURVE

The slow growth of demand for farm products reflected the slope of the Engel curve, named for nineteenth-century Prussian statistician Ernst Engel. Engel curves are usually based on samples of family budgets and show average expenditures on food (or other goods and services) at each level of income. Economic growth lifts the average family to higher income levels, but expenditures on food rise less rapidly, and the share spent on food falls. The farmer could retain his share of total spending only if the slope of the Engel curve for farm products were equal to the slope of the 45-degree line bisecting the figure.

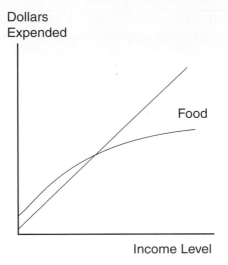

raised interest rates, manipulated the currency, and then foreclosed on farm mortgages; grain elevator operators who charged rates farmers could not afford; industrialists who charged high prices for farm machinery and consumer goods; railroads that charged monopoly rates on freight; and so on.

The evidence of these alleged sources of distress is largely unsupported, suggesting that farmers were attacking symptoms rather than causes. Figure 15.2 shows that the prices of industrial items in the West fell relative to the prices of farm products; Figure 15.3 shows

FIGURE 15.2
Price of Industrial
Goods in Terms of Farm
Products, West and East,
1870–1910

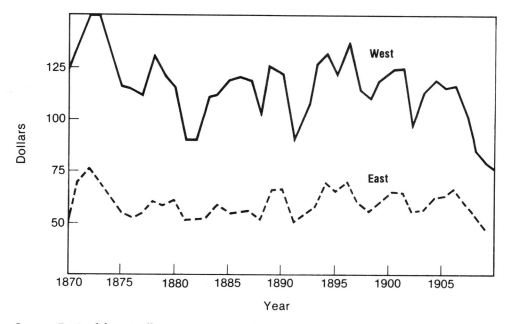

Source: *Derived from Williamson 1974, 149.*

FIGURE 15.3
Freight Costs on Wheat
from Iowa and Wiscon-
sin in New York as Per-
centage of Farm Price,
1870–1910

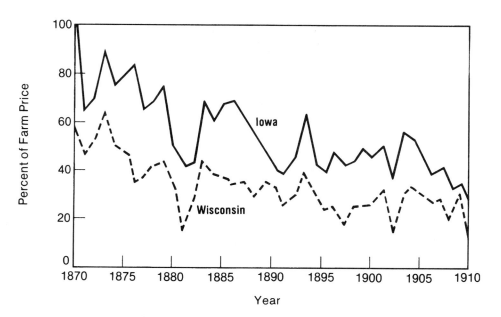

Source: *Derived from Williamson 1974, 261.*

that freight costs also fell as a percentage of farm prices. This does not mean, of course, that every complaint of every farmer was baseless. Although long-haul railroad rates fell dramatically relative to agricultural prices over the period, for example, certain monopolized sections of railroad permitted discriminatory monopoly pricing on short hauls (for more on this, see Higgs 1970).

Finally, both in nominal and in real terms, interest rates charged on midwestern farm mortgages declined over the decades, as shown in Table 15.5. Such rates were higher than in the East, where capital was more plentiful and investments typically less risky, but they declined more rapidly in the West. Indeed, to the extent that farmers were suffering from monopoly prices in credit markets, it was the small western bank rather than the eastern financier who was to blame. This point was first made by Richard Sylla (1969) and John James (1976). Even here, however, subsequent research has narrowed the potential role of local bank monopolies in the credit problems of farmers (see Keehn 1975; Smiley 1975; Binder and Brown 1991). Farm mortgage rates, as well as short-term rates, were high, especially in the 1870s, but appear to have been a product of high lending risks and other causes rather than monopoly power (for more on this issue, see Eichengreen 1984; Snowden 1987).

Part of the explanation for agricultural discontent in this era was the process of commercialization and globalization that created a world in which the farmer was subject to economic fluctuations that he could neither control nor even fully comprehend. As emphasized by Ann Mayhew (1972), to keep abreast of progress, the farmer needed more equipment—reapers, planters, harrows—as well as more land and irrigation facilities. This often meant greater indebtedness. When agricultural prices fell, foreclosures or cessation of credit extensions brought ruin to many farmers. Farm prices, moreover, were increasingly subject to international forces. Farm prices could rise despite good weather and abundant crops in the United States and fall despite bad weather and poor crops. Everything might depend on events abroad, which the farmer could not directly observe. Robert A. McGuire (1981) has shown a strong correlation between political agitation in various western states and the economic instability of these states, and that price fluctuations had a particularly important bearing on the income instability of farmers.

Even though modern research has rejected many of the analyses put forward in the late nineteenth century, we need to take a close look at the political forces spawned by the farmers' discontent, for the reforms proposed by the agrarian protesters helped shape the institutional framework of the American economy.

AGRARIAN POLITICAL ORGANIZATIONS

In what has been called the "Thirty Years' War" against the princes of privilege, a number of organizations, large and small, were formed to fight for the farmers.[10] Urban

TABLE 15.5 REAL (NOMINAL) INTEREST RATES ON MIDWESTERN FARM MORTGAGES, 1870–1900

YEAR	ILLINOIS		WISCONSIN		IOWA		NEBRASKA	
1870	17.0	(9.6)%	15.4	(8.0)%	16.9	(9.5)%	17.9	(10.5)%
1880	11.4	(7.8)	10.8	(7.2)	12.3	(8.7)	12.7	(9.1)
1890	7.6	(6.9)	6.6	(5.9)	7.7	(7.0)	8.5	(7.8)
1910	4.3	(5.8)	3.4	(4.9)	4.0	(5.5)	4.8	(6.3)

Note: The real rate is the nominal rate plus the rate of deflation or minus the rate of inflation.

Source: Derived from Williamson 1974, 152.

---

[10]For a most informative article providing a longer perspective on farm movements and political activity, see Rothstein (1988); also see Destler (December 1944).

industrial labor influenced some organizations and many of the ideas of the agrarians originated in the urban radicalism of the East. Farmers in the West and South dominated—if not entirely motivated—four rather clearly distinguishable movements.

The Grangers

The first farm organization of importance was the National Grange of the Patrons of Husbandry. Formally organized in 1867, the order grew rapidly. By 1874, it had 20,000 local branches and a membership of about 1.5 million. After seven years of ascendancy, a decline set in, and by 1880, membership had largely disappeared except in a few strongholds such as the upper Mississippi valley and the Northeast.

Although the organization's bylaws strictly forbade formal political action by the Grangers, members held informal political meetings and worked with reform parties to secure passage of regulatory legislation. In several western states, the Grangers were successful in obtaining laws that set an upper limit on the charges of railroads and of warehouse and elevator companies and in establishing regulation of such companies by commission, a new concept in American politics. The Supreme Court, in *Munn v. Illinois* (1877), held that such regulation was constitutional if the business was "clothed with the public interest." However, in 1886, the Court held that states could not regulate interstate commerce, so reformers had to turn to the federal government to regulate the railroads. The Interstate Commerce Commission (which will be discussed in chapter 16), established in 1887, was the result.

The Grangers developed still another weapon for fighting unfair business practices. If businesses charged prices that were too high, then farmers, it was argued, sensibly enough, ought to go into business themselves. The most successful type of business established by the Grangers was the cooperative, formed for the sale of general merchandise and farm implements to Grange member owners. Cooperatives (and conventional companies that

© CORBIS

In Granger Movement meetings like this one in Scott County, Illinois, members focused their discontentment on big-city ways, monopoly, the tariff, and low prices for agricultural products. From such roots grew pressures to organize support for agriculture.

sold stock) were established to process farm products, and the first large mail-order house, Montgomery Ward and Company, was established to sell to the Grangers.

The Greenback Movement

Some farmers, disappointed in the Grange for not making more decisive gains in the struggle to bolster farm prices, joined forces with a labor element to form an Independent National Party, which entered candidates in the election of 1876. This group was hopelessly unsuccessful, but a Greenback Labor Party formed by the same people made headway in the election of 1878. To finance the Civil War, the government had resorted to the issue of paper money popularly known as "greenbacks," and the suggestion that a similar issue be made in the late 1870s appealed to poor farmers. The Greenback Labor platform, more than any other party program, centered on demands for inflationary (they would have said "reflationary") action. Although Greenback Labor candidates were entered in the presidential campaign of 1880, they received a very small percentage of the popular vote because labor failed to participate effectively. Greenback agitators continued their efforts in the elections of 1884 and 1888 but with little success.

The movement is worth remembering for two reasons. First, Greenback agitation constituted the first attempt made by farmers to act politically on a national scale. Second, the group's central tenets later became the most important part of the Populists' appeal to the electorate in the 1890s.

The Alliances

At the same time that the Grangers were multiplying, independent farmers' clubs were being formed in the West and South. Independent clubs tended to coalesce into state "alliances," which, in turn, were consolidated into two principal groups—the Northwestern Alliance and the Southern Alliance. In 1889, an attempt to merge the Alliances failed, despite the similarity of their aims. The Alliances advocated monetary reforms similar to those urged by the Greenback parties and, like the Grangers, favored government regulation and cooperative business ventures. Alliance memberships, moreover, favored government ownership of transportation and communication facilities.

Each Alliance offered a proposal that had a highly modern ring. The Southern Alliance recommended that the federal government establish a system of warehouses for the storage of nonperishable commodities so that farmers could obtain low-interest loans of up to 80 percent of the value of the products stored. The Northwestern Alliance proposed that the federal government extend long-term loans in greenbacks up to 50 percent of the value of a farm. Because of their revolutionary nature, such ideas received little support from voters.

The Populists

After mild periods of prosperity in the late 1880s, economic activity experienced another downturn, and the hardships of the farmer and the laborer again became severe. In 1891, elements of the Alliances met in Cincinnati with the Knights of Labor to form the People's Party. At the party convention of 1892, held in Omaha, famed agrarian and formidable orator General James Weaver was nominated for the presidency. Weaver, an old Greenbacker, won 22 electoral votes in the election of 1892. Two years later, the party won a number of congressional seats, and it appeared that greater success might be on the way. Populism thus emerged from 30 years of unrest—an unrest that was chiefly agricultural but that had urban connections. To its supporters, populism was something more than an agitation for economic betterment: It was a faith. The overtones of political and social reform were part of the faith because they would help to further economic aims. The agitation against monopoly control—against oppression by corporations, banks, and capitalists—had come to a head. Along with the key principle of antimonopolism ran a strongly collectivist doctrine. Populists felt that only through government control of the monetary system and through government ownership of banks, railroads, and the means of communication could the evils of monopoly be put down. In fact, some Populists advocated operation of government-owned firms in basic industries so that the government would have the information to determine whether or not monopolistic prices were being charged. The government-owned firm would, in other words, provide a "yardstick" by which to measure the performance of private firms.

In older parts of the country, the radicalism of the People's Party alienated established farmers. Had the leaders of the 1896 coalition of Populists and Democrats not chosen to stand or fall on the issue of inflation, there is no telling what the future of the coalition might have been. But inflation was anathema to property owners with little or no debt, and when the chips were down, rural as well as urban property owners supported "sound" money.

THE BEGINNINGS OF FEDERAL ASSISTANCE TO AGRICULTURE

Although attempts by farmers to improve their condition through organization were unsuccessful as far as immediate goals were concerned, the way had been opened for legislation and federal assistance. Of course, the land acts of the nineteenth century had worked to the advantage of new farmers, but they can scarcely be considered part of an agricultural "program." Similarly, much regulatory legislation passed in the late nineteenth and early twentieth centuries, although originating in agrarian organizations, produced effects that were not restricted to agriculture. Federal assistance to agriculture before World War I was designed to compile and disseminate information to help the individual farmer increase productivity; it was not designed to alleviate distress, as was later New Deal legislation.

The Department of Agriculture

As early as 1839, an Agricultural Division had been set up in the Patent Office. Congress created a Department of Agriculture in 1862, but its head, who was designated the Commissioner of Agriculture, did not have Cabinet ranking until 1889.

Until 1920, the Department of Agriculture performed three principal functions: (1) research and experimentation in plant exploration, plant and animal breeding, and insect and disease control; (2) distribution of agricultural information through publications, agricultural experiment stations, and county demonstration work; and (3) regulation of the quality of products through the authority to condemn diseased animals, to prohibit shipment in interstate commerce of adulterated or misbranded foods and drugs, and to inspect and certify meats and dairy products in interstate trade. Pressure always fell on the department to give "practical" help to the farmers, as evidenced by the fact that throughout this period, the department regularly distributed free seeds. In retrospect, it seems that the chief contribution of the Department of Agriculture in these early years lay in its ability to convince farmers of the value of "scientific" farming.

Agricultural Education

Attempts to incorporate the teaching of agricultural subjects into the education system began locally, but federal assistance was necessary to maintain adequate programs.

Although colleges of agriculture had been established in several states by 1860, it was the Morrill Act of 1862 that gave impetus to agricultural training at the university level. The Morrill Act established "land-grant" colleges that gradually assumed statewide leadership in agricultural research. The Hatch Act of 1887 provided federal assistance to state agricultural experiment stations, many of which had already been established with state funds. The Hatch Act also provided for the establishment of an Office of Experiment Stations in the Department of Agriculture to link the work of the department with that of the states. After 1900, interest in secondary schools began to develop. The Smith-Hughes Vocational Education Act of 1917 provided funds to states that agreed to expand vocational training at the high-school level in agriculture, trades, and home economics.

These and other measures advanced by reformers nurtured the beginnings of federal involvement in the agricultural sector. As we shall see, such involvement would grow dramatically in the decades after 1920. Similarly, calls to "end the waste" of natural resources advanced the role of government in the control and use of land, timber, and other natural resources.

NATURAL RESOURCE CONSERVATION: THE FIRST STAGES

The waste of natural resources in North America as perceived by Europeans, contemporaries, and others dates as far back as colonial times. For instance, many colonial farmers ignored "advanced" European farming methods designed to maintain soil fertility, preferring to fell trees and plant around stumps and then move on if the land wore out. Because land was abundant, their concern was not with soil conservation but with the shortage of labor and capital.

Similarly, in the early nineteenth century, lumber was in great abundance, especially in the eastern half of the nation, where five-sixths of the original forests were located. Indeed, in most areas of new settlement, standing timber was often an impediment rather than a valued resource. As late as 1850, more than 90 percent of all fuel-based energy came from wood.

By 1915, however, wood supplied less than 10 percent of all fuel-based energy in the United States, and in the Great Plains and other western regions, timber grew increasingly scarce.[11] The western advance of the railroad (which devoured nearly one-quarter of the timber cut in the 1870s) and the western shift of the population brought new pressures on limited western and distant eastern timber supplies. Moreover, the price of uncut marketable timber on public lands was zero for all practical purposes. This fact and the lack of clear legal rights to timber on public lands provided incentive to cut as fast as possible on public lands (Economic Reasoning Proposition 3, incentives matter). As a result, much waste occurred, and various environmental hazards were made more extreme. These included the loss of watersheds, which increased the hazard of floods and hastened soil erosion. More important, the buildup of masses of slash (tree branches and other timber deposits) created severe fire hazards. In the late nineteenth century, large cutover regions became explosive tinderboxes. For example, in 1871, the Peshtigo fire in Wisconsin devoured 1.28 million acres and killed more than 1,000 people. Similar dramatic losses from fire occurred in 1881 in Michigan and in 1894 in Wisconsin and Minnesota. These and other factors, such as fraudulent land acquisitions, demanded legislative action and reform (for further detail, see Clawson 1979; Olmstead 1980).

---

[11]For an excellent account of the responsive process in the form and use of natural resources to changes in their costs and supplies, see Rosenberg (May 1973).

Theodore Roosevelt and naturalist John Muir at Yosemite. An enthusiastic outdoorsman, Roosevelt expanded the role of the federal government in preserving America's wilderness and natural resources.

Land, Water, and Timber Conservation

The first major step toward reform was the General Revision Act of 1891. As noted earlier, this law repealed measures that had been an open invitation to land fraud, making it more difficult for corporations and wealthy individuals to steal timber and minerals. Prevention of theft scarcely constitutes conservation, but one section of the 1891 act, which empowered the president to set aside forest reserves, was a genuine conservation measure. Between 1891 and 1900, 50 million acres of valuable timberland were withdrawn from private entry, despite strong and growing opposition from interest groups in the western states. Inadequate appropriations made it impossible for the Division of Forestry to protect the reserves from forest fires and from depredations of timber thieves, but a start had been made.

When Theodore Roosevelt succeeded to the presidency in 1901, there was widespread concern, both in Congress and throughout the nation, over the problem of conservation. With imagination, charm, and fervor, Roosevelt sought legislation during both his terms to provide a consistent and far-reaching conservation program. By 1907, he could point to several major achievements:

1. National forests comprised 150 million acres, of which 75 million acres contained marketable timber. In 1901, a Bureau of Forestry was created, which became the United States Forest Service in 1905. Under Gifford Pinchot, Roosevelt's able chief adviser in all matters pertaining to conservation, a program of scientific forestry was initiated. The national forests were to be more than just preserves; the "crop" of trees was to be continually harvested and sold such that ever-larger future crops were ensured.

2. Lands containing 75 million acres of mineral wealth were reserved from sale and settlement. Most of the lands containing metals were already privately owned, but the government retained large deposits of coal, phosphates, and oil.

3. There was explicit recognition of the future importance of waterpower sites. A policy of leasing government-owned sites to private firms for a stipulated period of years was established, while actual ownership was reserved for the government.

4. The principle was accepted that it was a proper function of the federal government to implement a program of public works for the purpose of controlling stream flows. The Reclamation Act of 1902 provided for the use of receipts from land sales in the arid states to finance the construction of reservoirs and irrigation works, with repayment to be made by settlers over a period of years. In reality, however, it was overwhelmingly taxpayers generally, rather than only western settlers, who paid for these water projects.

Although such achievements seem modest, it should be recalled that in the first decade of the twentieth century, many people bitterly opposed any interference with the private exploitation of the remaining public domain. Much of the growth of government expenditures in water control, dams, and irrigation systems awaited a second Roosevelt in the 1930s. But the precedents set by Theodore Roosevelt's administration set the stage for the engineering marvels of the present era, which freed western agriculture from the shackles of dry-land farming of basic grains and livestock feeding—at considerable cost to the taxpayer. They also set a new direction, however haltingly, toward more conservation of natural space, minerals, forests, and water.

SELECTED REFERENCES AND SUGGESTED READINGS

Arrington, Leonard. *Great Basin Kingdom.* Cambridge, Mass.: Harvard University Press, 1958.

Atherton, Lewis. *The Cattle Kings.* Bloomington: Indiana University Press, 1961.

Binder, John J., and David T. Brown. "Bank Rates of Return and Entry Restrictions, 1869–1914." *Journal of Economic History* 51 (1991): 47–66.

Bowman, John D., and Richard H. Keehn. "Agricultural Terms of Trade in Four Midwestern States, 1870–1900." *Journal of Economic History* 34 (1974): 592–609.

Clawson, Marion. "Forests in the Long Sweep of American History." *Science* 204 (June 15, 1979).

Danhof, Clarence H. "Agriculture," in *The Growth of the American Economy*, ed. H. F. Williamson. New York: Prentice Hall, 1951.

David, Paul. "The Mechanization of Reaping in the Antebellum Midwest." In *Technical Choice, Innovation and Economic Growth, Essays on American and British Experience in the Nineteenth Century.* Cambridge: Cambridge University Press, 1975.

Destler, Chester McArthur. "Western Radicalism, 1865–1901: Concepts and Origins." *Mississippi Valley Historical Review* 31 (December 1944): 335–368.

Eichengreen, Barry. "Mortgage Interest Rates in the Populist Era." *American Economic Review* 74 (December 1984): 995–1015.

Fogel, Robert, and Jack Rutner. "Efficiency Effects of Federal Land Policy, 1850–1900." In *Dimensions of Quantitative Research in Economic History*, ed. William Aydelotte et al. Princeton, N.J.: Princeton University Press, 1972.

Galenson, David. "The End of the Chisholm Trail." *Journal of Economic History* 24, no. 2 (June 1974): 350–364.

Gallman, Robert E. "The Agricultural Sector and the Pace of Economic Growth: U.S. Experience in the Nineteenth Century." In *Essays in Nineteenth Century Economic History*, eds. David Klingaman and Richard Vedder. Athens: Ohio University Press, 1975.

Gates, Paul. "An Overview of American Land Policy." In *Two Centuries of American Agriculture*, ed. Vivian Wiser, 213–229. Washington, D.C.: Agricultural History Society, 1976.

Higgs, Robert. "Railroad Rates and the Populist Uprising." *Agricultural History* 44 (July 1970).

Historical Statistics. Washington, D.C.: Government Printing Office, 1975.

James, John. "The Development of the National Money Market." *Journal of Economic History* 36 (1976): 878–897.

Keehn, Richard. "Market Power and Bank Lending: Some Evidence from Wisconsin, 1870–1900." *Journal of Economic History* 35 (1975): 591–620.

Kendrick, John W. *Productivity Trends in the United States.* Princeton, N.J.: Princeton University Press, 1961, 362–364.

Libecap, Gary D. "Economic Variables and the Development of the Law: The Case of Western Mineral Rights." *Journal of Economic History* 38 (1978): 338–362.

Libecap, Gary D., and Ronald N. Johnson. "Property Rights, Nineteenth-Century Federal Timber Policy, and the Conservation Movement." *Journal of Economic History* 39 (1979): 129–142.

Mayhew, Anne. "A Reappraisal of the Causes of Farm Protest in the United States, 1870–1900." *Journal of Economic History* 32 (1972): 464–475.

McGuire, Robert A. "Economic Causes of Late Nineteenth Century Agrarian Unrest." *Journal of Economic History* 41 (1981): 835–849.

Olmstead, Alan., "The Mechanization of Reaping and Mowing in American Agriculture, 1833–1870." *Journal of Economic History* 35 (June 1975).

_____. "The Costs of Economic Growth." In *The Encyclopedia of American Economic History*, Vol. 2, 863–881. New York: Scribner's, 1980.

Olmstead, Alan L., and Paul W. Rhode. "Beyond the Threshold: An Analysis of the Characteristics and Behaviors of Early Reaper Adopters." *Journal of Economic History* 55 (1995): 27–57.

_____. *Creative Abundance, Biological Innovation, and American Agricultural Development.* Cambridge: Cambridge University Press, 2008.

Previant Lee, Susan, and Peter Passell. *A New Economic View of American History.* New York: Norton, 1979.

Rosenberg, Nathan. "Innovative Responses to Material Shortages." *American Economic Review* 63 (May 1973).

Rothstein, Morton. "Farmers' Movements and Organizations: Numbers, Gains, Losses." *Agricultural History* 62, no. 3 (Summer 1988): 161–181.

Smiley, Gene. "Interest Rate Movements in the United States, 1888–1913." *Journal of Economic History* 35 (1975): 591–662.

Snowden, Kenneth A. "Mortgage Rates and American Capital Market Development in the Late Nineteenth Century." *Journal of Economic History* 47 (1987): 771–791.

Sylla, Richard. "Federal Policy, Banking Market Structure, and Capital Mobilization in the United States, 1863–1913." *Journal of Economic History* 29 (1969): 657–686.

Williamson, Jeffrey G. *Late Nineteenth Century American Development, A General Equilibrium History.* Cambridge: Cambridge University Press, 1974.

CHAPTER **16**

Railroads and Economic Change

CHAPTER THEME

Few developments have captured the attention of historians and contemporary observers quite like the railroad. Fast and powerful, reaching everywhere, the railroad came to dominate the American landscape and the American imagination. Trains became the symbol of modern America, epitomizing America's economic superiority in an industrializing world.

To stipulate the many important influences of the railroad would generate a list of unmanageable proportions. We will confine our attention to four main questions:

1. Were these continent-spanning investments built ahead of demand, or were railroads followers in the settlement process?
2. How did the builders get their capital? Large land grants, both federal and state, and other means of financial assistance were given. Were these land grants needless giveaways or prudent uses of empty spaces? How important were they in the overall picture?
3. Another factor of great importance was the growth of government intervention in the economy as manifested in railroad regulation, both at the state and federal levels. Key legal interpretations paved the way for new economic controls by government. Was there a capture of the regulatory process by railroad management, or did regulation primarily benefit users? (Recall Economic Reasoning Proposition 4, institutions matter, in Economic Insight 1.1 on page 8.)
4. Finally, what impact did the railroad have on the overall growth rate of the economy? Was it only marginally superior to other modes of transport, or was it indispensable to American prosperity? Was the pace of productivity advance observed for the railroad during the antebellum period (see chapter 9) sustained during the postbellum period?

These questions have been asked by every generation of economic historians since the railroads were built. As we shall see, the answers have sometimes changed as new sources of data have been exploited and as new tools of analysis have been applied (Economic Reasoning Proposition 5, evidence and theory give value to opinions).

THE TRANSCONTINENTALS[1]

The Gold Rush of 1849 yielded knowledge about the riches of the Pacific Coast and about the vast spaces that separated East from West. There were three ways to get to the Pacific Coast, all difficult. Wagon trains along trails to California and the Pacific

---

[1]Astute readers will note that we sometimes use the term loosely to cover railroads that might be better designated as western railroads.

Northwest were beset with blizzards in winter, thirst in summer, and Indian attacks in all seasons. The shorter sea route via the Isthmus of Panama could cut the six- to eight-month trip around Cape Horn to as little as six weeks. But from Chagres, the eastern port on the Isthmus, to Panama City was a five-day journey by native dugout and mule-back, and at Panama City, travelers might have a long wait before securing passage north. For those who could afford it, the best way to California was by clipper ship, which made the passage around the Horn in about 100 days.[2] Thus, it is hardly surprising that a safe rail connection with the Pacific Coast was eagerly sought.

From the outset, government participation was viewed as essential. It was assumed that while the profits to the nation would be enormous, the profits to private investors would be insufficient to compensate for the enormous uncertainty surrounding such a project. By 1853, Congress was convinced of the feasibility of a railroad to the West Coast and directed government engineers to survey practical routes. The engineers described five, but years passed before construction began because of rivalry for the eastern terminus of the line. From Minneapolis to New Orleans, cities along the Mississippi River vied for the position of gateway to the West, boasting of their advantages while deprecating the claims of their rivals. The outbreak of the Civil War removed the proponents of the southern routes from Congress, and in 1862, the northern Platte River route was selected because it was used by the pony express, stages, and freight wagons.

By the Pacific Railway Act of 1862, Congress granted a charter of incorporation to the Union Pacific Railroad, which was authorized to build a line from Council Bluffs, Iowa, to the western boundary of Nevada. The Central Pacific, incorporated under the laws of California in 1861, was at the same time given authority to construct the western part of the road from Sacramento to the Nevada border. The government furnished financial assistance in two ways: in the form of grants of public land and loans for each mile of track completed. Initially, the loans were to be secured by first-mortgage bonds. Because the act of 1862 failed to attract sufficient private capital, the law was amended in 1864 to double the amount of land grants and to provide second-mortgage security of government loans, thus enabling the railroads to sell first-mortgage bonds to the public. To encourage speed of construction, the Central Pacific was permitted to build 150 miles beyond the Nevada line; later it was authorized to push eastward until a junction was made with the Union Pacific. With the railroads receiving their loans based on how much track they completed, it is not surprising that they encouraged rapid construction by pitting their workers against each other in their famous races; it is also not surprising that the quality of the track left something to be desired. (Economic Reasoning Proposition 3, incentives matter.)

The last two years of construction were marked by a storied race between the two companies to lay the most track. With permission to build eastward to a junction with the Union Pacific, the directors of the Central Pacific wished to obtain as much per mile subsidy as possible. The Union Pacific, relying on ex-soldiers and Irish immigrants, laid 1,086 miles of track; the Central Pacific, relying on Chinese immigrants, laid 689 miles, part of it through the mountains. The joining of the Union Pacific and the Central Pacific occurred amid great fanfare and celebration on May 10, 1869, at Promontory Summit (commonly called Promontory Point), a few miles west of Ogden, Utah. By telegraph, President Ulysses S. Grant gave the signal from Washington to drive in the last spike. The hammer blows that drove home the golden spike were echoed by telegraph to waiting throngs on both coasts. The continent had at last been spanned by rail;

---

[2]The record between New York and San Francisco was 88 days, set in 1854 by the clipper *Flying Cloud*. This record was not broken until 1989, when a small, high-tech sailboat named *Thursday's Child*, with a crew of two, made the passage in 80 days.

PERSPECTIVE 16.1

THE RAILROAD AND MORMON HANDCARTERS

When the Pacific Union hooked up with the Central Pacific Railroad at Promontory Point, May 10, 1869, to form the first transcontinental railroad line, the nation was at last united by rail. In addition, the linkage ended the long-distance mail-passenger stage lines, the pony express, and one of the most unique forms of migration in U.S. history.

Even before the Mormon pioneers, fleeing from persecution in Illinois, first entered the Great Basin of Utah in 1847 and relocated their church there (Salt Lake City today), Mormon missionaries were laboring in Great Britain and northern Europe to recruit new members into the church. Before 1854, Mormons, moving west to their Land of Zion, came in wagon trains.

From 1854 to 1868, most new Mormon arrivals in Utah came from European shores to the United States by ship, then by train to the western railhead of Iowa City (later to Omaha), and then by foot, walking the last 1,000 miles. Known as *handcarters*, they carried their belongings on hand-pulled flatbed carts resembling Chinese rickshaws. Too poor to afford animal-drawn wagons, they walked west under the direction and financial assistance of the church. A momentous disaster struck in early November 1856 when two handcart companies of nearly 500 each, under the direction of Captain Willie and Captain Martin, left Iowa City "late in the season." These two separate companies hit early winter storms at nearly 8,000 feet near the great divide in western Wyoming. News of the storms and knowledge of the numbers of people exposed and worn down on the trail motivated a rapid dispatch of an advance rescue party. Twenty-nine men galloped east from Salt Lake. Most of the 1,000-plus people stranded were saved, but between 200 and 300 perished from starvation and freezing.

Today, two coves in Wyoming where the companies held up and waited for a break in the weather are museums open to the public in remembrance of the greatest disaster of voluntary western migration in U.S. history. Though later handcart companies learned and avoided the risks that bore down so harshly on the Willie and Martin Companies, the long walks of handcarters were not ended until the railroad's advantage eclipsed them in the spring of 1869.

although transcontinental train travel was not without discomfort and even danger, the terrible trials of the overland and sea routes were over. See Perspective 16.1 on this page.

TOTAL CONSTRUCTION: PACE AND PATTERNS

As the first transcontinentals pushed toward completion and others were added, settled regions were crisscrossed with rails for through traffic (see Map 16.1). All major lines tried to secure access to New York in the east and to Chicago and St. Louis in the west. On the more northerly routes, the New York Central completed a through line from New York to Chicago by 1877, and the Erie did the same only a few years later. After the mid-1880s, the trunk lines filled the gaps, gaining access to secondary railroad centers and building feeder lines in a north-south direction.

From 1864 to 1900, the greatest percentage of track, varying from one-third to nearly one-half of the country's total annual construction, was laid in the Great Plains states. Chicago became the chief terminus, the center of a web of rails extending north, west, and south. St. Louis, Kansas City, Minneapolis, Omaha, and Denver became secondary centers. The Southeast and the Southwest lagged both in railroad construction and in the combination of local lines into through systems. Sparseness of population and war-induced poverty accounted in part for the backwardness of the Southeast, but the competition of coastal shipping was also a deterrent to railroad growth. The only southern transmountain crossing utilized before 1880 was the Chesapeake and Ohio, and, except for the Southern, no main north-south line was completed until the 1890s.

MAP 16.1

Today's Basic Railroad Network

The modern railroad network of the United States reflects the great waves of railroad building that occurred in the nineteenth century.

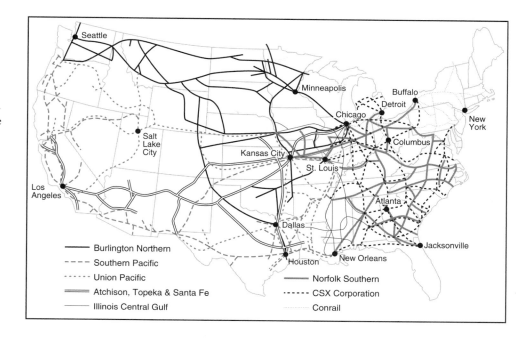

Legend:
— Burlington Northern
- - - Southern Pacific
······ Union Pacific
═══ Atchison, Topeka & Santa Fe
— Illinois Central Gulf
— Norfolk Southern
- - - CSX Corporation
······ Conrail

Table 16.1 on this page shows the expansion of total line mileage nationally. One feature is unsurprising: The eventual slowing in percentage jumps in mileage added. In pioneering work on economic development Nobel laureate Simon Kuznets (1929) and Arthur Burns (1934) showed that rapid industrial expansion was typically followed by a tapering off in the growth rate (and speed of productivity advance). All great innovations and industry growth patterns show these features, as we observed earlier in tobacco

TABLE 16.1 MAIN LINE RAILROAD TRACK IN OPERATION (IN THOUSANDS OF MILES)

YEAR	MILES	PERCENTAGE CHANGES (IN FIVE-YEAR INTERVALS)
1860	31	
1865	35	13
1870	53	63
1875	74	42
1880	93	26
1885	128	38
1890	167	30
1895	180	8
1900	207	15
1905	238	15
1910	266	12

Source: *Derived from* Historical Statistics *1960, Series Q15, 49–50.*

production, in cotton, and in steamboating. It is interesting to note, however, that the total absolute mileage doubled in the 25 years preceding 1910. Work by Albert Fishlow (1972a) reveals three major waves in the late nineteenth-century pattern of main track construction: 1868–1873, 1879–1883, and 1886–1892. These construction booms ended promptly with each of the major financial crises of the period: 1873, 1882, and 1893. As J. R. T. Hughes (1970) has argued, this is not terribly surprising when we recall that railroad construction depended heavily on borrowed money. Railroad construction had a strong influence on aggregate demand and business cycles. It accounted for 20 percent of U.S. gross capital formation in the 1870s, 15 percent of the total in the 1880s, and 7.5 percent of the total in each of the remaining decades until 1920. These investments reinforced and responded to swings in the business cycle. In 1920, railroad employment reached its peak, about 1 worker in 20.

Productivity Advance and Slowdown

The rapid but slowing pace of growth in construction is also seen in the gains in railroad productivity. As shown in Table 16.2, total factor productivity of the railroad somewhat more than doubled in the 40 years between 1870 and 1910. As in other maturing sectors and industries, the railroad experienced a continued but slowing advance. As observed in chapter 9, the pace of total factor productivity advance was so rapid between 1840 and 1860 that it doubled in this early 20-year period.

The sustained rapid growth of output relative to inputs was due primarily to two sources of productivity advance. First, as shown by Fishlow (1965, 2000), were additional gains from economies of scale in operation, accounting for nearly half of the productivity advance of the railroads at that time. The other half resulted from four innovations. In order of importance, these were (1) more powerful locomotives and more efficient freight cars, which tripled capacity; (2) stronger steel rails, permitting heavier loads; (3) automatic couplers; and (4) air brakes—these latter two facilitating greater speed and safety.

Despite the expected slowing of the railroad's productivity advance, it continued throughout the period up to World War I. It averaged 2 percent annually and exceeded the pace of productivity advance for the economy as a whole, which was approximately 1.5 per unit per annum. The railroads were not, in themselves, the cause of America's rapid economic progress in the nineteenth century, but for several generations of Americans, they symbolized the ceaseless wave of entrepreneurial energy and technological advance that was the cause of progress.

TABLE 16.2 PRODUCTIVITY IN THE RAILROAD SECTOR, 1870–1910
(1910 = 100)

YEAR	OUTPUT	LABOR	CAPITAL	FUEL	TOTAL INPUT	TOTAL FACTOR PRODUCTIVITY
1870	7	14	17	5	14	47
1880	14	25	32	12	26	54
1890	33	44	62	29	49	67
1900	55	60	72	46	63	87
1910	100	100	100	100	100	100

Note: To link these measures to similar ones before the Civil War, see Table 9.4 in chapter 9.

Source: *Adapted from Fishlow 1972b, 508.*

BUILDING AHEAD OF DEMAND?

Joseph Schumpeter, one of the leading economists of the early twentieth century, argued that many midwestern railroad projects "meant building ahead of demand in the boldest sense of the phrase" and that "Middle Western and Western projects could not be expected to pay for themselves within a period such as most investors care to envisage" (Fishlow 1965, 165–167). The implication of Schumpeter's argument was that government aid to the railroads was necessary to open the West.

Schumpeter's argument was a conjecture based on common sense. Albert Fishlow specified and tested the Schumpeter thesis rigorously, drawing the praise of fellow economists (Fogel 1967, 296; Desai 1968, 12). Fishlow reasoned that if railroads were built in unsettled regions, the demand for the railroad's services must have been low initially, with prices below average costs. As settlement occurred, the demand curve would shift upward so that average revenues would eventually exceed average costs. This provided him with three tests: (1) government aid should be widespread; (2) profit rates initially should be less than profit rates in alternative investments and should grow as the railroad aged; and (3) the number of people living near the railroad should initially be low compared with the number living near eastern railroads. On all three tests, Fishlow's findings failed to support Schumpeter's assertion that the railroads were built ahead of demand. Government aid to the railroads was often minimal, directed simply at getting a railroad already under construction to go through one town rather than another. Profit rates often started out relatively high and then fell over time. And the number of people living near the railroads when they began operations was typically similar to the number living near railroads in eastern rural areas. (Economic Reasoning Proposition 5, evidence matters, often because it contradicts what appears to be "common sense.")

What could explain such a paradoxical result? After all, it seems self-evident that farmers wouldn't move into an area before the railroads and that railroads couldn't be built until the farmers were in place. How could the market coordinate economic development in the Midwest? Fishlow discovered what he called "anticipatory settlement." Farmers and businessmen were well informed about the new territories being opened up by the railroads. They moved into a region, cleared the land, planted crops, and opened up ancillary businesses while a railroad was being constructed. By the time it was completed, crops were waiting to go to market. Fishlow concluded, however, that "a similar set of criteria casually applied to post–Civil War railroad construction in states farther West suggest that this constituted a true episode of 'building before demand'" (1965, 204).

The work to determine whether or not Fishlow's tentative answer was right about the post–Civil War's transcontinentals was done by Robert Fogel (1960) and Lloyd Mercer (1974).[3] Using Fishlow's criteria, they showed that indeed, the railroads were built ahead of demand; they had relatively low initial profit rates, and their profit rates grew over time. Finally, Fogel and Mercer tested for another interpretation of the notion of the railroads being built ahead of demand. Did the transcontinentals eventually earn high enough profit rates on operations to justify private investment without government subsidy? Alternatively stated, was their average rate of return (excluding revenues from land sales) over several decades above or below average rates of return on alternative investments? Mercer's findings showed mixed results. The Central Pacific and the Union Pacific (which formed the first transcontinentals) and the Great Northern (the last) had private rates of return above rates on alternative investments in the long run. Had private investors anticipated this result, they would have been willing to finance the

---

[3]Fogel's work came earlier and anticipated Fishlow's.

railroads without government assistance. Three others—the Texas and Pacific, the Santa Fe, and the Northern Pacific—did not. These findings show that the postbellum transcontinentals were all built ahead of demand, in the sense that initial profits were low. The necessity of government subsidies for the three high profit railroads could be questioned, because in the long run, these railroads made enough extra profits to compensate investors for their low early returns.

LAND GRANTS, FINANCIAL ASSISTANCE, AND PRIVATE CAPITAL

Subsidies for canals, as we observed, were common. States and municipalities, competing with one another for railroad lines they thought would bring everlasting prosperity, also helped the railroads, though on a smaller scale. They purchased or guaranteed railroad bonds, granted tax exemptions, and provided terminal facilities. Several states subscribed to the capital stock of the railroads, hoping to participate in the profits. Michigan built three roads, and North Carolina controlled the majority of the directors of three roads. North Carolina, Massachusetts, and Missouri took over failing railroads that had been liberally aided by state funds. Outright contributions from state and local units may have reached $250 million—a small sum compared with a value of track and equipment of $10 billion in 1880, when assistance from local governments had almost ceased.

In contrast to the antebellum period, subsequent financial aid from the federal government exceeded the aid from states and municipalities, although by how much we cannot be sure. Perhaps $175 million in government bonds was loaned to the Union Pacific, the Central Pacific, and four other transcontinentals, although after litigation, most of this amount was repaid. Rights-of-way grants, normally 200 feet wide, together with sites for depots and terminal facilities in the public domain and free timber and stone from government lands, constituted other forms of federal assistance. But the most significant kind of federal subsidy was the grant of lands from the public domain.

In this form, Congress gave a portion of the unsettled lands in the public domain to the railroads in lieu of money or credit. Following the precedent set by grants to the Mobile and Ohio and to the Ohio and Illinois Central in 1850, alternate sections (square miles) of land on either side of the road, varying in depth from 6 to 40 miles, were given outright for each mile of railroad that was constructed. The Union Pacific, for example, was granted 10 sections of public land for each mile of track laid; five on each side of the track alternating with sections retained by the government. The alternate-section provision was made in the expectation that the government would share in the increased land values that would result from the new transportation facilities. Land-grant subsidies to railroads were discontinued after 1871 because of public opposition, but not before 79 grants amounting to 200 million acres, reduced by forfeitures to just over 131 million acres, had been given.[4] This amounted to about 9 percent of the U.S. public domain accumulated between 1789 and 1904 and was slightly less than the amounts granted to the states.

Note, however, that aid to the railroads was not given unconditionally. Congress required that companies that received grants transport mail, troops, and government property at reduced rates. (In 1940, Congress relieved the railroads of land-grant rates for all except military traffic; in 1945, military traffic was removed from the reduced-rate

---

[4]Five great systems received about 75 percent of the land-grant acreage. These were the Union Pacific (including the Denver Pacific and Kansas Pacific); the Atchison, Topeka, and Santa Fe; the Northern Pacific; the Texas and Pacific; and the Central Pacific system (including the Southern Pacific Railroad).

category.) While land-grant rates were in effect, the government obtained estimated reductions of more than $500 million—a sum several times the value of the land grants when they were made and about equal to what the railroads received in land grants with an allowance for the long-run increase in the value of the land. The land grants, moreover, were in some ways a better incentive than alternative subsidies. A railroad could best realize the value of a land grant by quickly building a good track. In contrast, as we noted in the case of the Union Pacific, cash subsidies or loans based on miles of track completed or similar criteria encouraged shoddy construction (Economic Reasoning Proposition 3, incentives matter). Subsidies added to the profits and, thus, to the incentives of railroad builders until the early 1870s, but the bulk of both new and replacement capital came from private sources. The benefits of railroad transportation to farmers, small industrialists, and the general public along a proposed route were described in glowing terms by its promoters. Local investors responded enthusiastically and sometimes recklessly, their outlay of funds prompted in part by the realization that the growth of their communities and an increase in their personal wealth depended on the new transportation facility. Except in the industrial and urban Northeast, however, local sources could not provide sufficient capital, so promoters had to tap the wealth of eastern cities and Europe.

Thus, as the first examples of truly large corporations, railroad companies led the way in developing fundraising techniques by selling securities to middle-class investors. Even before 1860, railroads had introduced a wide range of bonds secured by various classes of assets.[5] After the Civil War, these securities proliferated as railroads appealed to people who had been introduced to investing through purchases of government debt during the war. Although conservative investors avoided the common stock of the railroads, the proliferation of such issues added tremendously to the volume of shares listed and traded on the floor of the New York Stock Exchange.

The modern investment banking house appeared as an intermediary between seekers of railroad capital in the South and the West and eastern and European investors, who could not easily estimate the worth of the securities offered them. From the 1850s on, the investment banker played a crucial role in American finance, allocating capital that originated in wealthy areas among those seeking it. J. Pierpont Morgan, a junior partner in the small Wall Street firm of Dabney and Morgan, joined forces in 1859 with the Drexels of Philadelphia to form Drexel, Morgan and Company. Along with Winslow, Lanier and Company and August Belmont and Company, Morgan's house grew rich and powerful by selling railroad securities, particularly in foreign markets. European interests eventually owned a majority of the stock in several railroads; English, Dutch, and German stockholders constituted important minority groups in the others. In 1876, European holdings amounted to 86 percent of the common stock of the Illinois Central, and at one time, two directorships of the Chicago and Northwestern were occupied by Dutch nationals. By 1914, Europeans, mostly English, owned one-fifth of all outstanding American railroad securities. We will discuss the role of these investment bankers in more detail in chapter 19.

UNSCRUPULOUS FINANCIAL PRACTICES

Railroad promoters sometimes indulged in questionable, even fraudulent, practices. Typically, these schemes involved the construction companies that built the railroads. Here is how it worked. The railroad contracted with a construction company to build a certain

---

[5]For extensive analysis see Chandler 1965, 43–94.

number of miles of road at a specific amount per mile. The railroad then met the costs by paying cash (acquired by selling bonds to the public) or transferring common stock to the construction company. In addition, government subsidies (land grants, state and local bonds, etc.) could be transferred to the construction company. Under one complicated but widely used system, common stock was transferred to permit its sale below par value, which was prohibited by law in some states. As long as the railroad corporation originally issued the securities at par, they could be sold at a discount by a second party, the construction company, without violating the law. The contract price was set high enough to permit the construction company, when selling the stock, to offer bargains to the investing public and still earn a profit. This method of financing, although cumbersome, provided funds that might not have been obtained otherwise, given the restrictions on the railroads' issue of common stock.

So far so good, but the system was easily abused. The owners of the construction company were often "insiders"—that is, officers and directors of the railroad corporation. The higher the price charged by the construction company, the lower the dividends paid to shareholders in the railroad and the greater the risk of bankruptcy because of the heavy indebtedness of the railroad, but the greater would be the profits that the insiders made on their investment in the construction company. The officers of the railroad, in other words, had a fiduciary duty to their investors to minimize the costs of construction, but they violated this duty to enrich themselves.

Although not all railroad construction was carried out by inside construction companies, this device was common—especially during the 1860s and 1870s—and all the transcontinentals used it. The most notorious inside company was the Crédit Mobilier of America, chartered under Pennsylvania statutes, which built the Union Pacific. During President Grant's second term, this company's operations caused a national scandal. Certain members of Congress bought stock (at favorable prices) or were given shares. It was a clear conflict of interest. By voting for grants of land and cash for the railroad, they were enriching themselves. Two congressmen were censured, and the careers of others (including outgoing Vice President Schuyler Colfax) were tarnished. Representative James A. Garfield was also implicated, but he denied all wrongdoing and was subsequently elected president. Huge profits accrued to the Crédit Mobilier. A congressional committee reported in 1873 that more than $23 million in cash profits had been realized by the company on a $10 million investment—and this cash take was over and above a $50 million profit in securities. By inflating the cost of construction, the insider construction companies saddled the railroads with large debt burdens that came back to haunt them, especially in the depressed 1890s.

GOVERNMENT REGULATION OF THE RAILROADS

The railroads engaged in a variety of discriminatory pricing policies that while understandable and sometimes justifiable from an economic point of view, nevertheless stirred considerable opposition from customers who felt victimized by discrimination. One of the most irritating forms of discrimination was the difference in long-haul and short-haul rates. Before 1870, each railroad usually had some degree of monopoly power within its operating area. However, as the railway network grew, adding more than 40,000 miles in the 1870s and 70,000 miles in the 1880s, the trunk lines of the East and even the transcontinentals of the West began to suffer the sting of competition. To be sure, major companies often faced no competition at all in local traffic and therefore had great flexibility in setting prices for relatively short hauls, but for long hauls between

Public land granted to the railroads as a subsidy and in turn sold to settlers was a continuing source of capital funds. Ads like this one appeared in city newspapers, luring thousands of Americans and immigrants westward. Note that each region of the state is carefully described so that farmers can buy land suitable for crops with which they have some experience.

major cities, there were usually two or more competing carriers. The consequence was a variance in the rates per mile charged between short and long hauls. The shipper paying the short-haul rate was understandably embittered by the knowledge that similar goods traveling in the same cars over the same track were paying a lower rate.

There were other forms of discrimination. Railroad managers were in charge of firms with high fixed costs, so they tried to set rates in ways that would ensure the fullest possible use of plant and equipment. Where it was possible to separate markets, managers set rates in a discriminating way. For example, rates per ton were set much lower on bulk freight such as coal and ore than on manufactured goods. If traffic was predominantly in one direction, shipments on the return route could be made at much lower rates because receiving any revenue was better than receiving nothing for hauling empty cars. For shippers, this common problem is called the "backhaul problem." Another form of rate discrimination arose when the same railroad was in a monopolistic position with respect to certain customers (a producer of farm machinery in the Midwest, for example) and a competitive position with respect to others (a favorably located producer of coal who could turn to water transport). Shippers not favored by these discriminatory rates or by outright rebates were naturally indignant at the special treatment accorded their competitors. Railroads also discriminated among cities and towns, a practice especially resented by farmers and merchants of one locality who watched those in another area enjoy lower rates for the same service.

There is a possible economic justification for these practices: By discriminating among customers, the railroad may have been able to increase its total output and lowered costs. Indeed, if forced to charge one price to all, a railroad may not have been able to cover its costs and remain in business. But the person paying the higher price generally didn't see things that way, and the pressure to regulate discriminatory practices grew rapidly (Economic Reasoning Proposition 2, choices impose costs).

Opposition to the railroads was heightened by the trend toward price fixing. By 1873, the industry was plagued by tremendous excess capacity. One line could obtain business by cutting rates on through traffic, but only at the expense of another company, which then found its own capacity in excess. Rate wars during the depressed years of the 1870s led to efforts to stop "ruinous competition" (as railroad owners and managers saw it). Railroads responded by banding together on through-traffic rates. They allocated shares of the business among the competing lines, working out alliances between competing and connecting railroads within a region. More often than not, though, these turned out to be fragile agreements that broke under the pressure of high fixed costs and excess capacity. To hide the rate cutting, shippers might pay the published tariff and receive a secret rebate from the railroad. Sooner or later, word of the rebating would leak out, with a consequent return to open rate warfare.

To provide a stronger basis for maintaining prices, Albert Fink took the lead in forming regional federations to pool either traffic or profits. The first was the Southern Railway and Steamship Association, which was formed in 1875 with Fink as its commissioner. Then, in 1879, the trunk lines formed the Eastern Trunk Line Association. But the federations eventually came unglued as weak railroads or companies run by aggressive managers or owners such as Jay Gould broke with the pool and began price cutting (Chandler 1965, 161). Shippers and the general public naturally resented pooling as well as price discrimination. The result was widespread support for government regulation of the railroads.

State Regulation

The first wave of railroad regulations came at the state level in the early 1870s, largely in response to increasing evidence of discrimination against persons and places. As the decade progressed, agrarian tempers rose as farm incomes declined. As emphasized in chapter 15, farmers in the Midwest blamed a large measure of their distress on the railroads. Many farmers had invested savings in railroad ventures on the basis of extravagant promises of the prosperity sure to result from improved transportation. When the opposite effect became apparent, farmers clamored for legislation to regulate rates. Prominent in the movement were members of the National Grange of the Patrons of Husbandry, an agrarian society founded in 1867. Thus, the demand for passage of measures regulating railroads, grain elevators, and public warehouses became known as the *Granger movement*, the legislation as the *Granger laws*, and the review of the laws by the Supreme Court as the *Granger cases.*

Between 1871 and 1874, Illinois, Iowa, Wisconsin, and Minnesota passed regulatory laws. Fixing schedules of maximum rates by commission rather than by statute was a feature of both the Illinois and Minnesota laws. One of the common practices that western farmers could not tolerate was charging more for the carriage of goods over a short distance. The pro rata clause in the Granger laws prohibited railroads from charging short shippers more than their fair share of the costs. Both personal and place discrimination were generally outlawed, although product discrimination was not. Finally, commissions were given the power to investigate complaints and to institute suits against violators.

Almost as soon as the Granger laws were in the statute books, attempts were made to have them declared unconstitutional on the ground, among others, that they were repugnant to the Fifth Amendment to the Constitution, which prohibits the taking of private property without just compensation. It was argued, for example, that limitations on the prices charged by the grain elevators restricted their earnings and deprived their properties of value. Six suits were brought to test the laws. The principal one was *Munn v. Illinois*, an action involving grain elevators. This case was taken to the U.S. Supreme Court in 1877 after state courts in Illinois found that Munn and his partner Scott had violated the state warehouse law by not obtaining a license to operate grain elevators in the city of Chicago and by charging prices in excess of those set by state law. From a purely economic point of view, the argument made by the grain elevator operators makes some sense. The loss of wealth may be the same whether the government takes a piece of land to build a road (the classic case requiring compensation) or imposes a maximum price.

But the Supreme Court saw the case (and five similar railroad cases before it) in a different light: it upheld the right of a state to regulate these businesses. Chief Justice Morrison Remick Waite stated in the majority opinion that when businesses are "clothed with a public interest," their regulation as public utilities is constitutional. The *Munn* case settled the constitutionality of the state regulation of railroads and certain other enterprises within the states—but not between states.

In 1886, a decision in the case of *Wabash, St. Louis and Pacific Railway Company v. Illinois*, however, severely limited what states could regulate. The state had found that the Wabash was charging more for a shorter haul from Gilman, Illinois, to New York City than for a longer haul from Peoria to New York City and had ordered the rate adjusted. The U.S. Supreme Court held that Illinois could not regulate rates on shipments in interstate commerce because the Constitution specifically gave the power to regulate interstate commerce to the federal government. In the absence of federal legislation, the *Wabash* case left a vast area with no control over carrier operation; regulation would have to come at the national level or not at all.

Federal Regulation[6]

Early in 1887, Congress passed and President Grover Cleveland signed the Act to Regulate Commerce. Its chief purpose was to bring all railroads engaged in interstate

---

[6]For an excellent survey of the issues of regulation, see McCraw (1975).

commerce under federal regulation. The Interstate Commerce Commission (ICC), consisting of five members to be appointed by the president with the advice and consent of the Senate, was created, and its duties were set forth. First, the commission was required to examine the business of the railroads; to this end, it could subpoena witnesses and ask them to produce books, contracts, and other documents. Second, the commission was charged with hearing complaints that arose from possible violations of the act and was empowered to issue cease-and-desist orders if unlawful practices were discovered. The third duty of the commission was to require railroads to submit annual reports based on a uniform system of accounts. Finally, the commission was required to submit to Congress annual reports of its own operations.

The Act to Regulate Commerce seemingly prohibited all possible unethical practices. Section 1 stated that railroad rates must be "just and reasonable." Section 2 prohibited personal discrimination; a lower charge could no longer be made in the form of a "special rate, rebate, drawback, or other device." Section 3 provided that no undue preference of any kind should be accorded by any railroad to any shipper, any place, or any special kind of traffic. Section 4 enacted, in less drastic form, the pro rata clauses of the Granger legislation by prohibiting greater charges "for the transportation of passengers or of like kind of property, under substantially similar circumstances and conditions, for a shorter than for a longer distance, over the same line, in the same direction, the shorter being included in the longer distance." Pooling was also prohibited.

The ICC was the first permanent independent federal regulatory agency. Its formation represented the beginning of direct government intervention in the economy on an expanding scale. The first decade and a half of the ICC, however, was filled with court challenges by the railroads. To clarify certain powers delegated by Congress, both the ICC and the railroads sought new legislation, especially regarding issues of price discrimination.

The Elkins Act of 1903 dealt solely with personal discrimination. The act made any departure from a published rate (giving a special rate to a favored customer) a misdemeanor. Until this time, the courts had overruled the commission in the enforcement of published rates by requiring that discrimination against or injury to other shippers of similar goods had to be proved. Convincing evidence suggests that the Elkins Act represented the wishes of a large majority of the railroad companies because it protected them from demands for rebates by powerful shippers and brought the government to their aid in enforcing the cartel prices set by the trunk line associates. The act stated that railroad corporations should be liable for any unlawful violation of the discrimination provisions. Up to this time, only officials and employees of a company had been liable for discriminatory actions; henceforth, the corporation itself would also be responsible.

To close remaining loopholes, Congress passed the Hepburn Act of 1906. This act extended the jurisdiction of the ICC to private-car companies that operated joint express, tank, and sleeping cars. Services such as storage, refrigeration, and ventilation were also made subject to the control of the commission. This was necessary because the management of the railroads could use such services to discriminate among shippers. For example, railroads normally charged for storage; if any shippers were not charged for this service, discrimination resulted. Perhaps most important was the change in the procedures for enforcement of the ICC's orders. Until 1906, the ICC had to prove before the court the case it had adjudicated. The Hepburn Act put the burden of proof on the carriers. The right of judicial review was recognized, but the railroads—not the commission—had to appeal, and the presumption was for—not against—the Commission.

Capturing the Regulators?

Initially, the ICC clearly endeavored to protect consumers from abuses, and, also initially, the railroad industry was clearly not pleased with the ICC. In 1892, Charles E. Perkins, president of the Chicago, Burlington and Quincy Railroad, wrote a letter to his lawyer Richard Olney (who later became attorney general of the United States) recommending that the embryonic five-year-old commission be abolished. Olney's shrewd reply is worth quoting:

> *My impression would be that looking at the matter from the railroad point of view it would not be a wise thing to undertake. ... The attempt would not be likely to succeed; if it did not succeed, and were made on the grounds of the inefficiency and uselessness of the Commission, the result would very probably be giving it the power it now lacks. The Commission, as its functions have been limited by the courts, is, or can be made of great use to the railroads. It satisfies the public clamor for a government supervision of railroads, at the same time that the supervision is almost entirely nominal. Further, the older such a commission gets to be, the more inclined it will be found to take the business and railroad view of things. It thus becomes a sort of protection against hasty and crude legislation hostile to railroad interests. . . . The part of wisdom is not to destroy the Commission, but to utilize it. (Fellmeth 1970, xiv–xv)*

To what extent did Olney's analysis prove to be an accurate prediction? Did the railroads capture the ICC and use it for their own ends? In 1965, the noted historian Gabriel Kolko (1965) suggested that railroad managers did use the ICC to stabilize profit rates and secure other advantages of cartel management. Although railroad managers openly supported the Elkins Act to ensure through regulation similar pricing among competing carriers, the scholarship of Robert C. Harbeson (1967) and Albro Martin (1971), which we find convincing, shows that the work of the ICC was largely for the benefit of users—shippers, especially the shippers of bulk commodities, and passengers. When the long period of falling prices reversed itself in 1896, the ICC disallowed rate increases sufficient to match rises in the general price level. Railroads reacted by slowing their repair and replacement of capital stock and equipment. This helped to some extent to slow the rising costs of railroad operations. By the outbreak of World War I, the railroads were physically decayed and financially strapped. If there was a management capture of the regulatory process, it is difficult to find in the events preceding the 1920s. Indeed, in 1917, the federal government scored the critical capture by nationalizing the railroads in the interests of the war effort. After the war, the railroads were returned to private ownership. As we shall see in later chapters, the "capture thesis" applies in other situations, but managers did not initially capture and control the regulation process in the case of early ICC activities. One reason the railroads failed to capture the ICC may be that many large shippers had nearly as much incentive to monitor the ICC and as much clout in Washington as the railroads. The capture thesis is most likely to apply when the costs of a decision favoring the regulated industry are widely diffused.

RAILROADS AND ECONOMIC GROWTH

Joseph Schumpeter (1949), whose argument that the railroads were built ahead of demand was noted earlier in this chapter, also believed that railroads had led the transition to modern economic growth. Schumpeter argued that growth was a dynamic process of applying major technological advances, both invention and innovation, and that the railroad epitomized these growth-generating forces. Walt Rostow (1960) later added to this view by arguing that the railroad was a "leading sector" in the nation's "take-off" to modern economic growth.

Within a year of each other in the mid-1960s, Robert Fogel (1964) and Albert Fishlow (1965) produced books that generated an avalanche of debate. Their objective was to pin down with actual numbers the contributions of the railroad to nineteenth-century U.S. economic growth. Although their classic works differed in style and approach, their goals were essentially the same: to measure the social savings of the railroad (amount of additional real gross national product [GNP] that could be attributed to the railroad) in 1859 (Fishlow) and in 1890 (Fogel). See Economic Insight 16.1 on this page concerning social savings from rail transport.

Fogel's work particularly drew fire, because of his willingness to explore what might have happened in the absence of the railroad. Fogel began his study by reviewing the evolution of the "axiom of indispensability," a term that became widely accepted in describing the role of the railroad. It was primarily in the late nineteenth-century battles over government control that "the indispensability of railroads to American economic growth was elevated to the status of an axiomatic truth" (Foel 1964, 7). The usefulness of this term, incidentally, confirms Deirdre McCloskey's (1985, chapter 6) claim that the wide influence of Fogel's work depended in part on his superb rhetorical skills. Until Fishlow's and Fogel's books were published, the most widely used texts in American economic history courses portrayed the railroads as having "the power of life and death over the economy" or as

ECONOMIC INSIGHT 16.1

SOCIAL SAVINGS FROM RAIL TRANSPORT

The figure below illustrates the measurement of social savings. The quantity of transport (measured, say, in a standardized ton-mile) is measured on the horizontal axis; the price charged is measured on the vertical axis. D is the demand curve. P_W is the price of transport via water, and P_R is the price of transport via the railroad. Q_R is the amount of transport actually supplied with railroads predominant. Q_W is the amount of transport that would be carried by the waterways in the counterfactual world in which railroads did not exist. For simplicity, it is assumed that over the relevant range, the costs of supplying water transport and rail transport are constant.

The social savings from the railroad are given by the shaded area P_W-A-B-P_R. Why? The area under the demand curve is derived from the demand for goods and services and represents the value of the transport used in producing those final products. With the higher costs of water transport, some use of transport either must be abandoned (the area A-B-C) or be produced by using more resources and thus reducing output in other sectors (the area P_W-A-C-P_R).

The trick, of course, is to estimate the position and elasticities of the actual curves. Only points near B are

likely to be observed directly; others must be estimated in some way. Controversy over the shape of the supply curve of water transport, for example, has been heated. But simply putting the issue in this way takes some of the steam out of the axiom of indispensability. Total railroad revenues were less than 10 percent of GNP in 1890, so it would take some extreme assumptions about the elasticity of demand and the increased costs of water transport to push the social saving to a significant share of GNP.

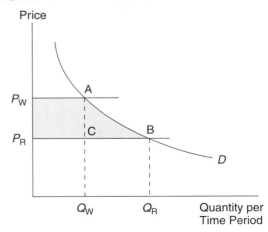

"essential to the development of Capitalism in America" (Fogel 1964, 9). Because of the efforts of Fishlow and Fogel and other scholars, those views are gone.

Fishlow measured the cost of moving all freight and passengers carried by rail in 1859 by the next-best alternative to railroads. In other words, the cost of carrying freight or passengers in 1859 was estimated as if the railroads had suddenly vanished and shippers had to rely on water or wagon. The higher costs of carrying railroad passengers and freight by these older technologies were figured to be about 4 percent of GNP in that year. Fogel selected 1890 to make his social savings estimate, picking a year in which the cost advantage of railroads over alternatives and the mix of output produced by the economy were particularly favorable to the railroads, and a year in which the railroads were at their peak in terms of their role in the transportation system. He wanted an upper-bound estimate of the social saving so that if the estimate nevertheless turned out to be small, there would be little argument that the axiom of indispensability had to go.

Fogel concentrated on the shipment of agricultural products. Surprisingly, when looking only at direct transport costs, one finds that the costs of shipping goods by water were often lower than shipping them by rail. In shipping wheat from Chicago to New York, for example, the average all-rail rate was $0.52 per ton-mile, while the average all-water rate was only $0.14 per ton-mile. Obviously, other costs made the total cost of shipping by water higher. Some of these were relatively easy to measure from existing commercial data. For example, grain shipped by water from Chicago to New York had to be shifted from lake steamers to canal barges at Buffalo; this cost must be added in to get the total cost of shipping by water.

The most important additional cost of shipping by water, however, was that it was slower in all seasons and not available at all in winter. How does one measure the cost of slowness? The answer is that with water transport, eastern merchants would be forced to keep larger inventories of grain. The advantage of fast, all-weather transport can be measured by estimating the reduction in eastern inventories.

Fogel also pointed out that in computing the true social savings, it is a mistake to assume that the same goods would have been shipped between the same places in the absence of the railroads. Instead, production would have been intensified in certain areas and cut back in others. Investments that were made in railroads would have gone into improving the canal and water network as well as into other areas of the economy. The true social savings compare actual real GNP with real GNP that has adjusted completely to the absence of the railroads. That is, social savings should be measured as the difference between GNP in the United States and GNP in a "counterfactual" United States (to use Fogel's evocative term) that had fully adjusted to the absence of the railroad. Fogel therefore investigated the effects on agricultural rents of investing in substitutes for rail services such as an extension of the canal network and improvements in the road network. Here he made creative use of the extensive plans made by Army Corps of Engineers and the Bureau of Public Roads to extend the canal and road networks. Fogel did find that the "boundary of feasible agriculture" had been pushed outward by the railroads. Some land would not have been farmed had the rail systems not been developed, but the theoretical reduction in the land under cultivation was much smaller than suggested by some of the rhetoric surrounding the railroads. Much of the prairies would have been farmed even if the railroads had never been invented.

Fogel's "counterfactual" world, in which canals are built and filled with water, roads improved, and the development of trucks and automobiles accelerated, proved to be an especially lively part of the debate and analysis that followed. Traditional historians did not like the idea of historians patiently investigating "imaginary" worlds. But a younger generation of economic historians trained in economics were enthusiastic about evaluating historical developments in terms of the relevant alternatives.

Overall, Fogel found that the railroad had saved at most only about 1.4 percent of GNP in the transportation of agricultural products after allowing for adjustment to a nonrail world. He did not launch a full-scale effort to measure the social savings for other types of freight or for passengers. His preliminary estimate for other kinds of freight, an estimate that did not allow for adjustments to a nonrail world, was 3.1 percent of GNP. Subsequently, J. Hayden Boyd and Gary Walton (1972) calculated the social savings of 1890 rail passengers, including the value of their time saved. The total extra costs of having rail passengers travel by water or stage figured to 2.8 percent of 1890 GNP. Overall, therefore, an upper-bound estimate of the social savings came to about 7.3 percent of GNP in 1890.

This measure of the direct effects of the railroad suggests that output per capita would not have reached its 1890 level until 1892 without the railroad. In short, the railroad accounted for about two years of growth, or alternatively stated, failure to build the railroads would simply have postponed growth for two years. Fishlow's and Fogel's pioneering classics debunked long-held myths about the indispensability of the railroad. Though it is difficult to think of any other single innovation that rendered economic gains of a similar magnitude, the railroads were nevertheless merely one among many developments that contributed to America's economic growth.

Fishlow and Fogel's work inspired a long running debate about the validity of their methodologies and accuracy of their calculations, and inspired studies of the contribution of the railroads in many other countries.[7] As students of this lively professional debate quickly learn, however, it was not so much the final calculations that were Fishlow's and Fogel's main contributions, significant though these were; rather, it was their ability to focus the argument, specify a testable hypothesis, and bring forth the evidence that narrowed the range of disagreement. In short, they advanced the level of analysis and the profession's understanding of an important issue in economic growth generally and in American economic history in particular.

SELECTED REFERENCES AND SUGGESTED READINGS

Boyd, J. Hayden, and Gary M. Walton. "The Social Savings from Nineteenth-Century Rail Passenger Services." *Explorations in Economic History* 9 (1972): 233–254.

Burns, Arthur F. *Production Trends in the United States Since 1870.* New York: National Bureau of Economic Research, 1934.

Chandler, Alfred D. *The Railroads: The Nation's First Big Business.* New York: Harcourt Brace Jovanovich, 1965.

David, Paul. "Transport Innovation and Economic Growth: Professor Fogel On and Off the Rails." *Economic History Review* 2, 2d series (1969): 506–525.

Desai, Meghnad. "Some Issues in Econometric History," *Economic History Review* 21, 2nd series (1968): 1–16.

Fellmeth, Robert C. *The Interstate Commerce Commission.* New York: Grossman, 1970.

Fishlow, Albert. *American Railroads and the Transformation of the Ante-bellum Economy.* Cambridge, Mass.: Harvard University Press, 1965.

_____. "The Dynamics of Railroad Extension into the West." In *Reinterpretation of American Economic History*, eds. Robert Fogel and Stanley Engerman. New York: Harper & Row, 1972a and b.

_____. "Internal Transportation." In *Economic Growth: An Economist's History of the United States,*

[7]The most influential early criticisms of Fishlow, and especially Fogel's work include Stanley Lebergott (1966), McClelland (1968), David (1969), and Williamson (1974, chapter 9). Fogel's (1979, 1–55) response to his critics was given in his presidential address to the Economic History Association. Leunig (2006) is a recent example of a study of social savings from the railroad in Britain. Leunig finds that the railroads produced substantial savings in Britain by reducing the travel time of passengers.

ed. Lance E. Davis et al., 508. New York: Harper & Row, 1972.

_____. "Internal Transportation in the Nineteenth and Early Twentieth Centuries." In *The Cambridge Economic History of the United States*, Vol. 2, *The Long Nineteenth Century*, eds. Stanley Engerman and Robert Gallman, 543–642. Cambridge: Cambridge University Press, 2000.

Fogel, Robert W. *The Union Pacific Railroad: A Case of Premature Enterprise.* Baltimore, Md.: Johns Hopkins University Press, 1960.

_____. *Railroads and American Economic Growth.* Baltimore, Md.: Johns Hopkins University Press, 1964.

_____. "The Specification Problem in Economic History," *Journal of Economic History* 27 (1967): 283–308.

_____. "Notes on the Social Saving Controversy." *Journal of Economic History* 39 (1979): 1–54.

Harbeson, Robert. "Railroads and Regulation, 1877–1916: Conspiracy or Public Interest?" *Journal of Economic History* 27 (1967): 230–242.

Historical Statistics. Washington, D.C.: Government Printing Office, 1960

Hughes, Jonathan. *Industrialization and Economic History: Theses and Conjectures.* New York: McGraw-Hill, 1970.

Kolko, Gabriel. *Railroads and Regulation, 1877–1916.* Princeton, N.J.: Princeton University Press, 1965.

Kuznets, Simon. "The Retardation of Industrial Growth." *Journal of Economic and Business History* (August 1929): 534–560.

Lebergott, Stanley. "United States Transport Advance and Externalities." *Journal of Economic History* 26 (1966): 437–461.

Leunig, Timothy. "Time Is Money: a Re-assessment of the Passenger Social Savings from Victorian British Railways." *Journal of Economic History* 66, no. 3 (2006): 635–673.

MacAvoy, Paul. *The Economic Effects of Regulation.* Cambridge, Mass.: MIT Press, 1965.

McCloskey, Deirdre. *The Rhetoric of Economics.* Madison: University of Wisconsin Press, 1985.

Martin, Albro. *Enterprise Denied: Origins of the Decline of American Railroads, 1897–1917.* New York: Columbia University Press, 1971.

McClelland, Peter D. "Railroads, American Growth, and the New Economic History: A Critique." *Journal of Economic History* 28 (1968): 102–123.

McCraw, Thomas K. "Regulation in America: A Review Article." *Business History Review* 49 (1975): 159–183.

Mercer, Lloyd. "Building Ahead of Demand: Some Evidence for the Land Grant Railroads." *Journal of Economic History* 34 (1974): 492–500.

Rostow, W. W. *The Stages of Economic Growth: A Non-Communist Manifesto.* New York: Cambridge University Press, 1960.

Schumpeter, Joseph. *The Theory of Economic Development.* Cambridge, Mass.: Harvard University Press, 1949.

Union Pacific Web site. http://www.uprr.com/aboutup/history/, historical section.

Williamson, Jeffrey G. *Late Nineteenth Century American Economic Development.* Cambridge: Cambridge University Press, 1974.

CHAPTER 17

Industrial Expansion and Concentration

During the half-century between the Civil War and World War I, the American economy assumed many of its modern characteristics. The most impressive changes were the shift from an agricultural to an industrial economy and the speed of productivity advance, especially in manufactures. Although this shift had been under way throughout the entire nineteenth century, agriculture remained the chief generator of income in the United States until the 1880s. The census of 1890, however, reported manufacturing output greater in dollar value than farm output, and by 1900, the annual value of manufactures was more than twice that of agricultural products. Our main concern in this chapter is with the technological and other productivity advances of the period, the expanding size and concentration of business enterprises, and the threat of monopoly that spurred new waves of government intervention and institutional change. In short, we are looking primarily at changes on the supply side, in production, in business organization, and in the public policy responses. The issues of product distribution, urbanization, and other market changes are assessed in chapter 20.

STRUCTURAL CHANGE AND INDUSTRY COMPOSITION

The continuing rise of manufacturing after the Civil War astonished contemporaries. It is a period that has come to be known for reasons we will discuss in more detail below as the Second Industrial Revolution.[1] One striking set of numbers is the exact flip-flop between agriculture and manufactures in the percentage distribution of commodities produced in 1869 and in 1899. In 1869, this distribution was 53 percent agriculture, 33 percent manufactures, and 14 percent mining and construction combined. Thirty years later, it was 33 percent, 53 percent, and 14 percent (Gallman 1960, 26).

As emphasized in chapter 15, agriculture expanded in these years but fell relatively because of more rapid increases elsewhere. Table 17.1 shows the 1910 labor force in several employments as multiples of their 1860 employment level. For example, in 1910, the total labor force of 37.5 million was approximately 3.4 times the 1860 level of 11.1 million. Agriculture's labor force grew only by a factor of 2, however, from 5.9 million to 11.8 million between 1860 and 1910. By comparison, total labor in manufacturing grew by a multiple of 5.4, and in railroads by 23.2.

Table 17.2 on page 299 shows multiples of output in several categories. The output multiples are far larger than the labor multiples in comparable categories. For example,

---

[1]The first Industrial Revolution began in England toward the end of the eighteenth century. Cotton textiles were the leading sector during the first Industrial Revolution.

TABLE 17.1 LABOR FORCE EXPANSION, 1860–1910: SELECT 1910 MULTIPLES OF 1860

Agriculture	2.0
Cotton textiles	3.0
Construction	3.7
Teaching	5.2
Total manufacturing	5.4
Trade	6.0
Mining	6.7
Primary iron and steel	7.1
Railroads	23.2
Total labor force	**3.4**

Source: Derived from Stanley Lebergott, Manpower in Economic Growth: The American Record Since 1800 (New York: McGraw-Hill, 1964), 510. Copyright © 1964 by The McGraw-Hill Companies, Inc. Reprinted by permission.

total manufactures output in 1910 was 10.8 times that of 1860, whereas the labor force in manufactures had grown by a multiple of only 5.4. The coal and cement multiples suggest the vast devouring of natural resources needed to industrialize the nation; they were far larger than the mining labor multiple. All of these selected categories reveal output multiples higher than the total labor force or sector labor multiples (Table 17.1). The reason for the difference is the great increase in productivity that occurred in these years.

American gains in manufacturing output were also phenomenal relative to the rest of the world. In the mid-1890s, the United States became the leading industrial power, and by 1910, its factories poured forth goods of nearly twice the value of those of its nearest rival, Germany. In 1913, the United States accounted for more than one-third of the world's industrial production.

Table 17.3 on page 300 lists the top 10 manufactures (by value added) in 1860 and again 50 years later. It is clear from this evidence that the "make-up" of manufactures altered significantly as industrial expansion unfolded over the period. The push and tug of market forces and a high degree of resource mobility rendered such change possible. In addition, the industrial products of the United States were sold in markets that were expanding both at home and abroad, as we shall see in detail in chapter 20. Most American manufacturers, however, did not aggressively seek major foreign outlets until late in the nineteenth century because the nation itself provided an expanding free trade arena.

TABLE 17.2 OUTPUT EXPANSION, 1860–1910: SELECT 1910 MULTIPLES OF 1860

Food and kindred products	3.7
Textiles and their products	6.2
Total manufacturing products	10.8
Iron and steel and their products	25.2
Bituminous coal	46.1
Cement	70.7
Railroad passenger miles[a]	17.1
Railroad freight ton miles[a]	98.1

[a]The railroad multiples are for 1859 to 1910.

Source: Derived from U.S. Bureau of the Census, Historical Statistics, 1960, Series M, 178, Part 1; Frickey 1947, 38–43, 54; and Fishlow 1966, 585.

TABLE 17.3 THE 10 LARGEST INDUSTRIES, 1860 AND 1910 (BY VALUE ADDED)

1860 VALUE ADDED (IN MILLIONS OF DOLLARS)		1910 VALUE ADDED (IN MILLIONS OF DOLLARS)	
Cotton goods	$ 55	Machinery	$ 690
Lumber	54	Lumber	650
Boots and shoes	49	Printing and publishing	540
Flour and meal	40	Iron and steel	330
Men's clothing	37	Malt liquors	280
Iron	36	Men's clothing	270
Machinery	33	Cotton goods	260
Woolen goods	25	Tobacco manufactures	240
Carriages and wagons	24	Railroad cars	210
Leather	23	Boots and shoes	180
All manufacturing	815	All manufacturing	8,529

Source: *U.S. Bureau of the Census 1861, 733–742; 1913, 40.*

Note also the prominence of Printing and Publishing in 1910, which was partly a result of the spread of primary schooling in previous decades.

A vast social transformation accompanied the changes shown in Table 17.3. Four industries—printing and publishing, malt liquor, tobacco, and railroad cars—were new to the top 10 list in 1910, whereas flour and meal, woolens, wagons and buggies, and leather goods had slipped into lower positions. The low-income elasticity of demand for flour products and woolens, plus new technologies (railroad cars instead of wagons) and other sources of productivity advance, explain much of this transition. Also, tastes were changing as cottons and linens, cigars and cigarettes, and store-bought alcoholic beverages added to or replaced other items, many previously homemade. (Remember Economic Reasoning Proposition 1, individual choices are the source of social outcomes, see page 8.)

New Technologies

Technological changes, investments in human capital, new energy sources that widened markets and brought new organizational business structures and economies of scale, and shifts in resources from lower to higher productivity uses (agricultural to manufacturing) all combined to cause these exceptional long-term trends.

Technological changes helped revolutionize industry after industry. No single industry is distinctly representative of the whole, but the advance of each was based on invention and innovation, the dual components of technological change. Invention signifies the discovery of something new, such as steam power or electricity. Innovation denotes the many ways found to use and adapt the new ideas to existing products and services.

The avalanche of technological change, especially in the 1870s and 1880s, was pervasive. The following sample of new technologies during these decades is by no means exhaustive: the roller mill to process oatmeal and flour; refrigerated cars for meat packing; sealed cans for meat, vegetables, and soup; steel-bottomed stills, long-distance pipelines, and steel tank cars for the petroleum industry; advances in Bessemer and open-hearth processes for steel making; advances in electrometallurgy for aluminum production; new varieties of machines and high-speed tools of all sorts; the typewriter, cash register,

© BETTMANN/CORBIS

Completed in 1883 at a cost of $15.1 million (about $2 billion today), the Brooklyn Bridge was a symbol of America's industrial and technological preeminence.

electrical streetcar, and so on (O'Brien 1988). (Economic Insight 17.1 on this page discusses the two new steel processes in more detail.) These new technologies permitted mass production and generated lower per-unit costs through economies of scale. Adding to these advances in plant size and productivity were the infrastructure of a transcontinental railroad and a national telegraph network. The outcome was a distribution system, by 1880, that was truly continental in scope.

ECONOMIC INSIGHT 17.1

STEEL INDUSTRY INNOVATIONS OF THE 1860s

New technologies often diffuse slowly. We illustrate this point by analyzing the steel industry in terms of two new and competing technologies—the Bessemer process and the open-hearth process—and linking these to other technological advances raising productivity and reducing per-unit costs in steelmaking.

The first successful method of making steel in quantity was invented in the late 1850s and early 1860s almost simultaneously by an Englishman, Henry Bessemer, and by an American, William Kelly.

Soon after, an alternative, the open-hearth method, reached experimental status. Inventors were trying to find a way of making cheap steel without infringing on Bessemer's patents. They were also trying to overcome some of the deficiencies of Bessemer's process. The most surprising deficiency was that the method was so quick there was not sufficient time to test the steel for carbon content, so the manufacturer could never be certain for what purposes a given batch would be suitable. The best work on the open hearth was accomplished by William and Friedrich Siemens in England and Emile and Pierre Martin in France. By 1868, the main features of the open-hearth or Siemens-Martin process had been

ECONOMIC INSIGHT 17.1

STEEL INDUSTRY INNOVATIONS OF THE 1860s, Continued

developed. Instead of a cylindrical converter that could be tipped like a huge kettle, the open-hearth method employed a furnace with a shallow, open container holding a charge of molten pig iron, scrap iron, limestone, and even some iron ore.

Several considerations made the open-hearth process more economical than the Bessemer process. A large charge required about 12 hours, compared with 10 to 15 minutes for a Bessemer "blow," but during the long refining period, open-hearth steel could be sampled and its chemical composition adjusted to exact requirements. The open-hearth furnace also had a cost advantage over the Bessemer converter in that scrap iron and iron ore could be charged with the more expensive molten pig iron. The regeneration principle, by which the open-hearth furnace used hot gases drawn from nearby coke ovens or blast furnaces to melt and refine the charge, was highly efficient.

Increases in furnace size and efficiency of operation followed these changes. In 1860, good blast furnaces produced 7 to 10 tons of pig iron a day; 25 years later, 75 to 100 tons a day was the maximum; and by 1900, a daily output of 500 tons or more, with markedly less coke consumption, was common. During these years, methods of handling material improved greatly, regenerative heating of the blast was developed, blowing equipment was strengthened, and coke entirely superseded anthracite and bituminous coal as a fuel.

Another major accomplishment was the integration of processes that produced great savings in heat. Coke ovens were placed close to blast furnaces to avoid heat loss. Blast furnaces, in turn, were placed near steel furnaces (either Bessemer or open hearth)

so that molten pig iron could be delivered directly to them. Finally, converters and open hearths were situated near the roughing mills so that the first rolling could be accomplished as quickly as possible with a minimum of reheating. Moreover, other economies were resulting from integration—notably, a savings in the handling of materials and in administration.

As shown in Table 17.4, by 1870 more than half of all steel was produced by the new methods. By 1880, the old methods of producing in pots and crucibles were fully eclipsed. Table 17.4 also indicates that, although introduced shortly after the Bessemer method, the open-hearth method lagged far behind until 1900. Bessemer steels were eminently satisfactory for rails, which constituted one of the first great demands for the new product. Eventually, however, engineers became convinced that plates and structural shapes made of Bessemer steel contained defects that did not appear in the open-hearth product. Because of this preference, some rolling mills had to build open-hearth furnaces to meet the new demand. Furthermore, the costs of open-hearth processing were much lower than those of the Bessemer process, not only because scrap could be used but also because small operators could build and operate plants far smaller than were needed for a Bessemer operation. Moreover, small owners did not have to fear being "held up" by the large companies that controlled the Bessemer ores. By 1910, the open hearth had clearly won out over the Bessemer converter: Of the 26 million tons of steel produced in that year, the open-hearth process accounted for 63 percent and the Bessemer process for only 36 percent; from this time on, the annual output of the Bessemer method decreased steadily (Temin 1964).

TABLE 17.4 STEEL PRODUCTION, 1870–1910

				PERCENTAGE	
YEAR	TOTAL[a]	BESSEMER[a]	OPEN-HEARTH[a]	BESSEMER	OPEN-HEARTH
1870[b]	69	38	1	55	2
1880	1,247	1,074	101	86	9
1890	4,277	3,689	513	87	12
1900	10,188	6,685	3,398	66	33
1910	26,095	9,413	16,505	36	63

[a]Calculations are rounded in thousands of long tons.
[b]In 1870, a substantial proportion of steel was still made by old technologies in pots and crucibles.

Source: *U.S. Bureau of the Census, Historical Statistics, 1960, Series P203-207.*

The effects of these new technologies, economies of mass production, and other sources of advances in labor productivity are shown in Table 17.5 on this page, which lists the growth in value added per worker in those six industries that were among the 10 largest in both 1860 and 1910. The cotton industry, which showed the slowest growth except for lumber in output per worker, was already maturing by 1860, and in no other field had power-driven machines already been so successfully applied. Therefore, most of the growth in value added in textiles after the Civil War was the result of innovation and greater automaticity. The industry listed in Table 17.5 with the most rapid advance per worker is men's clothing. During the Civil War, mechanization of men's clothing increased rapidly as standardized sizes were derived from measurements taken by the army for soldiers' uniforms. Beginning in the 1870s, rotary cutting machines and reciprocating knives made it possible to cut several thicknesses of cloth at once. By 1895, sewing machines had been improved to the point that, power driven, they could operate at speeds of 1,600, 2,200, and 2,800 stitches per minute.

The boot and shoe industry, the second-fastest growing in terms of value added per worker, was also markedly changed. Only in the decade or so before the Civil War were manufactured shoes shaped separately for the left and the right foot; consequently, many ladies and gentlemen had their footwear custom made and continued to do so for a long time. Manufacturers eventually realized that design, finish, and attention to size and fit were necessary to secure a broad market for factory-made shoes. In 1875, they introduced the Goodyear welt process, which enabled soles to be attached to uppers without allowing nails and stitches to penetrate the inside of the shoe. Within the next 20 years or so, machines were devised to do the work of lasting, eyeleting, heeling, and so on. By 1914, the industry was highly mechanized.

Improvements in steel processing and in nonferrous metals, especially copper and aluminum, made possible rapid advances in metalworking machinery, which jumped between 1860 and 1910 from the seventh largest to the largest manufacture. During the 1890s, there were two major technical advances: (1) machine tools became automatic or semiautomatic, and (2) compressed air and electricity were used to drive high-speed cutting tools and presses. The demands of the automobile industry and of the armament and aircraft industries during World War I brought the machine industry to maturity. Victor S. Clark (1928) reports that between the end of the Civil War and the end of World War I, precision in metalworking increased from a tolerance limit of 0.01 inch to

TABLE 17.5 REAL VALUE ADDED PER WORKER IN LEADING SELECT INDUSTRIES, 1860 AND 1910

	1860	1910	PERCENT CHANGE
Lumber	$710	$ 930	31%
Cotton goods	480	680	42
Machinery	810	1,290	59
Iron and steel	720	1,370	90
Boots and shoes	400	910	128
Men's clothing	320	1,180	269

Note: Value added measures the total value of output minus material costs; therefore, value added per worker reflects both labor and capital productivity.

Source: *Kuznets 1952, 30. Used by permission of the publisher.*

0.001 inch, and tolerances of 0.0001 inch had been achieved in small-scale production. By 1919, metalworking machinery had increased in power as well as precision. Electrically driven shears could cut steel slabs 12 inches thick and 44 inches wide, and huge presses could stamp out parts of automobile bodies rapidly enough to make "mass" production possible. Moreover, the industry played the central role in diffusing technical knowledge from its point of origin to other sectors of the economy. As Nathan Rosenberg has so cogently observed:

> The machine-tool industry was a center for the acquisition and diffusion of the skills and techniques uniquely required in a machinofacture type of economy. Its role was a dual one: (1) new skills and techniques were developed here in response to the demands of specific customers, and (2) once acquired, the machine-tool industry served as the main transmission center for the transfer of new skills and techniques to the entire machine-using sector of the economy. (1972, 98)

New Forms and Sources of Energy

Between 1860 and World War I, there was a remarkable transition from reliance on the power of wind and water and the physical exertion of humans and animals to other sources of energy. This transition had begun in the first half of the nineteenth century but dramatically gained momentum in the second half. In 1850, more than three-quarters of all power was furnished by animal energy, and human energy produced more power than machines did. On the eve of the Civil War, water power was far more important than steam power in the United States. During the 1870s, steam surpassed water as a source of power. Then two major additional influences hastened the phasing out of the ancient water wheel and the more recently developed water turbine: (1) the ever-increasing efficiency of the steam engine, along with the increased safety of high-pressure boilers and (2) the opening up of vast and apparently inexhaustible supplies of coal as a result of the transportation revolution. By 1890, relatively few factories —mostly in the textile and paper industries—used direct water power, although gristmills and sawmills were still powered by this source.

At the time when steam engines had gained an unquestioned ascendancy, electricity appeared on the scene. Like steam, electricity was not a new source of energy; it was a new means of using energy generated either by the flow of water or the burning of fuel. But electricity brought about a remarkable improvement in the utilization of the older sources of energy. Because electric power is flexible and divisible, the power plant could be separated from the manufacturing establishment by long distances, and the cumbersome devices required to change the to-and-fro motion of the steam engine into rotary motion and then to transmit this motion were no longer necessary: The energy required to turn either a small or large motor was readily "on tap."

By World War I, one-third of the nation's industrial power was provided by electricity, far more than in any other country. Nearly one-half of all urban dwellings had electric lights, although more than 98 percent of all farm families were burning kerosene lamps after dark.

The raw materials that produced energy were changing as well as the forms in which it was used. In 1890, coal was the source of 90 percent of the energy furnished to manufacturing; in the years just before 1920, coal remained the source of at least 80 percent of all industrial energy. But petroleum was rapidly growing more important, and hydropower was recovering. Within 25 years, petroleum and natural gas would become strategic fuels, although the transportation and manufacturing industries were planted squarely in the age of coal as late as 1920.

Steel manufacture required unprecedented amounts of capital in the form of great furnaces and mechanical aids as well as skilled workers who were able to judge when the time was ripe to tap Bessemer converters such as these.

MASS PRODUCTION

Two relatively new ideas spread like wildfire after the Civil War: continuous-flow production and scientific management. Continuous-flow production implies that materials move steadily through the factory where they are steadily transformed into finished products. Scientific management implies business procedures with a laboratory-like exactness. Let us consider each of these developments in turn.

Ever since Oliver Evans's first attempts at continuous-flow milling in the 1780s, entrepreneurs had understood the advantages of moving materials continuously through the production process. But it was after the Civil War that continuous-flow production revolutionized production. Indeed, for some students of the history of manufacturing, it is continuous-flow production that distinguishes the second industrial revolution from the first. One of the earliest applications was in meat packing. The famed Chicago meat packers, Gustavus Swift and Phillip Armour, set up long "disassembly" lines in which the carcasses were continuously moved past fixed stations where they were butchered and turned into a wide range of final products. Cigarettes were another early application that demonstrated the potential profitability of continuous-flow production. But it was Henry Ford, the great automobile entrepreneur, who devised the first progressive, moving assembly-line systems for large, complex final products. In 1914, a chassis that had formerly been assembled in 12 hours could be put together along a 250-foot line in a little over one and one-half hours. Before 1920, motor-driven conveyors were moving motors, bodies, and chassis at optimum heights and speeds to workers along greatly lengthened lines. By this time, the moving assembly line had spread throughout the automobile industry, the electrical industry, and the budding household-appliance industry.

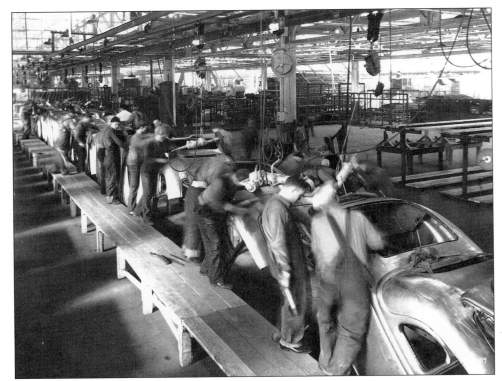

Mass production helped change the face of industry in the early part of the twentieth century.

The large scale of the new industrial giants required new forms of management. The railroads, the first of the huge employers, led the way (Chandler 1965). Before the railroad companies, most businesses, even the largest, were typically managed by single owners or partners on a day-to-day basis. Supervisors often were added, but owners usually oversaw the business operations and made key managerial decisions.

Faced with unmanageable size and complexity, the railroads developed a host of new management practices and concepts. Managerial innovations and organizational changes were essential to better coordinate the activities of thousands of employees who ran the trains, sold the tickets, loaded freight, repaired track and equipment, and performed endless other tasks. In the 1850s, Daniel McCallum of New York, president of the Erie Railroad, proposed a series of new management principles—with wide potential application. First, managers' authority to make decisions should match their level of responsibility. Internal reporting systems (accounting) should be used to identify trouble spots and allow prompt solutions. Performance evaluations, for employees and managers alike, should be routine. Other large businesses in the late nineteenth century soon adopted these and other management systems, and today, McCallum's concepts are routine in virtually all large business organizations.

With increases in size of plant and complexity of layout, the problems of efficiently handling a large labor force also became apparent. Frederick W. Taylor, ultimately the most famous contributor in this regard, argued that worker efficiency could be improved by (1) analyzing in detail the movements required to perform a job, (2) carrying out experiments to determine the optimum size and weight of tools and optimum lifts, and (3) offering incentives for superior performance. From such considerations, Taylor went on to develop certain principles pertaining to the proper physical layout of a shop or factory, the correct routing of work, and the accurate scheduling of the production of orders. Taylorism was and remains to this day a highly controversial subject (Noble 1977; Nelson 1980). Some observers saw it simply as a way of exploiting labor by speeding up and dehumanizing production. Others saw it as a way of using science to increase productivity and improve living standards for all. These productivity-enhancing improvements helped push real wages upward, softening somewhat workers' resentment to change and faster product processing. But competition kept the changes coming and the size of business growing.

ECONOMIES OF SCALE AND INDUSTRY CONCENTRATION

Central to the discussion of the rise of big business has been the debate over whether big business came about in response to technological changes and economies of scale, or whether the pursuit of monopoly power and market control was also a fundamental force.

Early Business Combinations

The first attempts at combination were two simple devices: (1) "gentlemen's agreements," usually used for setting and maintaining prices, and (2) "pooling"—dividing a market and assigning each seller a portion. In pooling, markets could be divided on the basis of output (with each producer free to sell a certain number of units) or territory (with each producer free to sell within his own protected area). Or sellers could form a "profits pool," whereby net income was paid into a central fund and later divided on a basis of percentage of total sales in a given period. Although pools had been formed even before the Civil War, they did not become common until after 1875. During the 1880s and 1890s, strong pooling arrangements were made in a number of important industries: producers of whiskey, salt, coal, meat products, explosives, steel rails, structural steel, cast-iron pipe, and certain tobacco products achieved great success with pooling agreements, as did the railroads in trunk-line territory. The pool resembled the European cartel. Germany was especially well known for these associations of producers in a particular industry that entered into agreements fixing prices and outputs. The American pool differed from its European counterpart, however, chiefly because in the United States such agreements were illegal (a heritage of English common law) and therefore not enforceable in the courts.

Although gentlemen's agreements and pooling both worked temporarily, they typically were not durable. If they were successful in raising prices and achieving a "monopoly" profit, they encouraged new firms to enter the field. The temptation to cheat, moreover, was strong. Individual firms could profit by exceeding their assigned outputs and encroaching on another's territory, and there was no legal recourse against violators.

Trusts and Holding Companies

To overcome these deficiencies, a new legal device was created: the trust, a perversion of the ancient device whereby trustees held property in the interest of either individuals or institutions. Under a trust agreement, the stockholders of several operating companies formerly in competition turned over their shares to a group of trustees and received "certificates of trust" in exchange. The trustees, therefore, had voting control of the operating companies, and the former stockholders received dividends on their trust certificates. This device was so successful as a means of centralizing control of an entire industry and so profitable to the owners of stock that trusts were formed in the 1880s and early 1890s to control the output of kerosene, sugar, whiskey, cottonseed oil, linseed oil, lead, salt, rubber boots and gloves, and other products (recall Economic Reasoning Proposition 4, institutions matter). But the trust had one serious defect: Agreements were a matter of public record. Once their purpose was clearly understood, such a clamor arose that both state and federal legislation was passed outlawing them, and some trusts were dissolved by successful common-law suits in the state courts.

Alert corporate lawyers, however, thought of another way of linking managerial and financial structures. Occasionally, special corporate charters had permitted a company to own the securities of another company, such provisions having been inserted to allow horizontal expansion. In 1889, the New Jersey legislature revised its general incorporation statutes to allow any corporation so desiring to hold the securities of one or more subsidiary corporations. When trusts were declared illegal in several states, many of them simply obtained charters in New Jersey as "holding companies."[2] The prime objective of centralizing control while leaving individual companies free to operate under their several charters, therefore, could be achieved by a relatively simple device. Theoretically, the holding company had to own more than 50 percent of the voting stock of its several subsidiaries to have control. In practice, especially as shares became widely dispersed, control could be maintained with a far smaller percentage of the voting stock. The holding company was here to stay, although it would have to resist the onslaughts of Justice Department attorneys from time to time.

---

[2]"Charter mongering" was also profitable for New Jersey, which derived a substantial proportion of its revenues from corporate fees. Later, other states—Delaware, in particular—undercut New Jersey's monopoly.

THE TWO PHASES OF THE CONCENTRATION MOVEMENT

Whatever the path to combination and whatever the form of organization finally selected, the large firm was typical of the American manufacturing industry by 1905. As we have seen, two forces propelled this transformation: (1) the rise of mass production as a result of continuous-flow production methods and new forms of management, and (2) the relentless search for monopoly profits that was often made possible by the development of new legal arrangements. The path, however, was not smooth. Combination occurred in two major phases. The first phase (1879–1893) was characterized by the horizontal combination of industries that produced the old staples of consumption. The second phase of the concentration movement (1898–1904) was characterized by the vertical combination of industries that produced producer-goods that manufactured new consumer goods for growing urban markets. Thanks to the work of Alfred Dupont Chandler, Jr. (1977, 1990), one of the founders of the field of business history, and scholars such as Naomi Lamoreaux (1985, 2000) who built on Chandler's work, we can now understand how these forces interacted to produce the concentration movement.

Phase 1: Horizontal Mergers (1879–1893)

Horizontal mergers, the type typical of the first phase, combine firms that produce identical or similar products. During the 1870s and 1880s, as the railroads extended the formation of a national market, many existing small firms in the consumer-goods industries experienced a phenomenal increase in the demand for their products. This was followed by an expansion of facilities to take advantage of the new opportunities. Then, in many areas, there was great excess capacity and "overproduction." When this occurred, prices dropped below the average per-unit production costs of some firms. To protect themselves from insolvency and ultimate failure, many small manufacturers in the leather, sugar, salt, whiskey, glucose, starch, biscuit, kerosene, and rubber boot and glove industries (to name the most important) combined horizontally into larger units. They then systematized and standardized their manufacturing processes, closing the least-efficient plants and creating purchasing, marketing, finance, and accounting departments to service the units that remained. By 1893, consolidation and centralization were well under way in those consumer-goods industries that manufactured staple household items that had long been in use. Typical of the large firms created in this way were the Standard Oil Company of Ohio (after 1899, the Standard Oil Company of New Jersey), the Distillers' and Cattle Feeders' Trusts, the American Sugar Refining Company, and the United States Rubber Company.

Of the firms that became large during the first wave of concentration, the most spectacular was the Standard Oil Company. From its beginnings in 1860, the petroleum-refining business had been characterized by a large number of small firms. By 1863, the industry had more than 300 firms, and although this number had declined by 1870 to perhaps 150, competition was vicious, and the industry was plagued by excess capacity. "By the most conservative estimates," write Harold Williamson and Arnold Daum, "total refining capacity during 1871–1872 of at least twelve million barrels annually was more than double refinery receipts of crude, which amounted to 5.23 million barrels in 1871 and 5.66 million barrels in 1872" (1959, 344). An industry with investment in fixed plant and equipment that can turn out twice the volume of current sales is one inevitably characterized by repeated failures (usually in the downswing of the business cycle) and highly variable profits in even the most efficient firms.

John D. Rockefeller, archetype of the nineteenth-century businessman, brought discipline and order to the unruly oil industry, parlayed a small stake into a fortune estimated at more than $1 billion (about $20 billion in today's money), and lived in good health (giving away some of his millions) until 96 on a regimen of milk, golf, and river watching.

John D. Rockefeller, the man who would become the symbol of America's rise to world industrial leadership, got his start in business at the age of 19, when he formed a partnership with Maurice B. Clark to act as commission merchants and produce shippers. Moderately wealthy even before the end of the Civil War, Rockefeller entered the oil business in 1862, forming a series of partnerships before consolidating them as the Standard Oil Company of Ohio in 1869. Rockefeller's company was perhaps the best managed in the industry, with two great refineries, a barrel-making plant, and a fleet of tank cars. Standard's holdings grew steadily during the 1870s, largely through the acquisition of refineries in Pittsburgh, Philadelphia, and New York, as well as in Ohio. Demanding and receiving rebates on oil shipments (and even drawbacks on the shipments of competitors), Standard Oil made considerable progress in absorbing independent refining competition. By 1878, Standard Oil either owned or leased 90 percent of the refining capacity of the country. The independents that remained were successful only if they could produce high-margin items, such as branded lubricating oils, that did not require high-volume, low-cost manufacture.

To consolidate the company's position, a trust agreement was drawn in 1879 whereby three trustees were to manage the properties of Standard Oil of Ohio for the benefit of Standard stockholders. In 1882, the agreement was revised and amended; stockholders of 40 companies associated with Standard turned over their common stocks to nine trustees. The value of properties placed in the trust was set at $70 million (about $9.5 billion in today's money using unskilled wages as the inflator), against which 700,000 trust certificates were issued.

ECONOMIC INSIGHT 17.2

STANDARD OIL AND PREDATORY PRICING

John D. Rockefeller was blessed with many critics, but the most effective by far was the crusading journalist (then known as a muckraker) Ida M. Tarbell. Tarbell's father had been a barrel maker in the early days of the oil boom, and blamed his eventual loss of employment on Standard Oil, which may well have been the inspiration for Tarbell's writings. In any case, Tarbell wrote a series of carefully documented and highly critical articles that were published in 1904 as *The History of the Standard Oil Company.* The public outcry against Standard Oil ignited by this book was one of the main forces behind the Supreme Court's decision to break up the company. Tarbell made many criticisms of Standard Oil, but one in particular has stirred considerable controversy among economists: that Standard Oil had engaged in "predatory pricing." The claim was that Rockefeller had systematically ruined his competitors by selling kerosene at a price below the average cost of production until his competitors were driven into bankruptcy. Rockefeller then bought them for a song, and made back everything he had lost by raising the price of kerosene to a higher level than would have been possible if he still faced competition. Many economists, however, have been skeptical. For one thing, the process seems to waste profits. Why not offer to buy the competitor at a price that includes part of the increased profits possible from monopoly? That way, prices could be increased to monopoly levels without going through a period of losses. John McGee (1958) made this point in a classic article that reexamined the testimony presented at the 1911 trial. McGee concluded that there was little evidence that

Rockefeller had engaged in predatory pricing. Still the claim that Standard Oil or other firms have at times engaged in predatory pricing continues to attract scholarly attention. Recently R. Mark Isaac and Vernon L. Smith (1985) used laboratory experiments to test the viability of predatory pricing. They concluded that predatory pricing was unlikely at least in the experimental formats they explored.

IDA M. TARBELL

The agreement further provided for the formation of corporations in other states sharing a similar name: Standard Oil Company of New Jersey, and of New York, and so on. After the Supreme Court of Ohio ordered the Standard Oil trust dissolved in 1892, the combination still remained effective for several years by maintaining closely interlocking directorates among the major refining companies. Threatened by further legal action, company officials changed the Standard Oil Company of New Jersey from an operating to a holding company, increasing its capitalization from $10 million to $110 million so that its securities might be exchanged for those of the subsidiaries it held. It secured all the advantages of the trust form, and, at least for a time, incurred no legal dangers. Thus, Standard Oil went from a trust to a holding company after the successful combination had long since been achieved.

Phase 2: The Vertical Mergers (1898–1904)

A vertically integrated firm is one in which each stage of the production process, from the production of raw materials to the marketing of the final product, is managed by different departments within one firm. In the latter part of the nineteenth century, industry after industry came to be dominated by giant vertically integrated firms. For example, Gustavus F. Swift and his brother Edwin, after experimenting with the shipment and storage of refrigerated meat, formed a partnership in 1878 that grew over the next two decades into a huge, integrated company. Its major departments—marketing, processing, purchasing, and accounting—were controlled from the central office in Chicago. Other meatpackers, such as Armour and Morris, built similar organizations, and by the late 1890s, a few firms dominated the meatpacking industry with highly centralized, bureaucratic managements. In a similar manner, James B. Duke set out in 1884 to establish a national, even worldwide, organization to market his machine-made cigarettes. In 1890, he merged his company with five competitors to form the American Tobacco Company. Less than 15 years later, American Tobacco, after a series of mergers, achieved a monopoly in the cigarette industry.

In steel, the Carnegie Company had by the early 1890s consolidated its several manufacturing properties into an integrated firm that owned vast coal and iron deposits. As the Carnegie interests grew, other businesspeople were creating powerful steel companies. In 1898, the Federal Steel Company was formed under the auspices of J. P. Morgan and Company. Its integrated operations and products greatly resembled those of the Carnegie Company, but it had the further advantage of having a close alliance with the National Tube Company and the American Bridge Company, producers of highly finished products. The National Steel Company, created by W. H. Moore, was the third-largest producer of ingot and basic steel shapes and was closely connected with other Moore firms that made finished products: the American Tin Plate Company, the American Steel Hoop Company, and the American Sheet Steel Company. When Carnegie, strong in coal and (through his alliance with Rockefeller) iron ore, threatened to integrate forward into finished products, he precipitated action toward a merger by the Morgan interests. The result was the United States Steel Corporation, organized in March 1901 with a capital stock of more than $1 billion and, by a substantial margin, the largest corporation in the world. Controlling 60 percent of the nation's steel business, United States Steel owned, in addition to its furnaces and mills, a large part of the vast ore reserves of the Lake Superior region, 50,000 acres of coking-coal lands, more than 1,100 miles of railroad, and a fleet of lake steamers and barges. While protecting its position in raw materials, the corporate giant was then able to prevent price warfare in an industry typified by high fixed costs.

The severe depression of 1893 brought all acts of combination to a virtual standstill. With the return of prosperity late in 1896, however, a new momentum developed. Between 1898 and 1904, more than 3,000 mergers were effected. In the four years before 1903, companies accounting for almost one-half of U.S. manufacturing capacity took part in active mergers, most of them vertically integrating.

Why did these giant, vertically integrated firms come to dominate so much of American manufacturing? Why, to use the provocative terms of Chandler (1977), did the *visible hand* of the giant corporation replace the *invisible hand* of the market? Chandler's answer starts with technology. Factories constructed to take advantage of continuous-flow technologies minimized costs of production when they could operate continuously; any interruption of the inflow of raw materials or the sale of the final products sent costs upward. Thus, to minimize costs, managers needed to schedule flows with meticulous care. Having raw materials and the process of distributing the final product under their complete control therefore allowed them to minimize costs. When a continuous-flow

Andrew Carnegie, a great salesman, built an integrated steel firm that combined with the Morgan and Moore interests to form the United States Steel Corporation in 1901. At that time, he sold out and became one of the world's leading philanthropists.

technology did not exist, the profits expected from vertical integration often proved chimerical. American Tobacco is a good example. A new machine, the so-called Bonsack machine, could produce good cigarettes with a continuous-flow technology. As a result, American Tobacco was able to build a vertically integrated firm that monopolized the cigarette industry. Conversely, no machine could be constructed that could produce good cigars on a continuous-flow basis, and American Tobacco's efforts to monopolize the cigar industry failed. Of course, minimizing costs was not the whole story. If a firm was successful in building a monopoly position in an industry, it could increase its profits further by restricting output and raising prices. As Lamoreaux (1985) has shown, monopoly profits were an important part of the story.

Continuous-flow facilities were being built elsewhere, but the process went further and faster in the United States. The United States led the way in the development of these giant corporations, in part because of its huge internal market, a market that was continually expanding due to the population growth and urbanization. Another reason, as Gavin Wright (1990) stressed, is that the successful new technologies required abundant natural resources: coal, iron, copper, petroleum, agricultural products, and so on. And abundant natural resources were America's great comparative advantage. Finally, as B. Zorina Khan and Kenneth Sokoloff (2001) stressed, America's patent system, which made it relatively inexpensive (compared with other industrial countries) for inventors to protect their intellectual property, also contributed to the surge in industrial activity.

THE SHERMAN ANTITRUST ACT

The rise of corporations such as Standard Oil produced pressures from several directions for government actions to regulate or eliminate these giants. The clamor from agrarian interests for legal action against monopolies is discussed in chapter 15. Gary Libecap (1992) has persuasively argued that cattlemen's associations provided the political muscle leading to the Sherman Antitrust Act of 1890. Their quarrel was with the "Chicago meat packing monopolists," the Swift brothers and Armour and Morris, who they believed soaked up all their profits from cattle raising. Small slaughterhouses selling fresh meat and other small businesses and farmers joined the cattlemen in urging antimonopoly legislation. A complementary argument to Libecap's, by Thomas Hazlett (1992), focused on Senator John Sherman (brother of General William Tecumseh Sherman), a high-tariff advocate who "traded" legislative votes with antimonopolists to secure the McKinley Tariff Bill of 1890, with its high average 51 percent rate on dutied goods. It seems that votes supporting anticompetitive practices (the higher tariffs) were being traded for votes supporting procompetitive policies (stronger antitrust legislation).

As interesting as the Sherman Act's origins were its effects. As a legal statute, the Sherman Antitrust Act of 1890 seemed simple enough. It declared illegal "every contract, combination in the form of trust, or otherwise, or conspiracy in restraint of trade among the several states." It prescribed punishment of a fine or imprisonment or both for "every person who shall monopolize, or attempt to monopolize, or combine or conspire … to monopolize any part of the trade or commerce among the several states." The attorney general was charged with enforcing the act by bringing either civil or criminal proceedings in the federal courts. Thus, how the law should be interpreted was left to federal judges.

The Supreme Court did much to discourage enforcement of the act by its decision in 1895 in *United States v. E. C. Knight Company*. The American Sugar Refining Company had acquired the stock of the E. C. Knight Company along with that of three other sugar refiners in the Philadelphia area, raising American's shares of the refining market from 65 to 98 percent. The attorney general brought an action against the sugar trust; but the Court would not apply the Sherman Act on the grounds that the company was engaged in manufacture—not in interstate commerce—and that Congress intended the prohibitions to apply only to interstate commerce. The business of sugar refining, the Court held, "bore no direct relation to commerce between the states or with foreign nations.…Commerce succeeds to manufacture, and is not a part of it." The Court further implied that the Sherman Antitrust Act did not preclude the growth of large firms by purchase of property—that is, by merger or consolidation.

Consequently, after 1895, mergers were widely viewed as legal and as the safer way to effectively eliminate cutthroat price competition. The post-1898 merger wave was launched in part by the 1898 ruling in the case of *United States v. Addyston Pipe and Steel Company*. Here the Court made it clear that the Sherman Act did apply to collusive agreements among firms supposed to be in competition with each other. But mergers were still apparently legal. George Bittlingmayer reports:

The trade publication for the iron, steel, and hardware industry, Iron Age, *ran a full-column editorial on the decision and concluded that merger might now replace price*

This 1890 drawing depicts a meeting of a company's board of directors—perhaps discussing how to deal with the passage of the Sherman Act.

fixing. "The new decision is one which may gravely affect some of the arrangements now in force among manufacturers in different lines, in which some control over prices is sought by concerns otherwise acting independently in the conduct of their business. At first sight it looks as though this decision must drive them to actual consolidation, which is really more apt to be prejudicial to public interests than the losses and temporary agreements which it condemns" [February 17, 1898]. A month later Iron Age reported that "quite a number of meetings of manufacturers have been held during the past week all looking to some scheme to take off the keen edge of unbridled competition" [March 17, 1898]. (1985, 90–91)

As this trade publication suggests, the interest of the law and the effect of the law are not always consistent. (Remember Economic Reasoning Proposition 4, institutions matter—but not always in the way we expect.) The law itself, in this instance, was a strong force in bringing about the combinations—through merger—that many people abhorred. Ironically, the available evidence strongly suggests that the first phase of the concentration movement (1879–1893), which led to the 1890 Sherman Antitrust Act, was less spurred by monopoly power seeking than was the second phase (1898–1904). As O'Brien (1988) informs us, factories grew in size much more rapidly in the 1870s and 1880s than in later decades because the pace of technological change was so exceptional in those decades. Lamoreaux (1985, chapter 4) concludes that the second phase of concentration was propelled mainly by the desire to suppress price competition. O'Brien agrees: "Increases in concentration during the merger wave were motivated more by the desire to reduce price competition than by the desire to exploit scale economies" (1988, 649). Whatever its primary source of motivation, the great merger wave of the turn of the century became an inviting political target.

The Supreme Court as Trustbuster

As early as 1902, Theodore Roosevelt sensed the political value of trust busting, and in the campaign of 1904 he promised vigorous prosecution of monopolies. During his administration, suits were filed against several great companies, notably the American Tobacco Company and the Standard Oil Company of New Jersey. These firms were the archetypes of monopoly in the public mind, and the judgment of the Supreme Court in the cases against them would indicate the degree of enforcement that might be expected under the Sherman Act.

In decisions handed down in 1911, the Supreme Court found that unlawful monopoly power existed and ordered the dissolution of both the Standard Oil Company and the American Tobacco Company. But it did so on rather narrow grounds. First, it gave great weight to evidence of intent to monopolize. The Court examined the predatory practices that had occurred during each company's growth period and the manner in which the companies exercised their monopoly power. The oil trust, so it was asserted, had achieved its powerful position in the market by unfairly obtaining rebates from the railroads and by acquiring refining companies brought to terms after price wars. Similarly, the tobacco trust was accused of bringing competing companies to heel by price wars, frequently closing them after acquisition by purchase. Moreover, the record showed that the old American Tobacco Company exerted a strong monopsonistic (single-buyer) power, beating down the prices of tobacco farmers when the crop was sold at the annual auctions. Second, the Court adopted a "rule of reason" with respect to restraints of trade; because action against all possible violators was obviously impossible, it became necessary for the Court to exercise judgment:

> Under this principle, combinations which restricted competition were held to be lawful as long as the restraint was not unreasonable. Since there is no precise economic standard by which the reasonableness of a restriction on competition can be measured, the courts examined the practices pursued by a corporate giant in achieving and maintaining its position in the market. Predatory practices were indicative of an intent to monopolize the market, and a corporate combination which achieved dominance by indulging in them might be dissolved. Those which behaved in a more exemplary manner, even though their size gave them power over the market, did not transgress the law. (Stocking 1954, 532–533)

Standard Oil and American Tobacco were the only companies that the Supreme Court dissolved, but even if the courts had continued ordering dissolution or divestiture, it is unlikely that competition in the classical sense would have been restored. The four major successor companies to the American Tobacco Company constituted a tight oligopoly with respect to cigarette manufacture. Stock in the 33 successor companies of the Standard Oil Company was ordered distributed pro rata to the stockholders of the holding company, but whatever the benefits of dissolution, an increase in price competition was not an obvious outcome.

In two decisions handed down at the close of World War I the Supreme Court made the position of large corporations even safer. In *United States v. United Shoe Machinery Company of New Jersey, et al.,* the court held that the company's power was not illegal because the constituent companies it had acquired had never been competitive. In *United States v. United States Steel Corporation,* the Court found that the corporation possessed neither the power nor the intent to exert monopoly control. The majority of the Court was impressed by the history of United States Steel, which revealed none of the predatory practices complained of in the oil and tobacco cases. The Court noted the splendid relations of the steel company with its rivals, noting that United States Steel's power "was efficient only when in cooperation with its competitors, and hence it concerted with them in the expedients of pools, associations, trade meetings, and finally in a system of dinners inaugurated in 1907 by the president of the company, E. H. Gary, and called 'The Gary Dinners.'"

> *But the corporation resorted to none of the brutalities or tyrannies that the cases illus-trate of other combinations.... It did not have power in and of itself, and the control it exerted was only in and by association with its competitors. Its offense, therefore, such as it was, was not different from theirs and was distinguished from theirs only in the leadership it assumed in promulgating and perfecting the policy. This leadership it gave up and it had ceased to offend the law before this suit was brought. (40 Sup. Ct. 251 U.S. 417, 295–296)*

The government's assertion that the size of the corporation made it a potential threat to competition in the industry was denied. On the contrary, said the Court, "the law does not make mere size an offense, or the existence of unexerted power an offense." After this decision, only the most optimistic Justice Department attorneys could see any point in bringing action against a firm simply because it produced a large share of the total output of an industry.

The Federal Trade Commission

In 1914, during Woodrow Wilson's first term, Congress passed the Clayton Act, which was intended to remove ambiguities in existing antitrust law and force the courts to take stronger actions against big corporations by making certain specific practices illegal. Price discrimination among buyers was forbidden, as were exclusive selling and tying contracts, acquiring the stock of a competitor, and interlocking directorates, if the effect was to lessen competition. The Federal Trade Commission (FTC) was established to en-force the act, and decisions of the FTC were to be appealed to the circuit courts. The commission could also carry out investigations, acting on its own initiative or on the complaint of an injured party. If a violation was found, the commission could issue a cease-and-desist order; offenders then had the right to appeal to the federal courts.

The Clayton Act, however, was so weakly drawn that it added little to the govern-ment's power to enforce competition. Once the existence of listed illegal practices was determined, the courts still had to decide whether their effect was to lessen competition or to promote monopoly. As we have just observed, by 1920, about the only practice the courts would consistently consider in restraint of trade was explicit collusion among in-dependent producers or sellers. "Reasonable" monopoly practices of huge firms on one hand and "weak" forms of collusion on the other were not subject to punishment. The useful functions of the FTC became the compiling of a massive amount of data helpful to economists and the elevation of the ethics of competition by acting against misbranding and misleading advertising. Not until it could take action on the basis of injury to con-sumers instead of on the basis of injury to a competitor would the public gain much advantage from the FTC's efforts.

Thus, the one great pre-1920 experiment in the social control of business, the Sherman Antitrust Act, achieved little. By the time a vigorous enforcement of the anti-trust laws was undertaken late in the 1930s, it was too late to do much about the prob-lem of big business in industry. But by then, it was clear that a kind of competition not envisioned by the framers of the Sherman Act helped protect consumers. The fall in communication and transportation costs wedded regional markets into national and international markets, thereby reducing local monopoly powers (Atack 1985). The effec-tiveness of these new competitive sources is examined in chapter 20.

SELECTED REFERENCES AND SUGGESTED READINGS

Atack, Jeremy. "Industrial Structure and the Emergence of the Modern Industrial Corporation." *Explorations in Economic History* 22 (1985): 29–52.

Bittlingmayer, George. "Did Antitrust Policy Cause the Great Merger Wave?" *Journal of Law and Economics* (April 1985): 90–91.

Chandler, Alfred D., Jr. *The Railroads: The Nation's First Big Business*. New York: Harcourt, Brace & World, 1965.

_____. *The Visible Hand: The Managerial Revolution in American Business*. Cambridge, Mass.: Harvard University Press, 1977.

_____. *Scale and Scope: The Dynamics of Industrial Capitalism*. Cambridge, Mass.: Belknap, 1990.

Clark, Victor S. *History of Manufacturing in the United States, 1607-1914*. Washington D.C: The Carnegie Institution, 1928.

Fishlow, Albert. "Productivity and Technological Change in the Railroad Sector, 1840–1910." In *Output, Employment and Productivity in the United States after 1800, Studies in Income and Wealth,* Vol. 30, 585. National Bureau of Economic Research. New York: Columbia University Press, 1966.

Frickey, Edwin. *Production in the United States, 1860–1914.* Cambridge, Mass.: Harvard University Press, 1947.

Gallman, Robert. "Commodity Output, 1839–1899." In *Trends in the American Economy in the Nineteenth Century*, National Bureau of Economic Research, Conference on Research in Income and Wealth. Princeton, N.J.: Princeton University Press, 1960.

Hazlett, Thomas W. "The Legislative History of the Sherman Act Re-examined." In a symposium: *Economics and 100 Years of Antitrust,* eds. George Bittlingmayer and Gary M. Walton. *Economic Inquiry* 30, no. 2 (April 1992): 263–276.

Isaac, R. Mark, and Vernon L. Smith. "In Search of Predatory Pricing." *The Journal of Political Economy* 93, no. 2 (April 1985): 320–345.

Khan, B. Zorina, and Kenneth L. Sokoloff. "History Lessons: The Early Development of Intellectual Property Institutions in the United States." *The Journal of Economic Perspectives* 15, no. 3 (Summer 2001): 233–246.

Kuznets, Simon. "Changes in the National Incomes of the United States of America Since 1870." *Income and Wealth Series II*. London: Bowes & Bowes, 1952.

Lamoreaux, Naomi R. *The Great Merger Movement in American Business, 1895-1904.* Cambridge: Cambridge University Press, 1985.

_____. "Entrepreneurship, Business Organization, and Economic Concentration." In *The Cambridge Economic History of the United States*, Vol. II, *The Long Nineteenth Century*, eds. Stanley L. Engerman and Robert E. Gallman, 403–434. New York: Cambridge University Press, 2000.

Libecap, Gary D. "The Rise of the Chicago Packers and the Origins of Meat Inspection and Antitrust." In a symposium: *Economics and 100 Years of Antitrust,* eds. George Bittlingmayer and Gary M. Walton. *Economic Inquiry* 30, no. 2 (April 1992): 242–262.

Lebergott, Stanley. *Manpower in Economic Growth: The American Record Since 1800.* New York: McGraw-Hill, 1964.

McGee, John. "Predatory Price Cutting: The Standard Oil (N.J.) Case." *Journal of Law and Economics* (1958): 137–169.

Nelson, Daniel. *Frederick W. Taylor and the Rise of Scientific Management.* Madison: University of Wisconsin Press, 1980.

Noble, David F. *America by Design: Science, Technology & the Rise of Corporate Capitalism.* New York: Knopf, 1977.

O'Brien, Anthony P. "Factory Size, Economies of Scale, and the Great Merger Wave of 1898–1902." *Journal of Economic History* 48 (1988): 639–649.

Rosenberg, Nathan. *Technology and American Economic Growth.* New York: Harper & Row, 1972.

Stocking, George W. "The Rule of Reason, Workable Competition, and the Legality of Trade Association Activities." *University of Chicago Law Review* 21, no. 4 (Summer 1954): 532–533.

Temin, Peter. *Iron and Steel in Nineteenth-Century America.* Cambridge, Mass.: MIT Press, 1964.

U.S. Bureau of the Census. *Census of the United States: 1860,* Vol. 3. Washington, D.C.: Government Printing Office, 1861.

U.S. Bureau of the Census. *Census of the United States: 1910,* Vol. 8. Washington, D.C.: Government Printing Office, 1913.

U.S. Bureau of the Census. *Historical Statistics.* Washington, D.C.: Government Printing Office, 1960.

Williamson, Harold F., and Arnold R. Daum. *The American Petroleum Industry*. Evanston, Ill.: Northwestern University Press, 1959.

Wright, Gavin. "The Origins of American Industrial Success, 1879–1940." *American Economic Review* 80 (1990): 651–668.

CHAPTER **18**

The Emergence of America's Labor Consciousness

CHAPTER THEME

Between the Civil War and World War I, the conditions of working Americans changed dramatically. The supply of labor grew rapidly because of immigration and natural increase. The demand for labor grew even faster because of capital accumulation and technological and other productivity advances in industry, agriculture, and the service sector. Real wages rose. But unemployment and real incomes rose and fell during the recessions that punctuated the era, and the gains for unskilled workers appeared to be agonizingly slow, bringing demands from labor and from the middle class for legislation to protect and improve the lot of the common worker.

Class consciousness was never as deeply felt in the United States as in Europe. Nevertheless, in the 50 years following the Civil War, the first national unions emerged and labor slowly developed a degree of political influence. The result was legislation and court decisions that gave greater weight to "labor's perspective."

DEMOGRAPHIC CHANGE AND THE SUPPLY OF LABOR

One reason that laborers as an organized group became more important was simple arithmetic. In 1860, there were about three farmers per manufacturing worker; by 1910, the ratio was one to one. Moreover, the number of workers as a percentage of the total population was rising, from 33 to 40 percent. Table 18.1 shows this relative growth: the population grew by a factor of 2.7 between 1870 and 1920, and the labor force grew by 3.2. Immigrants, as Table 18.1 shows, added substantially to the population and even more to the labor force since immigrants tended to be concentrated in the prime working years. But the main source of growth was the natural increase of the native and immigrant populations.

Birth and Death Rates

Fertility was high by modern standards, but the trend was down, as shown in Table 18.2, continuing the trend that had begun early in the nineteenth century. Live births per 1,000 people fell by almost half over the nineteenth century, from 55 in 1800 (for whites, data for blacks are not available) to 30.1 in 1900. By the turn of the century, Americans were increasingly viewing two children as the "normal" family (David and Sanderson 1987). This trend has continued, and as of the 1990s, the birthrate was less than half that of 1900. Urbanization has been a major source of this decline because the costs of raising an additional child are much higher in the city. Also playing their parts were declining infant mortality (which reduced the number of births needed to reach a desired family size), rising female employment (which increased the opportunity cost of

319

TABLE 18.1 POPULATION AND LABOR FORCE (IN MILLIONS), 1870–1920

YEAR	POPULATION	PERCENT INCREASE	TOTAL IMMIGRATION	LABOR FORCE	PERCENT INCREASE
1870	39.9			12.9	
1880	50.3	26	2.8	17.4	35
1890	63.1	25	5.2	23.3	34
1900	76.1	21	3.7	29.1	25
1910	92.4	21	8.8	37.5	29
1920	106.5	15	5.7	41.6	10

Source: Historical Statistics *1975, Series A6, C89, and D167.*

additional children), and compulsory schooling (which lengthened the time in which children depended economically on their parents).

Even this list of factors, however, cannot fully explain the fertility decline. Urbanization was important, but fertility dropped in rural areas as well as urban areas in the nineteenth century. Rising land prices that forced families to accumulate greater financial reserves or do with less land may be the answer. Fertility was generally lower, moreover, in the United States than in Europe (other than France), a surprising contrast if urbanization and restrictions on child labor were the crucial factors explaining the decline in fertility (Haines 1989, 1990). Meanwhile, death rates—indicated in Table 18.2 by the expectation of life at birth—began a long decline dating from the 1870s. Surprisingly, specific medical treatments were not a major quantitative factor until well into the twentieth

TABLE 18.2 BIRTHRATE AND EXPECTED LIFE, 1800–1990

YEAR	WHITE BIRTHRATE (PER 1,000)	BLACK BIRTHRATE (PER 1,000)	WHITE EXPECTATION OF LIFE AT BIRTH	BLACK EXPECTATION OF LIFE AT BIRTH
1800	55.0	n/a	n/a	n/a
1830	51.0	n/a	n/a	n/a
1860	41.4	56.8	40.9	n/a
1870	38.3	55.2	44.1	n/a
1880	35.2	53.7	39.6	n/a
1890	31.5	48.1	45.7	n/a
1900	30.1	44.4	49.6	n/a
1910	29.2	38.5	51.9	n/a
1920	26.9	35.0	57.4	47.0
1930	20.6	27.5	60.8	48.5
1940	18.6	26.7	65.0	53.9
1950	23.0	33.3	69.6	60.8
1960	22.7	32.1	70.6	63.6
1970	17.4	25.1	71.7	64.1
1980	14.9	22.1	74.4	68.1
1990	15.0	23.1	76.1	69.1
2004	11.5	15.7	78.3	73.1

Source: "Birthrate and Mortality," by Michael R. Haines, in The Reader's' Companion to American History, edited by Eric Foner and John A. Garraty. Copyright (c) 1991 by Houghton Mifflin Company. Reprinted by permission of Houghton Mifflin Harcourt Publishing Company. All rights reserved.

century. Instead, the key factor in the first phase of mortality reduction was improved sanitation, especially better water supplies and sewage disposal (Meeker 1972; Higgs 1979; Haines 1985; and Troesken 2004). America's biggest cities had been particularly unhealthful; but beginning in the 1890s, they began large-scale projects to provide piped water, filtration and chlorination of water, sewer systems, and public health administration. These improvements brought down the death rates from cholera, typhoid fever, gastrointestinal infections, and other diseases. Death rates fell more for African Americans and recent immigrants than for native born whites. Indeed, in some cases, as Werner Troesken (2004) shows, advocates of improved sanitation appealed to fears of contamination from poor groups to win public funding.

Immigration

Figure 18.1 traces the arrivals of immigrants in the context of economic fluctuations. Major waves began in the early 1880s and late 1890s. Between 1880 and 1920, more than 23 million immigrants came to make their homes in the United States. Their impact on labor markets was substantial. In 1920, immigrants accounted for 33 percent of railroad laborers, 22 percent of railroad foremen, 33 percent of jewelers and watchmakers, and 17 percent of policemen. More generally, immigrants accounted for 25 percent of the labor force in manufacturing, 35 percent in mining, 18 percent in transportation, and substantial shares in most other sectors (Niemi 1980, 262).

As shown in Figure 18.1, the number of immigrants rose in good times and fell in bad times. In times of rising economic activity and employment, the tug on immigrants increased tremendously; as depressions ensued and jobs disappeared, the attractiveness of American opportunity receded. Peak years of inflow coincided with or immediately preceded the onset of severe depressions. Peaks were reached in 1873, 1882, 1892, 1907, and

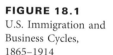

FIGURE 18.1

U.S. Immigration and Business Cycles, 1865–1914

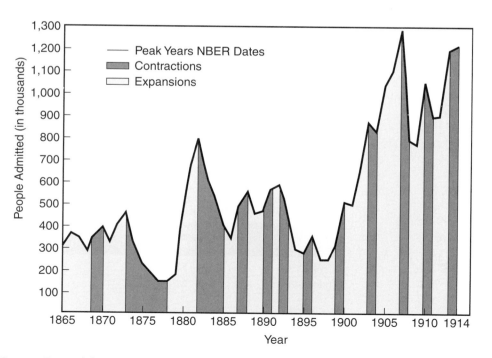

Source: *Derived from* Historical Statistics *1960, Series C88; business cycle dates from Burns and Mitchell 1947, 78.*

1914. Immigration declined greatly during the World War I years as shipping lanes were cut and people went about sterner business.[1]

The work of Brinley Thomas (1954) clarified underlying patterns. The inflow of immigrants—coupled with foreign capital inflows—helped push the American economy in its upswings and slowed the growth phase in the countries of departure. In effect, the growth surges in the United States coincided with slow expansion phases in much of Europe, and growth surges in Europe coincided with slower expansion periods in the United States.

IMMIGRATION: POLITICS AND ECONOMICS

Table 18.3 shows a striking alteration in the origins of immigrants from 1820 to 1920. In the 1880s, there was a decreasing flow of people from northern and western Europe and an increasing flow from southern and eastern Europe. It is usual to speak of the immigration from Great Britain, Ireland, Germany, and the Scandinavian countries as the "old" immigration, as distinguished from the "new" immigration composed of Hungarians, Poles, Russians, Serbs, Greeks, and Italians. In the 1870s, more than 80 percent of the immigrants came to America from northern and western Europe; by 1910, 80 percent of the total was arriving each year from southern and eastern Europe. The year 1896 marks the point at which a majority of those arriving annually were of the "new" nationalities.

Much was once made of the presumed economic significance of this geographic shift in the sources of immigration. In cultural characteristics, the Swedes and Germans of the old immigration were not unlike the Anglo-Saxons who colonized America. Slovaks and Magyars, on the other hand, along with Russians, Italians, and other people from the new areas, had unfamiliar customs, practiced strange religions, and spoke odd languages—and they looked different. To many native-born citizens of turn-of-the-century America, the new immigrants seemed inferior in skills, in cultural background, and in potential. The prejudice often went undisguised. Each immigrant group in its period of peak arrivals was deemed inferior: The "shanty Irish" and "dumb Swedes" of a previous generation were scorned as much as the "crazy Bohunks" who came later. Twentieth-century Americans seized on the assumed "inferiority" of southern and eastern Europeans as an argument for excluding them.

The new immigrants supplanted the old for two reasons. As economic opportunity grew in England, Germany, and Scandinavia, America became less attractive to the nationals of those countries. Also important was the rapid improvement in transportation during the 1860s and 1870s. The steamship put the Mediterranean much closer to Amer-

TABLE 18.3 ORIGINS OF IMMIGRANTS, 1820–1920 (IN PERCENT)

	NORTHERN AND WESTERN EUROPE	CENTRAL, EASTERN, AND SOUTHERN EUROPE	OTHER
1821–1890	82%	8%	10%
1891–1920	25	64	11

Source: Historical Statistics *1960, Series C88-114.*

---

[1]The ratio of foreign born to the total U.S. population rose only from 13.1 in 1860 to 14.6 in 1920. This curious fact is explained by the high rate of increase in the native population, the substantial emigration during depressions, and possibly by a bias in the statistics because persons for whom place of birth was not reported were counted as native born.

ica, and railroads from the interior of eastern Europe to Mediterranean ports gave mobility to southeastern Europeans. Vast differences existed between the economic opportunities offered an American laborer—even an unskilled one—and those available to the European peasant at home. The suction created by the removal of transportation barriers was irresistible; railroads, steamship companies, and American mill and factory managers hastened the movement by promotional advertising and financial assistance.

We can only guess whether immigrants arriving just after 1880 were less skilled and educated than earlier immigrants had been. It may be that their different political and cultural histories made their assimilation into American democracy and into the labor force more difficult. Nevertheless, the economic effects of the old and the new immigrations were roughly the same. New arrivals, whatever their national origins, usually filled the ranks of unskilled labor. Slovaks, Poles, and Italians replaced Irish, Germans, and Swedes in the coal fields and steel mills and, like their predecessors, took the lowest positions in the social strata.

Foreign Workers and American Labor

What was the impact of these foreigners on the American economy? The great majority of immigrants entered the labor markets of New England, the Middle Atlantic states, and the states of Ohio, Michigan, and Illinois, where they concentrated in the great industrial cities. Working for low wages in crowded factories and sweatshops and living in unsanitary tenements, immigrants complicated such urban social problems as slums, crime and delinquency, and municipal corruption.

For the most part, the difficulties of predominantly European immigrants did not result from discrimination in hiring or in wages. The relative earnings of native and foreign-born workers were approximately equal after adjusting for differences in schooling, experience, skills, and similar factors. Unskilled immigrants, in other words, earned about the same as unskilled American-born workers, and skilled immigrants about the same as skilled American-born workers (Hill 1975; Shergold 1976; Frauendorf 1978).

American business profited greatly from an inexhaustible supply of unskilled and semiskilled workers. The steamship companies that brought these immigrants to America and the railroads that took them to their destinations were the first to benefit. Manufacturing and mining companies profited most of all: Immigration enabled them to expand their operations to supply growing markets. The influx of immigrants also meant more customers for American retailers, more buyers of cheap manufactured goods, and a greatly enlarged market for housing. American consumers benefited from the increased supplies of goods and services.

The rapidly increasing supply of unskilled labor, however, kept wage levels for great numbers of workers from rising as fast as they would have otherwise. Therefore, some established American workers who could not escape from the unskilled ranks were adversely affected (see Economic Insight 18.1 on page 325). But supervisory jobs and skilled jobs were given to native white Americans, and the number of better jobs available increased as the mass of unskilled new immigrants grew. As William Sundstrom (1988) has shown, by the turn of the century, U.S. firms methodically recruited and trained existing employees for more advanced and skilled positions. Promotion ladders were common, especially in large firms. Moreover, the wages of craftsmen engaged in making equipment to be used by the unskilled and semiskilled masses doubtlessly rose. Native-born American workers gained as consumers of the lower-priced manufactured products made possible by cheap labor. The reality, and in some cases the fear that immigrants posed a threat to the wages of American workers led to repeated efforts to restrict immigration. These campaigns are discussed in Perspective 18.1 on page 326.

NEW VIEWS

CONTEMPORARY ISSUES AND LESSONS FROM HISTORY

In the 1980s more than 7 million immigrants entered the United States, and in the 1990s nearly 8 million more arrived, most of them from Mexico and Latin America. They are the latest waves of people into a nation that is most certainly a land of immigrants. Less than 1 percent of the U.S. population is Native American. Current citizens complain about new immigrants, their oddities, their differences from established residents, and, most often, their supposed inferiorities. Many pundits and critics argue that these new immigrants, legal and illegal, have not made the kinds of advances that past European immigrants made because of their resistance to assimilation (e.g., demands for bilingual education) frequent return trips to their native countries, and discrimination against them. The first and third of these arguments are perennial to the issue, no different than those expressed against the Irish (1840s and 1950s), the Italians, and others of southern European origin (1880s to 1910s).

The perception that Mexican and other Latin immigrants have assimilated into society and into the economy less effectively than did Europeans should not rest on opinion. This claim is a testable proposition, and as we assert in Economic Reasoning Proposition 5, evidence is needed to prove or refute a hypothesis. Using census data from the recent century, James Smith (2006) of the Rand Corporation has found that male immigrants from Mexico born between 1905 and 1910 had an average of 4.3 years of formal schooling. Their sons had 9.4 years, and their grandsons more than 12 years. European immigrants in the same period started with higher levels of formal schooling, nearly 9 years, with their grandsons having nearly 13.5 years. Salaries for Latino male immigrants around 1900 were about 55 percent of the salaries of native white males, but their grandsons' comparable earnings were nearly 90 percent of that of white males. In most respects, Latino immigrants have shared the same pattern of experiences with earlier immigrants, whether Irish, Italian, or eastern/southern European.

GAINS FOR WORKERS IN THE POSTBELLUM PERIOD

Hours and Wages

Despite the rapid growth in the supply of labor, workers made considerable progress between the end of the Civil War and the end of World War I. In 1860, the average number of hours worked per day in nonagricultural employment was close to 10.8. By 1890, the average workday in manufacturing was 10.0 hours, and people normally worked a six-day week (Long 1960, 3–12, 109–118). There were, of course, deviations from the average. Skilled craftsmen in the building trades worked a 10-hour day in 1860 and probably no more than an average of 9.5 hours per day by 1890. On the other hand, in the textile mills outside New England, 12- to 14-hour days were still common in 1890, and workers in steel milling, paper manufacturing, and brewing stayed on the job 12 hours a day, seven days a week.

By 1910, the standard work week was 55 hours in all industries; by 1920, it had dropped to about 50. A widespread standard week consisted of five 9-hour days and 4 to 5 hours on Saturday morning. Again, the skilled trades fared better, having achieved a 40-hour week by 1920. Unskilled laborers, on the other hand, were still working 9-hour days, six days a week, and the 12-hour day persisted in the metal-processing industries.

Both daily wages and annual earnings in manufacturing increased by about 50 percent between 1860 and 1890. Prices rose so rapidly during the Civil War that real wages fell drastically between 1860 and 1865. But from then on, the cost of living declined persistently, eventually returning the dollar to its prewar purchasing power. So real wages and earnings also increased by about 50 percent between 1860 and 1890 (Long 1960, 109).

ECONOMIC INSIGHT 18.1

IMMIGRATION IN TERMS OF SUPPLY AND DEMAND

Supply-and-demand models help to clarify the effects of immigration on the economy. Figures A and B display models of the market for unskilled and skilled labor in the late nineteenth century. In Figure A, we assume that all immigrants are unskilled. When immigration shifts the supply of labor to the right (L_1 to L_2), the real wage of unskilled labor (in the absence of any effect on demand) falls from W_1 to W_2. Area b is the income (the change in wage rate multiplied by the amount of labor) lost by the existing supply of workers. This amount is transferred to other factors of production (owners of land and capital and skilled

labor), and their share is further augmented by d as total production increases by e + d.

Is there no way to escape from the logic that immigration reduced the real wage of existing American workers? Figure B shows one possibility. If skilled labor was a complement to unskilled labor, then an influx of unskilled immigrants could raise the demand for skilled labor (D_1 to D_2). As drawn in Figure B, this effect raises the real wage of skilled labor to W_4, in contrast to the reduction in real wages of unskilled labor produced by immigration. An opposite wage effect occurs, however, when unskilled labor is a substitute for skilled labor. Probably most workers, skilled and unskilled, opposed immigration because they presumed that skilled and unskilled workers were substitutes in production.

Figure A

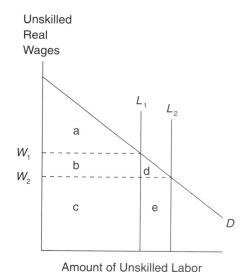

Figure B

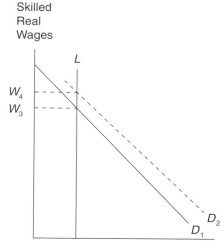

Daily wages in manufacturing rose from just over $1.00 in 1860 to $1.50 in 1890, and annual earnings increased from slightly less than $300 in 1860 to more than $425 in 1890. In the building trades, both real wages and real earnings rose a little higher, perhaps by 60 percent. If we take into account the shortening of the work week by about 7 percent, the net increase in hourly money or real wages over the 30-year period was about 60 percent, or 1.6 percent compounded annually.

Wage differentials among industries were great in both 1860 and 1890: the highest-wage industries paid more than twice as much as the lowest. These differentials reflected differences in skills and differences in the terms and conditions of work. Soft-coal miners, for example, earned a higher hourly wage than other industrial workers to compensate for the danger and disagreeable working conditions in the mines (Fishback 1992, chapter 6).

PERSPECTIVE 18.1

RESTRICTING IMMIGRATION

From the Civil War to the end of World War I, there was a constant struggle between the proponents and adversaries of immigration restriction. In 1864, when labor was in short supply because of the war, Congress passed the Contract Labor Law at the behest of the manufacturing interests. This law authorized contracts made abroad to import foreign workers and permitted the establishment of the American Emigrant Company to act as an agent for American businesses. The Contract Labor Law had the practical effect of bringing in laborers whose status could scarcely be distinguished from that of indentured servants, their cost of passage being repaid out of their earnings in the United States. The law failed, however, and was repealed in 1868. Few Europeans volunteered to work on contract; ocean passages had become much less costly, and many who did sign contracts left their employment early. Wage earners fought effectively for the repeal of the Contract Labor Law and continued to struggle for additional restrictions on immigration.

The first to feel the effects of the campaign for immigration restriction were the Chinese. Their influence on the labor market was localized on the West Coast, where nearly 300,000 Chinese had arrived between 1850 and 1882. Facing long-distance passage fares four times their annual wage, most of those laborers arrived in debt. Six large Chinese owned and Chinese-controlled companies held title to most of the debts and used or rented out the immigrants' labor, taking systematically from the workers' wages to ensure repayment. These immigrants typically worked in gangs (e.g., railroad building) under a foreman who oversaw repayment. Even if workers left the gangs, the six companies had agreements with the steamboat companies not to sell a return ticket to any migrant without a certificate from the companies declaring him free of debt. Threats of boycotts by the companies enforced the compliance of the steamship owners who handled the immigrants' passages coming and going. It was just short of actual indentureship, but no formal contracts existed or were exchanged. These informal but carefully controlled arrangements were legal, a peculiar system combining freedom and coercion that worked (Cloud and Galenson 1987).

Other laborers, especially in California, feared and despised what they regarded as cheap and unfair competition, and the Workingman's Party (also known as the "sand lotters") urged the exclusion of all Asians. With the Chinese Exclusion Act of 1882, the first victory of the restrictionists was won, and this unique system of bringing in Chinese workers stopped. Successful in their first major effort, the restrictionists pressed on to make illegal the immigration of anyone who could neither read nor write English. Acts requiring literacy tests passed Congress, but President Grover Cleveland, and later President William Howard Taft, vetoed them. For many years, labor had to be content with whittling away at the principle of unrestricted immigration. In succeeding laws, further restrictions were imposed on the immigration of the physically and mentally ill, vagrants, and anarchists. In 1917, Congress finally passed a literacy requirement—this time over President Woodrow Wilson's veto—and permanent bars to the free flow of migrants into the United States were erected in 1920.

In the decades after 1890, real wages continued to march upward. The real earnings of manufacturing workers advanced 37 percent (an annual compound rate of 1.3 percent) between 1890 and 1914 (Rees 1961, 3–5). Further gains were made during the war years, so the overall annual growth rate between 1891 and 1920 was only slightly less than that recorded during the preceding 30 years.

Figure 18.2 summarizes the growth of average real incomes of nonfarm workers—propelled by growing productivity in industry, agriculture, and the service sector—after the Civil War. The series beginning in 1870 assumes that the laborer worked a full year; the series beginning in 1900 takes unemployment into account. For that reason, the latter series shows the effects of the business cycle more clearly. But even the pre-1900 series is sharply marked by the severe depressions of the 1870s and the 1890s. Keep in mind that these averages for all nonfarm workers conceal the difficulties of unskilled laborers competing in markets constantly augmented by fresh immigrants.

Densely packed ships brought millions of workers to America, often under contracts that specified no wage increases during the first year of employment.

FIGURE 18.2
Real Earnings of
Nonfarm Employees

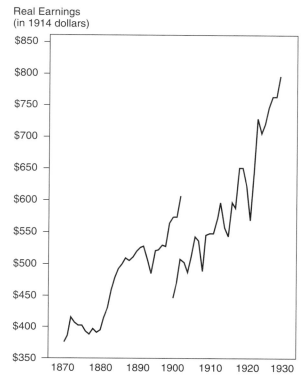

Source: *Stanley Lebergott, Manpower in Economic Growth: The American Record Since 1800 (New York: McGraw-Hill, 1964), 524. Copyright © 1964 by The McGraw-Hill Companies, Inc. Reprinted by permission.*

Women

The role of women in society and in the labor force changed considerably over the period. Near midcentury, state after state passed laws giving women clearer title to property, the right to engage in business, secure rights to their earnings, and property rights to patents and intellectual property. As Zorina Kahn's (1996) research on patents and commercial activities of nineteenth-century women shows, American women were highly responsive to legal and institutional changes that elicited their creativity and commercial and market participation. By 1880, 2.5 million women, constituting 15 percent of the workforce, were at work outside the home. By 1900, 5.3 million women, constituting 18 percent of the workforce, were at work outside the home. By 1920, 8.5 million women, or one-fifth of the gainfully employed, were involved in some pursuit other than homemaking.

Sales work in city stores and professional work, particularly teaching, became attractive alternatives to domestic service. The typewriter, which was introduced shortly after the Civil War, ushered in an office revolution that took hold in the 1890s. By the turn of the century, the typewriter and other office equipment had created a major field of employment for young women. As Elyce Rotella (1981b, 52) has shown, clerical workers as a percentage of the nonagricultural workforce grew from 1.2 to 9.2 percent between 1870 and 1920, while women as a percentage of all clerical workers grew from 2.5 to 49.2 percent over these 50 years.

The office workforce, however, remained segregated by sex. Women were confined to routine clerical jobs, while personal secretaries and other decision-making jobs remained a male province. The new clerical jobs were also segregated by race: Black women were rarely hired. Segregation of the office workforce by sex maintained the norm of the industrial workforce. Milliners (hatmakers) were generally women, whereas meatpackers were generally men; in cotton textiles, an industry in which about 50 percent of the workforce was female, spoolers (who transferred thread from the bobbins on which it was wound) were almost all women. The segregation of the labor force had some roots in economic differences between men and women: The labor force attachment of women was often less than for men. Thus, some firms that did not want to invest much in training workers who would soon leave found it convenient to treat women and men as separate classes, even though they sometimes made the error of promoting the less able worker by doing so. But the main sources of sex and race segregation were powerful social norms that dictated the work opportunities for women and African Americans.

These social norms, however, were being gradually eroded by economic forces and political opposition. Typing and sales work, for example, even as they confined women to subsectors of the labor force, changed traditional thinking about the role of women. World War I further shook the ideologies that underlay segregated hiring: Urged to employ women as replacements for men lost to the armed services, employers discovered that women performed a wide range of occupations as satisfactorily as men and that in some jobs their performance was often superior. It would take another half century, however, for the ideologies that segregated the workplace to begin to crumble on a major scale.

Statutes prescribing maximum hours and minimum wages for women were common by 1920. These were motivated in part by growing concerns about the physical surroundings in which women worked and the effects on their health and their ability to care for their children. The statutes were also supported by trade union leaders, who hoped that limiting the hours women could work would limit competition with male workers and, in some cases, also might limit the hours of male workers whose jobs were complementary with those of female workers. Indeed, empirical studies reveal that wage and hour

In 1886, limited demand and financial difficulties forced Philo Remington to sell his typewriter company. By 1890, the boom was on, remaking the office and bringing large numbers of women into the paid labor force.

restrictions for women served to limit the hours worked by both male and female workers. The effect on women's employment, moreover, was negligible: Few employers decided not to hire women simply because their hours were regulated (Goldin 1990, 195–199). In the pre–World War I years, concerns about the employment of children also increased sharply. In 1880, 1 million boys and girls between the ages of 10 and 15 were "gainfully occupied," and the number rose to a high of nearly 2 million by 1910. In 1910, one-fifth of all youngsters between 10 and 15 had jobs, and they constituted 5.2 percent of the workforce. But in 1920, the total number employed in this market was again less than 1 million; children made up only 2.6 percent of the workforce, and only one-twelfth of the 10- to 15-year age-group was at work. True, the proportion of children who worked was always small, except on the farm, and it was probably lower in the United States than in other industrial countries. But the conditions in which children worked were sometimes unsafe and harsh by modern standards.

Children

The employment of children decreased primarily because various advocates for children, including religious groups and trade unions, worked to obtain protective legislation at the state level. Massachusetts had a long history of ineffective child labor legislation, and the first stringent state regulation did not appear until 1903, when Illinois passed a

When publicized, bad working conditions like these among very young slate pickers in Pennsylvania at the turn of the century won middle-class sympathy for labor's cause.

law limiting child labor to an eight-hour day. State laws limiting hours of work, requiring minimum wages, and setting age limits were common by 1920, but additional protection was needed in certain states, such as in the cotton belt and some industrial states in the mid-South and East. In these states especially, the fight against child labor was waged indirectly through increases in compulsory education ages. Federal legislation that outlawed child labor was passed in 1916, but the Supreme Court struck it down on the grounds that the federal government had no power to regulate intrastate commerce. Child labor would not be effectively controlled by the federal government until the 1930s, when the Supreme Court reversed itself.

UNIONS, EMPLOYERS, AND CONFLICT, 1860–1914

Following the Civil War, unions grew in numbers and strength, but this growth was often punctuated by violent conflicts with business. Memberships in local unions reached nearly 300,000 nationally in 1872. Defeats at the polls in 1872 reduced union strength, but a new national union, the Knights of Labor, reached the unprecedented total of 750,000 members in 1885. When a general strike in May 1886 against the railroads failed to achieve an eight-hour day, members lost faith, and membership slipped to 100,000 by 1890. By then, the American Federation of Labor (AFL) had captured the leadership of most union workers. The AFL was an amalgamation of two federations: the Federation of Organized Trades and Labor Unions (printers, glassworkers, iron and steel workers, welders, and cigar makers) and the American Federation of Labor (composed of several

These pickets are helping to dramatize the case for labor's legislative agenda.

national unions spun off from the Knights). Under Samuel Gompers, the AFL's first president, membership rose to 1.5 million in 1905.

The AFL's unifying principle was to control job opportunities and job conditions in each craft. This principle implied an organizational unit composed of workers who performed the same job and who, in the absence of collective action, would have competed with one another to their economic detriment. Thus, the craft union could act quickly to exert economic pressure on the employer.

Labor's organizational gains were won as a result of serious and prolonged struggle, which was still unresolved by 1920. Strikes, though frequent even in the late nineteenth century, were not sanctioned legally nor were they always instigated by unions. Sometimes strikes erupted simply as the spontaneous responses of unorganized workers, and on certain occasions, successful strikes resulted in the formation of a union. In any case, employers, supported by middle-class opinion and by government authorities, took the position that their rights and the very institution of private property were threatened by the growing strength of the unions.

The most violent conflicts between management and labor occurred in the last quarter of the century. During the depressed years of the mid-1870s, much blood was shed when strikes were broken by force. The climax of this series of conflicts occurred in 1877, a zenith of turmoil that had begun with railroad strikes in Pittsburgh and had spread throughout the country. In the anthracite regions of Pennsylvania, a secret society of Irish American miners known as the "Molly Maguires" (named for the leader of an Irish antilandlord organization) was blamed for numerous murders and other outrages. What they did and didn't do is still a matter of heated dispute. Their power was finally broken after a trial that led to the hanging of 20 men on the basis of testimony provided by an agent from the Pinkerton detective agency who claimed to have infiltrated the organization.

The brutality was not all on one side. Often it was the laborer who had to fend off the physical assaults of paid thugs, state militiamen, and federal troops. Three incidents, purposely spaced over time, it would seem, to do the maximum damage to labor's cause stand out as symbols of the most severe disputes.

Labor leadership eventually became concentrated in the hands of Samuel Gompers, who sat on the first executive council of the American Federation of Labor in 1881.

The infamous Haymarket affair on May 4, 1886, was the tragic climax of efforts of the Knights of Labor to secure a general strike of workers in the Chicago area. A bomb thrown at police officers attempting to break up a mass meeting at Haymarket Square resulted in several deaths. The authorities and the press demanded action. Seven men, who were probably innocent, were executed for murder. Although the injustice of the punishment aroused great resentment among labor's sympathizers, antilabor agitators used the incident as a horrible example of what radicals and anarchists would do to undermine American institutions by violence.

Six years later, just as antilabor feeling was subsiding, the management of the Carnegie Homestead Works at Pittsburgh decided to oust the Amalgamated Association of Iron and Steel Workers, which was trying to organize the Homestead laborers. A strike was called, ostensibly because the company refused to come to an agreement on wage matters. Henry Frick, a close associate of Carnegie, brought in 300 Pinkerton detectives to disperse the strikers and maintain order. Turning the tables, the striking mob won a heated battle with the detectives, capturing several and injuring many severely. The state

Simultaneous strikes by various Chicago unions were met by strong police action, resulting in the Haymarket Riot of May 4, 1886.

militia was called out to restore order, and the union suffered a defeat that set the organization of labor in steel mills back several decades.

The adverse publicity received by the Homestead episode was exceeded only by that of the Pullman strike of 1894. Although the Pullman strike was led by the mild-mannered Eugene V. Debs, who had not yet embraced socialist doctrines, the strife was attributed to the un-American ideology of other radical leaders. Rioting spread over the entire Chicago area, and before peace was restored—this time by federal troops sent on the pretext of protecting the U.S. mails—scores of people had been killed or injured. Again, the seriousness of the labor problem became a matter for widespread concern and the basis of much immoderate opposition to labor's cause. On the other hand, the Pullman strike served as a warning to conservative union leaders that violence would only disrupt unions and damage them in the public regard. Furthermore, the dispatch with which Debs and other labor leaders were jailed on contempt proceedings for disobeying a court injunction against inciting union members to strike was a sobering blow. Any long-term strategy would have to include efforts both to pacify voters and to strengthen labor's position in the courts. Pre-1920 successes along both lines were limited, to say the least.

Beginning in 1902, employers changed their tactics. They began a serious drive to sell Americans on the benefits—to employers, workers, and the public—of the "open shop" (factories where workers are not required to join the union). To further their propaganda, several organizations were formed. The most prominent were the National Association of Manufacturers and the American Antiboycott Association, both of which were assisted materially by employers' trade associations.

In response, Samuel Gompers and other labor leaders began a counteroffensive against the employers through education and propaganda. Affiliating with the National Civic Federation—an association that included wealthy eastern capitalists, corporate officers, editors, professionals, and labor representatives—AFL leaders sought to elicit a more favorable attitude from the electorate. The National Civic Federation maintained a division for the mediation and conciliation of disputes, tried to secure wider acceptance of collective-bargaining agreements, and preached the doctrine that greater labor responsibility would mean fewer work stoppages and a better livelihood for all. How much good the National Civic Federation did is difficult to say. It doubtlessly served in part to offset the organized efforts of employers, but the alliance may have lulled job-conscious unionists into ultraconservatism at a time when more aggressive policies were called for. At any rate, the core of employer opposition remained almost as solid as ever, particularly among industrialists of the Midwest.

Union activity in the United States, in general, was largely apolitical, at least at the national level, especially in comparison with labor efforts in Europe. No National Labor Party emerged as a political entity, and until the New Deal, unions could rarely rely on help from the federal government. Why this was so has been the subject of considerable research. Attention has been drawn to many factors, such as the relatively high standard of living for workers in the United States compared with workers in Europe, without reaching a firm consensus (Sombart 1906; Perlman 1928; Lipset 1983; Wilentz 1984; Howe 1985). In any case, the main area of confrontation between employers and employees lay outside the political arena. For that reason, perhaps, strikes were longer in the United States, although they lacked the sanction of law, than they were in Europe (Friedman 1988).[2]

The Unions and the Courts

By the end of the nineteenth century, the right of labor unions to exist had been established; yet the right of employers to force employees to enter into antiunion contracts was upheld to the very end of this period. In this way, many employers maintained nonunion status as a condition of employment. For example, in the case of *Coppage v. Kansas* (1912), the Court overturned a state law passed to outlaw antiunion contracts—called at the time "yellow dog contracts" by workers, perhaps because they reduced a worker who signed one to the status of a mangy dog. Coppage, a railroad employee, had been fired for refusing to withdraw from a union. Because his withdrawal would have cost him $1,500 in insurance benefits, the Kansas Supreme Court held that the statute protecting him prevented coercion and was valid. But the U.S. Supreme Court reversed this decision, holding that an employer had a constitutional right to require an antiunion contract from employees; a statute contravening this right, the Court held, violated the Fourteenth Amendment by abridging the employer's freedom of contract.

As late as 1917, the U.S. Supreme Court decided that antiunion contracts, whether oral or written, could be protected by injunction (a court order). The Hitchman Coal and Coke Company, after winning a strike, had hired back miners on the condition that they could not be members of the United Mine Workers while in the company's employ. Later, union organizers tried to convince the miners to promise that, after a certain time had elapsed, they would again join the union. In a U.S. district court, the company asked for and obtained an injunction stopping further efforts to organize. The Supreme Court affirmed the decision, holding that, even though the miners had not yet joined the union, they were being induced by organizers to break a contract with the employer and that the employer was entitled to the injunction.

State and federal governments typically stood firmly on the side of business against labor unions. Calling out troops to break strikes was considered a legitimate use of police power. Such actions were condoned by the state and federal courts, which proved to be invaluable allies of management in the struggle to suppress collective action on the part

---

[2]Edwards (1981) provides a good historical account of strikes, violent and otherwise, in the United States.

of the laboring class. The injunction was especially effective as a device for restraining union action. Employers could go to court to have labor leaders enjoined from calling or continuing a strike. Failure to comply with an injunction meant jail for the offenders, and "government by injunction" proved to be one of the strongest weapons in the anti-union arsenal.

LABOR'S GAINS AND THE UNIONS

In 1920, the American factory worker could look back on 66 years of substantial improvement. Real wages had risen, hours were shorter, and laborers, children, and (to some extent) women were protected by law. The fundamental ideas of social security were being more generally discussed, and clear-cut legislative victories had been won to reduce the hardships caused by industrial accidents. In addition, urban dwellers of all kinds saw vast improvements that brought about sharp long-term reductions in mortality.

How many of these gains should be attributed to the labor movement? Clearly, the unions' ability to control the supply of labor and, thus, the conditions and terms of work, was limited throughout the period from the Civil War to the Great Depression by the inability of the labor movement, despite valiant efforts, to organize more than a small fraction of the labor force. The crucial figures are given in Table 18.4. At the nineteenth-century peak in 1886, unions had organized about 8 percent of the nonfarm labor force. Even at the peak after World War I, unions could claim only 17 percent of the nonfarm labor force. Hence, unions could do little directly to raise the average level of real wages or improve the typical conditions of work. Unions could raise wages in unionized sectors; but by restricting the supply of labor in those sectors, they had the undesired effect of increasing the supply of labor and lowering wages in nonunionized sectors.

On the eve of World War I, however, unions could lay claim to some other important gains for their members. As direct owner supervision declined and management became impersonal, the power of foremen indulging their personal whims increased. Unions

TABLE 18.4 UNION MEMBERSHIP, SELECTED YEARS

YEAR	TOTAL UNION MEMBERSHIP (thousands)	TOTAL MEMBERSHIP AS A PERCENT OF TOTAL LABOR FORCE	TOTAL MEMBERSHIP AS A PERCENT OF NONFARM LABOR FORCE
1860	5	0.1%	n/a
1870	300	2.4	4.6%
1880	50	0.3	0.5
1886	1,010	4.8	8.2
1890	325	1.4	2.3
1900	791	2.8	4.7
1905	1,918	5.9	9.3
1910	2,116	5.8	8.6
1917	2,976	7.4	10.0
1920	5,034	12.2	16.7
1929	3,625	7.6	9.7

Source: *Lebergott 1963, 220;* and Historical Statistics *1975, Series D4, D7, D8, D12, D17, D940, D943.*

helped offset and reduce arbitrariness in hiring and firing and other harsh treatment by supervising personnel. In addition, some particularly strong unions gained substantial wage differentials for their members. For example, a substantial differential was obtained in the bituminous (soft) coal industry, where union workers received wages some 40 percent higher than those of nonunion workers. For most unskilled work, though, the wages of union members were only slightly higher than those of nonunion workers, perhaps a few percentage points (Lewis 1963).

Finally, trade unions had become an important voice for labor in the political system. Labor Day as a national holiday was first celebrated in 1894; in 1913, cabinet-level status was given to the Department of Labor.

Perhaps the most important result of the growing political power of labor was the change in rules governing compensation to workers for injuries received on the job. Under the common law an injured worker could sue his employer for damages. But an employer who was sued had three powerful defenses that often prevented an injured worker from receiving compensation: (1) the worker had known and accepted the risk, (2) the worker had not been reasonably careful, and (3) the worker had been injured because of the negligence of a fellow worker. Between 1910 and 1930, however, labor won changes in state laws that first eliminated these defenses and eventually required that all injured workers be compensated.[3] In addition, insurance programs were established; employers and employees contributed to a common pool that compensated injured workers. The main result of these laws was that injured workers received more compensation. Employers, in many cases, also approved the new laws because they reduced conflict with workers and because the cost of insurance could sometimes be forced back on the workers in the form of lower wages. But, as Price Fishback and Shawn Kantor (2000), the leading historians of Workers Compensation, have pointed out, the side effects sometimes differed from what was intended. It was hoped that putting the burden on employers would make for a safer workplace, and often it did. The rate of fatal accidents in bituminous coal mining, however, increased because workers had a smaller incentive to avoid accidents and because employers found it cheaper to pay the additional claims than to try to reduce accident rates. Worker's compensation laws are a good example of Economic Reasoning Proposition 4, laws and rules matter, see page 8.

The power of organized labor's support for favorable legislation was destined to grow and, as we shall see, flower during the Great Depression. For labor as a whole, however, it is fair to conclude that labor's nineteenth-century progress owed more to economic growth and rising productivity than to the unions' strength.

SELECTED REFERENCES AND SUGGESTED READINGS

Burns, A. F., and W. C. Mitchell. *Measuring Business Cycles.* New York: National Bureau of Economic Research, 1947.

Cloud, Patricia, and David W. Galenson. "Chinese Immigration and Contract Labor in the Late Nineteenth Century." *Explorations in Economic History* 24 (1987): 22–42.

David, Paul A., and Warren C. Sanderson. "The Emergence of a Two-Child Norm among American Birth Controllers." *Population and Development Review* 13 (1987): 1–41.

Edwards, P. K. *Strikes in the United States 1881–1974.* New York: St. Martin's, 1981.

Fishback, Price V. *Soft Coal, Hard Choices: The Economic Welfare of Bituminous Coal Miners, 1890–1930.* New York: Oxford University Press, 1992.

Fishback, Price V., and Shawn Everett Kantor. *A Prelude to the Welfare State: The Origins of Workers'*

---

[3]Wahl (1993) provides a fascinating account of "worker's compensation" under slavery. Southern courts were quite willing to compensate the slaveowners when their slaves were injured because of the political power of the slaveowners and the ease with which the market values of slaves could be determined.

Compensation. Chicago: University of Chicago Press, 2000.

Friedman, Gerald. "Strike Success and Union Ideology: The United States and France, 1880–1914." *Journal of Economic History* 48 (1988): 1–25

Frauendorf, Martha Norby. "Relative Earnings of Native and Foreign-Born Women." *Explorations in Economic History* 15 (1978): 211–220.

Goldin, Claudia. *Understanding the Gender Gap: An Economic History of American Women.* New York: Oxford University Press, 1990.

Haines, Michael R. "American Fertility in Transition: New Estimates of Birth Rates in the United States, 1900–1910." *Demography* 26 (1989): 137–148.

_____. "Birthrate and Mortality." In *The Readers' Encyclopedia of American History,* eds. Eric Foner and John Garraty, 104. New York: Houghton Mifflin, 1991.

_____. "Inequality and Childhood Mortality: A Comparison of England and Wales 1911, and the United States, 1900." *Journal of Economic History* 45 (1985): 885–912.

_____. "Western Fertility in Mid-Transition: Fertility and Nuptiality in the United States and Selected Nations at the Turn of the Century." *Journal of Family History* 15 (1990): 23–48.

Higgs, Robert. "Cycles and Trends of Mortality in 18 Large American Cities, 1871–1900." *Explorations in Economic History* 16 (1979): 381–408.

Hill, Peter. "Relative Skill and Income Levels of Native and Foreign-Born Workers in the United States." *Explorations in Economic History* 12 (1975): 47–60.

Historical Statistics. Washington, D.C.: Government Printing Office, 1960.

Historical Statistics. Washington, D.C.: Government Printing Office, 1975.

Howe, Irving. *Socialism and America.* San Diego: Harcourt Brace Jovanovich, 1985.

Kahn, Zorina. "Married Women's Property Laws and Female Commercial Activity: Evidence from United States Patent Records 1790." *Journal of Economic History* 56 (1996): 356–388.

Lebergott, Stanley. *Manpower in Economic Growth: The American Record Since 1800.* New York: McGraw-Hill, 1964.

Lewis, H. Gregg. *Unionism and Relative Wages in the United States: An Empirical Inquiry.* Chicago: University of Chicago Press, 1963.

Lipset, Seymour Martin. "Radicalism or Reformism: The Sources of Working Class Protest." *American Political Science Review* 77 (March 1983): 1–18.

Long, Clarence D. *Wages and Earnings in the United States, 1860–1890.* Princeton, N.J.: Princeton University Press, 1960.

Meeker, Edward. "The Improving Health of the United States, 1850–1914." *Explorations in Economic History* 9 (1972): 353–374.

Niemi, Albert W. *U.S. Economic History,* 2nd ed. New York: University Press of America, 1980.

Rees, Albert. *Real Wages in Manufacturing, 1890–1914.* Princeton, N.J.: Princeton University Press, 1961.

Perlman, Selig. *A Theory of the Labor Movement.* New York: The Macmillan Company, 1928.

Rotella, Elyce J. *From Home to Office.* Ann Arbor, Mich.: UMI Research Press, 1981a.

_____. "The Transformation of the American Office: Changes in Employment and Technology." *Journal of Economic History* 41 (1981b): 51–57.

Sombart, Werner. *Why Is There No Socialism in America?* 1st ed. White Plains, 1906/1976.

Shergold, Peter R. "Relative Skill and Income Levels of Native and Foreign-Born Workers: A Re-examination." *Explorations in Economic History* 13 (1976): 451–461.

Smith, James P. "Immigrants and the Labor Market." *Journal of Labor Economics* 24 (April 2006): 203–33.

Sundstrom, William. "Internal Labor Markets before World War I: On the Job Training and Employee Promotion." *Explorations in Economic History* 25 (1988): 424–445.

Thomas, Brinley. *Migration and Economic Growth.* Cambridge: Cambridge University Press, 1954.

Troesken, Werner. *Water, Race, and Disease.* Cambridge, Mass.: MIT Press, 2004.

Wahl, Jenny B. "The Bondsman's Burden: An Economic Analysis of the Jurisprudence of Slaves and Common Carriers." *The Journal of Economic History* 53, no. 3 (1993): 495–526.

Wilentz, Sean. "Against Exceptionalism: Class Consciousness and the American Labor Movement." *International Labor and Working Class History* 26 (Fall 1984): 1–24.

CHAPTER 19

Money, Prices, and Finance in the Postbellum Era

CHAPTER THEME

The 50-year span between the Civil War and World War I was one of continuous, intense public controversy over the American monetary system. Two issues—deflation and banking panics—overshadowed all others and produced repeated attempts to reform the monetary system.

Deflation began after the Civil War and persisted with brief interruptions for three decades. Debtors suffered from the protracted deflation, and farmers were particularly hard hit. As one popular folksong from the 1880s put it: "The farmer is the man, lives on credit till the fall, with interest rates so high, it's a wonder he don't die, for the mortgage man's the one who gets it all" (Seeger 1961, 57). Farmers and other debtors were vocal in their opposition to deflation and supported a number of inflationary schemes. Many Americans had learned lessons, however, they would not soon forget, from the high inflations of Revolutionary times and the Civil War. Leaders in politics and finance insisted on "sound money." They were generally successful in resisting inflationary changes in the monetary system.

This was the era of the classical gold standard. It was almost an article of faith, at least in certain circles, that a nation's currency should be convertible into a fixed weight of gold. The leading industrial nations, the United States included, followed this policy. The benefits were clear: fixed exchange rates and confidence in the long-run value of money. But there were also costs: It was difficult to adjust the money supply in response to adverse trends in prices or income.

The deflation and rise in standards of living for most Americans were punctuated by financial crises in which banks closed, factories and railroads went bankrupt, and hundreds of thousands lost their jobs. The depressions of the mid-1870s and mid-1890s were especially severe. In April 1894, "Coxey's Army" of the unemployed arrived in Washington to demand federal relief. It portended a different future for the nation, one in which the government provided direct aid to the unemployed. Prices began rising after the depression of the mid-1890s, but another bank panic occurred in 1907.

Although the problems in the financial system were easy to identify, reaching agreement on solutions was far harder. Special interests used every means at hand to forestall change or force it in directions favorable to themselves. Silver producers, for example, jumped on the antideflation bandwagon and helped direct its course. Lobbying by country bankers shielded a system of thousands of isolated local banks, perpetuating a system that was vulnerable to banking panics.

These legal restrictions had an important impact on the growth of industrial firms hungry for financial capital. Investment bankers, essentially brokerage houses specializing in stocks and bonds, emerged to fill the void and take positions of dominance in the world of U.S. finance. This situation was quite different from the one in England, where large banking conglomerates were allowed and grew large enough to meet most of the financial needs of an industrializing nation.

Despite the conflicts among interest groups, by the end of 1913, the United States once again had a central bank based on arrangements different from those of earlier versions. These were codified in the Federal Reserve Act signed by President Woodrow Wilson. As the Great Depression of the 1930s proved, however, the Federal Reserve System was not a foolproof answer to the nation's hard-earned lessons about deflation and panics.

NEW FORMS OF CURRENCY

Before the Civil War, the amount of money in circulation was determined by flows of specie (money in the form of coin) into and out of the country through foreign trade and by flows from U.S. mines. By 1862, gold was flowing out of the country so fast that the government and banks were forced to suspend gold payments. Silver, which had been undervalued at the mint (the price in the market for bullion was higher than the price paid by the mint) ever since the Currency Act of 1834, had virtually no circulation.

Because sufficient revenues to wage the war were not obtained from sales of U.S. Treasury bonds (at least at interest rates the government was willing to pay), the Treasury in 1862 issued a new fiat currency, U.S. notes, nicknamed "greenbacks." In addition, in 1863 the National Bank Act was passed, creating a new set of banking institutions (national banks) and another new money (national bank notes). This avalanche of new paper money is shown in Figure 19.1, and the results are reflected in Figure 19.2 on page 341, which shows the upward zoom of prices during the war years. Collectively, greenbacks, national bank notes, and silver and gold specie or their certificates, plus small subsidiary coins, made up the currency. As shown in Figure 19.1, however, greenbacks supplied the monetary increases that sent prices skyrocketing during the Civil War years. Later, gold supplied increases in hand-to-hand money. These types of currency provided the base of the money supply. As shown in Figure 19.3 on page 341, however, most of the increase in the total money supply was created by the growth of bank deposits— savings and checking deposits created by loans. The new currency, however, was critical to the total because it constituted the reserves of the banking system. The growth of these reserves allowed the growth of bank deposits and the total money supply.

The greenbacks solved two problems: the immediate problem of providing additional revenue for the government during the war and the longer-run problem of providing a currency of uniform value throughout the country. In many parts of the country, especially in the West, where the state banks were having difficulties because they had invested heavily in Southern bonds, "Lincoln Green" was popular. Why then did Congress create the national banking system? Conservative Republicans worried that making the greenbacks permanent would create a temptation for weak administrations to issue too many notes. Hence, they created a new institution whose notes would be backed up by government bonds and would have uniform value throughout the country, thus solving the same problems that the greenback had solved. However, the issue of national bank notes would be in private hands, thus eliminating the danger of overissue.

To secure its note issue, each national bank was required to buy U.S. government bonds equal to one-third (later one-quarter) of the dollar amount of its paid-in capital stock, with the provision that no bank would have to buy more than $50,000 worth of bonds. Each bank was to deposit its bonds with the U.S. Treasurer and was to receive notes, engraved in a standard design but with the name of the issuing bank on the obverse side, in the amount of 90 percent of the par or market value (whichever was lower)

FIGURE 19.1

Forms and Values of Currency in the United States, 1860–1915

From the late 1870s to the early 1890s, substantial additions were made to the nation's monetary stocks of gold and silver, but it was not enough to prevent deflation. After 1895, however, the increase in the stock of gold became even more rapid, and deflation became inflation.

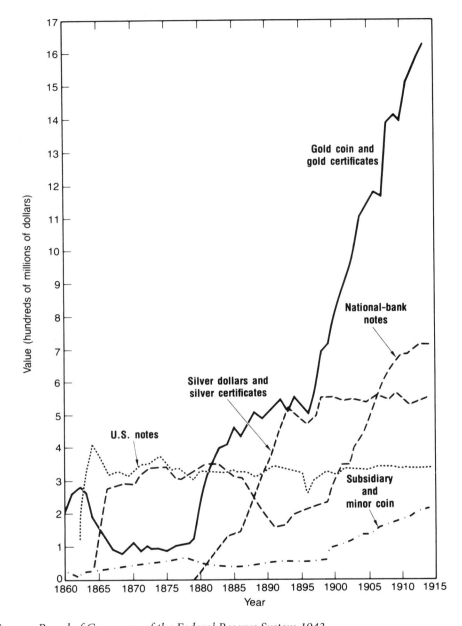

Source: *Board of Governors of the Federal Reserve System 1943.*

of the bonds deposited. A national bank could have any amount of government bonds in its portfolio, but the amount of its notes outstanding could not exceed its capital in dollar amount.

A Dual Banking System

Although the National Bank Act of 1863 created a new type of bank, it did not eliminate the older institutions chartered by the states. To make the national banks appear more sound than state banks, stiff legal reserve requirements were mandated, and double

FIGURE 19.2

Prices, 1860–1914
Prices generally fell from
the end of the Civil War
until the 1890s and then
rose until WWI.

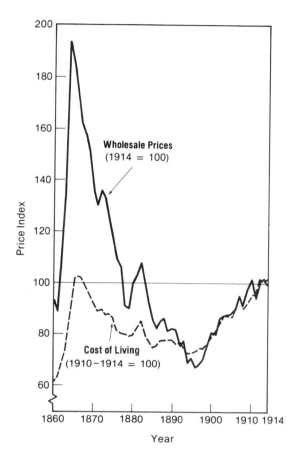

Source: Historical Statistics *1960, Series E1, 101, 157.*

FIGURE 19.3

Per Capita Deposits and
Currency in Circulation

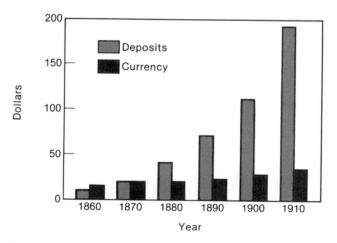

Source: *Data from* Historical Statistics of the United States
1947, 25, 262, 263, and 274.

liability was imposed on the stock of national banks (if the bank failed the stock holders would have to contribute a second time to reimburse the creditors of the bank).

Because the early pace of conversion from state to national status was slow, a tax of 2 percent was levied against state bank notes in June 1864, and this was raised to 10 percent in March 1865. Then the pace of conversion soared. A majority of the state banks immediately shifted to federal jurisdiction; in 1866, fewer than 300 state banks remained.

At that point, it might well have been assumed that the state banking system would soon wither and die, an assumption that proved to be spectacularly wrong. It was no longer necessary for a bank to issue notes to succeed; it could do quite well issuing only deposits. Often, moreover, the rules governing the operations of state banks were less onerous than those governing national banks. The revival in state banking began in about 1870. By 1914, as Table 19.1 shows, there were more state banks than national banks, and the state banks' total assets were larger. The United States ended up with a *dual banking system.* Bankers weighed the advantages of membership in the national system (prestige that attracted depositors and the right to issue notes) against the costs (stricter regulations) and chose the charter that promised the most profits. Legislators and regulators also had to choose. Should they make stricter rules with respect to reserves, capital, and so on? This would protect depositors and increase the prestige of their system, but it also would encourage bankers to choose a different charter. As Economic Reasoning Proposition 2 reminds us, choices impose costs—that is, rational choices are made by weighing costs and benefits (see page 8).

Granted, a bank could get by without issuing bank notes, but it still seemed intuitively (at least to the Populists) that the privilege of issuing notes was valuable, and that the national banks should be subject to more restrictions or higher taxes. True, the national banks had to back the notes with reserves and government bonds, but they could still print money. In the following years, however, economists investigated whether the privilege of note issue was valuable, and if so, why the banks did not take more advantage of

TABLE 19.1 COMMERCIAL BANKS IN THE UNITED STATES, 1860–1914

YEAR	NUMBER OF STATE BANKS[a]	ASSETS OF STATE BANKS[a] (millions of dollars)	NUMBER OF NATIONAL BANKS	ASSETS OF NATIONAL BANKS (millions of dollars)
1860	1,562	$ 1,000	0	$ 0
1863	1,466	1,192	66	17
1864	1,089	721	467	252
1865	349	231	1,294	1,127
1866	297	197	1,634	1,476
1867	272	180	1,636	1,494
1868	247	164	1,640	1,572
1869	259	171	1,619	1,564
1870	325	215	1,612	1,566
1880	1,279	1,364	2,076	2,036
1890	4,717	3,296	3,484	3,062
1900	9,322	6,444	3,731	4,944
1910	18,013	13,030	7,138	9,892
1914	20,346	15,872	7,518	11,477

[a]Includes mutual savings banks.

Source: Historical Statistics *1960, Series X20, X21, X42, X43, X64, and X65.*

it, without coming to a firm conclusion. Phillip Cagan and Anna J. Schwartz (1991) argued that the banks passed up some profits by not issuing more notes, but that the amounts were small, and not the kind of profits that conservative bankers wanted to pursue. On the other hand, Charles W. Calomiris and Joseph Mason (2004) have recently argued that a variety of regulations limited the profitability of issuing notes for most banks, and that the opportunity cost of the capital absorbed in issuing notes was high in some regions, a point originally made by John James (April 1976).

Barriers formed by high capital requirements of national banks, restrictions on mortgage loans, and other restrictions also protected many country national banks from competition from new national banks. This allowed many rural national banks to price discriminate: to restrict loans and charge higher interest rates to local borrowers. Rural national banks also sent their reserves to city banks. This practice, in combination with slower banking expansion rurally, helped finance urban-industrial growth. Richard E. Sylla, one of the leading writers on the banking history of the period, has concluded that the national banking system "raised barriers to entry into banking, and these had differential geographic impact which, when coupled with the increased mobility the National Banking System gave to interbank transfers of funds, worked very much to the advantage of industrial finance" (1972, 236).

Rural banks' discrimination created regional differences in lending rates that persisted, narrowing gradually, from the Civil War to 1900. The differences narrowed for a number of reasons. The recovery of the southern financial system after the Civil War gradually brought rates in that region in line with those in other regions. The spread of the commercial paper market (in which short-term business loans were sold directly to private investors) provided additional competition for the state banks. And, as John James (1978) has pointed out, the introduction of free banking in a number of states increased competition among the state banks. To some extent, as shown in recent work by Howard Bodenhorn and Hugh Rockoff (1992), the postwar integration of the capital market marked a return to the pre–Civil War status quo. This was especially true for the South.

GOLD, GREENBACKS, OR BIMETALLISM?

Between the Civil War and the end of the nineteenth century, Americans engaged in a long-running debate over their monetary system. Some people favored retention of the greenback, the paper money of the Civil War. Some favored a gold standard in which the dollar would be convertible into a fixed amount of gold. Others favored a bimetallic system in which the dollar would be convertible into a fixed amount of either gold or silver. Which system would solve the problems of deflation and banking instability?

Returning to the Gold Standard after the Civil War

During the Civil War, the United States was on the greenback standard. Greenbacks, which were legal tender, were not backed by either gold or silver. Indeed, as Americans liked to joke, they were "backed" only by the green ink on the back of the notes. Many people wanted to return to the situation that had existed before the war when the United States was on the gold standard and every dollar could be converted into 23.22 grains (a little less than 1/20th of an ounce) of pure gold. This was easier said than done, however.

Prices in the United States had risen substantially during the war relative to prices in Britain. In fact, as shown in columns (1) and (2) of Table 19.2, prices had risen 76 percent in the United States between 1861 and 1865 compared with only 5 percent in Britain. At the same time, the price of a British pound had risen, as shown in

	(1)	(2)	(3)
			PRICE IN U.S. DOLLARS OF A
	U.S. PRICES	**BRITISH PRICES**	**BRITISH POUND**
YEAR	**(GDP Deflator)**	**(GDP Deflator)**	
1861			
Beginning of the Civil War	100	100	$4.77
1865			
End of the Civil War	176	105	7.69
1873			
The Crime of 1873	129	113	5.55
1879			
Resumption	104	96	4.85

TABLE 19.2 RETURNING TO THE GOLD STANDARD

Source: *Johnston and Williamson 2003a and b; Officer 2001, 2003.*

column (3), from $4.77 to $7.69, about 61 percent. This increase offset much of the attractiveness of British goods. Suppose the U.S. Treasury in 1865 decided to make the dollar convertible into gold at the prewar rate? This decision would have reestablished the prewar exchange rate or "prewar parity" of about $4.85 per British pound because $4.85 could be converted into an amount of gold that could be converted into £1 at the Bank of England. This exchange rate would cause a rush to convert dollars into gold and the gold into pounds to buy the relatively cheaper British goods. The Treasury would soon find its stock of gold exhausted, and the United States would find that its gold coins were being exported.

Prices in the United States evidently had to come down before the United States could successfully resume the exchange of gold for greenbacks. Many Democrats, along with members of radical groups such as the Greenback Party, argued that returning to gold was not worth the economic pain that was sure to result. Debtors would suffer during the deflation, and working people would suffer from unemployment.

Republicans, who held the upper hand politically, argued, however, that resumption was necessary for several reasons. First, it was only fair that creditors, especially those who had lent to the government, be paid in gold. Bond prices had remained strong during the war, and, it was said, this was because bondholders had received an implicit promise that they would be repaid in gold. Indeed, the right of bondholders to gold was confirmed by the Public Credit Act of 1869. Second, to leave the monetary base tied permanently to paper money would be dangerous because the government could not be trusted with this power. Third, and perhaps most important, returning to the *prewar gold parity* (no reduction in the gold content of the dollar) was necessary to maintain the credibility of the United States abroad and access to foreign capital markets, especially London.

Treasury officials had recourse to two courses of action over the price level:

1. The price level could be forced down rather quickly by contracting the supply of paper money. This could be done by running a budget surplus and burning up the greenbacks as they came in.
2. A slower, less painful decline in prices could be achieved by holding the money supply constant and allowing the growth of the economy to bring about a gradual decline in prices (Timberlake 1964; Kindahl 1971)

The first alternative, a severe monetary contraction, was initiated by Hugh McCulloch, secretary of the treasury during the Andrew Johnson administration. Congress approved this strategy in December 1865 by passing of the Contraction Act. But the deflationary medicine was too bitter, and Congress ended contraction in February 1868. George S. Boutwell, President Grant's secretary of the treasury, followed a much easier policy: a general easing of the money markets rather than a tightening of them.[1] After Boutwell's resignation in 1873, Assistant Secretary William Richardson pursued a still more passive policy. The idea was that the price level would fall as the country "grew up" to its currency.

After the Democrats won control of Congress in the election of 1874, lame-duck Republicans hurriedly passed an act providing for a return to gold payments in four years. Continued deflation, as shown in the last row of Table 19.2, restored (approximately) the 1861 relationship between U.S. and British prices, and made it possible to resume conversion of greenbacks into gold on the appointed day. For a technical reason to be

© CULVER PICTURES, INC.

When gold fluctuated wildly in 1869, the Gold Room of the New York Stock Exchange was the nerve center of speculation. In its center, a bronze cupid sprayed water quietly; on the dais, the secretary of the room had to cup his ears to hear and record transactions.

---

[1]It was Boutwell who broke the dramatic corner (monopoly) on gold attempted by James Fisk and Jay Gould in September 1869 by selling $4 million of the money metal in the Gold Room of the New York Stock Exchange (Wimmer 1975).

The changing face of the American dollar—it reflected the search for a sound banking system and a stable price level. Reproduced here, starting from the top, are (1) a Federal Reserve Note, (2) a Federal Demand Note issued early in the Civil War, (3) a National Bank Note, and (4) a silver certificate.

discussed presently, the United States was not legally committed to a gold standard and would not be for another 21 years. Nevertheless, between 1879 and 1900, the government did maintain parity of all forms of money with gold, and, during these years, America was on a de facto gold standard.

The Crime of '73

Large denomination silver coins had gone out of circulation in the 1890s. During the Civil War and for several years afterward, even small denomination silver coins had gone out of circulation, having been replaced at first by ungummed postage stamps and later by fractional currency—paper notes issued by the government in denominations of 5, 10, 25, and 50 cents. Not surprisingly, when Congress sought to simplify the coinage in 1873, the silver dollar was omitted from the list of coins to be minted. Some farseeing officials feared an increase in the supply of silver that would flood the mint, increasing the money supply, raising prices, and thus delaying resumption. At a mint ratio of approximately 16 to 1, silver was worth more on the market than at the mint, and thus most of the Congress took little notice of the omission at the time. Scarcely three years later, the failure to include the silver dollar in the act of 1873 began a furor that was to last for a quarter century.[2]

The reason for the subsequent agitation over the "demonetization" of silver lay in the fact that the price of silver began falling in international markets. The increasing output of western silver mines in the United States and a shift of the bimetallic countries of western Europe to the gold standard had led to a growing surplus of silver. When the market value of the silver contained in a dollar actually fell below a dollar, silver producers took silver to the mint for coinage. To their dismay, they discovered that the government would take only as much silver as the Treasury needed for small subsidiary coins. The cry from the silver producers was horrendous.

A relatively small group such as the silver producers would not appear to have much power. But during the 1870s and 1880s, a number of western states were being admitted to the Union, each having two U.S. senators to represent their small populations, and silver producers concentrated in these states acquired political representation out of all proportion to their numbers. Opponents of deflation joined the silver producers in a clamor for the free and unlimited coinage of silver at the old mint ratio of 16 to 1. Silver advocates knew that at such a ratio, silver would be brought to the mint in great quantities and that the monetary reserves of the country, the total money supply, and the general price level would rise.

The opposition's cry that gold would be driven out of circulation meant nothing to the advocates of free silver except relief to the unemployed and lighter burdens for oppressed debtors. To the supporters of the free coinage of silver, the act that had demonetized silver became the "Crime of '73."

Ultimately, Congress passed a compromise between the positions of the "sound-money" and free-coinage forces. The first of several major silver bills was the Bland-Allison Act of 1878. This law provided for the coinage of silver in limited amounts. The secretary of the treasury was directed to purchase not less than $2 million and not more than $4 million worth of silver each month at the current market price. The conservative secretaries in office during the next 12 years purchased only the minimum amount of silver, but by 1890, the Treasury's monetary silver (not counting subsidiary coins) amounted to almost $380 million.

The silver question was by no means settled. In 1878, the average market value of the silver contained in a dollar was just over $0.89. For the next 12 years, silver prices, despite the purchases, consistently fell. Neither the producers of silver nor the debtors who wanted inflation were appeased. A new bill, the Sherman Silver Purchase Law of 1890,

---

[2]Inevitably, some critics of the "Crime of '73" charged that Congress had been bribed by foreign bankers. There was nothing to the charges of corruption, although some of the officials drafting the legislation were trying to protect a future commitment to gold.

If the Government stamps 412½ grains of silver with the words "One Dollar," and forces them upon the people when they are at 7 per cent. discount with gold and over 4 per cent below greenbacks, it stamps a lie upon the coin, and legalizes a cheat and fraud upon those whom it forces to accept it.—*Times.*

THE CURRENT QUESTION.

SILVER—"*You need not hold yourself so high. I'm as good as you are.*"
GOLD—"*You never were, and never will be, my equal.*"

Friends of silver saw in its monetization relief from depression and persistent grief and agony if gold continued to reign as the sole monetary metal in America.

was carefully prepared to avoid President Benjamin Harrison's veto. The secretary of the treasury was directed to make a monthly purchase, at the market price, of 4.5 million ounces of silver. To pay for this bullion, he was to issue a new type of paper money to be known as Treasury notes, which were to be redeemable in either gold or silver at his discretion. At the silver prices prevailing in 1890, the new law authorized the purchase of almost double the monthly amount of silver taken in under the previous law. Silver supplies kept expanding so rapidly that its market price resumed further sharp declines almost immediately.

Within three years, the dollar amount of silver being purchased was little more than it had been under the old act. In 1893, at the insistence of Democratic president Grover Cleveland—a "sound-money" man at odds with his party on this issue—the Sherman Act was repealed. President Cleveland believed that the act had undermined confidence in the dollar and produced a financial panic. In more than three years of purchasing under this law, more than $150 million of the Treasury notes of 1890 were issued; overall, between 1878 and 1893 (as shown in Figure 19.1), $500 million was added to the

ECONOMIC INSIGHT 19.1

THE FISHER EFFECT

As debtors, farmers would benefit from inflation, but perhaps not by as much as they hoped. Farm mortgages, particularly on the frontier, were for short durations, often five years or less. If a mortgage was renewed after silver inflation was expected, lenders would demand and get higher interest rates. American economist Irving Fisher published a detailed study of the relationship between price level changes and interest rates in 1894 in response to the debate over silver. He found that interest rates did go up

after inflation and down after deflation, but with a long lag. In his honor, the tendency of interest rates to reflect inflation is known as the "Fisher effect." It can be expressed by the following equation:

$$i = r + p$$

where i is the market rate of interest, r is the real rate of interest, and p is the rate of price change. Critics of the silverites maintained that an increase in p would produce an increase only in i, leaving r unchanged.

currency by silver purchases. This was a victory of sorts for the silver forces. But the Treasury's silver purchases were insufficient to prevent silver prices from falling, and the general price level continued its deflationary spiral (as shown in Figure 19.2 on page 341). Economic Insight 19.1 discusses the tendency of interest rates to reflect inflation and deflation.

The Commitment to the Gold Standard

As Figure 19.2 shows, prices continued to fall from the resumption of gold payment in 1879 to the mid-1890s. This was true not only in the United States but also in other countries on the gold standard. Only countries on the silver standard experienced rising prices.

Why did prices fall? The basic problem was that the demand for money (and ultimately for gold, which was the base of the monetary system) was growing faster than the supply. The rapid increase in economic activity, growing financial sophistication, and the addition of more countries to the gold standard all increased the demand for gold. Meanwhile, the supply, although growing at a good rate by historical standards, could not keep pace.

Although the silver acts of 1878 and 1890 made silver certificates redeemable in either gold or silver, in practice, Treasury authorities redeemed them in gold if it were demanded. After 1879, Treasury secretaries and the public came to believe that a minimum gold reserve of $100 million was necessary to back up the paper circulation. Just when the Treasury notes of 1890 were authorized, the government's gold reserve began declining toward the $100 million mark as the public presented Treasury notes and greenbacks for payment in gold. By early 1893, the gold drain had become serious, and the gold reserve actually dipped below $100 million toward the middle of the year.

Several times during the next three years, it appeared certain that the de facto gold standard would have to be abandoned. Two kinds of drains—"external" (foreign) and "internal" (domestic)—plagued the Treasury from 1891 to 1896. The difficulty was that when the danger of abandoning gold became apparent, people rushed to acquire gold, thus making it even more likely that the Treasury would have to abandon the gold standard. Chiefly by selling bonds for gold, the administration replenished the government's reserve whenever it appeared that the standard was about to be lost. The repeal of the Sherman Silver Purchase Law of 1893 reduced the number of Treasury notes, which the public was presenting along with greenbacks, for redemption. Increasing commodity exports at last brought an influx of gold from abroad in the summer of 1896, improving public confidence to the point that the gold standard was saved.

The election of 1896 settled the matter of a monetary standard for nearly 40 years. The Democrats, under the leadership of William Jennings Bryan, stood for free coinage of silver at a ratio of 16 to 1—even though the market ratio was then more than 30 to 1. At the Democratic national convention, Bryan inspired the inflationists and won the party's nomination with his famous "Cross of Gold" speech, which ended with this stirring call to arms:

> *Having behind us the producing masses of this nation and the world, supported by the commercial interests, the laboring interests and the toilers everywhere, we will answer their demand for a gold standard by saying to them: You shall not press down upon the brow of labor this crown of thorns, you shall not crucify mankind upon a cross of gold.*

The Republicans, with William McKinley as their candidate, stood solidly for the gold standard.[3] The West and the South supported Bryan; the North and the East supported McKinley. In the East, industrial employers brought every possible pressure, legitimate or not, to bear on employee voters. One genuine issue was the tariff. Bryan, like many of his supporters in the farm states, opposed a high tariff, but workers may have been persuaded that the tariff protected jobs. In any event, Bryan did not draw the great urban

© KEAN COLLECTION/GETTY IMAGES

In his 1896 campaign for the Presidency, Bryan crisscrossed the nation by rail. It has been called the first modern campaign. Although defeated by McKinley, many of Bryan's Populist ideas were adopted during the New Deal.

---

[3]McKinley, however, did promise to call an international conference to consider a bimetallic standard, a promise he honored.

vote, as Franklin Roosevelt would do 36 years later, and when well-to-do farmers in the older agricultural states deserted Bryan, the cause was lost.[4]

The Republican victory of 1896 was not followed immediately by legislation ending the controversy because free-silver advocates still held a majority in Congress. The return of prosperity, encouraged by new supplies of gold, however, made Congress receptive to definitive gold legislation. The new supplies of gold, although partly the result of the high real price for gold (the price paid by the mint relative to prices in general), were largely unanticipated. New gold fields were opened in many areas of the world, including the immensely rich gold fields of South Africa, and a new method for processing gold through the use of cyanide was developed. Ironically, the increase in the supply of gold accomplished the goal of the silverites: expansion of the money supply and inflation. Figure 19.1 clearly shows the rapid increase in monetary gold after 1896.

Under the Gold Standard Act of 1900, the dollar was defined solely in terms of gold, and all other forms of money were to be convertible into gold. The secretary of the treasury was directed to maintain a gold reserve of $150 million, which was not to be drawn on to meet current government expenses. To prevent a recurrence of the difficulties of the 1890s, a provision was made to keep redeemed silver certificates and greenbacks in the Treasury during times of stress for borrowing to meet deficits that might occur from time to time. The United States had at last committed itself by law to the gold standard.

Who was right, Bryan and the silverites or McKinley and the "gold bugs"? Economist Milton Friedman has provided the most convincing answer. He argues that eliminating the silver dollar in 1873 was a mistake that produced an unnecessary deflation, but that by Bryan's time, it was probably too late to do much about it (Friedman 1990). Friedman and Anna J. Schwartz (1963, 133–134) have pointed out that a firm commitment to either standard would have been better than the long, drawn-out battle that took place. The lessons to be drawn from this unique experience with deflation are discussed further in the accompanying New View 19.1.

The International Gold Standard

The years between 1896 and World War I were the heyday of the gold standard. As data in Figure 19.2 indicates, prices rose at a moderate rate, about 2 percent per year. International exchange rates among the industrial countries were fixed because most were on the gold standard. Indeed, it could well be said that there was really only one international currency—gold; it simply had a different name in each country. Fixed exchange rates and mildly rising prices encouraged the free flow of goods and capital across international borders. London was the financial center of the world. Bonds sold there sent streams of capital into the less-developed parts of the world. No wonder many economists still look to this period as a model for the world's monetary system.

However, the gold standard had costs as well as benefits. Resources were used to mine gold in South Africa and the Klondike and to dredge gold from the rivers of California. A paper standard would have permitted those resources to be used elsewhere. The rates of growth of the world's money supplies, moreover, were determined by the individual decisions of miners and chemists and by the forces of nature that had sewn the rare seams of gold into the earth. During the years after 1896, the net result was that the

---

[4]The battle over the standards was reflected, it has been argued, in L. Frank Baum's contemporary *The Wonderful Wizard of Oz*. Dorothy represents America; the Scarecrow, the farmer; the Tin Man, the working man; the Cowardly Lion, William Jennings Bryan; and so on. Dorothy seeks wisdom by following the yellow brick road (the gold standard) to the Emerald City (Washington, D.C.). But in the end, she discovers that she had the power to solve her problems with her entire time, her silver shoes (the ruby slippers were added by MGM) (Rockoff 1990, 739–760).

NEW VIEW 19.1

DEFLATION

For most of the years after World War II, inflation was the main worry of monetary economists. Today, the United States, as well as other industrial countries such as Japan, faces the prospect of deflation. Is deflation always a bad thing? Many people assume so, perhaps because of the correlation between falling prices and hard times during the 1930s. The experience of the United States after the Civil War shows that deflation, at least a mild form of it, may not be such a bad thing. Between 1865 and 1896, the price level in the United States fell at an annual rate of about 2.10 percent per year, but real GDP per capita rose at an annual rate of 1.35 percent per year, and total industrial production rose at 4.76 percent per year. Iron and steel

production rose an astonishing 6.38 percent per year as the United States became the world's leader. Of course, deflation did not affect everyone the same way. If a lender and a borrower entered into a contract without factoring in the deflation, the lender would receive an unanticipated profit at the expense of the borrower. And while the period as a whole was one of rapid economic growth, there were shorter periods of hard times, especially in the mid-1870s and early 1890s. Still, a look back at this period helps put the simple equation of deflation and economic stagnation into richer perspective.

Sources: *Prices and real GDP per capita: Johnston and Williamson 2003a and b. Industrial production and iron and steel:* Historical Statistics *1975, Series P17 and P270.*

world's stock of monetary gold grew at a satisfactory rate. But this was not true for the years before 1896. During financial crises, moreover, adherence to the gold standard made it difficult to supply additional money to financial markets. In any case, there was always the hope that central bankers backed by reams of scientific analysis could do a better job of controlling the money supply than an automatic mechanism such as the gold standard.

The debate over the net benefits of the gold standard continues unabated. Historical comparisons, however, can narrow the range of debate. Michael D. Bordo (1981) has shown that along many dimensions (most important, average unemployment), the gold standard was inferior to modern monetary standards. Only with respect to long-term price stability could the gold standard be declared clearly superior. Once again we see the value of testing conjectures with evidence (Economic Reasoning Proposition 5, evidence and theory give value to opinions).

THE RISE OF INVESTMENT BANKING

Lance Davis (1963) showed that British financial markets were quite different from American markets. British industrialists could visit their local branch banks—Lloyd's, or Westminster's, or Barclays—and draw capital from a huge international system. American firms, on the other hand, faced banks with more restricted resources.

Because of this limitation, investment banking in the United States emerged to serve the expansion of railroads, mining companies, and large-scale manufacturers. Unlike commercial banks, investment banks did not have the power to issue notes or create deposits. Instead they acted as intermediaries, bringing together lenders (stock and bond buyers) and borrowers (firms). J. P. Morgan and Company was a pioneer in investment banking, earning $3 million for services in advising and selling stocks for Vanderbilt and his New York Central Railroad in 1879. Charles Schwab, an employee of Andrew Carnegie, carried a note to Morgan in 1900 with an asking price of more than $400 million for Carnegie's steel holdings. Morgan promptly replied, "I'll take it"—thus giving birth to the United States Steel Corporation; it was by far the largest merger up to that time. Forty years earlier, when Carnegie tried to raise financial

© BETTMANN/CORBIS

Investment banker J. P. Morgan ruled the world of finance. In 1901 he formed the United States Steel Corporation, the world's first billion-dollar corporation. When asked what the market would do, he answered, "It will fluctuate."

capital of only a fraction of the sum Morgan promptly gave him in 1900, Carnegie had to go to England because no U.S. banks could supply his capital needs.

The close links between investment bankers and big business were forged even more strongly by the practice of placing representatives of the large investment houses on the boards of directors of the firms. Critics of the investment bankers complained that this practice stifled competition. Morgan and a few smaller investment banking firms such as Kuhn Loeb and Company in New York and Kidder Peabody and Company in Boston seemed to control both the distribution of securities and (through interlocking directorates) the business decisions of the major industrial firms. In 1912, Congress subjected this "money trust" to a detailed and highly critical examination by the Pujo committee. J. Bradford DeLong's (1991) research has shown that there was also a positive side to Morgan's links with industrial firms: Investment bankers helped inform investors about how best to invest their funds (Economic Reasoning Proposition 5, evidence matters).

Another important force helping finance industrial growth was the rapid, steady retirement of the national debt. The federal debt had been retired completely by 1835 (for the first and only time in our history), and only a small debt existed on the eve of the Civil War. By 1865, the debt was $2.32 billion, about 25 percent of gross domestic product (GDP); it was reduced to $648 million by 1877 before increasing for several years. By 1893, $1.73 billion had been retired. Sizably, collections of tariffs supplied government with continued surpluses that permitted the debt retirement. This inflow of government funds to buy up old bonds—a type of crowding in, as James has called it—lowered yields on private assets and stimulated capital formation in the private sector (James 1984).

BANK PANICS AND THE ESTABLISHMENT OF THE FEDERAL RESERVE SYSTEM

Despite the increased flexibility, the panic of 1893 and the depression of the mid-1890s were followed by the severe panic of 1907 and the ensuing recession. Once again, the American people were aroused to the need for basic reforms. One of the most painful aspects of economic crisis before World War I was the rush by individuals and business firms, as they became apprehensive about the economic future, to the banks to convert their deposits into cash. The banks, which operated on the "fractional reserve" principle, could not immediately meet the demands for their total deposit liabilities. Given time, any sound bank could be liquidated in an orderly fashion, and its depositors and stockholders could be paid in full. In panics, however, an orderly shifting of assets into cash was difficult, if not impossible. As many harried banks tried to sell bonds (their most liquid assets) at the same time, the prices of bonds fell drastically. For some banks, the consequent losses on bonds proved disastrous, even though "runs" were stopped. If, instead of selling its securities, a bank called in its loans or refused to renew loans as they came due, it transferred pressure to its customers. If these customers could not meet their obligations, the banks were forced into insolvency.

A common way to mitigate these difficulties was to suspend cash payments during crises. After the Civil War, suspension meant that banks ceased to pay out cash in any form: gold or gold certificates, silver or silver certificates, greenbacks, national bank notes, or subsidiary coins. As another option, a bank might restrict cash payments to a certain maximum sum per day or per withdrawal. During the panic of 1907, such suspensions were more general and for longer time periods (over two months in some cities) than ever before. In the Southeast and Midwest, the resulting shortage of cash was so serious that local clearinghouses issued emergency notes against collateral pledged by cooperating banks so that people could carry on business. These small-denomination "clearinghouse certificates" were not issued much elsewhere, but banks in cities all over the United States used large-denomination certificates to make up balances due one another. The issue of clearinghouse loan certificates, as Gary Gorton (1985) and Richard Timberlake (1978) have shown, went a long way toward softening the effects of a crisis, but it could not prevent them. A related, although less severe, problem occurred almost every year. The demand for money would rise in the fall because money was needed to pay harvest workers and purchase commodities from farmers and during the winter because extra money was needed for the Christmas buying season. Because the supply of money, and especially cash, was "inelastic," the result was an increase in interest rates in the fall and winter. To farmers, this seemed grossly unfair: Interest rates rose just when the farmers had the greatest need to borrow. Seasonal fluctuations in the demand for money were inherent in an agricultural economy, but they were aggravated by the national banking system, which made it hard for banks to accommodate changes in the desired ratio of deposits to bank notes. George Selgin and Lawrence H. White (1994) showed that in Canada, where banks had more freedom to convert deposits into notes, seasonal fluctuations in interest rates were much less severe. Thus, the farmers' demand that something be done about seasonal fluctuations in interest rates was added to the general demand that something be done about banking panics.

National Monetary Commission

Suspending cash payments and issuing clearinghouse certificates were better than allowing a panic to continue, but the public wanted a reform that would prevent suspensions altogether. In response, the Aldrich-Vreeland Act of 1908 provided for the organization of "national currency associations" to be composed of no fewer than 10 banks in sound financial condition. The purpose of these associations was to enable the banks that formed them to issue emergency bank notes against the security of bonds and commercial paper in their portfolios. Another provision established the National Monetary Commission, whose report in 1912 blasted the American banking system:

> *The methods by which our domestic and international credit operations are now conducted are crude, expensive and unworthy of an intelligent people.... The unimportant part which our banks and bankers take in the financing of our foreign trade is disgraceful to a progressive nation.... The disabilities from which our producers suffer in our foreign trade also apply largely to domestic transactions. (U.S. National Monetary Commission 1912, 28–29)*

The Commission's key recommendation was a new central bank: an institution to hold the reserves of the commercial banks and with the power to increase the commercial bank's reserves through its own credit-granting powers. A central bank was also needed to help the Treasury. After the demise of the second Bank of the United States, the federal government had to maintain its own fiscal agent in the form of the Independent Treasury, which was by law required to remain aloof from the banking system. Impossibly antiquated methods of handling government funds resulted. By 1912, the need for a modern, central fiscal agent was too great to be postponed further.

Federal Reserve Act

Two days before Christmas in 1913, President Wilson signed the bill that established the Federal Reserve System. The system was composed of 12 Federal Reserve Banks, one in each of 12 separate districts, to protect the interests of different regions. Unlike the 20-year charter of the first and second Banks of the United States, the charter of the Federal Reserve was permanent.

The system was to be headed by a Federal Reserve Board composed of seven members, including the secretary of the treasury, the comptroller of the currency ex officio, and five appointees of the president. Each Federal Reserve Bank was to be run by a board of nine directors. The Federal Reserve Board was to appoint three of the directors representing the "public"; the member banks of the district were to elect the remaining six. Three of the six locally elected directors could be bankers; the remaining three were to represent business, industry, and agriculture. Thus, the banking community had a minority representation on the Reserve Bank directorates in each district.

The Federal Reserve Act made membership in the system compulsory for national banks. Upon compliance with federal requirements, state banks might also become members. To join the system, a commercial bank had to purchase shares of the capital stock of the district Federal Reserve Bank in the amount of 3 percent of its combined capital and surplus. Thus, the member banks nominally owned the Federal Reserve Banks, although the annual return they could receive on their stock was limited to a

6 percent cumulative dividend. A member bank also had to deposit with the district Federal Reserve Bank a large part of the cash it had previously held as reserves. After 1917, all legal reserves of member banks were to be in the form of deposits with the Federal Reserve Bank.[5]

It was hoped that if the Federal Reserve Act were carefully followed, monetary disturbances would be nearly eliminated. As we will see in Part IV, however, despite the high hopes held for the Federal Reserve System, periods of inadequate leadership and lack of understanding at the "Fed" permitted catastrophic monetary disturbances, bank panics, and sharp business cycles. Indeed, the Great Depression—America's darkest economic period—was partly a result of failure at the Fed.

SELECTED REFERENCES AND SUGGESTED READINGS

Board of Governors of the Federal Reserve System (U.S.). *Banking and Monetary Statistics.* Washington, D.C.: Board of Governors of the Federal Reserve System, 1943.

Bodenhorn, Howard, and Hugh Rockoff. "Regional Interest Rates in Antebellum America." In *Strategic Factors in Nineteenth Century American Economic History: A Volume to Honor Robert W. Fogel,* eds. Claudia Goldin and Hugh Rockoff, 159–187. A National Bureau of Economic Research Conference Report. Chicago: University of Chicago Press, 1992.

Bordo, Michael D. "The Classical Gold Standard: Some Lessons for Today." *Federal Reserve Bank of St. Louis Review* 63 (1981): 1–17.

Cagan, Phillip, and Anna J. Schwartz. "The National Bank Note Puzzle Reinterpreted." *Journal of Money, Credit and Banking* 23, no. 3, Part 1 (August 1991): 293–307.

Calomiris, Charles W., and Joseph R. Mason. "Resolving the Puzzle of the Under Issuance of National Bank Notes." National Bureau of Economic Research, Inc., NBER Working Papers No. 10951, December 2004.

Davis, Lance E. "Capital Immobilities and Finance Capitalism: A Study of Economic Evolution in the United States." *Explorations in Entrepreneurial History* 1, no. 1 (Fall 1963): 88–105.

DeLong, J. Bradford. "Did J. P. Morgan's Men Add Value? A Historical Perspective on Financial Capitalism." In *Inside the Business Enterprise,* ed. Peter Temin. Chicago: University of Chicago Press, 1991.

Friedman, Milton. "The Crime of 1873." *Journal of Political Economy* 6 (1990): 1159–1194.

Friedman, Milton, and Anna J. Schwartz. *A Monetary History of the United States, 1867–1960.* National

Bureau of Economic Research. Princeton, N.J.: Princeton University Press, 1963.

Gorton, Gary. "Clearinghouses and the Origins of Central Banking in the U.S." *Journal of Economic History* 45 (1985): 277–283.

Historical Statistics of the United States, 1789–1945. Washington, D.C.: Government Printing Office, 1947.

Historical Statistics. Washington, D.C.: Government Printing Office, 1960.

Historical Statistics. Washington, D.C.: Government Printing Office, 1975.

James, John A. "The Conundrum of the Low Issue of National Bank Notes." *The Journal of Political Economy* 84, no. 2 (April 1976): 359–368.

_____. *Money and Capital Markets in Postbellum America.* Princeton, N.J.: Princeton University Press, 1978.

_____. "Public Debt Management Policy and Nineteenth-Century American Economic Growth." *Explorations in Economic History* 21 (1984): 192–217.

Johnston, Louis D., and Samuel H. Williamson. "The Annual Real and Nominal GDP for the United States, 1789–2002." Economic History Service, March 2003a. http://www.measuringworth.org/usgdp/.

_____. "Source Note for US GDP, 1789–Present." Economic History Services, March 2003b. http://www.measuringworth.org/usgdp/.

Kindahl, James K. "Economic Factors in Specie Resumption: The United States, 1865–1879." In *The Reinterpretation of American Economic History,* eds. Robert W. Fogel and Stanley L. Engerman. New York: Harper & Row, 1971.

---

[5]All required reserves were held on deposit with Federal Reserve Banks from June 1917 until late 1959, when, after a series of transitional steps, member banks could once again count vault cash as reserves.

Officer, Lawrence H. "Exchange Rate between the United States Dollar and the British Pound, 1791–2000." Economic History Services, 2001. http://www.measuringworth.org/exchangepound/.

———. "The Annual Real and Nominal GDP for the United Kingdom, 1086–2000." Economic History Services, June 2003. http://www.measuringworth.org/ukgdp/.

Rockoff, Hugh. "The Wizard of Oz as a Monetary Allegory." *Journal of Political Economy* 98 (1990): 739–760.

Seeger, Pete. *American Favorite Ballads.* New York: Oak, 1961.

Selgin, George A., and Lawrence H. White. "Monetary Reform and the Redemption of National Bank Notes, 1863–1913." *Business History Review* 68 (1994): 205–243.

Sylla, Richard. "The United States, 1863–1913." In *Banking and Economic Development: Some Lessons of Economic History*, ed. Rondo Cameron. New York: Oxford University Press, 1972.

Timberlake, Richard H. "Ideological Factors in Specie Resumption and Treasury Policy." *Journal of Economic History* 24 (1964).

———. *The Origins of Central Banking in the United States.* Cambridge, Mass.: Harvard University Press, 1978.

U.S. National Monetary Commission. *Report of the National Monetary Commission.* Washington, D.C.: Government Printing Office, 1912.

Wimmer, Larry T. "The Gold Crisis of 1869: Stabilizing or Destabilizing Speculation under Floating Exchange Rates?" *Explorations in Economic History* 12 (1975): 105–122.

CHAPTER **20**

Commerce at Home and Abroad

CHAPTER THEME

Between 1880 and 1920, the United States became the leading manufacturer in the world in terms of total production and output per worker. Both the quality and the quantity of goods and services increased. Rather than buying commodities in bulk for further processing within the home, as they had done in an earlier and simpler time, Americans increasingly relied on finished products. Dependable brand-name products, heavily promoted through advertising, played an increasingly important role in the distribution of goods. The new styles and number of goods lifted the material well-being of greater and greater proportions of the population. These developments resulted from underlying trends in urbanization and, as emphasized in chapters 16 and 17, from advances in transportation and technology.

URBANIZATION

The choice of city life over rural life was largely a nineteenth-century (and later) phenomenon. The long march to city dominance of where most Americans live is revealed in Table 20.1 on page 359, which shows that the percentage of the population living in urban centers nearly doubled between 1800 and 1840, doubled again between 1840 and 1860, and then again from 1860 to 1900. By 1910, nearly 10 percent of the total population lived in three cities—New York, Chicago, and Philadelphia—each having a million-plus residents.

Before 1860, the rapid pace of urbanization resulted primarily from the rapid growth of interregional trade spurred by the transportation revolution. Urban centers emerged as entrepôts of trade, and trade more than industry was the magnet pulling people into cities and towns (Clark 1929, 2). As Eric Lampard (1955) has shown, the 15 greatest cities in the nation in 1860 employed relatively small shares of their population in manufactures. What the cities in this early period provided was primarily transport and commercial and banking services for expanding long-distance trades.

Urbanization after the Civil War was different. Early industrial complexes, which had been tied to primary resources in city hinterlands, shifted to the city. The railroad and other advances in transportation and communication made factories and cities nearly synonymous by the late nineteenth century.

People, many from abroad, poured into the centers of trade and industrial activities. Between 1860 and 1910, more than half of new city residents came from overseas. About 10 percent of the urban growth resulted from natural increase, and a little over one-third came from domestic rural areas.

Cities in the Midwest and the South, long established as distributing centers for the manufactures of the East and now developing industry of their own, grew phenomenally

TABLE 20.1 URBAN PERCENTAGES OF THE POPULATION, 1800–1910

YEAR	POPULATION IN TOWNS OVER 2,500	POPULATION IN TOWNS OVER 100,000
1800	6%	0%
1840	11	3
1860	20	8
1880	28	12
1900	40	19
1910	46	22

Source: Historical Statistics, *1975, Series A2 and A57-72.*

as industrial workers flocked to them. Chicago and Detroit, Cleveland and Cincinnati, St. Louis and Kansas City, Memphis and New Orleans, and Atlanta and Birmingham originated shipments that went far beyond their own trade areas. By 1910, the West and the South originated half as much railroad tonnage of manufactures carried as the East did. Meanwhile, smaller cities within the trade areas of the metropolises and cities in the thinly populated region west of the Mississippi specialized in the mercantile functions. As automobiles came into common use after 1910, large towns and cities gained business at the expense of small towns and villages; by 1920, retailers in urban centers were attracting customers from distances that had been unimaginable just a few years earlier. These changes were reflected in new ways of distributing goods and in new marketing institutions, as Martha Olney (1991) has emphasized.

MARKETING AND SELLING

On the eve of the Civil War, the typical store was more devoted to processing sales than to promoting sales. Advertising was limited largely to local newspapers and some national magazines, with occasional outdoor ads in a few large cities. "Attracting customers" was not the main purpose of advertisements; the information conveyed was simple and direct. Newspaper ads wasted no space, listing the items for sale and the location, but usually not prices. Installment buying was known but uncommon until after the turn of the century (see Perspective 20.1). Cyrus McCormick sold his reaper "on time" at 20 percent down and four months to pay. Edward Clark of the Singer Sewing Machine Company had innovated consumer credit in 1856, selling $125 sewing machines for $5 down and $3 per month. McCormick and Singer, pioneers for direct sales to consumers before the Civil War, were rare exceptions. Most manufacturers sold directly to wholesalers or to commission agents who marketed the wares. Many wholesalers, in turn, hired "drummers," traveling salesmen who "drummed up" trade and solicited orders in the towns and countryside.

Wholesaling

The full-service wholesale houses that evolved after 1840 bought goods on their own account from manufacturers and importers to sell to retailers, frequently on credit. In the growing cities of the Midwest, successful retailers began to perform some wholesale functions along with the business of selling to consumers. As these houses grew, they sometimes dropped their retailing activities altogether and concentrated on handling the output of manufacturing centers in the East. A few wholesale firms, especially those located in major distributing centers such as Chicago and St. Louis, offered several lines of merchandise, but more often they specialized in a single "full line," such as hardware or dry goods.

From 1860 to 1900, full-line, full-service wholesale houses were without serious competitors in the business of distributing goods from manufacturers to retailers. Beginning in the 1880s and increasingly after 1900, however, they faced competition from the marketing departments of large manufacturers (Livesay and Porter 1971; Chandler 1977). Wholesale houses did not decline absolutely between 1900 and 1920—in fact, their sales continued to increase—but they handled an ever-smaller proportion of goods in the channels of distribution.

The reason for the relative decline in wholesaling lay in the structure of emerging large-scale producers. Firms in many industries were adopting "continuous process" technologies, in which raw materials moved in a steady flow through the factory rather

PERSPECTIVE 20.1

CREDIT, INSTALLMENT PURCHASES, AND RACE

Although purchase on credit from country stores was common in the nineteenth century, buying on installment was uncommon until the early twentieth century. Thanks to the research of Martha Olney (1998), an interesting racial profile has emerged on the use of store credit and installment payment for the purchase of goods. Table 20.2 shows the percentage of families who used merchant credit or installments to buy merchandise, and the relative uses of these debt forms by race. Blacks took on more debt than whites, and blacks were much more likely to use installment payments. Table 20.3 shows the use of installment payments for various common "durables." Although there is little difference between the races in the percentage of families buying each item listed (the first set of columns), blacks often nearly doubled their use of installment purchases compared with whites. Olney's analysis strongly suggests that this heavy

reliance on installment purchases by blacks was because merchants (mostly white) were reluctant to give blacks store credit. Such credit was informal and not tied to specific items that could be repossessed. Installment contracts were formal and could be used legally for repossession. Given high information costs about ability to pay and racial profiling, merchants reduced their risks of default by using installment methods. Especially for durables, Olney concludes:

Down payments were typically 10 to 25 percent of the goods' price. Contract maturities were typically 12 to 18 months, much shorter than the goods' expected service life. The value of the collateral therefore often exceeded the balance due, especially in the first few months of the installment contract. Whatever concerns a durable good merchant might have had regarding the creditworthiness of a family were easily allayed by the knowledge that valuable collateral could be repossessed if the family defaulted on the installment contract. (1998, 427)

TABLE 20.2 JOINT USE OF INSTALLMENT AND MERCHANT CREDIT

	WHITE	BLACK
Percentage of families using installment or merchant credit	38.6%	48.9%
Percentage of families using installment or merchant credit:		
Using only installment credit	35.2	55.6
Using only merchant credit	45.6	24.3
Using both installment and merchant credit	19.2	20.2

Source: *Olney 1998,* 412.

PERSPECTIVE 20.1

CREDIT, INSTALLMENT PURCHASES, AND RACE, Continued

TABLE 20.3 GOODS FAMILIES PURCHASED ON INSTALLMENT (1918–1919)

GOODS BEING PURCHASED	PERCENTAGE OF FAMILIES BUYING PRODUCT		PERCENTAGE OF PURCHASES MADE ON INSTALLMENT	
	WHITE	BLACK	WHITE	BLACK
Pianos and musical instruments	5.9%	5.5%	80.8%	93.6%
Phonographs	7.9	6.6	48.0	53.6
Furniture	45.9	47.9	20.7	52.8
Chair	21.0	24.6	26.5	56.2
Bedstead	18.4	21.7	26.6	57.3
Mattress	20.3	21.7	23.2	56.4
Appliances	62.8	69.0	14.6	23.8
Stove	24.5	24.7	20.1	40.3
Sewing machine	8.0	8.0	45.3	72.1
Refrigerator	6.2	8.4	19.8	40.3
Washing machine	3.0	0.6	15.9	40.0
Vacuum	5.1	1.2	7.7	20.0

Source: *Olney 1998,* 413.

than being processed in separate batches. This meant that any interruption in the distribution of the final product would cause a steep increase in production costs. These firms then sought to gain control over their distribution channels in some cases by dealing directly with retailers. James B. Duke's marketing of cigarettes illustrates the point. In 1884, Duke installed two Bonsack cigarette-making machines in his factory. Each machine could turn out 120,000 cigarettes per day, compared with the 3,000 that a skilled worker could produce by hand. Duke's machines, working continuously, easily could have saturated the cigarette market that existed in 1884. To create and maintain the market for these cigarettes, and to ensure that his output moved steadily to the consumer, Duke built an extensive sales network that kept an eye on local advertising and worked closely with other departments in the firm to schedule the flow of cigarettes from machine to consumer.

The marketing departments of firms like Duke's helped to establish and maintain the brand name of the product, particularly by stressing better quality or unique services. For example, producers requiring controlled temperatures during shipment, such as the Chicago meatpackers Armour and Swift, wanted to be certain that consumers would identify their product as the one that reached the market at the right temperature. Others, such as John H. Patterson, founder of National Cash Register (NCR), needed to ensure that consumers knew that NCR provided adequate instruction in how the product worked, proper service, and credit. Manufacturers urged buyers to ask specifically for their brand. Brand names were the way the market protected consumers, far removed from producers, from inferior merchandise. They were an alternative market-generated substitute to consumer protection legislation.

Retailing

At the same time that manufacturers were becoming bigger and more engaged in direct distribution, retailing was also undergoing a revolution. As cities became bigger and more congested, the convenience of being able to shop for all personal necessities in a single store had an increasing appeal. The response was the department store. At first, department stores bought merchandise through wholesalers. However, larger stores such as Macy's in New York, John Wanamaker's in Philadelphia, and Marshall Field's in Chicago took advantage of their growing size to obtain price reductions by going directly to manufacturers or their selling agents. Because of the size of their operations, large stores with numerous clerks had to set one price for all customers, and the old practice of haggling with merchants over the price of an article was soon a thing of the past. So successful was the department store concept that, by 1920, even small cities could usually boast one.

Smaller, specialized retail outlets, operating on their own lacked the buying power to match the department stores. But high sales volumes could be obtained by combining many spatially separate outlets in "chains" with a centralized buying and administrative authority. Current examples include Barnes & Noble, Home Depot, and Wal-Mart. One

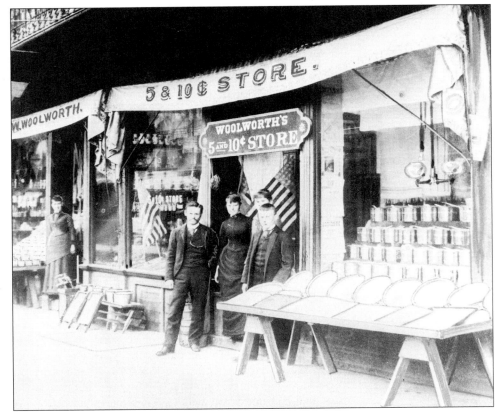

F. W. Woolworth—a pioneer in chain-store merchandising—opened his first store in 1879 in Lancaster, Pennsylvania. At today's prices, it would be a one and two dollar store.

of the early chains, still with us today, was the Great Atlantic and Pacific Tea Company, founded in 1859. From an original line restricted to tea and coffee, the company expanded in the 1870s to include a general line of groceries. In 1879, F. W. Woolworth began the venture that was to make him a multimillionaire when he opened variety stores carrying articles that sold for no more than a dime. By 1900, tobacco stores and drugstores were often organized in chains, and hardware stores and restaurants soon began to fall under centralized managements. By 1920, grocery, drug, and variety chains were firmly established as a part of the American retail scene. A few companies then numbered their units in the thousands, but the great growth of the chains was to come in the 1920s and 1930s—along with innovations in physical layout and the aggressive selling practices that would incur the wrath of the independents.

Although e-commerce has produced a tremendous resurgence of ordering goods by mail in the United States, it is probably difficult for the modern urban resident to imagine the thrill that "ordering by mail" once gave Americans. Indeed, for many American families in the decades before World War I, the annual arrival of a catalog from Montgomery Ward or Sears, Roebuck and Company was an event awaited with great anticipation. Although Montgomery Ward started his business with the intention of selling only to Grangers, he soon included other farmers and many city dwellers among his customers. Both Montgomery Ward and Sears, Roebuck experienced their great growth periods after they moved to Chicago—a vantage point from which they could sell, with optimum economies of shipping costs and time, to eager Midwestern farmers and to both coasts as well. Rural free delivery (1896) and the establishment of a parcel post system (1913) were godsends to mail-order houses. By 1920, however, towns were readily accessible to farmers, who could now make their own purchases. If the mail-order houses were to remain important merchandisers, they would have to modify their selling methods.

PRODUCT DIFFERENTIATION AND ADVERTISING

Merchants had advertised long before the Civil War, but as long as durable and semidurable goods were either made to order for the wealthy or turned out carelessly for the undiscriminating poor, and as long as food staples were sold out of bulk containers, the field of the advertiser was limited. In fact, the first attempts at advertising on more than a local level were directed largely toward retailers rather than consumers. Notable exceptions were patent medicine manufacturers, the first sellers in America to advertise on a national scale.[1]

After the Civil War, advertising on a national scale finally became a widely accepted practice. With the trusts, came truly national firms whose brand names and trademarks became impressed on the minds of consumers. Economic Insight 20.1 on page 365 discusses monopolistic competition resulting from the growth of brand names, advertising, and product differentiating. Wherever products such as tobacco, whiskey, kerosene, or shoes could be differentiated in terms of buyer thinking, the trusts attempted institutional advertising that was designed to reassure householders about the quality of the goods being purveyed. As the quality of nondurables improved, particularly in the case of clothing, manufacturers of leather shoes, hosiery, underwear, and men's suits and

---

[1]There is a strong suspicion that the popularity of patent medicines resulted in good part from their high alcohol content. Many customers may not have realized that the immediate sense of well-being derived from such medicines arose from alcohol instead of from other "beneficial ingredients." Others may have understood perfectly well, but thought that they could avoid the censure that went with drinking alcoholic beverages.

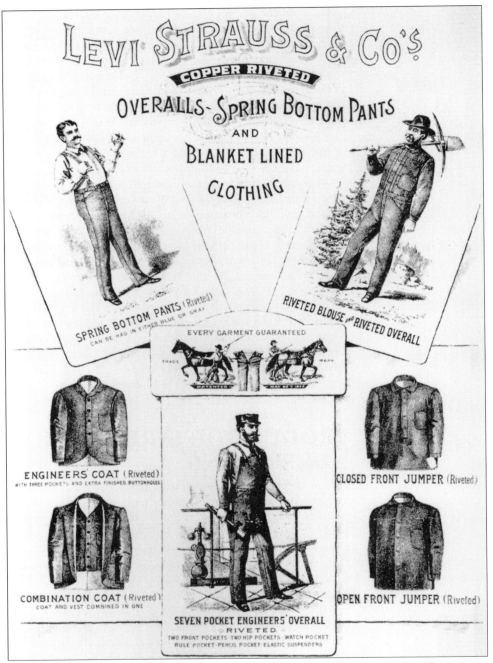

Measurements of American male sizes for Civil War uniforms marked the beginning of standardized clothing, and U.S. manufacturers of boots and shoes steadily improved the quality and fit of their product. Economies resulting from mass-production techniques drove down the cost of clothing, and mail-order solicitation helped to broaden markets.

overcoats found that a loyal, nationwide following could be won through brand-name advertising. By 1920, advertising was a billion-dollar industry. In some fields, the increasing size of a firm was an important factor in the growth of its national advertising, but advertising itself helped many firms to attain these large sizes.

ECONOMIC INSIGHT 20.1

MONOPOLISTIC COMPETITION

The growth of brand names, advertising, and product differentiation led economists to develop a new theory: monopolistic competition. In 1933, two books were published describing the new theory, Edward Chamberlin's *The Theory of Monopolistic Competition: A Re-orientation of the Theory of Value* and Joan Robinson's *Economics of Imperfect Competition*. The figure illustrates the famous "Chamberlinian tangency solution." The demand curve facing the firm (*dd*) is downward sloping, showing that the firm has some monopoly power. Even if it raises its price, it will not lose all of its customers because it produces a differentiated product. Some customers will remain loyal, for example, to Levi Strauss's overalls or Dr. C. V. Girard's ginger brandy even when the prices of these products are raised relative to alternatives. These firms will not be able to earn extraordinary profits for long. New entrants to the industry will capture some of the market, reducing demand, and force the existing firms into more advertising, raising costs. The long-run equilibrium price will be at *p*. Price will be equal to average cost, which includes only a normal profit.

There is, in one sense, excess capacity in a monopolistically competitive industry. If product differentiation could be eliminated, say, by prohibiting advertising and requiring firms to produce a simple, standardized product, the resulting competitive price would be lower, approximately at *p** (only approximately because cost curves would be affected as well as demand). There would be fewer firms in the industry, each producing more output. Critics of the theory of monopolistic competition have pointed out, however, that variety may be of real value to consumers. Although it is easy to make fun of Dewdrop Bitters, Levi Strauss's riveted overalls are another matter.

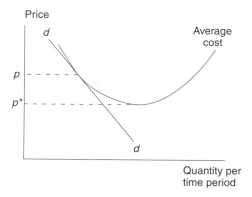

It became a well-accepted fact that a firm had to advertise to maintain its share of an industry's sales. It was also realized that as competing firms carried on extensive campaigns, the demand for a product might increase throughout the entire industry. Yet only a beginning had been made. Two changes were to loom large in the future of American advertising. One was the radio, which within a decade was to do the job of advertising far more effectively than it had ever been done before. The second was the change in the kind of consumer durables people bought. In 1869, half the output of consumer durables consisted of furniture and house furnishings; 30 years later, the same categories still accounted for somewhat more than half of the total. But after 1910, as first the automobile and then electrical appliances revolutionized American life, the share of furniture and household furnishings in the output of consumer durables declined rapidly. Household furnishings could not be differentiated in people's minds with any remarkable degree of success, although efforts were continually made to do so. On the other hand, automobiles and household appliances could be readily differentiated, presenting a wonderful challenge to the American advertising account executive.

THE FIRST STEPS TOWARD CONSUMER PROTECTION

The Pure Food and Drug Act and Meat Inspection Act, both passed on June 30, 1906, were dramatic interventions by the federal government into the economy to ensure quality standards of products for unwary customers. In 1906, Upton Sinclair's novel *The Jungle* was published and received the personal attention of President Theodore Roosevelt. Sinclair's descriptions of unsanitary production facilities for meat and his allegations of occasional processing of diseased animals stirred up sensational media and public reactions. Sinclair's book was timely, coming on the heels of the 1898 "embalmed beef" scandal, an event of the Spanish-American War in which adulterated beef was allegedly provided to the army.

The Pure Food and Drug Act was initially trivial in effect, calling simply for federal regulation of the content and labeling of certain food and medicinal products. The sum of $174,180 was allocated to the Bureau of Chemistry for its enforcement. In contrast, the 1906 Meat Inspection Act increased the Bureau of Animal Husbandry's budget for inspection purposes from $0.8 million to $3 million.

The 1906 Meat Inspection Act was not new. It was an amendment to the Meat Inspection Act of 1891, which had been passed in response to allegations by small local

Advertising helped to expand the consumer demand for new products such as this all-purpose potion.

The famous Sears, Roebuck and Company catalog, and that of its rival, Montgomery Ward, brought access to an abundance of reasonably priced merchandise to every farmer's door.

butchers and their organizations that dressed meat sent to distant markets by refrigerated railroad cars was unwholesome (Libecap 1992). Chicago meatpacking companies such as Armour, Swift, Morris, and Hammond dominated the interstate dressed-beef trade. In 1890, their market shares of cattle slaughtered in Chicago were 27, 26, 24, and 12 percent, respectively. Because the new refrigeration technology dramatically lowered the costs of shipments (dressed beef was roughly one-third of the weight of whole beef), these companies vastly undercut local butchers' prices. To fight back, local butchers attempted to discredit refrigerated beef, claiming it was unwholesome.

As Libecap informed us, although these claims were unfounded, the big packers welcomed the governmental response. The large Chicago packers had private quality controls for dressed beef and a substantial stake in protecting their brand-name reputations. They welcomed federal inspection of beef in interstate markets, first because federal inspection augmented their own quality assurances, and gave each firm clear and accurate public information on the shipments of every other firm. This publicly provided inspection system allowed the firms to engage in pooling and market-sharing arrangements with excellent assurances that no firm could cheat on sale-share agreements. The 1891 Meat Inspection Act for interstate trade was similar to an 1890 act on meat for export. Both acts largely benefited the producers by reinforcing each firm's quality control standards for shipment to markets at home and abroad. Whether or not consumers benefited from the acts is unsubstantiated, but the grounds and precedents for consumer protection were established by these first inspection acts, ostensibly on the consumers' behalf.

FOREIGN TRADE

By 1900, the United States had become the leading manufacturing country in the world in terms of total production. Great Britain (the world's first industrial nation) was second, and Germany was third. By 1913, the U.S. lead had increased, and Britain had fallen to third. The United States forged to the front in iron and steel production, and Germany and the United States became leaders in the electrical, chemical, and machine tool industries. This does not mean that output had declined in Britain. To the contrary, British output continued to increase. In terms of industrial output per capita, Britain was still the leader in 1900 and was only slightly below the United States in 1913 when the United States took the lead. Although many people in Britain were concerned about a failure of British entrepreneurship, what had happened to Britain was mainly that two large nations, well endowed with natural resources and possessing economic systems conducive to growth, had expanded their output more rapidly. During this period, the network of international trade assumed a form that would continue for decades. The industrial countries—the United States, Germany, Great Britain, and later several others—exported manufactured and semimanufactured products. In exchange, the less-industrial nations sent an ever-swelling flow of foodstuffs and raw materials to support the growing industrial populations and feed the furnaces and fabricating plants of industry.

Rapid improvement in methods of communication and transportation was the key to this system. Several examples follow. The first successful transatlantic cable began operations in 1866, a railroad line spanned the American continent in 1869, the Suez Canal was opened in the same year, and dramatic productivity gains in ocean transportation occurred over the last half of the nineteenth century. An extremely important improvement was the development of railroads in various parts of the world, making possible a flood of cheap grain from Canada, Australia, Argentina, Russia, and the Danube valley, as well as from the midlands of the United States. In the late 1870s and early 1880s, refrigeration on vessels made possible the shipments of meats, then dairy products, and finally fruits. To these were added the products of the tropics: rice, coffee, cocoa, vegetable oils, and tapioca.

Changing Composition of Exports and Imports

Figure 20.1 on page 369 shows the changing composition of U.S. foreign trade between 1850 and 1900. This transition portrays the shift in U.S. comparative advantage internationally, away from agriculture and toward manufactures. On the export side, Figure 20.1 shows that the most striking change was the decline of raw materials (such as cotton) from three-fifths to one-fourth of the total. Crude foodstuffs, which had swelled from about 1 percent in 1850 to nearly one-quarter of all exports in the late 1870s (reflecting the piercing of the West by the railroad), declined to 17 percent by 1900 and continued to fall until 1915. Manufactured foodstuffs, which also had climbed to about 25 percent of the total, held fairly steady. As shown, another important trend was the rise of semimanufactures and finished manufactures. (By the period between 1915 and 1920, these would account for almost half the total value of exports.)

Opposite movements, although not as remarkable, can be seen on the import side. Crude materials rose from one-twelfth the value of imports in 1850 to one-third by 1900. The chief crude materials imported—those that were necessary to a great industrial structure but that could not be found in the United States—were rubber, tropical fibers, and metals such as nickel and tin. Crude foodstuffs showed uneven ups and downs but did not change materially over the half-century as Americans imported coffee, tropical fruits, and olive and coconut oils, which could be produced domestically only at great cost, if at all. Imports of semimanufactures increased somewhat, but finished manufactures declined greatly in importance as American productive capacity grew.

Trade linkages altered as well. American exports to Europe began to decline relatively about 1885. During the 1870s and 1880s, Europeans were the recipients of more than four-fifths of all U.S. exports; by 1920, this share had dropped to three-fifths. In the

FIGURE 20.1
Composition of U.S. Foreign Trade, 1850 and 1900

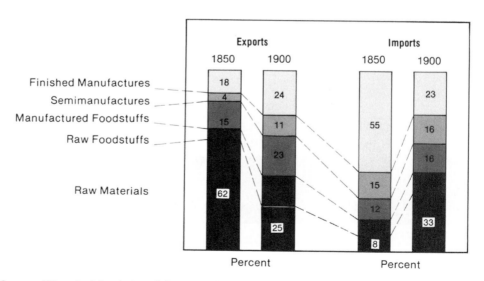

Source: Historical Statistics of the United States, Earliest Times to the Present, *2006, Table Ee446-457.*

meantime, the United States remained Europe's best customer. The sharp decline in the proportion of American imports from Europe between 1915 and 1920, a result of wartime disruption, however, permanently injured this trade.

In the first 20 years of the twentieth century, Americans found new customers in Asia and Canada, and their interest in the Latin American market was just beginning. On the import side, the Asian countries and Canada were furnishing a great part of the crude materials that were becoming typical U.S. imports. South America had already achieved a substantial position as a purveyor of coffee and certain key raw materials to the United States.

What was the source of the American preeminence in manufacturing achieved by 1900? As Gavin Wright's research has shown, America's preeminence resulted not so much from a relative abundance of capital or skilled labor or technological knowledge but from the relative abundance of nonreproducible natural resources. In 1913, the United States produced 65 percent of the world's petroleum, 56 percent of the copper, 39 percent of the coal, 37 percent of the zinc, 36 percent of the iron ore, and 34 percent of the lead, and the country was the world's leader in the production of each of these materials. It was the leader, or among the leaders, in the production of many other minerals (Wright 1990, 661). America's abundance of nonreproducible resources did not result from a series of lucky accidents of nature. The large and stable internal market for manufactures, combined with a flexible system for establishing property rights, promoted intensive exploration for and exploitation of natural resources.

It merits emphasis that this preeminence, founded in raw material abundance, did not lead to prosperity based on raw material dependence as it does in many oil-rich countries in the world today. The expansion of materials and institutions favoring many diverse production and distribution forms sustained growth even as national resources were being used up and dependence on oil and other raw material imports increased.

Changes in Balance of Trade

A good way to summarize the history of American foreign trade is to examine a series of international balance-of-payments statements. As Table 20.4 shows, Americans paid out a net total of $1.8 billion (columns 2 + 3) between 1850 and 1873. Residents of the United States could enjoy this net inflow of goods and services and pay interest and dividends on existing foreign investments largely because foreign nationals continued to make new investments in American businesses (column 4), especially in railroads. Another balancing item during this period was the $200 million in foreign currencies brought or sent to the United States and changed into dollars by immigrants and their families. Such payments are called *unilateral transfers* (column 5).

TABLE 20.4 UNITED STATES INTERNATIONAL PAYMENTS, BY PERIODS (IN BILLIONS OF DOLLARS)

(1) PERIOD	(2) NET GOODS AND SERVICES	(3) NET INCOME ON INVESTMENT	(4) NET CAPITAL TRANSACTIONS	(5) UNILATERAL TRANSFERS	(6) CHANGES IN MONETARY GOLD STOCK
1850–1873	–0.8	–1.0	1.6	0.2	–0.0
1874–1895	1.7	–2.2	1.5	–0.6	0.4
1896–1914	6.8	–1.6	–0.7	–2.6	–1.9

Notes: A minus sign indicates an addition to the U.S. monetary gold stock. Changes in the monetary gold stock includes errors and omissions.

Source: Historical Statistics, Colonial Times to 1970, *1975, 865–869.*

From 1874 to 1895, American agricultural commodities were available to the world market in rapidly increasing quantities. When we consider that the manufacturing industries of the United States were also becoming progressively more efficient, reflecting America's growing comparative advantage in the production of goods dependent on mineral resources, it is hardly surprising to find that exports increased as they did. During these years, the favorable trade balance was reduced by the growing tendency of Americans to use the services of foreigners. Even so, Americans had net credits on current account of $1.7 billion (column 2), and foreign investors poured another $1.5 billion into this country (column 4). Offsetting the credits were more than $2 billion in interest and dividend payments to foreigners, and on balance, unilateral transfers began to reverse themselves as immigrants sent substantial sums back to friends and relatives in their countries of origin. To make up the balance, the United States imported $400 million in gold (column 6).

During the prosperous years of 1896 to 1914, the United States came into its own as an economic power. The trade surplus shot up to more than $9 billion, although this figure was cut to less than $7 billion by purchases of services from foreigners. This surplus was offset by interest and dividend payments to foreign investors, remittances of immigrants to their families, foreign investments, and an inflow of gold. The reversal in the international capital flows, though small compared with domestic investment in the United States, nevertheless had considerable symbolic value. The United States had become a lender rather than a borrower, a sign of economic maturity.

THE ACCEPTANCE OF PROTECTIONIST DOCTRINES

The United States, which had long been protectionist (imposing high tariffs on imported goods to protect American industry), as had most of Europe but not Great Britain, became more so beginning with the Civil War. Setting up ever-higher tariff walls, Americans sought to control trade with other countries in the interests of national policy.

Figure 20.2 traces a 100-year history of tariffs, or customs duties, as a percentage of the value of (1) total imports and (2) dutiable imports (some imports were not taxed). In 1861, maximum U.S. tariffs were not more than 24 percent and averaged less than

FIGURE 20.2

Customs Duties as a Percentage of (1) Total Imports and (2) Dutiable Imports, 1821–1920

Tariffs slid steadily until the Civil War; then the new politics produced a sharp increase and new level that was maintained until the turn of the century.

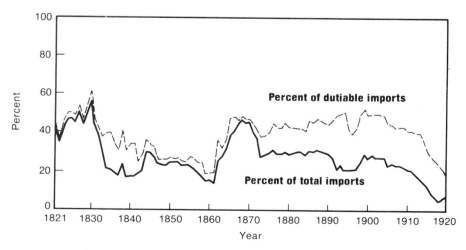

Source: Historical Statistics, Colonial Times to 1970, *1975, 888.*

20 percent on dutiable commodities. The national prosperity of the last 15 years before the Civil War seemed to refute protectionists' argument that a healthy economy required high duties. Yet by 1864, the trend of nearly three decades was reversed sharply to put the United States on a high protective-tariff basis for nearly three-quarters of a century. There was no widespread demand for such a change in policy; only in the manufacturing centers were the old arguments for protection advanced with enthusiasm. To win the votes of the industrial East, the Republicans advocated higher tariffs during the campaign of 1860. After the returns were in but before Lincoln's inauguration, Congress passed the Morrill Act of 1861, the first in a long series of laws levying ever-higher taxes on imports. Thus, Congress took the first step before the war but after the southern opponents of the tariff had left the Congress. The requirements of Civil War financing, at a time when import duties and domestic excises furnished the principal revenues, provided another reason for raising tariffs to unprecedented highs. By 1865, the average level of duties was 48 percent, and protection was granted to nearly any commodity for which it was requested.

For 25 years after the war, a few leaders in both political parties attempted to reduce the "war tariffs." In 1872, to ward off drastic downward reductions that appeared imminent, protectionist forces in Washington agreed to a flat 10 percent decrease in all protective duties. In 1875, however, the earlier levels were restored, and it appeared for a time that consumers and the electorate were resigned to permanently high import rates. Yet people were increasingly persuaded that protective tariffs were, in effect, a tax that raised consumer-goods prices—and there was a growing suspicion that high levels of protection fostered the rapid growth of business combinations. During his first administration, President Grover Cleveland placed the Democrats squarely on the side of greater freedom of trade, but two Democratic assaults on the protective system produced disappointingly modest results. Cleveland's defeat in 1888 blasted hopes of genuine reform. The McKinley tariff of 1890 raised the average level of protection to 50 percent of the value of the goods when they first reached American shores, increased the number of articles on the dutiable list, and reaffirmed the Republican commitment to the support of high tariffs. Following insignificant reductions during Cleveland's second term (1893–1897), the Dingley Act of 1897 raised duties above 50 percent. More goods, by value, were then taxed as imports than were admitted free. As might be expected, free goods were mostly raw and semifinished commodities requiring further processing, but even some farm products, raw wool, and hides were placed in a protected category.

The prosperity between 1897 and 1914 made it easy to defend high tariffs. Protectionists argued that the country was experiencing a high level of employment and economic activity *because* tariffs were high. Yet by 1900, American industry had obviously come of age. American manufacturers were competing in the markets of Europe; it was apparent, especially in the metal-processing industries, that most American firms needed no protection. The textile industries, which had enjoyed the benefits of high tariffs for a century, paid the lowest wages, had the highest unemployment, and suffered from the rigors of competition more than any other class of producers. Moreover, it was readily demonstrable by this time that import duties usually raised the prices of protected articles to consumers. As the populace felt the pressures of rising living costs in the first decade of the century, voters blamed the tariffs, and Democratic politicians exploited this political unrest. When the Payne-Aldrich bill of 1909 failed to bring any relief from high tariffs, widespread political protest resulted.

In the campaign of 1912, the Democrats promised a downward revision of import duties, which was carried out in the Underwood-Simmons Bill of 1913. It placed iron and steel on the free list, and sharply reduced duties on cost-of-living items such as cotton and woolen textiles. The result was a simplified tariff structure, still of protective significance, with average duties about half of what they had been for several decades. During President Woodrow Wilson's administration, the average level of the tariffs was slightly below 25 percent—almost the level that had prevailed just before 1860.

Economists have long wrestled with the idea that protection may be beneficial in the case of an "infant" industry. When a firm is first starting out, its productivity will be low because workers and managers do not have much on-the-job training, and the firm may not be able to survive competition from experienced foreign firms. Tariff protection will buy the domestic firm time to mature. Eventually, tariff protection can be removed. In the long run, the gains to the consumer from having a vigorous domestic producer may offset the short-term costs of protection. In recent years, this argument has been extended by a number economists working in the field of strategic trade theory (Helpman and Krugman 1989).

One potential problem with the infant-industry argument, and similar arguments calling for tariffs during the early phase of an industry's development (revealed in the long history of tariff protection after the Civil War), is that the "infants" may never grow up. As Bennett Baack and Edward Ray (1983) have shown, the structure of tariffs and subsequent levels of protection throughout the late nineteenth century were explained largely by the profit motives of established special interest groups rather than by a scientific determination of which infants needed protection based on costs and benefits to the economy as a whole.

Although we are justified in criticizing tariff protection for established industries, we should not exaggerate the costs to the American people. In many protected industries, vigorous domestic competition was a close substitute for foreign competition. At the turn of the century, imports were a little over 6 percent of GNP. The total loss to the United States from tariffs at the turn of the century was probably in the neighborhood of one half of one percent (Irwin 2007a). We should note, however, that while the overall loss was small, the gains and losses for particular industries' interest groups resulting from changes in the tariff could be large (Irwin 2007b).

THE INCOME TAX

Opposition to the tariff was strong, particularly in the South and West. But if tariffs were cut, where would federal revenues come from? The answer, according to the Populists and Progressives, was from an income tax. The income tax was not a new idea. Income taxes had been used sporadically before the Civil War at the state level and sometimes proposed for the federal level. The Civil War income tax, a federal tax, had been a successful moneymaker. It was allowed to lapse in 1872. In 1894, however, Congress passed income tax legislation, only to have it declared unconstitutional in 1895. Overcoming the Supreme Court decision would require an amendment to the Constitution, which became possible because support for the income tax continued to grow.

Two categories of spending proved extremely popular and increased support for a tax to fund them: more generous army pensions and increased military spending, particularly on the navy. Support for the naval buildup in turn is explained by the growing role of the United States in the world competition for colonies (which we will discuss below) and for naval supremacy. By 1907, when President Theodore Roosevelt sent the Great White Fleet of the United States around the world, the U.S. fleet, measured in battleship strength, was already second only to Britain's. Some states, moreover, that had opposed the income tax earlier saw that they would benefit from expenditures for naval construction.

In 1909, Congress passed an amendment to the Constitution providing for an income tax; it was ratified in 1913. The income tax, as Baack and Ray (1985) concluded in their classic study, did not cause the great expansion of government spending that occurred later in the century, but it did make it possible.

THE UNITED STATES IN AN IMPERIALIST WORLD

In the early 1880s, western Europeans, although never shy about extending their control over other peoples, became obsessed with a desire to own more of the earth's surface (Lebergott 1980). Africa's interior, which before 1875 had been almost entirely unexplored and unmapped by Europeans, was partitioned among the major European powers, with only Liberia and Ethiopia remaining independent. In Asia, the French took over all of Indochina, Britain added Burma to British India, and Britain extended its hold over the Malay states. Although it avoided physical disintegration, China nevertheless had to make humiliating economic concessions to the major European powers. By the end of the nineteenth century, not much of the world was left to colonize.

A detailed study by Lance Davis and Robert Huttenback (1988) has shown that the costs of the British Empire to the British people outweighed the economic benefits, although some citizens and enterprises benefited. Nevertheless, a combination of special interests, fears of other European powers, and exaggerated claims about potential economic gains kept the competition for colonies going full tilt.

Through most of the nineteenth century, the United States remained somewhat apart from the race to acquire colonies in other parts of the world. Before the Civil War, southern politicians had looked to Central and South America for colonies that might be incorporated as slaveholding areas within the United States, but these efforts came to naught. Americans concentrated on westward expansion in North America, wresting control when necessary from the European powers and from Native Americans. The U.S. war with Mexico (1846–1848) added valuable new territories, above all California. It was imperialism, to be sure, but not what Americans of the late nineteenth century had in mind when they debated the merits of an empire. The only major territory acquired before 1898 that did not border on the United States was Alaska (1867), which was presumed at the time to be almost worthless. In 1893, agitation to annex Hawaii began, but many Americans balked at the high-handed methods used to depose the existing Hawaiian government, and the islands were not finally annexed until 1898. A new phase of American imperialism, however, began with the Spanish-American War (1898).

American sympathy for the Cuban revolutionaries trying to win independence from Spain rose in the late 1890s, fueled in part by dramatic accounts of brutal Spanish attempts to suppress the revolution in the Hearst and Pulitzer newspapers. However, there was also considerable opposition to going to war, especially in the business and financial communities. J. P. Morgan and other business leaders were worried about the value of Spanish securities held by American banks and the value of American investments in the Cuban sugar industry. Perhaps most of all, they were worried that the war would be inflationary—the inflation of the Civil War was a personal memory for many business people—and that inflation would undermine America's commitment to the gold standard. All this changed, however, when a martial spirit was whipped up by the destruction of the U.S. battleship *Maine* in Havana Harbor on February 15, 1898. The quick and favorable outcome of the "splendid little war" (as Secretary of State John Hay described it to Theodore Roosevelt) that followed forced Americans to make decisions regarding expansion outside their continental borders.

© WILLIAM DINWIDDIE/HULTON ARCHIVE/GETTY IMAGES

American soldiers on the march in the Philippines. The war to annex the Philippines and "plant an American flag 500 miles from China" bitterly divided the American people.

The first decisions concerned disposition of the former Spanish colonies of Cuba, Puerto Rico, and the Philippines. Cuba was given nominal independence, and Puerto Rico received territorial status, but the Platt Amendment of 1901 so restricted Cuban independence that Cuba, in effect, became a protectorate of the United States. Instead of granting independence to the Philippines, the United States claimed that country as a colonial possession. Once American forces had entered the Philippines, the caution of the business community had evaporated: It was important to America's economic interests to maintain an "open door" in China and to have an American flag "only 500 miles from China." At first, the Philippine–American War (1899–1902) went well for the United States; Manila and the insurgent's capital at Malagos were captured quickly. But when the insurgents turned to guerilla warfare, the days of quick American victories ended. Ultimately, resistance was crushed after a series of long and often brutal campaigns.

With these islands in the Pacific and a growing interest in trade with the Orient, the United States insisted on economic opportunities in East Asia equal to those of the European powers. In the Western Hemisphere, the United States in 1903 acquired a perpetual lease of the Panama Canal Zone from the newly independent Republic of Panama, and the completion of the canal in 1914 ensured a lasting American interest in the Caribbean and Central America.

The policy known as the "Roosevelt Corollary" (to the Monroe Doctrine) was enunciated by President Theodore Roosevelt in a message to Congress in 1904. According to Roosevelt, the United States might be forced to exercise police power in "flagrant cases of wrongdoing or impotence" by countries in Latin America. Otherwise, the Europeans might intervene, and that could not be tolerated under the Monroe Doctrine. Europeans were not disturbed by such an assumption of international police power, but Latin Americans were—and they had reason to be—apprehensive.

The United States did not wait long to apply the Roosevelt Corollary. When the Dominican Republic could not meet its financial obligations, certain European states threatened to collect payments by force. Roosevelt's new doctrine required American intervention to forestall such moves. A treaty was signed in 1905 between the United States and the Republic, giving the United States authority to collect customs duties, of which 55 percent was to be paid to foreign creditors. In 1916, the Dominican government tried to escape American domination, and U.S. marines were sent in to quell the rebellion. In 1914, Haiti was made a protectorate of the United States, again with the aid of the marines. American forces landed so often in Nicaragua that the succession of episodes became a standing joke.

After the 1910 Mexican Revolution against the country's dictator, Porfirio Diaz, American and other foreign investors, who were heavily committed in railroads and oil, pressed for intervention and the restoration of order. For a time, President Wilson encouraged Latin Americans by declining to invade Mexico. But "watchful waiting" could last just so long amid the cries of outrage at the destruction of American property, and U.S. politicians were unable to tolerate these repeated affronts to American honor.

FIGURE 20.3

Military Spending,
1895–1914

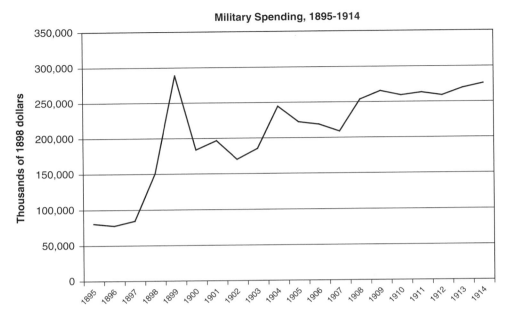

FIGURE 20.3

Military Spending, 1895–1914

Source: Historical Statistics of the United States, Earliest Times to the Present, *2006, series Ca13 and Ea 638-40.*

Troops crossed onto Mexican soil in 1914 and 1917—the second time, under the leadership of General John "Black Jack" Pershing—to seize the "bandit" Pancho Villa. With the adoption of the Mexican constitution in 1917, the turmoil subsided temporarily, only to begin again in the early 1920s.

Figure 20.3 shows American military spending (adjusted for inflation) from 1895 to 1914. The impact of the Spanish-American War, the Philippine-American war, and the Roosevelt Corollary are clearly visible. Spending ratchets upward with the Spanish-American War, but never falls back to what it was before.

Economic motives were invoked to justify America's imperialist adventures. America sought foreign colonies, some have said, to provide an outlet for American capital and a cheap source of raw materials. Little evidence, however, backs up such explanations. Only a small fraction of U.S. foreign investment went to areas under U.S. political control, and only a small fraction of raw materials imported from the rest of the world came from these areas (Zevin 1972; Lebergott 1980). A more satisfying economic explanation could be based on the role of special interests anxious to collect debts or protect particular interests. As Robert Zevin (1972) has argued, one of those special interests may well have been the military itself. Far-flung wars and colonies created opportunities to move up the ladder of command.

Clearly, however, noneconomic motives were also important in U.S. imperialism. Theodore Roosevelt, Senator Henry Cabot Lodge, and other supporters of American imperialism believed that the United States had to play a role in the "great game" of international power politics, and that to do so, the United States needed overseas bases and colonies, especially coaling stations for its fleets. Many Americans, however, remained unconvinced. The years from 1898 to 1918 were marked by an uncomfortable conviction that euphemisms such as "manifest destiny" and "extending the areas of freedom" could not long cover up the high-handed methods used to acquire America's growing empire. Nor would it be possible to maintain approval for a diplomacy that was devoted largely to promoting or protecting private financial or commercial interests. Critics of imperialism contended that investors seeking profits in the countries of Central America and the Caribbean should be willing to take the risks of venturing under unstable governments. Recall Economic Reasoning Proposition 4, laws and rules matter—that is, the "rules of the game" influence choices (see page 8).

The economic consequences of America's imperialistic ventures were relatively small, but the diplomatic consequences were important. These adventures forced the United States to turn its attention outside itself and increase its military strength. Offsetting these gains were the fears and hatreds built up among natural allies in central and South America, with whose aspirations Americans should have sympathized. It would take a new generation of Americans and a second world war to remove part of this emotional conflict. Even so, the harm of two decades of harsh diplomacy could not be easily undone.

SELECTED REFERENCES AND SUGGESTED READINGS

Baack, Bennett D., and Edward John Ray. "The Political Economy of Tariff Policy: A Case Study of the United States." *Explorations in Economic History* 10 (1983): 73–93.

_____. "Special Interests and the Adoption of the Income Tax in the United States." *Journal of Economic History* 45 (1985): 607–625.

Chamberlin, Edward Hastings. *Monopolistic Competition: A Reorientation of the Theory of Value.* Cambridge: Harvard University Press, 1933.

Chandler, Alfred D., Jr. *The Visible Hand: The Managerial Revolution in America.* Cambridge, Mass.: Belknap Press of Harvard University Press, 1977.

Clark, V. S. *History of Manufacturers in the United States,* Vol. 1. New York: McGraw-Hill, 1929.

Davis, Lance, and Robert Huttenback. *Mammon and the Pursuit of Empire: The Economics of British Imperialism.* New York: Cambridge University Press, 1988.

Helpman, Elhanan, and Paul Krugman. *Trade Policy and Market Structure.* Cambridge, Mass.: MIT Press, 1989.

Historical Statistics, Colonial Times to 1970, bicentennial edition. U.S. Bureau of the Census. Washington, D.C.: Government Printing Office, 1975.

Historical Statistics of the United States: Earliest Times to the Present, millennial ed. Eds. Susan B. Carter … [et al.]. New York: Cambridge University Press, 2006.

Irwin, Douglas A. "Trade Restrictiveness and Deadweight Losses from U.S. Tariffs, 1859-1961." NBER Working Paper No. 13,450. National Bureau of Economic Research, September 2007a.

_____. "Tariff Incidence in America's Gilded Age." *Journal of Economic History* 67 (September 2007b): 582–607.

Lampard, Eric. "The History of Cities in the Economically Advanced Areas." *Economic Development and Cultural Change* 3 (January 1955): 119.

Lebergott, Stanley. "The Return to U.S. Imperialism, 1890–1929." *Journal of Economic History* 40 (1980): 229–252.

Libecap, Gary D. "The Rise of the Chicago Packers and the Origins of Meat Inspection and Antitrust." *Economic Inquiry* 30, no. 2 (April 1992): 242–262.

Livesay, Harold, and Glenn Porter. *Merchants and Manufacturers.* Baltimore, Md.: Johns Hopkins University Press, 1971.

Olney, Martha L. *Buy Now—Pay Later.* Chapel Hill: University of North Carolina Press, 1991.

_____. "When Your Word Is Not Enough: Race, Collateral, and Household Credit." *Journal of Economic History* 58, no. 2 (June 1998): 408–431.

Robinson, Joan. *The Economics of Imperfect Competition.* London: Macmillan and Co., Ltd., 1933.

Wright, Gavin. "The Origins of American Industrial Success, 1879–1940." *American Economic Review* 80 (1990): 651–668.

Zevin, Robert B. "An Interpretation of American Imperialism." *Journal of Economic History* 32 (March 1972): 316–370.

War, Depression, and War Again: 1914–1946

ECONOMIC AND HISTORICAL PERSPECTIVES *1914–1946*

1. Two world wars engulfed the industrial nations, producing enormous costs in terms of labor, capital, and human suffering. The United States emerged from each conflict with its domestic capital intact and with an enhanced position relative to that of its economic rivals.

2. A communist government came to power in Russia. The Soviet Union engaged in a long rivalry, first with Germany and then with the United States that dominated worldwide big-power politics for most of the century.

3. The stock market boom of the late 1920s was based on widespread expectations that a new age of continuous prosperity had dawned. The great crash of 1929 dashed those hopes and ushered in a severe economic contraction.

4. The Great Depression of the 1930s was a cataclysm of unparalleled magnitude. The banking system collapsed, farm prices fell, and industrial production plummeted. At the lowest point, in 1933, one worker in four was unemployed.

5. As a result of the depression, the federal government took a much larger role in the economic life of the nation. Regulation of the private sector and expenditures for social welfare increased. In 1929, federal spending amounted to 3 percent of the gross national product (GNP); in 1947, it amounted to 15 percent.

6. The nation's financial system was changed radically as a result of the depression. Deposit insurance was introduced, the payment of interest on deposits was prohibited, and the Securities and Exchange Commission was set up to regulate the stock market. The world's monetary system, moreover, was radically altered. The gold standard disappeared, and at the end of World War II, a new system was established in which the dollar was given the central role.

CHAPTER 21

World War I, 1914–1918

CHAPTER THEME

The United States entered World War I in April 1917. Although the United States was actively engaged for only 19 months, labor and capital were quickly mobilized on an impressive scale. The armed forces increased from 180,000 in 1916 to nearly 3 million in 1918. Scores of new agencies attempted to regulate prices, set priorities, and allocate resources. To pay for the war taxes were raised, the money supply was expanded, and billions of dollars worth of bonds were sold to the public. At the start of the war, the national debt was equal to 3 percent of gross domestic product (GDP); by the end of the war, the national debt was equal to 32 percent of GDP. When the war ended, most wartime controls were abandoned, and most wartime agencies were dismantled. Nevertheless, the war provided a precedent for the federal government's increased role in the economy that emerged in the 1930s; the lesson that many people drew from the war, that the government could play a powerful positive role in meeting a crisis, would be remembered when the nation faced the Great Depression.

THE ORIGINS OF THE WAR

By 1914, Europe's armed forces had been built up in a sustained arms race, and her nations had been linked together in military alliances. Nationalistic and imperialistic rivalries had combined to produce a dangerous state of affairs. In France, many still sought revenge for the territory and reparations that France had been forced to give Germany as a result of the Franco-Prussian War of 1870–1871. In Austria-Hungary, fear of the restive Slavic minorities had increased. In Britain, Germany's attempt to challenge British naval supremacy had produced heightened tensions. Germany in turn feared being surrounded by hostile military alliances. And this list of fears and conflicts could be greatly expanded.

Even on the eve of war, however, there was still considerable optimism that the peace would hold. Europe had experienced several decades without a major war, and in the meantime, industrialization and relatively free international trade had produced rapidly rising standards of living. A war that would destroy the fruits of this progress seemed irrational. Many people believed, moreover, that the rising international solidarity of the labor movement would undermine support for a war entered into by imperialistic capitalist powers. Although financial markets were retrenching, they gave no sign that a cataclysm lay ahead. The optimists were wrong.

The assassination of Austrian Archduke Ferdinand by a Serbian revolutionary on June 28, 1914, set off a chain reaction that soon engulfed Europe in the bloodiest war the world had yet seen. On one side were the Allies: Britain, France, Italy, and Russia, and several smaller nations. On the other side were the Central Powers: Germany, Austria-Hungary, and their associates. Many believed that the war would end quickly as the Franco-Prussian War had done. But on the western front, a German advance into France became bogged down in trench warfare, producing a stalemate that could not be broken even with the loss of incredible numbers of lives. By one conservative estimate, 10 million people died in the war and another 20 million were wounded (Chickering and Forster 2000, 6).

The first economic reaction in the United States was a financial panic. The stock market was closed for four months, an unprecedented event that has never been repeated (Silber 2007), and banks experienced considerable pressure as depositors tried to convert their money into gold. But the crisis soon passed. Under the Aldrich-Vreeland Act, adopted after the crisis of 1907, banks had been authorized to issue emergency currency as a temporary substitute for gold, and the issue of this currency put an end to the crisis. At one point, this currency amounted to nearly one-quarter of the currency in the hands of the public (Friedman and Schwartz 1963, 172). It soon became clear that the period of American neutrality (from 1914 until 1917) would be immensely profitable for American business. German imports from the United States fell to practically nothing because of the British naval blockade; but Britain, France, and other European countries began to purchase large amounts of food and munitions at ever-rising prices from the United States. A wide gap opened between America's soaring exports to Europe and America's declining imports. The Europeans paid for these exports by extinguishing holdings of American debt, by shipping gold, and by incurring new debts. When the war began, the United States was a debtor, the normal status for a developing country. When the war ended, the United States was a creditor that held much of the world's stock of monetary gold. Before the war, the world's financial center was London; after the war, it was New York.

With the fighting so far away and so bloody, sentiment in the United States initially favored keeping out of the war, but eventually many forces and events combined to push the United States toward active involvement on the side of the Allies. Partly it was the close cultural and linguistic ties between Britain and the United States. But the crucial factor in turning public opinion against Germany was Germany's use of submarine warfare. In 1915, after the sinking without warning of the British ship *Lusitania* (with the loss of 1,198 lives, including 124 Americans), President Woodrow Wilson sent a series of strongly worded warnings to Germany. For a time, Germany moderated its use of submarines. In early 1917, however, the Germans returned to a policy of unrestricted submarine warfare in a desperate gamble to starve Britain into submission before intervention by the United States could turn the tide.

America's involvement in the war would be brief but decisive. The United States declared war on April 17, 1917. The armistice with Germany was signed on November 11, 1918, 19 months later. American forces were instrumental in winning a number of important victories. These victories and the prospect of enormous American reinforcements and victories to come forced the Germans, exhausted by years of war and blockade, to negotiate. The Germans believed, however, that they had agreed to end the fighting based on assurances from President Wilson of a just peace. When the war ended, the Central Powers still controlled large amounts of Allied territory from France to Crimea.

THE UNITED STATES GOES TO WAR

A military draft was instituted in April 1917, with a system of deferments for skilled workers. The armed forces of the United States, as noted in the chapter introduction, increased from 179,000 in 1916 to nearly 3 million in 1918. Some 2 million served overseas in the American Expeditionary Force, and about three-quarters of them saw combat. Americans took part in bitter fighting, and 117,000 Americans died in military service, more than half from disease. The United States produced vast amounts of arms and weapons, including a new instrument of war, the airplane, and launched a great ship-building program.

The financial reflection of the military effort was a tremendous increase in spending by the federal government, from 1.5 percent of GNP in 1916 to 24.2 percent in 1918. American involvement began with the country operating at close to full employment: The unemployment rate in 1916 was 5.1 percent. (This was in marked contrast to World War II, which America entered with reserves of underutilized labor and capital.) Therefore, it was not possible to increase the production of weapons and other military supplies without reducing civilian investment and consumption.

Financing the War

Governments can obtain the resources needed to fight a war in many ways: (1) commandeering, including drafting soldiers, confiscating food and other raw materials, and appropriating living quarters for soldiers; (2) capturing resources from the enemy; (3) receiving voluntary contributions from citizens or allies; (4) selling existing assets such as land owned by the government; (5) taxing; (6) borrowing; and (7) printing money. The latter three methods—taxing, borrowing, and printing money—are often singled out as the three ways of *financing* wars. They are by far the main ways that the United States has acquired the money required to mobilize its resources for war.

In 1916, Congress levied an estate tax to help finance rearmament. Populist reformers who wanted to redistribute the wealth of the "Robber Barons" had long advocated this tax. But at the federal level it had been successfully resisted on the grounds that it was needed only in wartime. World War I was the first time it was imposed since the Spanish American War. After its passage in 1916, however, the estate tax became a permanent but small part of the federal revenue system.

On October 3, 1917, after considerable wrangling, Congress passed the War Revenue Act. This act increased corporate and personal income taxes (the rate in the top bracket was raised to 70 percent) and established excise, excess profits (for business), and luxury taxes. Table 21.1 shows the total financial cost of the war and how it was distributed among various sources of finance. Taxation was important, but borrowing was far more important, accounting for 61 percent of total financing.

Why did Congress prefer to borrow? One reason may be that borrowing concealed some of the costs of the war. When taxes are raised, it is altogether too clear who is doing what to whom. It could also be argued that the war was an investment—"to make the world safe for democracy," in President Wilson's phrase. Since future generations would benefit, why should the current generation bear all the burden of the war? Raising taxes high enough to finance all of the war, moreover, would have reduced work effort. It is better, many economists now believe, to use borrowing to "smooth" taxes over time.

TABLE 21.1 FINANCING WORLD WAR I, 1917–1919

	TOTAL (BILLIONS)	PERCENT
War expenditures	$31.0	100.0%
Taxes	7.6	24.5
Borrowing from the public	19.0	61.4
Creating new money	4.4	14.1

Note: Total wartime expenditures were calculated as the sum of federal government expenditures in 1917 through 1919 less three times average expenditures in 1916.

Source: Historical Statistics *1975, Series Y336 (expenditures), Y335 (taxes), X594 (U.S. government obligations held by commercial banks), and X800 (U.S. government obligations held by the Federal Reserve).*

Wilson's Secretary of the Treasury William Gibbs McAdoo studied the financing of the Civil War and concluded that Salmon Chase, the Treasury secretary, had erred in not linking the purchase of war bonds more closely to patriotism. McAdoo launched an aggressive program to market bonds in World War I, to "capitalize patriotism" (Kennedy 1980, 105). Huge bond rallies were held, and the crowds were exhorted to buy war bonds by celebrities such as Mary Pickford and Douglas Fairbanks. Charlie Chaplin made a film showing how the purchase of war bonds helped finance the war. How much all of this helped is open to question. Despite all the hoopla and the considerable, often vicious anti-German propaganda, the government found that it could not sell bonds that paid much below the going market rate (Kang and Rockoff 2006). Evidently, Economic Reasoning Proposition 3, incentives matter (see page 8), applies in war as well as in peace.

The government also relied on creating new money. In earlier wars, the mechanism had been simple. In the Revolutionary War, the government had printed Continental dollars, in the Civil War, greenbacks. Now the mechanism was more complicated. When the Federal Reserve bought bonds on the open market, it did so by creating deposits that had not existed before. When lodged in the banking system, those deposits became the basis for a further expansion of money and credit by the banks. All told, as Table 21.1 shows, the Federal Reserve and the commercial banking system acquired more than $4 billion worth of government bonds, about 14 percent of total war finance. Even this figure understates the effect of money creation to some extent because the banks made personal loans, secured by government bonds, to purchasers of bonds. Although this transaction appeared on the books of the bank as a personal loan, it was really the indirect purchase of a government bond by the banking system and indirectly the result of the expansion of the money supply.

The net result of financing part of the war by creating money was a substantial increase in the stock of money and the price level. As Table 21.2 shows, the stock of money about doubled between 1914 and 1920, as did the level of prices. Note, however, that prices did not rise in the exact proportion as money per unit of real output, as a naïve version of the quantity theory of money would predict. See Economic Insight 12.1 on page 203. Prices rose more rapidly than money per unit of output between 1915 and 1918, more slowly from 1918 to 1919, and then more rapidly from 1919 to 1920. This pattern can be given a fairly straightforward explanation. During the years of threatened and actual war, the fear of inflation encouraged people to spend their money. The end of the war created expectations of a return to price stability, which reduced inflation. Finally, an unexpected postwar boom rekindled economic activity and expectations of inflation.

TABLE 21.2 MONEY AND PRICES IN WORLD WAR I

YEAR	STOCK OF MONEY (US$ BILLIONS)	MONEY PER UNIT OF REAL NNP (1914 = 100)	PRICES IMPLICIT NNP DEFLATOR (1914 = 100)
1914	$16.39	100.0	100.0
1915	17.59	104.1	103.1
1916	20.85	105.2	116.5
1917	24.37	126.3	143.9
1918	26.73	126.1	165.5
1919	31.01	140.5	168.0
1920	34.80	166.0	191.7

Note: NNP = Net National Product.

Source: *Milton Friedman and Anna J. Schwartz, Monetary Trends in the United States and the United Kingdom (Chicago: University of Chicago Press, 1982), 123–124.*

Movie star Charlie Chaplin selling war bonds.

When the real value of the cash in your pocket goes down in value because the government acquires real resources and drives up prices, inflation occurs, and inflation is a tax on money. Inflation due to money creation has the attractive political property of being a hidden tax. The public will blame profiteers rather than monetary policy for the inflation. All of this does not mean that there is no justification for finance through money creation. If the government can tax houses, tobacco, and alcohol, why not money? It does suggest, however, that money creation is likely to be overused because policymakers will not be held accountable to the same degree as with more visible taxes.

REPLACEMENT OF THE MARKET WITH A COMMAND SYSTEM

During World War I (unlike the Civil War), attempts were made to direct the economy from the top. This effort arose from the ideological temper of the times. The battle between those who favored and those who opposed organizing the economy through the market was sharp just prior to the war, and there were strong antimarket factions in both the Democratic and Republican parties. There was also the example of Germany, which was widely perceived to be both powerful and organized along centralizing lines.

Perhaps the most daring departure from the tradition of laissez-faire was the nationaliza-tion of the nation's railroads. By the end of the war, Washington was bulging with agen-cies set up to cope with a vast array of economic problems, including a Capital Issues Committee designed to limit issues of securities by the private sector, a War Trade Board with powers over imports and exports, an Emergency Fleet Corporation and a War Ship-ping Board designed to produce ships and to control their use, and about 150 others. Existing agencies, moreover, were often given new powers. How did the control and command system actually work? Space permits us to consider in detail only a few of the more important agencies.

The War Industries Board

In March 1918, responding to the mounting criticism that the mobilization was lag-ging, Wilson reorganized the most ambitious of the war agencies, the War Industries Board, and placed at its head Bernard Baruch. Baruch was a successful Wall Street speculator, but a loyal Democrat. He went to work immediately, personally negotiating prices of key industrial raw materials. Other industrial prices were set by a separate Price-Fixing Committee within the War Industries Board. The Committee often used a system called "bulkline pricing." Under this system, firms reported their costs of pro-duction, and the committee then set a price that would bring forth the "bulk" (say, 80 percent) of the maximum possible output. This system was designed to balance the need for raw materials against the need for overall price stability while limiting the profits of low-cost producers. Baruch also set up a system of priorities to guide business in filling the mounting volume of war contracts. Each contract was given a government priority rating: AA, A, B, C, or D. If a conflict arose, a producer had to fill an AA order before an B order, and so on. It sounded good. But when firms were given their own power to set priorities on subcontracts to save administrative resources, markets soon became choked with high-priority contracts. The natural ten-dency was to give everything the highest priority. (In World War II, "priorities infla-tion" led to the abandonment of the system.)

Baruch's stint at the War Industries Board was brief—about eight months—but he drew strong conclusions from his experience. In subsequent years, he repeatedly argued that the example of the War Industries Board pointed the way toward cooperation be-tween business and industry in peacetime and centralized administration (doing away with the market) in wartime.

The Food and Fuel Administrations

In August 1917, Congress passed the Lever Food and Fuel Control Act, establishing a wartime Food Administration and a Fuel Administration. Herbert Hoover was appointed the food administrator. Hoover enjoyed a reputation as a brilliant administrator—he was then serving as the director of the Commission for the Relief of Belgium—and his repu-tation grew with his performance as food administrator. His job was to maintain an ad-equate supply of food to the domestic market and to our allies while preventing excessive increases in prices. The tools given to Hoover were limited, and his philosophy of gov-ernment—which emphasized voluntary cooperation—discouraged him from seeking greater authority. Direct control of prices, with penalties for violation, was generally avoided, as was formal rationing, except in the case of sugar. (Economic Insight 21.1 on page 387 discusses the economics of rationing.) But the food administrator was given the power to license food dealers. This license could be revoked if the dealer failed to go along with Food Administration price policies.

Bernard Mannes Baruch in a less trying moment. A successful Wall Street investor and speculator and strong supporter of the Democratic Party, Wilson named him to head the War Industries Board in 1918.

In place of formal rationing, Hoover called for voluntary conservation. "Meatless Mondays" and "Wheatless Wednesdays" were promoted as ways of reducing domestic demand and leaving more for exports. Hoover clearly believed that appeals to moral principles could influence behavior. Retailers, moreover, were encouraged (or permitted, depending on how you look at it) to sell wheat flour along with what were then considered less desirable substitutes such as rye or potato flour. The resulting mixture could be baked into a loaf of "Victory bread." Of course, this was really a hidden price increase. The true price of the wheat flour was the direct amount paid plus the difference between what the buyer paid for the less desirable substitute and what he would have paid voluntarily. By such half-measures, food prices were controlled and output rationed.

ECONOMIC INSIGHT 21.1

THE ROLE OF RATIONING

This figure illustrates the role of rationing. The government has fixed the price at *P*. But at this price, the quantity demanded exceeds the quantity supplied by *AB*. This reduces output (compared with letting the price rise to the free market equilibrium, *P**). Some consumers will be frustrated by empty shelves. Time may be wasted waiting in line. The scramble among consumers may lead to bribes and various forms of concealed price increases such as reductions in quality.

Instead, consumers can be issued ration tickets. With each purchase, a consumer must turn over a ration ticket along with the money price. The ration tickets in this case reduce the effective demand curve from *D1* to *D2*. Because the government in this example has guessed exactly right (issued neither too few nor too many tickets), no excess demand occurs, and the problems created by price controls are reduced. Formal rationing was used for sugar (after long waiting lines became intolerable), but in many cases, the government permitted "socially desirable" forms of hidden price increases, such as the tie-in sales intended to promote the baking of Victory bread described in the text. The result was to move the true price toward the free market equilibrium, *P**.

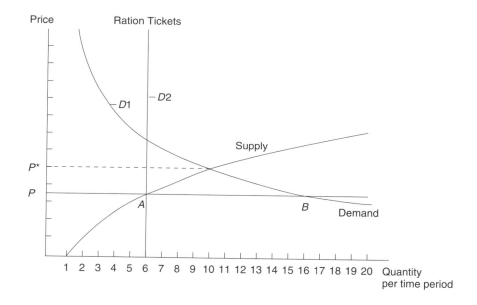

LABOR DURING THE WAR

The demand for labor was increased by government contracts and the supply of labor was reduced by the cutoff of immigration and by the drafting of men into the armed forces. By 1918, as Table 21.3 shows, real earnings were considerably above the level of 1914. Adjustments in the labor market, however, were far from smooth. In 1917 in particular, money incomes were up 14.5 percent over 1916, but consumer prices were up 16.1 percent—real wages had fallen. The situation was reminiscent of the Civil War. In the long run, we expect real wages to be determined by the productivity of labor, but in the short run, some wages may prove to be sticky and inflation or deflation can alter the real wage. It is not surprising, then, that 1917 was a year of strikes—4,450 of them, which was a record. Strikes were particularly acute west of the Mississippi, where a

The Food Administration used appeals to patriotism to relieve the pressure on the prices of commodities in short supply.

combination of low wages, harsh working conditions, uncompromising employers, and radical unions produced bitter labor disputes.

The Wilson administration's response was pragmatic. In a few cases, it threatened strikers through the draft and in other ways, but in most cases, it was more accommodating. War contracts generally included provisions calling for higher wages and better

TABLE 21.3 ANNUAL EARNINGS, 1914–1920

YEAR	MONEY EARNINGS OF ALL EMPLOYEES AFTER DEDUCTION FOR UNEMPLOYMENT	REAL EARNINGS OF ALL EMPLOYEES AFTER DEDUCTION FOR UNEMPLOYMENT (1914 DOLLARS)
1914	$ 555	$555
1915	547	541
1916	647	595
1917	748	586
1918	972	648
1919	1,117	648
1920	1,236	619

Source: Historical Statistics *1975, Series D723, D725.*

working conditions, though they did not provide the goal dearest to the heart of organized labor: the closed shop. When a strike of railroad workers threatened to disrupt the industry that was at the heart of the war effort, the administration nationalized the railroads. Under government control, the railroads provided improved working conditions and higher wages while raising shipping costs only modestly. The result was an operating deficit made up by the government. The railroads were finally returned to private ownership in 1920. According to Table 21.3, money earnings leaped upward in 1918 by some 22.6 percent, outrunning the cost of living. Although it is difficult to be certain about this because price controls distorted the meaning of price indexes, real earnings probably reached an all-time high.

Organized labor was extremely optimistic in the immediate postwar period. Labor union membership was up, as was the the public's view of the conservative wing of the labor movement under the leadership of Samuel Gompers. Gompers, the president of the American Federation of Labor, had served on Wilson's Council of National Defense during the war and had attended the Treaty of Versailles where he helped to organize the International Labour Organization. But the hopes of many labor leaders for a new era in labor relations soon came to an end. An industrial conference called by the president in 1919—with representatives from labor, management, and the public under Baruch's leadership—ended in failure. More important, an attempt to organize the steel industry, then the bellwether of American industry, was beaten back after a long and bitter strike.

Women were one potential source of labor tapped during the war. Some women served with the armed forces in Europe, usually as nurses or telephone operators. Women also made important contributions in industry, with about a million taking up war work. However, the war did not mean a breakthrough in the economic role of women. Few took jobs in heavy industry, and first-time hires were relatively few. Many married women who entered the labor force had been previously employed while single; they returned temporarily to help their families cope with war. When the war ended, the role of women in the labor force returned to what it had been before the war. Partly this was the result of pressure from labor unions and other sectors for women to make room for returning veterans; partly it was the result of older economic pressures. The labor force participation rates for married and single women were both a bit lower in 1920 than they had been in 1910. On the political front, the Wilson administration strongly supported the right of women to vote, calling their contributions "vital to the winning of the war." As a result, the Nineteenth Amendment to the Constitution, giving women the right to vote, was finally adopted in 1920.

Perhaps no group of workers seized the opportunities provided by the war more eagerly than African Americans. With factories operating at full capacity and deprived of a steady stream of immigrants from Europe, northern industry at last looked to African Americans for a supply of labor. Beginning in 1914, agents for northern industries fanned out across the South to recruit workers, who were often given free transportation north. There began a mass exodus of African American workers from the rural South: New York, Detroit, St. Louis, Cleveland, Chicago, and other industrial cities saw a steady stream of newcomers. In a few places in the South, the new shortage of labor actually led to improved race relations; but elsewhere, the South reacted in the old way, with harassment, detentions, and beatings. Some southerners also tried to prevent northern agents from recruiting black workers, but nothing could stem the tide: Northern industry provided higher wages, and northern cities a greater measure of freedom.

White workers, however, reacted negatively, sometimes violently, to the immigrants from the South. Competition between African American and white workers soon exploded in violent race riots: In East St. Louis in July 1917, nine whites and a larger but undetermined number of African Americans were killed; in Chicago in July 1919, 13 whites and 23 African Americans were killed. But the result was not always so negative. In Cincinnati, we know, thanks to the work of Warren Whateley (1990), that the employment of African Americans during the war led to permanent changes in employment practices—the war provided the chance for African Americans to, in Whateley's phrase, "get a foot in the door."

THE COSTS OF THE WAR

The major part of the war's cost was borne by the soldiers, sailors, and airmen, and their families. To some extent, we can think of these costs in economic terms. The draft can be thought of as a tax. The amount of the tax was the difference between what the government would have had to pay a soldier to get him to volunteer for military service and what it actually paid. When a soldier received a nonmortal wound (204,000) or died (117,000), there was a further loss: the discounted value of the lost future income (*Historical Statistics* 1975, Series Y879, Y880, Y882).

These losses, it was widely recognized, created an obligation of the United States to the veterans and their families. Partly, these obligations were made good through veterans' benefits paid after the war. The adequacy of compensation, however, was debated. The "fair" amount of compensation for death or dismemberment is hard enough to agree on, and the idea that war entails heavy psychological costs, shell shock, for example, was just gaining acceptance. There also were more subtle psychological effects, a disillusionment with American life and culture, for example, that sometimes affected the capacity of the veteran to earn a living. The writers who gave a voice to this disillusionment with war and traditional American values, including Ernest Hemingway, John Dos Passos, and F. Scott Fitzgerald, became known as the "Lost Generation."

Payments to veterans or their families do not change the loss of resources and output that the economy as a whole sustained. These payments merely redistribute the burden of the losses. All of these calculations and the inevitable debate about whether compensation was adequate should not be allowed to obscure the reality that, in the end, it is impossible to put dollar signs on all of the human costs, costs that were high for the United States and staggering for the European belligerents.

The most careful and detailed estimate of the cost of the war was made by John Maurice Clark (1931) in his classic book, *The Costs of the War to the American People*. Clark took into account many of the complications that one encounters in trying to measure the costs of a war. He made an adjustment, for example, to the wages of the men drafted into the army to account for their lower-than-market wages, and included money technically lent to the Allies but not expected to be repaid. Clark put the total cost at $31 billion. This was about 44 percent of average GDP during the war period (1917–1920). Today, a similar share of GDP would be about $6 trillion.

THE LEGACIES OF THE WAR

Demobilization followed the simplest possible path after the Armistice. Soldiers were mustered out of the army as fast as possible. War contracts were canceled. Government bureaus were closed. Despite the rapid demobilization, however, the economy never returned to what it had been before the war.

The Postwar Recession

The immediate effect of the Armistice was a slowdown in the economy. Prices remained roughly level for some months. Then, in 1919, a vigorous boom began, and prices began to rise rapidly. Monetary policy added to the boom. The Federal Reserve continued to follow a policy of keeping its discount rate (lending rate) below market rates. The Federal Reserve realized that this policy was adding to inflationary pressures: Banks were finding it profitable to borrow from the Federal Reserve and then expand their own lending. The Federal Reserve, however, was reluctant to raise its rates. One reason was that higher interest rates might have depressed the values of the large amount of government war loans in the market.

Finally, possibly because its own reserves of gold were becoming depleted, the Federal Reserve acted. In late 1919 and early 1920, the Federal Reserve raised its discount rate. The increase in January 1920 from 4.75 percent to 6 percent was the sharpest single increase in the short history of the system. On June 1, the discount rate was raised again, to 7 percent. These increases sent a strong signal to the market that credit would soon be tight. In addition, there were sharp breaks in other sectors of the economy. Agricultural prices, for example, fell throughout much of the world as European production recovered. As a result, the economy went into a severe recession. From 1920 to 1921, nominal net national product fell 18 percent, and real net national product fell 4 percent. But the recession was also brief: It resembled what has come to be called a "V-shaped" recession, straight down and straight back up again. One reason, perhaps, is that even though the number of bank failures rose substantially, there was no financial panic. (As we shall see, the sharp contraction in 1929–1930, which appeared at first to be a repeat of that in 1920–1921, produced a financial panic that drove the economy far deeper into depression.) After the economy recovered from the recession of 1920–1921, it entered a long period of economic expansion. So vigorous was this expansion that many people came to believe that a new age of continuous prosperity had arrived. The "roaring twenties" are the subject of the next chapter.

The Domestic Legacies

The war also left many domestic legacies, as shown by Robert Higgs in his book *Crisis and Leviathan* (1987, chapter 7). Some were financial, such as increased federal spending for interest on the national debt, veterans' benefits, and other longterm costs.

More important was the ideological legacy. Most Americans, it is true, were more than willing to return to the old ways of doing things after the war; a weariness with war had set in. President Warren Harding (1921–1923) captured this mood perfectly when, in his campaign for the presidency against democrat James M. Cox, Harding called for a "return to normalcy." Some war leaders, Bernard Baruch in particular, concluded that the economy would work better if the government played a larger role in coordinating economic activity than it had before the war. In retrospect, we can see that American involvement in the war was too brief to draw strong conclusions about the long-term effects of government interventions. But the glow of success that surrounded wartime government programs made them powerful examples in the debate over the appropriate role of government in the economy. The idea that an activist government could improve the functioning of the economy lay dormant during the prosperous twenties but would become important as the Great Depression took form. The New Deal's National Recovery Administration, for example, was modeled on Baruch's War Industries Board. The New Deal's Commodity Credit Corporation was modeled on the U.S. Grain Corporation, and controls exercised under the Agricultural Adjustment Acts, passed in the 1930s, were modeled on those exercised by the Food Administration. The complete list is much longer. Many of the individuals who were chosen to run New Deal programs, moreover, had worked for government agencies during the war. General Hugh S. Johnson, for example, who headed the National Recovery

Administration in 1933, had served under Baruch at the War Industries Board (Leuchtenburg 1966).

Reformers undoubtedly would have won many changes in the economy in the 1930s even if World War I had never occurred. But the perception in the 1930s that federal programs' control and regulation of markets had been a success in World War I increased the pace and depth of reform.

The International Legacies: The Treaty of Versailles

Some of the most important legacies of the war were in the international sphere. Shortly after the war ended, Wilson sailed for Europe to take part in the Paris peace conference that would negotiate the Treaty of Versailles to end the war. Ultimately, a treaty was hammered out by the Big Four: Britain, France, Italy, and the United States. The United States, however, never ratified the treaty. It was bottled up in the Senate, where Republicans insisted on changes to which Wilson would not agree. Under the treaty, Germany was forced to admit responsibility for the war, to transfer land and other resources to the allies, and to pay reparations that were later set at $56 billion in gold dollars.

John Maynard Keynes, who attended the conference as part of the British delegation, wrote a brilliant critique of the Treaty: *The Economic Consequences of the Peace* (1919), one of the most powerful tracts ever written by an economist and still well worth reading. Keynes argued that Allied demands for reparations went far beyond any that could be reasonably calculated on the basis of the understanding that had produced the Armistice. The treaty, in other words, was punitive and imposed excessive penalties on Germany and Austria. He argued, moreover, that Germany would never be able to make the reparation payments. To do so, Germany would have to run a persistent balance-of-payments surplus by decreasing its imports and increasing its exports. But Germany could not reduce its imports significantly, because they included necessities like food and fertilizer, and Germany could not increase its exports significantly, because its trading partners would erect tariff barriers to protect their domestic industries from competition. Keynes's argument started a long debate among economists over the "transfer problem" that still has not been resolved.

Keynes's argument was later answered in *The Carthaginian Peace: Or the Economic Consequences of Mr. Keynes*, a brilliant polemic by the French economist Etienne Mantoux (1946). Mantoux, who died in World War II, argued that Germany's ability to create a powerful military force in the 1930s proved that it had the capacity to make the required transfers if sufficient political will could be mustered. But few would argue today with Keynes's plea for a less punitive peace. The German belief that the peace was unjust contributed to what then seemed unthinkable—a second world war.

SELECTED REFERENCES AND SUGGESTED READINGS

Chickering, Roger, and Stig Forster. *Great War, Total War.* Cambridge: Cambridge University Press, 2000.

Clark, John Maurice. *The Costs of the War to the American People.* New Haven, Conn.: Yale University Press, 1931.

Friedman, Milton, and Anna J. Schwartz. *A Monetary History of the United States.* Princeton, N.J.: Princeton University Press, 1963.

_____. *Monetary Trends in the United States and the United Kingdom.* Chicago: University of Chicago Press, 1982.

Higgs, Robert. *Crisis and Leviathan: Critical Episodes in the Growth of American Government.* New York: Oxford University Press, 1987.

Historical Statistics. Washington, D.C.: Government Printing Office, 1975.

Kang, Sung Won, and Hugh Rockoff. "Capitalizing Patriotism: The Liberty Loans of World War I." NBER Working Paper 11919, National Bureau of Economic Research, 2006.

Kennedy, David M. *Over Here: The First World War and American Society.* Oxford, England: Oxford University Press, 1980.

Keynes, John Maynard. *The Economic Consequences of the Peace.* New York: Harcourt, Brace & World, 1919.

Leuchtenburg, William E. "The New Deal and the Analogue of War." In *Change and Continuity in Twentieth-Century America*, ed. John Braeman, Robert H. Bremner, and Everett Walters. New York: Harper & Row, 1966.

Mantoux, Etienne. *The Carthaginian Peace: Or the Economic Consequences of Mr. Keynes.* Oxford: Oxford University Press, 1946.

Silber, William L. *When Washington Shut Down Wall Street: The Great Financial Crisis of 1914 and the Origins of America's Monetary Supremacy.* Princeton: Princeton University Press, 2007.

Taussig, Frank W. "Price Fixing as Seen by a Price Fixer." *Quarterly Journal of Economics* 33 (1919): 205–241.

Whateley, Warren C. "Getting a Foot in the Door: Learning, State Dependence, and the Racial Integration of Firms." *Journal of Economic History* 50 (March 1990): 43–66.

CHAPTER 22

The Roaring Twenties

CHAPTER THEME

After World War I, the American public hoped for a "return to normalcy," as President Warren G. Harding put it. Wartime controls were removed, taxes were cut back, and the Republican administrations of the 1920s generally looked to market forces to produce economic growth. After a severe but brief recession in 1920 and 1921, the economy moved into a long expansion. A new American middle-class lifestyle emerged that relied on consumer durables, especially the automobile. The stock market surged, and the belief took hold that the economy had moved into a new era of continuous growth and prosperity that would eventually eliminate poverty. But the stock market crash in October 1929 and the fall into the depths of an unprecedented depression in the early 1930s made pessimists out of the most determined optimists.

A central question faced by economic historians is whether the disasters of the 1930s were the inevitable outcome of the prosperity of the 1920s and its reliance on a free market economy, or whether they were the result of shocks and policy mistakes in the 1930s. Was there, to put it somewhat dramatically, a fatal cancer growing in the economy of the 1920s that brought disaster ever closer, even as the economic physicians of the day continued to pronounce the patient in good health? Economic historians have suggested numerous problems carried over from the 1920s to the 1930s—changes in the distribution of income, the ongoing problems in agriculture, the stock market boom and bust, and so on. The vast research on this period shows, however, that the depression could have been prevented or at least ameliorated if the right policies had been followed in the early 1930s. The prestige of the market economy peaked with the stock market. In the depression, the nation turned from the free market model of 1920s to the central-planning model of the war years to restore prosperity and growth.

SOCIAL CHANGES IN THE AFTERMATH OF WAR

When World War I ended, a promising young songwriter named Harry Donaldson cast his lot with the just-organized Irving Berlin Music Company. His smash 1919 hit was at once a question and a prophetic answer: "How ya gonna keep 'em down on the farm after they've seen Paree?" How, indeed? Millions of young Americans had been wrested from the boredom of country life to serve in the war, marking the beginning of the end of an agrarian society. To be sure, only a fraction of them ever saw Paris, and some got no farther than Camp Funston. But country boy, small-town bookkeeper, and city mill-worker alike developed a taste for travel and adventure.

Lured by the availability of jobs, the excitement of city life, and advances in transportation, nearly 15 million people were added to the number of American urbanites between 1920 and 1930. Sometime near the end of World War I, the number of Americans living in urban centers of 2,500 people or more passed the 50 million mark. As the census of 1920 was to report, for the first time, more than 50 percent of the population, over 54 million people, were urban dwellers. Leading the migration to the city were southern African Americans, who had begun migrating northward in large numbers during the war. Especially magnetic to African Americans were New York City, Philadelphia, Washington, D.C., Chicago, St. Louis, and Los Angeles. By 1930, Harlem was the concentration point of nearly 300,000 African Americans. The term *Harlem Renaissance* refers to a remarkable flowering in literature and the arts, but its backbone was industrial jobs. This wave of migration was tied to the end of free immigration discussed later in the chapter. Unable to rely on a steady flow of unskilled and low-skilled immigrants from Europe, employers turned to immigrants from the South.

In a dreadful intrusion on the rights of the individual, a minority secured passage of the Eighteenth Amendment, prohibiting the manufacture, sale, or transport of "intoxicating liquors" and taking away a basic comfort of field hands, factory workers, and others, on the grounds that drinking was sinful and that poor people were not entitled to such a luxury anyway.[1] A swell of fear and hate was rising that would crest in the activities of the Ku Klux Klan, and by 1924, that organization's anti–African American, anti-Jewish, and anti–Roman Catholic persecutions had become a national scandal.

The future nevertheless held a bright promise of prosperity and more leisure time. Women had gained the right to vote, but their emancipation was broader than that. Young women in particular began to chisel away at the double standard of morality that had been typical of pre-1914 relations between the sexes; the "flapper" of the 1920s was already emerging in 1919 as the girl who could smoke men's cigarettes, drink men's whiskey, and play men's games. It might have been expected that these changes would be matched by changes in the workplace, especially among older married women (Goldin 1990, chapter 6). Increased education, a reduced birthrate, smaller families, the emergence of the clerical sector, and the demonstration effect of World War I all worked toward greater female participation in the labor force. Indeed, looking at the purely economic factors, one might have expected a rapid increase in the number of two-earner households of the sort that actually arrived in the 1980s. But this development was prevented by "marriage bars," policies followed by public and private employers that prohibited the hiring of married women and that forced female employees to leave when they married. In part, these bars simply reflected broader social norms maintaining that married women belonged at home with their children. They became more widespread in the 1920s with the growth of large firms that relied on personnel departments to make hiring and firing decisions and that preferred bureaucratic rules for making decisions to individualized hiring and firing.

NEW GOODS AND THE RISE OF THE MIDDLE CLASS

In the 1920s, the modern American standard of living became available to a broad segment of the middle class. Mass production, mass marketing, and spectacular advances in the production of consumer durables, electric power, new appliances, suburban housing, and city skyscrapers highlighted the decade.

---

[1]The authors confess their prejudice on this issue.

TABLE 22.1 PERCENTAGE OF AMERICAN FAMILIES OWNING VARIOUS APPLIANCES, 1920 AND 1930

	1920	1930
Inside flush toilets	20%	51%
Central heating	1	42
Home lighting with electricity	35	68
Mechanical refrigerators	—[a]	8
Washing machines	8	24
Vacuum cleaners	9	30
Radios	—[a]	40
Automobiles	26	60

[a]Less than 1 percent.

Source: *Lebergott 1976,* 248–299.

The extent of that revolution is indicated by the figures in Table 22.1, which were compiled by Stanley Lebergott (1976). At the beginning of the decade, only a little more than a third of American families lived in homes and apartments that were lit with electricity; by the end of the decade, only a little under a third lacked electric lighting. At the beginning of the decade, the automobile could still be regarded as a plaything of the wealthy; by the end of the decade, it had become a necessity for the middle class.

The Automobile

In many ways, the automobile was the economic symbol of the 1920s. Annual production rose from 1.5 million cars in 1921 to 4.8 million in 1929. By 1930, 60 percent of America's families owned an automobile (see Table 22.1).

One consequence of the automobile was the great construction boom of the 1920s. The automobile changed the location of residences, portending the heyday of suburbia. The automobile combined travel with entertainment and spotted the countryside with motels, hot dog stands, road signs, and gas stations. This remaking of the American landscape was largely unplanned and unregulated by government. As shown by Alexander Field (1992), it also left a residual of legal tangles that made recovery from the depression more difficult in the late 1930s.

The automobile also enlarged the demands on government for paved roads, as automobile clubs and especially farmers pressed for assistance to get out of the mud. With the passage of the Federal Aid Road Act of 1916, the development of a nationwide highway system began. Under the act, the government committed itself to spending $75 million to build rural post roads, with the money to be expended by the Department of Agriculture over a period of five years. The national contribution was not to exceed 50 percent of the total construction cost, exclusive of bridges and other major structures, and was conditional on the organization of state highway departments with adequate personnel and sufficient equipment to initiate the work and carry out subsequent maintenance. The Federal Highway Act of 1921 amended the original law by requiring the secretary of agriculture to give preference to states that had designated a system of highways to receive federal aid. The designated system was to constitute the "primary" roads of the state and was not to exceed 7 percent of the state's total highway mileage. Incidentally, in the Highway Act of 1921, Congress appropriated as much money for a single year's construction (1922) as it had for all of the preceding five years.

Henry Ford began mass production of the Model T in 1908; by 1916, he was producing 2,000 per day. In the 1920s, however, the Model T lost market share to more stylish, although more expensive, competitors. Production of the Model T was discontinued in 1926.

Buy Now, Pay Later

Another major growth sector was electric appliances such as ranges, vacuum cleaners, radios, and refrigerators. Over the decade, annual refrigerator production, for example, expanded from 5 thousand units in 1920 to nearly 1 million units in 1930. Although only 8 percent (see Table 22.1) of American families relied on mechanical refrigeration in 1930, the days of the "ice man" were numbered. Perhaps most spectacular was the rapid adoption of the radio. In 1920, when station KDKA in Pittsburgh became the first to broadcast commercially, radio was still a toy for the gadget minded; by the end of the decade, 40 percent of American families owned radios (see Table 22.1), which had transformed the cultural and political life of the nation.

The growth in the market for consumer durables was brought about by developments on both the supply side and the demand side. Mass production and technological advances lowered the cost for a given quality of service of many consumer durables. Henry Ford, for example, had pioneered the mass production of low-cost automobiles using the moving assembly line before the war. In the twenties, to meet stiff competition from General Motors, he introduced improved models that incorporated the self-starter, the windshield wiper, and improved brakes.

Thanks to the work of Martha Olney (1991), we now know that important developments also occurred on the demand side. One was the development of consumer credit —"buy now, pay later." Rather than saving up cash or interest-earning assets to buy a consumer durable, a consumer could make a down payment, take immediate possession

When Americans driving their new cars ended up stuck in the mud, they launched a national roadbuilding program.

of the durable, and pay for it on the installment plan. The finance company that made the loan was protected because it had a claim on the durable and could repossess it if the buyer failed to make the requisite payments. Originally, automakers established finance companies to help dealers purchase cars for inventories during the slow seasons and thus smooth the annual demand for automobiles. But the practice was quickly extended to the financing of automobile purchases by consumers.

The purchase of consumer durables was also promoted by the rapidly growing volume of advertising, which touted the benefits of the new lifestyle based on time and labor-saving consumer durables and pointed out how these improvements in one's standard of living could be realized immediately by buying on the installment plan. Advertising relied on newspapers and magazines, particularly those aimed at women, such as the *Ladies Home Journal*, but some advertising also relied on the new medium of radio. The National Broadcasting Company (NBC) was formed in 1926, and the Columbia Broadcasting System (CBS) in 1927. Polling systems by telephone were used to determine program ratings, and programs with low rating were canceled. Certain goods became tied to particular programs as producers sought any and all means to address the desires, fads, and fancies of the American public.

Government policies toward business did not cause these fundamental changes in the consumption patterns of Americans, but they did accommodate them. In the 1920s, the administrations of Presidents Warren G. Harding and Calvin Coolidge were openly dedicated to the principle that business should be free to grow without government's meddling or interfering. With little hindrance from government, businesses became even more consolidated than in earlier decades. Secretary of Commerce Herbert Hoover, among others, encouraged consolidations for reasons of efficiency; competing firms were allowed to form trade associations, not just to standardize tools and share technical information but also to set prices. Both Harding and Coolidge appointed men to the Federal Trade Commission who had little intention of enforcing the antitrust laws, either in letter or in spirit. As the years passed, banking, manufacturing, distribution, electronics, iron and steel, automobiles, and mining all became increasingly controlled by large conglomerates. Mass consumption, mass production, and the giant corporation thus became the trademark of the 1920s.

Mass production of consumer durables, often purchased with credit, characterized the boom of the 1920s.

Prohibition

One major attempt to remake the American lifestyle failed. Calls to prohibit the consumption of alcohol date from the nineteenth century. The Prohibition Party, in particular, although never large, waged a long and militant campaign. But it was not until 1917 that legislation was finally passed at the national level to prohibit consumption of alcohol. This was a wartime measure. Giving up alcohol was seen as a temporary sacrifice that would free resources in the brewing and distilling industries and keep workers at peak efficiency. Enforcement of the law was tightened in the Volstead Act of 1919, and prohibition was made permanent, or as permanent as such things can be, in 1920 when the Eighteenth Amendment to the Constitution was ratified.

Initially, prohibition had wide middle-class support. This included one of the leading economists of the era, Irving Fisher, who believed that prohibition had increased the savings of the working class and had raised industrial productivity. As is well known, however, opinions changed when crime soared despite an increase in the amount spent on enforcement from $6.3 million in 1921 to $13.4 million in 1930. Bootlegging became a major industry, and gangsters such as Al Capone and Legs Diamond became household names. Spectacular stories could be backed up with cold statistics: The homicide rate rose, and prohibition cases swamped the federal courts. By the time the Twenty-First Amendment to the Constitution ending prohibition was ratified in 1933, a majority of Americans had become disillusioned with the results of the "Noble Experiment." The economics of prohibition is discussed further in New View (on page 401).

THE LABOR FORCE IN THE TWENTIES

Overall, labor's advance, as measured by increased wages, at least for those in the city and in industry, was substantial in the 1920s. Perhaps more important from our perspective, however, were a number of forces that would reshape the American labor force for decades to come: the decline of labor unions (that would be temporarily reversed in the 1930s); the restriction on immigration (that would be partially reversed in the 1960s); and perhaps most important for the long run, the rise in high school attendance.

The Paycheck Rises

The consumer durables revolution produced a strong demand for industrial labor and, as a result, improvements in hours and wages. During World War I, many manufacturing industries accepted the 48-hour workweek, and by 1920, some agreements granted a half-day holiday on Saturday. Not until the very end of the decade, however, did a 48-hour week become standard for most occupations. Nevertheless, advance in leisure for many American workers was one of the important gains of the period. Another gain was the relative absence of cyclical unemployment. Except for the hard years of 1921 and 1922, the 1920s were generally free of mass joblessness. The first detailed unemployment rates for the 1920s were made by Stanley Lebergott (1964), whose estimates showed that unemployment averaged only 3.3 percent between 1923 and 1929. Further research led to a revised estimate of 5.1 percent (Coen 1973). But even these estimates are comparable to modern rates in good years. In short, the threat of unemployment was low, thereby contributing, along with added leisure, to the growing sense of prosperity.

Real annual earnings of nonfarm employees rose between 1919 and 1929 by about 23 percent; the increase over 1914 was about 33 percent. Not all sectors, however, fared as well. Further in the chapter, we look at agriculture, which had a tough time in the twenties. And when workers compared their gains with those of people higher on the economic ladder, they saw less reason to be content with the gains they had made.

The Unions Decline

Despite (or perhaps because of) the surge in the demand for industrial labor, the 1920s were not years of advance for organized labor. As Table 22.2 shows, the number of workers holding union membership fell from a peak of more than 12 percent of the

NEW VIEW 22.1

PROHIBITION

What happens when a society outlaws drugs such as marijuana, cocaine, heroin, anabolic steroids, and so on? The Noble Experiment can tell us a good deal about the potential costs and benefits of this action. As a result of Prohibition, consumption of alcohol fell, although perhaps not as much as its advocates had hoped. Prohibition reduced supply because producers faced the risk of legal prosecution. Prohibition probably reduced demand because of respect for the law, although there is some uncertainty about this because demand might have been increased as a result of the "forbidden fruit" effect.

Statistics on alcohol production are incomplete, of course, because so much was produced illegally. Economists such as Clark Warburton (1932) and, more recently, Jeffrey Miron and Jeffrey Zwiebel (1995) use related variables, such as deaths from cirrhosis of the liver, to infer consumption. According to their work, consumption of alcohol fell drastically at first but then rose to 60 or 70 percent of its preprohibition level. With both supply and demand falling, it is not

clear what the impact on the price would be. Evidence on prices is extremely sketchy but suggests that prices rose, although not a great deal.

Crime increased. Participants in the "black market" could not use the legal system to settle disputes between buyers and sellers or among competing sellers. Hence, sellers turned to crime, sometimes violent crime, to protect their property. Because their business was already illegal, moreover, the marginal costs of violence aimed at potential competitors was lower than it otherwise would have been. The homicide rate rose during this era by an amount that cannot be explained by other factors.

Deaths from overdose and accidental poisoning increased. Producers tended to make highly concentrated alcoholic beverages in order to better conceal their product from authorities. This increased the risk of accidental overdoses. Quality, moreover, tended to vary widely because producers could not establish and protect brand names and therefore had little incentive to maintain the quality of their product. In one case, an adulterant used to disguise alcohol as medicine led to thousands of poisonings.

civilian labor force in 1920 to less than 8 percent at the end of the decade. This fall is especially surprising in light of the rapid growth of manufacturing and the concentration of the population in urban areas. It is true that, throughout the 1920s, employers continued their effective use of the antiunion instruments developed before World War I. They

TABLE 22.2 UNION MEMBERSHIPS, 1919–1929

YEAR	TOTAL UNION MEMBERSHIP (in thousands)	TOTAL MEMBERSHIP AS A PERCENTAGE OF TOTAL LABOR FORCE	TOTAL MEMBERSHIP AS A PERCENTAGE OF NONFARM LABOR FORCE
1919	4,046	10.2%	14.8%
1920	5,034	12.2	16.3
1921	4,722	11.2	15.0
1922	3,950	9.3	12.4
1923	3,629	8.4	11.1
1924	3,549	8.0	10.6
1925	3,566	7.9	10.3
1926	3,592	7.9	10.3
1927	3,600	7.8	10.0
1928	3,567	7.6	9.7
1929	3,625	7.6	9.7

Source: Historical Statistics *1975, Series D4, D7, D8, and D940.*

discriminated in hiring and firing against employees who joined or organized unions. They used the hated "yellow-dog" contract, in which new employees promised not to join a union, to prevent union membership, and to serve as a basis of civil suits against unions that persuaded employees to violate the contracts. But the employers' most useful weapon was the injunction, by which a court could forbid, at least temporarily, such practices as picketing, secondary boycotts, and the feeding of strikers by the union. During the 1920s, except for legislation applying to railroads, government generally did not interfere with labor relations.

Although such policies slowed organized labor's progress, it is difficult to accept such actions as the primary cause of an absolute decline in union membership. It seems most likely that the upsurge in union membership associated with World War I had not been firmly established. The wartime increase in membership resulted in part from agreements by the unions to a nonstrike pledge in return for lessened opposition to union organization. The sharp recession of 1921 and 1922, which raised levels of unemployment to 11 percent, undermined labor's bargaining power. It is pertinent to note in Table 22.2 that most of the membership decline had occurred by 1923, after which time there was only minor attrition. In addition, beginning with the important strike against U.S. Steel in 1916, a host of strikes failed—except to anger employers. Company welfare programs designed to entice workers away from their own organizations also took their toll, but the inertia between 1924 and 1929 must be attributed primarily to two other causes. First, the increase in real wages left the greater part of the labor force generally satisfied. More important, the powerful American Federation of Labor (AFL) unions, whose members especially benefited from the building boom, took no interest in organizing the growing mass production industries. Added to this was a generally tired and unimaginative labor leadership.

Immigration Is Restricted

Labor did, however, finally achieve one of its most cherished objectives in the 1920s—limiting immigration. The restrictions on immigration imposed in the 1920s were part of a long-term trend. In 1882, for example, Chinese immigration was banned for 10 years, a restriction that was later renewed and strengthened. In 1885, the practice of prepaying the cost of an immigrant's voyage in exchange for future labor services was made illegal. In 1907, a financial test for immigrants was imposed, and in 1917, a literacy test. This trend, which was common in other countries receiving large numbers of immigrants such as Argentina and Australia, reflected the growing assertiveness of labor, which believed that free immigration was slowing the growth of the real wages of relatively unskilled labor. In the United States, sectional interests, as Claudia Goldin (1994b) has shown, also played a role. The South, for example, believed that its political power was being weakened by rapid population growth in other regions based on immigration. Until World War I, the door was still open; in 1921, legislation was finally passed that effectively limited immigration.

The Emergency Immigration Act of 1921 restricted the number of people to be admitted each year from any country to 3 percent of the number of people of that nationality residing in the United States in 1910. In 1924, a new law limited immigration to 2 percent of a nationality's 1890 U.S. population. This change further restricted immigration from southern and eastern Europe. Immigration from East Asia, moreover, was completely eliminated, reinforcing President Theodore Roosevelt's earlier "gentleman's agreement" with the Japanese. The law also set a maximum limit of slightly more than 150,000 immigrants with quotas based on 1920 to become effective in 1929. The effects of these restrictions on the flow of immigrants can be seen in Table 22.3. The contrast

TABLE 22.3 IMMIGRATION, 1910–1929

YEAR	NEW ARRIVALS	YEAR	NEW ARRIVALS
1910	1,041,570	1920	430,001
1911	878,587	1921	805,228
1912	838,172	1922	309,556
1913	1,197,892	1923	522,919
1914	1,218,480	1924	706,896
1915	326,700	1925	294,314
1916	298,826	1926	304,488
1917	295,403	1927	335,175
1918	110,618	1928	307,255
1919	141,132	1929	279,678

Source: Historical Statistics *1975, Series C89.*

between the prewar years (the war in Europe began in 1914) and the 1920s is obvious. The limit on immigration was clearly effective in cutting the number of legal immigrants.

Why were drastic restrictions placed on immigration at this time? In part, the restrictions were the result of growing hostility to the "new immigrants" from southern and eastern Europe who had constituted the bulk of the large influx of immigrants in the years leading up to the war. Racism, including the activities of the Ku Klux Klan, was on the rise, excited partly by wartime propaganda and patriotism. Sometimes racism was given a pseudoscientific veneer by writers who claimed that the new immigrants were less able and intelligent than native-born Americans. Sometimes, moreover, racism was combined with antiradicalism: the newcomers, it was said, filled the ranks of the anarchists and communists.

The war, moreover, had created the specter of a large influx of labor that would erode the real wages of unskilled labor. In the years preceding World War I, the economy of central Europe had grown rapidly; afterward it lay in ruins, saddled for years with heavy reparation payments. Farther east, the Russian economy had also been exhausted by years of war and revolution; now the communists controlled the economy, and no one could be sure what that would mean. The war, moreover, had created a vast new supply of shipping that could easily bring immigrants to the United States. Would not the country be swamped with immigrants from continental Europe once the war was over? These fears seemed to be confirmed by the resumption of a high level of immigration immediately after the war. Slightly more than 800,000 immigrants entered the United States between June 1920 and June 1921. Fear in turn bred legislation limiting immigration.

America Goes to High School

Another component of the modern American standard of living that arrived in the 1920s was the American high school, complete with 45-minute periods, diverse curricula, academic tracking, and, of course, bands and athletic teams. The increase in enrollment and graduation rates during the 1920s and 1930s was astonishing, as shown in Table 22.4. In 1910, less than 10 percent of American 17-year-olds had graduated from high school. By 1938, almost half were graduates. Graduating from high school had become a standard rite of passage. The United States, moreover, led the way internationally. By the middle of the twentieth century, a large gap in years of secondary schooling per capita had opened between the United States and the rest of the industrial nations.

TABLE 22.4 HIGH SCHOOL GRADUATION RATES

	HIGH SCHOOL GRADUATES (as a percentage of children age 17)	
	48 STATES	**32 NONSOUTHERN STATES**
1910	8.6%	11.1%
1920	16.2	19.9
1928	27.0	32.1
1938	48.2	55.9

Source: *Derived from Goldin 1994a, Table 1.*

Why did the "High School Movement" have so much success in the United States? Recent research by Claudia Goldin and Larry Katz (2008, chapters 5 and 6) has clarified the underlying forces. First, the rate of return from going to high school was extremely high (the extra income earned after graduation compared with the earnings forgone). In addition, communities were willing to build and staff high schools so that the children and grandchildren of the people living there would have more economic and social opportunities. The kinds of communities that had the most social cohesion, and therefore were most likely to vote for high taxes to finance high schools, were not located in the big cities with their diverse immigrant populations. Instead, it was the farming communities of the Midwest—in Iowa and Nebraska, for example—that led the way in establishing high schools. The high school movement provides a further illustration of Economic Reasoning Propositions 3, incentives matter (high rates of return encouraged young people to stay in school); and 4, laws and rules matter (local finance and control of public schooling encouraged the early adoption of the high school in the Middle West) (see on page 406).

ON THE LAND

The period between 1896 and 1914, sometimes called the "Golden Age of Agriculture," was one of rapid improvement in the economic position of the American farmer. Then the surge in international demand for American farm products during World War I amplified the rise in farm incomes. The 1920s, however, witnessed the return of hard times for many farmers. The result was the first tentative steps by the government toward the support of farm incomes.

Economic Distress in Agriculture

Agriculture lost a lot of ground during the 1920–1921 recession. In mid-1920, farm prices began a precipitous drop. By the end of 1921, despite a slight recovery, wheat that 18 months previously had sold for $2.58 per bushel was selling for $0.93, and corn was down to $0.41 from $1.86. Many commodities did not suffer quite as severe a decline, but prices seriously decreased in all lines of production. From an index of 234 in June 1920 (1909–1914 = 100), prices received by farmers fell to an index of 112 a year later. A gradual recovery followed, and the farm index stood at 159 in August 1925. After a small decline during 1926 and 1927, prices remained stable until the end of 1929. The deflation of 1920 and 1921 was severe in the industrial sector and overall economy, too, but not as great as in the agriculture sector. The terms of trade (the ratio of the prices received by farmers to the prices they paid) ran against agriculture during the break in prices. Then, however, they recovered, so that by 1925, they were not much below the 1920 level. This index fell a little during the next few years, but in 1929, it was still not far from the level of prosperous prewar years. The earnings of farm workers, moreover, rose only a bit slower than those of industrial workers during the 1920s (Alston and Hatton 1991). Moreover, research by Charles F. Holt (1977) suggested a rise in income for the average farmer in the 1920s. On the whole, then, it does not seem that agriculture should have suffered much in the middle and late 1920s. Yet great agitation for remedial farm legislation occurred during these years. Why?

The answer seems to be that many farmers, especially in the Midwest, had incurred fixed indebtedness at what turned out to be the wrong time. Land values had risen sharply between 1910 and 1920; at the height of the boom, the best lands in Iowa and Illinois sold for as much as $500 an acre—a fantastically high figure for the time. In those 10 years, many high-grade farms doubled in value. To buy such high-priced properties, farmers borrowed heavily. World War I added to the boom as many farmers rushed to increase the acreage they had under cultivation to take advantage of what they realized would be a temporary rise in prices (Alston 1983). Long-term debt rose from $3.2 billion in 1910 to $8.4 billion in 1920 and reached a high of nearly $11 billion in 1923. Deflation in the early 1920s turned farm debts into crushing burdens. Although a majority of American farmers may not have been burdened with fixed debt payments during these years, a large and extremely vocal minority were pushed toward bankruptcy. The number of farm mortgage foreclosures advanced sharply at the turn of the decade and then remained high throughout the 1920s. According to H. Thomas Johnson, the rate increased from 2.8 per 1,000 mortgaged farms foreclosed in 1918 to 3.8 in 1920, to 6.4 in 1921, to 11.2 in 1922, and to between 14 and 17 per 1,000 for the remainder of the decade (Johnson 1973–1974, 176).

First Steps toward Farm Subsidies

During the severe recession of 1920–1921 the War Finance Corporation made emergency loans to farmers. President Harding described the Corporation's actions as "helpful" and called for broadened powers. Although the Corporation gradually curtailed its activities after the emergency passed, it was a portent of much to come (Nash 1959, 458–460). Violent protests from farmers in late 1920 led Congress to create the Joint Commission of Agricultural Inquiry in 1921. The commission reported the obvious—that farm troubles were the result of general business depression and a decline in exports—and recommended measures to help cooperative marketing associations, improve credit facilities, and extend the Department of Agriculture's research activities. A more radical approach was advocated at the National Agricultural Conference, convened early in 1922 by Secretary of Agriculture Henry C. Wallace.[2] In its report, the idea of "parity" for agriculture was first made explicit, and the slogan "Equality for Agriculture" was offered. It was argued that agriculture was entitled to its fair share of the national income and that this would be achieved if the ratio of the prices farmers received to the prices they paid was kept equal to the ratio that had prevailed from 1910 to 1914.

Throughout the 1920s, various ideas were proposed aimed at securing "parity prices" or "fair-exchange values" for agricultural products. Most acceptable to professional farm supporters and politicians were the McNary-Haugen bills, which sought to determine the fair-exchange value of each farm product. The fair value was to be a price that would

---

[2] His son, Henry A. Wallace, one of the developers of hybrid corn, would serve as secretary of agriculture and vice president under Roosevelt and as commerce secretary under Truman.

have preserved pre–World War I purchasing power and was to be maintained in two ways: first, a tariff was to protect the home market from imports, and second, a private corporation chartered by the federal government (modeled on the War Finance Corporation) was to buy a sufficient amount of each commodity to force its price up to the computed fair value. The corporation could in turn sell the acquired commodities. It was proposed, moreover, that the surpluses be sold abroad at the world price, which presumably would be lower than the supported American price. Administrative expenses and operating losses would be shared among the producing farmers. For every bale of cotton or bushel of wheat sold, a tax called an "equalization fee" would be charged to the grower. These taxes would be used to defray all expenses of operating the price support plan. The farmer would gain insofar as the additional amount of income resulting from higher prices exceeded the tax. Refer to Economic Reasoning Propositions 1, scarcity forces us to make choices; 2, choices impose costs; and 4, laws and rules (institutions) matter.

The McNary-Haugen bills were twice passed by Congress and twice vetoed by President Calvin Coolidge. Despite this setback, the agitation of the 1920s did secure some special privileges for agriculture. For one, the Capper-Volstead law of 1922 exempted farmers' cooperatives from the threat of prosecution for violation of antitrust laws. The following year, the Federal Intermediate Credit Act provided for 12 intermediate credit banks that would rediscount agricultural paper for commercial banks and other lending agencies. Nonemergency short-term farm credit needs were fairly well taken care of with the passage of this act; the Federal Farm Loan Act of 1916 had already established 12 Federal Land Banks to provide long-term loans to farmers through cooperative borrowing groups.

To achieve the broader aims of price and income maintenance, there were two major efforts. A naïve belief in the tariff as a device to raise the prices of farm products (which had been traditionally exported, not imported!) led to "protection" for agriculture, culminating in the high duties of the Smoot-Hawley Tariff Act of June 1930. More significant was the Agricultural Marketing Act of 1929, which was passed to fulfill Republican campaign promises of the previous year. This law, the first committing the federal government to a policy of stabilizing farm prices, worked as much as possible through nongovernment institutions. The act established a Federal Farm Board to encourage the formation of cooperative marketing associations and to establish "stabilization corporations" to be owned by the cooperatives, which would use a $500 million fund to carry on price support operations.

Periods of distress in agriculture had occurred before. Why on a limited scale in the twenties were direct efforts made to aid farmers? Several things, as shown by Elizabeth Hoffman and Gary D. Libecap (1991), had changed. First, the experiments with price controls in World War I and the use of the War Finance Corporation to aid farmers in the 1920–1921 recession had convinced farmers and their advocates that direct federal intervention in agricultural markets would work. The federal government, moreover, had become far stronger than it had earlier been—in part because the passage of the income tax had given it a new source of revenue—and this made direct aid to farmers seem more realistic. Finally, the integration of national markets had made it clear that only federal intervention could help farmers.

Ultimately, the farm programs adopted in the 1920s provided only limited help to farmers. The supply of farm output was highly elastic. Without the means to control output, or buy it on a massive scale, federal legislation could not significantly alter farm incomes, especially those of poor farmers. Nevertheless, the policy discussions of the 1920s set the stage for the massive government intervention in agriculture that was to follow in the 1930s.

WERE THE RICH GETTING RICHER WHILE THE POOR GOT POORER?

Images of the wealthy during the 1920s often portray them as self-satisfied and self-indulgent—drinking champagne and ignoring the growing misery around them. Some historians, moreover, have seen a direct link between a growing concentration of income during the 1920s and the depression of the 1930s. Too much income, goes the argument, was going to the rich, who were not spending it fast enough to maintain aggregate demand. Early studies of the distribution of income to some degree confirmed that the rich had grown relatively richer. In his pioneering work published in 1953, Simon Kuznets showed that the share of disposable income received by the top 1 percent of the population increased from 11.8 percent in 1920 to 18.9 percent in 1929 (Kuznets 1953; *Historical Statistics* 1975, Series G341). Charles Holt (1977), working from Kuznets's data, moreover, argued that all of the increases in real income in the 1920s went to upper-income groups. More recent research, however, counters this view. Gene Smiley (1983) pointed out that the upward trend in the share of income going to the richest fractions of the population was biased upward because it was based on tax returns. Tax rates for the rich were lowered substantially in the 1920s, encouraging people to shift their wealth into assets yielding taxable income and to report income that previously had gone unreported. Jeffrey Williamson and Peter Lindert (1981, chapter 12), in a landmark study of American inequality, drew attention to the long-term dimension of the problem. A long trend toward increased inequality had been interrupted by World War I, so some increase in inequality in the 1920s was to be expected, as the economy returned to normal. The distribution of income was far from equal in 1929, but little evidence exists that something drastic and unexpected had occurred that could explain the depression that was to follow.

When discussing the distribution of income in the 1920s, moreover, it is important to keep in mind Lebergott's point: However much certain groups suffered, there were improvements in the standard of living of a large segment of the American people that can be seen in such statistics as the percentage of families with electric lighting, the percentage of families with washing machines, and even the percentage of families with inside flush toilets (see Table 22.1 on page 396). Economic Reasoning Proposition 5, evidence and theory give value to opinions, is well illustrated by this debate over the changes in the distribution of income in the 1920s. Evidence matters, but the discovery of one piece of evidence, however important it may seem to be, can be merely the beginning of a long journey.

MACROECONOMIC POLICIES

Fiscal and monetary policy were conducted in a conservative fashion in the 1920s. Tax rates were cut, the budget was balanced, and the Federal Reserve focused, at the end of the decade, on restraining the growing

Fiscal Policy

Fiscal policy in the late 1920s is best viewed as a long, drawn-out postwar readjustment. Although certain costs of the war, such as veterans' benefits and interest on the increase in the national debt, continued into the postwar period, demobilization nevertheless created considerable scope for cutting the high level of taxes imposed during wartime.

The debate over taxes in the twenties covered the same ground as the debate that began in the 1970s (under the banner of supply-side economics) and continues to the

TABLE 22.5 GOVERNMENT SPENDING AND DISTRIBUTION OF EXPENDITURES BY LEVEL OF GOVERNMENT, 1922 AND 1927 (IN PERCENT)

	1922	1927
Share of GNP		
Total government	12.6%	11.6%
Federal	4.9	3.5
State and local	7.7	8.1
Expenditure distribution by level		
Federal	39.2	30.4
State	11.7	12.9
Local	49.1	56.7

Source: *Niemi 1975, 117.*

present day. The White House favored reducing taxes by removing the steep progression in rates introduced during the war. Secretary of the Treasury Andrew Mellon argued that reducing high tax rates would encourage savings and growth and that the effects on tax revenues would be relatively small. The wealthy would shift their assets from tax-exempt municipal bonds to taxable assets, thus minimizing the effect on total revenues. Liberals in Congress did not oppose cutting taxes altogether. However, they favored reducing taxes by increasing exemptions for those in lower-income groups. The outcomes of this fight—the revenue acts of 1924, 1926, and 1928—swept away the system of wartime excise taxes, reduced the rates for personal and corporate taxes, and reduced estate duties. On the whole, the pride in their fiscal policies taken by successive administrations during the 1920s is understandable. Tax rates were cut, but revenues grew, and a budget surplus was maintained. Perhaps even more important for the long run, a federal budget system was introduced in 1921 under President Harding that would make it possible to cope, to some degree, with the massive expansion of the federal government that was to come in later decades.

Table 22.5 shows that federal spending was relatively small compared with the whole economy in the 1920s. Indeed, in 1927, the federal government was spending only 3.5 percent of gross national product (GNP), most accounted for by the traditional categories of national defense, the postal service, veterans' services, and interest on the national debt. Although more funds were being spent on health and welfare, these were still minor categories. The revolution in the budget would come in the thirties.

Monetary Policy

The 1920s were years of growing prestige for the Federal Reserve System. Table 22.6 shows that after the sharp but brief recession of 1920–1921, the economy advanced smoothly. Real income rose steadily year after year, as did the stock of money. Prices for the most part were stable.

What influenced the Fed's policy during these years? Surprisingly, one fact that did not influence policy was the large number of bank closings. Suspensions numbered in the hundreds each year, reaching a peak of 975 banks in 1926. The Federal Reserve concluded that these banks (mostly small banks in rural areas) were plagued by bad management, unrealistic loans to farmers made during the war boom, and increased competition due to the rise of the automobile. (The automobile increased the ability of borrowers and depositors to shop for favorable terms.) It followed that simply allowing

TABLE 22.6 MONEY, PRICES, AND REAL INCOME, 1920–1929

YEAR	STOCK OF MONEY (in billions of dollars)	IMPLICIT PRICE DEFLATOR (1929 = 100)	REAL NATIONAL INCOME (in billions of 1929 dollars)
1920	$34.80	121.7	$62.208
1921	32.85	103.7	59.567
1922	33.72	98.6	63.859
1923	36.60	100.9	73.460
1924	38.58	99.6	75.559
1925	42.05	101.6	77.343
1926	43.68	102.1	82.807
1927	44.73	99.4	83.623
1928	46.42	100.1	84.918
1929	46.60	100.0	90.308

Source: *Friedman and Schwartz 1982,* 125.

these banks to close strengthened the banking system as a whole. Although it is difficult to imagine the Fed taking such a callous position today, its analysis probably contained a good deal of truth. Unfortunately, this policy was carried into the 1930s when high numbers of bank failures under very different economic conditions undermined confidence in the banking system.

An important series of papers by Eugene White (1981, 1984, 1986) clarified the nature of the weakness in the rural banking system and its role in the breakdown of the banking system in the early 1930s. To a large extent, the problem stemmed from legislation that prohibited branch banking. Small unit banks were unable to diversify their loan portfolios and had no resources to draw on during periods of temporary illiquidity. The states tried various deposit insurance schemes to protect their systems, but these ended in failure. Eventually, most states began to eliminate crippling prohibitions against branch banking, but by then the damage had been done, and it was too late to build a system that could withstand the deflation of the 1930s.

The Fed, however, was deeply concerned about the growing speculation on Wall Street. Brokerage houses were lending money to their customers so they could buy stocks, and the brokerage houses were in turn borrowing from the banks in the form of call loans—loans that had to be repaid on demand, that is, when "called." Speculation, the Fed believed, diverted capital from more productive investments, and the inevitable retrenchment might cause widespread disturbances in the economy. But it was not clear how to slow the flow of funds to the stock market without simultaneously restricting the total supply of credit, thus risking a recession. At first, the Fed tried "moral suasion," pressuring the New York City banks into making fewer call loans. This policy was partly effective, but other lenders quickly moved into the gap left by the banks. Finally, frustrated by its inability to cool the market in any other way, the Fed raised its discount rate from 4.5 to 5.5 percent on August 9, 1929. The discount rate was still well below the call loan and other bank lending rates, so the increase itself did not remove the incentive to borrow, but it did signal the Fed's intention to restrict the supply of credit. Other central banks were taking similar actions: The Bank of England raised its discount rate from 5.5 to 6.5 percent in September. Perhaps as a result of these widespread harbingers of tighter credit, American stock prices reached their peak early in September. The exact role of the Fed's policy in subsequent events is a matter of considerable debate, as we will read in the next chapter. During the 1930s, however, the Fed was given the power to set margin requirements on stock purchases because it was recognized that the Fed's monetary policy had been distorted in the late 1920s by its efforts to control the stock market.

INTERNATIONAL DEVELOPMENTS

During the 1920s, the problems of Europe seemed far away to most Americans and unrelated to their lives. In retrospect, we can see that such an attitude was naïve and counterproductive. The future might have been different if Americans had given more thought to its role in the world economy. Nevertheless, America could not completely ignore two problems that dominated the international scene: German war reparations (and Allied war debts to the United States) and the reestablishment of the international gold standard.

As noted in chapter 21, the Treaty of Versailles, which formally ended World War I, called for Germany to make large payments to France and the other Allies to compensate for damages caused by German forces during the war. It quickly became apparent that Germany lacked the economic strength and political commitment to make its payments on schedule. The question of what to do about Germany's unpaid reparations would vex policymakers throughout the 1920s. In 1923, French and Belgian troops occupied the Ruhr valley because Germany had failed to make its scheduled payments. In 1924, under the Dawes plan—the commission that proposed the plan was headed by American Charles G. Dawes—France and Belgium left the Ruhr, Germany was given more time to pay its reparations, and a large loan, mostly from the United States, was floated to help Germany restore its economy and make its debt payments. In the late 1920s it became clear that the Dawes plan would not be enough. Under the Young plan of 1929—this commission was headed by American Owen Young—Germany's reparation payments were scaled back. During the early 1930s further attempts were made to relieve Germany's reparations burden, but the deteriorating economic situation and the rise of Hitler soon made these efforts irrelevant. Most historians now agree that trying to extract reparations from Germany was a mistake and that a wiser policy would have aimed at restoring the German economy as rapidly as possible, the policy followed after World War II.

It was taken for granted in the 1920s that restoration of the gold standard was necessary to achieve lasting prosperity. If each country made its currency convertible into gold, exchange rates would be fixed, monetary authorities would be forced to limit the amount of money they created (to avoid an outflow of gold), and inflation would be prevented. British bankers were particularly anxious to return to the gold standard at the prewar parity (i.e., the prewar price of pounds in terms of dollars) to help restore the position of London as the world's leading financial center. Britain finally did return to the gold standard in 1924, but it appears that the pound was overvalued at the prewar rate. (The rate was $4.86 per £1.00, but the equilibrium price where supply and demand for pounds would balance was probably less, say, $4.40.) The high rate made it hard for Britain to export goods and contributed to a long period of hard times in Britain. Winston Churchill was the chancellor of the exchequer (similar to our secretary of treasury) at the time and responsible for this decision. Just as John Maynard Keynes had warned against imposing reparations on Germany in *The Economic Consequences of the Peace* (1920), he now warned against restoring the pound at its prewar value in *The Economic Consequences of Mr. Churchill* (1925).

The pressure on British exports would have been lessened had the United States been willing to let the resulting influx of gold increase its price level, but the Federal Reserve chose instead to "sterilize" the gold inflows. In retrospect, considerable difficulties might have been avoided had American policymakers seen the importance of taking into account the international repercussions of their actions. American monetary and fiscal policies during the 1920s, however, were influenced primarily by domestic considerations, and (except in the agricultural sector) things seemed to be moving smoothly.

THE GREAT BULL MARKET

One event dominates the social memory of the twenties: the great stock market boom. Stock prices rose steadily in the early 1920s, but in 1928 and the first three-quarters of 1929, they rocketed upward. But before looking at the stock market, two other events illustrate the speculative temper of the times: the Ponzi Scheme and the Florida Land Boom.

The Ponzi Scheme

In late 1919 Charles Ponzi, an Italian immigrant with a checkered past, started a fraudulent investment plan that would add a new term to the language: the Ponzi Scheme (Zuckoff 2005). Ponzi promised his investors high rates of return, 50 percent in 45 days. He had a story to back up his claim: He would invest in a special kind of international postage stamp. It could be bought in Italy for lira and sold in the United States for dollars. Because the official prices of the stamp had not been adjusted to match wartime changes in exchange rates, it was possible to buy the stamps cheaply in Italy and sell them for a profit in the United States. The costs of arbitrage, however, were high, and Ponzi never seems to have followed his plan. Instead, as more and more people—many of them, like Ponzi, Italian immigrants—invested with Ponzi, he used income from recent investors to pay interest to earlier investors and to pay investors who wanted to cash in their investments. For a time large amounts of money flowed in to the bank where Ponzi had moved his operation, and he began to live the life of a wealthy man. Stories questioning Ponzi soon appeared in the press, the government investigated, and in August 1920 federal agents shut his operation. He was later imprisoned for mail fraud. Ponzi was not the inventor of the scheme—indeed, he seems to have learned it from another fraudulent banker for whom he worked in Canada—but he gave the language a new term. It would be used again and again. In March 2009 Bernard Madoff pleaded guilty to running a $50 billion Ponzi Scheme, the largest to that date. Ponzi's original scheme lasted only a short time and hurt a relatively small number of investors. The next speculative mania, the Florida Land Boom (in which an unrepentant Ponzi participated), would prove a clearer precursor of the stock market boom.

The Florida Land Boom

The real estate boom in the 1920s was nationwide (Field 1992). Suburbs, whose accessibility was increased by the automobile, were developed rapidly, but there was also a building boom in American cities. New York's skyline was penetrated by a bevy of new skyscrapers, including the world's tallest, the Empire State Building (nicknamed the Empty State Building in the depression). The real estate boom reached its most outlandish form, however, in Florida (Vanderblue 1927; Vickers 1994; Frazer and Guthrie, Jr. 1995). Prices for building sites rose rapidly, and hucksters of all types descended on Florida to make their fortunes buying and selling land. It was claimed, for example, that a property in Palm Beach, Florida, that sold for $800,000 in 1923 was broken into lots that were resold for $1.5 million, and that by 1925 the land was worth $4 million (Allen 1931, 276). The speculative frenzy was lampooned by the Marx brothers in the

© EVERETT COLLECTION

A scene from the movie Cocoanuts—a spoof of the Florida Land Boom—starring the Marx brothers.

movie *Cocoanuts* (1929). The pace of construction was dizzying. At one point the railroads embargoed nonperishables such as building materials so that they could transport sufficient food to feed the large number of people drawn to South Florida. The boom was based on fundamentals—Florida's wonderful climate, and the decline in travel costs brought about by the automobile—but things had clearly gotten out of hand. Finance was readily available. Florida banks, aided by lax bank regulation, provided much of the capital. It was possible, moreover, to finance new developments with tax-exempt municipal bonds made attractive by the rise in tax rates during the war. During the spring and summer of 1926, however, the bubble began to deflate. The winter tourist season had been disappointing and the signs of overbuilding were everywhere. In September 1926 a powerful hurricane devastated Miami, the heart of the boom, wrecking construction sites, and perhaps wrecking beliefs about an earthly paradise as well; the Florida land boom was over. In its wake, a devastated banking system was left that failed to recover before the depression. Still, the effects of the Florida Land Boom were limited. The next speculative extravaganza would be played on the biggest stage of all: Wall Street.

The Stock Market Boom

Table 22.7 shows what happened to stock prices between 1922 and 1929: In seven years, prices more than tripled. Between 1928 and 1929, the average stock rose 26.5 percent in value. It seemed that getting rich was easy—just put money in the stock market and sit back and wait. Typical of the times was an article by financier John Jacob Raskob in the *Ladies' Home Journal* with the optimistic title, "Everybody Ought to Be Rich" (Galbraith 1961, 57).

What caused the great bull market? One cause was the rise in earnings of and dividends paid by corporations in the 1920s. The rise in earnings in turn reflected the great surge in the demand, especially for automobiles and other consumer durables. General

TABLE 22.7 THE STOCK MARKET, 1922–1929

YEAR	STANDARD & POOR'S COMMON STOCK INDEX (ALL STOCKS)
1922	100
1923	102
1924	108
1925	133
1926	150
1927	182
1928	237
1929	309

Source: Historical Statistics *1975, Series X479 and X495.*

Motors, as a result of its strong earnings resulting from its successful challenge to Ford, was a market favorite. But stock prices rose even faster than earnings. Consider column 2 of Table 22.7, which shows the ratio of stock prices to dividends. In 1922, an investor had to pay $17.24 for each dollar of current dividends; by 1929, that figure had climbed to $28.74. Of course, people do not invest on the assumption that dividends will remain the same forever. One of the favorites of the bull market was Radio Corporation of America (RCA), which had never paid a dividend. People bought RCA stock on the assumption that it would pay large dividends in the future.

George Sirkin (1975), in an interesting comment on the bull market, argued that if earnings growth in the years immediately preceding the stock market crash were projected forward, then only relatively few stocks could be considered overvalued at the market's peak. But Eugene White (1989) pointed out that Sirkin's result depends on projecting earnings from a favorable period of years. In White's view, this begs the question: Why did the market choose to base its projections on the most favorable years rather than on a long run of experience? See Economic Insight 22.1 on page 414 for more detail. Part of the explanation seems to be that people convinced themselves that a "New Age" had dawned. Science and technology, now being pursued in large industrial laboratories, would produce much faster earnings growth than had been possible in the past.

What role was played by easy credit? During the boom, much stock was bought on margin. The buyer would put down, say, 50 percent of the value of the stock in cash and borrow the remaining 50 percent from the broker. Leveraging in this way means that when stock prices go up by, say, 10 percent, the speculator makes 20 percent on the initial investment. But what is true going up is also true going down. If stocks fall 10 percent, the speculator loses 20 percent. It is sometimes assumed that the margin requirements became very low during the 1920s—5 or 10 percent—but most brokers required 45 or 50 percent down (Galbraith 1961, 37). Sometimes an assumption is made that the boom arose because banks became more willing to make call loans to brokers. This, however, also appears not to have been the case (see Economic Insight 22.2 on page 415).

It does appear then, that there was a "bubble" in the stock market in the late 1920s—March 1928 is often suggested as the date when the bubble began—in the sense that the prices of stocks rose even more than what would be expected on the basis of "fundamentals," such as expected earnings and interest rates on alternative investments. The

ECONOMIC INSIGHT 22.1

PROJECTION OF FUTURE DIVIDEND GROWTH

Economic theory concludes that if investors are rational, the value of a stock (or group of stocks) will equal the discounted value of expected future dividends.

The formula is

$$(1) \quad P = \frac{D_1}{(1+i)} + \frac{D_2}{(1+i)^2} + \frac{D_3}{(1+i)^3} + \cdots$$

where P is the price of a stock or group of stocks; $D1$, $D2$, $D3$, and so on are the dividends expected next year, two years from now, three years from now, and so on; and i is the rate of interest at which investors discount the future.

If we make the additional assumption that dividends are expected to grow at the constant rate g, the equation reduces to:

$$(2) \quad P = \frac{D_1}{i-g}$$

In 1922, as shown in Table 22.8, the price-dividend ratio was 17.24. Suppose investors were using the prewar (1900–1914) rate of growth of dividends of 2.72 percent per year to project future dividend growth. This assumption would imply (from the second equation) a discount rate of about 8.52 percent per year. Let us suppose that in 1929 investors used the same discount rate but that they now used the postwar (1919–1929) rate of growth of dividends, 5.84 percent per year, to project the future growth of dividends. Then from the second equation, the expected price-dividend ratio would be 37.34, considerably above the actual market price-dividend ratio of 28.74. On these assumptions, stocks were still *undervalued* in 1929. But if we assume that a more reasonable rate of growth of dividends was 4.28, the average of the prewar and postwar growth rates, then the price-dividend ratio should have been around 23.58; stocks were *overvalued* in 1929.

TABLE 22.8 THE STOCK MARKET, 1922–1929

YEAR	RATIO OF STOCK PRICE TO DIVIDEND
1922	17.24
1923	16.84
1924	17.04
1925	19.27
1926	18.80
1927	20.96
1928	25.13
1929	28.74

Source: Historical Statistics *1975, Series X479 and X495.*

institutions that supplied credit to the market and perhaps many investors, expected a decline in prices. Money, however, kept pouring into the market because some investors thought that prices would continue to rise, and because others who believed that the market was overvalued thought that they could beat the crowd out the door before the market began to tumble.

The true explanation for the boom, if there ever is one, will have to be provided by social psychologists. It was an optimistic age. Business was booming. There seemed to be no reason that it could not keep on booming, providing an ever-higher standard of living for the average American. The stock market reflected that optimism.

ECONOMIC INSIGHT 22.2

CALL LOANS AND THE BULL MARKET

Some historians have thought that an increased willingness on the part of the New York banks to supply call loans caused the bull market (Galbraith 1961, 37). Eugene White's (1989) study of the market shows, however, that this was not the decisive factor. His analysis is illustrated in the following figure. The amount of call loans rose dramatically in the 1920s,

but interest rate on call loans also rose from 4.36 percent in 1922 to 7.74 percent in 1929. Evidently, as the figure illustrates, the market equilibrium moved toward the upper right, indicating that the demand for loans increased more than the supply. Had supply increased more than demand, the equilibrium call loan rate would have fallen. Credit, to put it somewhat differently, was being pulled into the stock market by the rising interest rate on call loans.

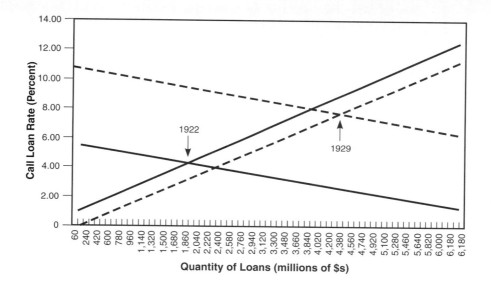

Should They Have Seen the Crash Coming?

In the uncommonly pleasant summer of 1929, Americans were congratulating themselves for having found a way to unending prosperity. The flow of U.S. goods and services had reached an all-time high, industrial production having risen 50 percent in a decade. Most businesses were satisfied with their profits, and workers were content with the gains in wages and earnings that enabled them to enjoy the luxury of automobiles and household appliances. Farmers grumbled about prices, but it was traditional that they should; anyone could see that mechanical inventions had made life on the farm easier and more productive than ever before. Besides, anyone who really wanted to become rich had only to purchase common stock. The political climate was favorable to the business venturer, then held high in public esteem as the provider of material well-being. Herbert Hoover, a successful businessman and a distinguished public servant, had been elected to the presidency, and people generally expected him to be a temperate and judicious leader. Equally reassuring was the stability of the economies of western Europe. War damage had been repaired, the gold standard had been restored, and the problem of reparations seemed to be near solution.

Irving Fisher was the greatest American economist of the day. A remarkable figure, Fisher made important contributions in areas of economics ranging from index numbers to monetary theory. His invention of a card index system made him a fortune, and his book on how to eat a healthy diet was a best seller. When journalists wanted to know whether the popular song title "Yes, We Have No Bananas" was good English, they asked Irving Fisher. (The answer, according to Fisher, was yes, if the question was "Have you no bananas?") Fisher was not shy in making predictions about the stock market. Just weeks before the crash, he argued that "stock prices have reached what looks like a permanently high plateau," adding that "there might be a recession in stock prices, but not anything in the nature of a crash." Even after the crash, Fisher wrote that for "the immediate future, at least, the outlook is bright" (Galbraith 1961, 91, 99, and 151).

It is easy now to laugh at such optimism. But should Fisher and others have known better? Were there signs of the impending disaster that should have been heeded? The long history of panics and crises in U.S. history (which Fisher knew well) should, perhaps, have given pause. There also were, of course, weaknesses in the economy, such as the banking system and the agricultural sector, but the economy had expanded rapidly for years despite these weaknesses. Ultimately, whether we believe that Fisher and other optimists were unwise or merely incredibly unlucky depends on what we believe caused the Great Depression, the subject of the next chapter.

SELECTED REFERENCES AND SUGGESTED READINGS

Allen, Frederick Lewis. *Only Yesterday: An Informal History of the Nineteen-Twenties.* New York, London: Harper & Brothers, 1931.

Alston, Lee J. "Farm Foreclosures in the United States During the Interwar Period." *The Journal of Economic History* 43, no. 4 (December 1983): 885–903.

Alston, Lee J., and T. J. Hatton. "The Earnings Gap Between Agricultural and Manufacturing Laborers, 1925–1941." *The Journal of Economic History* 51, no. 1 (March 1991): 83–99.

Coen, R. M. "Labor Force Unemployment in the 1920s and 1930s: A Re-examination Based on Postwar Experience." *Review of Economics and Statistics* 55 (1973): 46–55.

Field, Alexander J. "Uncontrolled Land Development and the Duration of the Depression in the United States." *Journal of Economic History* 52 (December 1992): 785–805.

Fisher, Irving. *Prohibition Still at Its Worst.* New York: Alcohol Information Committee 1928.

Frazer, William, and John J. Guthrie, Jr. *The Florida Land Boom: Speculation, Money and the Banks.* Westport, Connecticut: Quorum Books, 1995.

Friedman, Milton, and Anna J. Schwartz, *Monetary Trends in the United States and the United Kingdom.* Chicago: University of Chicago Press, 1982.

Galbraith, John Kenneth. *The Great Crash of 1929*, reissued with a new introduction. Boston: Houghton Mifflin, 1961.

Goldin, Claudia. *Understanding the Gender Gap: An Economic History of American Women.* New York: Oxford University Press, 1990.

_____. "How America Graduated from High School: 1910 to 1960." NBER Working Paper No. 4762. National Bureau of Economic Research, 1994a.

_____. "The Political Economy of Immigration Restriction in the U.S., 1890 to 1921." In *The Regulated Economy: A Historical Approach to Political Economy,* eds. Claudia Goldin and Gary Libecap. Chicago: University of Chicago Press, 1994b.

Goldin, Claudia, and Lawrence F., Katz. *The Race between Education and Technology.* Cambridge, Mass.: Belknap Press of Harvard University Press, 2008.

Historical Statistics of the United States, Colonial Times to 1957. U.S. Bureau of the Census. Washington D.C. Government Printing Office, 1960.

Historical Statistics, Colonial Times to 1970, bicentennial edition. U.S. Bureau of the Census. Washington, D.C.: Government Printing Office, 1975.

Holt, Charles. "Who Benefitted from the Prosperity of the Twenties?" *Explorations in Economic History* 14 (1977): 277–289.

Hoffman, Elizabeth and Gary D. Libecap. "Journal of Economic History, Institutional Choice and the Development of U.S. Agricultural Policies in the 1920s." *The Journal of Economic History* 51, no. 2 (June 1991): 397–411.

Johnson, H. Thomas. "Postwar Optimism and the Rural Financial Crisis of the 1920s." *Explorations in Economic History* 11 (Winter 1973–1974): 176.

Keynes, John Maynard. *The Economic Consequences of the Peace*. New York: Harcourt, Brace & World, 1920.

_____. *The Economic Consequences of Mr. Churchill*. London: Woolf, 1925.

Kuznets, Simon. *Shares of Upper Income Groups in Income and Savings*. New York: National Bureau of Economic Research, 1953.

Lebergott, Stanley. *Manpower in Economic Growth: The American Record since 1800*. New York: McGraw-Hill, 1964.

_____. *The American Economy: Income, Wealth and Want*. Princeton, N.J.: Princeton University Press, 1976.

Miron, Jeffrey A., and Jeffrey Zwiebel. "Economics of Drugs: Alcohol Consumption during Prohibition." *American Economic Review* 81, Papers and Proceedings (1991): 242–247.

_____. "The Economic Case against Drug Prohibition." *Journal of Economic Perspectives* 9 (Autumn 1995): 175–192.

Nash, Gerald D. "Herbert Hoover and the Origins of the Reconstruction Finance Corporation." *The Mississippi Valley Historical Review* 46, no. 3 (December 1959): 455–468.

Niemi, Albert W. *U.S. Economic History*. Chicago: Rand McNally, 1975.

Olney, Martha. *Buy Now Pay Later: Advertising, Credit, and Consumer Durables in the 1920s*. Chapel Hill: University of North Carolina Press, 1991.

Sirkin, Gerald. "The Stock Market of 1929 Revisited: A Note." *Business History Review* 49 (Summer 1975): 223–231.

Smiley, Gene. "Did Incomes for Most of the Population Fall from 1923 through 1929?" *Journal of Economic History* 42 (1983): 209–216.

Vanderblue, Homer B. "The Florida Land Boom." *Journal of Land and Public Utility Economics* 3, no. 2 (May 1927): 113–131, 252–269.

Vickers, Raymond. *Panic in Paradise: Florida's Banking Crash of 1926*. Tuscaloosa: University of Alabama Press, 1994.

Warburton, Clark. *The Economic Results of Prohibition*. New York: Columbia University Press, 1932.

White, Eugene N. "State-Sponsored Insurance of Bank Deposits in the United States, 1907–1929." *Journal of Economic History* 41 (September 1981): 537–557.

_____. "A Reinterpretation of the Banking Crisis of 1930." *Journal of Economic History* 44 (1984): 119–138.

_____. "Before the Glass-Steagall Act: An Analysis of the Investment Banking Activities of National Banks." *Explorations in Economic History* 23 (1986): 33–53.

_____. "When the Ticker Ran Late: The Stock Market Boom and Crash of 1929." In *The Stock Market Crash in Historical Perspective*, ed. Eugene Nelson White. Homewood, Ill.: Dow Jones–Irwin, 1989.

Williamson, Jeffrey, and Peter Lindert. *American Inequality: A Macroeconomic History*. New York: Academic Press, 1981.

Zuckoff, Mitchell. *Ponzi's Scheme: The True Story of a Financial Legend*. New York: Random House, 2005.

CHAPTER 23

The Great Depression

CHAPTER THEME

As the 1920s drew to a close, Americans were confident in their well-being and in the prospects of even better times ahead. On the election trail in the summer of 1928, presidential candidate Herbert Hoover boasted of America's optimism with these words:

We in America today are nearer to the final triumph over poverty than ever before in the history of any land. The poorhouse is vanishing from among us. We have not yet reached the goal, but, given the chance to go forward with the policies of the last eight years, we shall soon, with the help of God, be in sight of the day when poverty will be banished from this nation.

Hardly a voice in the wilderness, Hoover's words were typical of the confidence of the times; nearly everyone missed the emerging signs of a faltering economy. Indeed, many failed to recognize the magnitude of the decline even after the Great Depression was erupting in full force.

The Great Depression was the most important economic event of the twentieth century. Between 1929 and 1933, the economy of the United States collapsed. It is almost impossible to convey the sheer terror and misery that the depression produced, but numbers can suggest the dimensions. Real GDP fell 30 percent. Unemployment rose from 3.2 percent of the labor force in 1929 to 24.9 percent in 1933. Hunger and fear paralyzed the nation.

The central questions for economic historians are these: What caused this unprecedented collapse? Why did the economy remain depressed for so long? How can a repetition be avoided? As we shall see, scholars are still far from full agreement on all the issues. A consensus has been reached, however, on the key factors that contributed to the severity of the crisis, in particular the breakdown of the financial system. In this chapter, we concentrate on the dimensions and causes of the crisis. In the next chapter, we focus on the response of the Roosevelt administration to the depression and on the long-term consequences, particularly the emergence of the modern "mixed" economy in which the central government plays a major role in the allocation of resources.

DIMENSIONS OF THE DEPRESSION

It is utterly remarkable, even in hindsight, that an economic catastrophe of such magnitude could have occurred. In the four years from 1929 to 1933, the American economy simply disintegrated. The U.S. gross domestic product (GDP) in current prices declined 46 percent, from $104.4 billion to $56 billion. As shown in Figure 23.1, in constant (1929) prices, the decline was 27 percent. Industrial production declined by more than one-half, and gross investment, as indicated in Figure 23.2, came to a halt. By 1933, gross investment was below levels of capital depreciation. The nation's capital stock was

FIGURE 23.1

Gross Domestic
Product, 1929–1940

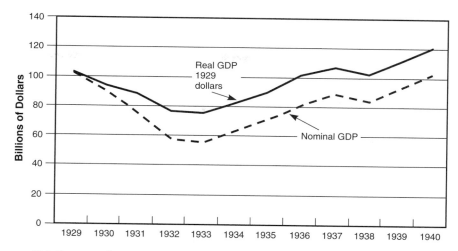

Source: *U.S. Bureau of Economic Analysis.*

actually declining. In the process, wholesale prices dropped one-third and consumer prices one-quarter. At the trough of the depression in March 1933, output of durables had fallen 80 percent; nondurables had fallen 30 percent.

The most horrible statistics were those for unemployment. Figure 23.3 graphically illustrates how unemployment soared. The number of unemployed rose from 1.5 million to 11.5 million. In 1933, the worst year, one-quarter of the civilian workforce was unemployed or had to get by on emergency "make work" jobs created by the federal government. Many of those employed were working fewer hours. Fully half of the nation's breadwinners were either out of work or in seriously reduced circumstances. There were fewer two-earner families and no unemployment insurance to cushion the blow.

The intensity of the Great Depression was agonizing, and its seeming endlessness brought frustration and despair. The depression of 1920 and 1921 had been sharp and nasty, with a decline in durable-goods output of 43 percent, but it had behaved as a depression should, coming and going quickly. In the Great Depression, on the other hand, durable-goods production did not regain the 1929 peak until August 1940, more than

FIGURE 23.2

Gross Private Domestic
Investment, 1929–1940

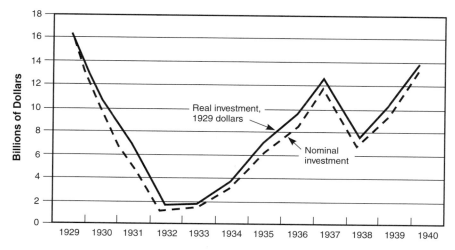

Source: *U.S. Bureau of Economic Analysis.*

FIGURE 23.3

Percentage of the Labor Force Unemployed, 1920–1940

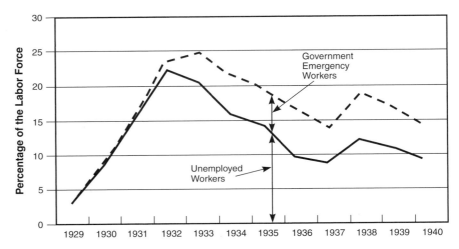

Source: *Michael Darby, "Three and a Half Million U.S. Employees Have Been Mislaid: Or an Explanation of Unemployment, 1934–41," Journal of Political Economy 84 (1976): 7, 8. Reprinted by permission of the University of Chicago Press.*

11 years after the beginning of the depression. Unemployment, as shown in Figure 23.3, remained stubbornly high a decade after the depression began.

It is difficult to overemphasize the deep imprint registered by the duration and depth of the collapse. The revolutionary impact—economically, politically, socially, and psychologically—of the events of that fateful decade were matched only by those of the Civil War.

CAUSES OF THE GREAT DEPRESSION

A satisfactory explanation of the Great Depression requires us to distinguish between the forces that brought a downturn in economic activity and those that turned a downturn into an utter disaster.

Hindsight enables us to detect two drags on the economy that prepared the way for a decline in economic activity. The most important was the decline from 1925 onward in both residential and nonresidential construction. The boom in building activity that began in 1918 had doubtlessly helped the economy out of the slump of 1920 and 1921; the downward phase of the same building cycle, coinciding as it did with other economic weaknesses, was a major depressing influence. What began as a gentle slide in construction from 1925 to 1927 became a marked decline in 1928. The second drag on the economy came from the agricultural sector, which was still important enough in the 1920s to exert a powerful influence on the total economy. As noted in chapter 22, farmers struggled throughout the decade with falling world prices and heavy indebtedness. In the great agricultural midlands, few manifestations of boom psychology appeared after 1926.

A mild downturn in durables output in the spring of 1929 and a drop in nondurable production in the summer of that year could well have been expected—but nothing catastrophic was forecasted. A series of devastating blows that turned a recession into the Great Depression then hit the economy.

The Stock Market Crash

The first blow was the break in the stock market during the last week in October 1929. Declines in the stock market, even substantial ones, do not inevitably cause declines in

Wall Street on Black Thursday, October 24, 1929. Investors and the curious milled around in confusion in the planked street (subway construction was going on) as the extent of the disaster inside the New York Stock Exchange (at right) became clear.

business. The 1987 crash is an example of one that did not. The 1929 break, however, significantly accelerated the mild downturn then under way because of the catastrophic magnitude of the decline and the uncertainty it created about the future course of the economy.

The *New York Times* index of 25 industrial stocks, which early in 1924 had stood at 110, had climbed by January 1929 to 338, and by September to 452. It was almost impossible to buy a common stock that did not rise rapidly in value, and investors quickly accumulated fortunes. The optimism engendered by these gains permeated the business community and led to the conclusion that permanent prosperity had arrived. Some investors and government officials, however, had become uneasy about the dizzying heights to which prices had risen. President Hoover and officials at the Federal Reserve worried about excessive speculation and the danger of a crash. In August, the Federal Reserve raised the discount rate (the rate at which it lent to member banks) to 6 percent in an attempt to stem the flow of credit into the stock market. The Bank of England and other central banks took similar actions for the same reason. For a short time, at least, these actions had no effect: Stock prices continued upward.

On September 5, the well-known investment adviser Roger Babson warned that a crash was coming, and the market staggered through the "Babson break." Prices declined through September, but as yet, there was no sign of panic. Then a sharp break occurred on October 23 and October 24 ("Black Thursday"), when a record 13 million shares traded (3 million was normal). Massive organized buying by banks and investment houses prevented a complete rout, but on October 28 ("Black Monday") and October 29 ("Black Tuesday"), the panic resumed. The slide continued until mid-November. By that time, stock prices had fallen to about one-half of what they had been in August.

Newspapers reported the painful details of Wall Street's Collapse.

Well into 1930, however, share prices remained above the levels reached in 1926. If all that was involved had been the loss of the extraordinary capital gains made by stock market investors in 1927 and 1928, it would be hard to blame the depression on the stock market crash—after all, "easy come, easy go." The unique psychological trauma produced by the crash was more significant than the direct effects of the loss of wealth. In the 1920s many Americans had come to believe that the economy had entered a "new era" of continuous and rapid progress that would carry them to higher and higher standards of living. The spectacular rise in the stock market was taken as proof that this view was widely shared by knowledgeable investors. When the market crashed, this optimistic view of the future crashed with it; almost overnight, uncertainty and pessimism about the future gripped the public. Purchases of consumer durables, in particular, which depended on consumer confidence about the future and which had increasingly been bought on the installment plan, declined drastically (Romer 1990). See New View 23.1 on page 423 on lessons the stock market crash could teach.

NEW VIEW 23.1

LESSONS FROM HISTORY FOR INVESTING IN THE STOCK MARKET

The following figure shows the value of stocks on the New York Stock Exchange from 1925 to 1955. If someone had invested at the peak in 1928, they would have had to wait until 1952, 24 years, to see the value of their investment recover. This might have seemed an acceptable wait for a young person, fresh out of college, and saving for retirement. But it would have seemed a tragedy for an older person nearing retirement in 1928. The right time to buy, of course, was at trough in 1932. Stocks bought in 1932 had nearly doubled in value by the end of the decade. The trick, of course, was knowing that the stock market had finally bottomed out and having the cash to invest.

FIGURE 23.4
The Cowles Commission/ Standard and Poor Index of Common Stock Prices, 1925–1955 (1928=100)

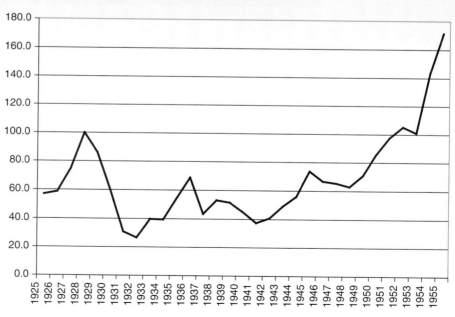

Source: Historical Statistics *2006, Series CJ800.*

The Banking Crises

The devastating impact of the stock market collapse came in the early stages of the depression. Morale might have improved, and the stock market and the economy might have regained some buoyancy had it not been for the structural weaknesses of the banking system.

The economy was repeatedly buffeted in the early 1930s by waves of bank failures. The first of these, as shown in Table 23.1 on page 424, began in October 1930 with the failure of banks in the South and Midwest. Although losses were heavy, these failures drew little attention from the Federal Reserve or the national media, perhaps because they were similar to the failures that had occurred in the 1920s (White 1984; Wicker 1996, chapter 2). Then on December 11, the Bank of the United States in New York failed. This failure was significant for several reasons. It was the largest failure, measured by deposits, in the history of the United States up to that time. Although it was an ordinary bank (chartered by the state of New York), its name may have led some people to believe that a bank having a particularly close association with the government had failed. Its location in New York City (although it was not a Wall Street bank), moreover, may have produced fears that the heart of the nation's financial system was now in danger.

The Federal Reserve at this point, most economic historians agree, should have acted as a *lender of last resort*. It should have lent generously to the Bank of United States and other failing banks to break the cycle of fear that was undermining the banking system. This was standard practice in financial crises: In financial panics central banks should

TABLE 23.1 A CHRONOLOGY OF THE FINANCIAL MELTDOWN, 1929–1933

DATE	EVENT	COMMENT
October 1929	The stock market crash	Optimism about the future becomes pessimism. Consumer durable purchases fall.
October 1930	Onset of the first banking crisis in the United States	Bank failures mount in the South and Midwest.
December 11, 1930	Failure of the Bank of the United States in New York City	The ratio of currency to deposits begins to rise.
March 1931	Onset of the second banking crisis in the United States	Bank failures reach new highs, and deposits fall.
May 1931	Failure of the Kreditanstalt, Austria's largest private bank	The crisis has become international.
July 1931	Closing of the German banks	Capital flows to the United States, but short-term obligations of U.S. banks are frozen.
September 1931	Britain's departure from gold standard	Is nothing sacred? Drain of gold from the United States.
April 1932	Beginnings of large-scale open-market purchases	Too little, too late.
March 1933	The banking panic of 1933	State bank holidays occur. President Roosevelt declares a national holiday on March 6.

Source: *Derived from Friedman and Schwartz 1965, 301–324, and other histories of the period.*

follow Bagehot's rule (see Economic Insight 12.1) and lend freely at high rates. For a variety of reasons that we will discuss in detail below, however, it did not do so. To the Federal Reserve, it seemed that the banks that were failing were simply badly managed banks that should be eliminated to make the system more efficient. At times a rumor that a bank was in trouble would send people running to the bank to try to get their money out before the bank closed its doors, the classic sign of a panic. More generally, the fear of bank failures led people to convert deposits into cash, depriving the banks of reserves. The banks, moreover, to build up their reserves refused to make new loans or renew old ones. The result was shrinkage in the amount of deposits and bank loans available. In retrospect, we can see that it was important to end this downward spiral, but the Federal Reserve did not recognize it at the time.

For a few months, things seemed calmer, but a second, more intense crisis began in the United States in March 1931 and continued throughout the summer. This time events abroad reinforced the crisis in the United States. In May 1931, the Kreditanstalt, a major bank in Vienna, failed. Because gold was the base of the money supply in most industrial countries, failures such as this one convinced people worldwide that it was time to convert paper claims to gold into the real thing. In July 1931 the panic had spread throughout central Europe, and the German government was forced to close the German banks. In September 1931, Britain, still one of the world's financial centers and a symbol of financial rectitude, left the gold standard. The British pound would no longer be convertible on demand into gold. This, in turn, increased the pressure on the dollar, which was still convertible into gold.

The final banking panic in the United States began in 1933. Between 1930 and 1932, more than 5,000 banks containing more than $3 billion in deposits (about 7 percent of total deposits in January 1930) had suspended operations. In 1933, another 4,000 banks containing more than $3.5 billion in deposits would close. The banks' weakened condition after years of deflation, uncertainties about how the new administration of Franklin D. Roosevelt would handle the crisis, and the general atmosphere of distrust and fear all contributed to the final crisis. By the time that Roosevelt took office on March 4, 1933, the financial system had ceased to function.

One of President Roosevelt's first acts was to announce a nationwide bank holiday beginning on March 6, 1933. This action, which followed a number of state bank holidays, closed all of the banks in the country for one week. How could such an action improve things? The public was told that during this period, the banks would be inspected and only the sound ones allowed to reopen. Questions have been raised about the way this was handled. Probably many sound banks were closed and unsound ones allowed to remain open. But the medicine seemed to work, even if it was only a placebo; the panic subsided.

In addition to the bank holiday, the federal government took a number of other actions that helped to restore confidence in the financial system. Gold hoarding was ended by the simple expedient of requiring everyone to turn their monetary gold over to the Federal Reserve in exchange for some other currency. Perhaps most important, the Federal Deposit Insurance Corporation (FDIC) was established to insure bank deposits. The insurance took effect on January 1, 1934, and within six months, almost all of the nation's commercial banks were covered. Deposit insurance dramatically changed the incentives facing depositors. No longer would a rumor of failure send people rushing to the bank to try to be first in line; they now knew that they would eventually be paid their deposits in any case. Together these policies drastically changed the rate of bank failures. The number of bank failures fell from 4,000 in 1933 to 61 in 1934 and remained at double-digit levels through the rest of the 1930s. (By way of contrast, the lowest number of bank failures in any year from 1921 to 1929 was 366 in 1922.) Although the Great

Depression was to drag on for the remainder of the decade, the banking crisis had been surmounted. The introduction of deposit insurance and the decline in bank failures that followed are a striking example of Economic Reasoning Proposition 3, incentives matter (see page 8).

The Smoot-Hawley Tariff

The Smoot-Hawley tariff has often been considered along with the stock market crash and the banking panics to have been a major cause of the Great Depression. Scholars for the most part now agree, however, that the tariff, although unwise, was a minor force driving the economy down. The tariff was passed in June 1930. It raised tariffs on a wide array of goods, especially agricultural products. There were vigorous protests against the bill, and 1,000 economists, including all the leaders of the profession, signed a petition urging President Hoover to veto it on the grounds that high tariffs would reduce imports, thus making it more difficult for other countries to earn the money needed to buy U.S. exports. It also was believed that high tariffs would provoke retaliation by other countries. Every country would raise its tariffs, and trade would decline. Soon, in fact, other countries did raise their tariffs, for example, Great Britain in 1932. It is difficult to say, however, whether other countries raised their tariffs in retaliation for the American tariffs or for other reasons, such as simply to raise revenues during the depression because normal sources of funds were drying up.

Trade, however, was less important to the U.S. economy than it is now. Exports were only 6 percent of GNP in 1930, and imports only 4.9 percent. The increases in the tariffs, moreover, applied only to a portion of the total array of U.S. imports; many goods were exempted. The increased tariffs did have some positive employment benefits in import-competing sectors. So at most, Smoot-Hawley made a bad situation slightly worse (Eichengreen 1989). Perhaps the greatest effect of the tariff was psychological: Controversy over the bill added to pessimism about the future, and dampened willingness to invest.

For many other countries more dependent on trade than the United States, the rounds of tariff increases that followed Smoot-Hawley in the thirties were more significant. Most experts at the time, and since, viewed the tendency to raise tariffs in the thirties as a self-defeating "beggar thy neighbor" policy. Partly as a result, the United States became a champion after World War II (although not always a consistent one) of lower tariffs and freer trade. The Smoot-Hawley tariff turned out to be the last of America's high "protective" tariffs.

THE ROLE OF THE FINANCIAL CRISIS

The financial and banking crises were clearly major disasters. However, that observation raises additional questions. What was their role in the Great Depression? Were they the cause of the depression or only a consequence of it? Exactly how did they contribute to the collapse of the real economy? To answer these questions, we can turn to the analyses of the leading financial historians.

Monetary Effects of the Financial Crises

To monetarists such as Milton Friedman and Anna J. Schwartz (1963), the primary cause of the Great Depression was the decline in the stock of money produced by the withdrawal of currency from the banking system and the decisions of banks to hold more reserves. The only way banks could maintain or increase their reserves was by decreasing their lending, a decision that led to a multiple contraction of bank credit and deposits. According to the quantity theory of money, when the stock of money contracts, people try to restore the relationship between their money balances and their incomes by spending less. The result is a fall in the GDP. Thus, monetarists believe that the fall in the stock of money from $47 billion in 1929 to $32 billion in 1933, as shown in Table 23.2, was a major *cause* of the fall in GDP from $104 billion to $56 billion. They blame the Federal Reserve for not acting as a lender of last resort to prevent the decline in the stock of money.

Monetarists do not claim that the fall in the stock of money was the only factor at work. Note that the ratio of money to GDP rose (see column 3 of Table 23.2), showing that people were hoarding rather than spending. During the first year of the depression, in particular, the ratio of money to GDP rose, probably because of the stock market crash, while the money supply fell only slightly. Nevertheless, monetarists insist that any decline in the money supply is significant, because the money supply normally rises from year to year.

It is difficult to believe that the collapse of the stock of money did the economy any good, and most financial historians now follow the monetarists in assigning a major role to the monetary collapse. There has been some controversy, however, over exactly how much weight to assign to the banking crisis compared with other causes. The most skeptical view about the role of the money was expressed by Peter Temin (1976). Temin claimed that, although there was a correlation between money and GDP, much of the causation ran from the fall in GDP to the fall in money. The collapse in consumer spending brought about by the stock market crash, according to Temin, produced a downward spiral in which profits fell, workers were laid off, and many borrowers could not repay their bank loans. This triggered the waves of bank failures and the decline in the money stock. This was a tragedy, to be sure, but in Temin's view it was another symptom of the depression rather than the cause. The key piece of evidence, according to Temin, is the behavior of the rate of interest. He contends that if the decline in the money stock were the initiating factor, we would have seen interest rates rising. After all, if there is a shortage of wheat, we expect the price of wheat to rise, and if there is a shortage of money, we expect the rate of interest to rise. But we observe just the opposite: Short-term interest rates (see column 4 in Table 23.2) fell from 5.78 percent in 1929 to 1.67 percent in 1933. (Economic Insight 23.1 provides a more detailed look at Temin's analysis.) To some extent, the debate centers

TABLE 23.2 MONEY AND INCOME, 1929–1933

YEAR	(1) MONEY SUPPLY (billions)	(2) GROSS DOMESTIC PRODUCT (billions)	(3) RATIO OF MONEY TO GDP	(4) COMMERCIAL PAPER RATE (percent)	(5) REAL RATE OF INTEREST (percent)
1929	$46.6	$103.7	0.45	5.78%	5.88%
1930	45.7	92.3	0.50	3.55	8.15
1931	42.7	76.6	0.56	2.63	15.46
1932	36.1	58.8	0.61	2.72	14.99
1933	32.2	56.4	0.57	1.67	3.03

Source: *Milton Friedman and Anna J. Schwartz, Monetary Trends in the United States and the United Kingdom (Chicago: University of Chicago Press, 1982), 124.*

ECONOMIC INSIGHT 23.1

TEMIN'S CRITIQUE OF THE MONETARIST INTERPRETATION OF THE GREAT DEPRESSION

These figures illustrate Peter Temin's famous critique of the monetarist interpretation of the Great Depression. They depict the supply of and demand for money, with the interest rate as the price of holding money. Temin's rendering of the monetarist interpretation is in Figure A and the Keynesian interpretation is in Figure B. If the monetarists were correct (according to Temin), the dominant shift would have been the supply curve to the left (Figure A). If the

Keynesians were right, the dominant shift would have been the demand curve to the left (Figure B). Because interest rates fell during the depression—as shown in column (4) of Table 23.2—Temin concluded that the Keynesians were right.

Monetarists countered that Temin neglected intermediate and longer-term effects of the decline in the quantity of money on the demand for money. Falling real income (caused by past decreases in the supply of money) reduced the demand for money. So part of the shift in the demand curve in Figure B could be attributed to the fall in the stock of money. Moreover, lower market rates were consistent with higher real rates.

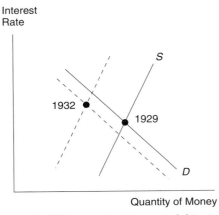

A. If the monetarists were right.

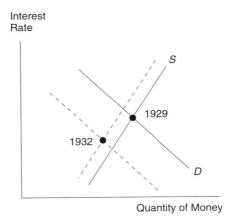

B. If the Keynesians were right.

on the years one stresses. Temin focuses on the events of 1929 and 1930, while Friedman and Schwartz concentrate more on 1930–1933.

Nonmonetary Effects of the Financial Crisis

Recent research has identified additional channels through which the financial crisis accelerated the decline in economic activity. The seminal research was done by Ben Bernanke (1983)—yes, the Ben Bernanke who later became chair of the Federal Reserve Board—who argued on the basis of a wide range of evidence that bank failures made it difficult for firms, particularly smaller firms, to get the credit they needed to remain in operation.

Bernanke's interpretation stressed the problem of "asymmetric information." When a borrower and lender negotiate, their access to key information differs. The lender cannot see into the mind of the borrower to learn the borrower's determination to repay. Normally, this problem can be overcome by forging long-term relationships between borrowers and lenders or through the use of collateral. When a bank failed, however, the long-term relationships between the bank and its borrowers was severed. A borrower

A scene from "It's a Wonderful Life." Mary Bailey (Donna Reed) turns over the money she has saved for a second honeymoon to George Bailey (Jimmy Stewart), so he can end the run on his savings bank. The Federal Reserve should have handled the crisis the way Mary did.

could approach another lender, but how would another lender know that in the past the borrower had struggled to faithfully repay loans or that the borrower was regarded by other members of the community as a good risk? In addition, Bernanke pointed out that the ongoing deflation increased the burden of debt carried by businesses and consumers and thus reduced their ability to qualify for credit. The decline in the value of stocks and land, both urban and rural, had a similar effect. Businesses and individuals did not have assets that they could offer as collateral. Although the role of nonmonetary effects of the crisis has received considerable attention in recent years, it has been thought about for a long time. Irving Fisher (1933), one of America's leading economists of the depression decade, blamed the depression on the rising real value of debt and its effect on spending.

In short, controversy continues over the exact role of the financial crisis in the Great Depression, but most economic historians now agree that the financial crisis was important, and the Federal Reserve deserves considerable blame for the disastrous path along which events unfolded (Temin 1989).

WHY DIDN'T THE FEDERAL RESERVE SAVE THE BANKING SYSTEM?

The Federal Reserve had been created in the wake of the panic of 1907 for the purpose of preventing future crises by acting as a lender of last resort. This was a well-accepted function of central banks. Walter Bagehot famously had argued that the banking system required a lender of last resort in his classic book, *Lombard Street* (1873) (see Economic Insight 12.1). For a number of reasons, however, the Federal Reserve failed to act as lender of last resort during the Great Depression.

One reason is that the members of the Federal Reserve Board simply failed to appreciate the magnitude of the crisis and the actions needed to combat it. In his diary entries during August 1931, Charles S. Hamlin, then a member of the Federal Reserve Board, wrote that the Open Market Committee voted 11 to 1 against open-market purchases of $300 million worth of government bonds—which would have pumped reserves into the banking system as bond sellers deposited the checks drawn on the Federal Reserve —substituting $120 million instead. The governors of the regional banks, who were still in control, simply could not grasp the magnitude of the crisis, and Governor Meyer of the Federal Reserve Board was even worried about inflation.

To some extent, the failure to appreciate the magnitude of the collapse was the result of the tendency at the Federal Reserve to look at the wrong indicators of monetary policy. Many officials at the Federal Reserve believed that low nominal interest rates— column (4) of Table 23.2—were a certain sign that financial markets were awash with money and that trying to pump in more would do little good. Had they looked at real interest rates—column (5) of Table 23.2—they would have reached a different conclusion. The Federal Reserve also misread the fall in the stock of money. The data were available to them, but Fed officials viewed the decline in the stock of money merely as a sign that the need for money had fallen (Steindl 1995).

In its 1932 annual report, the Federal Reserve Board argued that its power to purchase bonds was limited by the requirement that Fed notes be backed 40 percent by gold and 60 percent by either gold or eligible paper (loans sold by the banks to the Federal Reserve). The only "free gold" the Federal Reserve owned, to use the technical term, was the amount of gold that it held in excess of the amount it was legally required to hold. This amount, it argued, was simply too small to permit substantial open-market purchases. Such purchases would have led banks to cut their borrowing from the Fed (why borrow reserves at interest if reserves are already adequate?), depriving the Fed of loans that it could count against notes. The result would be that the Fed's free gold, then about $416 million, would disappear, violating the rules that committed the United States to the gold standard.

Friedman and Schwartz (1963) advance a number of arguments to show that the free gold problem was merely a rationalization, not the real reason for the Federal Reserve's reluctance to expand the stock of money. For one thing, when the rules defining what the Fed had to hold in reserve against notes were eased by the Glass-Steagall Act in February 1932, the Federal Reserve did not respond by increasing its open-market purchases of bonds commensurately. Concern about the maintenance of the gold standard, however, as Barry Eichengreen (1992) has shown, rather than technical concerns about the amount of free gold, may have been an important psychological constraint on Federal Reserve actions. Indeed, in his view, central banks throughout the world made the mistake of putting the maintenance of the gold standard above expanding the stock of money to fight the depression.

A shift of power within the Federal Reserve system identified by Friedman and Schwartz (1963, 407–419) was another important factor. In the 1920s, the Federal Reserve Bank of New York, under its charismatic president Benjamin Strong, had dominated the system. After Strong's death in 1928, the Federal Reserve Board in Washington tried to assert its authority by resisting pressures from New York. This power struggle took its toll in the 1930s, when the New York bank pushed for more expansionary monetary policies and the Federal Reserve Board resisted for internal political reasons.

The precise weight to be put on each of these factors is a matter of debate, but the important point is that as a result of them, the Federal Reserve, although created in 1913 to protect the nation's banking system in times of crisis, failed 20 years later to stop the greatest banking crisis in American history.

FISCAL POLICY IN THE 1930S

The popular belief that the Hoover administration did nothing to combat the depression is erroneous. In January 1932, he set up the Reconstruction Finance Corporation to borrow money by issuing securities guaranteed by the federal government and to relend it to banks, insurance companies, railroads, and other businesses experiencing financial difficulties. The very formation of such an agency in peacetime (it was a revival of the War Finance Corporation of World War I) marked a sharp break with tradition. Support of agricultural prices with production controls by the Federal Farm Board, which had been established in 1929, was equally revolutionary. The Hoover administration's major deficiencies were its persistent refusal to establish a desperately needed federal program of work relief, even if it meant deficits, and its failure to press the Federal Reserve to expand money and credit. Orthodox Keynesians would add that the administration should have deliberately raised spending for whatever purpose and cut taxes to generate "multiplier effects." Virtually all economic historians agree that too much reliance was placed on maintaining confidence through the public testimonials of business and government leaders but not enough on measures to raise incomes and correct the deflation.

Franklin D. Roosevelt and his staff were uncomfortable with deficits. During the campaign of 1932, Roosevelt promised to cut spending 25 percent and balance the budget. But once in office, the Roosevelt administration was willing to run large deficits by historical standards to finance its many new programs. How large were these deficits? Why did they not lift the country out of the depression, as Keynesian economic theory predicts?[1] The relevant numbers are given in Table 23.3. The federal budget was steadily in deficit during the depression. Relative to the traditional size of the federal government, the level of spending and the deficits seemed large indeed. Note that by 1938, federal spending was two and one-half times as high as it had been in 1927. Taxes had also been increased (despite the depression) by 75 percent from $4 billion to $7 billion. The resulting deficit of $0.2 billion ($7.2 − $7.0) in 1938, however, was more than offset by a surplus at the state and local levels of $1.1 billion ($10.0 − $11.1).

---

[1]The famous book by John Maynard Keynes, *The General Theory of Employment, Interest and Money*, was not published until 1936. Many economists, however, favored increased government spending financed by deficits. Some thought that increased spending would "prime the pump" and stimulate the natural expansionary powers of the economy.

TABLE 23.3 GOVERNMENTAL EXPENDITURES AND REVENUES, 1927–1940 (BILLIONS OF DOLLARS)

YEAR	FEDERAL		STATE AND LOCAL		PRIVATE INVESTMENT
	EXPENDITURES	REVENUES	EXPENDITURES	REVENUES	
1929	$2.9	$3.8	$ 7.8[a]	$ 7.8[a]	$14.5
1932	4.8	2.0	8.4	7.9	3.4
1934	6.5	3.1	7.8	8.4	4.1
1936	7.6	4.2	8.5	9.4	7.2
1938	7.2	7.0	10.0	11.1	7.4
1940	9.6	6.9	11.2	11.7	11.0

[a]This is for 1927; data for 1929 is not avaiable.

Source: Historical Statistics *1975, Series F53, Y335, Y336, Y339, Y340, Y652, and Y671.*

PARTIAL RECOVERY AND THEN A NEW DOWNTURN

The Price of Gold and the Stock of Money

During the bank holiday and the weeks that followed, the Roosevelt administration prohibited transactions in gold. On April 5, 1933, it took the extraordinary step of ordering all holders of gold to deliver their gold (rare coins and other specialized holdings were exempt) to the Federal Reserve. These actions took the United States off the gold standard. For several months, the price of gold, and therefore of foreign currencies still linked to gold, fluctuated according to the dictates of supply and demand. The federal government, however, made a determined effort to increase the price of gold by purchasing gold. The idea was to raise the dollar price of commodities, particularly agricultural commodities, set on world markets. To some extent, the policy was successful; some of the inflation that occurred in this period, otherwise surprising because of the depressed state of the economy, can be attributed to the manipulation of the exchange rate.

On January 31, 1934, the United States recommitted itself to a form of the gold standard by fixing a price of $35 per ounce (the predepression price had been $20 per ounce) at which the Treasury would buy or sell gold. The new form of the gold standard, however, was only a pale reflection of the classical gold standard because ordinary citizens were not allowed to hold gold coins. As a result of these policies, production of gold in the United States and the rest of the world soared in the 1930s. World production rose from 25 million ounces in 1933 to 40 million ounces in 1940. After all, costs of production such as wages had fallen, but the price at which gold could be sold to the U.S. Treasury had risen. The result was a rapid increase in the Treasury's stock of gold. When the government sets prices, it changes incentives and influences production. This is explained in Economic Reasoning Proposition 3, incentives matter. In addition, the rise of fascism in Europe created a large outflow of capital, including gold, seeking a safe haven and further augmenting U.S. gold holdings.

When the Treasury purchased gold, it created gold certificates that it could use as cash or deposit with the Federal Reserve. In effect, if the Treasury bought gold, it was allowed to pay for it by printing new currency. The result was a rapid increase in the monetary base, which, in conjunction with the redeposit of currency in the banking system, produced a rapid increase in the money supply.

Climbing Out of the Abyss

GDP rose from a low of $56 billion in 1933 to $92 billion in 1937, still well below the level of 1929 but sufficient to alleviate much hardship and to demonstrate the potential of the economy to recover. Over the same period, the implicit price deflator rose from 73.3 to 81.0 (1929 = 100). This boom was stimulated, orthodox Keynesians argue, by the expansion of government spending for relief of the unemployed and for other New Deal programs to be described in chapter 24. Recovery was also stimulated by the expansion of the money stock from $32.2 billion in 1933 to $45.7 billion in 1937.

The monetary expansion was not the result of a deliberate Federal Reserve policy of increasing the money stock. Rather, as confidence in the banking system took hold, people began to redeposit currency in the banking system. This led to an increase in the money stock because banks would create several dollars of loans and deposits on the basis of each additional dollar of currency redeposited. The fractional reserve system that had worked to destroy the monetary system from 1930 to 1933 now ran in reverse. Even more important, however, was an increase in the monetary base, primarily because of purchases of gold by the U.S. Treasury (Romer 1992).

Campaign promises to balance the budget and cut spending met head-on with the economic realities of the Great Depression. Some in the media chastised FDR for deficit spending to pay for his new programs.

The Recession within the Depression

By early 1937, total manufacturing output had exceeded the rate of 1929, and the recovery, though not complete, seemed to be going well. At that point, however, the expansion came to an abrupt halt. Industrial production reached a post-1929 high in May 1937 and then turned downward. Commodity prices followed, and the weary process of deflation began again. Retail sales dropped, unemployment increased, and payrolls declined. Adding to the general gloom, the stock market started a long slide in August that brought prices in March 1938 to less than half the peak of the previous year. The important setbacks of 1937 are revealed graphically in Figures 23.1 through 23.3.

Whatever merit this argument has, it is clear that fiscal and monetary policy also played a role in causing the downturn. Government officials were convinced in early 1937 that full employment and inflation were just around the corner. Expenditures for relief and public works were cut, and new taxes such as the Social Security tax (discussed in chapter 24) were imposed. The result was that the projected deficit for 1937 dropped significantly. Keynesian economists would not be surprised to find a recession.

Monetary policy also worked to create a recession. The excess reserves of the banks, as noted, had risen steadily after the banking crises of the early 1930s. The Federal Reserve interpreted these reserves simply as money piling up in the banks because it could not be profitably invested at the low interest rates then prevailing. The Fed then decided to raise legal reserve ratios to lock up the excess reserves and prevent them from being put into use during the anticipated not-too-distant inflation. This policy, however, proved to be a disastrous mistake. In fact, these reserves were not unwanted by the banks, which had been deliberately building up a cushion in the event of a replay of the banking crises. Their response to the Federal Reserve's decision to raise legal reserve ratios was to restore their margin of safety by acquiring more reserves. To do this, they reduced their loans and deposits. The money supply fell once again, although only slightly, in 1937.

The contraction from 1937 to 1938 was not as deep or as persistent as the contraction from 1929 to 1933. One reason is that the banking system did not collapse. The protection created by deposit insurance, along with the cautious behavior of the banks that survived the debacle of the early 1930s, prevented a repetition. In 1937 only 82 banks suspended operations, and in 1938 only 80, compared with 1,350 in 1930 and 2,293 in 1931. Nevertheless, the result of the recession within the depression was that the economy was still far from fully employed in 1939.

WHY DID THE DEPRESSION LAST SO LONG?

The United States had experienced many financial crises before 1929. At the start of the Great Depression, people remembered the panics of 1907 and 1893. On those occasions, the recession following the financial panic was sharp, but the recovery was rapid. The depression of the 1930s, however, dragged on and on. What had happened? Why did it last so long? This is the most controversial question about the depression. Part of the story, of course, is simply how far the economy had fallen. If you fall into a deep pit, it will take a long time to crawl out, even if you are climbing rapidly. The recession within the depression, moreover, delayed the final recovery by several years. Something more, however, seems to have been at work, and many economic historians have labored to figure out what it was.

Perverse Effects of the New Deal?

One factor, stressed by some economists at the time, including Joseph Schumpeter (1939, 1037–1050) in particular and more recently Robert Higgs (1997), was that the level of private investment spending remained depressed (see the last column in Table 23.3). They blame the political climate created by the New Deal for discouraging investment. Social Security and the new freedom granted to labor came in for some harsh words from the business community. The rhetoric of the New Deal, it must be admitted, was often antibusiness. In his State of the Union message of 1936, President Roosevelt had castigated "the royalists of the economic order" who, he said, opposed government intervention in economic affairs and received a disproportionate amount of national income. People of means especially resented the tax legislation in 1935 and 1936, directed at preventing tax avoidance and making the tax structure more progressive. In addition, estate and gift taxes were increased, as were individual surtaxes and taxes on the income of large corporations. The undistributed profits tax of 1936—a surtax imposed on corporations to make them distribute profits instead of holding them so that individual stockholders could avoid personal taxation—was also resented. Why would business undertake long-term investments, critics of the administration wondered, when the profits might all be taken away by future legislation? The argument is plausible, but difficult to prove or disprove. Higgs looked at a variety of evidence including opinion polls and found some support for the conjecture, but Thomas Mayer and Manojit Chatterji (1985) found no correlation between New Deal legislative actions and investment spending.

New Deal Policies such as the National Industrial Recovery Act (1933) and the National Labor Relations Act (1935), which are described in more detail in chapter 24, have also been criticized. These policies were intended to restore full employment by checking the downward spiral of wages and prices, even at the cost of allowing firms to collude to keep prices up, an action that was traditionally illegal under the Sherman Antitrust Act. Harold L. Cole and Lee E. Ohanian (2004), however, maintained that these policies had the unintended effect of inhibiting downward adjustments in wages and prices that would have produced a new full employment equilibrium. Michael D. Bordo, Christopher J. Erceg, and Charles L. Evans (2000) constructed a model in which "sticky" wages help explain the severity and persistence of the depression, although they remain open about the origins of sticky wages. These economists use calibrated general equilibrium models to make their case. One can get a taste of their arguments, however, by considering what would happen in a competitive labor market if the demand for labor fell, but the wage rate was prevented from falling by a government-enforced cartel or some other factor that inhibited adjustment. The result would be a supply of labor that exceeded demand: persistent unemployment.

Fiscal and Monetary Policy

Keynesian economists argue, as noted above, that New Deal fiscal policy, although hotly contested politically, was simply not strong enough to push the economy back to full employment. Keynesian theory suggests that the role of government spending is to offset decreases in autonomous private spending such as investment or consumption. It is clear that the fall in private investment spending alone, $7.1 billion between 1929 and 1938 (Table 23.3), was far greater than the increase in federal spending or the federal deficit. Indeed, the federal deficit was offset by surpluses at the state and local level. No wonder, then, that Keynesian economist E. Cary Brown concluded that "fiscal policy...seems to have been an unsuccessful recovery device in the thirties—not because it does not work, but because it was not tried" (Brown 1956, 879; Peppers 1973). What was needed,

© BETTMANN/CORBIS

Farm and home foreclosures and unemployment created a growing mass of homeless people during the depression. Shantytowns like this one were called "Hoovervilles."

according to Keynesian economists, was huge injections of federal spending of the type that finally came in World War II.

Similarly, monetarists blame the length of the depression on the failure of the Federal Reserve to use the monetary device with sufficient vigor. If the Federal Reserve had increased the money supply rapidly and steadily, rather than allow it to plunge during the Great Crash of 1929 to 1932 and in the recession within the depression, the depression would have never reached the proportions that it did. Ultimately, in the monetarist view, the depression was cured by the huge injections of new money that occurred in the late 1930s and World War II (Cole and Ohanian). Bernanke's analysis (1983) of the financial system also helps explain why the depression lasted so long. He believes that bank lending was often based on long-term relationships between banks and their customers. When the banking system collapsed, it took a long time for the surviving banks to forge new relationships with borrowers. Had the banking system been saved in 1929 to 1933, lending could have been restored much sooner.

CAN IT HAPPEN AGAIN?

No one can say for certain that such a depression cannot happen again. As this is written (Spring 2009) the United States is passing thorough the worst economic crisis since the Great Depression, and many people are afraid that we are at the beginning of another Great Depression; that unemployment rates may rise from the current level of 8 or 9 percent to 25 percent.

There are many reasons, however, for thinking that a collapse on the scale of the Great Depression is unlikely. One reason is that we are not likely to repeat the same mistakes. The Federal Reserve, with better data at hand and with the monetary history of the Great Depression laid out in many books and articles, is unlikely to permit a collapse of the banking system. The Federal Reserve's aggressive actions to halt the current crisis are a far cry from its passivity in 1929–1933. The same is true of fiscal policy. In the 1930s, especially the early 1930s, the Roosevelt administration was unwilling to run huge deficits, even as it increased spending for emergency relief. Today's crisis has been met by a massive economic "stimulus package." Many sorts of spending such as unemployment benefits — the so-called automatic stabilizers— are increasing without specific congressional actions.

The private economy, too, is less vulnerable to economic collapse. The industrial sector, particularly producers of consumer durables, is the most susceptible to sudden shifts in demand that produce massive layoffs. This is true today, as it was in the 1930s. This sector, however, is now relatively much smaller compared with the service sector than it was in the. 1930s. The rapid increase in two-earner households, moreover, has reduced the likelihood for many families that an economic downturn will completely deprive them of an income. Finally, there exists a vast network of government programs that would alleviate suffering and, simply by being there, reduce the chance of a paralyzing fear. These include the FDIC, the Pension Guarantee Corporation, and others. However much we may be aware of these facts, it is nevertheless true that when the crisis of 2007 – 2009 hit, the nightmare of the Great Depression came back to haunt us.

WHAT DOES THE DEPRESSION TELL US ABOUT CAPITALISM?

Rexford Tugwell, a member of President Roosevelt's "brain trust" (a group of advisers who suggested many new programs to combat the depression), remarked:

> *The Cat is out of the Bag. There is no invisible hand. There never was. If the depression has not taught us that, we are incapable of education....We must now supply a real and visible guiding hand to do the task which that mythical, nonexistent, invisible agency was supposed to perform, but never did. (Gruver 1972, 936)*

Tugwell's forthright remark addresses a fundamental question raised by the Great Depression: Doesn't the depression prove that unguided by government, a free market economy has the potential to run off the rails and produce an economic disaster? Why should we leave the allocation of capital to a stock market that goes through ridiculous boom-and-bust cycles? And why should we leave the allocation of agricultural products to Adam Smith's "invisible hand" when it drives farmers off the land while people in cities go hungry? To many thoughtful observers in the 1930s, the clear answer to these questions was the one given by Tugwell: Do not leave things to the free market; common sense tells us that government regulation makes things better.

Most mainstream economists and economic historians, however, have not been entirely persuaded. John Maynard Keynes, who agreed that the depression revealed fundamental weaknesses in the economic system, nevertheless concluded that it did not justify across-the-board intervention in the market. He believed that the depression was a problem of aggregate demand and that this was separate from the problem of individual markets. As he wrote:

> *To put the point concretely, I see no reason to suppose that the existing system seriously misemploys the factors of production which are in use. There are, of course, errors of foresight; but these would not be avoided by centralizing decisions. When 9,000,000 men are employed out of 10,000,000 willing and able to work, there is no evidence that the labor of these 9,000,000 men is misdirected. The complaint against the present system is not that these 9,000,000 men ought to be employed on different tasks, but that tasks should be available for the remaining 1,000,000 men. It is in determining the volume, not the direction, of actual employment that the existing system has broken down. (Keynes 1964 [1936], 379)*

More conservative economists have given the most negative answer to Tugwell. In their view, the Great Depression was a monetary-financial crisis. Government regulation had produced a weak, crisis-prone banking system. The Federal Reserve, the agency created to prevent banking crises, failed to save it when confidence in the banking system collapsed. Eliminate these weaknesses by allowing the banking system to strengthen itself through competition and by forcing the Federal Reserve to maintain the stock of money, and a recurrence of the Great Depression could be prevented. All government programs introduced in the 1930s, in their view, served merely to undermine confidence, discourage private investment, and delay recovery. During the 1930s, Tugwell's position prevailed. As we shall read in chapter 24, the depression led to a vast increase in the extent to which the federal government attempted to influence individual markets.

SELECTED REFERENCES AND SUGGESTED READINGS

Bagehot, Walter. *Lombard Street.* London: H.S. King, 1873.

Bernanke, Benjamin. "Nonmonetary Effects of the Financial Crisis in the Propagation of the Great Depression." *American Economic Review* 73 (1983): 257–276.

Bordo, Michael D., Christopher Erceg, and Charles L. Evans. "Money, Sticky Wages, and the Great Depression." *American Economic Review* 90 (2000): 1447–1463.

Brown, E. Cary. "Fiscal Policy in The Thirties: A Reappraisal." *American Economic Review* 46 (December 1956): 857–859.

Cole, Harold L., and Lee E. Ohanian. "New Deal Policies and the Persistence of the Great Depression: A General Equilibrium Analysis." *The Journal of Political Economy* 112, no. 4 (August 2004): 779–816.

Darby, Michael. "Three and a Half Million U.S. Employees Have Been Mislaid: Or an Explanation of Unemployment, 1934–41." *Journal of Political Economy* 84 (1976): 7, 8.

Eichengreen, Barry. "The Political Economy of the Smoot-Hawley Tariff." In *Research in Economic History,* Volume 12, eds. Roger Ransom, Peter H. Lindert, and Richard Sutch, 1–43. Greenwich, Conn.: JAI, 1989.

———. *Golden Fetters: The Gold Standard and the Great Depression, 1919–1939.* New York: Oxford University Press, 1992.

Fisher, Irving. "The Debt Deflation Theory of Great Depressions." *Econometrica* 1 (1933): 337–357.

Friedman, Milton, and Anna J. Schwartz. *A Monetary History of the United States.* Princeton, N.J.: Princeton University Press, 1963.

———. *Monetary Trends in the United States and the United Kingdom.* Chicago: University of Chicago Press, 1982.

Gruver, Rebecca. *An American History.* New York: Appleton-Century-Crofts, 1972.

Higgs, Robert. "Regime Uncertainty: Why the Great Depression Lasted So Long and Why Prosperity Resumed after the War." *Independent Review* 1 (Spring 1997): 561–590.

Historical Statistics, Colonial Times to 1970, bicentennial edition. U.S. Bureau of the Census. Washington, D.C.: Government Printing Office, 1975.

Historical Statistics of the United States, millennial edition. Eds. Susan B. Carter, et. al. Cambridge: Cambridge University Press, 2006.

Keynes, John Maynard. *The General Theory of Employment, Interest and Money*. New York: Harcourt, Brace & World, 1964 (reprint of 1936 edition).

Mayer, Thomas, and Monojit Chatterji. "Political Shocks and Investment: Some Evidence from the 1930s." *The Journal of Economic History* 45, no. 4 (December 1985): 913–924.

Peppers, Larry C. "Full Employment Surplus Analysis and Structural Changes: The 1930s." *Explorations in Economic History* 10 (Winter 1973): 197–210.

Romer, Christina. "The Great Crash and the Onset of the Great Depression." *Quarterly Journal of Economics* 105 (1990): 597–624.

_____. "What Ended the Great Depression?" *Journal of Economic History* 52 (December 1992): 757–784.

Schumpeter, Joseph. *Business Cycles*. New York: McGraw-Hill Book Company, Inc., 1939.

Steindl, Frank G. *Monetary Interpretations of the Great Depression*. Ann Arbor: University of Michigan Press, 1995.

Temin, Peter. *Did Monetary Forces Cause the Great Depression?* New York: Norton, 1976.

_____. *Lessons from the Great Depression*. Cambridge, Mass.: MIT Press, 1989.

U.S. Bureau of Economic Analysis. http://www.bea.gov/.

White, Eugene N. "A Reinterpretation of the Banking Crisis of 1930." *Journal of Economic History* 44 (1984): 119–138.

Wicker, Elmus. *The Banking Panics of the Great Depression*. New York: Cambridge University Press, 1996.

CHAPTER **24**

The New Deal

The presidential campaign of 1932 was fought in an atmosphere of fear and discontent. Herbert Hoover, nominated for a second term, blamed events in Europe for the nation's troubles and promised that prosperity would soon return. Tampering with our basic economic institutions, Hoover argued, could only lead to even worse disasters. Franklin D. Roosevelt, the warm and yet forceful Democratic candidate, generally was not specific about what measures he would take if elected, although he did promise to balance the budget. There was no mistaking his willingness to use the power of the government to try to solve the nation's problems. In his acceptance speech at the Democratic convention, Roosevelt promised a "New Deal" if he were elected. Few people at the time realized how fully these words would be put into practice in the years to come.

Between Roosevelt's election and his inauguration, economic conditions deteriorated. No president since Abraham Lincoln had faced a greater crisis at the moment he assumed power. One-quarter of the nation's workers were unemployed. In his inaugural address, delivered on March 4, 1933, Roosevelt rallied the nation's spirits, declaring, "Let me assert my firm belief that the only thing we have to fear is fear itself—nameless, unreasoning, unjustified terror which paralyzes needed efforts to convert retreat into advance."

THE FIRST NEW DEAL

The New Deal unfolded in two phases. In the *First New Deal* (1933–1934), in particular in the first "100 days," a wide range of legislation designed both to provide immediate relief and to promote recovery was passed. It was a time of experimentation in which any idea that offered hope might get a trial. The Civilian Conservation Corps (March 1933), the Agricultural Adjustment Act (May 1933), and the National Industrial Recovery Act (June 1933) were among the landmarks that were created in this phase of the New Deal. The *Second New Deal* (1935–1941) was marked by a more conscious turn toward the political left. Although relief and recovery efforts continued, the administration now pushed for reforms that it believed would permanently improve and protect the standard of living of the working class. The Social Security Act (1935) and the Fair Labor Standards Act (1938) are among the major achievements of the Second New Deal. Although the New Deal occupied only a short span of time, we must consider it in detail because it is the origin of many of the institutions and ideas that shape our daily lives.

Relief

The most pressing problem for the new administration was to provide relief for destitute families. One of the first actions of the Roosevelt administration, therefore, was to create

Photographers for the Works Progress Administration took now classic pictures of poverty-stricken Americans to build support for the New Deal.

the Federal Emergency Relief Agency. Through this agency, the federal government pumped a half billion dollars into bankrupt state and local relief efforts. The agency was directed by Harry Hopkins, a social worker and administrator from New York; already a friend, he would become one of Roosevelt's most trusted advisors and confidants during the depression. In 1935, the federal government set up the Works Progress Administration (later the name was changed to Works Projects Administration to avoid the left-wing associations of the term "Progress"), also under Hopkins's direction. This agency employed millions of people in road building, flood control projects, and similar programs. Its most famous and controversial projects employed writers, photographers, and other creative artists. Critics complained, with some justice, that these projects often pushed strong left-wing political messages. Some of the projects, however, such as recording the recollections of the last generation of former slaves, also had lasting value. Under Hopkins's direction, the main emphasis of the Works Projects Administration was creating employment; the contribution of these projects to the infrastructure of the economy was secondary. Another well-known agency with a similar purpose was the Civilian Conservation Corps, which created camps for young men and employed them in refurbishing national parks and similar activities. All of these relief efforts reflected Hopkins's philosophy of relief: It was not enough to give the unemployed cash payments. The government also had to create work for the unemployed to help them maintain their self-respect as well as maintain and build skills that could be used in the private sector when jobs again became available.

The Public Works Administration undertook larger construction projects. It spent more than $6 billion over the course of the depression on dams, low-cost housing, airports, warships, and other projects. Its director, Harold Ickes, earned an enviable reputation for honesty and for his efforts to secure employment for African Americans, but he was sometimes criticized for taking too much time to plan projects. The most ambitious and controversial of all was the Tennessee Valley Authority, a multifaceted project designed to promote economic development in a large region that had been poverty stricken for decades. The Authority built dams in a seven-state area (see Map 24.1), supplied low-cost electric power to farmers (a policy that created considerable opposition from private power companies), engaged in flood control, created inland navigation routes, and promoted farmer education and related projects.

MAP 24.1
Public Power

The Tennessee Valley Authority—the New Deal's major experiment in publicly financed power—ranges through portions of seven states. Its supporters call it a splendid monument to "regional planning"; its foes denounce it as a noxious example of "creeping socialism."

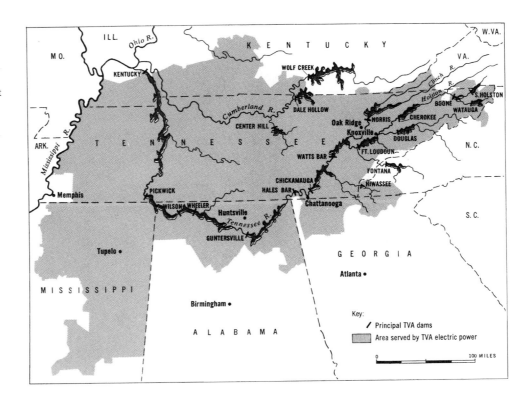

NEW VIEW 24.1

SHOULD THE GOVERNMENT BE THE EMPLOYER OF LAST RESORT?

When the unemployment rate rises, should the federal government step in and hire the unemployed? After all, if the banks can have a lender of last resort to bail them out, why can't the workingman or woman have an employer of last resort? Supporters of this proposal argue that the government has a moral obligation to relieve the enormous suffering caused by unemployment. Critics of this proposal warn that such a policy would be enormously expensive, would undermine the work ethic of the unemployed, and might well become political patronage, the breeding ground of corruption. The text discusses historical examples that one could study to see how such a system might work. The New Deal instituted a number of job creation programs. One of the most famous and most controversial was the Civilian Conservation Corps. Modeled on the army, the Corps, at its peak in 1935, employed 500,000 men in building national park facilities, cleaning and enlarging reservoirs, planting trees (as shown in the photo), and similar activities.

© AP PHOTO

These work-eager lads of the Civilian Conservation Corps go at it with axe and saw as they start their first duties of the forestry army in George Washington National Park, near Luray, Va., April 18, 1933. Here they are shown clearing trees to make their camp site.

One measure of the impact of the emergency relief measures is shown in Table 24.1. In 1933, the first year of the New Deal, federal, state, and local emergency work programs employed more than 2 million workers (4.3 percent of the labor force). The peak year was 1936, when 3.7 million people (7 percent of the labor force) were employed. To put the point somewhat differently, had the relief programs not existed, and had the workers not been able to find employment in the private sector, the percent of the labor force without jobs would not have been 9.9 percent in 1936 (itself a very high rate) but 16.9 percent. Indeed, the official figures, the figures usually quoted in history textbooks and newspaper, listed 16.9 percent of the workforce as unemployed. Because it was

TABLE 24.1 EMERGENCY WORKERS DURING THE GREAT DEPRESSION

YEAR	UNEMPLOYED (in thousands)	UNEMPLOYED (percent of labor force)	EMERGENCY WORKERS (in thousands)	EMERGENCY WORKERS (percent of labor force)
1929	1,550	3.2%	0	0.00%
1930	4,320	8.7	20	0.04
1931	7,721	15.3	299	0.6
1932	11,468	22.5	592	1.2
1933	10,635	20.6	2,195	4.3
1934	8,366	16.0	2,974	5.7
1935	7,523	14.2	3,087	5.8
1936	5,286	9.9	3,744	7.0
1937	4,937	9.1	2,763	5.1
1938	6,799	12.5	3,591	6.6
1939	6,225	11.3	3,255	5.9
1940	5,290	9.5	2,830	5.1
1941	3,351	6.0	2,209	3.9
1942	1,746	3.1	914	1.6
1943	985	1.8	85	0.2

Source: *Michael Darby, "Three and a Half Million U.S. Employees Have Been Mislaid: Or, an Explanation of Unemployment, 1934–1941," Journal of Political Economy 84 (1976): 7, 8. Reprinted by permission of the University of Chicago Press.*

believed that these workers would be unemployed in the absence of these jobs, this figure emphasized the severity of the depression.

Recovery

One of the most dramatic advances in government intervention came with the National Industrial Recovery Act (NIRA). Its chief purposes were to raise prices and wages, spread work by reducing hours, and prevent price cutting by competitors trying to maintain volume. The National Recovery Administration, under the direction of General Hugh Johnson, supervised the preparation of a "code of fair practice" for each industry. These were really agreements among sellers to set minimum prices, limit output, and establish minimum wages and maximum hours of work. Pending the approval of basic codes, the president issued a "blanket code" in July 1933. Sellers signing the blanket code agreed to raise wages, shorten the maximum work week, and abstain from price cutting. In return, they could display a "blue eagle" and avoid being boycotted for not doing their part.

By 1935, 557 basic codes had been approved. Although in theory the codes were supposed to be the product of labor, consumer, and employer representatives, in practice, labor representatives participated in the construction of fewer than 10 percent of the codes, and consumer representation was negligible. Employer representatives worked through their national trade associations and manufacturers' institutes, with the consequence that prices were set to maximize profits. The possibility of such an outcome was recognized in the NIRA by suspending the antitrust laws.

Was the NIRA effective? It appears, for the most part, the codes redistributed rather than expanded incomes. Manufacturing output jumped after the institution of the NIRA as merchants added to their inventories in anticipation of price increases. Production lapsed again, however, and by midsummer 1935, it was no higher than it had been after

Roosevelt's broad grin, in evidence above, center, at the 1936 Democratic convention, made his theme song, "Happy Days Are Here Again," believable to a shaken nation. His charm and buoyancy did much in itself to soften the Great Depression's psychological impact.

the initial spurt. Unemployment, although reduced, was still incredibly high, and most manufacturing firms were operating at far less than capacity. Other factors may account for the slowdown (as well as for the spurt), but in any case enthusiasm for the NIRA waned. It was with little regret, then, that New Dealers saw the passing of the NIRA, which the Supreme Court declared unconstitutional in 1935 on the grounds that Congress had illegally delegated legislative powers to the president.

REFORM OF THE FINANCIAL SYSTEM

The financial system lay in ruins after the contraction from 1929 to 1933. The Roosevelt administration, with allies in both parties, set out to revive and reform the system. Profound changes occurred in four main areas: the banking system, the securities markets, the international financial system, and the Federal Reserve System.

A Safety Net for the Banking System

Perhaps the most important reform in the banking system was the introduction of deposit insurance. The Federal Deposit Insurance Corporation (for commercial banks) and the Federal Savings and Loan Insurance Corporation (for savings banks) were established in 1934. Roosevelt was somewhat skeptical about deposit insurance, fearing that it would encourage lax banking practices, but he bowed to strong support for deposit insurance in Congress (Calomiris and White 1994). For many years, deposit insurance was viewed as an unalloyed success.

In their classic *A Monetary History of the United States*, Milton Friedman and Anna J. Schwartz argued that "Federal insurance of bank deposits was the most important structural change in the banking system to result from the 1933 panic, and, indeed, in our view, the structural change most conducive to monetary stability since state bank note issues were taxed out of existence immediately after the Civil War" (1963, 434). A major part of their evidence (see Economic Reasoning Proposition 5, evidence and theory give value to opinions, page 8) was the tremendous fall in the annual number of bank failures and losses borne by depositors once deposit insurance was introduced. Even in the relatively prosperous 1920s, annual bank suspensions numbered in the hundreds; however, from 1934 on, this number never reached 100 (Friedman and Schwartz 1963). During the savings and loan crisis of the 1970s, however, a number of economists pointed out that deposit insurance had come with a long-run cost: Depositors no longer had an incentive to regulate the banking system by withdrawing funds from risky banks and placing them in safer banks.

There were a number of other important reforms of the banking system. Under the Glass-Steagall Act, commercial banking (taking deposits from the public and making short-term loans) was separated from investment banking (buying and selling securities). Banks could do one or the other, but not both. This reform reflected the belief that combining the two activities had undermined the banking system in the late 1920s: Banks had taken the hard-earned savings of their depositors and used them to finance loans to stock market speculators. Research by White (1986), Kroszener and Rajan (1994), and Ramírez (1996), however, shows that these charges were largely baseless. (Recall Economic Reasoning Proposition 5, claims must be tested; evidence matters.) Another reform prohibited the payment of interest on bank deposits. The argument here was that in the 1920s competition to pay high interest rates on deposits had led banks into reckless lending. Both of these restrictions, separation of commercial banking from investment banking and the prohibition of interest on deposits, have since been removed on the grounds that they inhibited competition and punished bank customers.

Increased Regulation of Securities Markets

The collapse of the stock market left many investors reeling from losses and with a deep suspicion they had been duped by Wall Street. A congressional investigation led by Ferdinand Pecora seemed to provide the evidence for widespread fraud. The result was the establishment of the Securities and Exchange Commission in 1934. This agency was given wide powers to supervise the stock exchanges, their trading practices, and the issue of new securities. Joseph P. Kennedy, father of President John F. Kennedy, was its first chair.

The End of America's Commitment to the Gold Standard

On April 5, 1933, a presidential executive order required that all holders of gold coins to turn in their gold (except for rare coins) to the Federal Reserve in exchange for Federal Reserve Notes. America's commitment to the gold standard was over. The gold standard was discarded for two reasons. First, it was thought that the attempt to convert assets into gold was undermining the banking system. Second, by breaking the fixed link to other currencies that were on the gold standard, the United States could devalue the dollar (make it cheaper in terms of foreign currency) and so make U.S. exports, particularly of farm products, more attractive. Although an attempt was made to reestablish fixed exchange rates and a role for gold after World War II, Americans would never again hear the jingle of gold coins.

Centralization of Monetary Power in the Federal Reserve Board

The Federal Reserve system clearly had failed to stem the tide of bank closures and failures. The response of the Roosevelt administration was to centralize power in Washington. This was somewhat ironic, to say the least, because the board in Washington had done the most to resist calls from some of the district banks for more vigorous action. But by centralizing authority and putting its own people in charge, the administration believed that it could secure more vigorous action from the Federal Reserve. In 1935 the Federal Reserve Board became the Board of Governors, all of whose members the president appointed. The Board of Governors was given control of the system's most powerful economic tool, the ability to buy or sell securities on the open market. Marriner S. Eccles, a Utah banker, who believed strongly in using federal deficit spending and monetary policy to stimulate the economy, was the first chair of the newly empowered board. The district banks, which had been important in the 1920s, would now serve only an advisory role in making monetary policy.

Although some of the financial reforms introduced by the New Deal were later abandoned, many, such as the Federal Deposit Insurance Incorporation and the Securities and Exchange Commission, continue to this day. There are few better examples of how institutions created in the heat of an emergency (Walton 1979) may continue to influence economic actions for decades to come (Economic Reasoning Proposition 4, institutions matter).

REFORM OF THE AGRICULTURAL SECTOR

With the onset of the Great Depression, farm people began to suffer a severity of economic distress that only a few would have believed possible. In three years, the average price of corn at central markets fell from $0.77 to $0.19 per bushel, and the average price of wheat dropped from $1.08 to $0.33 per bushel. Table 24.2 shows the key averages. Between 1929 and 1932, prices received by farmers declined 56 percent. True, prices farmers paid declined as well. Even taking this into account leaves the farmer's "terms of trade"—prices received by farmers divided by prices paid—down 37 percent. The net income of farm operators fell from a total of $6.2 billion in 1929 to $2 billion in 1932. Again, adjusting for the price change helps a little, but net real income fell from $6.2 billion to $3 billion in constant 1929 dollars.

Farmers with fixed indebtedness were particularly hard hit: In 1932, 52 percent of all farm debts were in default. From the previous record high of 15 farm foreclosures (lenders taking back properties because mortgages were not being paid) per thousand farms in 1929, foreclosures jumped to 18 per thousand farms in 1930 and 27.8 per thousand in 1931, finally peaking at 38.1 per thousand in 1932 (Johnson 1973–1974, 176). Mortgage foreclosures sometimes reduced the owners of farms that had been in the family for generations to the status of tenants or, in the depths of the depression, forced them on to relief rolls. Many states, under aggressive pressure from farm organizations and concerned about threats of violence by farmers, imposed moratoriums on foreclosures (Alston 1984; Alston and Rucker 1987). The foreclosures have often been blamed on

TABLE 24.2 FARM PRICES AND INCOMES IN THE DEPRESSION, SELECTED YEARS

YEAR	PRICES RECEIVED BY FARMERS	PRICES RECEIVED BY FARMERS RELATIVE TO PRICES PAID	TOTAL NET INCOME OF FARM OPERATORS FROM FARMING (millions)	NET INCOME OF FARM OPERATORS 1929 PRICES (millions)
1929	100	100	$6,152	$6,152
1932	44	63	2,032	2,956
1937	82	101	6,005	7,206
1938	66	85	4,361	5,509
1939	64	83	4,414	5,726

Source: Historical Statistics *1975, Series K344, K347, K352, and K137.*

the overexpansion of agriculture in World War I. Farmers went into debt to acquire land, it is said, and ended up defaulting when the postwar economy failed to sustain the high prices of the war years. A careful study by Lee J. Alston (1983) shows, however, that this problem, although important in the 1920s, had been worked out by 1929. The high levels of foreclosures in the early 1930s were mainly the result of the fall in agricultural prices.

It did not help that most farm mortgages were often short-term "balloon" mortgages: The entire principal was due back after the end of, say, five years. This worked as long as prices were stable and banks were willing to "roll over" loans, that is, replace maturing loans with new ones. If the bank was in trouble and demanded its money, and prices were low, a farmer could do little to avoid bankruptcy. The replacement of short-term balloon mortgages with long-term "amortized" mortgages, in which a little bit of the principal was paid off each year, became a high priority of the Roosevelt administration, one that it achieved through a variety of measures.

Farmers had long pushed for government measures to maintain "fair" prices for farm products, but these demands were frustrated by opposition to the large expenditures or far-reaching government controls on production that it would take to achieve this goal. Most federal aid for farmers had been for disease control, the provision of information about best practice, and so on. Things began to change, however, with the passage of the Agricultural Marketing Act of 1929, which was the outcome of Republican campaign promises in 1928 (Libecap 1998). This predepression law committed the government to a policy of farm price stabilization and established the Federal Farm Board to encourage the formation of cooperative marketing associations. The board was also authorized to establish "stabilization corporations" to be owned by the cooperatives and to use an initial fund of $500 million for price support operations. With the onset of the depression in 1930, the Federal Farm Board strove valiantly to support farm prices, but between June 1929 and June 1932, the board's corporations bought surplus farm products only to suffer steadily increasing losses as prices declined. The board itself took over the operation and accepted the losses, expending some $676 million. Meanwhile, however, farmers faced with catastrophically falling prices increased output. At the time, it seemed that prices could not be supported without production controls.

The Roosevelt administration was prepared to go much further than its Republican predecessors. But initially it was unwilling to undertake the enormous outlays that would be required to raise prices by increasing demand through government purchases. Consequently, the Agricultural Adjustment Act, passed in May 1933, provided for an Agricultural Adjustment Administration, the AAA, which was given the responsibility of raising farm prices by restricting the supply of farm commodities. The AAA's most important tool was "acreage allotment." The AAA would determine a total acreage of certain major crops to be planted in the next growing season. The total acreage would then be subdivided into state totals, which in turn were allotted to individual farms on the basis of each farm's recent crop history. To secure the cooperation of the individual farmer, an "adjustment payment" was made. The payment was made by check from the federal Treasury, but in these early New Deal days, it still seemed too much to expect the taxpayer to foot the bill—at least directly. The benefit payments were financed, therefore, by taxes paid by the first processor of any product (millers, for example, had to pay a tax for each bushel of wheat that was ground into flour), although it was assumed that the tax would be shifted forward to the consumer.

The original AAA scheme experienced a setback in 1936 when the Supreme Court, in the *Hoosac Mills* case, declared the Agricultural Adjustment Act unconstitutional because it attempted to regulate agricultural production—a power reserved to the states. The

Agricultural poverty sent thousands fleeing from the Midwest to California, with belongings piled in the family jalopy. America had become, as beloved humorist Will Rogers said, A nation that "drove to the poor house in an automobile."

decision, however, did not end acreage allotments. The administration quickly found a way around the decision by basing allotments on the need for soil conservation.

The severe drought of 1936, with its attendant dust bowl conditions provided the rationale. The dust storms in the Midwest were so severe that many people were forced to flee. In particular, the migration of the "Okies" created both fear and sympathy in California and focused attention on the need for such measures as soil conservation to deal with the underlying problem. (Their plight is eloquently described by John Steinbeck in *The Grapes of Wrath,* and in an Oscar-winning 1940 movie based on the novel, staring Jane Darwell and Henry Fonda.)

The result was passage of the Soil Conservation and Domestic Allotment Act. Under this act, the secretary of agriculture could offer benefit payments to farmers who would reduce their acreage planted in soil-depleting crops and take steps to conserve or rebuild the land withheld from production.

Farm production in 1937 was very high, and there was pressure to supplement acreage reduction with even more vigorous measures to raise prices. In 1938, Congress passed a new Agricultural Adjustment Act, which placed greater emphasis on supporting prices by increasing demand. Since 1933, the Commodity Credit Corporation (CCC) had performed the minor function of "cushioning" the prices of corn, wheat, and cotton by making loans to farmers on the security of their crops. Most of these loans were made "without recourse." If the CCC extended a loan against a commodity and the price of that commodity fell, the farmer could let the CCC take title to the stored product and cancel the debt. If the price of the commodity rose, the farmer could sell the commodity, pay back the loan, and keep the profit. Thus, CCC support prices became minimum prices in the marketplace (see Economic Insight 24.1).

The Agricultural Adjustment Act of 1938 increased the role of the CCC by making it mandatory that the directors extend loans on corn, wheat, and cotton at "parity" prices. These prices were defined as farm prices adjusted to have the same purchasing power as

ECONOMIC INSIGHT 24.1

EFFECTS OF COMMODITY CREDIT CORPORATION PRICE SUPPORTS

The figure illustrates the effects of CCC price supports. In the absence of government intervention, the price would be P_0 and the quantity produced Q_0. Intervention raises the price to P_1 and the quantity produced to Q_1. The higher price reduces consumption to Q_2 and leads to the accumulation of Q_1-Q_2 stocks by the government. Farm incomes (net of production costs) are raised by the sum of areas $A + B + C$. Total expenditures by the government are $(Q_1-Q_2) \times P_1$. Area A is paid directly by consumers in the form of higher prices. $B + C + D$ are paid by consumers indirectly through taxes. The change in direct expenditures by consumers is $Q_2 \times P_1 - Q_0 \times P_0$. (Whether consumers spend more or less than before depends on the elasticity of demand.)

A number of losses are associated with this program. First, the resources used to produce Q_1-Q_2 are wasted. Storage costs for the surplus (not shown) are also incurred. Second, consumers are deprived of farm products that they value more than the costs of production. Their loss on this account is measured by area B. The attempt to minimize these losses then leads to other programs described in the text: production quotas, surplus removal programs, and export subsidies.

Economists often recommend direct income supplements to farmers combined with a free market in agricultural products as a way to help farmers without incurring these losses. For a number of reasons, however, farmers usually prefer price supports. Three are worth noting: (1) direct income supplements may be viewed as demeaning, (2) direct income supplements may go mostly to poor farmers, and are therefore opposed by rich and influential farmers, and (3) direct income supplements tend to remain fixed over time. The subsidy delivered through price supports may grow as technological advances shift the supply curve to the right.

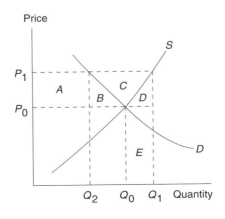

© BETTMANN/CORBIS

Adding to the farmer's woes during the depressed 1930s were several years of intense heat and drought. The subsequent blowing of previously eroded land created dust storms like this one in the Texas panhandle. Government land policies also contributed, as Hansen and Libecap (2004) have shown, by limiting homesteaders to small plots.

those prevailing in 1910–1914, a time when farm prices relative to other prices were exceptionally high. The Populist dream of "fair" prices determined by the government had become a reality.

Two other means of raising farm prices were used during the 1930s: (1) marketing agreements and (2) surplus removal programs. Marketing agreements, which became important for milk and certain fruits and vegetables, are contracts (which require the approval of the Department of Agriculture) between an association of producers and the processors of a product. These agreements may set minimum prices, total quantities to be marketed, and allotments of marketings among processors. In other words, firms in the industry may legally set up cartels to reduce output and raise prices.

The most acceptable and enduring surplus removal programs proved to be the nutrition programs, such as the food-stamp plans, low-cost milk distribution plans, and school lunch programs. The Food Stamp Plan, in operation from 1939 to 1942, won enthusiastic support. Stamps given to low-income families were used to purchase food from regular retail outlets. Thus, surplus commodities were given to those who presumably had the greatest need for them. In addition they helped offset the effect on the poor of artificially high prices created by the crop restrictions. In 1961, after almost two decades, advocates finally secured reactivation of this program.

By 1937, thanks to the recovery of the economy and to the New Deal's farm programs, the farmer's terms of trade were back to where they had been in 1929, and total net real income of farmers was above the 1929 level (see Table 24.2). Farmers were then hit by the "recession within the depression," and by 1939, the farmer's terms of trade and total real net income were again well below the levels of 1929.

The most concrete steps taken by government to raise farm incomes during the early 1930s were production controls. It was a mistake, however, to restrict output in agriculture and raise prices of food and fiber when the major national problems were massive unemployment and hunger. Far better ways were available to help farmers. This is easy to see now, but was not so easy to see at the time. Many of Roosevelt's early advisers were convinced that restoring the "balance" among the sectors of the economy would restore full employment. In truth, the primary outcome of the New Deal's farm policies, as with other types of New Deal legislation aimed at helping particular groups, was to redistribute income rather than end the depression.

Clearly, Roosevelt's New Deal for farmers was far removed from President Harding's policy advice that "the farmer must be ready to help himself." The acceptance by the American people of the principle that the government ought to bolster the economic fortunes of particular occupational groups or classes was momentous. Farmers have not been the only beneficiaries of this philosophy, but we cannot find a better example of the way in which legislation, passed at first in an effort to relieve emergency distress, has become accepted as a permanent part of the economic system (Walton 1979) (Economic Reasoning Proposition 4, institutions matter).

LABOR AND THE NEW DEAL

The New Deal transformed the relationship between the American worker and the federal government. Before the New Deal, the dominant assumption was that most of the time the labor market would provide adequate opportunities for the poor to advance. If they failed to do so, it was because of individual failure: laziness, ignorance, bad habits, and so on. The Great Depression changed this attitude. The dominant assumption came to be that if the opportunities provided by the market were inadequate, it was up to the federal government to make sure that those able to work could find work, and with decent wages and working conditions.

A New Institutional Framework for Labor Markets

Whatever the impact of government programs on real wages and employment, the establishment of government relief programs and the new powers given to labor unions—most important were the right to strike and to organize free of employer interference—created a strong bond between organized labor and the New Deal. Union membership had declined sharply from more than 5 million in 1920 to 3.5 million in 1923. It remained steady around this level until 1930, when it began falling again before reaching bottom in 1933. Before the new administration had been in power a year, the more vigorous union leaders sensed that the government would encourage organization and that the attitude of the nation toward unions had changed because people were disillusioned with business.

Especially successful were the powerful and able leaders of the industrial unions that had evolved within the American Federation of Labor (AFL): John L. Lewis of the United Mine Workers, Sidney Hillman of the Amalgamated Clothing Workers, and David Dubinsky of the International Ladies Garment Workers. By the mid-1930s, a conflict within the union movement between the older craft unions and the newer industrial unions had grown to major proportions. The drive to organize the mass production industries (steel, automobiles, rubber, and electrical equipment) was inevitable, but the older unions hampered the effort by insisting that their craft jurisdictions remain inviolate and by raiding the membership of the new industrial unions. In 1935, eight industrial unions formed the Committee for Industrial Organization within the AFL. In 1936 these unions were suspended from the federation; three years later, it became a separate entity, the Congress of Industrial Organizations (CIO). Relations between these two great federations were bitter. CIO leaders made no secret of their contempt for the AFL's lack of militancy, and AFL leaders viewed the CIO's violent break with conservative unionism with concern. However, complacency and inertia no longer beset the labor movement. Union membership increased rapidly in the 1930s (see Table 24.3). Government's new

TABLE 24.3 WAGES DURING THE GREAT DEPRESSION

YEAR	NOMINAL WAGE (the hourly wage in manufacturing)	GROSS NATIONAL PRODUCT DEFLATOR	REAL WAGE
1929	$0.56	100	100
1930	0.55	97	101
1931	0.51	89	103
1932	0.44	79	99
1933	0.44	78	101
1939	0.63	85	132

Note: The real wage is the nominal wage divided by the gross national product deflator. The result was set equal to 100 in 1929 so that the trend could be observed easily.

Source: Historical Statistics *1975, 169–170, D802; 197, E1.*

prolabor attitude, clearly revealed in the labor legislation of the New Deal, played an important role. Between 1930 and 1939, union membership increased from 6.8 to 15.8 percent of the labor force. Eventually, the split in the labor movement would end. In 1955, the AFL and the CIO, prodded into unity by hostile public opinion and labor legislation, merged to form the AFL-CIO. Roughly 50 percent of the total membership was in AFL affiliates, 30 percent in CIO unions, and the remainder in unaffiliated unions.

Except for legislation that applied only to the railroad industry, Congress had seldom interfered with labor relations before 1932. The Norris-LaGuardia Act of 1932 was the first step toward removing barriers to free organization. The act greatly restricted the ability of the courts to issue labor injunctions. It made the "yellow-dog contract"—an employment contract in which a worker agrees not to join a union—nonenforceable in federal courts. In addition, it permitted nonemployee boycotting and picketing. The Norris-LaGuardia Act granted workers the opportunity to organize but did not intercede to ensure that they could secure the benefits of collective bargaining.

The first positive assertion of the right of labor to bargain collectively was in Section 7a of the NIRA, but no means of enforcing the statement of principle were provided. Two years later, when the NIRA was declared unconstitutional, Congress replaced Section 7a with a much more elaborate law, the National Labor Relations Act (usually called the Wagner Act). This new act established the principle of collective bargaining as the cornerstone of industrial relations and stated that it was management's obligation to recognize and deal with a bona fide labor organization in good faith. The act further guaranteed workers the right to form and join a labor organization, to engage in collective bargaining, to select representatives of their own choosing, and to engage in concerted activity. In addition, the Wagner Act outlawed a list of "unfair" managerial practices.

Henceforth, employers could not—

- *Interfere with, restrain, or coerce employees in the exercise of their rights of self-organization and collective bargaining.*
- *Dominate or interfere with the formation or administration of any labor organization or contribute financial or other support to it.*
- *Encourage or discourage union membership by discrimination in regard to hiring or tenure of employment or condition of work, except such discrimination as might be involved in a closed-shop agreement with a bona fide union enjoying majority status.*
- *Discharge or otherwise discriminate against an employee for filing charges or testifying under the act.*
- *Refuse to bargain collectively.*

The Wagner Act was more than a mere statement of principles. It established a National Labor Relations Board with powers of enforcement. When the Supreme Court declared the Wagner Act constitutional in 1937, there were no remaining legal barriers to the rapid organization of labor. Before the question of constitutionality was settled, however, many employers openly violated the act, producing increasing turbulence in labor relations. Animosity between the suspended CIO unions and the AFL grew, leading to jurisdictional conflicts that the National Labor Relations Board had to spend much time settling. As industrial strife seemed to be increasing rather than decreasing, there were public demands for amendments to the act, and employers complained bitterly of the one-sidedness of the law. From labor's view, however, the Wagner Act was its Magna Carta.

The Fair Labor Standards Act of 1938, which replaced and extended provisions of the NIRA, was the beginning of federal regulation of the workplace. Among other things, the law set a minimum wage of $0.25 per hour (scheduled to rise eventually to $0.40), fixed a maximum work week of 44 hours (scheduled to fall to 40) with extra pay for overtime work, and prohibited the employment of children under 16 years of age. (Average hourly earnings in manufacturing were then about $0.62 per hour.) The Wages and Hours Division of the Department of Labor was created to enforce the act. Agriculture was exempt, and other exemptions reduced the share of nonagricultural workers initially covered by the law to about 44 percent. The goal was to protect workers and to increase employment. The hope was, for example, that requiring extra pay for overtime would encourage firms to hire more workers at the lower rate that applied up to 44 hours. The rules and regulations introduced by the Fair Labor Standards Act shaped labor markets for decades to come (Economic Reasoning Proposition 4, institutions matter).

The Congressional fight over the first national minimum wage—there had been some legislation at the state level—was not a simple fight between politicians who supported labor and therefore supported minimum-wage laws and politicians who supported business, and therefore opposed minimum-wage laws. Many Southern Democrats who had supported other aspects of the New Deal opposed the Fair Labor Standards Act. To be sure, southern legislators were influenced by their political party (Democrats favored the minimum wage) and by their ideology (left-wing politicians favored the minimum wage). They were also influenced, however, by what they perceived to be the interests of their constituents. Southern firms that were less well capitalized and who employed less well educated workers than their Northern rivals feared that a uniform national minimum wage law would inhibit their ability to compete by paying lower wages (Seltzer 1995, 2004; Sobel 1999; Fleck 2002, 2004). Despite opposition, however, the legislation passed and the South had to adjust. It did so in a variety of ways. In some industries the imposition of the minimum wage produced a substitution of capital for labor, in others, attempts to circumvent or evade the law (Seltzer 1997).

Why Was Unemployment So High for So Long?

Despite all the legislation designed to help the worker, the New Deal failed to accomplish what labor wanted most: the restoration of full employment. Not only did unemployment rise to unprecedented heights after 1930, but high unemployment persisted throughout the decade. Unemployment had risen sharply during the recession of 1920–1921, and earlier recessions, but then it had ebbed quickly. The persistence of high unemployment despite the best efforts of the Roosevelt administration to promote recovery was the most frustrating reality of the 1930s.

Could New Deal policies themselves have contributed to the persistence of high unemployment? One possibility was that New Deal relief policies had discouraged employment. But research by John Wallis (1987) showed that private employment was largely unaffected by the presence of relief programs, although later work by Robert Margo (1991) suggested that the availability of relief may have had some impact on the duration of unemployment.

Many economists, however, have argued that the persistence of high unemployment was the result of "sticky" wages. As you can see in Table 24.4, real wages (wages divided by prices) did remain high. Of course, this was cold comfort for those who had lost their jobs or had their weekly hours cut; but perhaps in some economic sense these real wages were too high.

Why did real wages remain so high? Government policy is part of the explanation. In the first two years of the depression, as Anthony Patrick O'Brien (1989) has shown, the Hoover administration successfully pressured large corporations to maintain wages, a policy that the administration and business leaders thought would help maintain demand. During the early years of the New Deal, the NIRA continued the policy of maintaining wages. Economic forces were at work keeping real wages high. Unemployed workers are not likely to suddenly slash their "reservation wage" (the minimum they would take) to the bone. Instead, they are likely to slowly adjust their reservation wage as they search the market for jobs (Economic Reasoning Proposition 1, scarcity forces us to make choices). The adjustment process therefore took a considerable time. During the latter part of the New Deal, the Wagner and Fair Labor Standard Acts and the associated growth of labor unions (discussed below) helped maintain wages.

Would a policy of encouraging competition in labor markets have restored full employment? Even today, economists are far from a consensus on this contentious issue. Many economists continue to follow John Maynard Keynes, who argued, in his famous book *A General Theory of Employment, Interest, and Money* (1936), that wage cuts would have simply fed a downward spiral of expectations, investment, national income, and employment. In Keynes's view, only government spending on a massive scale could have cured the depression, and this simply did not happen before World War II. Recently, however, a number of economists, in particular Michael Bordo, Christopher J. Erceg, Charles L. Evans (2000) and Harold L. Cole, and Lee E. Ohanian (2004), have

TABLE 24.4 UNION MEMBERSHIP, 1930–1955

YEAR	NUMBER (in thousands)	PERCENT OF LABOR FORCE	YEAR	NUMBER (in thousands)	PERCENT OF LABOR FORCE
1930	3,401	6.8%	1943	13,213	20.5%
1931	3,310	6.5	1944	14,146	21.4
1932	3,050	6.0	1945	14,322	21.9
1933	2,689	5.2	1946	14,395	23.6
1934	3,088	5.9	1947	14,787	23.9
1935	3,584	6.7	1948	14,300	23.1
1936	3,989	7.4	1949	14,300	22.7
1937	7,001	12.9	1950	14,300	22.3
1938	8,034	14.6	1951	15,900	24.5
1939	8,763	15.8	1952	15,900	24.2
1940	8,717	15.5	1953	16,948	25.5
1941	10,201	17.7	1954	17,022	25.4
1942	10,380	17.2	1955	16,802	24.7

Source: Historical Statistics *1975, 178, Series D948-949.*

argued that New Deal policies that promoted high real wages inhibited adjustment in labor markets and prolonged high unemployment.

THE SUPREME COURT AND THE NEW DEAL

Many opponents of the New Deal hoped that the Supreme Court would declare much of Roosevelt's legislation unconstitutional. Among other things, opponents were hopeful that the Fifth and Fourteenth Amendments to the Constitution, which prohibit the taking of private property without compensation and due process, would be invoked to limit the expansion of economic regulation. After all, whenever the government imposes controls—for example, by setting minimum wages or maximum prices—the value of someone's property is reduced. If each such taking must be adjudicated in court and properly compensated, regulation would be severely hampered.

The Supreme Court itself was deeply divided on the New Deal. As a result, some early New Deal legislation won the Court's approval; while other New Deal legislation, including its most ambitious initiatives, were struck down. In *A.L.A Schechter Poultry Corp. et al. v. United States* (1935), the Supreme Court unanimously ruled the National Recovery Act unconstitutional on the grounds that the law delegated too much arbitrary authority to the executive branch and that it attempted to regulate intrastate commerce. In *United States v. Butler* (1936), the Agricultural Adjustment Act was ruled unconstitutional on the grounds that it was financed by improper taxes. (The press knew it as the "sick chicken case" because it was alleged that the company had sold diseased chickens.)

Buoyed by his landslide victory in 1936, Roosevelt tried to change the Court's direction by proposing legislation that would permit him to appoint additional justices. Opposition to Roosevelt's attempt to "pack" the Court, however, was widespread, and he suffered one of his few political defeats. Nevertheless, in the end he got what he wanted. The moderates on the Court, perhaps reading the election returns, shifted to the left. Over the next few years, moreover, a number of conservative justices retired, permitting Roosevelt to appoint additional liberals. In *United States v. Darby* (1941), the Court ruled in favor of the Fair Labor Standards Act; in *Wickard v. Fillburn* (1942), it ruled in favor of the new Agricultural Adjustment Act. Thus, legal doctrines that had stood in the way of federal (and state) control of the economy, such as the idea that the federal government could regulate only what was clearly interstate commerce, and the idea that federal and state governments could not interfere arbitrarily with private contracts, were overturned. The legal path to increased government regulation of the economy had been cleared.

THE SECOND NEW DEAL: THE WELFARE STATE

Before 1932, a worker's loss of income from any cause other than industrial accident posed a great hardship. Workers had to rely on their savings, or help from friends and relatives, organized charities, and state and local government. The burden of relief during the Great Depression overwhelmed these institutions, while the federal government rapidly expanded its relief efforts. This experience convinced the majority of Americans, on both economic and ethical grounds, of the need for a permanent federal plan to cope with severe losses in income.

The idea was not new. A few leaders in government, business, and academia had long argued that a comprehensive program of social insurance, including old age pensions and unemployment insurance, was needed. Such programs had long been common in Europe, Canada, and Australia, and learned journals contained glowing reports about these programs. Yet as late as 1930, there was little public sentiment in favor of social legislation in the United States. Americans believed that the individual ought to be self-reliant and objected to compulsory government support.

Various interest groups voiced their opposition. Private insurance companies sought to prevent, or at least modify, government insurance of social risks. In agriculture where the need for social insurance was not so pronounced, there was opposition to additional taxes for such insurance. In fact, organized labor itself did not support social insurance (except worker compensation) before the Great Depression: As late as 1931, a national AFL convention refused to endorse unemployment insurance legislation.

Four years of economic disaster removed all serious obstacles to major legislation. The Social Security Act of 1935 provided for a federal old-age and survivors' insurance program based on workers' payments of 1 percent of earnings up to $3,600. It further provided for assistance to the needy aged, dependent children, and the blind. Subsequent amendments have added other groups.

The act was structured as an "insurance" plan in which the worker "contributed" half and the employer "contributed" the other half of the insurance premium. The language in which a bill is written, however, does not determine its economic effect. The premium payment is part of its wage cost. Therefore, over time, this resulted in lower wages to workers. In the long run, it seems likely that employers shifted most of the premiums to employees. By presenting Social Security as an insurance program rather than as a welfare program financed by a tax on workers, the administration hoped to overcome the negative image of welfare and build long-run support for the program. Roosevelt famously remarked that "we put those payroll contributions there so as to give contributors a legal, moral, and political right to collect their pensions....With those taxes in there no damn politician can ever scrap my social security program."

The insurance idea, however, did not last long. Pressure by seniors to start paying benefits as soon as possible led to an amendment in 1939 that converted the system into one in which payments were not saved but instead promptly transferred to those receiving Social Security checks, a pay-as-you-go system. Although highly controversial at the time, the American people quickly accepted Social Security. Controversies continued over who should be covered, what the level of benefits should be, and how the system should be financed, but the existence of the system itself was not challenged.

The program of unemployment insurance was less extensive in its aim than Social Security, but it has provided important short-run help to discharged workers. Largely to circumvent legal difficulties, unemployment insurance is provided through state systems. The Social Security Act of 1935 secured state action by levying a 3 percent tax on the first $3,000 of wages paid by employers in all except a few business occupations. Similar to changes in Social Security, recent trends have made unemployment insurance laws more liberal—partly in recognition of the fact that unemployment compensation is a highly dependable automatic stabilizer. This automatic stabilizing effect occurs through the timely increase in unemployment compensation payments when unemployment levels increase.

THE CRITICS OF THE NEW DEAL

Then, as now, the New Deal was heavily criticized. Conservative critics complained that Roosevelt was creating an "alphabet soup" of new programs and agencies that was turning the United States into a bureaucratic state. They also complained that the jobs created by the Civilian Conservation Corps and other agencies were merely "leaf-raking jobs" that undermined the character of America's worker.

Conservatives also complained that funds were not being spent simply with the idea of providing relief for the destitute but also to maximize political support for the New Deal. This criticism has received considerable attention from economic historians because it is subject to empirical investigation. Leonard Arrington (1969) was the first to study the issue systematically. Arrington found that New Deal per capita spending was higher in the West even though the South was the region in greatest need. Later, other scholars, including Gavin Wright (1974) and Gary Anderson and Robert Tollison (1991) confirmed that the New Deal appeared to be allocating funds to maximize its political support. Wallis (1987), however, pointed out that some of what appeared to be political allocation could be explained by the provision in many New Deal programs that required matching grants from the states. This provision tended to reward people living in wealthier states. Nevertheless, it appears that even when considering matching grants, some evidence supports the political allocation theory. Even though political considerations influenced spending, it is still true that many disadvantaged people benefited. Recent research by Price V. Fishback, Michael R. Haines, and Shawn Kantor (2007) shows that New Deal relief spending lowered infant mortality rates, suicide rates, and other forms of premature mortality.

Perhaps the most damning conservative criticisms were those that claimed that the Roosevelt administration's policies, although intended to help the poor, prolonged the depression. Some economists today, echoing a criticism made at the time, blame the prolongation of high rates of unemployment on New Deal labor policies designed to keep wages high and strengthen organized labor. Many critics at the time, including Joseph Schumpeter (1939) one of the leading economists of the day, argued that Roosevelt's antibusiness rhetoric and his constant addition of new regulations and taxes had discouraged private investment, and that lack of investment had inhibited recovery. Without this break on private investment they argued, the economy might have recovered quickly as it had in 1921 under conservative Warren Harding and his regime of tax cuts and laissez-faire. This criticism remains controversial because determining the effect of the political regime on private investment is extremely difficult. Michael Bernstein (1984, 1987) showed that investment spending was depressed during the 1930s, but argued that this owed little to New Deal rhetoric—after all some sectors recovered quickly—and more to changing patterns of investment demand. Thomas Mayer and Monojit Chatterji (1985) used econometric methods to examine the determinants of investment spending in the 1930s and concluded that there was no evidence that the antibusiness rhetoric and actions of the Roosevelt administration had reduced investment. Their results were challenged by O'Brien (1990), to which they replied (Mayer and Chatterji 1990), reasserting their basic claim. Robert Higgs (1997) reinvigorated the Schumpeterian criticism, citing both opinion polls and financial market data to show that New Deal policies had discouraged investment.

The New Deal was criticized from the left as well as the right. Dr. Francis E. Townsend, a California physician, attracted a considerable support for his plan to give everyone over the age of 60 a federal pension of $150 per month ($5,000 in today's money). Sung Won Kang (2006) showed that Social Security was influenced by the Townsend movement: Members of Congress who voted against the Townsend plan then voted for the liberalization of Social Security to remain in good standing with constituents who supported the plan. Reverend Charles E. Coughlin, a radio priest, advocated Populist monetary reforms, including abolition of the Federal Reserve. An early supporter of the New Deal, he later became a bitter opponent. Perhaps the most influential of the radicals was Huey Long, the political boss and senator from Louisiana. His "Share-the-Wealth" plan would have presented every American family with a $5,000 house, a $2,000 annual income (about $67,000 in today's money), and other benefits, financed by a capital levy on great fortunes.

The critics from both the right and the left, however, were in the minority. There can be no doubt that a large majority of the public approved of the administration's aggressive and experimental yet constrained response to the crisis, as revealed by Roosevelt's overwhelming reelection victories in 1936 and 1940.

THE LEGACY OF THE NEW DEAL

The New Deal, as we have seen, was a mixture of sometimes-conflicting programs: some aimed at relieving distress, some aimed at restoring full employment, and some aimed at preventing a recurrence of the Great Depression. In retrospect, the New Deal might have done better had it followed Keynes's advice and concentrated on relieving distress and maximizing the aggregate monetary and fiscal stimulus rather than trying to reform individual markets. In any case, the New Deal left an indelible imprint. First, it created a wide array of institutions and programs that continue to shape our economic life: the Securities and Exchange Commission, the Federal Deposit Insurance Corporation, minimum wages and other workplace regulations, Social Security, unemployment compensation, and so on. Some of these institutions were small and achieved their goals mainly by imposing rules and regulations; others such as Social Security and agricultural price supports meant vast new expenditures. Big government arrived in the 1930s and the role of state and especially local government shrank in relative terms (Wallis 1984). Second, the New Deal created an idealistic spirit among young people that would bear fruit in the form of additional liberal legislation passed years later, especially during the Kennedy-Johnson years. Third, the New Deal created the presumption that people could look to Washington for solutions to their economic difficulties. True, people had often turned to Washington for help before 1929—for example, to reduce foreign competition, to subsidize railroad construction, to relieve the victims of fire, and so on. But before the New Deal potential reforms had to overcome the presumption that the existing political and economic institutions, including the free market, were fundamentally sound. The New Deal reversed the burden of proof, leaving it to the defenders of the status quo to show that market forces could solve a problem to which the attention of the public had been drawn by a crisis.

The fourth and perhaps most important legacy of the New Deal is, paradoxically, what it did not do: It did not try to overthrow capitalism. With the nation in turmoil and its economy in ruins, socialism or at least widespread nationalization of commerce and industry might have been instituted in 1933. The basic instinct of the New Deal, however, was to reform and conserve the system. Americans like to think of themselves as good poker players. In 1932 they did not want to play a fundamentally different game, they just wanted a New Deal.

SELECTED REFERENCES AND SUGGESTED READINGS

Alston, Lee J. "Farm Foreclosures in the United States during the Interwar Period." *Journal of Economic History* 43 (1983): 885–903.

_____. "Farm Foreclosure Moratorium Legislation: A Lesson from the Past." *American Economic Review* 74 (1984): 445–457.

Alston, Lee J., and Randal R. Rucker. "Farm Failures and Government Intervention: A Case Study of the 1930's." *American Economic Review* 77 (September 1987): 724–730.

Anderson, Gary M., and Robert Tollison. "Congressional Influence and Patterns of New Deal Spending,

1933–1939." *Journal of Law & Economics* 34 (1991): 161–75.

Arrington, Leonard J. "The New Deal in the West: A Preliminary Statistical Inquiry." *Pacific Historical Review* 38 (August 1969): 311–316.

Bernstein, Michael. "A Reassessment of Investment Failure in the Interwar American Economy." *Journal of Economic History* 44 (1984): 479–488.

Bordo, Michael D., Christopher J. Erceg, and Charles L. Evans. "Sticky Wages, and the Great Depression." *American Economic Review* 90 (December 2000): 1447–1463.

Cole, Harold L., and Lee E. Ohanian. "New Deal Policies and the Persistence of the Great Depression: A General Equilibrium Analysis." *The Journal of Political Economy* 112, no. 4 (August 2004): 779–816.

Calomiris, Charles W., and Eugene N. White. "The Origins of Federal Deposit Insurance." In *The Regulated Economy: A Historical Approach to Political Economy*, eds. Claudia Goldin and Gary D. Libecap, 145–188. National Bureau of Economic Research Project Report Series. Chicago and London: University of Chicago Press, 1994.

Darby, Michael. "Three and a Half Million U.S. Employees Have Been Mislaid: Or, an Explanation of Unemployment, 1934–1941." *Journal of Political Economy* 84 (February 1976): 1–16.

Fishback, Price V., Michael R. Haines, and Shawn Kantor. "Births, Deaths, and New Deal Relief during the Great Depression." *Review of Economics and Statistics* (February 2007): 1–14.

Fleck, Robert K. "Democratic Opposition to the Fair Labor Standards Act of 1938." *The Journal of Economic History* 62 (March 2002): 25–54.

_____. "Democratic Opposition to the Fair Labor Standards Act of 1938: Reply to Seltzer." *Journal of Economic History* 64: (March 2004): 231–235.

Friedman, Milton, and Anna Jacobson Schwartz. *A Monetary History of the United States, 1867-1960.* National Bureau of Economic Research. Studies in Business Cycles, Vol. 12. Princeton: Princeton University Press, 1963.

Hansen, Zeynep K., and Gary D., Libecap. Small farms, externalities, and the dust bowl of the 1930s. *Journal of Political Economy* 112 (June 2004): 665–694.

Higgs, Robert. "Regime Uncertainty: Why the Great Depression Lasted so Long and Why Prosperity Resumed after the War." *Independent Review* 1, no. 4 (Spring 1997): 561–590.

Historical Statistics. Washington, D.C.: Government Printing Office, 1975.

Johnson, H. Thomas. "Postwar Optimism and the Rural Financial Crisis of the 1920's." *Explorations in Economic History* 11, no. 2 (Winter 1973–1974): 173–192.

Kang, Sung Won. *The Political Economy of Social Security Expansion: From 1935–1983.* Rutgers University, 2006.

Keynes, John Maynard. *The General Theory of Employment, Interest and Money.* London: Macmillan, 1936.

Kroszner, Randall S., and Raghuram G. Rajan. "Is the Glass-Steagall Act Justified? A Study of the U.S. Experience with Universal Banking before 1933." *The American Economic Review* 84, no. 4 (September 1994): 810–832.

Libecap, Gary D. "The Great Depression and the Regulating State: Federal Government Regulation of Agriculture, 1884–1970." In *The Defining Moment: The Great Depression and the American Economy in the Twentieth Century*, eds. Michael D. Bordo, Claudia Goldin, and Eugene N. White, 181–224. Chicago: University of Chicago Press, 1998.

Margo, Robert. "The Microeconomics of Depression Unemployment." *The Journal of Economic History* 51 (June 1991): 333–342.

Mayer, Thomas, and Monojit Chatterji. "Political Shocks and Investment: Some Evidence from the 1930s." *Journal of Economic History* 45 (December 1985): 913–924

_____. "Reply to O'Brien." *Journal of Economic History* 50 (December 1990): 942–944.

O'Brien, Anthony Patrick. "A Behavioral Explanation for Normal Wage Rigidity during the Great Depression." *Quarterly Journal of Economics* 104 (1989): 719–735.

_____. "Were Businessmen Afraid of FDR? A Comment on Mayer and Chatterji." *The Journal of Economic History* 50 (Dec., 1990): 936–941.

Seltzer, Andrew J. "The Political Economy of the Fair Labor Standards Act of 1938." *Journal of Political Economy* 103, no. 6 (December 1995): 1302–1342.

_____. "The Effects of the Fair Labor Standards Act of 1938 on the Southern Seamless Hosiery and Lumber Industries." *The Journal of Economic History* 57, No. 2 (June 1997): 396–415.

_____. "Democratic Opposition to the Fair Labor Standards Act: A Comment on Fleck," *The Journal of Economic History* 64, no 1 (March 2004): 226–230.

Schumpeter, Joseph. *Business Cycles: A Theoretical, Historical, and Statistical Analysis of the Capitalist Process.* 1939.

Sobel, Russell S. "Theory and Evidence on the Political Economy of the Minimum Wage." *The Journal of Political Economy* 107, no. 4 (August 1999): 761–785.

Wallis, John Joseph. "The Birth of the Old Federalism: Financing the New Deal, 1932–1940." *Journal of Economic History* 44 (1984): 139–159.

———. "Employment, Politics, and Economic Recovery during the Great Depression Employment, Politics, and Economic Recovery during the Great Depression." *The Review of Economics and Statistics* 69 (August 1987): 516–520.

Walton, Gary M., ed. *Regulatory Change in an Atmosphere of Crisis: Current Implications of the Roosevelt Years*. New York: Academic Press, 1979.

White, Eugene Nelson. "Before the Glass-Steagall Act: An Analysis of the Investment Banking Activities of National Banks." *Explorations in Economic History* 23, no. 1 (January 1986): 33–55.

Wright, Gavin. "The Political Economy of New Deal Spending: An Econometric Analysis." *Review of Economics and Statistics* 56 (1974): 30–38.

CHAPTER **25**

World War II

CHAPTER THEME

In 1939, only 21 years after the end of World War I, the world was once more engulfed in global war. Ultimately, the war took an enormous human toll. The United States suffered 405,000 deaths in World War II, 292,000 in battle. In addition, 671,000 suffered nonmortal wounds. The American death toll was four times that of World War I and two-thirds that of the Civil War. For the other belligerents, the tolls were much higher. All told, about 40 million people died in World War II.

America's primary economic goal was to supply sufficient arms to her own military forces and to those of her allies to overwhelm the Axis (Germany, Japan, and their allies), to become, as President Roosevelt put it, the "Arsenal of Democracy." This goal was achieved with astonishing speed. In a few short years, the factories of the United States were turning out more weapons than any other nation and more than all the Axis powers combined, even though the Axis had begun converting to a war footing years before the United States.

In the short run, the war effort alleviated the need for many of the New Deal's emergency measures. Work relief was no longer necessary because the nation's factories were humming at full capacity; emergency funds were no longer needed to bail out firms faced with bankruptcy because profits were surging. In the long run, the war effort reinforced the restructuring of the economy that had taken place in the 1930s. The association of large federal deficits and low unemployment convinced many economists and the public at large that Keynes's cure for unemployment was effective. The government's management of the mobilization convinced economists and the public at large that the federal government had the ability to successfully manage large-scale projects.

MOBILIZING FOR WAR

World War II began in September 1939, when German forces attacked Poland. Britain and France, who had guaranteed Poland's independence, then declared war on Germany. In the United States, a brief surge occurred in industrial production as manufacturers anticipated a repeat of the heady days of 1916 when a neutral America had made enormous profits by supplying a Europe at war. Industrial production sagged during the "phony war," however, when it appeared that Britain, France, and Germany, although officially at war, would avoid a major clash of arms. The phony war ended in May 1940 when Germany launched a *blitzkrieg* (lightning war) attack against the Low Countries, swept around France's Maginot Line, and conquered France. American manufacturers began building up inventories in anticipation of future shortages, Britain and her remaining allies began placing large orders for American war materials, and the United States launched a vastly expanded program of military procurement.

Initially, Britain was asked to pay for arms on a cash-and-carry basis. It paid by transferring gold and by requisitioning American bank deposits and securities owned by British nationals. This policy soon stripped Britain of much of its overseas investment. When these sources of funds began to run out, President Roosevelt succeeded in establishing the Lend-Lease program in March 1941. The name "Lend-Lease" was calculated to deflect attention from the simple fact that the U.S. government would now be paying for the arms sent to Britain and its other allies.

At first, prices remained relatively stable because millions of American workers were still unemployed and underemployed and because industrial capacity was underutilized. The United States had not yet reached its production possibilities curve, to use the economist's term. By the autumn of 1940, however, supply had become less elastic and wholesale prices had begun to rise. In 1941, the American economy was moving into high gear despite some pockets of unemployment. Production of steel ingots and castings, for example, had already reached 59.8 million long-tons in 1940, exceeding the previous peak of 56.4 million reached in 1929; in 1941, production reached 74 million long-tons. Sulfuric acid, a chemical having a wide variety of industrial applications, was also being produced in unprecedented quantities: 6.8 million short-tons in 1941 compared with 5.3 million in 1929. The Federal Reserve Board's index of industrial production reached a level of 139 in 1941 compared with 100 in 1929. Although American industry was moving into high gear, many Americans still doubted the wisdom of aid to Britain and its allies. All doubts vanished, however, on December 7, 1941. To quote President Roosevelt's famous war message:

Yesterday, December 7, 1941—a date which will live in infamy—the United States of America was suddenly and deliberately attacked by the naval and air forces of the Empire of Japan.... The facts of yesterday speak for themselves. The people of the United States have already formed their opinions and well understand the implications to the very life and safety of our nation.

America was now fully committed to war against the Axis powers (Germany had quickly declared war against the United States after the Japanese attack and the United States reciprocated), but many military and economic questions still had to be answered.

Under President Roosevelt's leadership, the United States adopted a bold plan of economic mobilization. America would use its vast industrial might to mass-produce arms and overwhelm the Axis with sheer firepower. Characteristically, President Roosevelt called for the unheard-of total of 50,000 airplanes, although at the time no one knew how such a vast number of planes could be produced. Economic mobilization involved many trade-offs. The most important question was how far to reduce civilian consumption—the choice, as it was often put, between "guns and butter."[1] See Economic Insight 25.1 on page 464.

Table 25.1 shows, in very broad terms, how America allocated its resources to the war effort: In 1929, the federal government was spending a small fraction of gross national product (GNP), 2.6 percent. Even in 1940, after years of expansion in the role of the federal government under the New Deal, the federal government was spending about 8.2 percent of GNP. The war changed things dramatically. The maximum effort occurred in 1944, when the federal government spent some $722.5 billion (at 1982 prices), about 52.3 percent of total GNP.

---

[1]The term "guns or butter" is usually attributed to German Field Marshal Hermann Goering, who in the 1930s demanded "cannon instead of butter." In the United States, civilian consumption of butter did fall during the war, but this appears to have been simply part of a long-term trend toward lower consumption. Consumption of ice cream, on the other hand, was higher during the war, also part of a long-term trend.

ECONOMIC INSIGHT 25.1

"GUNS OR BUTTER" 1939–1949

The production possibilities curve shows the trade-off between guns (military spending), measured on the horizontal axis, and butter (civilian spending), measured on the vertical axis. The figure shows the actual combinations of guns and butter produced annually during the war years and a hypothetical curve drawn through the combinations achieved in 1944 and 1948.

Some of the combinations lie inside the production possibilities curve (1939, 1940, 1941, and 1942, in particular); these points indicate that the economy was still operating below its maximum possible output. Thus, in general, the United States increased its war output mainly by moving horizontally toward the production possibilities curve rather than moving along it.

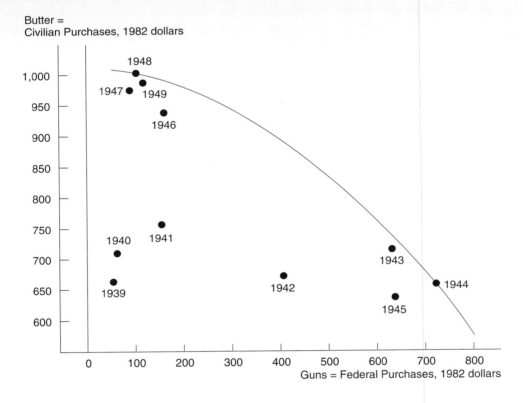

Butter =
Civilian Purchases, 1982 dollars

Guns = Federal Purchases, 1982 dollars

Another way to analyze these figures is also of interest. Between 1940 and 1944, total real federal spending increased by $658.9 billion ($722.5 in 1944 – $63.6 in 1940), while total real GNP increased by $607.7 billion ($1,380.6 – $772.9). Thus, 92.2 percent of the increase in spending ($607.7 ÷ $658.9) was paid by the increase in real GNP; the remaining 7.8 percent of the increase was offset by a decline in production for the civilian sector. The great bulk of the resources for the war effort was obtained by employing previously unemployed resources and by using already employed resources more intensively. Remarkably enough, Germany was also able to sustain civilian consumption well into the war, although not throughout. In other countries, though, where the capacity to expand was lower, the need to sacrifice current consumption or investment to make available resources for the military effort was correspondingly greater.

TABLE 25.1 REAL GROSS NATIONAL PRODUCT (IN BILLIONS OF 1982 DOLLARS)

YEAR	GNP	TOTAL FEDERAL PURCHASES OF GOODS AND SERVICES	PREVIOUS COLUMN AS A PERCENTAGE OF GNP	TOTAL CIVILIAN PURCHASES OF GOODS AND SERVICES[a]	PREVIOUS COLUMN AS A PERCENTAGE OF GNP
1929	$ 709.6	$ 18.3	2.58%	$ 691.3	97.42%
1939	716.6	53.8	7.51	662.8	92.49
1940	772.9	63.6	8.23	709.3	91.77
1941	909.4	153.0	16.82	756.4	83.18
1942	1,080.3	407.1	37.68	673.2	62.32
1943	1,276.2	638.1	50.00	638.1	50.00
1944	1,380.6	722.5	52.33	658.1	47.67
1945	1,354.8	634.0	46.80	720.8	53.20
1946	1,096.9	159.3	14.52	937.6	85.48
1950	1,203.7	116.7	9.70	1,087.0	90.30

[a]Includes state and local government spending.

Source: Economic Report of the President *1987, 246–247.*

Trade-offs

While the decision about how much to reduce civilian consumption and investment was the most important, other more subtle trade-offs were also involved in wartime mobilization. Economic Reasoning Proposition 2, choices impose costs (see page 8), stresses the importance of trade-offs in war as well as in peace. One such trade-off occurred in the area of industrial safety. Industrial accidents, often resulting in serious injury or death, increased dramatically during the war. The official figures show an increase in the number of disabling injuries per million hours worked in manufacturing from 15.3 in 1940 to 20 in 1943, the all-time peak. To some extent this was to be expected, with so many more men and women working so many more hours in dangerous jobs.

Should greater efforts have been made to maintain safety? Possibly, but the problem was always one of the trade-off between safety and production. Well-rested workers are safer workers, but more rest breaks may mean lower output. More work space in shipping yards reduces the risk of accidents, but more work space means higher construction costs and fewer resources available for building other facilities.

Another subtle trade-off lay between the quality and quantity of arms produced. Changing technology and battlefield experience were constantly suggesting modifications of existing weapons. Making these modifications often meant tearing down and rebuilding an assembly line, thereby losing valuable production time. This trade-off was often a bone of contention between military leaders, who would argue for the most sophisticated weapon possible, and the civilians in charge of military production, who were more mindful of the potential loss in production. When Hitler's troops attacked the Allied invasion force in the Battle of the Bulge, Germany's tanks, the famous panzers, were as good as or better than any tank in the hands of the Allies, but they were vastly outnumbered.

On the whole, America's decision to mass-produce the weapons of war turned out to be a brilliant success. America by itself produced more arms than the Axis countries combined. Not only were supplies such as small arms and ammunition mass-produced, but also planes and even ships to carry the arms to the theaters of war. At Henry Kaiser's shipyards in Portland, Oregon, where some of the most innovative techniques were used, one of the famous Liberty ships was produced in a record eight days. To some extent, as Henry A. Gemery and Jan S. Hogendorn (1993) have shown, mass-production techniques were used even in producing destroyers.

TABLE 25.2 COMBAT MUNITIONS PRODUCED BY THE MAJOR BELLIGERENTS (IN BILLIONS OF DOLLARS AT 1944 U.S. MUNITIONS PRICES)						
	1933–1939	**1940**	**1941**	**1942**	**1943**	**1944**
United States	$ 1.5	$1.5	$4.5	$20	$38	$42
United Kingdom	2.5	3.5	6.5	9	11	11
U.S.S.R.	8	5	8.5	11.5	14	16
Germany	12	6	6	8.5	13.5	17
Japan	2	1	2	3	4.5	6

Source: *Harrison 1998, 172.*

Overwhelming Firepower

Table 25.2 shows the annual production of munitions (cumulatively for 1933–1939) by the five major powers. By 1939, Germany and Japan had accumulated considerable stocks of munitions. They hoped to win against countries with greater long-term economic capacities by employing these munitions in blitzkrieg attacks before their opponents had time to arm. Although they won numerous initial battles, eventually their paths of expansion were blocked, and the war became one of attrition. The United States launched a huge program to build both arms and the means of producing them, and its production surged. By 1942, U.S. munitions production exceeded that of Germany and Japan combined. Despite the ability of Germany and Japan to increase their production in the face of heavy air attacks (see Economic Insight 25.2 for a discussion of strategic

U.S. planes leaving the production line. By 1944 the United States was producing 100,000 per year.

ECONOMIC INSIGHT 25.2

THE ECONOMICS OF STRATEGIC BOMBING

Tactical bombing uses the air force as an aid to the ground or sea forces. Strategic bombing, however, attacks the enemy's civilian population. Often the purpose is economic: to reduce the enemy's ability to equip and support its armed forces. During World War II, all of the belligerents used strategic bombing, but the United States and Britain relied on it the most. Initially, Britain and the United States emphasized striking at "sensitive points" in the German economy such as transportation, steel, ball bearings, and so on. The campaigns based on destroying sensitive points, however, ran into trouble because the Germans could protect these points with massive antiaircraft defenses, and because the Germans found ways to harden sensitive sites and disperse facilities. The Germans also found substitutes for items in short supply. In general, the attempt to destroy sensitive points in the enemy economy proved frustrating, although the attacks on oil production and rail transport at the end of the war were fairly successful. So the Allies turned to mass destruction—destroying as much of the enemy's industrial base as possible—as a way to end the war. This was truer for the British

who bombed at night than for the Americans who bombed by day and continued to pay some attention to the theory of striking at sensitive points. Nevertheless, in the end, both countries followed a policy of mass destruction. To be effective such a policy has to be, and was, horrific. The loss of civilian lives in Germany and Japan was staggering. After the war, the U.S. Strategic Bombing Survey, led on the civilian level by economist John Kenneth Galbraith, found that strategic bombing had not been effective in the sense of reducing German or Japanese munitions production to very low levels (Galbraith 1981). On the contrary, production of munitions continued to rise in Germany and Japan until very near the end of the war. This finding encouraged Galbraith to become a vigorous opponent of bombing in the Vietnam era. There is, however, a vigorous debate about the effectiveness of strategic bombing. Richard Overy is one of the leading voices on the other side. In *Why the Allies Won* (1995), he argues that strategic bombing was important from a military perspective because it opened a second front against Germany. One-third of German artillery production was for antiaircraft protection, and most of the planes produced in Germany went up to fight the British and American bombers. This diversion of resources eased the burden of the Soviets fighting Germany on the Eastern Front.

The results of strategic bombing. The Allied air forces devastated thousands of acres in cities in Germany and Japan in an attempt to destroy their ability to wage war.

BETTMANN/CORBIS ©

The Liberty ship, mass produced during World War II, helped the United States multiply the total tonnage of its merchant marine fleet by a factor of 5.

bombing), and despite the advantage of fighting behind defensive lines, the final outcome was no longer in doubt. The enormous weight of the combined munitions production of the United States and her allies meant that Germany and Japan would be defeated sooner or later.

Several agencies, the most important being the War Production Board, tried to manage the vast expansion of munitions production. One tool was the priority, essentially a rating placed on contracts to guide manufacturers in scheduling production. The reallocation of resources was so rapid and so huge that the total volume of new contracts outstanding was said to exceed the GNP. Munitions production was reaching its peak when the War Production Board finally solved the problems—such as "priority inflation" (too many contracts having the highest priority)—that had developed soon after mobilization began. In the end, the profit motive was the primary allocator of resources.

FISCAL AND MONETARY POLICY

The United States relied on the same methods to mobilize resources in World War II that it had relied on in World War I. To mobilize labor, it relied on the draft; to mobilize financial resources, it relied on taxes, borrowing, and creating money. The war radically changed the income tax. The exemptions for single and married persons were lowered. In 1943, the payroll deduction system for collecting income taxes was introduced, and the term *take-home pay* entered the language. Together, these innovations meant that the income tax had become a mass tax for the first time. Corporate tax rates were also

TABLE 25.3 FINANCING WORLD WAR II

	BILLIONS OF DOLLARS, 1941–1946	PERCENTAGE OF EXPENDITURES
Total federal expenditures for war[a]	$320.2	100.0%
Tax revenues	129.8	40.5
Borrowing from the public	115.8	37.0
Creating new money	74.6	22.5

[a]Total expenditures 1941–1946, less six times 1940 expenditures.

Source: *Friedman and Schwartz 1970, 33–37.*

increased, and an excess profits tax was introduced. As a result of these tax increases and the rapid increase in the tax base, the United States was able to finance about 40 percent of the war with taxes (see Table 25.3). This was a larger share of total spending on the war than had been financed by taxes in the Civil War or World War I. Nevertheless, the United States still had to borrow large sums to help finance the conflict (refer to New View 25.1).

Conceivably, all wartime deficits could have been financed by sales of securities to the general public, but (despite highly publicized war bond drives) it is likely that the interest rates required to market those bonds would have been very high by historic standards. Therefore, the Federal Reserve took the extraordinary step of "pegging" the rate of interest on government securities. It accomplished this by pledging to buy government securities whenever their price fell below predetermined support levels. On the surface, selling bonds to the Fed seems to be a free ride because it minimizes the future interest costs that the government incurs. The fly in the ointment (or rat in the soup, depending

NEW VIEW 25.1

HOW SHOULD WARS BE FINANCED?

The World War II debate over whether to rely mainly on taxes or debt to finance the war (no one thought that relying on printing money was a good idea) continues to be relevant when the United States goes to war. The Roosevelt administration, reflecting one school of thought, proposed financing the greater part of the war by raising taxes. According to the administration, doing so would avoid burdening the younger generation (including those doing the fighting) with having to pay the interest and principal on a large debt in future years. Getting Congress to raise taxes, however, is never easy. Republican congressmen complained that high tax rates discouraged work, and they supported only partial financing through increased taxation. Today, many neoclassical economists, for example Robert J. Barro (1989) agree that "smoothing taxes"—raising them only a bit during

wars and relying mainly on debt—is the most efficient way to finance a war. Supporters of deficit finance can also point out that the federal debt reached $259 billion in 1945, 121 percent of gross domestic product (GDP), without causing an obvious crisis, as evidence that the economy can tolerate very high levels of debt.

In thinking about this debate, it is perhaps relevant to remind ourselves of what Adam Smith, a proponent of tax finance, had to say:

Wars [if financed by taxes rather than debt] would in general be more speedily concluded, and less wantonly undertaken. The people feeling, during the continuance of the war, the complete burden of it, would soon grow weary of it, and the government, in order to humor them, would not be under the necessity of carrying it on longer than it was necessary do so. (Smith 1976 [1776], 925)

	UNEMPLOYMENT (percent of the	GNP (in billions	FEDERAL BUDGET DEFICIT (in billions of	FEDERAL BUDGET DEFICIT AS A PERCENTAGE	STOCK OF MONEY (in billions of
YEAR	labor force)	of dollars)	dollars)	OF GNP	dollars)
1929	3.2%	$103.9	$ 0.7	0.67%	$ 46.6
1933	20.6	56.0	−2.6	−4.64	32.2
1939	11.3	91.3	−2.8	−3.07	49.2
1944	1.2	211.4	−47.6	−22.52	106.8

TABLE 25.4 DEFICIT SPENDING AND THE FALL IN UNEMPLOYMENT

Sources: Economic Report of the President 1987, *244, 280, and 331; and Darby 1976, 8. The last column is derived from Friedman and Schwartz 1982, 124–125.*

on one's view of things) is that the Federal Reserve must create new money to purchase these securities, and this adds to the inflationary pressures facing the economy.[2]

In 1939, unemployment remained at the stubbornly high level of 11.3 percent of the labor force. Keynesians claimed that unemployment could be cured with a sufficient increase in government spending, particularly deficit-financed spending. True, the deficit was 3.07 percent of GNP in 1939 (see Table 25.4). What was needed, according to the Keynesians, was simply a much bigger deficit. By 1944 the deficit had been vastly increased, to 22.5 percent of GNP, and unemployment was virtually gone (1.2 percent), one of the lowest rates on record. Most economists, particularly those of the younger generation such as future Nobel Prize winners Paul Samuelson and James Tobin, found this demonstration of the effectiveness of the Keynesian remedy for unemployment convincing.

A number of economists at the time, as well as a growing number since, were still skeptical about Keynes's cure. For one thing, the data are also consistent with the monetarist claim that a large increase in the money supply would cure the depression. Consider the last column of Table 25.4. The stock of money in 1939 was only slightly higher than that of 1929, but by 1944, it had more than doubled. Some economists have pointed out that the drafting of large numbers of young men into the armed forces removed many individuals who had a high probability of being unemployed from the labor force. As in so many cases, the lessons of history are ambiguous because in the natural experiments of history other factors are seldom as constant as we would like. Whatever reservations economists may now entertain about this demonstration of the Keynesian message, there is no doubt that it had a profound impact on economic policy making during and in the decades following the war. Even at the time, however, some Keynesians worried that the inflationary pressures produced by wartime policies of deficit spending had been checked only by a set of wage and price controls that would be unacceptable in peacetime.

WAGE AND PRICE CONTROLS

Early in the war, the Roosevelt administration decided that it would combat rising prices with direct controls. It would try to persuade firms not to raise prices by appealing to their patriotism; if persuasion failed, it would simply make price increases illegal.

---

[2]The interest rate paid on a bond is determined by the relationship between the fixed annual payments promised by the bond and the market value of the bond. High market values imply low interest rates.

In May 1940, President Roosevelt set up the National Defense Advisory Committee and chose Leon Henderson, a crusty, cigar-smoking New Dealer, to head its Price Stabilization Division. Henderson sought voluntary agreements from producers in key areas of the economy not to raise prices, a policy that met with little success. Prices continued to rise. In April 1941, Roosevelt strengthened Henderson's hand by creating the Office of Price Administration and Civilian Supply (OPA). Eventually, OPA would become the civilian agency most familiar to the average American because it set the prices and determined the quantities of the goods and services consumed every day. Of special interest to economists was the creation of the Price Division of OPA under the direction of John Kenneth Galbraith. In the postwar period, Galbraith would become a leading advocate of the liberal view that America's social and economic problems could be solved by expanding the role of the federal government. Undoubtedly, his experience at the OPA, with its enormous—and in Galbraith's (1952) view favorable—effect on the economy, profoundly influenced his thinking.

Initially, the OPA hoped to control the general price level by applying controls in only selected sectors, but uncontrolled prices continued to rise, and at an increasing pace. In April 1942, OPA issued the General Maximum Price Regulation, affectionately known as General Max, which put a ceiling on most prices. Even this measure was only partially successful. One problem was that each seller was responsible for setting its own prices according to the rules issued by the government. It was altogether too easy for a firm to justify charging a high price by pointing to an unusually high base period price or an unusually high price set by a competitor. Effective price control required that the OPA set specific dollars-and-cents prices that its employees or its boards of volunteer price watchers could check.

In April 1943, President Roosevelt issued his famous "hold-the-line" order requiring OPA to refuse all requests for price increases except in extremely limited circumstances. This approach, economically suspect because it did not provide for the adjustment of relative prices, but easy to defend in the court of public opinion, worked surprisingly well for the remainder of the war. The official consumer price index rose only 1.6 percent per year from April 1943 until February 1946, when the policy began to come apart.

Hidden Price Increases and the Black Market

The official index alone, however, does not tell the whole story. A basic proposition of economics is that if a price ceiling is set below the free-market equilibrium, a scramble for supplies will occur that will produce attempts to evade the ceiling. There were innumerable examples during the war. In some cases, evasion took the form of quality deterioration: Fat was added to hamburger, coarse fabrics were substituted for finer ones, and maintenance on rent-controlled apartments was reduced. Quality deterioration could be limited by regulations that specified the exact content of a product, such as the specified butterfat content of milk, but such regulations tended to get longer and longer and became a problem in themselves. In one famous case, Lou Maxon, an OPA official, resigned in 1943, complaining about what he saw as the antibusiness atmosphere at OPA. Many of Maxon's charges were exaggerated, but the six-page regulation specifying the content of fruit cakes, which he used to dramatize his charges, spoke to a real problem.

"Forced uptrading" was another problem caused by price controls. Before the war, manufacturers often offered buyers a choice between low-priced, low-quality items and high-priced, high-quality items. Typically, the high-priced lines carried higher profit margins but sold in smaller volumes. With wartime demand in all lines exceeding supply, manufacturers eliminated the lower-priced lines. This was fine for those consumers who wished to move up to the higher-priced item anyway, but for those who were forced to trade up, the difference between what they would have voluntarily paid for the high-priced line and what they were forced to pay because the low-priced line was eliminated was a hidden price increase.

The most startling form of evasion, although not the most frequent, was the black market. Here, buyers willing to pay more than the official price and sellers willing to sell for more would meet away from the prying eyes of the OPA. The black market took many forms, depending on the product and the enforcement effort being made by the OPA. In New York, there were "meat-easies," much like the speakeasies that had flourished during prohibition, where one could buy extra meat but at prices much higher than those set by the OPA. After production of automobiles resumed at the end of the war, evasion of automobile price controls was widespread. Some of it occurred in the dealer's showroom, where cash payments were often made on the side while official documents showed that the car had been sold at the OPA ceiling. A true black market also developed. In Leesville, South Carolina, for example, cars recently purchased from dealers were brought from all over the country to a huge lot where they would be resold at black-market prices.

Rationing

Rationing is one way to reduce evasion when prices are held below their free-market equilibrium. A consumer who is assured at least a bare minimum is less likely to enter the black market than a consumer who is in danger of being left without anything in a mad scramble for supplies. Moreover, a company that must be able to show the authorities ration tickets corresponding to the output it has sold will find it more difficult to divert supplies to the black market. In some cases, rationing was undertaken to achieve particular policy goals. Gasoline was rationed, for example, to reduce the use of automobile and truck tires, which were in short supply because of the rubber shortage. The real purpose of government programs, thus, was sometime difficult for the public to understand. A well-publicized campaign to save and recycle cooking fat, for example, led consumers to believe that the fat was needed to make a chemical crucial to the war effort. The real purpose, however, was to increase the supply of fat for making soap because manufacturers of soap feared that if soap was rationed during the war some consumers would continue to buy less afterward (Rockoff 2007).

The simplest form of rationing was a ticket entitling the holder to buy a certain quantity of a certain good that was surrendered when the good was purchased. Tires, the first commodity rationed, were handled in this way. Under the red-point system for meats and fats, however, the consumer was periodically supplied with a certain number of points. Each good was assigned a point price, and the consumer could choose among rationed items as long as he or she had enough ration points.

Balancing the supply of goods and the number of ration tickets or points was no easy matter. To make the red-point system operate more smoothly, the OPA issued red-point tokens that could be taken as change and stored for use at a later date. By late 1944, surveys showed that consumers had stored up large quantities of these tokens, and the OPA feared a run on the stores that would leave shelves bare and confidence in the rationing program shaken. To regain control, OPA canceled all outstanding ration tokens, a move that cost the agency a great deal of public support. In 1945, as the war came to a close, most of the rationing programs were discontinued, a highly popular decision.

When legislation authorizing price controls expired in June 1946, Congress passed a new law. It was so riddled with loopholes that President Truman vetoed it in the hope that a strong dose of inflation would force Congress to pass a stiffer measure. Eventually, legislation was passed that permitted the recontrol of selected prices. When meat prices were recontrolled, ranchers withheld their animals from the market—after all, it was clear that price controls were on the way out and that prices could only go higher—and the result was a meat shortage. Faced with outraged consumers on one hand and recommendations that he nationalize the nation's cattle herds on the other, Truman decided to terminate price controls for good.

WARTIME PROSPERITY?

If we look at a graph of real GDP per capita, as shown in Figure 25.1, the war years stand out as a unique achievement. Apparently, real per capita income was higher during the war than it was before or after. The statistics are matched by personal memories of the war and by historical accounts that single out the war years as a uniquely prosperous period. Robert Higgs (1992), however, has recently challenged this view of the war and claimed that the war was not a period of unique prosperity, but rather a period of continued depression. Real prosperity, according to Higgs, did not come until after the war. In other words, Higgs asserts that the story illustrated so eloquently in Figure 25.1 is spurious.

First, Higgs (1992) points out that many problems created by price controls and rationing, as mentioned, make measurement of output and especially civilian consumption during the war problematic. If price indexes are understated because they miss hidden price increases or because the price of rationed goods understates the difficulty of acquiring them, output will be overstated. Higgs also points out that war output did not contribute directly to consumption, either at the time or in the future. In his view, war production should be omitted altogether from GDP.

FIGURE 25.1

Real per Capita Income in 1987 Dollars

Official estimates of real GDP per capita reached an extraordinary peak in 1944. But can we really compare the output of the economy during the war with the output before or after?

Source: *U.S. Bureau of Economic Analysis, 1992*

One can take issue with Higgs's arguments. Any measurement of the extent of hidden price increases during the war is bound to have a large margin of error. Higgs's claim that war output should be omitted from GDP is also debatable. After all, we include categories, such as medical care, that raise many of the same issues in GDP. An operation for cancer, like fighting a battle against a determined enemy, is costly and painful. Indeed, we often use the same language: "He is battling for his life against cancer." Cancer operations and battles may be good investments because they protect our ability to enjoy life in the future.

Nevertheless, Higgs's (1992) arguments do help us understand the nature of "wartime prosperity." For many people, the war did mean an increase in their current real consumption compared with that during the grinding poverty of the Depression. For others, the important thing was not consumption during the war but the availability of jobs for the asking through which one could earn money that would be valuable in the years to come, even if it couldn't be spent during the war because of shortages and rationing. Economic Reasoning Proposition 5, evidence and theory give value to opinions, reminds us that evidence matters. Higgs's analysis reminds us that we must question and probe the evidence for its real meaning.

LABOR DURING THE WAR

Real wages rose during the war, at least when official price indexes are used to deflate wages. But the rise was not uniform. The gap between the wages earned by managers and workers, and the gap between the wages earned by skilled and unskilled workers, narrowed. The "Great Compression" in wage differences persisted for some years into the postwar era (Goldin and Margo 1992), although it eventually disappeared. Wartime wage controls, which were tougher at the high end of the wage distribution, and the strong demand for unskilled labor seem to be the main factors behind this important, albeit temporary, increase in wage equality.

The war put relations between labor and management on hold. The Roosevelt administration had been supporting labor's efforts to organize, bargain collectively, and strike; now labor was expected to cooperate with the effort to maximize production. Labor took a no-strike pledge, paralleling management's no-lockout pledge. For the most part, labor kept its pledge. The major exception was the United Mine Workers, under their charismatic leader John L. Lewis. As the result of public indignation over strikes in the coalfields, Congress passed the Smith-Connally War Labor Disputes Act in 1943, which provided for government takeover of mines and factories in essential war industries that were hampered by strikes. Despite this case, however, the conflict between labor and management was generally kept in check during the war by labor's patriotism and by the government's extraordinary powers.

The real crunch came at the end of the war. As workers' overtime disappeared and real earnings were eroded by rising prices, labor leaders were under pressure to secure wage increases, which were not forthcoming without a struggle. Meanwhile, the widespread work stoppages of 1945 and 1946, shown vividly in Figure 25.2, alienated large segments of the electorate.

During this period, employers complained that they were being caught in the jurisdictional disputes of rival unions and that labor itself was guilty of unfair practices. A belief was growing that union power was being used to infringe on the rights of individual workers. In fact, employers often used strikes to pressure the OPA to grant a price increase. Labor, of course, realized that this avenue was open to employers, and this entered into their strike calculations. The OPA, in many cases, claimed that higher wages

FIGURE 25.2

Five-Year Moving Average of Number of Strike Days per Thousand Nonagricultural Employees, 1929–1973

Source: *Edwards 1981, 18.*

could be paid without granting higher prices, but the path of least resistance often was to grant a round of wage and price increases in an industry experiencing a strike.

After the Republicans won control of Congress in 1946, they lost no time in drawing up a long, technical bill that significantly amended the Wagner Act. The new law, passed in 1947 over President Truman's veto, was officially called the Labor Management Relations Act but became known familiarly as the Taft-Hartley Act. The act reflected the belief that individual workers should be protected by public policy not only in their right to join a labor organization but also in their right to refrain from joining. The closed-shop agreement, under which the employer hires only union members, was outlawed. Union shop agreements, which permit nonunion members to be employed but require them to join the union within a certain time period after starting to work, were permitted. However, the enforcement of union security provisions was limited to cases of nonpayment of dues. More important, the law permitted individual states to outlaw all forms of union security, including the union shop.

The Taft-Hartley Act, unlike the Wagner Act, assumed that the interests of the union and individuals in the union were not identical, taking the view that many union members were "captives" of the labor bosses—a position offensive to a great part of organized labor.

The most important features of the Taft-Hartley Act were those purporting to regulate unions in the "public" interest. A union seeking certification or requesting an investigation of unfair labor practices had to submit to a scrutiny of its internal affairs by filing statements, and its officers were required to sign affidavits stating that they were not members of the Communist Party. The right to strike was modified by provision of a cooling-off period after notice of termination of contract, and the president of the United

States was given authority to postpone strikes for 80 days by injunction. More significant was the outlawing of certain unfair union practices. After 1947, it was unfair for a union to do the following:

1. Restrain or coerce employees regarding their right to join or refrain from joining a labor organization, or restrain or coerce employers in the selection of employer representatives for purposes of collective bargaining or adjustment of grievances.
2. Cause or attempt to cause an employer to discriminate against an employee.
3. Charge, under a valid union shop agreement, an excessive initiation fee.
4. Refuse to bargain collectively with an employer when the union involved is the certified bargaining agent.
5. "Featherbed" the job—that is, cause an employer to pay for services that are not performed.
6. Engage in, or encourage employees to engage in, a strike where the object is to force one employer to cease doing business with another employer (the secondary boycott).

After 12 years of almost complete freedom, labor found the Taft-Hartley Act harshly restrictive. Dire warnings were voiced about the coming decline of trade unionism in America. Labor's leadership was incensed at the offensive language and punitive spirit of the act. Many of the provisions looked worse in print, however, than they proved in practice. The injunction clause, for example, stirred memories of the days when the courts granted injunctions at the request of private parties; however, in the hands of a president of the United States, acting in an emergency, the injunction was no longer a destructive weapon. Moreover, although union problems persist today, they have arisen primarily from sources other than the Taft-Hartley Act.

WARTIME MINORITY EXPERIENCES

World War II had a significant effect on all Americans, but especially certain minorities. Women entered the workforce to fill job vacancies left by soldiers (see Perspective 25.1 on page 478). The wartime boom accelerated the long-term movement of poor whites and African Americans out of southern agriculture. Both groups responded to similar economic facts of life. Altogether, almost a million African Americans moved from southern farms to industrial centers in the South, the Northeast, the Midwest, and the Pacific Coast (Vatter 1985, 127). The forced relocation and internment of more than 100,000 Japanese Americans caused them enormous hardships (Broom and Reimer 1949; Robinson 2001).

Rosie the Riveter

One of the most dramatic developments during the war was the change in the role of women in the labor force. Some 200,000 women entered the military services. Mainly they served in the Women's Army Corps (WAC) and Women Accepted for Volunteer Emergency Services (WAVES), with smaller numbers in the Marine Corps, Coast Guard, and the Women's Auxiliary Ferrying Service. Women also entered the civilian labor force in large numbers. Many entered jobs that women had filled before the war, but many others, as symbolized by "Rosie the Riveter," entered jobs traditionally filled by men. Women became toolmakers, crane operators, lumberjacks, and stevedores. About 14 percent of the women who had been out of the paid labor force before Pearl Harbor went to work. High wages and a desire to serve their country encouraged women to take jobs. Government propaganda urged women to work in industry and to help supply the weapons needed to defeat the Axis (Rupp 1978). This propaganda also encouraged

"Debbie the Driller" kept the production lines moving.

women to think of these jobs as temporary, to be turned back to returning soldiers after the war was over. Perhaps somewhat more surprisingly, 34 percent of the women who had been working before Pearl Harbor left the labor force. Increased wages earned by other family members, and a decline in the availability of household workers explain this phenomenon (Goldin 1991).

Women's participation in the labor force had seen a long-term upward trend throughout the twentieth century, but the war decade stands out as a period of especially rapid growth. In 1940, only 13.8 percent of married women participated in the paid labor force. In 1950, that figure stood at 21.6 percent, an increase in the participation rate of 5.65 percent per year, a higher rate of increase than in any other decade. This was partly the result of changes in attitudes brought about by the war. Women who went to work temporarily (or so they or others may have thought) developed a taste for working in the paid labor force, as well as useful skills, which encouraged them to remain in the labor force after the war was over. Some employers, moreover, after seeing women performing well in jobs traditionally reserved for men, may have revised their ideas about the productivity of working women.

African Americans

The movement of the African American population had dramatic social and political consequences. In 1940, the African American population was about evenly divided between urban and rural areas; in 1950, it was predominantly urban. This rural exodus continued in the 1950s and 1960s. By 1970, three-quarters of the African American population lived in urban areas. The urbanization of the African American population contributed importantly to the Civil Rights movement and to the ending of legal discrimination. To some extent, that movement began during the war.

The military forces remained segregated for the duration of the war, but in 1940, officer's candidate schools (except those for the air force) were desegregated. Moreover, the outstanding record compiled in the military by African Americans, along with the growing demand by the African American community for equal justice, contributed to President Harry S. Truman's decision to issue an executive order desegregating the armed forces in 1948. Progress was also made on the home front. In February 1941, A. Philip Randolph, head of the Brotherhood of Sleeping Car Porters, organized a march on Washington to protest discrimination in defense industries. The Roosevelt administration prevailed on the Randolph group to call off the march in exchange for an executive

PERSPECTIVE 25.1

WOMEN IN THE LABOR FORCE: WAR OR LONG-TERM TRENDS?

We should not jump to the conclusion that all of the changes that occurred during the war or in subsequent decades were the result of women working in war production plants. Recent research by Claudia Goldin (1991) has shown that fundamental changes in the labor market were even more important than the changes in attitudes brought about by the war.

Investigating a sample of women workers over the war decade, Goldin found that more than half of the Rosies who had entered the paid labor force between 1940 and 1944 (the peak year) had dropped out by 1950. Many lost their jobs as a result of seniority rules and social pressures that favored returning servicemen. Others chose to leave because economic circumstances permitted them to do so. Although many of the Rosies left the labor force after the war ended, many other women decided to enter in the late 1940s. Overall, Goldin found that about half of the women who entered the labor force between 1940 and 1950 were Rosies who had entered during the war and continued to work afterward, and about half were women who had not worked during the war but who had entered the labor force between the end of the war and 1950.

What factors brought women into the labor force in the immediate postwar years? One was the growing demand for women workers. Full employment meant more demand for all types of labor, and the clerical sector, which employed many women, was growing especially rapidly. Table 25.5 shows the increase in jobs held by women between 1940 and 1950. The importance of clerical and sales jobs, which accounted for 47 percent of the increase, is evident. Increased education also helped fit women for more jobs. The supply of younger unmarried women was shrinking as a result of low birthrates of the 1930s, and the supply of younger married women was also declining due to the increase in family formation during the postwar period. These changes opened the market for older married women. By 1950, these fundamental forces had pushed the labor force participation of women, and especially that of older married women, above the wartime peak.

TABLE 25.5 JOBS HELD BY WOMEN IN 1940 AND 1950 (IN THOUSANDS)

OCCUPATION	1940	1950	INCREASE	PERCENTAGE OF TOTAL INCREASE
Professional, technical	1,608	2,007	399%	8.25%
Managers, officials, proprietors	414	700	286	5.91
Clerical	2,700	4,502	1,802	37.26
Sales	925	1,418	493	10.19
Manual	2,720	3,685	965	19.95
Craftswomen, forewomen	135	253	118	2.44
Operatives	2,452	3,287	835	17.27
Laborers	133	145	12	0.25
Service workers	3,699	3,532	−167	−3.45
Farm workers	508	601	93	1.92

Source: Historical Statistics *1975, 132.*

order forbidding discrimination in defense work and the establishment of the Federal Committee on Fair Employment Practices. The committee, although lacking in enforcement powers, worked with employers to end discrimination. Research by William Collins (2000, 2001) shows that these efforts had a positive impact on African American employment levels in war-related industries and that continued employment in such industries was associated with a significant wage premium for blacks.

The Committee on Fair Employment had to work, moreover, within a context in which violence was always possible. White–African American violence was not as frequent during World War II as in World War I, but in the early summer of 1943, a violent outburst near Detroit left 25 African Americans and 9 whites dead.

One of the worst examples of racial bigotry occurred in 1942. Some 110,000 Japanese Americans (75,000 of them citizens) were forced to leave their homes on the West Coast and were placed in internment camps until 1945. Many were forced to sell farms and other businesses at "fire-sale" prices, thus being deprived of property built up over decades. Meanwhile, Japanese Americans distinguished themselves in the armed forces, fighting valiantly on the Italian front and serving as interpreters and translators in the Pacific theater. In 1988, Congress formally apologized and granted each of the survivors of the internment $20,000 as compensation.

AGRICULTURE DURING THE WAR

As demand expanded, agricultural production, aided by exceptionally good weather, climbed at the remarkable rate of 5 percent per year. This figure may be compared with the average during World War I, when agricultural production increased at 1.7 percent per year. Price controls during the war were purposely made less effective for agricultural than for nonagricultural commodities; consequently, the prices of farm products rose more rapidly during the war than the prices of the things that farmers had to buy.

During 1942, emphasis was placed on the necessity of stimulating particular kinds of output, notably meats and the oil-bearing crops, and avoiding a repetition of the price collapse that followed World War I. Legislation of October 1942 set final policy for the war period and for two postwar years. The 1942 act provided minimum support rates of 90 percent of parity for basic commodities; the supports were to remain in effect for two full years, beginning with the first day of January following the official end of the war. Price ceilings on farm products were set at a maximum of 110 percent of parity.

Cotton supports, however, were set at 92.5 percent of parity. Draft exemptions were provided for workers producing long-fiber cotton, which was demanded for a number of war-related uses (Maines 1993). The secretary of agriculture, at his discretion, could leave wheat and corn supports at 85 percent of parity if he felt that higher prices would limit available quantities of livestock feed. It is not entirely beside the point to note that cotton and beef interests were strongly represented by congressmen, some of whom had reached powerful positions through their seniority.

Over the war period and during the first two postwar years, price supports were not generally required. Because of the great demand for most products, agricultural prices tended to push against their ceilings. For some meats and dairy products, it was even necessary to roll back retail prices in an effort to "hold the line" against inflation. In such cases, to prevent a reduction in the floor prices received by farmers, meatpackers and creameries were paid a subsidy equal to the amount of the rollback on each unit sold.

The war enabled the Commodity Credit Corporation (CCC) to unload heavy inventories that had built up between 1939 and 1941. From 1944 to 1946, loans extended by the CCC were small. Foreign demand through the United Nations Relief and Rehabilitation Administration and military governments and an unexpectedly high domestic demand led to highly favorable postwar prices and lightened CCC loan and purchase commitments. Indeed, contrary to the predictions of many experts, the demand for food, feed, and fiber was exceptionally high after the war. The removal of price controls in the summer of 1946 permitted all prices to shoot up, but the rise in agricultural prices was steeper than the price rise in other areas. Most production restrictions on crops were canceled before or during World War II, and by the spring of 1948, only tobacco and potatoes were still controlled.

DEMOBILIZATION AND RECONVERSION

Would the Depression Return?

The Great Depression was widely expected to return once the war was over. After all, it seemed as if the enormous level of government spending during the war was the only thing that had gotten the country out of the Depression; cut spending and the economy would sink back into depression. Many, perhaps most, economists agreed with this analysis. Economists and policy makers therefore pressed for a commitment by the government to maintain the high level of employment after the war. The result was the Employment Act of 1946.

According to the act, the federal government's responsibility was to "promote maximum employment, production and purchasing power." The adjective *maximum* was purposely ambiguous, but the entire statement was generally understood to mean that the government would act quickly to shore up the economy if a severe recession threatened. The Council of Economic Advisers, with an adequate professional staff, was added to the Executive Office of the President. The president, assisted by the council, was directed to submit to Congress at least annually a report on current economic conditions, with recommendations for legislative action. The statute further provided that the House and the Senate were to form a standing Joint Economic Committee, which would study the report of the president and the Council of Economic Advisers, hold hearings, and report, in turn, to Congress. Although no "investment fund" was provided to make up for shortfalls in private spending when unemployment was high as many liberal economists had hoped, a watchdog agency was established to keep Congress and the president systematically informed about economic conditions. A compromise piece of legislation, the act acknowledged the government's role in maintaining full employment but did not say how the government would prevent depressions.

The expected depression did not materialize. During the war, people had accumulated large stores of financial assets, especially money and government bonds. They did so partly because they could not buy consumer durables during the war and partly because they were saving for the bad times they thought lay ahead. Once the war was over, these savings created a surge in demand that contributed to a postwar rise in prices and to the reintegration of workers from the armed forces and from defense industries into the peacetime labor force.

The GI Bill of Rights

Government policy also played a role in smoothing the transition of servicemen into the workforce. The so-called GI Bill of Rights provided returning servicemen a number of benefits, including financial aid for veterans returning to school. This legislation delayed the reentry of many former servicemen into the labor force and provided them with improved skills.

Planning for veterans started in a serious way when President Roosevelt appointed the Postwar Manpower Committee, which issued a report in June 1943 recommending a generous package of benefits for veterans. Pushed by the Veterans of Foreign Wars and the American Legion, Congress was also inclined to be generous for a number of reasons beyond the simple gratitude that Americans felt toward the people who had sacrificed to defend them. There was a general perception that demobilization had gone badly after World War I and that veterans had not been treated well. There were also the examples of generous veterans' packages emphasizing education that had been provided by Wisconsin after World War I and by Canada during World War II. Finally, there was the fear that the depression would return after the war and that, without an adequate package of veterans benefits, returning servicemen and -women would go straight from "the battle lines to the bread lines." The resulting legislation, the Servicemen's Readjustment Act of 1943, has generally been known since by its popular name: the GI Bill of Rights. The GI Bill provided a wide range of benefits, including mustering-out pay; health care; assistance with job placement; low-interest loans to buy a home, farm, or business; unemployment benefits; reemployment rights; employment preferences; and education benefits.

The GI Bill's education provisions have been considered the most revolutionary parts of the legislation. Among other education benefits, the GI Bill provided money for tuition, fees, and living expenses for veterans enrolling in colleges and universities. Partly as a result of the GI Bill, enrollment in higher education boomed after the war. The peak year in terms of the influence of the original GI Bill was 1947, when about 1.7 million veterans were enrolled in college, making up 71 percent of the student body. (The Vietnam Era peak in 1977 was about 2 million.) The GI Bill cannot be given all the credit for increasing the percentage of young Americans attending colleges and universities in the postwar period. Enrollment continued to grow, and the percentage of young people attending colleges and universities continued to rise, long after the veterans of World War II had moved on. The emphasis on higher education was a natural outgrowth of the high school movement that had occurred earlier in the century. The GI Bill, however, did play a role in jump-starting the postwar expansion of higher education. It demonstrated that Americans from all sorts of backgrounds could succeed on the college campus. It also transformed many colleges and universities. Rutgers, now the State University of New Jersey, for example, had to hire professors and learn to "mass-produce" education, to accommodate the veterans.

Birth of the Consumer Society

The postwar surge in demand ushered in a new consumer-oriented society that to some Americans represented the fulfillment of the American dream and to others the creation of an unthinking, materialistic culture. Builders such as Levitt and Sons adapted mass-production techniques developed during the war to provide housing for war workers, to mass-produce suburban homes, even creating entire new communities such as Levittown, New York. Aided by advances from the Federal Housing Administration and the Veterans Administration, the Levitts offered attractive terms to returning servicemen and other buyers.

Balladeer Malvina Reynolds expressed the feelings of many critics of the new "tract" housing in a popular folksong:

> *Little Boxes on the hillside, little boxes made of ticky tacky,*
> *Little Boxes on the hillside, little boxes all the same.*
> *There's a green one and a pink one and a blue one and a yellow one,*
> *And they're all made of ticky tacky and they all look just the same. (Reynolds 1983, 378–380)*

Defenders of the new construction techniques argued that by achieving the economies of long production runs, builders were able to lower the unit cost of housing and permit people to buy homes who otherwise could not afford them. No one, however, was able to put that into an enduring folksong. These years witnessed the beginning of the "baby boom" as birthrates surged in the late 1940s and 1950s. The image of a baby boom following shortly after the reuniting of soldiers with their loved ones is romantic and undoubtedly valid in many individual cases, but the baby boom was a much broader phenomenon that continued into and peaked in the late 1950s. In fact, this unusual deviation from the long-term trend toward smaller families (Haines 1994) may be due to the development of a range of labor-saving devices for the home that lowered the costs of having children (Greenwood, Seshadri, and Vandenbroucke 2005).

The war, in short, ushered in a period in which millions of Americans could take part for the first time in a middle-class lifestyle. Government programs for veterans such as the GI Bill helped, but the key factor was the thing that did not happen—a return to the depressed economic conditions of the 1930s.

SELECTED REFERENCES AND SUGGESTED READINGS

Barro, Robert J. "The Neoclassical Approach to Fiscal Policy." In *Modern Business Cycle Theory*, ed. Robert J. Barro, 178–235. Cambridge, Mass.: Harvard University Press, 1989.

Broom, Leonard, and Ruth Reimer. *Removal and Return: The Socio-economic Effects of the War on Japanese-Americans.* Berkeley: University of California Press, 1949.

Collins, William J. "African-American Economic Mobility in the 1940s: A Portrait from the Palmer Survey." *Journal of Economic History* 60 (September 2000): 756–781.

———. "Race, Roosevelt and Wartime Production: Fair Employment in World War II Labor Markets." *American Economic Review* 91 (March 2001): 272–286.

Darby, Michael. "Three and a Half Million U.S. Employees Have Been Mislaid: Or, an Explanation of Unemployment, 1934–1941." *Journal of Political Economy* 84 (February 1976): 1–16.

Economic Report of the President, 1987. Washington, D.C.: Government Printing Office, 1987.

Edwards, P. K. *Strikes in the United States, 1881–1974.* New York: St. Martin's Press, 1981.

Friedman, Milton, and Anna J. Schwartz. *A Monetary History of the United States, 1867–1960.* Princeton, N.J.: Princeton University Press, 1963.

———. *Monetary Statistics of the United States.* New York: National Bureau of Economic Research, 1970.

———. *Monetary Trends in the United States and the United Kingdom.* Chicago: University of Chicago Press, 1982.

Galbraith, John Kenneth. *A Theory of Price Control.* Cambridge, Mass.: Harvard University Press, 1952.

———. *A Life in Our Times.* Boston: Houghton Mifflin, 1981.

Gemery, Henry A., and Jan S. Hogendorn. "The Microeconomic Bases of Short-Run Learning Curves: Destroyer Production in World War II." In *The Sinews of War: Essays on the Economic History of World War II*, eds. Geofrey Mills and Hugh Rockoff. Ames: Iowa State University Press, 1993.

Goldin, Claudia D. "The Role of World War II in the Rise of Women's Employment." *American Economic Review* 81 (1991): 741–756.

Goldin, Claudia, and Robert A. Margo. "The Great Compression: The Wage Structure in the United States at Mid-century." *Quarterly Journal of Economics* 107 (February 1992): 1–34.

Greenwood, Jeremy, Ananth Seshadri, and Guillaume Vandenbroucke. "The Baby Boom and Baby Bust." *The American Economic Review* 95, no. 1 (March 2005): 183–207.

Haines, Michael R. "The Population of the United States, 1790–1920." In *Cambridge Economic History of the United States,* Vol. 2, *The Long Nineteenth Century,* eds. Stanley L. Engerman and Robert E. Gallman, 143–205. Cambridge: Cambridge University Press, 1994.

Harrison, Mark, ed. *The Economics of World War II: Six Great Powers in International Comparison.* Cambridge: Cambridge University Press, 1998.

Higgs, Robert. "Wartime Prosperity: A Reassessment of the U.S. Economy in the 1940s." *Journal of Economic History* 52 (1992): 41–60.

———. "Private Profit, Public Risk: Institutional Antecedents of the Modern Military Procurement System in the Rearmament Program 1940–1941." In *The Sinews of War: Essays on the Economic History of World War II*, eds. Geofrey Mills and Hugh Rockoff. Ames: Iowa State University Press, 1993.

Historical Statistics. Washington, D.C.: Government Printing Office, 1975.

Maines, Rachel. "Twenty-Nine Thirty-Seconds or Fight: Goal Conflict and Reinforcement in the U.S. Cotton Policy, 1933–1946." In *The Sinews of War: Essays on the Economic History of World War II*, eds. Geofrey Mills and Hugh Rockoff. Ames: Iowa State University Press, 1993.

Overy, Richard J. *Why the Allies Won*. London: Jonathan Cape, 1995.

Robinson, Greg. *By Order of the President: FDR and the Internment of Japanese Americans*. Cambridge, Mass.: Harvard University Press, 2001.

Rockoff, Hugh. "Keep on Scrapping: The Salvage Drives of World War II." NBER Working Paper No. 13418, September 2007.

Reynolds, Malvina. "Little Boxes." In *The Ballad of America: The History of the United States in Song and Story*, ed. John Anthony Scott, 378–380. Carbondale: Southern Illinois University Press, 1983.

Rupp, Leila J. *Mobilizing Women for War: German and American Propaganda, 1939–1945*. Princeton, N.J.: Princeton University Press, 1978.

Smith, Adam. *An Inquiry into the Nature and Causes of the Wealth of Nations*. The Glasgow Edition of the Works and Correspondence of Adam Smith. Oxford: Clarendon Press, 1976 [1776].

U.S. Bureau of Economic Analysis. *National Income and Product Accounts of the United States*, Vol. 2, 1959–1988. Washington, D.C.: Government Printing Office, 1992.

Vatter, Harold G. *The U.S. Economy in World War II*. New York: Columbia University Press, 1985.

PART 5

The Postwar Era:
1946 to the Present

ECONOMIC AND HISTORICAL PERSPECTIVES *1946 TO THE PRESENT*

1. The depression that was widely expected after World War II failed to materialize. Economists credited Keynesian fiscal policy with the maintenance of high employment. For the first time in the nation's history, however, inflation became a chronic peacetime problem.

2. The role of the federal government in the economy continued to expand, especially during the first three decades of the postwar era. In 1950, federal spending amounted to 16 percent of GDP; by 1980, it amounted to 22 percent. However, a reaction to the growth of government set in. In 2007, federal spending was 20 percent of GDP.

3. The structure of the economy changed dramatically in the postwar era: manufacturing and agriculture declined relative to the service sector.

4. In the 1960s, a civil rights revolution shook the nation. Efforts were made through the government, and through direct action, to secure greater economic progress for women, African Americans, and other disadvantaged groups.

5. The pace of economic growth was the subject of only minor complaints in the first two decades after the war; but in the 1970s, concern mounted as productivity growth slowed and troubling signs of social deterioration emerged.

6. In the late 1970s and early 1980s, a reaction to government involvement in the economy set in. The airlines, the banks, and other sectors were deregulated; and marginal tax rates were cut. In 1996, an attempt was made to reform the welfare system.

CHAPTER 26

The Changing Role
of the Federal Government

CHAPTER THEME

One of the most profound changes in the American economy in the first three decades after World War II was the continued growth in the size and influence of government, especially at the federal level. Government grew not only in dollars spent but also in power to control the private sector through legal regulations and bureaucratic decisions. Liberal economists thought that this was all to the good. The unstable free market economy of the past had been replaced by the "modern mixed economy" that combined the flexibility of markets and the stability of government controls. This growth was sustained until the late 1970s, when growing dissatisfaction with big government, as well as the growing menace of inflation, led to successful calls by conservatives for reduced spending and deregulation. This chapter discusses in broad terms the dimensions of the growth in government, the causes, and the eventual disillusionment.

THE SIZE OF GOVERNMENT IN THE POSTWAR ERA

As Economic Reasoning Proposition 5 (evidence and theory give value to opinions, see page 8) stresses, opinions about important historical issues such as the growth of the federal government must be based on evidence. Here we explore three measures of the growth of the federal government: (1) total federal spending relative to GDP, (2) federal purchases of goods and services relative to GDP, and (3) federal employment relative to the total labor force. Looking at all three is necessary to provide a nuanced answer to the question of how much government grew in the postwar era.

Total Federal Spending

Total spending by the federal government relative to the gross domestic product (GDP) is shown by the upper line in Figure 26.1. Evidently, federal spending grew relative to the size of the economy until 1980, when it reached one-fifth of GDP. In the early 1980s, however, this ratio peaked and began to decline. After 2001 it began to move up again. Below we will discuss the origin of these trends in detail, tracing them to domestic trends, particularly to the ideological battle between liberals and conservatives, and to international developments. Although the movements have been important, especially in terms of politics, it is important to note that these movements have been limited and have tended to cancel out. Today this ratio is about the same as it was in the late 1950s.

Federal Purchases of Goods and Services

Total federal spending relative to GDP is the most commonly used measure of the size of government, but it tells only part of the story. Government spending includes not only

FIGURE 26.1

Two Measures of the Size of the Federal Government, as Percentages of GDP, 1934–2007

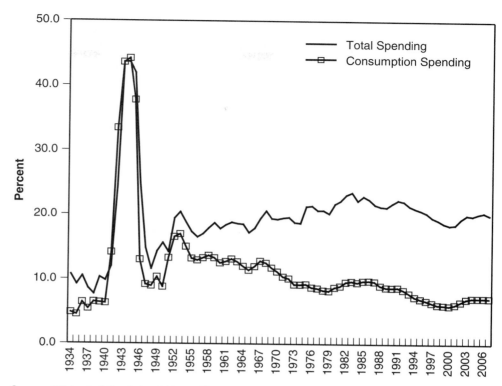

Source: Historical Statistics *2006, table Ca120-134;* Economic Report of the President 2009, *table B-79.*

purchases of goods and services (such as paper clips, tanks, dams, and the salaries of Supreme Court justices and army privates) but also transfer payments (such as welfare expenditures and subsidies for state and local governments). This is an important distinction because transfer payments do not directly reduce total spending in the private sector. For example, an increase in spending on welfare financed through an increase in taxes might mean that people on welfare bought more goods and services, while people who paid higher taxes bought less. The lower line marked by squares in Figure 26.1 excludes transfer payments; it includes only purchases of goods and services relative to GDP. This measure of the size of the federal government generally trended downward after the Korean War. It was strongly influenced by defense spending and the downward trend was clearly interrupted by the Vietnam War, the defense buildup pushed by President Ronald Reagan, and the recent wars in Iraq and Afghanistan.

Because considerable economic activity takes place at the state and local levels, it is important to compare the trends at these levels with the trends at the federal level. As the upper panel of Table 26.1 on page 488 indicates, purchases of goods and services at the state and local levels (mostly for police, fire, and education) exceeded purchases of goods and services at the federal level from 1970 on. This was a result of a small increase at the state and local level and the decline in the federal level due to the relative (to GDP) fall in defense spending. The most recent figure shows that purchases of goods and service at the state and local level was about 1.7 times purchases at the federal level. When looking at the trend in total government spending relative to GDP in the lower

TABLE 26.1 SPENDING AT ALL GOVERNMENT LEVELS

YEAR	PURCHASE OF GOODS AND SERVICES RELATIVE TO GDP		
	FEDERAL	STATE AND LOCAL	TOTAL
1940	6.3%	8.6%	14.9%
1950	8.8	7.1	15.9
1960	12.2	9.0	21.2
1970	10.9	11.6	22.5
1980	8.7	11.6	20.3
1990	8.8	11.6	20.3
2000	5.9	11.6	17.5
2006	7.1	12.1	19.1
	TOTAL SPENDING RELATIVE TO GDP		
1940	9.8%	11.1%	20.9%
1950	15.6	7.1	22.7
1960	17.8	9.6	27.4
1970	19.3	12.6	31.9
1980	21.7	13.7	35.4
1990	21.8	14.6	36.4
2000	18.4	15.7	34.1
2005	20.2	16.3	36.5

Note: Grants from the federal government to state and local governments are deducted from the grand total to avoid double counting.

Source: Historical Statistics *1975, series Y533, Y590, and Y671;* Economic Report of the President, *various years.*

panel of Table 26.1 (thus adding transfers to purchases of goods and services), it is evident that the ratio increased until about 1980 but then leveled off. Since 2000 there has been an increase reflecting the wars in Afghanistan and Iraq. So the overall trends are similar to the trends in federal spending.

Although transfers do not directly reduce production in the private sector, they may do so indirectly. Each time the government imposes a tax it affects incentives to work and invest. People who receive as much in transfers as they pay in taxes still have an incentive to reduce their taxes. If they respond by working less or by investing their capital in less productive uses, the total product of the economy will be reduced. (Never forget Economic Reasoning Proposition 3, incentives matter, even for a moment!)

Almost all economists agree with this analysis of the direction of the effects of tax and transfer policies, but one of the major controversies of the postwar period concerns the magnitude of these effects. Some experts, including prominently Peter Lindert (2004), argue that the disincentive effects of high taxes were not important and pointed out that total taxes in the United States, measured as a fraction of GDP, appeared relatively low compared with other developed countries, where work effort and savings seem to be satisfactory. For example, in 2007, total taxes at all levels of government in the United States were 34.4 percent of GDP. This was about the same as in Australia (35.4 percent), Japan (33.4 percent), and Switzerland (34.3 percent), but it was lower than in Canada (40 percent), the United Kingdom (41.7 percent), Germany (43.8 percent), and France (49.7 percent) (*Statistical Abstract of the United States 2009,* table 1315).

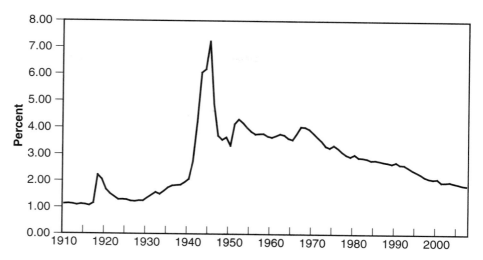

Source: Historical Statistics *2006, table Ea894-903;* Statistical Abstract of the United States *2009, table 478.*

FIGURE 26.2

The Ratio of Federal Civilian Employment to the Total Labor Force 1910–2007 (percent)

Federal Employment

Another frequently used measure of the size of the federal government is the share of federal civilian employment (including civilian employment by the Department of Defense) in total employment, shown in Figure 26.2. This series ratchets upward dramatically in the 1930s because of the many new federal agencies created by the New Deal. (Federal emergency workers are not included.) It ratchets up again in the 1940s largely because of the expansion of civilian employment at the department of defense and at the Veterans Administration. The share of federal employment in the total labor force peaked briefly above 4 percent during the Korean War, and then began a steady decline. In recent years it has reached a level about the same as that reached in the late 1930s. How can the share of federal spending in GDP increase or remain stable while the number of employees relative to the labor force falls? Recall that the dynamic element in the growth of the federal government was transfer payments. This source of growth did not require an equally large expansion of the federal bureaucracy. One bureaucrat can write many checks.

Winners in the Federal Budget

Figure 26.3 provides a bird's-eye view of how budget priorities changed in the postwar era. It is a "stacked line" chart. The bottom line shows real (adjusted for prices) defense spending from 1960 to 2007 in billions of dollars at 1950 prices. The defense buildup in the 1980s under President Ronald Reagan, which we will discuss in more detail below, is the dominant feature. The distance between defense spending and the line above it marked by squares shows spending on health care including Medicare. The rapid growth in this area was partly the result of the Medicare program adopted in 1965, which became more costly as more people became eligible. The distance to the next line, marked by triangles, shows the amount spent on income security. This category also grew rapidly as more people became eligible for Social Security. The distance to the next line, marked by x's, shows the interest on the national debt, and the distance to the final line shows all other federal spending, so the distance of the top line from the x-axis shows total federal spending. The figure as a whole, therefore, reveals that growth of federal spending on

FIGURE 26.3

Real Federal Spending by Major Category, 1960–2007 (billions of dollars at 1950 prices)

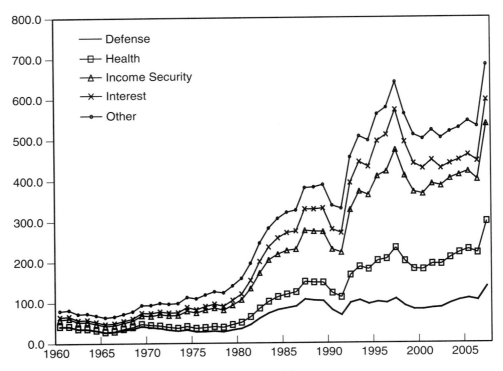

Source: Economic Report of the President 2009, *table B-90.*

health and income security has been the most important factor in the growth of federal spending overall. The figure also shows how difficult it would be to significantly reduce federal spending without cutting these sacrosanct areas of the budget. Even very large percentage cuts in "all other" spending would mean very small percentage cuts in the federal budget.[1]

THE LIBERAL ERA, 1945–1976: CONTINUED EXPANSION OF GOVERNMENT

In retrospect, we can divide the period after the war into two distinct ideological eras. No precise dividing line can be given; however, it is clear that the period from the end of the war to, say, 1976 was a liberal era; an era in which arguments to expand federal government programs, especially its civilian programs, or to create new ones received a sympathetic hearing from the general public. Even Republican presidents had to accommodate themselves to a dominant liberal ideology. Then, for a variety of reasons—the war in Vietnam, the slowing of economic growth, and the acceleration of inflation—sentiment turned toward the conservatives. Politicians, whether Democrats or Republicans, had to respond to the public's concern about the costs of expanding government.

---

[1]Although, as the late Senator Everett Dirksen of Illinois is credited with saying, "A billion here, a billion there, and pretty soon you are talking about real money."

During the liberal era, Democrats pressed hard for an expansion of the welfare state and other New Deal reforms while conservatives fought a rearguard action, delaying the advance of the welfare state when they could, and retreating to new positions when they could not. The first postwar president, Democrat Harry S. Truman, favored a major expansion of the New Deal. Truman's program, which he named the Fair Deal, called for a wide range of economic legislation, including repeal of the Taft-Hartley Act, increased Social Security benefits, a higher minimum wage, federal subsidies for housing, compulsory federal health insurance, and authority to build industrial plants to overcome "shortages."[2]

Some parts of Truman's program, those that were extensions and modifications of existing programs, were enacted—Social Security benefits were extended, and the minimum wage was raised—but new programs were blocked by a congressional coalition of Republicans and southern Democrats. Special interest groups played an important role in lobbying Congress to oppose legislation they considered contrary to their interests. The American Medical Association, for example, lobbied vigorously against Truman's health insurance proposals, which they denounced as the forerunner of "socialized medicine."

The philosophy of Republican Dwight D. Eisenhower's administration generally opposed new initiatives in the economic sphere. The administration's motto, "less government in business and more business in government," summed up its philosophy, but existing programs around which a consensus had formed continued to expand. For example, Social Security benefits increased and extended to more workers, the minimum wage was raised from $0.75 to $1.00 per hour, more money was provided for housing, and a greatly expanded program of highway building was introduced: the replacement of America's congested single-lane highways with two-lane interstate "super highways."

The "Little New Deal"

The breakthrough in welfare legislation occurred during the presidencies of Democrats John F. Kennedy and Lyndon B. Johnson. Kennedy's New Frontier was similar to Truman's Fair Deal, but in many ways it did not go as far. Kennedy's narrow victory over Vice President Richard Nixon, moreover, hardly seemed a mandate for radical change. The program called for federal medical insurance for the elderly, aid to education, and more federal money for housing and "urban renewal." As in previous administrations, existing programs were expanded. Social Security benefits were increased, the minimum wage was raised from $1.00 to $1.25 (over a four-year period) and was made applicable to more workers, and, as promised, more money was made available for federal housing projects. There were also new initiatives. Legislation provided aid for medical education, college construction projects, and relief for areas adversely affected by federal projects. Kennedy's proposals for medical care for the aged and federal aid for public schools, however, were defeated.

The civil rights movement, however, was drawing attention to the plight of African Americans and other disadvantaged groups. On college campuses, students were drawn to Kennedy's faith in big government. For a time it seemed that Joseph Schumpeter's

---

[2]The tradition is for each administration to sum up its legislative programs in a single grand phrase. Franklin Roosevelt gave us the New Deal; Harry S. Truman, the Fair Deal; Dwight D. Eisenhower, the Great Crusade; John F. Kennedy, the New Frontier; and Lyndon B. Johnson, the Great Society. Or as one wag put it: "Roosevelt gave us the New Deal, Truman gave us the Fair Deal, but Johnson gave us the Ordeal" (Morris and Morris 1971, 397).

Lyndon Johnson signing the Medicare bill. Former President Harry S. Truman looks on.

prediction that capitalism would be undermined by the children of the bourgeoisie, who would lose faith in the system that had created the basis for their own high standard of living, had begun to come true (Schumpeter 1950, 415–424).

When Lyndon B. Johnson took office in 1963 after the assassination of President Kennedy, he proclaimed his intention of fighting a "War on Poverty." The result was the Economic Opportunity Act of 1964, which established training camps in rural and urban areas, provided grants for farmers and small businesses, and helped communities fund their own antipoverty programs. In 1964, President Johnson was reelected by a large majority; this mandate, and Johnson's long experience in Washington, helped him in pushing programs through Congress that were going to be, according to Johnson, the basis for a "Great Society."

A wide range of important legislation followed. Indeed, there had been nothing like it since the New Deal, and in some respects, it was even more radical. A medical care program for those age 65 or over (Medicare) was at last added to Social Security. Legislation was passed to fund $1 billion for improvements in Appalachian land and highways and to provide health centers. A Department of Housing and Urban Development was created, and its head was made a cabinet-level secretary. A new housing act provided, among other things, for federal rent subsidies for the poor, a new departure in welfare legislation. The minimum wage, a familiar part of liberal Democratic programs, was raised and extended to cover farm laborers, workers in small retail shops, and hospital workers. A mass transportation act provided money to improve rail transportation, and the Department of Transportation, the twelfth cabinet-level department, was created. These and other reforms substantially expanded the role of government in American life.

The New Regulation

One of the most dramatic developments of the postwar period was the passage of major pieces of legislation designed to protect the consumer from the purchase of dangerous or otherwise unsatisfactory goods and services. Consumer protection is by no means unique to the postwar period. As early as 1838, Congress created the Steamboat Inspection Service to check the safety of steamboats, but the rate of passage of consumer protection legislation accelerated in the liberal phase of the postwar era.

Many pieces of consumer protection legislation are the result of highly visible public tragedies. The Steamboat Inspection Service was enacted after a series of explosions killed many passengers and crew. The Food, Drug, and Cosmetic Act of 1938 followed the Elixir Sulfonamide tragedy. The form in which this drug was sold proved to be toxic and left more than 100 dead, many of them children. But the producer was held, under existing law, to be guilty of no more than mislabeling his product. The Flammable Fabrics Act of 1953 is another example. This act followed in the wake of a number of tragic accidents involving children. The industry, it should be noted, did not resist this legislation. By being able to show that their fabrics met federal safety standards, manufacturers hoped to increase demand and provide a basis for defense in lawsuits. The Kefauver-Harris amendments to the Food, Drug, and Cosmetic Act (1962) followed in the wake of the thalidomide tragedy. In Europe this drug produced severe birth defects when given to pregnant women. Similar outcomes were largely avoided in the United States, mainly because of the resolute behavior of one public official, Dr. Frances Kelsey of the Food and Drug Administration, who had resisted enormous pressure to license the drug. It was believed that without additional legal safeguards, future situations might emerge in which the absence of such an extraordinary regulator would lead to tragedy.

Tragic events, however, are not the whole story. The passage of consumer protection legislation was also related to swings in public opinion between liberal and conservative views. Notice in Table 26.2 that eight major pieces of consumer-protection legislation were passed between 1965 and 1972, including the Fair Packaging and Labeling Act, the National Traffic and Motor Vehicle Safety Act, and the Consumer Product Safety Act. This burst of legislative activity was related not so much to individual tragedies as to a general lack of faith in the market. Later, however, the liberal faith in government's ability to improve on the outcome of market forces was placed on the defensive. Presidential candidate Ronald Reagan cited the penchant of the Occupational Safety and Health Administration (1970) for issuing regulations costly to business as a prime example of how "government is the problem." No major pieces of consumer legislation were passed during the administrations of Ronald Reagan or George H. W. Bush. More recently, during the first administration of Bill Clinton, a massive overhaul of the health care system was planned, but despite the administration's backing, the overhaul failed to achieve the level of public support needed to overcome opposition.

Weighing the costs and benefits of regulatory legislation is a difficult task, and economists are far from agreement even on individual regulations, let alone the whole trend. The benefits of regulation are relatively easy to see: Consumers may be protected from consuming a dangerous food, using a dangerous drug, or driving a dangerous car. Regulation also has costs, however: It may raise prices by requiring expensive additions to a product or by requiring a firm to amass evidence that its product is safe. Regulation may also have the effect of limiting competition by preventing price competition or stifling innovation by raising the costs of introducing new products. It has been contended, for example, that regulation of the drug industry has limited the number of new drugs being brought to market (Asch 1988, chapter 7).

TABLE 26.2 MAJOR CONSUMER SAFETY LAWS OF THE UNITED STATES, 1900–1980

YEAR	LAW	MAIN PROVISIONS
1906	Food and Drug Act	Prohibits misbranding and adulteration of foods and drugs. Requires listing of medicine ingredients on product labels.
1906	Meat Inspection Act	Provides for federal inspection of slaughtering, packaging, and canning plants that ship meat interstate.
1938	Food, Drug, and Cosmetic Act	Defines as "adulterated" any food or drug that contains a substance unsafe for human use. Requires application for introduction of new drugs supported by tests of safety.
1938	Wheeler-Lea Amendment to Federal Trade Commission Act (1914)	Extends prohibitions of FTC Act to "unfair or deceptive acts or practices."
1953	Flammable Fabrics Act	Prohibits manufacture, import, or sale of products so "flammable as to be dangerous when worn by individuals."
1958	Food Additives Amendment to Food, Drug, and Cosmetic Act (1938)	Prohibits use of food additives shown to cause cancer in humans or animals.
1960	Hazardous Substances Labeling Act	Requires labeling of hazardous household substances.
1962	Kefauver-Harris Amendments to Food, Drug, and Cosmetic Act (1938)	Requires additional tests of both safety and efficacy for new drugs.
1965	Cigarette Labeling and Advertising Act	Requires use of health warnings on cigarette packages and in advertising.
1966	Fair Packaging and Labeling Act	Requires listing of product contents and manufacturer.
1966	Child Protection Act (Amendment to Hazardous Substances Labeling Act of 1960)	Prohibits sale of hazardous toys and other items used by children.
1966	National Traffic and Motor Vehicle Safety Act	Provides for establishment of safety standards for vehicles and parts, and for vehicle recalls.
1967	Amendments to the Flammable Fabrics Act (1953)	Extends federal authority to establish safety standards for fabrics, including "household" products.
1970	Public Health Cigarette Smoking Act	Prohibits broadcast advertising of cigarettes.
1970	Poison Prevention Packaging Act	Provides for "child-resistant" packaging of hazardous substances.
1972	Consumer Product Safety Act	Establishes the Consumer Product Safety Commission, with authority to set safety standards for consumer products and to ban products that present undue risk.
1977	Saccharin Study and Labeling Act	Requires use of health warnings on products containing saccharin; postpones saccharin ban.
1980	Comprehensive Environmental Response Compensation and Liability (Superfund) Act	Provides funds for cleaning up toxic waste sites.

Source: Asch 1988, passim.

THE CONSERVATIVE ERA: 1976–2000, DEREGULATION AND REAGANOMICS

After Jimmy Carter's election in 1976, there were few new attempts at the federal level to regulate economic activity, and a number of significant attempts at deregulation. The underlying reasons were the disillusionment with government produced by the long and futile war in Vietnam, the failure of some liberal programs to deliver benefits consistent with optimistic forecasts, and the deterioration in the performance of the economy. Productivity growth slowed, inflation accelerated, and unemployment remained at high levels. The belief that the economy could easily generate a large surplus with which the government could do good works now appeared naïve.

Deregulation

In previous years, the 1976 election of Democrat Jimmy Carter would have signaled a new round of New Deal legislation, but the Carter administration, although it supported many traditional Democratic programs, emphasized economy and efficiency in government and, surprisingly, deregulation in a number of areas of the economy. The administration argued that these regulations were no longer needed or that the original intent of the legislation had been subverted by the very groups that the legislation was intended to control.

In addition, some academics had long argued that regulatory agencies were often "captured" by a regulated industry. The public would become aroused by the revelation of an abuse in a certain industry and a regulatory agency would be created, staffed initially by people responsive to the public interest or at least highly critical of the industry. Eventually, however, public attention would turn to other problems, and only the regulated industry itself would maintain an interest in who was appointed to the agency and what decisions it rendered. The result, naturally enough, would be that in the long run people sympathetic to the regulated industry would be appointed to the regulatory agency, and rulings would be made in the interest of the industry rather than that of the public. Partly as a result of such ideas, President Carter supported decontrol of natural gas prices and deregulation of the airlines, trucking, railroads, and the financial services industry, including the elimination of ceilings on deposit interest rates.

Alfred E. Kahn, whom Carter chose to deregulate the airlines, was both symbolic of the new era and a major player in it (McCraw 1984, chapter 7). Kahn was a liberal Democrat by upbringing and sentiment, but he had come to believe that the general interest would best be served if regulators put more emphasis on increasing competition and marginal cost pricing. To take a simple example, marginal cost pricing held that airline seats should be priced at the low cost of actually carrying one more passenger rather than at a high average cost (Kahn 1988). At a time when many airline seats were going unfilled, important segments of the industry welcomed Kahn's emphasis on marginal cost pricing.

Reaganomics

Although the Carter administration undertook a number of reforms aimed at freeing markets from excessive regulation, it was Republican Ronald Reagan, first elected in 1980, who attempted to alter the basic ideological thrust of the postwar era. Reagan put it simply in his inaugural address: "Government is not the solution to our problems; government is the problem." His economic policy, often referred to as "Reaganomics," had several elements. One was the reduction in taxes, particularly the reduction of marginal rates (the rates applied to additional income). The Reagan administration claimed that such cuts were necessary to create incentives to work and invest. Its critics complained that such cuts were a giveaway to the rich.

The Reagan administration wanted to alter budget priorities radically, increasing defense expenditures and reducing civilian expenditures. It had little trouble increasing defense spending. Between 1980 and 1983, defense expenditures rose from $134 billion to $210 billion, but spending cuts on the civilian side, although some were made, were harder to get through Congress. Between 1980 and 1983, all spending other than national defense increased from $457 billion to $598 billion. Prices were rising over the same period (the rise in civilian expenditures was 27 percent, while the rise in the GNP deflator was 19 percent), and certain areas of the civilian budget were cut in nominal terms (the budget category of "education, training, employment, and social services" fell from $32 billion to $27 billion). On the whole, however, it was extremely difficult to make cuts, particularly after Reagan's initial "honeymoon" with Congress ended. Reagan's budget director, David Stockman, was in charge of proposing the cuts to be made and selling them to Congress. His book, *The Triumph of Politics* (1986), describes in case after case how difficult it was to cut programs, even those having little justification, once the affected interests and their allies in Congress and the government bureaucracy were alerted for battle.

The 1988 election of George H. W. Bush promised a slowdown of the Reagan policies, especially on the regulatory front. Bush did say, in his speech accepting the Republican nomination, "Read my lips: no new taxes," thus laying claim to the most popular part of the Reagan legacy. Two years later, however, under intense pressure to do something about the mounting federal deficit, Bush accepted tax increases. The resulting loss of political capital from breaking a clear and dramatic promise far outweighed any gains from reducing the deficit.

In 1992, Democrat Bill Clinton was elected president after promising to reverse the Reagan-Bush approach by raising taxes on the wealthy, spending more on the poor and on urban areas, spending less on defense, and increasing the federal government's role in health care. After his health initiative failed and a conservative Congress was elected in 1994, however, he retreated from attempts to expand the welfare state. In 1996, he became the first Democrat since Franklin Roosevelt to win reelection, but in the course of the campaign, he supported legislation that limited welfare and that in some cases cut off benefits, a far cry from his initial goal of preserving and extending the New Deal. In 2000, George W. Bush, a conservative Republican, won a narrow and controversial election. His first legislative victory, a substantial tax cut, showed that the conservative tide had not yet run its course. As this is written, Barack Obama has taken office. Many observers believe (hope?) that this will be the start of a new liberal era in which the federal government will expand its role in the economy.

THE COLD (AND SOMETIMES HOT) WAR AGAINST COMMUNISM

Our discussion to this point has been about the role of the federal government in the civilian economy. Defense spending followed a somewhat different course. Through much of the postwar era, defense spending was dominated by the long war to contain communism. There were outbreaks of hard fighting in Korea and Vietnam. But in the long years between and after those wars, the period known as the cold war, defense spending was elevated far above what had been typical before World War II. This war began as soon as World War II ended and continued until the collapse of the Soviet Union in 1991. Then after a short interregnum of peace in the 1990s, the effort to increase domestic security in the wake of the terrorist attacks of September 11, 2001, and the wars in Afghanistan and Iraq produced a new surge in defense spending. Figure 26.4 shows the key figures for the War against Communism. The continuous line shows defense and international spending as a share of GDP from 1947 to 2001. International spending is included because much "foreign aid" in those years was part of the cold war against the Soviet Union. International affairs was, in any case, a secondary source of spending. Over the years 1947 to 1991, spending on international affairs averaged about 10 percent of defense spending. Evidently, defense spending generally used a significant share of GDP, although that share declined as diplomatic efforts, including formal treaties to end the nuclear arms race, lowered tensions. The line marked with squares shows the average share from 1997 to 2001. This period begins five years after the end of the cold war and can be taken to represent the post-cold-war equilibrium. The difference between the lines is a measure of the resource cost of the wars, hot and cold, to contain communism. Surprisingly, in terms of resources used (the area between the lines) the War against Communism was the most costly war of the twentieth century, exceeding even World War II. The total sum of shares for World War II was about 1.32. In other words, fighting World War II required about one and a third years' worth of GDP. For the cold war alone, the figure is about the same, 1.3 years. If we add the Korean War and Vietnam War to get the total cost of the War against Communism, the resource cost comes to 2.03 years' worth of GDP. Resource use was more intense during World War II, but the War against Communism lasted far longer.

What was the long-term impact of the cold war on the economy? The answer to this difficult question depends on which categories of spending were reduced to maintain a high level of defense spending. Did the decrease come in other kinds of government spending? Private consumption? Private investment? Careful studies by Michael Edelstein (1990) and Robert Higgs (1994) showed that increases in defense spending came mainly at the expense of private consumption rather than private investment or nondefense government spending, suggesting that the long-term effects of defense

FIGURE 26.4

Federal Spending on Defense and International Affairs as a Share of GDP, 1947–2001

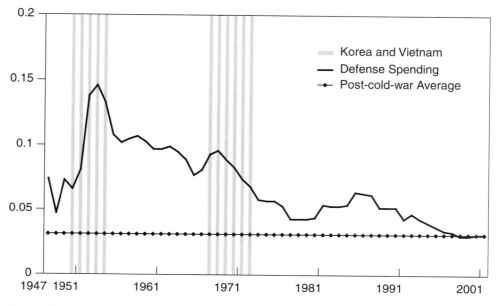

Source: Economic Report of the President 2009, *table B-80.*

spending on growth were small. We are entitled, however, to consider what might have been: the medical research, conservation efforts, and so on, that might have been undertaken with the resources devoted to the War against Communism. In the end, deciding whether this was money well spent is beyond the capacity of the historian or economist to answer, but the amounts were clearly enormous. To see the liberal and conservative eras more clearly, we review two sectors of the economy that show the changes with particular clarity: agriculture and the environment.

AGRICULTURE

During the postwar period agriculture continued to decline relative to other sectors of the economy. In part because it had become relatively less important, agriculture was able to maintain the price supports and subsidies that it had won during the 1930s.

The Relative Decline of Agriculture

A decline in the number of agricultural workers relative to the total workforce is a common feature of economic development. It is estimated that in 1800 about three-fourths of the workforce was employed in agriculture. By 1850, that proportion had fallen to 55 percent. By 1950, it had fallen to 12 percent. And by 1999 (the most recent figure), only 2.5 percent. Similar declines were recorded throughout the industrial world. Indeed, the declines were larger in countries undergoing rapid industrialization. In Italy, for example, agricultural employment, measured as a share of the total labor force, fell from more than 30 percent in 1960 to about 9 percent in 1990; in Japan, the change was similar, a fall from just less than 30 percent in 1960 to about 7 percent in 1990.

The decline in the agriculture's share of the workforce was the result of two phenomena. First, the demand for agricultural products did not grow as rapidly as real income.

© CHARLES BRUTLAG/ISTOCKPHOTO.COM

Large farms with heavy investments in modern technology increasingly dominated the farm sector. Compare the grain harvester shown here with the reaper shown in Chapter 15.

The income elasticity of demand for agricultural products, to use the technical term (the percentage change in the demand for an agricultural product produced by a given percentage change in real income), is typically less than one. Second, rapid technological progress in agriculture reduced the number of workers it took to produce a given amount of agricultural product. Technological progress came on several fronts. Farm machinery evolved rapidly. Tractors became larger, and sensitive electronic equipment was added that could monitor plowing, seeding, and harvesting. New herbicides and pesticides were developed, and scientific breeding of plants and animals and genetic modification further expanded output. In some cases, these developments were linked. Chemicals were used to defoliate cotton plants to make mechanical harvesting easier, and new strains of tomatoes were developed with tough skins that could withstand mechanical harvesting and cross-country—eventually international—transport. These innovations came from private companies producing farm machinery, chemicals, and seeds, and from federal and state laboratories and experiment stations. So successful were federal and state agencies in finding ways to increase output that liberals used the agricultural sector as an example of how the federal government could produce important technological advances.

The number of farms, as well as the number of farm workers declined. This is shown in Table 26.3, which includes some earlier years for comparison. In 1950, there were 5.39 million farms in the United States; by 2007, that number had fallen to 2.08 million, fewer than in 1870. The amount of land in farms also fell, but at a slower rate, from 1.16 billion acres in 1950 to 347 million in 2007. The result was that average farm size, shown in the final column of Table 26.3, rose over the long term from 216 acres in 1950 to 461 acres in 1990. It was the farmer working a small or medium-size farm who gave up the business. Much of the land went into larger farms owned by individual owner-operators or corporations. Indeed, the rise of corporate farm ownership was a striking and controversial feature of the postwar period, although many corporate farms were

TABLE 26.3 CHANGING STRUCTURE OF U.S. AGRICULTURE

YEAR	FARMS (in thousands)	TOTAL LAND IN FARMS	
		MILLIONS OF ACRES	AVERAGE FARM SIZE IN ACRES
1850	1,449	294	203
1870	2,660	408	153
1880	4,009	536	134
1900	5,740	841	147
1920	6,454	959	149
1940	6,109	1,065	175
1950	5,388	1,161	216
1960	3,962	1,177	297
1970	2,954	1,108	373
1980	2,440	1,039	426
1990	2,140	987	461
2000	2,172	943	434
2007	2,075	931	449

Note: The definition of a farm changed in 1993 to include some smaller farm operations, so later figures are not strictly comparable to earlier figures.

Source: *1850–1990:* Historical Statistics *2006, table Da14-27; 2000–2007:* Statistical Abstract of the United States 2009, *table 797.*

simply family farms converted to corporate status for tax purposes. In recent years average farm size has been relatively stable. In 2007 it was 449 acres.

What had provoked these changes? The operators of small and medium-size farms were both pushed and pulled from the farm. Typically, only those farm operators who could farm on a large scale and achieve the high productivity possible through massive investments in farm equipment could make farming pay. Alan Olmstead and Paul Rhode (2001) estimated that the tractor alone accounted for the disappearance of 956,000 farms between 1910 and 1960. In the cotton-growing South, for example, many landholders terminated small tenancies and consolidated their land so that they could make use of large-scale machinery. People were also pulled from agriculture by the possibility of earning higher incomes elsewhere. Tenant farmers in the South, for example, moved to industrial centers in the Mississippi Valley, the Midwest, and the Pacific Coast. While leaving farming generally meant earning more money, it was not a decision taken lightly, for it meant leaving family and friends behind and giving up a cherished way of life.

Why did farmers continue to leave the land despite substantial efforts by the federal government to aid them? Partly, this was because the lion's share of assistance went to those who were already at the top of the heap. When the government supported farm prices, those with the most bushels or bales to sell received the chief benefits; when acreage restrictions were put into effect, those who were in a position to reduce acreage the most received the largest checks. In 1989, for example, the top 15 percent of farm families by income received 62 percent of all government payments.

Price Supports and Subsidies

After World War II, the major agricultural problem was how to deal with the large farm surpluses created by farm price supports. To correct this problem, in 1949, Secretary of Agriculture C. F. Brannan announced the plan of "compensatory payments" to which the press and public quickly attached his name, although its central ideas had been developing for many years in academic writings. The Brannan plan would have allowed prices to seek their own level in the marketplace, with the difference between the market price and a "modernized" parity price to be paid to the farmer (up to a maximum amount) with a check from the Treasury. The potential benefits of the Brannan plan were obvious. Surpluses would be eliminated, saving storage costs; and the public, the poor in particular, would be able to buy food cheaply (see Economic Insight 26.1). After months of heated debate, during which the National Grange and the American Farm Bureau Federation opposed the plan, the House of Representatives refused to give the Brannan plan a trial run. Typical of political debates at the time, opponents of the Brannan plan won by castigating it as "socialism." Of course, if the Brannan plan was socialism, so was the existing system. The real objection to the Brannan plan was that unconcealed subsidies might be more difficult to defend in the court of public opinion than price supports focused on raising market prices to parity prices.

After the Brannan plan's failure, reformers turned their attention to less radical measures. For example, with surpluses still at controversial levels, Congress turned again to a depression-era solution. The Soil Bank Act of 1956 was devised to reduce supplies of basic commodities by achieving a 10 to 17 percent reduction in plowland through payments to farmers who shifted land out of production into the "soil bank." The diversion payments were based on the old formula of multiplying a base price for the commodity by normal yield per acre by the numbers of acres withdrawn. Although the soil bank idea had been linked at its creation in the 1930s with the dust bowl in the Plains states, the plan remained what it had always been: an attempt to raise farm prices thinly disguised as a conservation program.

ECONOMIC INSIGHT 26.1

ECONOMICS OF THE BRANNAN PLAN

This figure illustrates the economics of the Brannan plan. In a free market, the price of an agricultural product would be P and output produced would be Q, determined as usual by the intersection of the supply and demand curves. This price is considered, however, to be unfair to farmers.

Under the traditional support system, the government wishes to raise the price to P^*, the modernized parity price. At this price, consumers are willing to buy only Q^*; but farmers produce Q^{**}. To hold the price in the market at P^*, the government must purchase the excess supply, $Q^{**} - Q^*$. This will cost the government (the taxpayer) $P^* \times (Q^{**} - Q^*)$. The surplus, $Q^{**} - Q^*$, will have to be stored, so storage costs will be incurred in future years. The gain to farmers (compared with the free market equilibrium) will be the area P^*BCP.

Under the Brannan plan, the government simply allows the surplus to be sold in the marketplace. The price falls to P^{**}, the price at which Q^{**} can be sold. The Treasury then writes a check to each farmer for the difference between the parity price P^* and the new market price P^{**}. In this case, the total cost to the government is given by the area $Q^{**} \times (P^* - P^{**})$.

Consumers clearly benefit from switching to the Brannan plan: They pay a lower price for farm products. No resources are wasted simply producing food and then storing it in government warehouses. Even under the Brannan plan, however, there is an efficiency loss given by the triangle CBE: Resources are employed in farming that could better satisfy consumer demands elsewhere in the economy.

The impact on the government budget depends on whether area $Q^{**} \times (P^* - P^{**})$, the costs under the Brannan plan, exceed or fall short of area $P^* \times (Q^{**} - Q^*)$, the costs under the traditional purchase-for-storage system plus the storage costs. In general, this will depend on the elasticities of the supply and demand curves. The more elastic the supply and demand curves, the less costly will be the Brannan plan compared with the purchase-for-storage plan.

Financially, farmers fare the same under the two plans. They produce Q^{**} output and receive P^*Q^{**} total income. Under the Brannan plan, however, farmers receive a part of the income in the form of a "welfare" check. Some farmers will find this demeaning. Direct payments also will be obvious to the public and make it more difficult for farmers to defend and increase their subsidies.

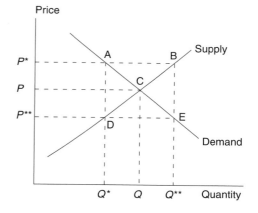

The results were unexpected, but easy to understand in retrospect. Farmers placed their least productive land in the soil bank and cultivated the remainder more intensively. Surpluses went right on mounting, reaching astronomical heights in 1961 after nine consecutive years of increase.[3] The Emergency Feed Grain Bill of 1961 encouraged drastic reductions in acreages devoted to corn and grain sorghums by offering substantial payments to farmers who reduced their acreage by 20 percent; even higher payments were offered for the diversion of an additional 20 percent of feed-crop acreage. On the whole, this plan worked because the reduction was large enough to offset attempts by farmers to minimize its effects. For the first time in a decade, feed grain carryover dropped.

---

[3]In a comment on a previous draft of the chapter Deirdre McCloskey pointed out another unintended consequence of the soil bank program: Iowa farms were once wooded on the edges of their fields, but the wooded borders (a habitat for animals and birds and a source of lumber) were cut down in an effort to get around the acreage restrictions.

As inflation and concern about government spending mounted in the 1970s, Congress found it more difficult to respond unilaterally to farm interests. The Democratic Congress and President Jimmy Carter, who was well versed in agricultural subsidies—he was a prosperous peanut farmer in Georgia before entering politics—made an effort to lower support prices in the Food and Agriculture Act of 1977. This monument to complication set support prices within specified ranges on wheat, cotton, feed grains, and many other commodities. Farmers, however, protested bitterly and crowded into Washington, D.C., to make known their opposition to lower prices. In the winter of 1978, they obtained higher support prices through the Emergency Act of 1978.

President Ronald Reagan's Farm Bill, passed in late 1981, exceeded $22.6 billion in expenditures, with more than $10 billion of it being allocated for the food stamp program; price supports were continued on peanuts, sugar, wheat, feed grains, rice, soybeans, cotton, and wool, although these supports were reduced from their levels during the Carter years. As expected, both Democratic and Republican farm interests claimed that the administration dictated the cutbacks, leaving no effective protection for farmers facing severely depressed incomes.

In subsequent years, the incentives offered to farmers improved somewhat. Under the deficiency payments system used for grains, which had elements of the Brannan plan, farmers received a subsidy based on the difference between a "target" price and the market price or support price, whichever of the latter two was higher. The quantity to which this deficiency payment was applied was based on historical yields and acreages under cultivation, so farmers could not increase their deficiency payment by cultivating their land more intensively. An important change also occurred in the acreage restriction system. In 1985, the Conservation Reserve Program was set up, allowing farmers to enter into long-term contracts with the Agriculture Department to retire land from production. This program was designed to combine the goal of protecting the environment by retiring environmentally sensitive land (a point system determined the importance of the land for this purpose) with the goal of restricting output.

It seemed in the early 1990s that farming would escape deregulation. Even agriculture, however, could not hold out forever against the free market tide. In 1996 Congress passed the Federal Agriculture Improvement and Reform Act, known colloquially as the "Freedom to Farm Bill." This legislation swept away the government's policy of setting a floor under agricultural prices in return for controls over production or acreage. As compensation, farmers were guaranteed annual payments through 2002 to aid the transition to free market agriculture. Although many farmers were opposed to the measure, others supported it. Prices for many agricultural products were at historical highs, and it seemed to some farmers that the stream of assured payments under the transition program would be higher than what might be forthcoming under traditional programs. Once the act was passed, however, agricultural prices began to fall. In 1998 and again in 1999, Congress provided emergency payments to help farmers cope with the sudden fall in their incomes. The system of price supports and direct subsidies was soon reinstated. The experiment with free market agriculture, in other words, did not last long. Under the Food, Conservation and Energy Act of 2008 farmers will benefit from price supports for major crops and from direct payments based on historic crop acreage and yield. Thus some farmers may receive payments based on the yield from land planted in cotton in the past, even though the land is now planted in another crop, or no crop at all.

Why are farmers so heavily subsidized in the United States and other developed countries? The sympathy that most of us feel for people who attempt to maintain a cherished way of life in the face of hard economic realities is part of the explanation. The main part, however, is the political economy of farming. Farmers are a well-organized special interest with considerable influence in the House of Representatives and especially in the Senate (where representation is independent of a state's population). The subsidies farmers receive, moreover, while crucial to them, are only a minor irritant to the average taxpayer. It does not pay for consumers to take the time to fight hard against price-increasing policies and tax-raising subsidies that reduce their incomes by only a small amount.[4]

THE ENVIRONMENT

The environment became a major concern of the public during the postwar era; and that concern led to the creation of the Environmental Protection Agency in 1970. Below we will take a look at the "conservation movement" that flourished during the progressive era and then at the post–World War II environmental movement.

The Conservation Movement

The roots of the conservation movement reach back into the nineteenth century. In 1832 a federal "reservation" was established at Hot Springs, Arkansas, to protect its mineral springs. In 1872, Yellowstone, perhaps the most famous national park, was established to preserve its natural wonders. There was little fear at the time that the land in Yellowstone would be exploited for agricultural or other commercial purposes if transferred to private hands. Rather, the concern in Congress was that if a private entrepreneur controlled access to Yellowstone, its natural beauties would be degraded by access roads and advertising, as had happened at some natural wonders in the East.

A major change in policy took place under President Theodore Roosevelt (1901–1909) who believed that natural resources would be depleted too rapidly if the rate of depletion was left to the market and that the federal government should, therefore, take an active role in preserving depletable resources, particularly timber and minerals. Roosevelt publicized the cause of conservation and, aided by Gifford Pinchot, the dynamic head of the Forest Service (then the Division of Forestry of the Department of Agriculture), converted some 150 million acres of western land in the public domain into national forests so that access could be controlled by the Forest Service.

The conservation movement languished in the 1920s but surged during the administration of Franklin D. Roosevelt, which undertook several important initiatives. First, during the New Deal the first systematic efforts were made to conserve agricultural land. These efforts began in 1933 with the establishment of the Soil Erosion Service in the Department of the Interior. (In 1935, as the Soil Conservation Service, it became part of the Department of Agriculture.) Originally, contracts were made with individual farmers; the service furnished technical assistance and some materials, and the farmers furnished labor and the remaining materials. Early in 1937, President Roosevelt wrote the state governors requesting that their legislatures pass acts enabling landowners to form soil conservation districts. By 1954, about 2,500 soil conservation districts, including 80 percent of all U.S. farms, had been organized.

Second, the New Deal attempted conservation through its efforts to control water distribution in river valleys in programs of great scope, such as the Tennessee Valley Authority. The main goals, reflecting the depressed condition of the economy, were providing construction jobs and cheap power that would lead to economic development,

---

[4]In a discussion of these issues Gary Libecap pointed out that in some special cases there are "consumers" who appear to have a large financial stake in reforming agricultural policies. Candymakers, for example, would seem to have a strong interest in reducing sugar prices. Nevertheless, even in these cases, it appears that it does not pay the consumer to participate in farm policy reform.

but conservation was also a goal. Some supporters of such programs argue that nothing less can produce permanently successful conservation. The evidence, however, is not conclusive. The Tennessee Valley Authority has unquestionably done a remarkable job of upgrading an entire region, but the costs of building this huge project were also substantial.

The Rise of the Environmental Movement

During the 1960s, an important segment of the public was persuaded that the environment had become polluted with many dangerous by-products of industry. Making the environment whole again, many argued, was important, for some more important than rapid economic growth. The environmental movement did not break completely with the earlier emphasis on conservation, but the two movements had important differences. The conservationists had emphasized the management of resources to sustain long-term yields of timberland, farmland, water, and mineral resources; the environmentalists put more emphasis on the preservation of natural resources for future aesthetic enjoyment. The conservationists emphasized individual resources; the environmentalists emphasized the interdependence of different parts of the environment. It was not sufficient, in their view, simply to preserve patches of the environment in national parks; the whole environment had to be protected from the destructive side effects of economic development.

Other developed countries, particularly those in western Europe, experienced the same phenomenon. Countries just beginning the process of industrialization often displayed what appeared to more developed countries to be a frustrating and cavalier attitude toward the environment. A clean and well-preserved environment, in other words, appears to be a luxury good: As income rises, consumers wish to spend a larger fraction of their income on preserving the environment.

Although concern about the environment remained a constant, public attention in the United States shifted from problem to problem, depending on the events of the day. In the early 1960s, Rachel Carson's book *Silent Spring* (1962) heightened concern about the danger of indiscriminate pesticide use, and, as a result, the Department of Agriculture banned the use of DDT (*Dichloro-Diphenyl-Trichloroethane*) completely in 1969. It was a major breakthrough for the environmental movement. That same year, a major oil spill off the coast of Santa Barbara, California, raised concerns about the danger of offshore oil drilling, and similar fears were raised about the impact of the proposed Alaska Pipeline.

Responding to these and other environmental concerns, Congress passed the Clean Air Act and Water Quality Improvement Act in 1970 and established the Environmental Protection Agency (EPA). Since then, the EPA has produced a flood of regulations. Typically, it sets a maximum level of pollution allowed based on the "best available technology." In many cases, the EPA must set literally hundreds of standards for each pollutant. For example, the EPA works out a separate standard for each model of automobile. Measuring the costs versus benefits of the EPA standards is exceedingly difficult and controversial, but no one doubts that the direct costs of complying with EPA standards are very high. By one estimate, these were $100 billion in 1988, about 2 percent of GDP. The reach of the EPA has been increased since its founding in response to new information about the dangers faced by the environment and specific crises. In 1980, for example, Congress established what became known as the "Superfund," a program for cleaning up toxic waste sites. This addition to the job of the EPA was brought about in part by the revelations concerning the dangerous pollution at the Love Canal in New York State near Niagara.

Marine biologist Rachel Carson. Her book, Silent Spring, *published in 1962, spelled out the dangers of certain insecticides and helped launch the modern environmental movement.*

Recently concern about global warming has taken center stage. This concern illustrates the environmental movement's emphasis on the way in which environmental problems are linked, and the way that environmental concerns lead to the expansion of government. The accumulation of certain gases (carbon dioxide, methane, and chlorofluorocarbons among them) produces the "greenhouse effect" in the atmosphere: These gases absorb infrared radiation reflected from the earth (much as does the glass over a greenhouse) and thus raise temperatures worldwide. The greenhouse effect is a good illustration of the problem of externalities. Individual producers, even entire nations, may have no financial incentive to control the gases they release into the atmosphere because the costs generated by their emissions will be shared worldwide.

The economic effects to be expected from global warming are uncertain and controversial. They are likely to be greatest for the developing countries, where agriculture (which is a large share of GDP) may be adversely affected and where debilitating parasitic diseases might become more widespread. The melting of polar ice, moreover, might raise ocean levels and cause extensive shore damage. On the other hand, some areas that would experience longer growing seasons might actually improve their agricultural productivity.

Various solutions to the problem of global warming have been proposed. As usual, there are two approaches. Liberal economists favor explicit emission targets reached through international negotiations and detailed government plans for reaching those targets. Market-oriented economists favor taxes on emissions, and some favor creating tradable rights. Countries would be assigned maximum emission levels, and if they exceeded their assigned level, they would have to buy the right to emit more from other countries that had managed to hold their emissions below their targets. Perhaps the main issue to be resolved in years to come is whether environmental protection will rely more heavily on market mechanisms or on direct government controls.

CHANGING IDEOLOGICAL TIDES

We have seen that the growth of government in the postwar period was the outcome of a battle between liberal and conservative philosophies of political economy. Historian Arthur Schlesinger, Jr. (1986, chapter 2) described this as an alteration between periods when the dominant ideology stresses "public purpose" and periods when the dominant ideology stresses "private interest." In the long run, according to Schlesinger, government will grow because programs initiated by liberals may be cut, but are unlikely to be eliminated, by the conservatives who follow. The appropriate image is that of government as a spiral that widens during periods of liberal dominance but that never contracts. In Schlesinger's view, the alteration between liberalism and conservatism is perpetual. Politically active young people adopt the ideology dominant in their formative years. As time goes by, they reach higher and higher levels of influence in government, the private sector, academia, and the media. Eventually, they take power and attempt to reimpose the liberal or conservative ideology of their youth. The Little New Deal is a good example. John F. Kennedy and Lyndon B. Johnson attempted to realize the liberal vision of the 1930s. Bill Clinton's presidency also illustrates Schlesinger's theory: Clinton and many of his close advisers were college students and antiwar activists during the liberal Kennedy-Johnson era.

Economists Milton Friedman and Rose D. Friedman (1983, 41–51) share with Schlesinger the view that new government bureaus and programs tend to survive subsequent administrations, liberal or conservative, but the Friedmans tell a different story about why this is so. In their view, federal programs become permanent because of the "tyranny of the status quo." An "iron triangle" of bureaucrats (see Economic Insight 26.2), politicians, and private sector beneficiaries of government programs protect programs even when it has been shown that these programs are detrimental to the public interest. Measured across all voters the gain from eliminating a given program may be large; but for each voter separately, the gain may be too small to make fighting to eliminate the program worthwhile.

In his book, *Crisis and Leviathan* (1987), Robert Higgs agreed that the dominant ideology is the crucial factor determining the growth rate of government but emphasized the role of economic or social crises in making the liberal interventionist ideology acceptable. A mild recession in 1931 might have led to a Democrat replacing Herbert Hoover; but the Great Depression persuaded people to accept a wide range of radical new programs. John F. Kennedy and Lyndon B. Johnson would have pushed for new programs in any case, but the social and political upheavals of the 1960s stemming from the civil rights movement persuaded the public to accept a much broader range of new legislation and programs, particularly those designed to solve the problems of poverty and racial discrimination.

ECONOMIC INSIGHT 26.2

WHY DOES BUREAUCRACY HAVE NEGATIVE CONNOTATIONS?

Maximizing the Size of the Bureau

Why do government bureaucracies often seem so big and inefficient? Why, to put it somewhat differently, does the term *bureaucracy* carry such negative connotations? Economist William Niskanen (1971) provided one still-controversial answer based on the relationship between Congress and the bureaus. The S curve in the figure represents a government bureau's cost of supplying units of "output"—acres of land irrigated, recommendations made to farmers, grants awarded, power plants inspected, or the like. The D curve shows the marginal valuation of each additional unit of output. The efficient output would be OG at that level of output; every unit would be produced for which the marginal value exceeded the marginal cost. At OG, the cost of producing the last unit, BG, would exactly equal the value placed on it. This is, of course, what would happen if the product were produced by private firms and sold in a competitive market.

Niskanen believes, however, that the budget-making process in Congress works differently. Bureaucrats are not interested in minimizing costs or maximizing profits. Their goal is to preside over as large a budget as possible—from which comes prestige in Washington. Because they are likely to be a monopoly and to have all available information about costs of producing a somewhat difficult-to-measure output, they will make it extremely difficult to judge the shape of the S curve. Instead, they will provide the congressional committee overseeing the bureau a single request for the money needed to carry out the bureau's "mission." The congressional committee is also likely to be happy with an output larger than OG because committee members will be receiving campaign contributions from the interest groups that benefit from the bureau's work. If, however, the agency's total costs were to grow to the point at which they exceeded the total benefits, questions would be raised by other members of Congress on other committees, by the press, and by the executive branch, which takes the heat when total taxes are raised. The result is that the bureau will produce output OF at a total cost of OCF and that these costs will be equal to total benefits of OAEF. The bureau will be too big.

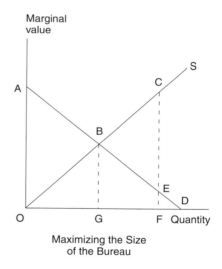

Maximizing the Size
of the Bureau

WAGNER'S LAW

Beneath these changing ideological tides a number of historians and economists have pointed to more fundamental economic forces that determine the size of government. Writing in the 1880s, German economist and economic historian Adolph Wagner wrote that the growth of modern industry would produce increasing political "pressure for social progress" and thereby continuous expansion of the public sector. In part, this would happen because competitive nation-states would find it in their interest to appease labor and to meet, at least partially, its demands for social justice. Wagner's prediction has proved accurate in many cases, and the idea that the public sector will inevitably expand relative to the private sector has come to be known as Wagner's Law.

A number of American economists have accepted Wagner's Law but emphasized a different underlying force: the increase of real per capital income. Government programs that help the disadvantaged, protect the environment, and the like may be luxury goods:

We buy disproportionately more of them when income rises. The slowdown in the growth of the demand for government after 1969 is consistent with this thesis. To the extent that voting patterns reflect views about long-term incomes, the belief that productivity growth had slowed produced a substantial decrease in the demand for government expenditures. Other long-term trends may also influence the demand for government. Population growth and urbanization, for example, may have increased the demand for programs to preserve the environment or provide mass transportation (Fabricant 1952).

What about pure transfer payments? A poor person could be expected to vote for heavy taxes on the rich. We might expect, therefore, that in a democracy in which the rule of one adult, one vote was followed, income tax rates would be highly progressive, and after-tax incomes would tend toward equality. Indeed, the surprising thing about most industrial democracies is not that they have progressive income taxes but that those taxes are not even *more* progressive.

Economists Allan H. Meltzer and Scott F. Richard (1978, 1981, 1983) devised a rational theory of transfer payments. In their model, people vote for programs that redistribute income in their favor but take into account the disincentive effects of higher taxes—the tendency of high marginal tax rates to discourage work and savings. The poor do not automatically vote for "soak-the-rich" taxes because they think that, as a result, the whole economy will be less productive and that they will end up with less than they had before. Economist Sam Peltzman (1980) developed a related theory. Based on international comparisons, he argued that a more-equal distribution of income generated by the market, paradoxically, accelerates the growth of government because it increases the political strength of the group that favors further redistribution through the government. When the poor are very poor, they are not able to produce political pressures that advance their interests. Economic growth empowers the poor and makes them a political force to be reckoned with.

It is common for an academic writer to push his or her own theory as if it were the one and only cause of the trends observed. Product differentiation is as useful to academics as it is to producers of automobiles or insurance policies. The theories of the growth of government that we have examined, however, seem to complement one another. Schlesinger's emphasis on the allegiance of political leaders for the ideologies of their youth, the Friedmans' emphasis on the iron triangle of bureaucrats, legislators, and narrow economic interests, and Higgs's emphasis on the role of crises all contribute to our understanding of the complex process that produced first an expansion and later a (limited) retrenchment in the role of government in the economy during the postwar era.

SELECTED REFERENCES AND SUGGESTED READINGS

Asch, Peter. *Consumer Safety Legislation: Putting a Price on Life and Limb.* New York: Oxford University Press, 1988.

Carson, Rachel. *Silent Spring.* Boston: Houghton Mifflin, 1962.

Economic Report of the President 2009. U.S. Council of Economic Advisors. http://www.gpoaccess.gov/eop/.

Edelstein, Michael. "What Price Cold War? Military Spending and Private Investment in the US, 1946–1979." *Cambridge Journal of Economics* 14 (1990): 421–437.

Fabricant, Solomon. *The Trend of Government Activity in the United States since 1900.* New York: National Bureau of Economic Research, 1952.

Friedman, Milton, and Rose D. Friedman. *Tyranny of the Status Quo.* San Diego: Harcourt Brace Jovanovich, 1983.

Higgs, Robert. *Crisis and Leviathan: Critical Episodes in the Growth of American Government.* New York: Oxford University Press, 1987.

_____. "The Cold War Economy: Opportunity Costs, Ideology, and the Politics of Crisis." *Explorations in Economic History* 31 (July 1994): 283–312.

Historical Statistics of the United States Colonial Times to 1970, bicentennial edition. Washington D.C.: Government Printing Office, 1975.

Historical Statistics of the United States: Earliest Times to the Present, Millennial Edition. Eds. Susan B. Carter, et al. Cambridge: Cambridge University Press, 2006.

Kahn, Alfred E. "Surprises of Airline Deregulation." *American Economic Review, Papers and Proceedings* 78 (1988): 316–322.

Lindert, Peter H. *Growing Public: Social Spending and Economic Growth since the Eighteenth Century.* Cambridge; New York: Cambridge University Press, 2004.

McCraw, Thomas K. *Prophets of Regulation.* Cambridge, Mass.: Harvard University Press, 1984.

Meltzer, Allan H., and Scott F. Richard. "Why Government Grows (and Grows) in a Democracy." *Public Interest* 52 (Summer 1978): 111–118.

———. "A Rational Theory of the Size of Government." *Journal of Political Economy* 89 (October 1981): 914–927.

———. "Tests of a Rational Theory of the Size of Government." *Public Choice* 41 (1983): 403–418.

Morris, William, and Mary Morris. *Morris Dictionary of Word and Phrase Origins.* New York: Harper & Row, 1971.

Niskanen, William A. *Bureaucracy and Representative Government.* Chicago: Aldine-Atherton, 1971.

Olmstead, Alan L., and Paul Rhode. "Reshaping the Landscape: Impact and Diffusion of the Tractor in American Agriculture, 1910–1960." *Journal of Economic History* 61 (September 2001): 663–980.

Peltzman, Sam. "The Growth of Government." *Journal of Law and Economics* 23 (October 1980): 220–285.

Schlesinger, Arthur M., Jr. *The Cycles of American History.* Boston: Houghton, Mifflin, 1986.

Schumpeter, Joseph. *Capitalism, Socialism, and Democracy,* 3rd edition. New York: Harper & Row, 1950.

Statistical Abstract of the United States 2009. U.S. Bureau of the Census. http://www.census.gov/compendia/statab/.

Stockman, David A. *The Triumph of Politics: How the Reagan Revolution Failed.* New York: Harper & Row, 1986.

CHAPTER 27

Monetary Policy, Fiscal Policy, and the Business Cycle after World War II

CHAPTER THEME

When World War II ended, there was a widespread fear that the Great Depression would return, but fear gave way to optimism when the expected economic collapse failed to materialize. Academic economists were especially optimistic because of the belief that John Maynard Keynes, the famous English economist, had shown how a modern industrial economy could be kept on even keel through the judicious use of fiscal policy. The confidence of economists that the business cycle could be tamed reached its peak during the Kennedy-Johnson years, but then the weakness of the Keynesian regimen (as it was applied in practice), and its bias toward inflation, began to make itself felt (see Figure 27.1 on page 511).

Depression-level unemployment rates were never approached, even in the most severe postwar recessions after World War II. Instead, inflation became the primary problem. Inflation tended to fall and unemployment tended to rise in each recession (see Figure 27.2 on page 512), but inflation did not fall as much in each recession as it had risen in the previous expansion, so that the core, or base, rate of inflation moved steadily upward during the 1960s and 1970s. Similarly, the unemployment rate did not fall as much in each expansion as it rose in each recession; the core, or natural, rate of unemployment, as some called it, also increased during these years. By the late 1970s, "stagflation" (high unemployment combined with high inflation) seemed to be as perplexing as depression had been to an earlier generation.

Stagflation presented a fundamental challenge to Keynesian economics. As a result, economists and policymakers began to pay more attention to the ideas of Milton Friedman, the free market economist at the University of Chicago. Friedman stressed several points that had a profound influence on policy from the 1970s through the remainder of the century: (1) the trade-off between inflation and unemployment was temporary, (2) inflation was a monetary problem best solved by increasing the stock of money at a slow and stable rate, and (3) freely floating exchange rates worked better than fixed exchange rates. The attempt to apply monetarist ideas (as the school of thought established by Friedman came to be called), although not always faithful to the original doctrine, became the basis for monetary and fiscal policy in the 1980s and early 1990s. Inflation was arrested in the early 1980s, but at the cost of a severe recession. Although inflation was never reduced to zero, it was kept under control for the remainder of the century.

THE KEYNESIAN ERA

Keynes's masterwork, *The General Theory of Employment, Interest, and Money*, appeared in 1936. It is often listed among the most influential books of the twentieth century. For more than three decades, the ideas advanced in *The General Theory* dominated macroeconomic policymaking in the United States and other industrial countries.

FIGURE 27.1

The Rate of Inflation in the United States, 1950–2007

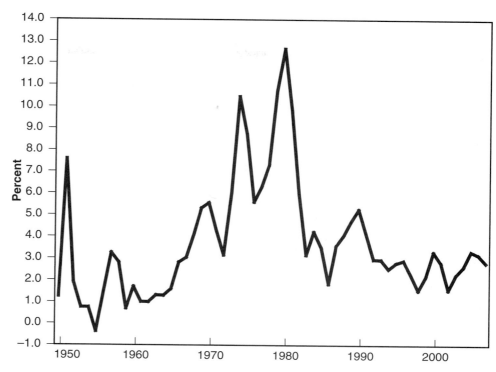

Source: Historical Statistics of the United States, *2006, Table Cc1-2;* Economic Report of the President 2009, *Table B-60.*

The General Theory is a complex book, and considerable controversy exists about how to interpret it. Several key points, however, come through clearly: (1) no natural tendency exists for the economy to return to full employment after a recession; investment demand might be insufficient to soak up all the savings that people wish to accomplish at full employment income; (2) monetary policy is unlikely to be effective in restoring investment and full employment when the economy is below full employment; and (3) to restore full employment after a recession, it may be necessary to control private investment and supplement it with government spending on public works. The last point—stressed by Keynes's American disciples such as Alvin Hansen, Abba Lerner, and Paul Samuelson—was taken to mean that the economy could be kept on even keel by increasing government spending, or cutting taxes, or both during recessions and by reversing these actions when, after reaching full employment, inflation threatened.

The success of deficit spending in eliminating unemployment during World War II seemed to confirm the value of the Keynesian medicine for treating severe depressions. This mood of optimism was strengthened by the handling of the first postwar recession, which lasted (as shown in Table 27.1) from November 1948 to October 1949. After industrial production dropped 10 percent and the gross domestic product (GDP) fell 4 percent, the Truman administration moved quickly to award military contracts in "distressed areas," and although unemployment rose above 5 percent for several months, revival came so quickly that public clamor for action never became loud. The Keynesian medicine seemed to work on mild recessions and without creating dangerous side effects requiring other treatments (see Economic Insight 27.1).

FIGURE 27.2
The Civilian Unemployment Rate, 1950–2007

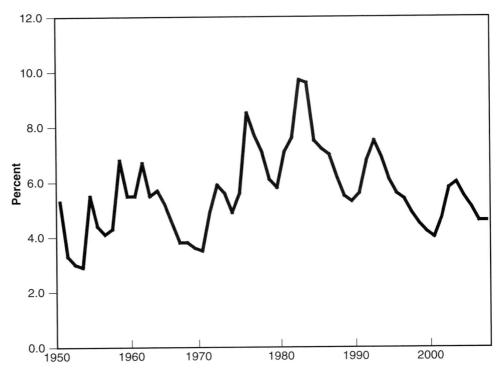

Source: Economic Report of the President 2009, *Table B35.*

John Maynard Keynes (1883–1946), architect of the theory that full employment could be maintained by appropriate changes in government spending and taxation and through control of private investment. His theories gained increasing acceptance during the 1940s, 1950s, and 1960s.

TABLE 27.1 BUSINESS CYCLES AFTER WORLD WAR II

PEAK	TROUGH	LENGTH OF THE EXPANSION FROM PREVIOUS TROUGH TO THIS PEAK (months)	LENGTH OF THIS CONTRACTION FROM PEAK TO TROUGH (months)
February 1945	October 1945	80[a]	8
November 1948	October 1949	37	11
July 1953	May 1954	45	10
August 1957	April 1958	39	8
April 1960	February 1961	24	10
December 1969	November 1970	106	11
November 1973	March 1975	36	16
January 1980	July 1980	58	6
July 1981	November 1982	12	16
July 1990	March 1991	92	8
March 2001	November 2001	120	8
December 2007		73	

[a]From June 1938—the World War II expansion.

Source: *The dates and a description of how they are determined are available from the National Bureau of Economic Research, 2009.*

The Korean War and the Treasury-Fed Accord

On June 25, 1950, North Korean forces crossed the thirty-eighth parallel and attacked South Korea. President Truman responded immediately by authorizing the use of U.S. forces to repel the attack. Less than five years after the end of World War II, the United States found itself at war again.

At home, consumers responded by stocking up on items that had been scarce during World War II: sugar, automobile tires, consumer durables, and so on. Inflation accelerated (see Figure 27.1). The government responded swiftly to the threat of inflation; the lesson drawn from World War II was that half-measures don't work. First, the Revenue Act of 1950, which provided for higher personal and corporate tax rates, was enacted in September 1950. The Revenue Act of 1951, although less comprehensive than the Truman administration wanted, provided for additional increases in individual and corporate taxes. Second, price and wage controls were imposed. A debate quickly developed between those who favored a gradual approach to controlling prices and those who favored an immediate across-the-board freeze. This time, unlike World War II, the advocates of a freeze won, and a freeze was announced in late January 1951. Michael V. DiSalle, the director of the Office of Price Stabilization and a major advocate of a freeze, explained his position this way. Controlling prices was like "bobbing a cat's tail"—it was better to do it all at once, close to the body; doing it bit by bit produced "a mad cat and a sore tail."

Third, the government imposed a restrictive monetary policy. During World War II, the Fed pegged interest rates (i.e., placed a ceiling on them), even though this forced the Fed to purchase more federal debt than it wanted, thus expanding money and credit. Pegging was continued in the early postwar years at the request of the Treasury despite the Fed's growing resentment. The Korean War brought the conflict into the open. After discussions conducted at the urging of President Truman, the Fed and the Treasury announced that they had reached an agreement on March 4, 1951. This

ECONOMIC INSIGHT 27.1

DEFINING THE BUSINESS CYCLE

The business cycle is illustrated in the following diagram.

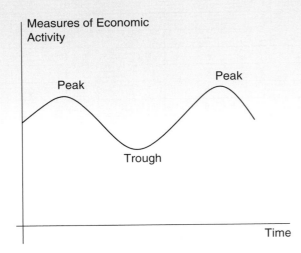

An economic contraction (recession) is the time between the peak of the business cycle and the trough; an expansion is the time between a trough and a peak. By tradition, the peaks and troughs of the business cycle are chosen by a committee established by the National Bureau of Economic Research, a private think-tank. The Bureau was founded by Wesley Clair Mitchell, one of the pioneers in the study of the business cycle; one of its early resident scholars was Simon Kuznets, who won the Nobel Prize for his work on national income accounting. The Bureau examines a range of data, emphasizing data that are available on a monthly basis, such as employment, and chooses particular months for the peaks and troughs of the cycle. A rule of thumb, a recession that is two-quarters of shrinking real GDP works well in practice and is often described in the press as the definition of a recession. The term cycle implies a regular ebb and flow, like the tides. Many economists, however, believe that the expansions and contractions are a random process reflecting random positive and negative shocks to the economy.

agreement came to be known as the Treasury-Fed Accord because the joint statement issued by the two agencies said that they had reached "full accord." The main point of the accord was that the Fed would be allowed to limit its purchase of government debt even if the result was higher interest rates. This was a victory for the Fed, although the Treasury won some minor points. There were predictions that financial markets would be sent into shock by the Accord, but in fact financial markets adapted quickly to the new regime. The Accord permitted the Fed to follow a noninflationary monetary policy during the war; for the entire period of the war, money per unit of real GDP actually fell slightly.

The anti-inflation program worked well. Consumer prices rose at an annual rate of only 2.1 percent from the price freeze in January 1951 to the termination of controls in February 1953. When controls were terminated, many prices were below their ceilings, and no postcontrol price explosion occurred. Consumer prices rose at a rate of only 2.6 percent from the termination of controls until the postwar price peak.

As we shall discuss, controls were used again in the 1970s, partly because they had seemed to be such a success in the Korean War. In the 1970s, however, the other parts of the Korean War program—monetary and fiscal restraint—were rejected, and the result was that controls were a failure.

Dwight D. Eisenhower: The Conservative Approach to the Business Cycle

During 1953, the key economic indicators took an unfavorable turn. In about nine months, industrial production fell 10 percent, the GDP declined 4 percent, and manufacturing employment dropped 10 percent. Keynesian economists had widely forecast this contraction. (See Economic Insight 27.1 on page 514 for a definition of the business cycle.) National defense spending and, therefore, total government spending declined $11 billion between the second quarter of 1953 and the second quarter of 1954. There was also a $10 billion drop in gross investment, mostly in inventories. In short, there was a sharp drop in "exogenous" spending, which in the Keynesian model is the source of major fluctuations in the economy as a whole.

This recession aroused great concern. Unemployment in several areas of manufacturing exceeded 10 percent of the local workforce, and many families exhausted their unemployment insurance benefits before any clear signs of improvement were visible. The administration took no drastic steps to combat the recession. A moderate fiscal deficit, partly the result of a reduction in federal income tax rates effective January 1, 1954, had a stimulating effect, and the Fed adopted the policy of "active ease." The "automatic stabilizers," unemployment insurance payments, a reduction in the total tax bill as incomes declined, and price supports for agriculture helped to cushion the decline in aggregate spending.

Prices began a steady rise in mid-1955 that continued until early 1957. Inflation became the pressing domestic problem of the day. The Fed responded with a restrictive monetary policy that continued until well past the point of economic downturn in the late summer of 1957. A recession of substantial proportions followed, the deepest of the postwar period thus far. By the spring of 1958, unemployment was at 7.5 percent of the civilian labor force. A rebound began in April 1958, but the recovery through 1959 was disappointing, and when the indicators took another turn for the worse at the end of the year, the frustration of policymakers was evident.

Many liberal economists believed that the performance of the economy in the Eisenhower years could have been improved with more vigorous use of the Keynesian medicine. With this view in mind, the next economic team to assume power attacked unemployment.

John F. Kennedy and Lyndon Johnson: The New Economics

The economy was a major issue in the election of 1960. Democrat John F. Kennedy promised to get the economy moving, placing more emphasis on full employment and economic growth and (presumably) less on price stability. Although the recession in 1959 and 1960 was mild and short, it was an important factor in Kennedy's narrow victory over Vice President Richard Nixon.

The economy began its resurgence in February 1961 but at a rate that disappointed the Kennedy team. Therefore, the Council of Economic Advisers, under the guidance of Chairman Walter Heller, laid plans for an experimental tax cut in 1964. After Kennedy's shocking assassination in November 1963, the politically astute Lyndon B. Johnson assumed the presidency and promptly guided the tax cut through Congress and into law. This tax cut was historic. The federal budget was then in deficit; orthodox economic theory called for tax increases to balance the budget, but President Kennedy's advisers believed in the "new economics" of John Maynard Keynes. They argued that as long as the economy was operating at less than full employment, a tax cut was justified because it would leave more income in the hands of the public, creating more demand for goods and services. As they pointed out, a budget that was in deficit when the economy was at less than full employment might turn out to be balanced or in surplus at full employment because tax revenues rise and certain categories of Federal spending fall (e.g., unemployment benefits) as the economy approaches full employment.

In an often-quoted passage from *The General Theory*, Keynes had written the following:

The ideas of economists and political philosophers, both when they are right and when they are wrong, are more powerful than is commonly understood. Indeed the world is ruled by little else. Practical men, who believe themselves to be quite exempt from any intellectual influences, are usually the slaves of some defunct economist. Madmen in authority, who hear voices in the air, are distilling their frenzy from some academic scribbler of a few years back. I am sure that the power of vested interest is vastly exaggerated compared with the gradual encroachment of ideas. (Keynes 1936, 383)[1]

Less than 30 years after the publication of *The General Theory*, Keynes's ideas were having a profound effect on U.S. fiscal policies. The Kennedy tax cut was widely regarded as a great success. Unemployment fell from 5 percent of the labor force in 1964 to 4.4 percent in 1965 and to 3.7 percent in 1966. The Vietnam War buildup that followed closely on the tax cut had not been part of the calculations, however, when Kennedy's advisers had first planned a cut. The change in conditions encouraged Walter Heller and other creators of the tax cut to urge President Johnson to raise taxes, but he did not take this advice. An important political weakness of the Keynesian system then became apparent. Cutting taxes is easy; raising them is hard. Inflationary pressures began to build, and (as Figure 27.1 shows) the rate of inflation turned upward late in 1965. At the time, it was thought that the Kennedy tax cut had ushered in a new era of active fiscal policy; as it turned out, the Kennedy tax cut was the last example of a major change in fiscal policy based on Keynesian ideas.

For a time, the Kennedy administration relied on "wage-price guideposts" to control inflation. In an early and controversial test, President Kennedy publicly castigated the steel industry when it raised prices more than the guideposts allowed, threatening a transfer of federal purchases to companies that remained within the guideposts and other sanctions. Eventually, the steel industry backed down, but the government could not, of course, treat every price increase that violated the guideposts as a major crisis. When inflation accelerated in 1965, the guideposts fell into disuse.

Not until the last quarter of 1969 was there more than a brief pause in the rate of expansion of the economy. Indeed, the expansion from February 1961 to November 1969 was, until that time, the longest sustained rise in the postwar period. The recession that followed the boom, in 1969 and 1970, was brief, with the major indicators showing a trough in the fourth quarter of 1970.

Richard M. Nixon: Price Controls and the End of Bretton Woods

In 1971 the rate of inflation was around 4 percent per year, and the rate of unemployment around 6 percent. Although inflation was down from the prerecession peak and was probably coming down more, the public was bitter about what seemed to be a very high price for a small reduction in inflation. In addition, the United States was awakening to the seriousness of its international financial position.

---

[1]The passage is quoted, it should not surprise us, mostly by economists.

After World War II, the world's major trading countries had adopted what came to be known as the *Bretton Woods system*, named after the New Hampshire resort where the meeting to establish the system was held in 1944. At that conference it was decided that the world would adopt a system of fixed exchange rates with all currencies fixed in terms of dollars. Various rules were set up that allowed countries, under certain circumstances, to devalue their currencies. The International Monetary Fund was also set up to provide short-term liquidity for countries experiencing balance-of-payments deficits; and the World Bank was created to provide long-term investment funds.

The system was, in some ways, like the gold standard, except that the base of the world's monetary system was the dollar rather than gold, although the dollar itself was then tied to gold. Immediately after World War II, the central problem had been the "dollar shortage": Countries devastated by the war had difficulty earning the dollars they desperately needed to buy food and capital equipment. Gradually, as Europe and Japan recovered from the war, the dollar shortage turned into a dollar surplus: U.S. imports regularly exceeded U.S. exports. Inflation in the United States contributed to the dollar surplus by making U.S. exports and U.S. goods that competed with imports more expensive. As a result of the U.S. balance-of-trade deficit, foreign countries built up short-term dollar claims on the United States. Foreign central banks held the bulk of these claims. Some of these claims were converted into gold, raising fears that the U.S. balance-of-trade deficit would eventually force the United States to devalue the dollar, and that this action would undermine the world's monetary system. Indeed, conversions into gold would have been even greater had the United States not exerted diplomatic pressures on central banks to hold dollars.

The U.S. balance-of-payments problem became acute in the second half of the 1960s. Private holders and foreign central banks were accumulating far more dollars than they wanted. America was faced with a run on its gold reserve. On August 15, 1971, the Nixon administration simultaneously "closed the gold window" and imposed a system of wage and price controls. Closing the gold window simply meant refusing to exchange dollars for gold. This action freed the dollar from its "golden anchor" and allowed its value to fluctuate. A brief attempt to reestablish fixed rates, the Smithsonian Agreement, was reached in December 1971; it called for fixed exchange rates, with the price of gold raised from $35 per ounce to $38 (an 8 percent devaluation of the dollar). The growing worldwide inflation made it difficult to stick to fixed exchange rates, however, and one country after another began to float its currency against the dollar. This sequence of events was reinforced by the ideas of free market economists led by Milton Friedman, who argued that the prices of foreign currencies should be set in the marketplace like the prices of wheat, automobiles, and computers. For a time, some economists hoped that the world would get back to fixed exchange rates, but this did not happen. The resulting system is frequently described as a "dirty float." Private supplies and demands are the main determinants of exchange rates, but governments often intervene, buying or selling currencies when the outcome of market forces is not to their liking.

The wage and price controls were intended to show the public that something was being done about one of the most pressing economic problems facing the nation. Controls also addressed what was happening to the dollar in international markets. The U.S. balance-of-payments problem was caused partly by the inflation because inflation made imports more attractive and exports less attractive. Controls, it was hoped, would buy time while the United States put its house in order by adopting appropriate monetary and fiscal policies.

Price controls went through a series of phases. The first three-month period, known as Phase I, was a price freeze. Because prohibiting all price increases could not work for long without producing shortages requiring rationing and evasions, a system with greater

© BETTMANN/CORBIS

Milton Friedman, staunch defender of free markets. His advocacy of slow and steady expansion of the stock of money, flexible exchange rates, an all-volunteer military, and free trade gained increasing acceptance during the 1970s, 1980s, and 1990s.

flexibility had to be introduced. In Phase II, prices were set by the Price Commission and wages by the Pay Board. These bureaus were given considerable discretion so that individual markets could be addressed. Inflation in 1972 under Phase II was only 3.3 percent, lower than it had been since 1967, and lower than it would be again until 1983. Price controls got much of the credit, although some economists believe that inflation would have slowed in any case. The time seemed right to begin dismantling controls before they became a permanent part of the economy. In Phase III, which began in January 1973, the rules were eased, and their administration was placed in the hands of businesses. Inflation accelerated from 3.3 percent in 1972 to 6.2 percent in 1973. Worse still, the volatile food index increased at an astonishing 14.5 percent annual rate.

Price controls were subjected to considerable criticism. Conservatives complained that inflation was rising because the inflation repressed in previous phases could no longer be kept in check. Liberals complained that the Nixon administration had deliberately undermined the program because it was working all too well. In response to the critics and to the acceleration of inflation, meat prices were frozen in March 1973 and a freeze on all prices was imposed again in June. A shortage of meat resulted; meat counters in many supermarkets were literally empty. The shortage was aggravated by the announcement of a future date when controls would be lifted; ranchers held their animals off the market in the almost certain knowledge that they would get a higher price later. This sequence is a dramatic illustration of Economic Reasoning Proposition 3, incentives matter (see page 8). Note that here the incentive is the possibility of future large gains. With meat shortages, distortions in other sectors, evasions, and rising prices, the control program was in a sorry state. Phase IV replaced Freeze II in August 1973. (It was really Phase V, but by that time, no one was counting.) During this phase, prices were decontrolled sector by sector.

What was the control program's overall effect on prices? In 1974, consumer prices rocketed upward at a 12.2 percent annual rate. Some observers have seen this as the release of inflationary pressures built up under controls. Others doubt that much repressed inflation was left after Phase III and look to other factors—such as supply-side shocks in oil and food and the lagged response to previous increases in the stock of money—to explain the acceleration of inflation. Most statistical studies agree that controls were successful in repressing inflation for a time, but they differ on how much and for how long.

If the calm created by Freeze I and Phase II had been used to impose restrictive monetary and fiscal policies, the economy might have emerged from this experiment with controls as it had from the Korean War experiment with controls, that is, with stable prices. This, however, was not to be. The stock of money rose at the unprecedented peacetime rate of 13.5 percent from December 1970 to December 1971 and at 13 percent from December 1971 to December 1972.[2] The inflation of 1974 was to some extent the result of these increments to the stock of money working through the economy. Fiscal policy was also inflationary. Deficits of $23 billion and $23.4 billion were run up in 1971 and 1972. In only one previous year during the postwar period had the deficit been larger, but typically it had been far smaller. It is not clear why monetary and fiscal policies were so expansionary in these years, but it is possible that the controls themselves were partly to blame. By creating the false impression that inflation was under control (and creating a new set of people to blame if it accelerated), the existence of controls encouraged the Fed to concentrate on reducing unemployment. In any case, it is clear that an opportunity to return to a stable price level, bought at considerable expense, was lost.

Jimmy Carter: The Great Inflation Reaches a Climax

When President Jimmy Carter took office, his administration had an excellent opportunity to stamp out the long-building inflationary forces. Instead, it went about the business of stimulating the economy. Political pressure for increases in Social Security benefits, veterans' benefits, farm subsidies, civil service pensions, grants to states, welfare programs, and other spending advances found a warm welcome with the Carter administration and Congress. Meanwhile, monetary policy was strongly expansionary. From 1975 to 1976, the stock of money increased at an annual rate of 13.7 percent, and from 1976 to 1977, it increased at 10.6 percent. By the fall of 1978, inflation was advancing at a rate twice that of two years earlier.

With the polls showing that inflation was "public enemy number one," Carter felt compelled to act. Carter's anti-inflation program eventually included the following: (1) a commitment to lower the increase in government spending, (2) a commitment to reduce the federal deficit, (3) a call to increase labor productivity and efficiency, and (4) a set of "voluntary guidelines" for wage and price increases. Within a year, it was clear that the program was an act of futility. The voluntary controls proved particularly unsettling. Some large corporations and unions were allowed to ignore the guidelines, while smaller, less politically potent groups were forced to conform. In effect, the voluntary controls became mandatory controls selectively applied. Meanwhile, inflation continued to rise.

An atmosphere of confusion prevailed as key members of the Carter team made conflicting public statements. Upon hearing that prices had risen 1.1 percent in one month, Alfred Kahn, the president's "anti-inflation chief," said, "The government can do some

---

[2]There are various definitions of money, depending on which financial assets are included. The figures here are for M2, which includes currency and deposits subject to check in commercial banks. This measure was widely used at the time, although not all economists agreed that it was the best measure.

things, but not a helluva lot; for the most part it rests with the consumer." Unlike Nixon, who could claim that the Organization of Petroleum Exporting Countries' (OPEC) price increases in oil and other external shocks were behind inflation during the years between 1973 and 1976, the Carter team could find no one to share the blame other than the nation's private sector.[3]

Throughout these years, the news media promoted this misplaced emphasis. Routinely, reporters would say that this month most of the inflation was *caused* by the rise in the price of housing, or food, or energy, or whatever price rose the most that month. Such advances were the result of inflation; however, they did not cause it. The inflation is shown in detail in Figure 27.3. The figures may tempt one to blame those sectors revealing the most rapid rise in prices. Clearly, however, the general rise of prices did not stem from any one sector. All sectors, albeit with variation, responded to the underlying inflationary forces.

In 1979 and 1980, inflation (Figure 27.1) reached double-digit levels, causing widespread fear of economic disaster. Creditors who had not foreseen rising prices lost. A retiree, for example, who had patiently saved by buying government bonds, saw the real value of a lifetime of savings being washed away. The wages of some workers kept pace, but for many there was the constant fear that the next pay increase would not keep pace with the raging inflation.

One of the most troubling aspects of the inflation of 1976 to 1980 was the rise in interest rates. Interest rates had moved irregularly upward after 1965, falling in recessions but then more than making up the lost ground during the subsequent expansions. During the remarkably volatile year of 1980, the prime rate (the rate charged by banks to their lowest-risk customers on short-term unsecured loans) tickled 20 percent in April, fell to 11 percent by midsummer, and reached the all-time record high of 21 percent by Christmas. High interest rates were continued throughout 1981 and into early 1982. Inflation was clearly an important factor in the rise of interest rates. Economists have long maintained that in a rational world, an inflation premium would be incorporated in the rate of interest. If a lender and a borrower could agree on a rate of 10 percent when no price increases were expected, they should set a rate of 15 percent if prices were expected to rise 5 percent. Inflation would wipe out 5 percent of the value of the principal and interest, leaving the lender and borrower in the same real position as when no inflation was expected. Historically, the relationship between inflation and interest rates has not been as exact as this example suggest, but as inflation persisted year after year, credit markets learned to pay close attention to inflation, and the relationship between inflation and the rate of interest grew closer and closer. Economists were to some extent the teachers in this learning process.

As interest rates and housing prices rose, many people found themselves unable to purchase the new home that had seemed within their grasp only a few years before. In the first decades of the postwar era, the idea that each generation would live a life of greater material comfort than had the preceding generation had come to be taken for granted. Now this view became problematic; many parents feared a bleak future for their children. As the young increasingly found housing difficult to obtain, the old were becoming concerned over the plight of the Social Security system: Would payment increases linked to inflation bankrupt the system?

---

[3]Although the large shift in wealth caused by Organization of Petroleum Exporting Countries (OPEC) is beyond dispute, its impact on inflation is less clear. West Germany and Switzerland were far more vulnerable to the real shocks produced by OPEC and failing agricultural crops than was the United States, yet they managed, by a determined effort, to reduce their monetary growth and lower their inflations to the vanishing point between 1972 and 1976.

FIGURE 27.3
(top) Producer Price Indexes, 1967–1980 (1967 = 100)
(bottom) Consumer Price Indexes, 1967–1980 (1967 = 100)

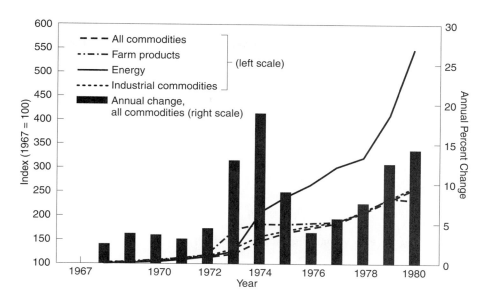

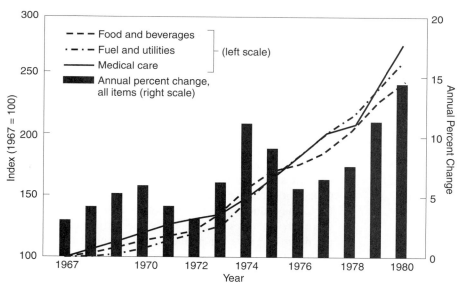

Source: *Charts prepared by the U.S. Bureau of the Census.*

As during the Great Depression, many government policies were initiated or enlarged in the 1970s to provide relief for needy individuals and families. For instance, as food prices rose, food stamps were distributed more liberally, but these measures could not prevent the public from losing confidence in the ability of the government to protect its future.

The decline in public confidence revealed in the polls would not have surprised John Maynard Keynes. In his 1919 book, *The Economic Consequences of the Peace,* he wrote:

> *Lenin is said to have declared that the best way to destroy the Capitalist System was to debauch the currency. By a continuing process of inflation, governments can confiscate, secretly and unobserved, an important part of the wealth of their citizens. By this*

method they not only confiscate, but they confiscate arbitrarily; and, while the process impoverishes many, it actually enriches some. The sight of this arbitrary rearrangement of riches strikes not only at security, but at confidence in the equity of the existing distribution of wealth. Those to whom the system brings windfalls, beyond their deserts and even beyond their expectations or desires, become "profiteers," who are the object of the hatred of the bourgeoisie, whom the inflation has impoverished, not less than of the proletariat. As the inflation proceeds and the real value of the currency fluctuates wildly from month to month, all permanent relations between debtors and creditors, which form the ultimate foundation of capitalism, become so utterly disordered as to be almost meaningless; and the process of wealth-getting degenerates into a gamble and a lottery.

Lenin was certainly right. There is no subtler, no surer means of overturning the existing basis of society than to debauch the currency. The process engages all the hidden forces of economic law on the side of destruction, and does it in a manner which not one man in a million is able to diagnose. (Keynes 1919, 235–236)

WAS THE ECONOMY MORE STABLE DURING THE KEYNESIAN ERA THAN BEFORE THE DEPRESSION?

Through much of the Keynesian era, economists believed that the economy had become more stable, certainly in comparison with the Great Depression but also in comparison with the predepression era. Greater stability was the result, they believed, of changes in the economy's structure (the relative decline of manufacturing and agriculture and the rise of services) and improved policy, especially fiscal policy. That view was certainly eroded by the Great Inflation, but many Keynesian economists believed that at least in terms of real magnitudes, their policies had stabilized the economy.

Christina Romer (1986a, 1986b) challenged this view. She pointed out that the amount and reliability of raw data available in the postwar period on unemployment, GDP, and similar variables were much greater than what it had been earlier in the century. The reduction in the variability of the key macroeconomic indicators, she argued, was merely the result of having better estimates: The improvement was a "figment" of the data. To prove her point, Romer extended the prewar estimates forward in time. In other words, she estimated postwar unemployment, GDP, and so on, as if she had to make do with only the "bad" prewar raw data. An example of what she found can be seen in Table 27.2. The official estimates for 1948–1982 are shown on the second line, and Romer's estimates are shown below them in parentheses. The key change is in the standard deviation of the unemployment rate. The conventional data shows a dramatic fall from 2.38 to 1.58 percent, indicating greater stability. Romer shows that if the prewar technique for estimating unemployment had been used in the postwar period, the fall

TABLE 27.2 ALTERNATIVE MEASURES OF THE UNEMPLOYMENT RATE

YEARS	MEAN	STANDARD DEVIATION
1900–1930 (Official)	4.84%	2.38%
1948–1982 (Official)	5.41	1.58
1948–1982 (Romer)	(5.52)	(2.24)

Source: *Computed from Romer 1986b, 3, 12.*

would have been from 2.38 to 2.24 percent, indicating little improvement in stability. Romer's work has been challenged (Weir 1986), but it has made economists more cautious about their claims for modern policymaking.

THE MONETARIST ERA

"Stagflation," high unemployment combined with high inflation, also undermined economists' confidence in Keynesian economics. In the 1960s, economists had believed in a stable Phillips (1958) curve: Unemployment could be permanently lowered at the cost of permanently higher inflation (see Economic Insight 27.2 on page 524). Now they realized that the Phillips curve represented only a temporary trade-off. Once workers and employers began to adjust to the new higher rate of inflation, unemployment would begin moving back to its "natural" rate.

A number of economists contributed to the new view of the relationship between inflation and unemployment; perhaps most influential was Milton Friedman. His address to the American Economic Association in 1967, "The Role of Monetary Policy," explained that increasing money growth reduced unemployment for a time because prices would initially rise faster than wages, and real wages would fall. Once workers caught on, however, they would demand wage increases in line with price increases, and unemployment would return to its "natural rate." Economists of all persuasions began to accept Friedman's analysis, but liberal economists preferred the term "nonaccelerating inflation rate of unemployment" (NAIRU) to natural rate because the former leaves open the question of whether it is a "good" rate. (This is also an example of the kind of humor that appeals to economists: The Nehru suit was fashionable at the time.) The policy implications were clear. Governments should not try to reduce unemployment to the lowest possible rate through monetary and fiscal policy because that would lead to ever higher rates of inflation (remember Economic Reasoning Proposition 2, choices impose costs). Better would be a stable monetary and fiscal framework. As Keynes noted in the passage just quoted, new ideas are rarely implemented immediately; rather, they gradually encroach upon policymakers.

A Monetarist Experiment?

Recognizing that President Carter's policies were not working and that the American people were becoming increasingly cynical about the prospects of reining in inflation, the Federal Reserve finally took dramatic steps. On October 6, 1979, the Federal Reserve announced a fundamental shift in policy. Henceforth, interest rates were going to assume less importance in their decision making. More attention would be paid to the monetary aggregates (different measures of the money stock), and new techniques would be introduced to control the growth of the money stock.

This shift appeared to be a triumph for the doctrines of Milton Friedman and other monetarists, who had long been making four principal points based on their reading of monetary history. (1) Inflation is primarily a monetary phenomenon—"too much money chasing too few goods." Therefore, to reduce inflation, the Fed had to reduce the growth of the stock of money. (2) Money affects the economy with a long and variable lag. Therefore, the best policy was the simplest: Gradually reduce the rate of growth of the stock of money to a low rate and then hold it. Attempts to fine-tune the economy might end up making matters worse. (3) The trade-off between inflation and unemployment is temporary. Again, the conclusion was don't try to fine-tune the economy. (4) Interest rates are a misleading guide to monetary policy. During the Great Depression, low interest rates had given the misleading signal that money was easy. Now, high interest rates were giving the misleading signal that money was tight.

ECONOMIC INSIGHT 27.2

THE PHILLIPS CURVE

The figure below shows the Phillips curve, which describes the relationship between unemployment (on the horizontal axis) and inflation (on the vertical axis). Originally, it was believed that the trade-off was stable. Policymakers, for example, could choose a low level of unemployment. The result would be a high rate of wage increase (unions would naturally be militant when replacement workers were few) and, as wage increases were passed along, a high rate of price increases. Policymakers, in the language of the time, were faced with a stable "menu of choices" and could choose the combination of inflation and unemployment that suited their preferences. Republicans, concerned about the value of the dollar, would choose high unemployment and low inflation; Democrats, concerned about the working poor, would choose low unemployment and high inflation.

The figure shows what happened to this tidy view: The Phillips curve shifted steadily upward. Economists responded with new theories about the curve: Perhaps more young workers were entering the workforce, or perhaps young people were less willing to work. As the shift continued, however, the curve was subjected to a more searching scrutiny. Economists Milton Friedman and Edmund Phelps (1967) argued persuasively that not the rate of inflation, but only the gap between actual and expected inflation increases profits and reduces unemployment. Successively higher Phillips curves were produced by successively higher rates of expected inflation. Moreover, because expectations always adapted in the end to actual inflation, no permanent trade-off occurred. Later, economists led by Robert Lucas (1976, 1977) argued that because people formed their expectations rationally, the trade-off might not exist even in the short run. What had once appeared to be a stable downward-sloping curve had become a cloud surrounding a vertical line.

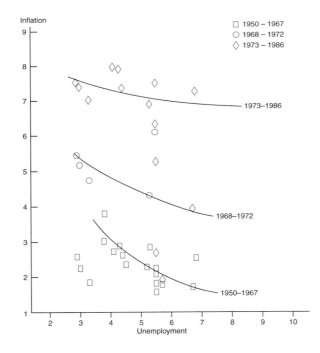

A related but distinct line of thought concerning "rational expectations" held that the costs of disinflation, unemployment, and reduced output were largely the result of mistaken expectations. If workers continued to demand high wage increases based on expectations of high inflation and those expectations were disappointed, the workers would end up pricing themselves out of the market. The policy implication of this line of thought was also clear: Even an abrupt change in monetary policy would cause little damage if people truly believed that the Federal Reserve would hold true to its new policy.

Once more, policymakers were turning to academic economists for ideas about how to manage the economy. Of course, policymakers could not be forced to carry out the experiment in the way that monetarists would have liked. Monetarists complained that rather than smoothly and slowly reducing the growth rate of the money stock, the fluctuations in the growth rate were becoming greater than ever. As in the Kennedy-Johnson years, policymakers could pay lip service to ideas and adopt the part of the program that suited them while ignoring the advice they did not want to hear. In this case, moreover, adopting a new set of doctrines had the advantage that if the policy did not work or if the costs of disinflation were high, the monetarists could be blamed.

Under the leadership of chairman Paul Volcker, the Fed curtailed the growth rate of the money stock, and inflation dropped dramatically. Inflation had fallen from 13.3 to 8.9 percent between 1980 and 1981, and rates were below 6 percent through the first half of 1982. Seizing the opportunity to eradicate inflation, Volcker tenaciously held to his policy throughout 1981 and early 1982. He did so despite an increase in unemployment from 5.8 percent in 1979 to 9.5 percent in 1982, the highest rate since the Great Depression.[4] The political pressure to relax the tight money policy was intense, but the Federal Reserve held to its course. President Ronald Reagan, elected in 1980, strongly and publicly supported Volcker, and this support allowed Volcker to maintain his tight money policies even as opposition to his policies mounted. In 1982, inflation was 3.9 percent. The cost of disinflation, however, was high, despite the predictions of some economists that once the Fed's commitment to stable prices was taken seriously, the real adjustments would be small. Of course, on this occasion, there was little reason based on past experience to take the Fed seriously.

© HARRITY/AP PHOTO

Paul Volcker, the cigar-smoking chairman of the Federal Reserve Board, was one of the principal leaders advocating tight money to reduce double-digit inflation in the 1970s and early 1980s.

---

[4]The frequent repetition of this fact in the media misled many people into thinking that the unemployment rate was almost as high as it had been during the Great Depression. This, of course, was not the case. See chapter 23.

Beginning in 1982, the economy began the longest peacetime expansion up to that time on record (refer to Table 27.1). Unemployment gradually declined, and inflation remained at tolerable levels through the remainder of the Ronald Reagan's presidency. After two terms, Reagan left the presidency in 1989 as one of the most popular presidents of the postwar period. Much of that popularity rested on the contrast between economic conditions as he found them and as he left them.

One of the ironies of the period is that the economy seemed able to absorb a considerable amount of new money without experiencing a return to high rates of inflation. From December 1980 to December 1986, the stock of money grew at an annual rate of 9 percent. Some observers considered this natural as long as the economy was emerging from the deep trough of the early 1980s. Others suggested that deregulation of the banking system and, particularly, the payment of interest on bank deposits had independently increased the demand for money. In any case, with the stock of money growing rapidly, frequently in excess of the targets proclaimed by the Fed, and with little evidence of unacceptably high rates of inflation, the Fed gradually abandoned its emphasis on monetary growth and began to pay attention again to interest rates.

Ronald Reagan: Supply-Side Economics

Ronald Reagan's landslide victory in the 1980 election and the dramatic shift in power in Congress—particularly in the Senate—to the Republicans provided both a mandate for change and the coalition to realize it. As soon as the Reagan administration was formed, it moved swiftly to implement Reagan's economic campaign promises. These centered on a large tax cut achieved by lowering marginal tax rates (especially for very high incomes), elimination of the federal deficit, a reduction in the role of the federal government in terms of spending and regulation, and a buildup of the armed forces.

Once again, a new school of economic thought was influential in altering the course of economic policy. "Supply-side" economists such as Arthur Laffer argued that high tax rates were inhibiting economic growth. Lowering rates would give people more incentive to work, invest, and innovate. Lowering rates would even produce more tax revenue by expanding the tax base, thus helping to balance the budget. The relationship between tax rates and tax revenues became known as the *Laffer curve*: Over some range, raising rates would increase revenues, but at some other point, additional increases would lead to reductions in work effort and increases in tax evasion; then total tax revenue would fall. Laffer and other supply-side economists believed that the economy had already entered this range. Although most economists agreed that high tax rates tended in some degree to discourage productive effort—this is after all Economic Reasoning Proposition 3, incentives matter—many doubted that the effects of cutting rates would be as large as the supply-siders thought. In the campaign for the Republican nomination, George Bush, then Reagan's rival, spoke for many ordinary citizens and many economists when he denounced the idea of balancing the budget through tax cuts as "voodoo economics," a term that gained wide currency among critics of supply-side economics.

After the election, Congress moved swiftly to reduce income taxes and other taxes by 23 percent over a three-year period, but reductions in spending were much harder to achieve.[5] As David A. Stockman, who was in charge of planning the Reagan spending cuts, tells us in his memoir, *The Triumph of Politics* (1986), even the most commonsense cuts were strongly resisted by an "iron triangle": the direct beneficiaries of government spending in the private sector, the government bureaucrats who administered the program, and the members of Congress who were particularly beholden to the beneficiaries.

---

[5]This is usually referred to as a 25 percent decrease, but it was phased in over three years in cuts of 10 percent, 10 percent, and 5 percent. These cumulate to 23 percent: $1 - (1 - 0.10) \times (1 - 0.10) \times (1 - 0.05) = 0.23$.

**TABLE 27.3 THE FEDERAL GOVERNMENT'S SURPLUS (+)
OR DEFICIT (−), 1940–2008, SELECTED YEARS**

YEAR	BILLIONS OF DOLLARS	AS A PERCENTAGE OF GDP
1940	−3.5	−3.0
1950	−4.7	−1.1
1960	+0.5	0.1
1970	−8.7	−0.3
1975	−54.1	−3.4
1980	−73.1	−2.7
1985	−221.5	−5.1
1990	−277.6	−3.9
1995	−226.4	−2.2
2000	+86.4	2.4
2005	−493.6	−2.6
2008 (estimated)	−602.2	−2.9

Source: Economic Report of the President 2008.

Tax cuts, the failure to make extensive spending cuts, increases in the military budget, and the recession (which also reduced tax revenues) produced deficits in the federal budget unprecedented in peacetime. Table 27.3 reveals both the acceleration of growth in the deficit under President Reagan and the long-term nature of the problem. As Table 27.3 shows, the deficit reached 5.1 percent of GDP in 1985, a peacetime record, and remained a high, although declining, proportion of GDP for the following decade.

© REUTERS/CORBIS

Alan Greenspan was appointed chairman of the Fed Board in 1987. His deft handling of monetary policy was given much of the credit for the economic expansion of the 1990s.

© DENNIS COOK/AP PHOTO

Ben Bernanke replaced Alan Greenspan as chair of the Federal Reserve Board in February 2006. An academic economist famed for his studies of the banking crisis of the 1930s, Bernanke faced the real thing when a severe financial panic hit in 2008.

What were the consequences of such deficits? Some economists predicted that large federal deficits would lead to skyrocketing real interest rates (the market rate less inflation) because deficits meant that a much-augmented demand for credit would face the same supply. But the supply of credit proved more elastic than had been anticipated. Foreign lenders rushed into the U.S. market, purchasing government bonds, private securities, real estate, and other assets. Real interest rates did not rocket upward, and the dollar remained strong (worth a large number of units of foreign currency) despite a growing gap between exports and imports. There was always the possibility that foreign lenders would some day lose confidence in the U.S. economy, but the "day of reckoning" proved to be longer in coming than many had expected.

There was, then, much concern about the federal deficit when President George H. W. Bush took office in January 1989. During the campaign, Bush had promised to continue Reagan's policies. He laid down the gauntlet to the Democrats by declaring, "Read my lips: no new taxes." He abandoned this pledge, however, when the recession of 1990 and 1991 helped drive the budget deficit higher. The deficit was still a major issue when Bill Clinton took the oath of office in January 1993. Rapid economic growth, however, solved the problem. By 2000, as Table 27.3 shows, there was a large surplus and the new worry (that proved to be fleeting) was how to spend the surplus rather than how to pay for the deficit.

From Greenspan to Bernanke at the Federal Reserve

In 1987, President Ronald Reagan appointed economist Alan Greenspan to head the Federal Reserve Board. Greenspan would go on to serve under Democrat Bill Clinton and Republican George W. Bush. His would become the longest tenure of any chair. He was tested quickly. Only a few months after taking charge, the stock market took a sudden and extreme plunge. Fear was widespread that the entire financial system would collapse (see Perspective 27.1).

Greenspan arranged a large temporary injection of money into financial markets that helped quell fears and restore order. There would be other financial crises: a Mexican

PERSPECTIVE 27.1

DO STOCK MARKET CRASHES CAUSE DEPRESSIONS?

For reasons that are still not entirely clear, a severe stock market crash occurred in 1987. The Dow Jones Industrial Average, a widely used index (shown in Figure 27.4 as the solid line measured against the right value axis) fell 26 percent between September and October 1987. In the immediate aftermath of the crash, many people expected a repeat of the events that had occurred in 1929 and 1930: a rapid slide into severe depression. This did not happen, however; the real economy, for example, as represented by the unemployment rate

(shown in the figure as the dashed line measured against the left value axis) remained stable. Alan Greenspan and the Federal Reserve received considerable credit for responding immediately by pumping additional liquidity into financial markets. There is also a lesson to be learned from this case about the danger of jumping to conclusions based on limited evidence. Conclusions such as "stock market crashes cause depressions" cannot be based safely on a hasty reading of one historic event, however compelling. As Economic Reasoning Proposition 5, evidence and theory give value to opinions, reminds us, conclusions must be tested by a wide range of facts.

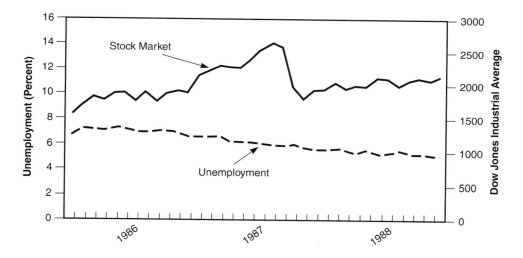

Debt Crisis in 1995 and an East Asian Debt Crisis in 1997. In both cases, Greenspan took measures to help contain the crisis. Greenspan's overall approach to monetary policy is depicted in Figure 27.4, which shows the Federal Funds rate from 1987 to 2008. The Federal Funds rate—the interest rate at which banks lend reserves to each other overnight—is the chief operating target of the Federal Reserve Board. If the Federal Reserve wants to make credit more available it adds reserves until the Federal Funds rate falls; if it wants to restrict credit, it withdraws.

The recessions defined by the National Bureau of Economic Research are shown as the short distances between the vertical dashed lines in Figure 27.4. When the economy went into a recession, Greenspan cut rates aggressively and then held them down until the all-clear was sounded, that is until there was widespread agreement that an economic expansion had firmly taken hold and there was no danger of a relapse.

The economic expansions on Greenspan's watch were remarkable. In March 1991 (see Table 27.1), the economy reached a trough from which began the longest economic boom in U.S. history. It did not end until March 2001, a full decade later. The expansion was driven by a huge investment boom as the use of personal computers and the Internet spread through the economy and changed the way Americans worked and played. To use

FIGURE 27.4

The Federal Funds Rate, 1987–2008.

Under Alan Greenspan, the Federal Reserve responded to economic downturns by lowering the Federal Funds rate.

Source: *Federal Reserve System.*

the colloquial expression, America was "getting wired." A stock market boom was a concomitant of the investment boom, as it had been in earlier investment booms, such as in the 1920s. From a level of 3,018 in March 1991, the Dow Jones Industrial Average nearly quadrupled to a peak of 11,750 in January 2000. The NASDAQ (National Association of Securities Dealers Automated Quotations) index, which contained more of the high-technology stocks that were so much in favor, rose even more. During this period, Greenspan received considerable credit for keeping the expansion going without driving the economy into an inflationary spiral. A well-received biography of Greenspan was titled *Maestro* (Woodward 2000). The stock market boom, however, was a continuing worry: Some observers worried that when the bubble burst there would be a major calamity. Greenspan attempted to use some of his immense prestige to talk the market down to what he believed was a more sustainable level. His characterization of the stock market as succumbing to "irrational exuberance" was widely quoted. Nevertheless, for a time, the market ignored even the famous chair of the Federal Reserve Board. All good things, at least all economic expansions, must end. At the beginning of the 2000s, the stock market tumbled, real investment tumbled, and unemployment rose. In March 2001, the unemployment rate was 4.2 percent; by the end of the year, it was 5.8 percent. According to the official dating, the recession that followed the great boom of 1990s was not especially long; only eight months from March 2001 to November 2001 (Table 27.1). Once again the Federal Reserve followed a policy of lowering interest rates in a recession and keeping them low until the recovery was well under way. Once again Greenspan was praised for his wise handling of the economy. Two worrisome problems, however, emerged.

First, the expansion that followed this recession was somewhat anemic despite a major tax cut pushed through by President George W. Bush. Unemployment remained stubbornly high. It was, to use the term favored by critics of the administration, a "jobless recovery." Second, the United States (as well as a number of other countries) experienced a tremendous real estate boom. Housing prices rose dramatically. Many home purchases, moreover, were financed with so-called subprime mortgages. Borrowers with low incomes and wealth were were encouraged to take out mortgages. Often they could afford the payments because the initial "teaser rates" were low. The stock market, moreover, climbed even higher than in the previous boom. Once again, some economists and pundits worried about what would happen when the stock market and real estate bubbles burst.

On January 31, 2006, Ben Bernanke was appointed chair of the Federal Reserve Board to replace Greenspan. An academic economist, Bernanke is an expert on monetary and financial policy in the Great Depression. His views on the Depression, you will recall are discussed in chapter 23. Bernanke was soon tested. In the spring and summer of 2007 a major financial panic hit the economy. It was centered on subprime lending and the confusing financial instruments based on subprime loans (Gorton 2008). The newspapers were filled with stories about financial firms suffering losses, writing down the value of their assets, drawing on emergency lines of credit, and closing. There were also bank runs reminiscent of the runs that had occurred in the Great Depression and earlier crises. In August 2007 there was a run on Countrywide Financial Corporation and in September a run on a British bank, Northern Rock. In December 2007, the U.S. economy entered a recession from which, as this is written, it has not emerged. The Federal Reserve responded vigorously to the crisis by cutting the Federal Funds rate, expanding credit, and underwriting lending in a variety of markets. Perhaps Bernanke remembered the criticisms leveled at the Federal Reserve by Milton Friedman, Anna J. Schwartz, and many other financial historians, including Bernanke himself, for not responding with sufficient vigor to the banking crises of the early 1930s. However, whether the measures taken to shore up the financial system will prove to be sufficient, and how long and deep the recession will be is yet to be determined.

SELECTED REFERENCES AND SUGGESTED READINGS

Economic Report of the President 2009. U.S. Council of Economic Advisors. http://www.gpoaccess.gov/eop/.

Federal Reserve System. Board of Governors. "Federal Funds Rate," 2009. http://www.federalreserve.gov/econresdata/default.htm.

Gorton, Gary B. "The Panic of 2007." NBER Working Paper No. 14358, National Bureau of Economic Research, September 2008.

Historical Statistics of the United States: Earliest Times to the Present, Millennial Edition. Eds. Susan B. Carter, et al. Cambridge: Cambridge University Press, 2006.

Keynes, John Maynard. *The Economic Consequences of the Peace.* New York: Harcourt Brace, 1919.

_____. *The General Theory of Employment, Interest, and Money.* New York: Harcourt Brace, 1936 (first Harbinger ed., 1964).

Lucas, Robert E., Jr. "Econometric Policy Evaluation: A Critique." In *The Phillips Curve and Labor Markets,* eds. K. Brunner and A. H. Meltzer. Carnegie-Rochester Conference Series on Public Policy, Vol. 1. Amsterdam: North Holland, 1976.

_____. "Understanding Business Cycles." In *Stabilization of the Domestic and International Economy,* eds. Karl Brunner and Allan Meltzer. Carnegie-Rochester Conference Series, Vol. 5. Amsterdam: North Holland, 1977.

National Bureau of Economic Research. "Historical Recessions and Recoveries." 2009. http://www.nber.org.

Phelps, Edmund S. "Phillips Curves, Expectations of Inflation and Optimal Unemployment Policy over Time." *Economica* 34 (1967): 254–281.

Phillips, A. W. "The Relation between Unemployment and the Rate of Change of Money Wage Rates in the United Kingdom, 1861–1957." *Economica* 25 (November 1958): 283–299.

Romer, Christina. "Is the Stabilization of the Postwar Economy a Figment of the Data?" *American Economic Review* 76 (1986a): 314–334.

_____. "Spurious Volatility in Historical Unemployment Data." *Journal of Political Economy* 94 (1986b): 1–37.

Stockman, David A. *The Triumph of Politics: How the Reagan Revolution Failed.* New York: Harper & Row, 1986.

Weir, David R. "The Reliability of Historical Macroeconomic Data for Comparing Cyclical Stability." *Journal of Economic History* 46 (June 1986): 353–365.

Woodward, Bob. *Maestro: Greenspan's Fed and the American Boom.* New York: Simon & Schuster, 2000.

CHAPTER 28

Manufacturing, Productivity, and Labor

CHAPTER THEME

Although many other nations aspired to increased industrialization, the manufacturing sector in the United States declined (relative to other sectors) throughout much of the twentieth century. In 1950 manufacturing as shown in Table 28.1 on page 534 accounted for 28 percent of gross domestic product (GDP); by 2007 manufacturing accounted for 12 percent. The decline in the manufacturing sector was the result of the faster growth in the demand for services, the increasing ability of consumers to purchase manufactured goods more cheaply from abroad, and the increasing productivity in the manufacturing sector.

A portrait of relative decline, however, should not lead to the idea that the sector was stagnant. The manufacturing sector changed dramatically during the postwar era. New industries arose and displaced old ones. New production techniques were adopted. Waves of mergers and acquisitions eliminated old firms and created new giants. An energy crisis forced firms to alter long-established practices. "Downsizing" altered the relationship between employer and employee. Antitrust policies were increasingly modified by the ideas of economists.

The American labor market underwent a profound transformation during the postwar era. The decline in the importance of manufacturing in total output was mirrored in employment. In 1950 manufacturing employed a quarter of the labor force; by 2007 it employed less than 10 percent. In addition to this and other changes on the demand side of the labor market, there were also important changes on the supply side. A moral awakening in the 1960s reshaped the labor market. Discriminatory barriers that had confined many women, African Americans, and members of other minorities to the margins of American economic life were reduced, and immigration laws were changed to eliminate quotas that restricted immigration from certain parts of the world. Partly as a result of the decline in restrictive barriers, the labor force participation rate of women, including women with young children, rose dramatically.

One consequence of these changes was the decline of the unions, which reached a peak in power and membership in the 1950s only to see their influence wane in the following decades. Finally, in the later part of the century, these changes produced a slowdown in the growth of real wages, particularly for workers with relatively low skills, that threatened to leave a disturbing legacy for the twenty-first century.

GALES OF CREATIVE DESTRUCTION

Long ago, economist Joseph Schumpeter observed that capitalism moves forward, for better or worse, through the introduction of new products and services that destroy the market for older products and services. In his famous phrase, the economy moves forward through "gales of creative destruction" (Schumpeter 1935; Rosenberg 1976, chapter 4).

TABLE 28.1 THE CHANGING ROLE OF MANUFACTURING

YEAR	EMPLOYMENT IN MANUFACTURING (millions)	EMPLOYMENT AS A SHARE OF THE LABOR FORCE (percent)	MANUFACTURING OUTPUT AS A SHARE OF GDP (percent)
1950	15.1	25.6%	28.0%
1960	15.4	23.5	26.9
1970	17.8	22.8	23.9
1980	18.7	18.9	20.0
1990	17.7	14.9	16.3
2000	17.3	12.6	14.5
2007	14.0	9.6	11.7

Source: Economic Report of the President 2008, *and previous years.*

The postwar era provides abundant evidence for Schumpeter's generalization. In the 1940s and 1950s, the antibiotics industry exhibited the highest average growth rate—a phenomenal 118 percent per year. Output of television sets was almost as great; home freezers and clothes dryers were close behind. At the other end of the spectrum, production of tractors, locomotives, and rayon and acetate slowed. Changes in consumer tastes accounted for some of these declines, as in the cases of pipe and chewing tobacco and mutton. For the most part, however, the retrogressing industries had fallen victim to competition from new products. Television hurt the motion picture industry, changed radio production, raised problems in spectator sports, and affected book sales and restaurant dining. Older methods of producing a given commodity may also be displaced by newer methods. Steel-reinforced aluminum cable, which is both stronger and lighter than an electrically equivalent copper cable, captured the high-voltage transmission line business. As the 1960s progressed, central air conditioning and electric heating systems vied with color television sets for a rapidly increasing share of household outlays. In the 1970s, recreational and vocational expenditures on new designs of old products rose spectacularly as families turned to cameras, stereos, boats, campers, and other leisure-time equipment. In the 1990s and 2000s the Internet revolutionized communication and marketing.

© D. G. ARNOLD

Plant closings, particularly in the "smokestack industries" of the northeastern and midwestern "rustbelt," produced significant job losses in the 1970s and 1980s.

Steve Jobs with an early version of the Apple personal computer. Being a pioneer, however, does not ensure one's place in an industry. At the beginning of the 21st century, Apple was struggling to catch up with rival Microsoft.

Today, as in the past, American manufacturers endlessly strive to develop new products and services. Schumpeter believed that the central justification for monopolies and oligopolies is that they develop large research departments that institutionalize the process of research and innovation. In Schumpeter's view, a firm with market power would be able to maintain or increase it by introducing new products, whereas competitive firms or independent laboratories may be hard pressed to raise capital to invest in research and development. Subsequent research, however, has challenged the central role of monopolies and oligopolies in research and development. For one thing, it appears that firms with market power often focus on minor innovations designed to protect their monopoly power. New products such as intermittent windshield wipers and Web browsers often come from smaller firms or independent inventors (Scherer 1984, chapter 11).

Above all, computers illustrate the role of different types of firms in the innovative process. For a time it looked as if the mainframe computer business dominated by IBM would be the norm. Next the personal computer revolution upset consensus predictions and left IBM scrambling to catch up. Then for a time it looked as if the Apple computer and its operating system would become dominant, but shortly it was overtaken by Microsoft and its Windows operating system. See Perspective 28.1 on page 536 for a comparison of the wealth of Bill Gates, Microsoft founder, and John D. Rockefeller, the wealthiest entrepreneur of the Gilded Age.

Some economic historians believe that these "gales of creative destruction" produce the most efficient allocation of resources. Others argue that the outcome is "path dependent." According to economic historians who emphasize path dependence, a few chance events can determine which product or service will dominate the market. Believers in path dependence often argue that government intervention is required to offset the effects of these chance events and to ensure that the "best" product or service wins out. (See Economic Insight 28.1 for more about path dependence.)

PERSPECTIVE 28.1

IS BILL GATES AS "RICH AS ROCKEFELLER"?

John D. Rockefeller, the founder of Standard Oil, was the richest person of his day. Although estimates differ, it is frequently said that Rockefeller's fortune peaked at about $1 billion in 1913. How does that figure compare with the fortune of Bill Gates, the largest in our day, estimated to have been about $43 billion in 2003 when it was near its peak? Obviously, we cannot directly compare 1913 dollars with 2003 dollars. We need, in economists' words, to inflate the 1913 dollars. The consumer price index was about 18 times higher in 2003 than it was in 1913, so by this criterion, Rockefeller's fortune would have been worth about $18 billion in 2003. In 2007 it would have been worth even more, about $22 billion. Using the consumer price indicator as an inflator shows that Bill Gates was richer. However, we can make the comparison in many other ways. For example, we can compare their fortunes using GDP. Rockefeller's fortune was equal to 2.73 percent of GDP, but Gates's fortune was equal to only 0.41 percent of GDP. To put it somewhat differently, in 2007 the Rockefeller fortune was the equivalent of $374 billion and the Gates 2003 fortune the equivalent of $57 billion. Using GDP as the inflator, therefore, shows that Rockefeller was richer. How can this be? There is no single "right" way to compare the two fortunes. To understand how much in goods and services could be purchased by philanthropic organizations financed with these fortunes, the consumer price index would be the better measuring rod, but to understand how much power and influence each man had, and how much fear they inspired, the GDP would be better. The appropriate measure really depends on the question we want to ask. More information about how to put things into today's money can be found at the Web site of the Economic History Association at http://www.eh.net.

Bill Gates, founder of the computer software giant Microsoft. Would the company founded by "the modern Rockefeller" endure? It's hard to say, but note that Exxon is the descendant of Rockefeller's Standard Oil.

ECONOMIC INSIGHT 28.1

PATH DEPENDENCE

Sometimes economic historians find it helpful to focus on a simple example that abstracts from the complexities surrounding historical processes. For example, many economic historians suspect that the triumph of Microsoft and the Windows operating system was *path dependent*. If Bill Gates had some bad luck early in the computer revolution and Steve Jobs, or some other pioneer, had some good luck, we might have ended up with a different, and possibly better, standard operating system. The problem with discussing path dependence in the context of Microsoft is that one must untangle this issue from so many others, including business practices, intellectual property rights, and so on. For that reason many economic historians have discussed path dependence in the context of a much simpler case. The six keys at the top left of a computer keyboard spell QWERTY. It has been alleged that the keys were originally assigned these letters to slow typists down and prevent the keyboards of the first mechanical typewriters from jamming. Now, according to this story, consumers are stuck with this inefficient design because the wrong path (from our perspective) was chosen in the nineteenth century when computers were unknown. This example was first brought to the attention of economic historians by Paul A. David in his famous paper "Clio and the Economics of Qwerty" (1985). Stanley J. Liebowitz and Stephen E. Margolis challenged David's view in a paper entitled "The Fable of the Keys" and in other works (Liebowitz and Margolis 1990, 1995, 1999). Liebowitz and Margolis argued that the advantages of alternative keyboards were not as great as claimed and that the suggestion of some that it would be in the interests of society for the government to force a transition to a new keyboard may well be a mistake. You can read a fascinating discussion among economic historians about path dependence and QWERTY at http://eh.net/lists/archives/eh.res/.

Productivity Growth

The wave of new products that hit the market after World War II was accompanied by rapid productivity growth. Indeed, growth was so rapid that some observers began to talk about another Industrial Revolution. After 1970, however, productivity growth slowed (as illustrated in Figure 28.1 on page 538). Figure 28.1 plots the growth of output per labor hour in the nonfarm business sector by showing the average annual percentage change for the previous five years. (The previous five years are used, rather than just the most recent year, to clarify the longer-term trends.) The exact date when the slowdown began (or the years of transition) are a matter of debate—you can make your own judgment as you look at the diagram—but the contrast between the early years of the postwar era and the middle years is dramatic. The slowdown in productivity growth was a major concern of policymakers because in a market economy, productivity is one of the fundamental determinants of real wages, a theme we will return to below.

Why did productivity growth slow down in the 1970s? A number of factors were at work. First, the shift of production away from manufacturing toward the service sector was one important factor. Productivity growth may be harder to achieve in services than in other sectors. Quality improvements, moreover, are extremely difficult to measure in the service sector, so output growth may have been understated. Second, as Michael Darby (1984) argued, changes in the structure of the labor force accounted for much of the slowdown. As a result of the earlier baby boom, many young and, therefore, inexperienced workers were entering the labor force for the first time in the 1970s. Third, the growth of capital per unit of labor input also slowed in the 1970s. To some extent, this may have been the result of rising inflation that disrupted financial markets and discouraged saving. Fourth, the highly variable rate of inflation in the 1970s also may have distorted price signals and prevented the reallocation of resources to their most efficient uses. When inflation varies dramatically from month to month, it is difficult for workers

FIGURE 28.1

The Growth of Output per Hour in the Non-farm Business Sector: Average Annual Percent Change Per Year for the Previous Five Years, 1950–2007

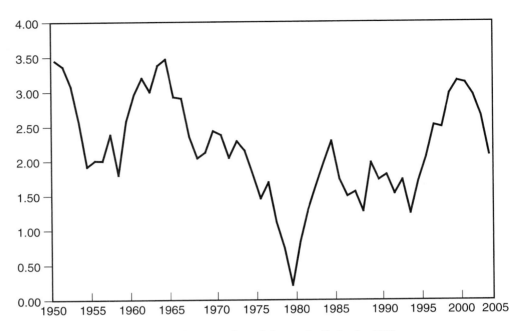

Note: The growth of labor productivity slowed dramatically in the 1970s.

Source: Historical Statistics of the United States Colonial Times to 1970 *1975, Series D-684; and* Economic Report of the President, 2008, *Table B–49.*

or owners of capital to know whether their real income has fallen because they are in a declining sector or because their nominal income has temporarily lagged behind prices. Fifth, some blame probably should be attached to the high cost of complying with new government regulations stemming from legislation passed in the 1960s and 1970s, perhaps because some credit should be given to deregulation for the rebound of manufacturing productivity in the 1980s. Six, when oil prices rose sharply, industries and agricultural producers that had relied on cheap and abundant oil suddenly were forced to adjust to higher prices. Large investments were required to replace older equipment with more energy-efficient equipment, even when the new equipment produced the same output per labor hour. Toward the end of the century, productivity growth began to rise, as is evident in Figure 28.1. Adjustment to higher energy prices, the computer revolution, and corporate restructuring all contributed to a rise in productivity growth that was as unexpected as was the preceding decline.

The Energy Crisis

Beginning in 1973, the Organization of Petroleum Exporting Countries (OPEC), which at that time controlled a substantial share of the world oil market, began to flex its muscles. Particularly disruptive was the oil embargo that followed the 1973 Arab-Israeli War. In response, the United States adopted price controls to protect consumers from the price increases. The result, as many economists predicted, was long lines at gas pumps: rationing by waiting time rather than by price.

This experience touched off a debate about how to meet the "energy crisis." Should it be through government actions—rationing, subsidies for the poor, and federal expenditures for new sources of energy—or through the price mechanism? The bureaucratic approach was tried. The Federal Energy Administration was established in 1974 (mainly through the merger of a number of existing agencies), and a cabinet level Department of Energy followed in 1977. Spending on a wide range of federal energy projects was increased. But in the end, much of the painful adjustment was the response to higher prices. Americans cut their energy consumption by buying smaller cars (many of them from foreign producers), insulating their homes, and investing in more fuel-efficient productive processes. On the supply side, higher prices produced a rapid increase in oil production in countries outside of OPEC, undermining OPEC's monopoly power. The price system worked much as many of its advocates had suggested it would, although not perhaps as quickly and painlessly as some of them had expected.

The dimensions of the energy crisis and its the results can be read from the data in Table 28.2. The first column shows what happened to the price of crude oil. As you can see, it rose dramatically and by 1980 was 6.76 times as high as it had been in 1970. The real price of oil (the price of oil divided by average prices), shown in the second column, also rose substantially, although not as much. During the 1990s, the nominal price of crude oil leveled off, and the real price fell. An average of the prices of crude oil, natural gas, and coal, shown in the third column, also rose as a result of the energy crisis but by a smaller proportion. The oil price shocks created an incentive to substitute less costly forms of energy for oil, but as demand shifted toward these sources, their prices rose as well.

The result of the increase in the price of energy is shown in the last column of Table 28.2, which shows the amount of energy used per dollar of real GDP. This measure fell from 18 British thermal units (BTU) per thousand dollars in 1970 to 15 in 1980 in response to rising energy prices. At first the response was limited, disappointing the hopes of some that rising prices would quickly reduce consumption, but eventually the reduction in energy use was substantial. Perhaps the most a car owner could do in the short run was to eliminate less important trips. In the long run, however, more adjustments were possible: a consumer could buy a smaller, more fuel-efficient car, move close to work or public transportation, and so on. By 2007, energy use per dollar of real GDP was half of what it had been in 1970. Although reducing energy use created a number of benefits for the economy, including reducing the damage caused by economic activity to the environment, making these adjustments also took their toll on the economy. Savings that might have financed investments that increased output were used instead to finance investments that conserved energy or developed alternative sources. The energy

TABLE 28.2 THE ENERGY CRISIS

YEAR	PRICE OF CRUDE OIL (current dollars per million BTU)	PRICE OF CRUDE OIL (year 2000 dollars per million BTU)	AVERAGE PRICE OF ENERGY FROM FOSSIL FUELS (year 2000 dollars per million BTU)	ENERGY CONSUMPTION (thousands of BTU per year 2000 dollar of GDP)
1960	0.50	2.36	1.35	18.0
1970	0.55	1.99	1.15	18.0
1980	3.72	6.89	3.78	15.1
1990	3.45	4.23	2.26	11.9
2000	4.61	4.61	2.60	10.1
2007	11.47	9.58	4.17	8.8

Source: Statistical Abstract of the United States *2009, table 883.*

crisis is a classic illustration of Economic Reasoning Propositions 2, choices involve trade-offs, and 3, incentives matter (see page 8).

CHANGES IN THE ORGANIZATION OF INDUSTRY

Mergers among firms, acquisitions of one firm by another, and divestitures are among the main ways that firms try to increase their productivity and, ultimately, their profitability. A combination of several firms producing the same product, for example, may allow the combined firm to achieve economies of scale that each firm separately could not. Even if the firms are producing different products, it may be more profitable to combine them to take advantage of an elite management.

Looking back, we can see that mergers and acquisitions come in waves that crested, typically, during periods of intense economic activity. The 1920s, for example, brought a wave of business consolidation that was comparable, in some respects, to the great merger movement of 1897 to 1904. These waves, moreover, typically produced a public backlash motivated by fear that giant corporations were taking over the economy. The backlash against the merger movement in the twenties was strengthened by the belief that the existence of widespread monopoly had contributed to the Great Depression. The postwar period witnessed three waves of mergers: (1) a wave of conglomerate mergers that was particularly marked during 1966 to 1969, (2) a wave of hostile takeovers that was particularly marked during 1977 to 1989, and (3) a wave of mergers to achieve economies of scale in the 1990s.

Conglomerate Mergers

In the first post–World War II wave of mergers, the dominant form was the conglomerate, which combined companies that produced unrelated commodities or services. Between 1964 and 1972, the peak of the wave, about 80 percent of all mergers were conglomerations. This type of merger's fundamental purpose was to reduce the adverse effects of the business cycle or unexpected shocks in individual markets by diversifying the activities the company undertook. A characteristic of the conglomerate was its management organization. A small, elite headquarters staff attended to general matters such as financial planning, capital allocations, legal, and accounting tasks.

Ling-Temco-Voight (LTV), one of the first and most successful conglomerates, began in 1958 as a small firm called Ling Electronic, with annual sales of less than $7 million. During the next 10 years, Ling acquired or merged with Temco Aircraft, Chance-Voight, Okonite, Wilson and Company, Wilson Sporting Goods Company, the GreatAmerica Corporation, and some 24 other companies. Its revenues in 1968 were nearly $3 billion. When LTV acquired the Jones and Laughlin Steel Company in 1969, the merger meant that two corporations in the list of the nation's 100 largest companies were combining to make LTV the fourteenth-largest company in the United States.

Comparable results were achieved by other conglomerates such as Gulf and Western Industries, International Telephone and Telegraph, Litton Industries, Boise Cascade, and the Automatic Sprinkler Corporation. These and other conglomerate mergers created much of the glamour and fast-paced financial action that characterized the first merger wave. This wave peaked in 1969. During the 1970s, many of the conglomerates failed to perform as expected. Diversified companies proved more difficult to manage than expected, and diversification failed to isolate the conglomerates from the troubles experienced by more conventional companies.

Hostile Takeovers

In the late 1970s and early 1980s, merger activity accelerated again. The number of merger and acquisition announcements increased by more than 30 percent between 1975 and 1985, and the value of merged firms rose (at 1975 prices) from $12 billion to $90 billion. New terms such as *junk bonds* and *leveraged buyouts* and new personalities such as T. Boone Pickens, Carl Icahn, and Michael Milken dominated the financial pages.

In the typical case, corporate raiders such as Pickens and Icahn targeted a firm believed to be undervalued. They then issued junk bonds (high-risk and, hence, high yield bonds), offering some combination of these bonds and cash to the holders of the stock of the firm being acquired. Milken (of the investment banking firm of Drexel, Burnham, Lambert) was instrumental in bringing together entrepreneurs who wished to use junk bonds in takeovers with buyers. Milken contended, based on the historical record of junk bonds, that these bonds rarely proved to be as risky in the long run as conventional wisdom would have it. What he and his buyers often forgot was that through his own actions, Milken had so reshaped the market that his crop of junk bonds could not correctly be compared with those issued in the past.

How could acquiring firms afford to pay more for a common stock than it currently sold for in the market? Ultimately, each leveraged buyout (leverage is the ratio of debt to equity) depended on the belief that income generated by the firm acquisition could be increased by an amount sufficient to cover the interest on the new debt and still leave an ample return for shareholders. The many ways of increasing income included replacing incompetent management, exploiting underutilized holdings of natural resources, and reducing "excessive" contributions to pension funds.

Defenders of leveraged buyouts and junk bonds argued that these techniques increased economic efficiency. Critics argued that leveraged buyout artists simply stripped firms of valuable assets for short-term gains and deceived foolish purchasers of junk bonds. The critics charged, moreover, that the debt-to-equity ratio for many of the resulting firms was dangerously high and that they would be unable to meet their interest payments during the next recession.

The fall of the junk bond market was as rapid as its ascent. In 1986 Drexel became a target in the ongoing investigation of insider trading by arbitrager Ivan Boesky.[1] In 1989 Drexel was forced to dismiss Milken, who later served time in jail for his part in the scandal. A few months later, Campeau Corporation, a large issuer of junk bonds in the retail field, encountered a liquidity crisis, sending the junk bond market into a tailspin. Legislation prohibiting U.S. savings institutions from holding junk bonds also contributed to the slide, although only a few savings banks had ever acquired large positions in junk bonds. In 1990 Drexel, which itself held a large inventory of junk bonds, declared bankruptcy. The issuing of new junk bonds and their use in corporate takeovers had ended for a time.

In retrospect, the spectacular rise and fall of the junk bond market was a symptom rather than a cause of the high interest rates and volatile financial markets of the late 1970s and early 1980s, which sent investors in search of new and more flexible forms of finance.

---

[1]"Insider trading" occurs when securities are bought or sold based on information from the management of the firm that has not been released to the public.

In Search of Economies of Scale and Scope

The third wave of postwar mergers began in the early 1990s. This time, companies sought to achieve economies of scale by merging with or acquiring companies that filled out their "core competencies." The union of Chemical Banking and Chase Manhattan in 1996 produced a leaner firm with a much larger share of the New York consumer market. In other cases, companies sought economies of scale through marketing. This seems to have been the motive behind Gillete's acquisition of Duracell, the battery maker. The largest merger in American history to date was the merger of America Online (AOL) with Time Warner in 2000. At the time it was hoped that the combination of Time Warner's media companies with AOL's access to the Internet would create a far more creative and efficient entity. In subsequent years, however, the merged company struggled. What was behind the third wave of mergers? A roaring stock market was one factor. Companies found it relatively easy to raise funds by issuing stock. An indulgent antitrust environment was another.

ANTITRUST POLICY

Antitrust policy has gone through two distinct phases since the 1920s. In the first, beginning in the late 1930s, the Justice Department and the courts were hostile to mergers and business practices that appeared to limit competition. During this phase, the courts generally followed *per se rules*. For example, they usually held that control of a large share of the market was per se (intrinsically) illegal. It was no excuse that the firm had obtained a large share because it supplied a high-quality product or it had charged "fair" prices.

A second phase of antitrust policy began in the 1970s when the courts began to pay attention to critics of *per se* rules, who argued that they were often inconsistent with sound economic analysis and, because of this, often did more harm than good. Many of the most prominent critics, such as Robert Bork, Harold Demsetz, and Richard Posner, were associated with the famous Law and Economics program at the University of Chicago. The law-and-economics school of antitrust stressed several points. First, large market shares are usually the result of efficient management or innovation. Breaking up such firms may create losses in efficiency that outweigh the benefits from greater competition and (possibly) lower prices. In the *Alcoa* decision (1945), Judge Learned Hand had viewed Alcoa's practice of building new capacity well ahead of demand as a dangerous practice tending toward monopoly. The law-and-economics school viewed it from the other side, as an example of foresight that should be congratulated rather than punished. Second, even if the deconcentrated industry can achieve high efficiency in the long run, high transition costs may be incurred. Third, splitting up monopolies or oligopolies, moreover, may discourage other firms from undertaking product innovation and cost cutting. Fourth, competition can be effective even when there are few firms in an industry because attempts to collude tend to break down quickly and because the number of potential entrants may be large.

Thus, the wave of mergers at the end of the twentieth century resembled the wave of mergers at the end of the nineteenth century. In both cases, companies sought economies of scale by merging with or acquiring companies in the same or closely related fields. In both cases, a buoyant stock market played a role. And in both cases, regulatory policy was a factor: at the end of the nineteenth century, mergers were driven by the fear that a loose alliance of companies would be attacked under the Sherman Antitrust Act, while at the end of the twentieth century, mergers were driven by confidence that mergers that created more efficient companies would ultimately survive court challenges.

THE RISE OF THE SERVICE SECTOR

The most important change in the demand for labor was the growth of the "white-collar" (service) sector, a diverse grouping that includes retail trade, finance, education, medicine, entertainment, and so on. Table 28.3 shows this expansion. In 1955, the service sector provided about 41 percent of all jobs; by 2002, it provided almost 64 percent. The major declining sectors were agriculture, manufacturing, mining, and construction; their combined share fell from 44.5 percent in 1946 to 20.2 percent in 2002. Agriculture declined most rapidly in the period before 1970; manufacturing, on the other hand, held its own until 1970 and then began to decline. As Deirdre McCloskey put it when commenting on this chapter, production of "things" declined relative to production of "words."

The rise and fall in sectors can be explained by the changing structure of demand. As real incomes rose, the demand for certain products, such as consumer durables, increased slowly while demand for certain services increased rapidly. For example, rapid improvements in medical technology and increased federal funding produced rapid growth in the number of health-related jobs. Inflation and deregulation encouraged firms in the financial sector to offer an array of new products.

Historically, productivity growth in the service sector has been slow compared with productivity growth in manufacturing and agriculture, although productivity in the service sector is notoriously difficult to measure. To illustrate the latter point, Phillip Coehlo has asked the following question: How much would one pay to use the services of a dentist today to fill a cavity in comparison with a dentist using the techniques available in 1950? We do not know the precise answer, but we know it is a lot. The slowdown in the growth of real wages that we will discuss in more detail below was partly the result of the shift to the service sector. This does not mean, however, that the economy would grow faster if the public invested more in other sectors. Expansion of some sectors has favorable effects on others. For example, productivity growth in education may be relatively slow, but an expansion of the education sector contributes to the manufacturing sector by supplying new techniques and better educated workers.

The growth of the service sector has also contributed to economic stability. In the manufacturing sector, a decrease in demand often leads quickly to unemployment. In the white-collar sector, however, employers are often willing to continue to employ workers because they have specialized knowledge or long-term relationships with customers. For this reason, the rise of the service sector has dampened the impact of recessions on employment in the postwar period.

TABLE 28.3 DISTRIBUTION OF JOBS, 1955–2002, AS A PERCENTAGE OF TOTAL EMPLOYMENT

YEAR	AGRICULTURE	MANUFACTURING, MINING, AND CONSTRUCTION	SERVICES	GOVERNMENT
1955	11.3	35.9	40.7	12.1
1960	9.2	34.3	42.6	14.0
1970	4.7	31.7	46.7	16.9
1980	3.6	27.4	51.7	17.3
1990	2.9	22.1	58.8	16.3
2000	2.4	19.0	63.2	15.3

Source: Economic Report of the President, 2003, *Table B46.*

THE CHANGING ROLE OF WOMEN IN THE LABOR FORCE

The most dramatic trend in the supply of labor after World War II was the increase in the proportion of women, particularly married women, who participated (worked or actively sought work) in the paid labor force. Table 28.4 shows the key ratios at decade-long intervals. The proportion of women participating in the paid labor force (and therefore excluding women who work, for example, at home caring for children) increased from 38 percent in 1960 to 59 percent in 2007. The pundits were fond of pointing out (accurately) that classic television comedies, such as *Leave It to Beaver* (originally shown from 1957 to 1963), that portrayed a family in which the mother did not work outside the home no longer represented the typical American family. The proportion of men in the labor force, on the other hand, fell substantially, in some cases because the additional income earned by their wives made this choice feasible. The figures are shown in the second column of data in Table 28.4. Labor force participation of men fell from 83 percent in 1960 to 73 percent in 2007. But the opposite trends did not offset each other. The overall rate of participation in the paid labor force rose from 59 percent in 1960 to 66 percent in 2007.

Increased participation of women in the paid labor force was the result of a number of economic, political, and cultural trends (Goldin 1990, 138–149). Both Economic Reasoning Proposition 3, incentives matter, and Economic Reasoning Proposition 4, institutions matter, explain the change in the role of women in the labor force. Let us consider first the economic forces working to increase the labor force participation of women.

1. *Real wages rose.* Real wages of men rose, which tended to discourage the labor force participation of married women, but the effect of higher real wages available for women dominated.
2. *Years of schooling increased dramatically over the course of the twentieth century.* About 10 percent of the nonwhite women born in 1900 and about 30 percent of the white women born in 1900 would graduate from high school; by 1970, those figures had increased to 80 and 90 percent. The increased incomes made possible by additional schooling encouraged women to join the paid labor force. This factor, of course, operated with a long lag. For some women, the full effects of education on labor force participation were not seen until they had passed the age when child-rearing demands were greatest.

TABLE 28.4 PARTICIPATION OF MEN AND WOMEN IN THE PAID LABOR FORCE, 1960–2001

YEAR	WOMEN	MEN	TOTAL
1960	37.7%	83.3%	59.4%
1970	43.3	79.7	60.4
1980	51.5	77.4	63.8
1990	57.5	76.4	66.5
2000	59.9	74.8	67.1
2001	59.3	73.2	66.0

Source: *Statistical Abstract 2009.*

3. *The average number of children in a family declined from three or four at the beginning of the century to one or two in the 1980s, and the average life expectancy of women increased.* Together, these demographic trends meant that women had many more years to pursue a career after the burdens of rearing a family moderated.

4. *An increased rate of divorce encouraged women to invest in a career outside the home.* The interaction of these trends was complicated. For example, although a rising divorce rate encouraged women to work outside the home, the rising participation rate of women in the paid labor force encouraged some women to choose divorce who would have been unable to afford it in earlier periods. Causation, in other words, ran both ways.

5. *The rapidly growing service sectors, especially the clerical and education sectors, were particularly attractive to women.* Until 1950, the growth of these sectors affected mainly the participation rates of white single women because of discrimination against married and minority women. As discriminatory hiring practices were broken, the effects of growth in these sectors spread more widely.

6. *The growing availability and technological sophistication of consumer durables affected labor needs in home maintenance.* Electric washing machines and refrigerators, low-maintenance fabrics, telephone answering machines, and other labor-saving devices reduced the labor input in home maintenance.

But in addition to these economic forces, the feminist movement helped overcome discrimination against women workers through moral suasion and political action. Some barriers were broken during World War II. Before the war, many firms had "marriage bars." These firms simply did not hire married women and forced women who married while on the job to leave. Marriage bars became particularly widespread during the Great Depression as a way to ration scarce jobs. One rationale was that it was unfair for a married woman who might already have a breadwinner in the family to work and thus take a job away from a man who was the sole support of his family. By 1950, marriage bars had virtually disappeared (except for flight attendants), and some personnel managers were singing the praises of married women.

Another burst of activity occurred in the 1960s. President Kennedy's appointment of a Presidential Commission on the Status of Women in 1961, with the venerable Eleanor Roosevelt as its honorary chair, was the starting point. Partly as a result of the commission's recommendations, Congress passed the Equal Pay Act of 1963, which called for equal pay for equal work. Title VII of the Civil Rights Act, passed in the following year, barred discrimination in hiring, promoting, or firing workers on the basis of race, color, religion, national origin, or sex and set up the Equal Employment Opportunity Commission to help enforce the law. The word sex, incidentally, did not appear in the bill until the day before it was passed. It has been claimed that it was originally inserted with the idea of making the bill unacceptable to a majority, but the matter remains unclear (Goldin 1990, 201). In 1965, President Johnson created the Office of Federal Contract Compliance to require the submission of affirmative action plans by employers doing business with the federal government. Affirmative action is more than a color-blind, sex-neutral labor policy; it requires positive efforts to find workers traditionally discriminated against. The National Organization for Women was founded in 1966, partly to pressure the government into vigorous enforcement of its new antidiscriminatory legislation.

During the 1970s the feminist movement experienced further successes. Title IX of the Educational Amendments Act of 1972 extended the Civil Rights Act to educational institutions; one consequence of Title IX was to increase the participation of women in high-school and college sports. In the late 1970s and 1980s, the feminist movement

TABLE 28.5 THE GENDER GAP—RATIOS OF FEMALE TO MALE EARNINGS

OCCUPATION	1890	1930	1970	2007[a]
Professional	0.26	0.38	0.71	0.74
Clerical	0.49	0.71	0.69	0.69
Sales	0.59	0.61	0.44	0.69
Manual	0.54	0.58	0.56	0.64
Service	0.53	0.60	0.56	0.65
Farm	0.53	0.60	0.59	0.62

[a]Because this column is based on a different source, only rough comparisons can be made with the other columns.

Source: *1890–1970: Goldin 1990, 64; 2007:* Statistical Abstract of the United States, 2007, *Table 627.*

seemed to lose momentum and was unable to win major legislative victories. The institutions created in the 1960s and 1970s continued, however, to press for the removal of discriminatory barriers.

The Gender Gap

Despite federal legislation, increased education and experience, and better understanding by employers of the abilities of women, a considerable gap remained between the earnings of men and women in a variety of occupations. Table 28.5—based on work by Claudia Goldin, one of the leading experts in the field—shows the gender gap in six broad occupational classifications in 1890, 1930, 1970, and, although the data are not strictly comparable, 2007. The surprising thing is the persistence of the gender gap and its tendency to increase in every class of occupations except "professional" between 1930 and 1970. It appears, however, that since 1970, progress toward equal pay has occurred in most sectors. A considerable gap, however, remains.

The main factors that produced the increase in the relative earnings of women over this long period were the increase in the education of women and the breakdown of discriminatory social norms through persuasion and legislation. The increase in the participation rate of women, however, has kept the gender gap from closing even more. Increasing participation means that women's average years of experience in the labor force remains relatively low because so many have just entered the labor force. Moreover, because discrimination often blocks them from entering or advancing in certain fields, women entering the labor force have crowded into areas open to them, thereby preventing wages in those areas from rising as fast as in the rest of the economy. As the labor force participation rate of women stabilizes and the entire array of jobs created by the economy are opened to women, the gender gap should decline even further.

The Baby Boom

Decisions about entering the labor market were closely related to decisions about family formation and child bearing. The birth rate plunged during the Great Depression. For example, for women between the ages of 15 and 44, the prime child-bearing years, the rate fell from 89.3 births per 1,000 women in 1929 to a low of 75.8 in 1936. With the return of prosperity during the war, the rate increased again. In 1942, the birth rate reached 91.5, surpassing 1929, although the birth rate fell in 1944 and 1945.

In 1946, the baby boom began. Undoubtedly, the baby boom owed part of its existence in its early years to the reuniting of couples separated by war, but it continued long beyond the time when this was an important factor. The baby boom, as shown in

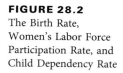

FIGURE 28.2

The Birth Rate,
Women's Labor Force
Participation Rate, and
Child Dependency Rate

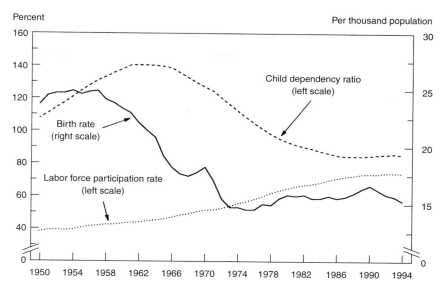

Source: Economic Report of the President, 1996, *57*.

Figure 28.2, lasted until the late 1950s. The birth rate then plunged to historically low levels. Indeed, natural fertility rates were so low that in the absence of immigration, the population might have declined. The child dependency ratio (the ratio of children under 14 to women between 20 and 54) peaked a few years after the baby boom began to taper off. The labor force participation rate of women climbed as the child dependency ratio fell and then leveled off when the child dependency ratio leveled off.

The baby boom was a complex phenomenon, but expectation of future economic conditions were undoubtedly important. The 1950s were the economic reverse of the 1930s: A strong economy and optimism about the future encouraged Americans to start or enlarge families. The birth rate declined for a number of reasons. Again, the rise in uncertainty about the future that prevailed in the 1960s and 1970s, like the uncertainty that prevailed in the 1930s, discouraged family formation and child bearing. The fall in the birth rate was also related, as shown in Figure 28.2, to the increasingly frequent decision by women to enter the paid labor force. Access to highly effective oral contraceptives, beginning in the 1960s, also contributed to the reduction in the birth rate (Goldin and Katz 2002).

MINORITIES

Efforts by African Americans, Hispanic Americans, and other minority workers to move into the economic mainstream met important but limited success during the postwar period. Table 28.6 shows the ratios of median family incomes of African Americans to whites, and Hispanics to whites, at 10-year intervals from 1950 to 2000. These numbers are not adjusted for other differences between the groups that affect family earnings: parents' age and work experience, number of children, the family's geographic location, and so on. This ratio nevertheless provides a rough indicator of the success of the search for economic equality. For African Americans there is some evidence of a narrowing gap: The ratio rose from 0.54 in 1950 to 0.65 in 2006. For Hispanic Americans there is no clear trend. There has been some deterioration in the ratio for both groups since 2000.

TABLE 28.6 RATIO OF AFRICAN AMERICAN AND HISPANIC FAMILY TO WHITE FAMILY INCOMES, 1950–2000

YEAR	AFRICAN AMERICAN	HISPANIC AMERICAN
1950	0.54[a]	NA
1960	0.55[a]	NA
1970	0.61	NA
1980	0.58	0.73
1990	0.60	0.71
2000	0.69	0.76
2006	0.65	0.66

Note: NA = not available. aIncludes other races.

[a]Includes other races.

Source: Statistical Abstract, *various years.*

African Americans

Two economic factors might have been expected to produce rapid African American progress in the postwar era: (1) the increase in the number of years of schooling and (2) the geographic redistribution of the African American labor force. It may be difficult for today's college students, aware of the overcrowding and underfunding of predominantly African American schools, to believe that much progress has been made. The reason is that it is difficult now to imagine how bad things were in, say, 1940. In that year, 80 percent of the African American male workforce had only elementary schooling, and 40 percent had less than five years of schooling. As shown in Table 28.7, the gap in the

TABLE 28.7 PERCENT OF POPULATION AGE 25 OR MORE HAVING COMPLETED 12 OR MORE YEARS OF EDUCATION BY RACE OR ETHNICITY AND GENDER, 1940–2000

YEAR	WHITE	AFRICAN AMERICAN	HISPANIC
		MALES	
1940	24.2	6.9	NA
1950	34.6	12.6	NA
1960	41.6	20.0	NA
1970	57.2	35.4	NA
1980	72.4	51.2	44.9
1990	81.6	65.8	50.3
2000	88.5	79.1	56.6
		FEMALES	
1940	28.1	8.4	NA
1950	38.2	14.7	NA
1960	44.7	23.1	NA
1970	57.7	36.6	NA
1980	71.5	51.5	44.2
1990	81.3	66.5	51.3
2000	88.4	78.7	57.5

Note: NA = not available.

Source: National Center for Education Statistics *2002, chapter 1, table 8.*

amount of schooling obtained by African American men narrowed considerably during the postwar period. In 1940 only 6.9 percent of African American men over 25 years old had completed high school compared with 24.2 percent of white men. By 2000, 79.1 percent of African American men were high school graduates, compared with 88.5 percent of white men. Similar improvements were recorded for African American women. The gap in quality of education, although more difficult to measure, probably also narrowed substantially.

African Americans also benefited, at least initially, from the geographic redistribution of their population. In 1940, a large gap in the wages for whites and African Americans existed in the North and South, and the gap for African Americans was much larger. The rapid migration of African Americans from the low-wage South was motivated in part by this disparity and tended to lessen it. In 1940, 75 percent of African American men lived in the South; by 1980, that figure had fallen to 53 percent.

Despite these trends, gains were slow and halting because of discrimination. The fight against discrimination has been a long and difficult one. In 1947, one of the most famous milestones occurred when Jackie Robinson broke the color barrier in major league baseball. This was important not only for African Americans who would earn their living in professional sports in the postwar period but also for the effect it would have on white stereotypes about the abilities of African Americans.

One of the main goals of the civil rights movement was the passage of fair employment laws. These laws, passed after World War II by a number of states, set up commissions that could issue cease-and-desist orders against firms that discriminated. By the time of the Civil Rights Act of 1964, 98 percent of African Americans outside the South were covered by these laws. Recent research by William Collins (2003) shows that these laws had some success in improving the wages and working conditions of African American women but little success in improving the wages and working conditions of African American men.

In 1954 the Supreme Court ruled in *Brown v. Board of Education of Topeka* that segregated schools were unconstitutional. This decision would have far-reaching consequences for U.S. education. Although many school districts then claimed that they were providing a separate but equal education for African Americans (a formula ordered by the Supreme Court in *Plessy v. Fergusson* in 1896), this was not actually the case. As Robert Margo (1982, 1986, 1990) documented, African American schools were systematically underfunded, and African Americans entered the labor force with a severe handicap. *Brown v. Board of Education* did not bring about change overnight. Many school districts dragged their feet, and not until the late 1960s, when courts began to order busing to achieve racial integration, was significant progress made in many areas.

Other visible signs of discrimination, such as segregated transportation, were also crumbling as a result of the civil rights movement. The culmination of that movement was the march on Washington in August 1963, where the young leader of the movement, Dr. Martin Luther King, Jr., gave his memorable "I Have a Dream" speech. Less than a year later, the Civil Rights Act was passed, which, among other things (as noted earlier), made it illegal to discriminate in employment. This law and the federal enforcement efforts that followed from it seem to have had a positive effect in breaking down discriminatory barriers, especially in the South. See New View 28.1 for some dramatic evidence.

The civil rights movement itself brought about change. As Gavin Wright explained in his thoughtful book, *Old South, New South* (1986), southern political and business leaders were trying to attract new businesses to the South during this era. They soon realized that a quick resolution of civil rights turmoil was necessary if they were to continue

NEW VIEW 28.1

MEASURING THE IMPACT OF THE CIVIL RIGHTS ACT

As John H. Donohue III and James Heckman (1991) show, federal pressure to end discrimination was directed at the South, where social norms, backed by state and local legislation, limited employment of African Americans. This pressure was successful. The graph below, showing employment in the South Carolina textile industry, is a dramatic piece of evidence. Notice that the share of African Americans (who were confined to the most menial jobs) was low and stable until 1965. To some extent, employers may have welcomed federal pressure. For example, employers in South Carolina who wanted to take advantage of relatively cheap African American labor could use the threat of federal sanctions as an excuse for breaking with established racial norms.

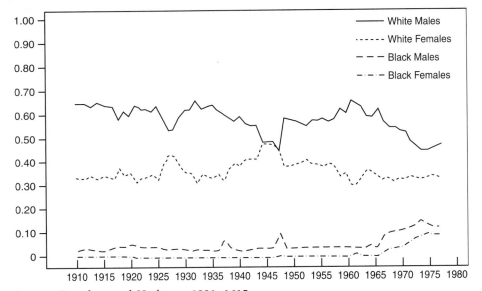

Source: *Donohue and Heckman 1991, 1615.*

to compete successfully for outside capital. In 1970, the president of Allis-Chalmers Corporation visited Jackson, Mississippi, and expressed doubts about locating a plant there because of the violent ongoing confrontation between African American students at Jackson State University and local police. As a result, the deadlock over school integration, then seven years old, was broken, and Allis-Chalmers announced construction plans.

In subsequent decades, however, progress toward equality slowed. One reason is that when the fight against discrimination moved from the South, where the targets were explicit laws, to the North, where the targets were implicit social norms, progress based on legal proceedings proved more difficult to achieve. In addition, as William Julius Wilson showed in *The Truly Disadvantaged* (1987), the loss of manufacturing jobs in a number of older northern cities hit the African American community, which had been drawn to those cities by those jobs, especially hard.

The Reverend Martin Luther King Jr. acknowledges the crowd at the "March on Washington for Jobs and Freedom" in 1963.

Native Americans

Despite the erosion of discriminatory barriers that followed the moral awakening of the 1960s, the effects of past and present discrimination continue to take a heavy toll. The postwar economic history of Native Americans is a clear illustration.

In the 2000 census, about 4.1 million people, 1.5 percent of the total population, identified themselves (either alone or in combination with other races) as American Indian or Alaskan Native. About 3.1 million identified themselves as belonging to a particular tribe. Median household income was $32,116, about 60 percent of the median household income for whites, and about 800,000 American Indians and Alaskan Natives had incomes that fell below the poverty line.

The current reservation and trust territories are, of course, only a small remnant of even the small amount that still belonged to Native Americans in the nineteenth century. In 1887 Congress passed the Dawes Act, which provided that each registered American Indian would receive 160 acres that would be held in trust for 25 years. In theory, the idea was that by "privatizing" the land, an efficient economy of prosperous farmers would be created. Leonard A. Carlson (1983) and a number of other economic historians, however, maintained that the program was structured to hinder the development of farming by Native Americans and to facilitate the transfer of American Indian properties to whites. Between 1887 and 1920, the land held by Native Americans fell from 138 million acres to 50 million acres. The allotment program was replaced in 1934 by the Indian Reorganization Act, which finally sought to preserve reservation and trust lands.

Many Native Americans choose to live their lives in accord with traditional values that reject the market, but many examples of an entrepreneurial spirit also exist. Often entrepreneurial initiatives have been deliberately frustrated by government policies intended to benefit white Americans at the expense of Native Americans. Lee Alston and Pablo Spiller (1992) reanalyzed a famous example from the nineteenth century, the *Cherokee Outlet* case. As early as 1867, the Cherokee had leased part of their land to white cattlemen. The leasing arrangement was backed by the federal government, which used the cavalry to keep squatters off the land. In 1888 the government ended the arrangement. The Cherokee were offered $30 million by some of the cattlemen for the land. Instead, the government, acting on behalf of white settlers, forced the Cherokee to sell the land to the government for $8.7 million.

More recently, the most visible sign of American Indian entrepreneurship has been gaming, which has been increasing at a rapid pace. In 2002, about 200 tribes nationwide sponsored gaming. In 1998 gaming revenues were a substantial $8.5 billion; in 2002, they were $14.5 billion; in 2007 they were $20 billion. However, much of the revenue is generated in a few large facilities. In 2007, the top 6 percent of Indian gaming operations produced 40 percent of the total revenue.[2] In addition, serious questions have been raised about the extent to which gaming revenues "trickle down" and relieve the economic distress experienced by the entire Native American community. Despite the prominence of gaming, it is wrong to assume that this is the only successful form of Native American entrepreneurship. Native Americans have engaged successfully in manufacturing, agriculture, tourism, and other industries, and have done so in widely diverse parts of the country. The Mississippi Choctaws, the White Mountain Apaches in Arizona, the Salish and Kootenai Tribes of the Flathead Reservation in Montana, and the Cochiti Pueblo in New Mexico have been cited as successful examples of reservation-based economic entrepreneurship.

THE NEW IMMIGRATION

Little change occurred in the immigration laws from the establishment of the quota system in the 1920s until 1965. The major exception to this generalization was a program under which Mexican agricultural workers (*braceros*) could work temporarily in the United States. This program began during World War II (although it is doubtful that it contributed to the war effort) and ended in 1965, another result of the wave of liberal legislation of the mid-1960s (Alston and Ferrie 1993).

At that time, a new immigration system was instituted. President John F. Kennedy and his allies in Congress were strongly opposed to national quotas, which they believed reflected racial and ethnic prejudice. Kennedy in fact had published a book, *A Nation of Immigrants* (1964), that celebrated the contribution of immigrants to American life and argued against limitations based on national origin. The new law, enacted after Kennedy's death, eliminated quotas based on the ethnic composition of the population in favor of a complex system of priorities that gave very high priority to uniting families. A limit was placed on the total number of immigrants, but that limit did not include spouses, minor children, or parents of American citizens. In 1980, a separate program for admitting political refugees was created. As a result of these changes, the number of immigrants increased, many coming from "new" areas—Latin America and the Caribbean. In the 1960s, 37 percent of immigrants came from Europe, 39 percent from Latin America and the Caribbean, and 13 percent from Asia. By 1990, 7 percent came from Europe, 67 percent from Latin America and the Caribbean, and 22 percent from Asia.

Table 28.8 shows total immigration to the United States since 1901. The acceleration of the rate of immigration after the 1965 change in the law is obvious in the table; the

---

[2]See the National Indian Gaming Commission Report at http://www.nigc.gov.

TABLE 28.8 IMMIGRATION, 1901–2007

YEAR	TOTAL (in thousands)	RATE (annual per thousand U.S. population)
1901–1910	8,795	10.4
1911–1920	5,736	5.7
1921–1930	4,107	3.5
1931–1940	528	0.4
1941–1950	1,035	0.7
1951–1960	2,515	1.5
1961–1970	3,322	1.7
1971–1980	4,493	2.1
1981–1990	7,338	3.1
1991–2000	9,095	3.4
2000–2007	7,984	3.9

Source: Statistical Abstract of the United States, *various years.*

rate increased from 1.5 per 1,000 between 1951 and 1960 to 3.4 between 1991 and 2000. Even the latter rate, however, was still well below the average of 10.4 per 1,000 between 1901 and 1910. The figures in Table 28.8 make no allowance for illegal immigration. Evidence suggests that the volume of such immigration, although difficult to measure, is large. In 1990, for example, some 1.2 million illegal aliens were apprehended attempting to cross into the United States from Mexico. Some experts believe that the number of illegal immigrants in the 1980s may have totaled as much as 40 percent of the legal immigration. Pressure to do something about illegal immigration led to the Immigration Reform and Control Act of 1986, which put tough new controls on illegal immigration (making it illegal, for example, for employers to hire undocumented workers) while creating an amnesty program for illegal immigrants who had put down roots in this country.

Many Americans benefit from immigration: those who own firms that employ immigrants (including those who own firms indirectly through retirement funds), those who possess special skills that become more valuable when unskilled labor is widely available, those who consume the products and services that immigrants help produce, those who provide the services consumed by immigrants, and those who own property in neighborhoods in which immigrants settle. On the other hand, native-born workers who compete directly with immigrants in the labor force—unskilled workers in urban areas, for example—face lower real wages and fewer job opportunities. It is difficult to say how large these effects have been. Some labor economists have stressed the substitutability between immigrants and native workers that implies lower wages for native workers (Grossman 1982; Briggs 1986). But others have found evidence of complementarity, which implies higher wages for native workers (Borjas 1983). A study by Francisco Rivera-Batiz and Selig Sechzer (1991) found evidence of both effects, depending on the group being considered, but stressed that both effects have been small

The countries from which the United States receives its immigrants also experience a variety of effects. In the first decades after World War II, for example, considerable concern was expressed about the "brain drain," the tendency of the United States to draw down the supply of engineers, scientists, physicians, and similar personnel in developing countries.

In the 1990s and 2000s, high immigration rates produced much the same political response as high rates of immigration in the early 1900s: exaggerated claims about the impact of immigrants on wages and the social welfare system, met by exaggerated denunciations of even moderate critics of immigration, although so far attempts to restrict immigration have been thwarted. Whether criticism of immigration will produce severe restrictions in the future seems to depend on whether the economy can deliver new jobs and rising real incomes.

UNIONS

Membership in labor unions increased sharply during the Great Depression and World War II. The percentage of the nonagricultural labor force that was unionized rose from 14.7 percent in 1933 to 20.4 percent in 1938, and from 22.5 percent in 1940 to 31.6 percent in 1950, stabilizing in the 1950s. At its peak, in 1953, nearly one-third of the nonagricultural labor force was enrolled in labor unions. Since that time, however, there has been a decline that has become precipitous since 1970. This can be seen in Table 28.9. By the mid-1990s, the percentage of the labor force enrolled in unions had fallen back to the level of the late 1920s.

A number of economic trends go far in explaining the deterioration in the strength of organized labor. First, the increasingly important service sector, where employee groups are usually small, has proved difficult to organize, although unions have had some success in recent years in organizing government workers. Moreover, within the goods-producing sector, a steady shift has occurred from blue-collar to white-collar employment that has slowed the pace of union growth because white-collar workers are less prone to organize. Second, the shift of manufacturing to the South and West, areas traditionally hostile to the labor movement, has also undermined union power. Third, foreign industrial competition, which has made workers in traditional bastions of union strength (such as automobiles) fearful of layoffs and plant closings, has further undermined organized labor. The high rate of immigration of unskilled workers, who often fear taking part in union activities, and who may oppose union attempts to control the supply of labor, has also undermined union strength.

In addition to these economic trends, changes in the legal environment (recall Economic Reasoning Proposition 4, institutions matter) have worked against the unions. Because of opportunities for legislation established by the Taft-Hartley Act, numerous states passed "right-to-work" laws. In 2003, 19 states, many of them in the South, had right-to-work laws. These laws, by making it illegal to enforce the union-shop provisions of an agreement within the state concerned, hamper efforts to unionize and are a source of friction between union and nonunion workers.

TABLE 28.9 UNION MEMBERSHIP, 1950–2001

YEAR	TOTAL UNION MEMBERSHIP (thousands)	AS A PERCENTAGE OF THE TOTAL CIVILIAN LABOR FORCE
1950	14,294	23.0%
1960	15,516	22.3
1970	20,990	25.4
1980	20,968	19.6
1990	16,740	13.5
2000	16,258	11.5
2007	15,670	10.7

Source: *1950–1980: Troy and Sheflin 1985; 1990–2007:* Statistical Abstract of the United States, *various years.*

Intraunion squabbles have also hurt the labor movement. At the peak of union strength, the American Federation of Labor (AFL) and the Congress of Industrial Organizations (CIO) merged in 1955, with George Meany becoming the first president. The radical dream of uniting all workers in one big union seemed near at hand, but harmony could not be maintained. Labor unity suffered a particularly severe blow in 1968 when the United Automobile Workers (UAW), under their dynamic leader Walter Reuther, left the AFL-CIO in a dispute over politics. At the same time, many of the organizational gains were being made by independent unions such as the Teamsters, who had been ousted from the AFL-CIO. Thus, it may well be true that critics who blame mainstream union leadership for part of the decline in labor's influence have a point.

Can organized labor regain some of its former influence? The economic trends we have been examining in connection with the union movement seem likely to continue. On the other hand, it has been noted that in Canada, where the industrial structure is in some ways similar to our own—although other policies, such as immigration policies, differ—the labor movement has remained far more influential than in the United States. It is best to remember that unionism in the United States has traditionally grown in spurts that were never predicted by the experts.

REAL WAGES

What was the net result of all the forces—birth rates, immigration, changes in labor force participation, and so on—operating on the labor market throughout the postwar era? Figure 28.3 on page 556 shows what happened to the productivity of labor and to real wages from 1960 to 2006. From the end of the war until the 1970s, both output per hour and real compensation per hour grew steadily, creating dreams of a future characterized by widespread affluence. Then, in the 1970s, as discussed above, labor productivity growth and real wage growth shifted to slower trends. The growth of output per worker then recovered somewhat, but the growth of real compensation per hour continued to lag. Over the whole period, real 1960 to 2006 real output per hour rose at an annual rate of 2.23 percent per year, while real compensation per hour rose only 1.47 percent per year.

What explains the stagnation in productivity and especially real-wage growth? Many conjectures about the causes of the slowdown have been put forward, each of which can probably account for some part of the phenomenon. First, some economists argued that the data are misleading. The price indexes used to measure real wages have been criticized, for example, for not properly accounting for the quality improvements in electronics, medicine, and other areas. Although this criticism undoubtedly holds some truth, it appears that there is nonetheless a real difference in real wage growth between the years from the end of World War II to the 1970s and the years that followed. Second, some economists accepted the data but claimed that the early postwar decades were exceptional. After all, the U.S. economy then enjoyed a unique position as the only industrial economy that had escaped the destructive effects of World War II. Perhaps the rates of productivity growth and real wage growth since the 1970s are more typical of what to expect in the long run. This observation is useful for policymakers, but it is cold comfort to workers. Third, after the 1970s, the savings rate was relatively low, holding down increases in the capital-to-labor ratio. Fourth, changes in the labor market, such as increases in immigration and in the labor force participation rate of women also held down increases in the capital-to-labor ratio. Fifth, the shift toward the service sector, the energy crisis, and, some would argue, the cost of complying with government regulations also reduced productivity. New View 28.2 discusses two additional factors: automation and downsizing.

ECONOMIC INSIGHT 28.2

COBB-DOUGLAS PRODUCTION FUNCTION

According to economic theory, the real wage should equal the marginal physical product (MPP) of labor.

$$(1) \text{ Real wage} = MPP$$

The cost of hiring one more worker, measured in goods and services, should equal the additional amount produced. This equation tells us that productivity is an important determinant of wages, but what factors will determine the marginal productivity of labor? Consider the Cobb-Douglas production function, one of the simplest and most frequently used:

$$(2) \ Y = AK^{a}L(1 - a)$$

where Y is output, A is the level of technological efficiency, K is the amount of capital, L is the amount of labor, a is the share of capital, and $(1 - a)$ is the share of labor. With this production function, the marginal physical product of labor is given by

$$(3) \ MPP = (1 - a) \ A \ (K/L)^{a}$$

This equation indicates that the marginal physical product of labor is determined by A, the general level of efficiency in the economy, and (K/L), the ratio of capital to labor. What is the relationship between the labor productivity measured by the Labor Department and reported in the press (the ratio of the amount of output produced to the amount of labor employed) to the marginal physical product of labor? In this model, the relationship is given by

$$(4) \ MPP = (1 - a) \ (Y/L)$$

In other words, if the a coefficient is stable, a stable relationship exists between the average product of labor, (Y/L), and the marginal product of labor. If equations (1) and (4) both hold, a close relationship should exist over time between real wages and the average product of labor. Percentage changes in the MPP, and hence the real wage, will equal percentage changes in output per unit of labor input. But as the graph below shows, this relationship does not seem to have held in recent years. We may need an alternative production function to describe the economy.

FIGURE 28.3
Productivity and Compensation, 1960–2006.

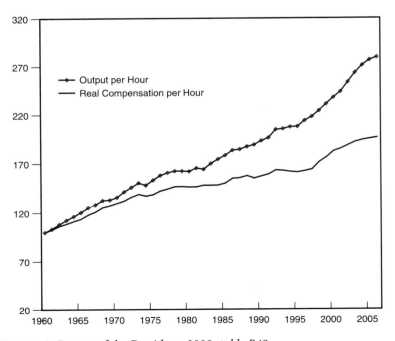

Source: Economic Report of the President, 2008, *table B49.*

NEW VIEW 28.2

AUTOMATION AND DOWNSIZING

The implementation of various new technologies of the 1980s resulted in the loss of many jobs. For example, the rapid advances in computer-based technologies enabled telephone companies to increase the number of daily calls from 1.2 billion in 1984 to 9.5 in 1990, while reducing their labor force from 742,000 in 1984 to 648,000 in 1990. The use of these technologies is one factor in the "downsizing" or reducing of the work force in many other industries. The reduction at General Motors from 1979 to the early 1990s was from 800,000 to 450,000; at General Electric, it was 402,000 to 298,000 during the same time period. As some firms quickly learned, however, the loss of the specialized knowledge provided by experienced laid off employees proved more costly than anticipated.

Are jobs that are lost when new technology is introduced eventually replaced by new jobs? This is one of the oldest questions in economics, and it resurfaces when unemployment rises. In the nineteenth century, David Ricardo, one of the founders of economics, argued that the introduction of the new machines could lead, at least for a considerable period, to higher unemployment, and Karl Marx described the plight of the handloom weavers who were displaced by weaving machines. Today, most economists believe that the jobs lost eventually will be replaced because the cost savings that result from technological innovations will be passed on to consumers in the form of lower prices, leaving consumers with more money to spend on other goods and services. Thus, technological progress need not produce mass unemployment. The great economic expansion of the last decade of the twentieth century (the longest on record) in which employment rose from 118 million in 1992 to 135 million in 2000 and unemployment fell from 7.5 percent of the labor force to 4 percent, helped to confirm the idea that the economy could create jobs in the face of rapid technological progress.

The confidence that new jobs will replace old ones, however, should not make us insensitive to the suffering that arises from technological progress. Workers whose skills once brought premium rates, typically older workers, may find themselves competing for low-paying jobs. It is little comfort to them to know that in the aggregate the number of jobs is increasing.

Inevitably, stagnant real wage growth produces demands that the government do something about it. An economic historian is reminded of the beginning of the twentieth century. In those years, slow growth in real wages produced militant unions and demands from a broad segment of the population that the government break up large corporations, limit immigration, and protect the wages of American workers from foreign competition. Young people who enter the labor market in the twenty-first century face a very different reality from the future envisioned in the early decades of the post–Word War II era.

SELECTED REFERENCES AND SUGGESTED READINGS

Alston, Lee J., and Joseph P. Ferrie. "The Bracero Program and Farm Labor Legislation in World War II." In *Sinews of War: Essays on the Economic History of World War II*, eds. Geofrey T. Mills and Hugh Rockoff. Ames: Iowa State University Press, 1993.

Alston, Lee, and Pablo Spiller. "A Congressional Theory of Indian Property Rights: The Cherokee Outlet." In *Property Rights and Indian Economies: The Political Economy Forum,* ed. Terry L. Anderson. Baltimore: Rowman & Littlefield, 1992.

Borjas, George J. "The Substitutability of Black, Hispanic and White Labor." *Economic Inquiry* 21 (1983): 93–106.

Briggs, Vernon M., Jr. "The Imperative of Immigration Reform." In *Essays on Legal and Illegal Immigration*, ed. S. Pozo. Washington, D.C.: W. E. Upjohn Institute, 1986: 43–71.

Carlson, Leonard A. "Federal Policy and Indian Land: Economic Interests and the Sale of Indian Allotments, 1900–1934." *Agricultural History* 57 (1983): 33–45.

Chiswick, Barry R. "The Effect of Americanization on the Earnings of Foreign-Born Men." *Journal of Political Economy* 86 (October 1978): 897–921.

Collins, William J. "The Labor Market Impact of State-Level Anti-discrimination Laws, 1940–1960." *Industrial and Labor Relations Review* 56, no. 2 (January 2003): 244–272.

Darby, Michael R. "The U.S. Productivity Slowdown: A Case of Statistical Myopia." *American Economic Review* 74 (June 1984): 301–322.

David, Paul A. "Clio and the Economics of Qwerty." *American Economic Review* 75 (1985): 332–337.

Donohue, John H., III, and James Heckman. "Continuous versus Episodic Change: The Impact of Civil Rights Policy on the Economic Status of Blacks." *Journal of Economic Literature* 29 (1991): 1603–1643.

Economic Report of the President, 1996. U.S. Council of Economic Advisors. Washington, D.C.: Government Printing Office, 1996. http://www.gpoaccess.gov/eop/

Economic Report of the President, 2003. U.S. Council of Economic Advisors. Washington, D.C.: Government Printing Office, 2003. http://www.gpoaccess.gov/eop/.

Economic Report of the President, 2008. U.S. Council of Economic Advisors. Washington, D.C.: Government Printing Office, 2008. http://www.gpoaccess.gov/eop/.

Goldin, Claudia. *Understanding the Gender Gap: An Economic History of American Women.* New York: Oxford University Press, 1990.

Goldin, Claudia, and Lawrence F. Katz. "The Power of the Pill: Oral Contraceptives and Women's Career and Marriage Decisions." *The Journal of Political Economy* 110, no. 4 (August 2002): 730–770.

Grossman, Jean Baldwin. "The Substitutability of Natives and Immigrants in Production." *Review of Economics and Statistics* 64 (1982): 596–603.

Historical Statistics of the United States Colonial Times to 1970, bicentennial edition. U. S. Bureau of the Census. Washington D.C.: Government Printing Office, 1975. http://www.census.gov/prod/www/abs/statab.html.

Kennedy, John F. *A Nation of Immigrants.* New York, Harper & Row, 1964.

Liebowitz, Stanley. J., and Stephen E. Margolis. "The Fable of the Keys." *Journal of Law & Economics* 33 (April 1990): 1–25.

_____. "Path Dependence, Lock-in, and History." *Journal of Law, Economics, and Organization* 11 (1995): 205–226.

_____. *Winners, Losers and Microsoft: Competition and Antitrust in High Technology.* Oakland, Calif.: Independent Institute, 1999.

Margo, Robert. "Race Differences in Public School Expenditures: Disenfranchisement and School Finance in Louisiana, 1890–1910." *Social Science History* 6 (Winter 1982): 9–33.

_____. "Educational Achievement in Segregated Schools: The Effects of Separate But Equal." *American Economic Review* 76 (September 1986): 794–801.

_____. *Race and Schooling in the South, 1880–1950.* Chicago: University of Chicago Press, 1990.

National Center for Education Statistics. *Digest of Education Statistics.* 2002. http://www.nces.ed.gov.

Rivera-Batiz, Francis L., and Selig L. Sechzer. "Substitution and Complementarity between Immigrant and Native Labor in the United States." In *U.S. Immigration Patterns and Policy Reform in the 1980s,* eds. Ira Gang, Francisco L. Rivera-Batiz, and Selig L. Sechzer. New York: Praeger, 1991.

Rosenberg, Nathan. *Perspectives on Technology.* Cambridge: Cambridge University Press, 1976.

Scherer, Frederic M. *Innovation and Growth: Schumpeterian Perspectives.* Cambridge, Mass.: MIT Press, 1984.

Schumpeter, Joseph. "The Analysis of Economic Change." *The Review of Economic Statistics* 17, no. 4 (May 1935): 2–10.

Statistical Abstract of the United States, 2007. U.S. Bureau of the Census. 2007. http://www.census.gov/compendia/statab/.

Statistical Abstract of the United States, 2009. U.S. Bureau of the Census. 2009. http://www.census.gov/compendia/statab/.

Troy, Leo, and Neil Sheflin. *U.S. Union Sourcebook.* West Orange, N.J.: Industrial Relations Data and Information Services, 1985.

Wilson, William Julius. *The Truly Disadvantaged: The Inner City, the Underclass, and Public Policy.* Chicago: University of Chicago Press, 1987.

Wright, Gavin. *Old South, New South: Revolutions in the Southern Economy Since the CivilWar.* New York: Basic Books, 1986.

CHAPTER **29**

Achievements of the Past, Challenges for the Future

In the first chapter we described some of the incredible changes in the U.S. economy during the twentieth century. To take an interesting example, since the early 1900s, college football and basketball players at the University of Wisconsin became substantially heavier and taller. Now you realize that constant change characterized every sector of the U.S. economy since colonial times, and you have an idea of how the U.S. economy has gotten from there to here. You know something about British colonial policy, slavery, railroads, tariffs, banking, the Great Depression, stagflation, and many other topics. We will not try to summarize all of those arguments in this chapter. Instead, we will focus on identifying the most important achievements of the U.S. economy and some of the important challenges for the future. History does not provide us with a crystal ball. At best it provides us with lessons that are useful in meeting an unpredictable future. As this is written, the United States faces the enormous uncertainties created by the wars in Iraq and Afghanistan, and by a financial and economic crisis that reminds some observers of the first years of the Great Depression. There will be events that cannot be forecasted and problems that cannot be solved on the basis of experience, but the economic history of America's responses to wars, to the Great Depression, and to similar forms of adversity provides important lessons to light the way.

ACHIEVEMENTS OF THE PAST

The achievements of the American economy are real and measurable. Here we cannot recount all of the achievements noted in the preceding 28 chapters, but we will describe four developments that are the culmination of those achievements: (1) the rise in real per capita income, the conventional measure of economic success; (2) the convergence of per capita incomes among regions, particularly the integration of the South into the economic mainstream; (3) the improvement in a variety of biomedical indicators of well-being that increasingly have been used by economic historians to document economic progress; and (4) the increase in the levels of education achieved by Americans.

Real Incomes Have Grown Rapidly

We judge the performance of our economy, first of all, by its ability to generate a rising level of real income for the American people. Figure 29.1 reveals the enormous increase in real per capita income since 1870. Although there are several large fluctuations around the trend—notably the decrease during the 1930s, and the increase in the 1940s (which is debatable because of the problems in measuring gross domestic product [GDP] in a war economy)—the long-term trend is clearly upward. We have, moreover, grown steadily: as Figure 29.1 shows, a 2 percent per year trend line fits the data extremely well. If history is any guide, future generations will be better off than past generations.

FIGURE 29.1

Real Gross Domestic
Product per Capita,
1870–2007

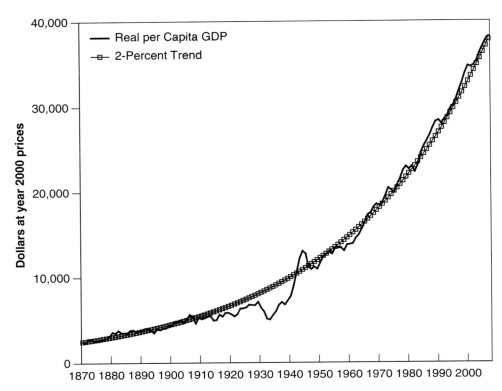

Sources: *1870–1958: Historical Statistics of the United States, 2006, series Ca11; 1959–2007:*
Economic Report of the President 2008, *Table B-31.*

The possibility that other countries may surpass the United States economically wor-
ries many Americans. A look at the data, however, shows that the United States has done
about as well as could be expected compared with other industrial countries. Table 29.1
compares the level of real per capita income in the United States with the levels in some
of our leading rivals. Such comparisons are inherently fraught with several difficulties.
The exchange rates used to convert incomes in foreign currencies into dollars may not
adjust for the true differences in prices in different countries. The income comparisons,

TABLE 29.1 REAL GROSS DOMESTIC PRODUCT PER CAPITA—SELECTED COUNTRIES AS A PERCENTAGE OF THE UNITED STATES				
COUNTRY	**1980**	**1990**	**2000**	**2006**
United States	100%	100%	100%	100%
Canada	84	83	80	81
France	79	76	72	74
Germany	69	78	73	72
Italy	71	73	69	69
Japan	67	87	79	73
Sweden	78	75	70	80
United Kingdom	67	71	69	80

Source: Statistical Abstract of the United States *2009, Table 1306.*

moreover, do not take into account differences in noneconomic variables that affect the standard of living, and do not take into account differences in the distribution of income. Nevertheless, the figures in Table 29.1 are an improvement over, or at least a supplement to, anecdotal evidence based on the accounts of travelers who have visited these countries. As you can see, most other industrial nations still have lower per capita real products than the United States. Indeed, the relative positions of different nations have not changed much since 1980. It is important, moreover, to remember that U.S. levels of consumption need not fall simply because other countries' consumption is rising. The global economy is not like a football game; in the economic game, all teams can come out ahead.

Lagging Regions Have Caught Up

Figure 29.2 shows regional incomes in the United States from 1840 until today. It summarizes in a single picture much of the story laid out in previous chapters. At the earliest date the West South Central (which includes Louisiana) had the highest per capita income. Of course, high average per capita income was consistent with huge disparities among individuals—there were rich planters and impoverished slaves. Average income in that region then fell drastically as a result of the Civil War and began a long slow process of catching up with the rest of the country, a process that has still not been completed. The earliest observation for the Pacific region shows it having an income twice the national average. The natural resources of the Pacific region help explain these high entry-level incomes.

Over the long run, however, as shown in Figure 29.2, per capita incomes in different regions of the United States have gradually converged. Convergence has been brought about mainly by market forces, although government policies that redistributed resources from one region to another played a role. Labor has migrated from labor-abundant regions such as the South to labor-poor regions such as the Pacific Coast, raising the growth rate of per capita income in the labor-exporting regions and lowering the growth

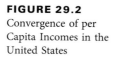

FIGURE 29.2
Convergence of per Capita Incomes in the United States

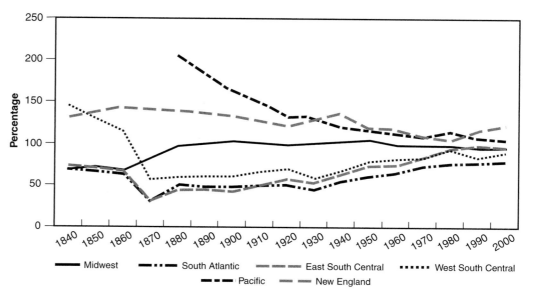

Source: *Easterlin 1971, 40;* Statistical Abstract of the United States 2002 *and previous editions.*

rate of per capita income in the labor-importing regions. The advice of Horace Greeley, a famous nineteenth-century newspaperman and politician, to "Go West Young Man, and Grow up with the Country," made good economic sense and was followed by millions of Americans. Similarly, capital migrated from capital-rich regions such as the Northeast to capital-poor regions such as the South, lowering the growth rate of per capita income in the capital-exporting regions and raising the growth rate of per capita income in the capital-importing regions.

Government policies contributed to regional convergence. Since the New Deal, government transfer programs, such as Social Security, and agricultural price supports have shifted incomes from high-income to low-income states. Perhaps the most important government policy was what it did not allow: individual states to impose barriers to trade. The United States was a free trade area: A business that could make a product at a favorable cost was free to sell it anywhere in the country that it chose. As railroads and other means of transport lowered the costs of transportation, interregional "product competition" contributed to the convergence of regional incomes.

Biomedical Measures of Well-Being Show Improvement

The measures of real income we have been discussing are imperfectly correlated with personal happiness, the ultimate goal of economic activity. One difficulty is what economists call the "index number problem." Typically, real income is computed by dividing money income by a weighted average of prices, where the weights are determined by the amounts consumed in a base period. This works fine for commodities that are consumed in the same amounts now as in the base period. But what happens when consumption of a commodity declines because it is replaced by something new and better? In that case, the use of the price index based on the old weights tends to understate the increase in real income. The government agencies that compute price indexes are well aware of the problem and have begun using "chain indexes," which update the weights annually, to minimize the problem. Nevertheless, it is still difficult to compare real income today with real income decades ago because of the introduction of new products. The computer revolution is a case in point. Pocket digital assistants, personal computers, digital video discs, electronic chess partners, video games, cell phones, and so on have added to our well-being but are only imperfectly reflected in our measures of real income, victims of the "index number problem."

Real income, moreover, is only one of many determinants of personal happiness. For that reason, economic historians increasingly have turned to biomedical measures of health and well-being to supplement their understanding of the achievements and challenges of economic growth. (See Economic Insight 29.1 on page 563 for a discussion of the insights provided by height.) These measures reveal that life in the United States was spent in better physical health in the postwar period as revealed by the statistics on death rates from specific diseases and broader measures of health such as infant mortality and life expectancy.

Striking gains have been made in the postwar period in reducing the death rates from numerous diseases, as shown in Table 29.2 on page 564. The age-adjusted death rate from influenza and pneumonia fell from 53.7 per 100,000 in 1960 to 20.3 per 100,000 in 2005 in part because of the development and widespread use of antibiotics.[1] Perhaps the most dramatic improvement was in the death rate from diseases of the heart, which dropped from 559 per 100,000 in 1960 to 211.1 per 100,000 in 2005. Rapid improvements in

---

[1]Certain diseases are more common among people of a certain age, for example, heart disease among the elderly. Statisticians, therefore, adjust the death rate so that it always refers to a hypothetical population with a constant distribution of people by age.

ECONOMIC INSIGHT 29.1

HEIGHT AS AN INDICATOR OF WELL-BEING

One of the most sensitive vital statistics is height. Height is the result of a number of factors, including nutrition and disease, and is closely related to the level and distribution of income. Height can supplement income as a measure of well-being and can help us understand periods or places for which conventional measures of income are of low quality or not available. Partly through the influence of Robert W. Fogel (1994, 2000), John Komlos (1987), Richard Steckel (1995), and other leading scholars, studies of height by age have become a "hot topic" in economic history.

Figure 29.3 here shows the adult height of white males in the United States by year of birth from colonial times to the present. The data come from a variety of sources. Men are measured, for example, when they enter the military. As you can see, the figure tells an interesting story, one that is different from Figure 29.1, which shows a steady rise in per capita real GDP. Evidently, heights of American men reached a fairly high level, although one below

modern standards, during the colonial era. Then heights fell from the 1840s to the turn of the century, when adult male heights began a long climb to modern levels.

The reasons for the depression in heights is not yet well understood. Urbanization does not seem to have been the whole story because heights declined in rural as well as urban areas. Growing inequality of income is one possibility now under study: the poor may not have been able to get enough to eat. Another possibility is that increased movements of people—between urban and rural areas, between regions, and between other countries and the United States—spread infectious childhood diseases that prevented many people from reaching their full adult height.

One important lesson we can derive from the study of height by age is that while per capita real GDP is a useful summary measure of how productive the economy is, we need other measures to get a well-rounded picture. Economic historians have long used measures such as industrial production and consumer prices. Now they are beginning to realize that additional measures drawn from other disciplines, such as height by age, can provide important insights.

FIGURE 29.3

Average Height of Adult, Native Born, White Males by Year of Birth

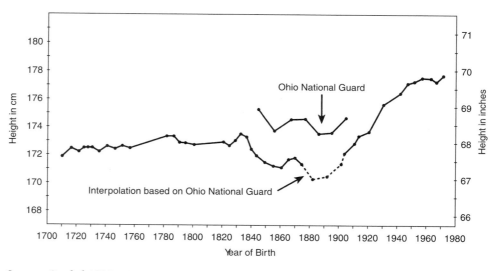

Source: *Steckel 1995, 1920.*

TABLE 29.2 AGE-ADJUSTED DEATHS FROM SELECTED DISEASES PER 100,000, 1960–2005

	1960	1980	1990	2000	2005
Chronic liver disease and cirrhosis	13.3	15.1	11.1	9.5	9.0
Influenza and pneumonia	53.7	31.4	36.8	23.7	20.3
Diabetes	22.5	18.1	20.7	25.0	24.6
Diseases of the heart	559.0	412.1	321.8	257.6	211.1
Cancer	193.9	207.9	216.0	199.6	183.8

Source: Statistical Abstract of the United States 2009, *Table 112.*

medical technology, improved living standards, and the adoption of more healthful life-styles among the elderly produced these improvements. The number of active physicians per 100,000, moreover, climbed from 153 in 1970 to 251 in 2000, in part because of the increase in the number of active physicians educated abroad. By the end of the period, physicians were plainly more efficient (if less personal) in treating patients than they had ever been in the history of medical science. Not all diseases, however, have shown such dramatic improvements: The death rate from diabetes was actually somewhat higher in 2005 than in 1960.

Infant mortality is a sensitive indicator of the overall health of the population. Table 29.3 shows infant mortality rates between 1940 and 2005. The decline in infant mortality has been dramatic. Improvements in medicine, such as the development of antibiotics, and improvements in income—because income governs access to nutrition and medical care—account for the downward trend. We are still very far, however, from the lowest levels that could be achieved given the current state of medical knowledge. The infant death rate for African Americans was 13.7 per 1,000 live births in 2005, more than twice the infant death rate for whites, 5.7. Some foreign countries, moreover, do better than the United States, showing that more progress could be made. In 2001, the infant mortality rate was 4.5 per 1,000 in France, 5 in Canada, and 5.5 in the United Kingdom. Another indicator of the potential for progress is the wide variance in infant mortality rates in the United States, from 4.5 per 1,000 in Utah in 2005, the lowest in the United States, to 14.1 in the District of Columbia, the highest.

TABLE 29.3 INFANT MORTALITY, 1940–2005 (PER 1,000 LIVE BIRTHS)

YEAR	TOTAL INFANT MORTALITY (birth to one year)		
	TOTAL	WHITE	AFRICAN AMERICAN
1940	47.0	43.2	73.8
1950	29.2	26.8	44.5
1960	26.0	22.9	43.2
1970	20.0	17.8	30.9
1980	12.6	10.9	20.2
1990	9.2	7.6	15.5
2000	6.9	5.7	14.1
2005	6.9	5.7	13.7

Source: *1940–1970:* Historical Statistics of the United States Colonial Times to 1970, *Series B 136–B147; 1980–2005:* Statistical Abstract of the United States 2009, *Table 112.*

TABLE 29.4 LIFE EXPECTANCY AT BIRTH, 1940–2005 (IN YEARS)

	WHITE			AFRICAN AMERICAN[a]		
	TOTAL	MALE	FEMALE	TOTAL	MALE	FEMALE
1940	64.2	62.1	66.6	53.1	51.5	54.9
1950	69.2	66.5	72.2	60.8	59.1	62.9
1960	70.6	67.4	74.1	63.6	61.1	66.3
1970	71.7	68.0	75.6	64.1	60.0	68.3
1980	74.4	70.7	78.1	68.1	63.8	72.5
1990	76.1	72.7	79.4	69.1	64.5	73.6
2000	77.6	74.9	80.1	71.9	68.3	75.2
2005	78.3	75.7	80.8	73.2	69.5	76.5

[a]The figures for 1940–1960 include other minorities.

Source: *1940–1960*, Historical Statistics *1970, Series B110-B115; 1970–2005, Statistical Abstract of the United States 2009, Table 100.*

Life expectancy at birth is another sensitive indicator of a population's health and well-being. This measure also reveals a steady improvement in the standard of living. For the United States, life expectancy in 1850 for a white baby at birth was 40 years; for an African American baby, it was only 23 years. By 1900, life expectancy had risen to 52 years for white babies and to 42 years for African American babies (Haines 2000). By 1940, life expectancy was 64 years for whites and 53 years for African Americans. Considerable additional progress has been made since 1940 (see Table 29.4). Between 1940 and 2005, life expectancy at birth for white Americans rose from 64 years to 78 years, an increase of 22 percent. Although African Americans still had a lower life expectancy at birth than whites, the increase for African Americans was even larger, from 53 years to 73 years, an increase of 38 percent. The overall increase is a testimony to improved public heath, increased access to medical care, and improved standards of living; although the continuing gap between whites and African Americans is also testimony to continued inequality in these areas. See Perspective 29.1 regarding the life expectancy of people with Down Syndrome.

PERSPECTIVE 29.1

GAINS IN THE LIFE EXPECTANCY OF THE MENTALLY RETARDED

The civil rights movement of the 1960s affected a wide range of groups that traditionally had been excluded from the mainstream of American economic and cultural life. Mentally retarded people were among them. A recent study (Friedman 2001), for example, reveals a startling increase in the life expectancy of people with Down Syndrome, a genetic defect that produces retardation. For white people, the increase in median age at death went from 2 years in 1968 to 50 years in 1997. There was also a startling increase in the life expectancy of African American people with Down Syndrome, but as with other measures of well-being, a gap between the rate for the two groups remained. In 1968, most African Americans born with Down Syndrome died before their first birthday. By 1997, however, median age at death had risen to 25 years. For white people, progress was steady throughout the period. For African Americans, progress began about 1982, with most of the improvement coming after 1992.

Although all reasons for the increase in life expectancy of people with Down Syndrome are not yet known, it seems probable that the increase in the frequency with which children with Down Syndrome are being reared at home rather than being institutionalized has led to improved supervision, nutrition, medical care, and emotional support. An important component of the improvement in medical care was the development and employment, often at an early age, of surgical techniques for remedying a congenital heart defect that afflicts a significant minority of people with Down Syndrome.

The increase in health and well-being in the United States (and the lack of progress when viewed from the perspective of other industrial countries or the most successful American states) can be traced to a variety of factors, including nutrition, lifestyle, and access to medical care. As late as 1940, only about 7 percent of the U.S. population had any kind of hospital insurance (e.g., any kind of prepayment of hospital costs that one day nearly everyone must pay). That percentage has risen dramatically in the postwar period as a result of new government programs—the most important being Medicare and Medicaid—and of the extension of private insurance, usually provided by employers. In 2000, 86 percent of the population was covered by private or public heath insurance. However, a worrisome segment of the population concentrated among poor people remained uncovered by health insurance. In 2000, only 70 percent of individuals living in families in which family income fell below the poverty line had any form of health insurance (Statistical Abstract 2002, 102). Many people who had some form of insurance worried about its adequacy. A major concern, for example, was that Medicare had not covered the cost of drugs until 2004.

Education Levels Reached by Americans Have Increased Steadily

As Claudia Goldin and Lawrence F. Katz (2008) demonstrate in their recent book *The Race between Education and Technology*, the United States was a world leader in education through much of its history. In the nineteenth century, the United States led the way in providing free and accessible elementary education. In part this reflected the American ideal that every citizen should be educated so that they could participate in the political life of the nation; in part it reflected an economic reality that education led

The Central High School Class of 1890, Dayton Ohio. The young man to the right of the entrance is Paul Lawrence Dunbar who would win international acclaim for his poetry and prose. The young man in the center of the entrance is Orville Wright who would win international acclaim as a pioneer aviator. America's investment in education paid dividends.

to higher paying jobs. To be sure, there were important exceptions, such as the provisions for schooling African Americans, but most native white families had access to "free" public educations for their children, usually financed by property taxes and supplied by local governments. In the first part of the twentieth century, Americans went to high school. In 1900 the typical young native-born American had a grade-school education, and by 1940 a typical young native-born American was a high school graduate (Goldin and Katz 2008, 164). Most of this had been financed at the local level. Parents demanded high schools for their children because it was clear that high school was a good investment: High school graduates earned more than young people with only a grade school education. Employers, moreover, could see that more education led to a more productive workforce, and the public could see that it led to a better informed and more productive democracy. America's thirst for education did not stop there. After World War II a college education became part of the American way of life for most people in the middle class, as well as for those who were aspiring to be middle-class Americans. The famous GI bill after World War II contributed to this trend, but the college movement persisted long after that generation of Americans had passed through college. Finally, American universities became world leaders in the sciences, social sciences, and other academic disciplines. College graduates from the United States and around the world sought advanced degrees in American universities. It is a triumphant story, but in the last part of the twentieth century, there were disturbing signs of retrogression in American education that we will take up in the next section.

CHALLENGES FOR THE FUTURE

The achievements of the American economy in the twentieth century would have seemed like science fiction to someone looking forward in the year 1901. However, we also will face challenges in the years ahead. Here, we consider four of the most important: (1) the deterioration in the distribution of income, (2) the aging of the population, (3) winning the race between education and technology, and (4) the search for a meaningful life.

Improving the Distribution of Income

Many Americans, particularly college students, worry that even though the economy is growing, they may not be able to share in that growth because the distribution of income is becoming less equal. The rich are hogging all the gains. Stories about the fabulous incomes of Internet entrepreneurs or top sports figures seem to confirm the impression that the rich are getting richer and the poor, poorer. What do the numbers show? Table 29.5 shows the distribution of household incomes from 1947 through 2005. This table is common way of presenting information about income or wealth inequality. If every household had the same income, then the poorest 20 percent of families would have the same share of total income as everyone else—20 percent. But of course the share of the poorest 20 percent is much less than the share of the richest 20 percent. Clearly, the distribution of family incomes has not changed radically over the postwar period. The shares in 2005 are in the vicinity of what they were in 1947. Just as clearly, however, the distribution has become less equal since the 1970s. The share of the lowest fifth fell from 4.3 percent in 1980 to 3.4 percent in 2005. To put it more dramatically, the share of the poorest fifth fell almost 25 percent $[(4.3 - 3.4)/((4.3 + 3.4)/2) = 0.23]$. While the share of the poorest households was falling, moreover, the slice of the pie going to the richest 20 percent of Americans rose from 43.7 percent in 1980 to 50.4 percent in 2005.

Although the evidence shown in Table 29.5 of a worsening distribution is clear, the reasons for this change, as thoughtful analysts such as Robert W. Fogel (2000, 217–222)

TABLE 29.5 DISTRIBUTION OF HOUSEHOLD INCOMES BY QUINTILE (IN PERCENT)

YEAR	LOWEST FIFTH	SECOND FIFTH	THIRD FIFTH	FOURTH FIFTH	HIGHEST FIFTH
1947	3.5%	10.6%	16.7%	23.6%	45.6%
1950	3.1	10.5	17.3	24.1	45.0
1960	3.2	10.6	17.6	24.7	44.0
1970	4.1	10.8	17.4	24.5	43.3
1980	4.3	10.3	16.9	24.7	43.7
1990	3.9	9.6	15.9	24.0	46.6
2000	3.6	8.9	14.8	23.0	49.8
2005	3.4	8.6	14.6	23.0	50.4

Source: *1947–1990:* Historical Statistics of the United States, *2006, Series Be2–Be6; 2000–2005:* Statistical Abstract of the United States 2009, *Table E1.*

have pointed out, are complex. He and other analysts make a number of important points based on their analysis of the underlying determinants of the distribution of income that we will discuss below. Once again, remember the importance of Economic Reasoning Proposition 5, opinions must be based on a careful examination of all the evidence (see page 8).

1. A change in the distribution of work hours has had a major effect on the distribution of income. In 1890 poor people generally worked more hours than rich people. Now poor people work fewer hours than the professionals who make up a substantial proportion of the highest paid fifth. Two-earner families, in which both family members are highly paid professionals, once a rarity, have become commonplace. Table 29.6 shows how different types of families have fared since 1950. Median real incomes of "two-earner" households rose 1.07 percent per year, but median real incomes for households in which the wife was not in the paid labor force rose only 0.13 percent per year. These results were mirrored by the median real incomes for households headed by a single women or single man. Median real income for a household headed by a single woman rose 0.82 percent per year; median real income for a household headed by a single man actually fell 0.04 percent per year.

2. The mobility of people moving from one income class to another must be taken into account. Families in the lowest category may be there for temporary reasons: a proprietor of a small business who had a bad year or an executive of a large corporation who was laid off and is temporarily experiencing a low income. Highly

TABLE 29.6 MEDIAN REAL FAMILY INCOME BY TYPE OF FAMILY (IN 2006 DOLLARS)

FAMILIES	1950	1980	1990	2000	2006	ANNUAL GROWTH RATE 1980–2006
Married couple families	$ 24,646	$ 53,919	$ 59,661	$ 69,194	69,404	0.97%
Wife in the paid labor force	27,923	62,619	69,953	81,062	82,788	1.07
Wife not in the paid labor force	23,709	44,198	45,260	46,812	45,757	0.13
Male householder, no wife present	22,279	42,307	43,437	44,171	41,844	−0.04
Female householder, no husband present	13,746	23,314	25,321	30,109	28,829	0.82
All families	22,493	48,976	52,869	59,398	58,407	0.68

Source: Statistical Abstract of the United States 2009, *Table 677.*

skilled and ambitious immigrants may enter the lowest category but steadily work their way up.

3. Public policy should focus first on the people who are chronically poor and who year in and year out are unable to consume more than poverty-level incomes. These individuals and families constitute perhaps 4 percent of all households; they are what William Julius Wilson (1987) has referred to as "the truly disadvantaged." The capacity of the United States to help these people achieve a decent material standard of living is without question.

4. Almost all observers agree that a major reason for the widening of the gap between rich and poor has been the enormous increase in the demand for highly trained personnel compared with the stagnant demand for personnel with only a high school education. Mostly this was due to changes in the demand for labor: Demands increased for highly trained personnel in medicine, computers, finance, and similar fields. Partly, it was due to policy mistakes. In the 1970s, fear of oversupply led to cutbacks in government support for the education of highly skilled professionals. The number of medical degrees conferred, for example, declined after 1984. Improving the distribution of income may require a major push by the government to fund additional education.

Caring for an Aging Population

One of the major challenges that Americans face in this new century is caring for an increasingly elderly population. As Table 29.7 on page 569 shows, the percentage of individuals over 65 years of age increased steadily from 1960 to 2000. This trend has created severe strains for the Social Security system and doubts about its future. In 1999, 12.7 percent of the population was 65 and older; projections indicate a rise of the age-group eligible for Social Security to 19.4 percent in 2030. Whereas in 1994 there were about 3.2 covered workers per beneficiary, by 2030, it is projected, there will be only 2 workers per beneficiary.

Initially, Social Security was an insurance system, based on the principle that an interest-earning fund should be built up from the premiums collected from individuals and that the fund should be adequate to meet future obligations. Taxes were collected beginning in 1937, but no benefits were paid until 1942 to accumulate a reserve. The pressure to increase benefits, especially given the threat of more radical plans for redistributing income to the elderly, became too great to resist. In 1939 legislation was passed that converted Social Security into a pay-as-you-go system, with beneficiaries being supported by those currently paying into the system.

In the ensuing years, social security benefits increased rapidly for several reasons: the population aged, more workers were covered, and benefits were indexed to the price level. Inevitably, the tax rate had to be increased: from 2 percent in 1937 to 15.3 percent today. The maximum tax payment rose from $60 in 1937 (about $750 in today's money) to $11,659 today. From a legal point of view, half the tax is paid by the employer, and

TABLE 29.7 THE ELDERLY POPULATION, 1960–2000

PEOPLE AGE 65 AND OVER	1960	1970	1980	1990	2000
Total in millions	16.7	20.1	25.6	31.1	35
As a percentage of the total population	9.2%	9.8%	11.3%	12.5%	12.4%
As a percentage of the population age 18–64	17.0%	17.0%	19.0%	20.0%	21.0%

Source: *1960–1990:* Statistical Abstract of the United States 2000, *Table 12.; 2000:* Statistical Abstract of the United States 2002, *Table 12.*

half is paid by the employee. Economists recognize, however, that the economic locus of the tax may be different from the legal locus, and many economists believe that in reality workers pay most of the tax through direct contributions or by accepting lower wages. In 1950 there were 43.3 million workers paying into the system and 2.9 million beneficiaries, a ratio of 16.5 workers per beneficiary. By 1975, there were 100.2 million covered workers and 31.1 million beneficiaries, a ratio of 3.2 workers per beneficiary. Today there are 152.9 million covered workers and 45.2 million beneficiaries, for a ratio of 3.4 workers per beneficiary.

The Social Security system has come perilously close to bankruptcy. On April 1, 1982, the system's trustees reported that "Social Security will be unable to pay retirees' and survivors' benefits on time starting in July 1983 unless Congress takes corrective action." Congressman Claude Pepper of Florida, a leading spokesperson for the elderly and chair of the House Select Committee on Aging, said that the trustees' report "confirms my belief that the poor performance of the economy is robbing the Social Security trust funds." For the seventeenth straight year, the combined old-age and disability trust funds paid out more than they took in, and soon they would be depleted. Legislation based on a presidential commission headed by Alan Greenspan rescued the system. Nevertheless, concerns about the future of Social Security continue. A major question for the future is how will we pay the "unfunded" liabilities of Social Security and other government transfer programs: through higher taxes or lower benefits? In principle we should be making plans for meeting these future obligations now. If history is any guide, however, it will take a crisis, like the 1982 trustees report, to goad the Congress and the executive branch to action.

Winning the Race between Technology and Education

As noted above, the twentieth century witnessed great improvements in American education. In the 1970s, however, growth of American education measured by graduation rates and maximum years of schooling slowed (Goldin and Katz 2008). Troubling evidence emerged, moreover, that the quality of American education was declining, or at least failing to keep pace with improvements in other parts of the world. Technology, however, was advancing rapidly and creating increased demands for highly skilled college graduates. The result was a rise in "skill premiums" that contributed to the growing disparities in income. Potential college students, however, often found that they were thwarted at some point by a lack of proper preparation at the high school level and by the financial costs of higher education. The cost of a college education rose more rapidly than incomes. Many students, even well-prepared students, have found that they must combine work and education, an often daunting task. The challenge for the future is how to provide America's young people with the skills they need to prosper in the twenty-first century.

The Search for a Meaningful Life

Many social indicators of well-being began to "deteriorate" in the 1960s and 1970s. Between 1950 and 1980 births to unmarried women as a percentage of all births rose from 3.9 percent to 18.4 percent; the divorce rate per 1,000 people rose from 2.6 to 5.2; and the murder rate per 100,000 rose from about 5 to 10.2. Admittedly, the exact meanings of these changes was hard to determine. The increase in the proportion of births to unmarried women, for example, may partly reflect changes in social norms. We can see the effect of differences in social norms by looking at the international variance in this measure. In 1992, the U.S. proportion stood at 30 percent, less than Sweden (50 percent) but more than the Netherlands (12 percent) or Japan (1 percent). Social norms may also influence the reporting of variables as well as the true levels. Indeed, in some cases, one could argue that part of the trend represented an increase in well-being—some people may be happier divorcing than remaining married merely because of strong social pressures to do so. But for many people, these trends signaled a deterioration in values that was deeply disturbing.

In an important book addressed to this concern, *The Fourth Great Awakening* (2000), economic historian Robert W. Fogel has argued that the attempt to ensure that all citizens have the spiritual resources to achieve a meaningful life may be the greatest challenge of the twenty-first century.[2] By *spiritual* Fogel does not mean only religious values, although they are part of what he has in mind. He means to include as well other values and cultural traditions that help people cope with life and find a meaningful path.

What are some of the issues that the nation will face that will require spiritual as well as material resources to solve? The truly disadvantaged will require material resources to meet the demands of daily living. Will that be enough? Will they also need help finding a meaningful role in society? Retirement for most people will probably lengthen. How will society provide for meaningful activities for retirees, and how will it address the depression that often afflicts older people? On the other hand, in some sectors of the economy, such as academia, retirement may be delayed. How will young people in these sectors cope with years of delay before they take their place in the sun? As more women and minorities enter the workplace, how will society break the glass ceilings that prevent them from reaching the highest levels in business and government? As Americans become increasingly aware of the world outside the boundaries of the United States, how will Americans cope with the great international disparities in material income? Not one of these questions is easily answered; all of them require new ways of thinking about our economy and society.

PROPHETS OF DECLINE

What of the future? The slowdown in the growth of real wages for lower-skilled workers, the increase in the inequality of wealth and income, the deterioration of the environment, and the increase in various indicators of social malaise, such as the murder rate, brought to center stage a series of pundits who claimed that Americans faced a long-term decline in their living standards if they did not quickly shape up. Some focused on the lack of savings and the government deficit; others stressed America's dependence on foreign oil; still others decried the spoiling of the environment.

In his widely acclaimed book, *The Rise and Fall of the Great Powers* (1987), Paul Kennedy, one of the most thoughtful prophets of decline, stressed the tendency of great empires of the past to decline once they had reached a preeminent position because they had exhausted their resources in foreign adventures. It was natural for Americans who had witnessed the destructive domestic consequences of the war in Vietnam to see the force of his point.

Most students are familiar with prophecies of decline based on environmental dangers, such as global warming. The problems addressed by the prophets of decline are real ones. Solving them will not be easy. It is important to remember, however, that prophecies of decline are not unique to our age. For the British, especially, it is an old story. Writing in 1798, Thomas Robert Malthus, in his celebrated *Essay on Population* (1914), predicted that

---

[2]The title refers to Fogel's view that the United States is now undergoing a religious revival comparable to similar revivals that have reshaped economic and social institutions in the past.

eventually Britain's growing population would run into its declining ability to produce food. After all, the amount of agricultural land was limited, but the population could, if the food supply was adequate, grow without limit. Wages, Malthus argued, would eventually fall until they reached the minimum necessary to sustain life.[3] Disaster could be avoided only if the population could somehow be held in check. Nearly 200 years later, the population and standard of living of England is far higher than Malthus could have imagined. William Stanley Jevons was another prophet of inevitable decline. In his famous book, *The Coal Question* (1865), Jevons predicted that England would eventually be forced into decline because its reserves of coal (then its chief source of industrial power) would be exhausted. England would face not only economic decline but also "moral and intellectual retrogression" (Engerman 1993). This catastrophe never came to pass: more reserves of coal were found, technological change permitted other sources of power to be used, and the development of world trade made it possible to escape from the confines of a theory based on the premise that Britain was the only industrial nation.

We cannot say that the Jeremiahs of the current generation are wrong. The economic historian, looking at the long record of growth achieved by the American economy, however, is likely to be skeptical. The point was well put long ago by English historian Thomas Babington Macaulay:

We cannot absolutely prove that those are in error who tell us that society has reached a turning point, that we have seen our best days. But so said all who came before us, and with just as much apparent reason. (Macaulay 1881, Vol. 1, ii, 186)[4]

SELECTED REFERENCES AND SUGGESTED READINGS

Easterlin, Richard A. "Regional Income Trends, 1840–1950." In *The Reinterpretation of American Economic History*, ed. Robert W. Fogel and Stanley L. Engerman. New York: Harper & Row, 1971.

Economic Report of the President 2008. U.S. Council of Economic Advisors. Washington, D.C.: Government Printing Office, 2008. http://www.gpoaccess.gov/eop/.

Engerman, Stanley. "Chicken Little, Anna Karenina, and the Economics of Slavery: Two Reflections on Historical Analysis, with Examples Drawn Mostly from the Study of Slavery." *Social Science History* 17 (1993): 163.

Friedman, J. M. "Racial Disparities in Median Age at Death of Persons with Down Syndrome—United States, 1968–1997." *Morbidity and Mortality Weekly Report*, June 8, 2001, 463–465.

Fogel, Robert W. "Economic Growth, Population Theory, and Physiology: The Bearing of Long-term Processes on the Making of Economic Policy." *American Economic Review* 84 (1994): 369–395.

_____. *The Fourth Great Awakening and the Future of Egalitarianism.* Chicago: University of Chicago Press, 2000.

Goldin, Claudia, and Lawrence F. Katz. *The Race Between Education and Technology.* Cambridge, Mass.: Harvard University Press, 2008.

Haines, Michael. "The Population of the United States, 1790–1920." In *The Cambridge Economic History of the United States*, Vol. II, eds. Stanley L. Engerman and Robert E. Gallman. New York: Cambridge University Press, 2000.

Historical Income Inequality Tables. U.S. Bureau of the Census. 2009. http://www.census.gov/hhes/www/income/histinc/ineqtoc.html.

Historical Statistics of the United States Colonial Times to 1970, bicentennial edition. U. S. Bureau of the Census. Washington D.C.: Government Printing Office, 1975. http://www.census.gov/prod/www/abs/statab.html.

---

[3]Malthus refined his essay a number of times. In later versions he recognized that moral restraints on population growth would prevent the real wage from falling to the minimum needed to sustain life.

[4]We thank Deirdre McCloskey for suggesting this quotation.

Historical Statistics of the United States: Earliest Times to the Present, Millennial Edition. Eds. Susan B. Carter, et al. Cambridge: Cambridge University Press, 2006.

Jevons, William Stanley. *The Coal Question.* London: Macmillan, 1865.

Kennedy, Paul. *The Rise and Fall of the Great Powers: Economic Change and Military Conflict from 1500 to 2000.* New York: Random House, 1987.

Komlos, John. "The Height and Weight of West Point Cadets: Dietary Change in Antebellum America." *Journal of Economic History* 47 (1987): 897–927.

Macaulay, Thomas Babington. "Southey's Colloquies." In *Macaulay's Essays.* 1860 ed.; American ed. Boston: Riverside, 1881.

Malthus, Thomas R. *An Essay on Population,* 2 vols. London: J. M. Dent, 1914.

Statistical Abstract of the United States 2000. U.S. Bureau of the Census. 2000. http://www.census.gov/compendia/statab/.

Statistical Abstract of the United States 2002. U.S. Bureau of the Census. 2002. http://www.census.gov/compendia/statab/.

Statistical Abstract of the United States 2009. U.S. Bureau of the Census. 2009. http://www.census.gov/compendia/statab/.

Steckel, Richard H. "Stature and the Standard of Living." *Journal of Economic Literature* 33 (1995): 1903–1940.

Wilson, William Julius. *The Truly Disadvantaged: The Inner City, The Underclass, and Public Policy.* Chicago: University of Chicago Press, 1987.

Subject Index

Name Index